THE LONG PATROL

THE LONG PATROL

25 YEARS OF WRITING FROM THE WORK OF NORMAN MAILER
EDITED BY AND WITH AN INTRODUCTION BY ROBERT F. LUCID

WORLD PUBLISHING
TIMES MIRROR
NEW YORK

ACKNOWLEDGMENTS

The texts of all excerpts are taken from the orignal hardback editions. Acknowledgment is made here to Holt, Rinehart and Winston for permission to reprint from *The Naked and the Dead*, Copyright © 1948 by Norman Mailer, and *Barbary Shore*, Copyright © 1951 by Norman Mailer; to G. P. Putnam's Sons for permission to reprint from *The Deer Park*, Copyright © 1955 by Norman Mailer, *Advertisements for Myself*, Copyright © 1959 by Norman Mailer, *Deaths for the Ladies*, Copyright © 1962 by Norman Mailer, *The Presidential Papers*, Copyright © 1960, 1961, 1962, 1963 by Norman Mailer, and *Why Are We in Vietnam?*, Copyright © 1967 by Norman Mailer; to the Dial Press of Dell Publishing Co. to reprint from *An American Dream*, Copyright © 1964, 1965 by Norman Mailer, *The Deer Park, a Play*, Copyright © 1959, 1960, 1967 by Norman Mailer, and *Cannibals and Christians*, Copyright © 1966 by Norman Mailer; to New American Library, Inc., to reprint from *The Armies of the Night*, Copyright © 1968 by Norman Mailer, and *Miami and the Siege of Chicago*, Copyright © 1968 by Norman Mailer; and to Little, Brown & Co. to reprint from *Of a Fire on the Moon*, Copyright © 1969, 1970 by Norman Mailer.

Published by The World Publishing Company. Published simultaneously in Canada by Nelson, Foster & Scott Ltd. First printing — 1971. Text Copyright © 1948, 1951, 1955, 1959, 1960, 1961, 1962, 1963, 1964, 1965, 1966, 1967, 1968, 1969, 1970 by Norman Mailer. Introduction and Editor's Notes Copyright © 1971 by Robert F. Lucid. All rights reserved. Library of Congress catalog card number: 72–159589. Printed in the United States of America.

WORLD PUBLISHING
TIMES MIRROR

"I wanted to write a short novel about a long patrol. . . . When I started writing *The Naked and the Dead* I thought it might be a good idea to have a preliminary chapter or two in which to give the reader a chance to meet my characters before they went on patrol. But the next six months and the first 500 pages went into that, and I remember in the early days I was annoyed at how long it was taking me to get to the patrol."

Norman Mailer, in a *Paris Review* Interview

Contents

Introduction

I wonder what it would be like to be coming to read Norman Mailer for the first time. Usually the "introduction" to a collection like the present one is an occasion for the editor to press his particular critical case, aiming his argument toward an audience he assumes to be not only familiar with the author's work but in search of some comprehensive frame of reference by which extensive reading can now be pulled together. Such audiences exist, of course, and it is proper enough to address them, but there is another audience that is perhaps more suitably the target for an introduction like the present one. It is an audience composed of readers who had heard of Mailer—impossible not to have heard his name, one supposes—and had perhaps seen one or two short things by him in magazines or newspapers, but was now for the first time prepared to make, as it were, a long patrol into the territory of Mailer's writing. What an enviable situation.

It is enviable because it so seldom happens that one gets the chance to experience a writer as exciting as Mailer so dramatically. Most of us came to know his work piecemeal, which is after all the way he wrote it, and our pleasure was the strong but fragmentary gratification of accumulating, over a period of years, a gradual sense that we had grown along with a writer. But one of course knows the other kind, the dramatic pleasure of large, immediate discovery, and the design of the present volume is to offer such discovery to the reader. So far there are at least thirteen volumes of Mailer, and *The Long Patrol* represents not so much "the best" of those volumes—Mailer is a major writer, and there wasn't enough room to include anything like all of his "best"—as it is a chart to help guide an exploration. Apart from three collections of shorter writings, a play, and a volume of verse, Mailer has so far written five novels and three full-length non-fiction narratives. All are represented here with excerpts, and the job of excerpting is poor indeed if the effect is not to lead the reader out of this book and back to the original. Different readers will doubtless move to different rhythms, some going out after each excerpt to find its source, then returning as to a base for further direction, then out again. Others might go straight through, curving back after the final excerpt into the larger Mailer terrain, ready now to test the microcosm that was offered here. But whatever his particular style may be, the new Mailer reader is an object of envy because everyone can surely recall being as fortunate as he at least once.

Every reader has taken the plunge, has submerged into volume after volume of an artist whose vision enlarged and took him in like a personal fantasy, has raced through each book yet lingered in each at the same time, greedy not to leave, nervous as a drinker is nervous when he senses he will eventually run out, but still more nervous to go on and get more. Every reader knows what it is like to be bombed on some writer—Thomas Wolfe, it often used to be, or Joyce or Fitzgerald or Hemingway or of course Salinger. All know that gone feeling of astonishment: my God, it seemed to say, I am seeing in print something utterly secret, something I had thought no one ever felt but me. Mailer can easily have such an effect on a reader coming to him for the first time, and so this book and this introduction are for him, the new reader, who has his pleasure before him. If he wants it he can obtain here some measure of orientation in anticipation of the experience, and at least he can pick up some useful background and context.

II

Newness itself, combined with the impulse to explore, may well be all the orientation a reader needs as he crosses into Mailer's world. It is indeed one of Mailer's favorite notions that the best guide for an individual as he moves into any unfamiliar experience is a sense operating below the conscious level, some "navigator at the seat of being" he once called it. Presumably though, readers of such seismographic empathy with Mailer's mind have already abandoned this introduction, if they ever began it, and are somewhere far ahead in any case, happily free of compass and chart. The rest of us might safely begin with examining our title, *The Long Patrol.*

The phrase derives, of course, from the *Paris Review* excerpt that serves as the epigraph to this book. In 1964 Mailer was looking back on his early days, a career which had a very modest beginning in college in 1941, was interrupted by military service during the war, and which then landed running in 1948 with the publication of his best-selling novel *The Naked and the Dead.* Reminiscent in many respects of Dos Passos, that first novel is a construct of at least three lines of action, lines which intersect and interrupt each other and which themselves are interrupted by "time machine" flashbacks into the history of individual characters. The total action eventuates, after 433 pages, in the factorial dramatization of a long patrol undertaken by a platoon of infantrymen on a Pacific island during the war, and at least in a sense the patrol provides the rationale for the rest of the novel. Thus Mailer's "long patrol" in the *Paris Review* is a literal point toward which he had been trying to move in composition, a rational goal that at first appeared realistically within his reach, but which seemed mysteriously to recede as he moved toward it.

Here, however, the phrase seeks to invoke the metaphorical implication of what Mailer remembers having experienced back in 1946. While the creation of *The Naked and the Dead* was an important proximate goal for its author, in a larger sense it really served only as the first step in a much longer-range effort: Mailer was seeking to launch a major career as a novelist, was seeking to discover and evolve powers in himself that would allow him to create something far beyond the work of art immediately at hand. Considering the actual and potential strength revealed in *The Naked and the Dead,* this seemed a rational goal, realistically within his reach. In his novel and in the critical reception to it there was everything to encourage him to hope for real stature: both the artist and his critics conceived that he might mold his imagination into the forms of the novel, and thus over the years bring forth a canon of fiction which, in its rich variety and depth, would represent and do justice to that imagination. If all went as planned Mailer's novels were to be, in Fitzgerald's phrase, objects commensurate with his capacity for wonder.

But all did not go as planned. Whether choked by the knowledge that the literary community was waiting for him to "prove" the promise of his first book, or for more intricate causes, Mailer seemed to falter. Over a period of three years he worked at fiction: first on a manuscript he called "Mrs. Guinevere," then on a strike novel which died after fifty pages, then, armed with a few characters from the strike novel, back to "Mrs. Guinevere," and in 1951 he emerged with his second published novel, *Barbary Shore*. Its departure from *The Naked and the Dead* was so radical and so total as virtually to constitute a repudiation.

The first book had been almost a model of structural competence in the tradition of the pre-war naturalists. Mailer's 1943 S. B. from Harvard was in Engineering Sciences, and he was later to call the book an engineer's book, put together with spot-welding and rivets, a structural accomplishment on the order of the Eiffel Tower. Its limitation, on the other hand, was that though it was innovative and adept, it revealed an imagination that was uncomfortably close to predictable. The causes of war, of economic collapse, of institutional viciousness, of personal violence, and even of natural depravity were all available within the world of the book, and were all presented as rationally if not mathematically ascertainable. *Barbary Shore*, by contrast, is close to inept structurally. Its single line of action and simple setting are barely sustained by an author who, three years earlier, had been proclaimed the heir-apparent of Dos Passos in the realm of technical virtuosity. The imaginative vision of the book, however, is to *The Naked and the Dead* what Van Gogh's "Starry Night" is to a professionally executed illustration in an astrology text. Its young hero is an amnesiac, burning both to remember and to create, but with no way of knowing how he got into his wounded and driven condition. The action consists of his nightmarish wandering through the maze of a surrealistic Brooklyn boarding house, a place tenanted by half-mad victims and agents of the world's great institutional powers. The book shows us an imagination almost ripped by the murderous dialectics of known and unknown, rational and irrational, political and psychological, external and internal. The truth, if ascertainable at all, must be got not by mathematics but more nearly by miracle. It is an imagination whose character foreshadowed, as it turned out, most of the salient characteristics of post-war American art; but the book's total unexpectedness, combined with its almost poignant failure to develop a form commensurate to its imaginative wildness, doomed it critically. Mailer was suddenly in the position — both in his own eyes and those of his critics — of having to make a comeback if he was to realize that goal which, after *The Naked and the Dead*, had seemed his for the taking.

With varying degrees of pain or pleasure, readers of the later Mailer often report having observed a certain quality of the Napoleonic in his vision. Their report is certainly accurate, and it may be that the quality first surfaced in Mailer during the period between *Barbary Shore* and the publication of his 1955 novel, *The Deer Park*. After 1951, badly bruised by the experience of *Barbary Shore*, he tried his hand at shorter fiction and wrote a few interesting political essays, but at center he was trying to bring into balance his vision of how a novel should be shaped, on the one hand, and his vision of how the life of the modern individual could best be understood, on the other. As a way of affirming his faith in the novel as a key to understanding, he hit upon the act of almost apostolic commitment to the form. He recalls the moment:

> I was done with short stories and markets and editors and agents and thoughts of making my way back as some sort of amateur literary politician, done with trying to write less than I knew, rather than getting ready for something too large. I woke up in the morning with the plan for a prologue and an eight-part novel in my mind, the prologue to be the day of a small frustrated man, a minor artist manqué. The eight novels were to be eight stages of his dream later that night and the books would revolve around the adventures of a mythical hero, Sergius O' Shaugnessy. . . .

He launched into his comeback with a style — Grand — and a sound — Boom — that were to become his familiar trademarks. His prologue was written and is reprinted in this collection as "The Man Who Studied Yoga," and the eight novels coalesced into *The Deer Park*. Sergius O'Shaugnessy is its hero, a young pilot fleeing from the Korean war, a desert city like Palm Springs is its setting, and its denizens are an incredible range of damned or doomed or struggling people who in one way or another have been created by Hollywood.

The history of publishing-house intrigue and personal crisis that goes with *The Deer Park* is too much to summarize here, and the reader is invited to see Mailer's essay on the subject — "Fourth Advertisement for Myself" — reprinted in this book. Here, however, it is more important to observe that though the novel moved impressively toward correlating Mailer's command of his art with the expanding reaches of his imagination — much farther than any fiction he had hitherto written — it still gave off the nagging sense of saying much less than its author knew and was trying to say.

Mailer's secret weapon has for years been a promise he seems to give to his audience: if they will read him very carefully they may hope for an illumination of an almost magical order. What might be illuminated is the relationship between the world of affairs, institutions, society, realism, Marx, Tolstoy — between that world and the world of mood, hallucination, projection, surrealism, Freud, Dostoyevsky. If *The Naked and the Dead* was the virtual embodiment of the first world, and *Barbary Shore*, for all practical purposes, a quagmire of the second, *The Deer Park* is Mailer's first major effort to create a world out of the dialectic between the two. In and out of his fiction it is an effort he has been engaged upon ever since, and this, his third novel, stakes out an impressive range of what will come to be identified as basic Mailer material. The realm of sexuality is crucial to him here, permitting the artist as it does to penetrate the inner workings of both society and the private individual in sexual terms. The realm of art becomes hardly less crucial, and he uses it as a track into the imagination of his individuals and also, startlingly, into the character of institutions. The technical brilliance which seemed at first to have deserted him has impressively returned, and he manipulates two extremely complex lines of dramatic action with deceptive ease. Further, he mines into a new and very strong vein of the comic. This and much more enriches *The Deer Park*, and a good number of critics have argued that as of 1971 it is his finest fictional achievement. But the most ardent of the novel's admirers would not claim that in it Mailer has reached the long patrol at last. If anything, *The Deer Park* made the dénouement of Mailer's fictional career seem farther away than ever, for through its pages one hears the rustle of that Napoleonic fantasy which inspired it, hears the promise, or surely the need, for a novel which would capture Time and Space, Depth and Height, the Cosmos itself. "Not," as Mailer said at the time, "a modest novel — one would need the seat of Zola and the mind of Joyce to do it properly." No less a union than that is what Mailer's imagination reaches for, and it should thus come as no surprise to discover that on the next stage of his campaign toward his objective, he devises a radical new strategy.

III

The new strategy was to try for the long patrol through indirection, and the tactics were two: the use of non-fiction and the use of personal public display. Up to this time, after all, although he had written a few essays for low-circulation magazines and was into his second marriage, Mailer had concentrated directly on fiction and had pretty well kept his name out of the newspapers. In 1956 he broke both patterns by becoming a weekly columnist for *The Village Voice* (of which he had been a co-founder the year before) and by making his own personality the armature, as it were, of the column he wrote. The column came to a stormy conclusion after a few months, with Mailer at public odds with both publisher and audience, but he had found a line to follow. Mailer was on the track of disruption.

By the summer of 1957 the track had led him to writing "The White Negro," perhaps the most influential single American essay to be published in the decade. In it Mailer identifies a new revolutionary, a figure innocent of the doctrine of either Marx or Freud, but profoundly and explosively subversive of the culture's moral foundations. He is the Hipster, a man who follows his "navigator" not to the barricade or the analyst's chamber but into the most dangerous of the Negro underworlds. With no insulation to protect him, this questing individual moves through to those experiential truths about himself and about society which are to be learned in the realms of sex, drugs, and violence. Replying to accusations that such a figure is less a revolutionary than a neurotic, Mailer denied that the solution to the Hipster's problems lay with the analyst, and his tone was characteristic of his emerging new style:

> But the analyst, this middle-class and usually pampered son, is he the one to make the imaginative journey into the tortured marijuana-racked mind and genitalia of a hipster daring to live on the edge of the most dangerous of the Negro worlds? Or is it not finally a matter of courage, courage not necessarily nor uniquely before violence, but courage to accept telling blows to the ego? For what would the analyst do, and what would become of his tidy, narrow, other-directed little world if he were to discover, and may God help him, that the hipster way out by the lip of danger may conceivably know more of the savor and swing in the damn dialectic of the orgasm than he, the doctor, the educated ball-shrinker who diagnoses all joys not his own as too puny.

The tone was aggressive, the style highly charged and rhythmic, the ideas like sauce to the appetite of the imagination. It was a major breakthrough for Mailer, and he was to use the world of Hip and his role as the Hipster's champion centrally in his next attempt to achieve the long patrol.

The attempt was *Advertisements for Myself*, one of the most unusual books in American literature. It is first of all a showcase of all of Mailer's work, moving through the early fiction and essays, through the Hipster material, and on into the area of current fiction-in-progress. Mailer's personality is indeed the book's armature, and is revealed in an extended autobiographical essay, one whose chapters take the form of "advertisements" introducing and explaining each piece of work and showing the relationship of each to his life. Presenting himself as an artist whose struggle to achieve creativity is a mirror of the struggle of all individuals to come to self-realization, Mailer shapes his book into the form of a public promise. The epic that had been conceived with "The Man Who Studied Yoga" is ready at last to be hazarded. If luck and health hold it will be done in ten years, an underground novel as huge and fine as the Cosmic need for greatness in our perishing culture would require. Mailer spells it out like a man determined to risk every cent he owns on a single, apocalyptic turn of the card:

> If it is to have any effect, and I can hardly look forward to exhausting the next ten years without hope of a deep explosive effect, the book will be fired to its fuse by the rumor that I once pointed to the farthest fence and said that within ten years I would try to hit the longest ball ever to go up into the accelerated hurricane air of American letters.

Earlier in the book he had said that if he is wrong in his estimate of his own power "then I'm the fool who will pay the bill," and here the price is fixed. That Hipster courage he admired, "courage to accept telling blows to the ego," is the central moral quality displayed by *Advertisements*, and the emergence of it reveals the strategy Mailer has been evolving since *The Deer Park:* he will place himself in a public position where he must create fiction as great as his potential promises, because failure to do so would extract a price in humiliation too vast to be borne. The character of the act illustrates precisely what Mailer meant by the term "existential," and he clearly intended that the pressure generated by his commitment would explode him in the direction of his goal. Whether it did or not is still an unresolved question, but it seems fair to say that if Mailer's purpose was served by *Advertisements*, it was served in a much more complicated way than he had originally envisioned. His initial conception of how he would spend the next decade had been clear—he would work on his novel, breaking only for "a side effort or two to pick up some money." But the decade and more which has passed since his original announcement has revealed a canon of work not to be explained in terms of "side efforts" around a single, central main endeavor.

Mailer's statement of intention in *Advertisements* was so dramatic and so complex that the intention itself, by comparison, seemed rather uncomplicated: he simply wanted to become a great novelist, as Joyce and Zola and Proust were great. Thus critics, who were cautiously respectful in their reaction to the book, stood back to watch for the results of Mailer's efforts the way one might watch from the rail at a racetrack, wondering if that longshot might actually pull into the lead when they came turning for home. Many of the more adventurous had a small bet on him—nothing they couldn't afford to lose, but enough to make it interesting. For Mailer watchers, however, the 1960's turned out to offer a spectacle a little more intricate than had been anticipated.

It was less a horse race than a three-ring circus, with clowns, pratfalls, dazzling spectacle, some beautiful ladies, some savagery, and a few stop-your-heart high-wire acts—excitement for young and old. A Mailer marriage ended in the newspapers with a very loud bang and was followed shortly by a book of verse, *Deaths for the Ladies (and other disasters)*. For rail watchers the thing seemed almost an outrage—a book of *verse?* The short poems in it he called "short hairs," for which he supplied a versified explanation:

> The art of
> the
> short hair
> is that
> it
> don't
> go on
> for
> too long.

The poems weren't all like that, but a tough frivolity was probably the book's dominant tone, broken now and again by a touch of lyric sadness which at first was almost as distressing as it was effective. As one leafed through the eccentric, unpaginated book a disturbingly familiar thought began to form: while he's no poet, went the thought, and he certainly has got to find a line he can follow, it is still impressive to see the *variety* of his imagination. The thought was disturbing, of course, because one had had it so often before and had been led to believe, after *Advertisements*, that Mailer's imagination—its richness, variety, and promise—was not in question. One had granted him all that. The question now was supposed to be what was he going to do with with that imagination. Instead the verse offered the insight that Mailer might, under utterly different circumstances, have become an interesting lyric poet.

The note struck by *Deaths for the Ladies* turned out to be symptomatic of much of the decade, and the tone of downright petulance that characterized so much of Mailer's critical reception was to a certain extent predictable. Between 1961 and 1965 he published a really tremendous amount of shorter writings—regular readers of *Esquire* and *Commentary* must have felt almost like collaborators—so much in fact that the title of his virtuoso essay on the 1962 Patterson–Liston fight, "Ten Thousand Words a Minute," seemed a metaphorical reference to his own creative pace. But the writing was scattered widely in kind and in place, so that when he assembled a collection in 1963 and called it *The Presidential Papers*, the thing most people saw was just a kind of brilliant fragmentation.

Mailer in fact had woven the pieces into a mosaic of communication with President Kennedy (whose assassination that autumn cast the book into a critical limbo anyway), and the collection certainly had its unity, but what it really demonstrated was the startling, perhaps even dismaying fact that Mailer was capable of a much greater variety of things than anyone had heretofore realized. A Platonic dialogue, no less—"The Metaphysics of the Belly"—envisioned the relationship between the creative individual and the food he eats in such a way as positively to foreshadow the whole organic food movement, but most centrally he showed a really dazzling command of the cultural essay. "Superman Comes to the Supermarket," the first of what turned out to be a series of treatments of American political conventions, and the "Ten Thousand Words a Minute" fight essay reveal a prose style which Mailer simply hadn't commanded up to this point, and which was surely possessed by none of his contemporaries. They reveal, further, an ability to follow a focal event as it reverberates on out to the farthest edges of cultural implication with an all but seismographic sense of institutional tremor. Critical though it was as a genetic source for ideas and frames of reference, "The White Negro" is not to be compared with this later material. Some of the shorter work, like "The Big Bite" essay on the Cuban missile crisis, reaches so surely and so successfully for lyric intensity that abruptly one is reminded that Mailer discovered this power only after having passed through his much lamented foray into writing verse. The book contains only a fragment of fiction, however, and it was after all fiction which the literary community had been promised. No one wanted further disseminating lines of force from the Dynamo of the Mailer imagination; all demanded the pure unity of the Virgin novel, and most commentators felt that by creating the brilliance of *The Presidential Papers* Mailer had failed yet again.

In the December 1963 issue of *Esquire*, Mailer published a story in the form of a screen "treatment" called "The Last Night." The story, reprinted in this collection, depicted the collapse of the world order in a welter of pollution and infectious decay, the attempts of a desperately united humanity to discover some base for regeneration within our solar system, the failure of those attempts, and a final world decision. We would launch a spaceship manned by an expedition of a few hundred elected members, and when it had penetrated far enough out into the solar system we would detonate from the ship a core of hydrogen explosive planted at the center of the earth. The explosion of the planet would affect the spaceship as a breaking wave accelerates a surfboard rider, hurling it out of the polluted solar system in which it would otherwise have been helplessly locked, and into "the oceans of mystery, and the dark beyond." It is a stunning story and, reprinted as the concluding piece in Mailer's next collection of shorter writings, *Cannibals and Christians*, it gave that volume perhaps even greater authority than *The Presidential Papers* to claim that Mailer was continuing to multiply his creative powers at an amazing rate. But the central image of the story—the image of explosive escape from circumscribing dimensions—is strangely and hauntingly evocative with respect to Mailer's own literary situation. One recalled the imagery of explosion with which he presented the plan for his big novel in *Advertisements* and the indeed explosive character of much of his celebrated public life, and there was certainly something explosive about the way he returned to the novel. In the same issue of *Esquire* that carried "The Last Night," Mailer announced that starting with the next issue he would begin serializing a new novel. It was not to be the big book announced in *Advertisements*, that work was to be "put aside again," but would be new and would be composed as the serialization went forward. Mailer had created a set of circumstances which would build up to blast him out into the galaxy of the novel, and his audience could judge for themselves how close he was to his long-sought goal.

An American Dream came out as Mailer had promised, in eight consecutive installments, and it divided the critics almost evenly. Those who were certain the book proved that Mailer was merely inept as a novelist quarreled publicly with critics who argued that Mailer had created a whole new sense of novelistic proportion, that in fact the sequence of episodes made clear at last the meaning of what Mailer had so often referred to as existential moments. The novel's hero, Stephen Rojack, murders his wife in the first chapter and goes on to experience a series of consequences which to some critics demonstrated that Mailer had neither a sense of common moral decency nor an insight into the psychological situation which would be created in a man who had committed such an act. The same evidence convinced others that while Mailer might not have mastered the whole problem, he had gone far toward creating a fictional reality in which individual situations, moods, and even moments in time existed independently of and in complete separation from the situations, moods, and moments which came before and after them. But the basic quarrel, after all, was not about whether Mailer had finally managed to match the greatness of his imagination with a proportionately great single novel—not even he thought he had done that—it was really the same old quarrel about whether he had given significant promise of one day achieving that long patrol. The novel was officially published in 1965; the next year came *Cannibals and Christians* and its further pyrotechnical display of multiple talents; and then appeared the most recent work of fiction to date—in 1967 Mailer published a novella called *Why Are We in Vietnam?*

The very fact that the book was a novella, of course, argued against it as a major novelistic effort, but it was still true that more than a few Mailer watchers ranked it among the best of his best work. It was completely fresh, gusty as the wind blowing in from a brand-new fictional talent. The comic style resembled nothing that he had ever tried before; he manipulated a drama between the world of nature and the world of society which seemed deep as Faulkner, tight as Hemingway; and the hero was an adolescent— an age Mailer had never before been very successful in handling. Fine as it was, though, the book was really almost a prologue, and indeed we heard the rumor that Mailer had originally conceived a much larger book, a book dramatizing the way a band of adolescents had laid siege to a small American town, but in the end we heard that he had decided to settle for the prologue. In a poem called "The Executioner's Song" he wrote "You see: I am bad at endings," and if his admirers were not ready simply to agree, it did seem fair to say that he was no supplier of the kind of endings which we were conventionally led—partially by Mailer himself—to anticipate. As if to document the complexity of this fact, the next year he produced two full-length books which no one could have expected: *The Armies of the Night* and *Miami and the Siege of Chicago*.

It is not to minimize the extraordinary accomplishment of *Armies* to suggest that part of the reason the critical community greeted it with such a cry of acclaim was that it caught everybody flat-footed. It resists generic classification in the same way and for the same reason as *The Education of Henry Adams*, but its subtitle gives a clue to its design: "History as a Novel/The Novel as History." The book is an account of Mailer's experiences when he participated in the October 1967 anti-Vietnam march on the Pentagon. Book One, which constitutes at least the first two-thirds of the volume, views the historical event of the march as a novelist would see it: through the focus of a protagonist who in this case happens to be a comic figure named Norman Mailer. The last one-third of the book is a consideration of the historical event itself, maximally wide focus now, but with the overall intent of producing, as a novelist would produce (or as Henry Adams would) a metaphor whose analysis would cut through to the source of historical causality. It was not the Dynamo and the Virgin, but was in fact the metaphor of a woman with child: "She is America, once a beauty of magnificence unparalleled, now a beauty with a leprous skin." With more the voice of a prophet than either novelist or historian he extends it: Will her child be "the most fearsome totalitarianism the world has ever known? or can she, poor giant, tormented lovely girl, deliver a babe of a new world brave and tender, artful and wild?" There was nothing unfinished about this strange new book, but it seemed a beginning nevertheless, the beginning of a new or virtually new genre, and in honor of the achievement Mailer was given both the National Book Award and the Pulitzer Prize.

Miami and Chicago was also nominated for the National Book Award, and if it was not altogether as realized an effort as *Armies*, it helped make clear that Mailer had all along in his non-fiction, whatever his situation as a novelist, been moving toward a new form. In his earlier essays analyzing the political conventions of 1960 and 1964, it could now in retrospect be seen, he had been trying to use the theater of the political convention as a microcosm of cultural dialectics, but it was not until 1968 that he was able to obtain a large enough control of the sociology of the event and a narrative focus — the converting of "himself" into a third-person participant — to move his treatment beyond the stage of the essay form. This of course was true also of his handling of the Pentagon march in *Armies;* the earlier cultural essays of the sixties had been a preparation for him, getting him ready to handle an event like the march, or, for that matter, an event like the flight of a rocket to the moon.

The arrival of *Armies* and *Miami*, both so enthusiastically received, brought the assayers of the Mailer mission to a curious pause. Elsewhere he had spoken of himself as a sort of prospector, whose work added up to "various drillings, diggings, tests and explosions on the way to finding a certain giant mine, well-advertised over the years." Had he found the mine at this point, and was it to be not the novel after all but this new hybrid form, combining history, autobiograpy, and fiction? A case could certainly be made that he had. Even his old enemy *Time* magazine buried the hatchet, terminating seventeen years of steady vilification by welcoming him as a writer who had found his future at last, and Mailer himself gave the notion credence by staying with the new form in his next book.

Of a Fire on the Moon centers around the Apollo 11 moonshot in July, 1969, and is an attempt to open up a method of analyzing the cultural relationship between the creators of our technology and the creators of our art. Combining techniques from the cultural essay, history, autobiography and fiction once again, Mailer presents himself as "Aquarius," the questing artist in search of the origins from which American technology springs. Carried all the way, perhaps such an inquiry would produce the book of the century, doing for the space age what *Das Kapital* did for the industrial age, and though Mailer's book is hardly so ambitious—it is more like a foray in the direction that, should he arise among us, the new Marx would take—many critics felt that it was an exciting effort and received it most respectfully. In the midst of the respect, however, an extremely interesting and for Mailer a quite new critical note was struck. Richard Poirier, one of the most attentive of Mailer's readers, sounded it in *The New Republic:* Mailer was starting to repeat himself, Poirier said, and rather testily the critic called for something new, a fresh approach now, as he put it, "that Mailer's standard routines have become obsolete." Obsolete? After twenty years of searching Mailer comes up with a full-length form which might even serve as an alternative to the novel. Working the changes on it in *Armies* and *Miami*, he then focuses on what is to the artist probably the most unavailable territory in the whole culture, the territory of technology, moves over a spectrum of inquiry that ranges from the psychology of machines to the psychology of Provincetown poets, in this way produces his second major effort in the form, and the result is that one of his most intelligent and instinctively accurate critics responds that it is all very well but he had better get out of the rut. It is perhaps necessary to remind ourselves that this is the one thing that even Mailer's most hostile critics have never accused him of—on the contrary, most of his detractors have endlessly complained that he never settles down long enough to complete anything, let alone repeat himself—and the implications of such a response are provocative indeed.

A redefinition of the concept of the long patrol is implicit in the suggestion that Mailer is becoming too set in his ways. So far we, like most of Mailer's critics, have treated the concept as the metaphorical equivalant of Kafka's castle, a place where plenty dwells and fevers of search cool into the satisfactions of creation. In its literal, grammatical meaning, however, the long patrol is neither a place nor an objective but a process, an ongoing activity, and it is the virtue of Poirier's essay that it reminds us of this fact. The excellence of *Of a Fire on the Moon* is not really the issue — it is a fine piece of work, probably the only book of its kind ever written by a serious artist — what we are really drawn to at this point is a consideration of the pace of Mailer's overall career. Our first concern, we note, is not to examine it for signs of having come to some long-sought conclusion; on the contrary, it is suddenly clear that for all of our surface acceptance of the notion of movement toward a goal, it was the movement itself that had mattered to us. All of those false starts, colorful abortions, the innovations and schemes to breach the castle walls — all of this is precisely the substance of Mailer's artistic accomplishment. The notion that he was trying to get to some specific place, and if he got there he would be good and if he failed he would be bad, now seems about as real as a plot-summary of, say, *The Deer Park*, would be really an account of the book's power. What is now clear for us all to see is that Mailer's bursting effort to get to his long patrol has itself *been* the patrol, as it will continue to be, and he has been there all along.

IV

Mailer's original statement in the epigraph concerning the goal he had set for himself in *The Naked and the Dead* was of course consciously ironic, and he was quite aware of the fact that the writing he did in the novel in preparation for getting to his patrol was itself the very substance of his creative achievement. The basic misconception had been in his conscious intention to "write a short novel about a long patrol." Presumably it is less likely that he was always so conscious of the real nature of his ongoing achievement as he fought to get to his goal of "the big novel" over these years, but if in retrospect it is now clear how great an accomplishment it has been, one has still to consider the fact that Mailer's career is not over. "Not over," indeed, would be regarded by many Mailer readers as an almost insulting understatement, for the magic of his achievement so far is precisely that it seems always to promise a still greater stage to come. There is no reason to infer, however, that "the big novel," or the art of fiction generally, is merely the mechanical rabbit, hare to the hounds of his imagination, always and by the nature of things beyond him. In 1959 he said that he aspired to write a novel so fine that it would be admired by Dostoyevsky, Marx, Joyce, Freud, Stendhal, Tolstoy, Proust, Spengler, Faulkner "and even old moldering Hemingway," because it would have carried what they had to tell another part of the way forward. In 1971 we can say that while he has not written a single work that could make such claims, he has accumulated a body of work which can be taken to have an overall unity — Mailer himself has often remarked on this unity — and which so considered is fine enough to be called an actual realization of Mailer's soaring aspiration. But unlike the gods listed in his pantheon he has still not been acknowledged to be the master of a particular form, and unlike them also, of course, he is not dead. A huge novel, vast as his imagination is demonstrably vast, or even a shelf of huge novels, is not an unthinkable eventuality, or maybe there will be some new form still unimagined. But if it comes out that way, splendid though such a thing would be, perhaps one may conclude this introduction by reflecting on a paradox: if Mailer wins it all, we his loyal audience will have one thing taken away from us, for he then would join his pantheon for fair; have his picture, no doubt in an oval frame, on the walls of public school classrooms, and be thought of by the students in those classrooms as an object of the taxidermist's art. As we have him today, still in the pantheon's limbo, it is very different, for he is so far from being a god as to be in fact one of us, an admirer of the gods and their achievements, but with certain deep-felt reservations.

After all it is the case that what Mailer has always given his readers is the connection of closeness, of shared sympathy between at least would-be outlaws — "and I suspect that what has been true for me has been true for a great many of you," he said in *Advertisements*, angry and a comrade. The man who said that is our Mailer, and he is very far from being any god. Quite the opposite. No god himself, he stole their thunder; impudent Prometheus, he took their fire; and then he brought it all back for us and put on that sacrilegious display that made the worst of the best commentators worry about what the literary world was coming to — and he has been loved for that.

If Mailer finally comes up with the seat of Zola and the mind of Joyce and all those other ingredients which would make the biggest magic work at last and produces the greatest thing in the world, then they will certainly take him from us — the mandarin critics who have despised and ridiculed and demeaned him, and through him us, for all these years. They will claim that all along they saw the greatness too — or, worse, they will claim that his miserable admirers had liked him for the wrong reasons, and that his attackers had been right in their sneering because through it they forced him out onto the high road and into the company of the gods. Probably it doesn't matter, and it may even be that the new reader of Mailer (who it will be remembered is supposed to be the recipient of this introduction) thinks that Mailer is in the pantheon already, that he is one of those Great Writers, and that all this passionate talk about "them" and "us" and pantheons and mandarins is crazy. And it probably is. But it may be proper to say in closing that while Mailer's new reader has what old readers can't have—the blast of new discovery and all joys attendant—he still can't have everything. He can't have our pride in having always known.

ROBERT F. LUCID

March, 1971

THE NAKED
AND THE DEAD

The novel was published in 1948 by Rinehart and Company and became an immediate best seller. It remains available in the hardback edition, in Modern Library, and in the New American Library's Signet paperback edition. The excerpt here does not involve "the long patrol" mentioned in the epigraph, and, in fact, focuses on only one of the book's three central figures. In the novel, General Cummings, who is the commanding officer of the American forces in the invasion, and Lieutenant Hearn, a young, middle-class outsider, and Sergeant Croft, a career soldier, are the three central figures. Here we see Croft taking ashore his platoon in the invasion, and later taking them into combat. Of the three focal characters, Croft is perhaps the one who foreshadows most clearly the direction which Mailer's later work will take, for, in fact, the sergeant is a psychopath.

Part I, Chapter 2

At 0400, a few minutes after the false dawn had lapsed, the naval bombardment of Anopopei began. All the guns of the invasion fleet went off within two seconds of each other, and the night rocked and shuddered like a great log foundering in the surf. The ships snapped and rolled from the discharge, lashing the water furiously. For one instant the night was jagged and immense, demoniac in its convulsion.

Then, after the first salvos, the firing became irregular, and the storm almost subsided into darkness again. The great clanging noises of the guns became isolated once more, sounded like immense freight trains jerking and tugging up a grade. And afterward it was possible to hear the sighing wistful murmur of shells passing overhead. On Anopopei the few scattered campfires were snubbed out.

The first shells landed in the sea, throwing up remote playful spurts of water, but then a string of them snapped along the beach, and Anopopei came to life and glowed like an ember. Here and there little fires started where the jungle met the beach, and occasionally a shell which carried too far would light up a few hundred feet of brush. The line of beach became defined and twinkled like a seaport seen from a great distance late at night.

An ammunition dump began to burn, spreading a rose-colored flush over a portion of the beach. When several shells landed in its midst, the flames sprouted fantastically high, and soared away in angry brown clouds of smoke. The shells continued to raze the beach and then began to shift inland. The firing had eased already into a steady, almost casual, pattern. A few ships at a time would discharge their volleys and then turn out to sea again while a new file attacked. The ammo dump still blazed, but most of the fires on the beach had smoldered down, and in the light which came with the first lifting of the dawn there was not nearly enough scud to hide the shore. About a mile inland, something had caught fire on the summit of a hill, and back of it, far away, Mount Anaka rose out of a base of maroon-colored smoke. Implacably, despite the new purple robes at its feet, the mountain sat on the island, and gazed out to sea. The bombardment was insignificant before it.

In the troop holds, the sounds were duller and more persistent; they grated and rumbled like a subway train. The hold electric lights, a wan yellow, had been turned on after breakfast, and they flickered dully, throwing many shadows over the hatches and through the tiers of bunks, lighting up the faces of the men assembled in the aisles and clustered around the ladder leading up to the top deck.

Martinez listened to the noises anxiously. He would not have been surprised if the hatch on which he was sitting had slid away from under him. He blinked his bloodshot eyes against the weary glare of the bulbs, tried to numb himself to everything. But his legs would twitch unconsciously every time a louder rumble beat against the steel bulkheads. For no apparent reason he kept repeating to himself the last line from an old joke, "I don't care if I do die, do die, do dy." Sitting there, his skin looked brown under the jaundiced light. He was a small, slim and handsome Mexican with neat wavy hair, small sharp features. His body, even now, had the poise and grace of a deer. No matter how quickly he might move the motion was always continuous and effortless. And like a deer his head was never quite still, his brown liquid eyes never completely at rest.

Above the steady droning of the guns, Martinez could hear voices separating for an instant and then being lost again. Separate babels of sound came from each platoon; the voice of a platoon leader would buzz against his ear like a passing insect, undefined and rather annoying. "Now, I don't want any of you to get lost when we hit the beach. Stick together, that's very important." He drew his knees up tighter, rolled back farther on his haunches until his hipbones grated against the tight flesh of his buttocks.

The men in recon looked small and lost in comparison to the other platoons. Croft was talking now about the landing craft embarkation, and Martinez listened dully, his attention wavering. "All right," Croft said softly, "it's gonna be the same as the last time we practiced it. They ain't a reason why anything should go wrong, and it ain't goin' to."

Red guffawed scornfully. "Yeah, we'll all be up there," he said, "but sure as hell, some dumb sonofabitch is going to run up, and tell us to get back in the hold again."

"You think I'll piss if we have to stay here for the rest of the war?" Sergeant Brown said.

"Let's cut it out," Croft told them. "If you know what's going on better than I do, _you_ can stand up here and talk." He frowned and then continued. "We're on boat-deck-station twenty-eight. You all know where it is, but we're goin' up together just the same. If they's a man here suddenly discovers he's left anythin' behind, that'll be just t.s. We ain't gonna come back."

"Yeah, boys, don't forget to take your rubbers," Red suggested, and that drew a laugh. Croft looked angry for a second, but then he drawled, "I know Wilson ain't gonna forget his," and they laughed again. "You're fuggin ay," Gallagher snorted.

Wilson giggled infectiously. "Ah tell ya," he said, "Ah'd sooner leave my M-one behind, 'cause if they was to be a piece of pussy settin' up on that beach, and Ah didn't have a rubber, Ah'd just shoot myself anyway."

Martinez grinned, but their laughter irritated him. "What's the matter, Japbait?" Croft asked quietly. Their eyes met with the intimate look of old friends. "Aaah, goddam stomach, she's no good," Martinez said. He spoke clearly, but in a low and hesitant voice as if he were translating from Spanish as he went along. Croft looked again at him, and then continued talking.

Martinez gazed about the hold. The aisles between the bunks were wide and unfamiliar now that the hammocks were lashed up, and it made him vaguely uneasy. He thought they looked like the stalls, in the big library in San Antonio and he remembered there was something unpleasant about it, some girl had spoken to him harshly. "I don't care if I do die, do die," went through his head. He shook himself. There was something terrible going to happen to him today. God always let you know things out of His goodness, and you had to . . . to watch out, to look out for yourself. He said the last part to himself in English.

The girl was a librarian and she had thought he was trying to steal a book. He was very little then, and he had got scared and answered in Spanish, and she had scolded him. Martinez's leg twitched. She had made him cry, he could remember that. Goddam girl. Today, he could screw with her. The idea fed him with a pleasurable malice. Little-tit librarian, he would spit on her now. But the library stalls were still a troop hold, and his fear returned.

A whistle blew, startling him. "Men for boat-deck fifteen," a voice shouted down, and one of the platoons started going up the ladder. Martinez could feel the tension in everyone around him, the way their voices had become quiet. Why could they not go first? he asked himself, hating the added tension which would come from waiting. Something was going to happen to him. He knew that now.

After an hour their signal came, and they jogged up the ladder, and stood milling outside the hatchway for almost a minute before they were told to move to their boat. The decks were very slippery in the dawn, and they stumbled and cursed as they plodded along the deck. When they reached the davits which held their landing boat, they drew up in a rough file and began waiting again. Red shivered in the cold morning air. It was not yet six A.M., and the day had already the depressing quality which early mornings always had in the Army. It meant they were moving, it meant something new, something unpleasant.

All over the ship the debarkation activities were in different stages. A few landing craft were down in the water already, filled with troops and circling around the ship like puppies on a leash. The men in them waved at the ship, the flesh color of their faces unreal against the gray paint of the landing craft, the dawn blue of the sea. The calm water looked like oil. Nearer the platoon, some men were boarding a landing craft, and another one, just loaded, was beginning its descent into the water, the davit pulleys creaking from time to time. But over most of the ship men were still waiting like themselves.

Red's shoulders were beginning to numb under the weight of his full pack, and his rifle muzzle kept clanging against his helmet. He was feeling irritable. "No matter how many times you wear a goddam pack, you never get used to it," he said.

"Have you got it adjusted right?" Hennessey asked. His voice was stiff and quivered a little.

"Fug the adjustments," Red said. "It just makes me ache some-where else. I ain't built for a pack, I got too many bones." He kept on talking, glancing at Hennessey every now and then to see whether he was less nervous. The air was chill, and the sun at his left was still low and quiet without any heat. He stamped his feet, breathing the curious odor of a ship's deck, oil and tar and the fish smell of the water.

"When do we get into the boats?" Hennessey asked.

The shelling was still going on over the beach, and the island looked pale green in the dawn. A thin wispy line of smoke trailed along the shore.

Red laughed. "What! Do ya think this is gonna be any different today? I figure we'll be on deck all morning." But as he spoke, he noticed a group of landing craft circling about a mile from them in the water. "The first wave's still farting around," he reassured Hennessey. For an instant he thought again of the Motome inva-sion, and felt a trace of that panic catching him again. His fingertips still remembered the texture of the sides of the rubber boat as he had clung to it in the water. At the back of his throat he tasted salt water again, felt the dumb whimpering terror of ducking underwa-ter when he was exhausted and the Jap guns would not stop. He looked out again, his shaggy face quite bleak for a moment.

In the distance the jungle near the beach had assumed the naked broken look which a shelling always gave it. The palm trees would be standing like pillars now, stripped of their leaves, and blackened if there had been a fire. Off the horizon Mount Anaka was almost invisible in the haze, a pale gray-blue color almost a compromise between the hues of the water and the sky. As he watched, a big shell landed on the shore and threw up a larger puff of smoke than the two or three that had preceded it. This was going to be an easy landing, Red told himself, but he was still thinking about the rub-ber boats. "I wish to hell they'd save some of that country for us," he said to Hennessey. "We're gonna have to live there." The morning had a raw expectant quality about it, and he drew a breath, and squatted on his heels.

Gallagher began to curse. "How fuggin long we got to wait up here?"

"Hold your water," Croft told him. "Half the commo platoon is coming with us, and they ain't even up yet."

"Well, why ain't they?" Gallagher asked. He pushed his helmet farther back on his head. "It's just like the bastards to have us wait up on deck where we can have our fuggin heads blown off."

"You hear any Jap artillery?" Croft asked.

"That don't mean they ain't got any," Gallagher said. He lit a cigarette and smoked moodily, his hand cupped over the butt as though he expected it to be snatched away from him any moment.

A shell sighed overhead, and unconsciously Martinez drew back against a gunhousing. He felt naked.

The davit machinery was complicated, and a portion of it hung over the water. When a man was harnessed into a pack and web belt and carried a rifle and two bandoliers and several grenades, a bayonet and a helmet, he felt as if he had a tourniquet over both shoulders and across his chest. It was hard to breathe and his limbs kept falling asleep. Climbing along the beam which led out to the landing craft became an adventure not unlike walking a tightrope while wearing a suit of armor.

When recon was given the signal to get into its landing boat, Sergeant Brown wet his mouth nervously. "They could've designed these better," he grumbled to Stanley as they inched out along the beam. The trick was not to look at the water. "You know, Gallagher ain't a bad guy, but he's a sorehead," Stanley was confiding.

"Yeah," Brown said abstractedly. He was thinking it would be a hell of a note if he, a noncom, were to fall in the water. My God, you'd sink, he realized. "I always hate this part," he said aloud.

He reached the lip of the landing craft, and jumped into it, the weight of his pack almost spilling him, jarring his ankle. Everyone was suddenly very merry in the little boat which was swaying gently under the davits. "Here comes old Red," Wilson yelled, and everybody laughed as Red worked gingerly along the beam, his face puckered like a prune. When he reached the side he looked over scornfully at them and said, "Goddam, got the wrong boat. They ain't no one stupid-looking enough here to be recon."

"C'mon in, y'old billygoat," Wilson chuckled, his laughter easy and phlegmy, "the water's nice and cold."

Red grinned. "I know one place on you that ain't cold. Right now it's red-hot."

Brown found himself laughing and laughing. What a bunch of good old boys there were in the platoon, he told himself. It seemed as if the worst part were over already.

"How's the General get into these boats?" Hennessey asked. "He ain't young like us."

Brown giggled. "They got two privates to carry him over." He basked in the laughter which greeted this.

Gallagher dropped into the boat. "The fuggin Army," he said, "I bet they get more fuggin casualties out of guys getting into boats." Brown roared. Gallagher probably looked mad even when he was screwing his wife. For an instant he was tempted to say so, and it made him laugh even more. In the middle of his snickering he had a sudden image of his own wife in bed with another man at this exact moment, and there was a long empty second in his laughter when he felt nothing at all. "Hey, Gallagher," he said furiously, "I bet you even look pissed-off when you're with your wife."

Gallagher looked sullen, and then unexpectedly began to laugh too. "Aaah, fug you," he said, and that made everyone roar even more.

The little assault craft with their blunt bows looked like hippopotami as they bulled and snorted through the water. They were perhaps forty feet long, ten feet wide, shaped like open shoe boxes with a motor at the rear. In the troop well, the waves made a loud jarring sound beating against the bow ramp, and already an inch or two of water had squeezed through the crevices and was sloshing around the bottom. Red gave up the effort to keep his feet dry. Their boat had been circling for over an hour and he was getting dizzy. Occasionally a cold fan of spray would drop on them, shocking and abrupt and a trifle painful.

The first wave of soldiers had landed about fifteen minutes ago, and the battle taking place on the beach crackled faintly in the distance like a bonfire. It seemed remote and insignificant. To relieve the monotony Red would peer over the side wall and scan the shore. It still looked untenanted from three miles out but the ornament of battle was there—a thin foggy smoke drifted along the water. Occasionally a flight of three dive bombers would buzz overhead and lance toward shore, the sound of their motors filtering back in a subdued gentle rumble. When they dove on the beach it was difficult to follow them, for they were almost invisible, appearing as flecks of pure brilliant sunlight. The puff their bombs threw up looked small and harmless and the planes would be almost out of sight when the noise of the explosions came back over the water.

Red tried to ease the weight of his pack by compressing it against the bulkhead of the boat. The constant circling was annoying. As he looked at the thirty men squeezed in with him, and saw how unnaturally green their uniforms looked against the blue-gray of the troop well, he had to breathe deeply a few times and sit motionless. Sweat was breaking out along his back.

"How long is this gonna take?" Gallagher wanted to know. "The goddam Army, hurry up and wait, hurry up and wait."

Red had started to light a cigarette, his fifth since their boat had been lowered into the water, and it tasted flat and unpleasant. "What do you think?" Red asked. "I bet we don't go in till ten." Gallagher swore. It was not yet eight o'clock.

"Listen," Red went on, "if they really knew how to work these kind of things, we woulda been eating breakfast now, and we woulda got into these crates about two hours from now." He rubbed off the tiny ash which had formed on his cigarette. "But, naw, some sono-fabitchin' looey, who's sleeping right now, wanted us to get off the goddam ship so he could stop worrying about us." Purposely, he spoke loud enough for the Lieutenant from the communications platoon to hear him and grinned as the officer turned his back.

Corporal Toglio, who was squatting next to Gallagher, looked at Red. "We're a lot safer out in the water," Toglio explained eagerly. "This is a pretty small target compared to a ship, and when we're moving like this it's a lot harder to hit us than you think."

Red grunted. "Balls."

"Listen," Brown said, "they ain't a time when I wouldn't rather be on that ship. I think it's a hell of a lot safer."

"I looked into this," Toglio protested. "The statistics prove you're a lot safer here than any other place during an invasion."

Red hated statistics. "Don't give me any of those figures," he told Corporal Toglio. "If you listen to them you give up taking a bath 'cause it's too dangerous."

"No, I'm serious," Toglio said. He was a heavy-set Italian of about middle height with a pear-shaped head which was broader in the jaw than the temple. Although he had shaved the night before, his beard darkened all of his face under his eyes except for his mouth, which was wide and friendly. "I'm serious," he insisted, "I saw the statistics."

"You know what you can do with them," Red said.

Toglio smiled, but he was a little annoyed. Red was a pretty good guy, he was thinking, but too independent. Where would you be if everybody was like him? You'd get nowhere. It took co-operation in everything. Something like this invasion was planned, it was efficient, down to a timetable. You couldn't run trains if the engineer took off when he felt like it.

The idea impressed him, and he pointed one of his thick powerful fingers to tell Red when suddenly a Jap shell, the first in half an hour, threw up a column of water a few hundred yards from them. The sound was unexpectedly loud, and they all winced for a moment. In the complete silence that followed, Red yelled loud enough for the whole boat to hear, "Hey, Toglio, if I had to depend on you for my safety, I'd a been in hell a year ago." The laughter was loud enough to embarrass Toglio, who forced himself to grin. Wilson capped it by saying in his high soft voice, "Toglio, you can figger out more ways to make a man do something, and then it turns out all screwed up anyway. Ah never saw a man who was so particular over nothin'."

That wasn't true, Toglio said to himself. He liked to get things done right, and these fellows just didn't seem to appreciate it. Somebody like Red was always ruining your work by making everybody laugh.

The assault boat's motors grew louder suddenly, began to roar, and after completing a circle, the boat headed in toward shore. Immediately the waves began to pound against the forward ramp, and a long cascade of spray poured over the troops. There was a surprised groan and then a silence settled over the men. Croft unslung his rifle and held one finger over the muzzle to prevent any water from getting into the barrel. For an instant he felt as though he were riding a horse at a gallop. "Goddam, we're going in," someone said.

"I hope it's cleaned up at least," Brown muttered.

Croft felt superior and dejected. He had been disappointed when he had learned weeks before that recon was to be assigned to the beach detail for the first week. And he had felt a silent contempt when the men in the platoon had shown their pleasure in the news. "Chickenshit," he muttered to himself now. A man who was afraid to put his neck out on the line was no damn good. Leading the men was a responsibility he craved; he felt powerful and certain at such moments. He longed to be in the battle that was taking place inland from the beach, and he resented the decision which left the platoon on an unloading detail. He passed his hand along his gaunt hard cheek and looked silently about him.

Hennessey was standing near the stern. As Croft watched his white silent face, he decided that Hennessey was frightened and it amused him. The boy found it hard to be still; he kept bobbing about in his place, and once or twice he flinched noticeably at a sudden noise; his leg began to itch and he scratched it violently. Then, as Croft watched, Hennessey pulled his left trouser out of his legging, rolled it up to expose his knee, and with a great deal of care rubbed a little spittle over the irritated red spot on his knee. Croft gazed at the white flesh with its blond hairs, noticed the pains with which Hennessey replaced his trouser in the legging, and felt an odd excitement as if the motions were important. That boy is too careful, Croft told himself.

And then with a passionate certainty he thought, "Hennessey's going to get killed today." He felt like laughing to release the ferment in him. This time he was sure.

But, abruptly, Croft remembered the poker game the preceding night when he had failed to draw his full house, and he was confused and then disgusted. You figure you're getting a little too smart for yourself, he thought. His disgust came because he felt he could not trust such emotions, rather than from any conviction that they had no meaning at all. He shook his head and sat back on his haunches, feeling the assault boat race in toward land, his mind empty, waiting for what events would bring.

Martinez had his worst minute just before they landed. All the agonies of the previous night, all the fears he had experienced early that morning had reached their climax in him. He dreaded the moment when the ramp would go down and he would have to get out of the boat. He felt as if a shell would swallow all of them, or a machine gun would be set up before the bow, would begin firing the moment they were exposed. None of the men was talking, and when Martinez closed his eyes, the sound of the water lashing past their craft seemed overwhelming as though he were sinking beneath it. He opened his eyes, pressed his nails desperately into his palms. "Buenos Dios," he muttered. The sweat was dripping from his brow into his eyes, and he wiped it out roughly. Why no sounds? he asked himself. And indeed there were none. The men were silent, and a hush had come over the beach; the lone machine gun rapping in the distance sounded hollow and unreal.

A plane suddenly wailed past them, then roared over the jungle firing its guns. Martinez almost screamed at the noise. He felt his legs twitching again. Why didn't they land? By now he was almost ready to welcome the disaster that would meet him when the ramp went down.

In a high piping voice, Hennessey asked, "Do you think we'll be getting mail soon?" and his question was lost in a sudden roar of laughter. Martinez laughed and laughed, subsided into weak giggles, and then began laughing again.

"That fuggin Hennessey," he heard Gallagher say.

Suddenly Martinez realized that the boat had ground to a stop. The sound of its motors had altered, had become louder and a little uncertain, as if the propeller were no longer biting the water. After a moment he understood that they had landed.

For several long seconds, they remained motionless. Then the ramp clanked down, and Martinez trudged dumbly into the surf, almost stumbling when a knee-high wave broke behind him. He walked with his head down, looking at the water, and it was only when he was on shore that he realized nothing had happened to him. He looked about. Five other craft had landed at the same time, and the men were stringing over the beach. He saw an officer coming toward him, heard him ask Croft, "What platoon is this?"

"Intelligence and reconnaissance, sir, we're on beach detail," and then the instructions to wait over by a grove of coconut trees near the beach. Martinez fell into line, and stumbled along behind Red, as the platoon walked heavily through the soft sand. He was feeling nothing at all except a conviction that his judgment had been delayed.

The platoon marched about two hundred yards and then halted at the coconut grove. It was hot already, and most of the men threw off their packs and sprawled in the sand. There had been men here before them. Units of the first wave had assembled nearby, for the flat caked sand was trodden by many feet, and there was the inevitable minor refuse of empty cigarette packs and a discarded ration or two. But now these men were inland, moving somewhere through the jungle, and there was hardly anyone in sight. They could see for a distance of about two hundred yards in either direction before the beach curved out of view, and it was all quiet, relatively empty. Around either bend there might be a great deal of activity, but they could not tell this. It was still too early for the supplies to be brought in, and all the troops that had landed with them had been quickly dispersed. Over a hundred yards away to their right, the Navy had set up a command post which consisted merely of an officer at a small folding desk, and a jeep parked in the defilade where the jungle met the beach. To their left, just around the bend an eighth of a mile away, the Task Force Headquarters was beginning to function. A few orderlies were digging foxholes for the General's staff, and two men were staggering down the beach in the opposite direction, unwinding an eighty-pound reel of telephone wire. A jeep motored by in the firm wet sand near the water's edge and disappeared beyond the Navy's CP. The landing boats which had beached near the colored pennants on the other side of Task Force Headquarters had backed off by now and were cruising out toward the invasion fleet. The water looked very blue and the ships seemed to quiver a little in the midmorning haze. Occasionally one of the destroyers would fire a volley or two, and half a minute later the men would hear the soft whisper of the shell as it arched overhead into the jungle. Once in a while a machine gun would start racketing in the jungle, and might be answered soon after with the shrill riveting sound of a Japanese light automatic.

Sergeant Brown looked at the coconut trees which were shorn at the top from the shelling. Farther down, another grove had remained untouched, and he shook his head. Plenty of men could have lived through that bombardment, he told himself. "This ain't such a bad shelling, compared to what they did to Motome," he said.

Red looked bitter. "Yeah, Motome." He turned over on his stomach in the sand, and lit a cigarette. "The beach stinks already," he announced.

"How can it stink?" Stanley asked. "It's too early."

"It just stinks," Red answered. He didn't like Stanley, and although he had exaggerated the faint brackish odor that came from the jungle, he was ready to defend his statement. He felt an old familiar depression seeping through him; he was bored and irritable, it was too early to eat, and he had smoked too many cigarettes. "There ain't any invasion going on," he said, "this is practice. Amphibious maneuvers." He spat bitterly.

Croft hooked his cartridge belt about his waist, and slung his rifle. "I'm going to hunt for S-four," he told Brown. "You keep the men here till I get back."

"They forgot us," Red said. "We might as well go to sleep."

"That's why I'm going to get them," Croft said.

Red groaned. "Aaah, why don't you let us sit on our butts for the day?"

"Listen, Valsen," Croft said, "you can cut all the pissin' from here on."

Red looked at him warily. "What's the matter?" he asked, "you want to win the war all by yourself?" They stared tensely at each other for a few seconds, and then Croft strode off.

"You're picking the wrong boy to mess with," Sergeant Brown told him.

Red spat again. "I won't take no crap from nobody." He could feel his heart beating quickly. There were a few bodies lying in the surf about a hundred yards from them, and as Red looked a soldier from Task Force Headquarters began dragging them out of the water. A plane patrolled overhead.

"It's pretty fuggin quiet," Gallagher said.

Toglio nodded. "I'm going to dig a hole." He unstrapped his entrenching tool, and Wilson snickered. "You just better save your energy, boy," he told him.

Toglio ignored him and started digging. "I'm going to make one too," Hennessey piped, and began to work about twenty yards from Toglio. For a few seconds the scraping of their shovels against the sand was the only sound.

Oscar Ridges sighed. "Shoot," he said, "Ah might as well make one too." He guffawed with embarrassment after he spoke, and bent over his pack. His laughter had been loud and braying.

Stanley imitated him. "Waa-a-aaah!"

Ridges looked up and said mildly, "Well, shoot, Ah just cain't help the way Ah laugh. It's good enough, Ah reckon." He guffawed again to show his good will, but the laughter was much more chastened this time. When there was no answer, he began to dig. He had a short powerful body which was shaped like a squat pillar, for it tapered at neither end. His face was round and dumpy with a long slack jaw that made his mouth gape. His eyes goggled placidly to increase the impression he gave of dull-wittedness and good temper. As he dug, his motions were aggravatingly slow; he dumped each shovelful in exactly the same place, and paused every time to look about before he bent down again. There was a certain wariness about him, as though he were accustomed to practical jokes, expected them to be played on him.

Stanley watched him impatiently. "Hey, Ridges," he said, looking at Sergeant Brown for approbation, "if you were sitting on a fire, I guess you'd be too lazy to piss and put it out."

Ridges smiled vaguely. "Reckon so," he said quietly, watching Stanley walk toward him, and stand over the hole to examine his progress. Stanley was a tall youth of average build with a long face which looked vain usually and scornful and a little uncertain. He would have been handsome if it had not been for his long nose and sparse black mustache. He was only nineteen.

"Christ, you'll be digging all day," Stanley said with disgust. His voice was artificially rough like that of an actor who fumbles for a conception of how soldiers talk.

Ridges made no answer. Patiently, he continued digging. Stanley watched him for another minute, trying to think of something clever to say. He was beginning to feel ridiculous just standing there, and on an impulse kicked some sand into Ridges's foxhole. Silently, Ridges shoveled it out, not breaking his rhythm. Stanley could feel the men in the platoon watching him. He was a little sorry he had started, for he wasn't certain whether the men sided with him. But he had gone too far to renege. He kicked in quite a bit of sand.

Ridges laid down his shovel and looked at him. His face was patient but there was some concern in it. "What you trying to do, Stanley?" he asked.

"You don't like it?" Stanley sneered.

"No, sir, Ah don't."

Stanley grinned slowly. "You know what you can do."

Red had been watching with anger. He liked Ridges. "Listen, Stanley," Red shouted, "wipe your nose and start acting like a man."

Stanley swung around and glared at Red. The whole thing had

gone wrong. He was afraid of Red, but he couldn't retreat.

"Red, you can blow it out," he said.

"Speaking of blowing it out," Red drawled, "will you tell me why you bother cultivating that weed under your nose when it grows wild in your ass-hole?" He spoke with a heavy sarcastic brogue which had the men laughing before he even finished. "Good ol' Red," Wilson chuckled.

Stanley flushed, took a step toward Red. "You ain't going to talk to me that way."

Red was angry, eager for a fight. He knew he could whip Stanley. There was something which he was not ready to face, and he let his anger ride over it. "Boy, I could break you in half," he warned Stanley.

Brown got to his feet. "Listen, Red," he interrupted, "you weren't spoiling that damn hard to have a fight with Croft."

Red paused, and was disgusted with himself. That was it. He stood there indecisively. "No, I wasn't," he said, "but there ain't any man I won't fight." He wondered if he had been afraid of Croft. "Aaah, fug it," he said, turning away.

But Stanley realized that Red would not fight, and he walked after him. "This ain't settled for me," he said.

Red looked at him. "Go blow, will ya."

To his amazement Stanley heard himself saying, "What's the matter, you going chickenshit?" He was positive he had said too much.

"Stanley," Red told him, "I could knock your head off, but I ain't gonna fight today." His anger was returning, and he tried to force it back. "Let's cut out this crap."

Stanley watched him, and then spat in the sand. He was tempted to say something more, but he knew the victory was with him. He sat down by Brown.

Wilson turned to Gallagher and shook his head. "Ah never thought old Red would back down," he murmured.

Ridges, seeing he was unmolested, went back to his digging. He was brooding a little over the incident, but the satisfying heft of the shovel in his hand soothed him. Just a little-bitty tool, he told himself. Pa would get a laugh out of seein' somethin' like that. He became lost in his work, feeling a comfortable familiarity in the labor. They ain't nothin' like work for bringin' a man round, he told himself. The hole was almost finished, and he began to tamp the bottom with his feet, setting them down heavily and evenly.

The men heard a vicious slapping sound like a fly-swatter being struck against a table. They looked around uneasily. "That's a Jap mortar," Brown muttered.

"He's very near," Martinez muttered. It was the first thing he had said since they had landed.

The men at Task Force Headquarters had dropped to the ground. Brown listened, heard an accelerating whine, and buried his face in the sand. The mortar shell exploded about a hundred and fifty yards away, and he lay motionless, listening to the clear terrifying sound of shrapnel cutting through the air, whipping the foliage in the jungle. Brown stifled a moan. The shell had landed a decent distance away, but . . . He was suffering an unreasonable panic. Whenever some combat started there was always a minute when he was completely unable to function, and did the first thing that occurred to him. Now, as the echo of the explosion damped itself in the air, he sprang excitedly to his feet. "Come on, let's get the hell out of here," he shouted.

"What about Croft?" Toglio asked.

Brown tried to think. He felt a desperate urgency to get away from this stretch of beach. An idea came to him, and he grasped it without deliberation. "Look, you got a hole, you stay here. We're gonna head down about half a mile, and when Croft comes back, you meet us there." He started gathering his equipment, dropped it suddenly, muttered, "Fug it, get it later," and began to jog down the beach. The other men looked at him in surprise, shrugged, and then Gallagher, Wilson, Red, Stanley and Martinez followed him, spread out in a long file. Hennessey watched them go, and looked over at Toglio and Ridges. He had dug his hole only a few yards away from the periphery of the coconut grove, and he tried to peer into the grove now, but it was too thick to be able to see for more than fifty feet. Toglio's foxhole on his left was about twenty yards away but it seemed much farther. Ridges, who was on the other side of Toglio, seemed a very great distance away. "What shall I do?" he whispered to Toglio. He wished he had gone with the others, but he had been afraid to ask for fear they would laugh at him. Toglio took a look around, and then crouching, ran over to Hennessey's hole. His broad dark face was sweating now. "I think it's a very serious situation," he said dramatically, and then looked into the jungle.

"What's up?" Hennessey asked. He felt a swelling in his throat which was impossible to define as pleasant or unpleasant.

"I think some Japs sneaked a mortar in near the beach, and maybe they're going to attack us." Toglio mopped his face. "I wish the fellows had dug holes here," he said.

"It was a dirty trick to run off," Hennessey said. He was surprised to hear his voice sound natural.

"I don't know," Toglio said, "Brown's got more experience than

I have. You got to trust your noncoms." He sifted some sand through his fingers. "I'm getting back in my hole. You just sit tight and wait. If any Japs come, we've got to stop them." Toglio's voice was portentous, and Hennessey nodded eagerly. This was like a movie, he thought. Vague images overlapped in his mind. He saw himself standing up and repelling a charge. "Okay, kid," Toglio said, and clapped him on the back. Crouching again, Toglio ran past his own hole to talk to Ridges. Hennessey remembered Red's telling him that Toglio had come to the platoon after the worst of the Motome campaign. He wondered if he could trust him.

Hennessey squatted in his hole and watched the jungle. His mouth was dry and he kept wetting his lips; every time there seemed to be a movement in the bushes, his heart constricted. The beach was very quiet. A minute went by, and he began to get bored. He could hear a truck grinding its gears down the beach, and when he took a chance and turned around, he could see another wave of landing craft coming in about a mile from shore. Reinforcements for us, he told himself, and realized it was absurd.

The harsh slapping sound came out of the jungle and was followed by another discharge and another and another. That's the mortars, he thought, and decided he was catching on fast. And then he heard a screaming piercing sound almost overhead like the tearing squeals of a car braking to avert a crash. Instinctively he curled flat in his hole. The next instants were lost to him. He heard an awful exploding sound which seemed to fill every corner of his mind, and the earth shook and quivered underneath him in the hole. Numbly he felt dirt flying over him, and his body being pounded by some blast. The explosion came again, and the dirt and the shock, and then another and another blast. He found himself sobbing in the hole, terrified and resentful. When another mortar landed, he screamed out like a child, "That's enough, *that's enough!*" He lay there trembling for almost a minute after the shells had stopped. His thighs felt hot and wet, and at first he thought, I'm wounded. It was pleasant and peaceful, and he had a misty picture of a hospital bed. He moved his hand back, and realized with both revulsion and mirth that he had emptied his bowels.

Hennessey froze his body. If I don't move, I won't get any dirtier, he thought. He remembered Red and Wilson talking about "keeping a tight ass-hole," and now he understood what they meant. He began to get the giggles. The sides of his foxhole were crumbling, and he had a momentary pang of anxiety at the thought that they would collapse in the next shelling. He was beginning to smell himself and he felt a little sick. Should he change his pants?

he wondered. There was only one other pair in his pack, and he might have to wear them for a month. If he threw these away, they might make him pay for them.

But no, that wasn't true, he told himself; you didn't have to pay for lost equipment overseas. He was beginning to get the giggles again. What a story this would make to tell Pop. He saw his father's face for a moment. A part of him was trying to needle his courage to look over the edge of his hole. He raised himself cautiously, as much from the fear of further soiling his pants as from an enemy he might see.

Toglio and Ridges were still beneath the surface of their slit-trenches. Hennessey began to suspect he had been left alone. "Toglio, Corporal Toglio," he called, but it came out in a hoarse croaking whisper. There was no answer; he didn't ask himself whether they had heard him. He was alone, all alone, he told himself, and he felt an awful dread at being so isolated. He wondered where the others were. He had never seen combat before, and it was unfair to leave him alone; Hennessey began to feel bitter at being deserted. The jungle looked dark and ominous like a sky blacking over with thunderclouds. Suddenly, he knew he couldn't stay here any longer. He got out of his hole, clutched his rifle, and started to crawl away from the hole.

"Hennessey, where you going?" Toglio shouted. His head had suddenly appeared from the hole.

Hennessey started, and then began to babble. "I'm going to get the others. It's important, I got my pants dirty." He began to laugh.

"Come back," Toglio shouted.

The boy looked at his foxhole, and knew it was impossible to return to it. The beach seemed so pure and open. "No, I got to go," he said, and began to run. He heard Toglio shout once more, and then he was conscious only of the sound of his breathing. Abruptly, he realized that something was sliding about in the pocket his pants made as they bellied over his leggings. In a little frenzy, he pulled his trousers loose, let the stool fall out, and then began to run again.

Hennessey passed by the place where the flags were up for the boats to come in, and saw the Navy officer lying prone in a little hollow near the jungle. Abruptly, he heard the mortars again, and then right after it a machine gun firing nearby. A couple of grenades exploded with the loud empty sound that paper bags make when they burst. He thought for an instant, "There's some soldiers after them Japs with the mortar." Then he heard the terrible siren of the mortar shell coming down on him. He pirouetted in a little circle, and threw himself to the ground. Perhaps he felt the explosion before a piece of shrapnel tore his brain in half.

Red found him when the platoon was coming back to meet Toglio. They had waited out the shelling in a long zigzag trench which had been dug by a company of reserve troops farther along the beach. After word had come that the Jap mortar crew had been wiped out, Brown decided to go back. Red didn't feel like talking to anybody, and unconsciously he assumed the lead. He came around a bend in the beach and saw Hennessey lying face down in the sand with a deep rent in his helmet and a small circle of blood about his head. One of his hands was turned palm upward, and his fingers clenched as though he were trying to hold something. Red felt sick. He had liked Hennessey, but it had been the kind of fondness he had for many of the men in the platoon—it included the possibility that it might be ended like this. What bothered Red was the memory of the night they had sat on deck during the air raid when Hennessey had inflated his life belt. It gave Red a moment of awe and panic as if someone, *something*, had been watching over their shoulder that night and laughing. There was a pattern where there shouldn't be one.

Brown came up behind him, and gazed at the body with a troubled look. "Should I have left him behind?" he asked. He tried not to consider whether he were responsible.

"Who takes care of the bodies?"

"Graves Registration."

"Well, I'm going to find them so they can carry him away," Red said.

Brown scowled. "We're supposed to stick together." He stopped, and then went on angrily. "Goddam, Red, you're acting awful chicken today, picking fights and then backing out of them, throwing a fit over . . ." He looked at Hennessey and didn't finish.

Red was walking on already. For the rest of this day, that was one part of the beach he was going to keep away from. He spat, trying to exorcise the image of Hennessey's helmet, and the blood that had still been flowing through the rent in the metal.

The platoon followed him, and when they reached the place where they had left Toglio, the men began digging holes in the sand. Toglio walked around nervously, repeating continually that he had yelled for Hennessey to come back. Martinez tried to reassure him. "Okay, nothing you can do," Martinez said several times. He was digging quickly and easily in the soft sand, feeling calm for the first time that day. His terror had withered with Hennessey's death. Nothing would happen now.

When Croft came back he made no comment on the news Brown gave him. Brown was relieved and decided he did not have to blame himself. He stopped thinking about it.

But Croft brooded over the event all day. Later, as they worked on the beach unloading supplies, he caught himself thinking of it many times. His reaction was similar to the one he had felt at the moment he discovered his wife was unfaithful. At that instant, before his rage and pain had begun to operate, he had felt only a numb throbbing excitement and the knowledge that his life was changed to some degree and certain things would never be the same. He knew that again now. Hennessey's death had opened to Croft vistas of such omnipotence that he was afraid to consider it directly. All day the fact hovered about his head, tantalizing him with odd dreams and portents of power.

Part II, [From] Chapter 5

The truck convoy ground sullenly through the mud. It was over an hour since recon had left its bivouac area, but it seemed much longer. There were twenty-five men packed inside the truck and, since there were seats for only twelve, over half the men sat on the floor in a tangle of rifles and packs and arms and legs. In the darkness everyone was sweating and the night seemed incomparably dense; the jungle on either side of the road exuded moisture continually.

No one had anything to say. When the men in the truck listened they could hear the front of the convoy grinding up a grade before them. Occasionally the truck to their rear would creep up close enough for the men to see its blackout lights like two tiny candles in a fog. A mist had settled over the jungle, and in the darkness the men felt disembodied.

Wyman was sitting on his pack, and when he closed his eyes and let the rumble of the truck shake through him he felt as if he were in a subway. The tension and excitement he had felt when Croft had come up and told them to pack their gear because they were moving forward had abated a little by now and Wyman was drifting along on a mood which vacillated between boredom and a passive stream of odd thoughts and recollections. He was thinking of a time when he had accompanied his mother on a bus trip from New York to Pittsburgh. It was just after his father died, and his mother was going to see her relatives for money. The trip had been fruitless and, coming back on a midnight bus, he and his mother had talked about what they would do and decided that he would have to go to work. He thought of it with a little wonder. At the time it had been the most important night of his life, and now he was going on another trip, a far more eventful one, and he had no idea what would happen. It made him feel very mature for a moment; these were things which had happened just a few years ago, insignificant things now. He was trying to imagine what combat would be like, and he decided it would be impossible to guess. He had always pictured it as something violent, going on for days without halt. And here he had been in the platoon for over a week and nothing had happened; everything had been peaceful and relaxed.

"Do you think we'll see much tonight, Red?" he asked softly.

"Ask the General," Red snorted. He liked Wyman, but he tried to be unfriendly to him because the youth reminded Red of Hennessey. Red had a deep loathing of the night before them. He had been through so much combat, had felt so many kinds of terror, and had seen so many men killed that he no longer had any illusions about the inviolability of his own flesh. He knew he could be killed; it was something he had accepted long ago, and he had grown a shell about that knowledge so that he rarely thought of anything further ahead than the next few minutes. However, there had been lately a disquieting uncomfortable insight which he had never brought to the point of words, and it was bothering him. Until Hennessey had been killed, Red had accepted all the deaths of the men he knew as something large and devastating and meaningless. Men who were killed were merely men no longer around; they became confused with old friends who had gone to the hospital and never come back, or men who had been transferred to another outfit. When he heard of some man he knew who had been killed or wounded badly, he was interested, even a little concerned, but it was the kind of emotion a man might feel if he learned that a friend of his had got married or made or lost some money. It was merely something that happened to somebody he knew, and Red had always let it go at that. But Hennessey's death had opened a secret fear. It was so ironic, so obvious, when he remembered the things Hennessey had said, that he found himself at the edge of a bottomless dread.

Once he could have looked ahead to what he knew would be bad combat with a repugnance for the toil and misery of it, and a dour acceptance of the deaths that would occur. But now the idea of death was fresh and terrifying again.

"You want to know something?" he said to Wyman.

"Yeah?"

"They ain't a thing you can do about it, so shut up."

Wyman was hurt and lapsed into silence. Red felt sorry immediately afterward, and drew out a bar of tropical chocolate, bent out of shape and covered with tobacco grains from the silt of his pockets. "Hey, you want some chocolate?" he asked.

"Yeah, thanks."

They felt the night about them. In the truck there was no sound except for an occasional mutter or curse as they hit a bump. Each vehicle by itself was making all the noises that trucks can make; they creaked and jounced and groaned over the bogholes, and their tires made wet singing sounds. But, taken all together, the line of trucks had a combined, intricate medley of vibrations and tones which sounded like the gentle persistent lapping of surf against the sides of a ship. It was a melancholy sound, and, in the darkness, the men sprawled uncomfortably on the floor, their backs propped against the knees of the man behind them, their rifles pitched at every odd angle or straddled clumsily across their knees. Croft had insisted they wear their helmets, and Red was sweating under the unaccustomed weight. "Might as well wear a goddam sandbag," he said to Wyman.

Encouraged, Wyman asked, "I guess it's gonna be rough, huh?"

Red sighed, but repressed his annoyance. "It won't be too bad, kid. You just keep a tight ass-hole, and the rest of you'll take care of itself."

Wyman laughed quietly. He liked Red, and decided he would stay near him. The trucks halted, and the men moved around inside, shifting their positions and groaning as they flexed their cramped limbs. They waited patiently, their heads dropping on their chests, their damp clothing unable to dry in the heavy night air. There was barely a breeze and they felt tired and sleepy.

Goldstein was beginning to fidget. After the trucks had remained motionless for five minutes, he turned to Croft and asked, "Sergeant, is it all right if I get out and take a look at what's holding us up?"

Croft snorted. "You can stay right here, Goldstein. They ain't none of us gonna be getting up and getting lost on purpose."

Goldstein felt himself flush. "I didn't mean anything like that," he said. "I just thought it might be dangerous for us to be sitting here like this when there might be Japs around. How do we know why the trucks stopped?"

Croft yawned and then lashed him in a cold even voice. "I tell you what, you're going to have enough things to worry about. Suppose you just set down and beat your meat if you're gettin' anxious. I'll do all the goddam masterminding." There was a snicker from some of the men in the truck, and Goldstein was hurt. He decided he disliked Croft, and he brooded over all the sarcastic things Croft had said to him since he had been in the platoon.

The trucks started again, and moved jerkily in low gear for a few hundred yards before they stopped. Gallagher swore.

"What's the matter, boy, you in any hurry?" Wilson asked softly.

"We might as well get where we're goin'."

They remained sitting there for a few minutes, and then began to move again. A battery they had passed on the road was firing, and another one a few miles ahead also had gone into action. The shells whispered overhead, perhaps a mile above them, and the men listened dully. A machine gun began to fire far away, and the sound carried to them in separate bursts, deep and empty, like a man beating a carpet. Martinez took off his helmet and kneaded his skull, feeling as though a hammer were pounding him. A Japanese gun answered fire with a high penetrating shriek. A flare went up near the horizon and cast enough light for them to see one another. Their faces looked white and then blue as though they were staring at each other across a dark and smoky room. "We're gettin' close," someone said. After the flare had died, it was possible to see a pale haze against the horizon, and Toglio said, "Something's burning."

"Sounds like a big fight going on," Wyman suggested to Red.

"Naw, they're just feeling each other out," Red told him. "There'll be a helluva lot more noise if something starts tonight." The machine guns sputtered and then became silent. A few mortar shells were landing somewhere with a flat thudding sound, and another machine gun, much farther away, fired again. Then there was silence, and the trucks continued down the black muddy road.

After a few minutes they halted again, and somebody in the rear of the truck tried to light a cigarette. "Put the goddam thing out," Croft snapped.

The soldier was in another platoon and he swore at Croft. "Who the hell are you? I'm tired of just waiting around."

"Put that goddam thing out," Croft said again, and after a pause, the soldier snuffed it. Croft was feeling irritable and nervous. He had no fear but he was impatient and overalert.

Red debated whether to light a cigarette. He and Croft had hardly spoken to each other since their quarrel on the beach, and he was tempted to defy him. Actually he knew he wouldn't, and he tried to decide whether the real reason was that it was a bad idea to show a light or because he was afraid of Croft. Fug it, I'll stand up to that sonofabitch when the time comes, Red told himself, but I'll damn sure be right when I do.

They had begun to move once more. After a few minutes they heard a few low voices on the road, and their truck turned off and wallowed through a muddy lane. It was very narrow and a branch from a tree swept along the top of the truck. "Watch it!" someone shouted, and they all flattened themselves. Red pulled some leaves out of his shirt and pricked his finger on a thorn. He wiped the blood on the back of his pants and began searching for his pack, which he had thrown off when he first got into the truck. His legs were stiff and he tried to flex them.

"Don't dismount till you're told," Croft said.

The trucks came to a halt, and they listened to the few men circling around them in the darkness. Everything was terribly quiet. They sat there, speaking in whispers. An officer rapped on the tail gate and said, "All right, men, dismount and stick together." They began to jump out of the truck, moving slowly and uncertainly. It was a five-foot drop into darkness and they didn't know what the ground was like beneath them. "Drop the tail gate," someone said, and the officer snapped, "All right, men, let's keep it quiet."

When they had all got out, they stood about waiting. The trucks were already backing away for another trip. "Are there any officers here?" the officer asked.

A few of the men snickered. "All right, keep it down," the officer said. "Let's have the platoon noncoms forward."

Croft and a sergeant from the pioneer and demolition platoon stepped up. "Most of my men are in the next truck," the noncom said, and the officer told him to move his men together. Croft talked in a low voice to the officer for a minute and then gathered recon around him. "We got to wait," he said. "Let's stick around that tree." There was just enough light for them to notice it, and they walked over slowly. "Where are we now?" Ridges asked.

"Second Battalion headquarters," Croft said. "What've you been working on the road for all this time if you don't even know where you are?"

"Shoot, Ah just work, Ah don' spend mah time lookin' around," Ridges said. He guffawed nervously, and Croft told him to be quiet. They sat down around the tree and waited silently. A battery fired in a grove about five hundred yards away and it lit up the area for a moment. "What's the artillery doin' up this close?" Wilson asked.

"It's cannon company," someone told him.

Wilson sighed. "All a man does is sit around an' get his tail wet."

"It seems to me," Goldstein said formally, "that they're managing this thing very poorly." His voice was eager as if he were hoping for a discussion.

"You bitching again, Goldstein?" Croft asked.

The anti-Semite, Goldstein thought. "I'm just expressing my opinion," he said.

"Opinion!" Croft spat. "A bunch of goddam women have opinions."

Gallagher laughed quietly and mockingly. "Hey, Goldstein, you want a soapbox?"

"You don't like the Army any more than I do," Goldstein said mildly.

Gallagher paused, then sneered. "Balls," he said. "What's the matter, you want some gefüllte fish?" He stopped, and then as if delighted with what he had said, he added, "That's right, what Goldstein needs is some of that fuggin fish." A machine gun began to fire again; because of the night it sounded very close.

"I don't like the way you express yourself," Goldstein said.

"You know what you can do," Gallagher said. He was partially ashamed, and to drown it he added fiercely, "You can go blow it . . ."

"You can't talk to me that way," Goldstein said. His voice trembled. He was in a turmoil, revolted by the idea of fighting, yet recognizing the deep necessity for it. The goyim, that's all they know, to fight with their fists, he thought.

Red stepped in. He had the discomfort a display of emotion always roused in him. "Let's take it easy," he muttered. "You guys'll be getting plenty of fight in a minute." He snorted. "Fightin' over the Army. As far as I'm concerned, it's been a goddam mess ever since they put Washington on a horse."

Toglio interrupted him. "You've got the wrong attitude, Red. It ain't decent to talk about George Washington that way."

Red slapped his knee. "You're a regular Boy Scout, ain't you, Toglio? You like the flag, huh?"

Toglio thought of a story he had read once, *The Man Without a Country*. Red was like the man in that, he decided. "I think some things aren't fit for kidding," he said severely.

"You want to know something?"

Toglio knew a crack was coming, but against his judgment he asked, "What?"

"The only thing wrong with this Army is it never lost a war."

Toglio was shocked. "You think we ought to lose this one?"

Red found himself carried away. "What have I got against the goddam Japs? You think I care if they keep this fuggin jungle? What's it to me if Cummings gets another star?"

"General Cummings, he's a good man," Martinez said.

"There ain't a good officer in the world," Red stated. "They're just a bunch of aristocrats, *they* think. General Cummings is no better than I am. His shit don't smell like ice cream either."

Their voices were beginning to carry above a whisper, and Croft said, "Let's keep it down." The conversation was boring him. It was always the men who never got anywhere that did the bitching.

Goldstein was still quivering. His sense of shame was so intense that a few tears welled in his eyes. Red's interruption frustrated him, for Gallagher's words had pitched Goldstein so taut he needed some issue desperately now. He was certain, however, that he would start weeping with rage if he opened his mouth, and so he remained silent, trying to calm himself.

A soldier came walking toward them. "Are you guys recon?" he asked.

"Yeah," Croft said.

"Okay, you want to follow me?"

They picked up their packs and began walking through the darkness. It was difficult to see the man ahead. After they had gone a few hundred feet, the soldier who was leading them halted and said, "Wait here."

Red swore. "Next time, let's do it by the numbers," he said. Cannon company fired again, and the noise sounded very loud. Wilson dropped his pack and muttered, "Some poor sonsofbitches are gonna catch hell in 'bout half a minute." He sighed and sat down on the wet ground. "You'd think they had somepin better to do than have a whole squad of men walkin' around all night. Ah can't make up m' mind if Ah'm hot or cold." There was a wet heavy mist over the ground, and alternately they shivered in their wet clothing and sweltered in the airless night. Some Japanese artillery was landing about a mile away, and they listened to it quietly.

A platoon of men filed by, their rifles clanking against their helmets and pack buckles. A flare went up a short distance away, and in its light the men looked like black cutouts moving past a spotlight. Their rifles were slung at odd angles, and their packs gave them a humped misshapen appearance. The sound of their walking was confused and intricate; like the truck convoy, it resembled the whisper of surf. Then the flare died, and the column of men passed. When they were some distance away, the only sound that still remained was the soft metallic jingle of their rifles. A skirmish had started at some distance and Jap rifles were firing. Red turned to Wyman and said, "Listen to them. Tick-boom, tick-boom. You can't miss it." A few American rifles answered, their fire sounding more powerful, like a leather belt slapped on a table. Wyman shifted uneasily. "How far away do you figure the Japs are?" he asked Croft.

"Damned if I know. You'll see 'em soon enough, boy."

"Hell he will," Red said. "We're going to be sitting around all night."

Croft spat. "You wouldn't mind that, would you, Valsen?"

"Not me. I'm no hero," Red said.

Some soldiers walked past in the darkness, and a few trucks pulled into the bivouac. Wyman lay down on the ground. He was a little chagrined that he would spend his first night in combat trying to fall asleep. The water soaked through his shirt, which was already wet, and he sat up again, shivering. The air was very sultry. He wished he could light a cigarette.

They waited another half hour before receiving the order to move. Croft stood up and followed their guide while the rest trailed behind. The guide led them into a patch of brush where a platoon of men was grouped around six antitank guns. They were 37s, small guns about six feet long with very slender barrels. One man could pull one gun without too much difficulty over level hard ground.

"We're going along with antitank up to First Battalion," Croft said. "We got to pull two of them guns."

Croft told them to gather around him. "I don't know how muddy the damn trail is going to be," he began, "but it ain't too hard to guess. We're going to be in the middle of the column, so I'm going to cut us into three groups of three men each, and they'll be one group restin' all the time. I'll take Wilson and Gallagher, and Martinez can take Valsen and Ridges, and Toglio, you got what's left — Goldstein and Wyman. We're scrapin' the barrel," he added dryly.

He went up to talk to an officer for a few seconds. When he came back, he said, "We'll let Toglio's group have the first rest." He got behind one of the guns and gave it a tug. "The sonofabitch is going to be heavy." Wilson and Gallagher started pulling it with him, and the other platoon, which had already divided into a few men on each gun, began to move out. They tugged the guns across the bivouac area, and passed through a gap in the barbed wire where there was a machine gun emplacement. "Have a good time, men," the man at the machine gun said.

"Blow it out," Gallagher answered. The gun was beginning to drag on his arms already.

There were about fifty men in the column, and they moved very slowly down a narrow trail through the jungle. After they had moved a hundred feet, they were no longer able to see the men in front of them. The branches of the trees on either side of the trail joined overhead, and they felt as though they were groping through an endless tunnel. Their feet sank into the deep mud and, after a few yards, their boots were covered with great slabs of muck. The men on the guns would lunge forward for a few feet and then halt, lunge forward and halt. Every ten yards a gun would bog down and the three men assigned to it would have to tug until their strength seeped from their fingers. They would wrestle the gun out of its rut and plunge it forward for fifteen feet before their momentum was lost. Then they would pull it and lift it for another few yards until it sank into a hole once more. The entire column labored and stumbled at a miserable pace along the trail. In the darkness they kept ganging up on each other, the men on one gun sometimes riding it up onto the muzzle of the one ahead, or falling behind so far that the file at last broke into separate wriggling columns like a worm cut into many parts and still living. The men at the rear had the worst of it. The guns and men that preceded them had churned the trail until it was almost a marsh, and there were places where two teams would have to combine on one gun and carry it above the ground until they had passed the worst of the slime.

The trail was only a few feet wide. Huge roots continually tripped the men, and their faces and hands became scratched and bleeding from the branches and thorns. In the complete darkness they had no idea of how the trail might bend, and sometimes on a down slope, when they could let the gun roll a little distance, they would land at the bottom with the field piece completely off the trail. Then they would have to fumble in the brush, covering their eyes with their arms to protect them from the vines, and a painful struggle to bring the gun back on the path would begin.

Some Japanese might easily have been waiting in ambush, but it was impossible to keep silent. The guns squeaked and lumbered, made sucking sounds as their tires sank into the mud, and the men swore helplessly, panted with deep sobbing sounds like wrestlers at the end of a long bout. Voices and commands echoed hollowly, were lost in a chorus of profanity and hoarse sobbing, the straining sweating noises of men in great labor. By the time an hour had passed, nothing existed for them but the slender cannon they had to get down the track. The sweat drenched their clothing and filled their eyes, blinding them. They grappled and blundered and swore, advanced the little guns a few feet at a time with no consciousness any longer of what they were doing.

When one team was relieved by another, they would stagger alongside the guns trying to regain their wind, falling behind sometimes to rest for a little while. Every ten minutes the column would stop to allow the stragglers to catch up. During the halts the men would sprawl in the middle of the trail not caring how the mud covered them. They felt as though they had been running for hours; they could not regain their breath, and their stomachs retched emptily. Some of the men began to throw away their equipment; one after another the men threw their helmets aside or dropped them on the trail. The air was unbearably hot under the canopy of the jungle, and the darkness gave no relief from the heat of the day; if anything, walking the trail was like fumbling through an endless closet stuffed with velvet garments.

During one of the halts, the officer leading the file worked his way back to find Croft. "Where's Sergeant Croft?" he shouted, his words repeated by the men along the trail until it reached Croft.

"Here, sir." They stumbled toward each other through the mud.

"How're your men?" the officer asked.

"Okay."

They sat down beside the trail. "Mistake trying this," the officer gasped. "Have to get through."

Croft, with his lean ropy body, had borne the labor comparatively well, but his voice was unsteady and he had to talk with short quick spates of words. "How far?" he asked.

"Have to go one mile . . . one mile yet. More than halfway there, I think. Never should have tried it."

"They need the guns bad?"

The officer halted for a moment and tried to speak normally. "I think so . . . there's no tank weapons there . . . up on the line. We stopped a tank attack two hours ago . . . at Third Battalion. Orders came to move some thirty-sevens over to First Battalion. Guess they expect attack there."

"Better get them through," Croft said. He was contemptuous because the officer had to talk to him. The man ought to be able to do his own job.

"Have to, I guess." The officer stood up and leaned for a moment against a tree. "If you get a gun stuck, let me know. Have to cross a stream . . . up ahead. Bad place, I think."

He began to feel his way forward, and Croft turned around and worked his way back to the gun he was pulling. The column was over two hundred yards long by now. They started to move, and the labor continued. Once or twice a flare filtered a wan and delicate bluish light over them, the light almost lost in the dense foliage through which it had to pass. In the brief moment it lasted, they were caught at their guns in classic straining motions that had the form and beauty of a frieze. Their uniforms were twice blackened, by the water and the dark slime of the trail. And for the instant the light shone on them their faces stood out, white and contorted. Even the guns had a slender articulated beauty like an insect reared back on its wire haunches. Then darkness swirled about them again, and they ground the guns forward blindly, a line of ants dragging their burden back to their hole.

They had reached that state of fatigue in which everything was hated. A man would slip in the mud and remain there, breathing hoarsely, having no will to get to his feet. That part of the column would halt, and wait numbly for the soldier to join them. If they had breath, they would swear.

"Fug the sonofabitchin' mud."

"Get up," somebody would cry.

"Fug you. Fug the goddam gun."

"Let me lay here. I'm okay, they ain't a thing wrong with me, I'm okay, let me lay."

"Fug you, *get up!*"

And they would labor forward a few more yards and halt. In the darkness, distance had no meaning, nor did time. The heat had left their bodies; they shivered and trembled in the damp night, and everything about them was sodden and pappy; they stank but no longer with animal smells; their clothing was plastered with the foul muck of the jungle mud, and a chill dank rotting smell somewhere between leaf mold and faeces filled their nostrils. They knew only that they had to keep moving, and if they thought of time it was in so many convulsions of nausea.

Wyman was wondering why he did not collapse. His breath came in long parched shudders, his pack straps galled, his feet were ablaze, and he could not have spoken, for his throat and chest and mouth seemed covered with a woolly felt. He was no longer conscious of the powerful and fetid stench that rose from his clothes. Somewhere deep inside himself was a wonder at the exhaustion his body could endure. He was normally a sluggish youth who worked no more than he was obliged to, and the sensations of labor, the muscle strains, the panting, the taste of fatigue were things he had always tried to avoid. He had had vague dreams about being a hero, assuming this would bring him some immense reward which would ease his life and remove the problems of supporting his mother and himself. He had a girl and he wanted to dazzle her with his ribbons. But he had always imagined combat as exciting, with no misery and no physical exertion. He dreamed of himself charging across a field in the face of many machine guns; but in the dream there was no stitch in his side from running too far while bearing too much weight.

He had never thought he would be chained to an inanimate monster of metal with which he would have to grapple until his arms trembled helplessly and his body was ready to fall; certainly he had never imagined he would stumble down a path in the middle of the night with his shoes sucking and dragging in slime. He pushed at the gun, he lifted it with Goldstein and Toglio when it became mired in a hole, but the motions were automatic by now; he hardly even felt the added pain when they had to pull it out by the wheel hubs. His fingers were no longer able to close, and often he would tug helplessly until his hands slipped away with the gun still mired.

The column was proceeding even more slowly than it had at the start, and sometimes fifteen minutes would elapse before a gun could be moved a hundred yards. Every now and then a man would faint, and would be left by the side of the trail to make his way back alone when he recovered.

At last a message began to carry back along the trail, "Keep going, we're almost there," and for a few minutes it served as a stimulant so that the men labored with some hope again. But when each turning in the trail discovered only another ribbon of mud and darkness, the men began to feel a hopeless dejection. Sometimes for as much as a minute they would not move at all. It became harder and harder to pitch themselves against the guns again. Every time they stopped they felt like quitting.

There was a draw they had to cross a few hundred feet before they reached 1st Battalion, and its banks sloped very steeply down to a little stony brook, then ascended again abruptly to about fifteen feet above the bottom. This was the stream the officer had mentioned. When the men reached it, the column stopped completely, and the stragglers caught up. Each team of soldiers waited for the men and gun in front of them to cross the stream. In the night it was an extremely difficult business at best and took a long time. The men would go sliding down the bank trying to restrain their field piece from turning over at the bottom, and then they would have to lift it over the slippery rocks of the brook before attempting to wrestle it up the other side. The banks were slimy, and there was no foothold; time and again a team would force their gun up almost to the top of the draw only to slip back again futilely.

By the time Wyman and Toglio and Goldstein had to move their gun, a half hour had passed and they were a little rested. Their wind had returned and they kept shouting instructions to each other as they nosed the gun over the edge of the bank. It began to pull away from them, and they had to resist desperately to keep it from crashing to the bottom. The exertion drained most of the strength they had recovered, and after they had carried the piece across the stream, they were as exhausted as they had been at any time during the march.

They stopped for a few moments to gather whatever force was left in them and began the struggle up the bank. Toglio was wheezing like a bull, and his commands had a hoarse urgent sound as if he were wrenching them from deep inside his body. "Okay, PUSH . . . PUSH," he growled, and the three of them strove numbly to roll the gun. It resisted them, moved sluggishly and treacherously, and the strength began to flow out of their trembling legs. "HOLD IT!" Toglio shouted. "DON'T LET IT SLIP!" They braced themselves behind the gun, trying to wedge their feet into the wet clay of the bank. "PUSH AGAIN!" he shouted, and they forced it upward a few more feet. Wyman felt a band was stretching dangerously inside his body, and would snap at any moment. They rested again, and then shoved the gun another few yards. Slowly, minute by minute, they came closer to the top. They were perhaps four feet from the crest when Wyman lost the last reserves of his strength. He tried to draw some few shreds of effort from his quivering limbs, but he seemed to collapse all at once, and just lay stupidly behind the gun supporting it with no more than the weight of his sagging body. The gun began to slip, and he pulled away. Toglio and Goldstein were left at each of the hubs. When Wyman let go, they felt as though someone were pushing down against the gun. Goldstein held on until the sliding wheels pulled his fingers loose, one by one, and then he just had time to shout hoarsely, "WATCH IT!" to Toglio, before the gun went crashing down to the bottom. The three men fell after it, rolling in its wake. The gun struck some rocks at the bottom, and one of the wheels was knocked completely awry. They felt for it in the darkness like pups licking the wounds of their mother. Wyman began to blubber with exhaustion.

The accident caused a great deal of confusion. Croft's team was on the gun waiting behind them, and he began to shout, "What's holdin' you up? What's happening down there?"

"We had . . . trouble," Toglio shouted back. "Wait!" He and Goldstein succeeded in turning the gun on its side. "The wheel's shot," Toglio shouted. "We can't move the gun."

Croft swore. "Get her out of the way."

They tried, and couldn't budge it.

"We need help," Goldstein shouted.

Croft swore again, and then he and Wilson slid down the bank. After a while they were able to tumble the gun over enough times to move it down the creek bed. Without saying anything, Croft went back to his gun, and Toglio and the others climbed up the far bank and went staggering down the trail till they reached 1st Battalion's bivouac. The men who had arrived before them were lying on the ground motionless. Toglio stretched out in the mud, and Wyman and Goldstein lay down beside him. None of them spoke for ten minutes. Occasionally, a shell might burst somewhere in the jungle about them and their legs might twitch, but this was the only sign they gave of being conscious. Men were moving about constantly, and the sounds of the fighting were closer, more vicious. Voices kept coming to them out of the darkness. Someone would shout, "Where's the pack train for B Company?" and the answer would be muffled to the men lying on the ground. They hardly cared. Occasionally they would be aware of the sounds of the night; for a few instants they might concentrate on the constant thrumming that emanated from the jungle, but they always relapsed into a stupor, thinking of nothing once more.

Croft and Wilson and Gallagher brought their gun in a short while later, and Croft shouted for Toglio.

"What do you want? I'm here," Toglio said. He hated to move.

Croft came toward him in the darkness and sat down beside him. His breath was coming in long slow gasps like a runner after a race. "I'm going to see the Lieutenant . . . tell him about the gun. How the hell did it happen?"

Toglio propped himself on an elbow. He loathed the explanations that were to come, and he was confused. "I don't know," he said. "I heard Goldstein yell 'Watch out' and then it just seemed to rip out of our hands." Toglio hated to give excuses to Croft.

"Goldstein yelled, huh?" Croft asked. "Where is he?"

"Here I am, Sergeant." Goldstein's voice came out of the darkness beside them.

"Why'd you yell 'Watch out'?"

"I don't know. I felt suddenly as if I couldn't hold it any more. Something pulled it away from me."

"Who was the other man?"

Wyman roused himself. "I guess I was." His voice sounded weak.

"Did you let go?" Croft asked.

Wyman felt a trace of fear as he thought of admitting that to Croft. "No," he said. "No, I don't think so. I heard Goldstein yell, and then the gun started to come down on me. It was rolling back so I got out of the way." Already he was uncertain exactly how it had occurred, and a part of his mind was trying to convince him that he spoke the truth. With it, however, he felt a surprising flush of shame. "I guess it was my fault," he blurted out honestly, but his voice was so tired that it lacked sincerity, and Croft thought he was trying to protect Goldstein.

"Yeah," Croft said. A spasm of rage worked through him, and he turned on Goldstein and said, "Listen, Izzy."

"My name isn't Izzy," Goldstein said angrily.

"I don't give a damn what it is. The next time you pull a goddam trick like that, I'm going to put you in for a court-martial."

"But I don't think I let go," Goldstein protested weakly. By now, he too was no longer sure. The sequence of his sensations when the gun had begun to pull out of his hands was too confused for him to feel righteous. He had thought that Wyman stopped pushing first, but when Wyman declared he was to blame, Goldstein had a moment of panic. Like Croft, he believed Wyman was protecting him. "I don't know," he said. "I don't think I did."

"You don't think," Croft cut him off. "Listen, for as long as you've been in the platoon, Goldstein, you've done nothing but have ideas about how we could do something better. But when it comes down to a little goddam work, you're always dicking off. I've had enough of that bullshit from you."

Once again Goldstein was feeling a helpless anger. A reaction he could not control, his agitation was even greater than his resentment and choked him so that he could not speak. A few tears of frustration welled in his eyes, and he turned away and lay down again. His anger was now directed toward himself and he felt a hopeless shame. Oh, I don't know, I don't know, he said.

Toglio had a mingled relief and pity. He was glad the onus of losing the gun was not his, and yet he was unhappy anyone should be blamed. The bond of common effort that the three men had known while struggling with the weapon was still with him, and he said to himself, poor Goldstein, he's a good guy; he just had hard luck.

Wyman was too exhausted to think clearly. After he declared it was his fault, he was relieved to discover he was not to be blamed after all. He was actually too depleted to think consecutively about anything, or indeed remember anything. By now, he was convinced it was Goldstein who had deserted the gun, and his main reaction was one of comfort. The image still most vivid to him was the agony he had felt in his chest and groin as they had started up the embankment, and he thought, I would have let go two seconds later if he didn't. For this reason, Wyman felt a dulled sense of affection for Goldstein.

Croft stood up. "Well, that's one gun they ain't going to rescue for a little while," he said. "I bet it stays there for the whole campaign." He was enraged enough to strike Goldstein. Without saying anything more, Croft left them and went in search of the officer who had led the column.

The men in the platoon settled down and began to sleep. Occasionally a shell would burst in the jungle nearby, but they hardly cared. The battle had been threatening all evening like a thunderstorm which never breaks, and by now it would have taken a barrage to move them. Besides, they were too weary to dig holes.

It took Red longer to fall asleep than any of the others. For many years his kidneys had bothered him whenever he had too much exposure to dampness. They were throbbing now, and he turned several times on the wet ground, trying to decide if it would be less painful to sleep with his back against the moist earth or exposed to the night air. He lay awake for a long time thinking, his mood turning through a small gamut from weariness to sadness. He was thinking of a time when he had been caught in a small town in Nebraska with no jobs to be had, and had had to wait until he could catch a boxcar out of town. It had seemed very important to him then not to beg for something to eat, and he wondered if he still had that pride. "Oh, I've been tough in my time, he muttered to himself. "Lot of good it does me." The air was cold on his back, and he turned over. It seemed to him that all his life he had been sleeping in bare wet places, seeking for warmth. He thought of an old hobo saying "Half a buck in your pocket and winter coming," and felt some of the gloom he had known on cold October twilights. His stomach was empty, and he got up after a while and rummaged through his pack. He found a K ration and chewed the fruit bar, washing it down with water from his canteen. His blanket was still wet from the evening storm, but he wrapped it about him and found a little warmth. Then he tried to go to sleep again, but his kidneys were aching too much. At last he sat up, fumbled in the first-aid kit on his cartridge belt, and withdrew the little paper bag of wound tablets. He swallowed half of them and drank about half the water remaining in his canteen. For a moment he thought of using them all, but then remembered that he might be wounded and need them. It brought back his dejection, and he stared solemnly into the darkness, being able to discern after a time the bodies of the sleeping men around him. Toglio was snoring, and he heard Martinez mutter softly in Spanish and then cry out, "I no kill Jap, God, I no kill him." Red sighed and lay down again. What men sleep easy? he thought.

A trace of an old anger passed through him. I don't give a damn about anything, he said to himself, and listened uneasily to a shell sighing overhead. This time it sounded like the branches of a tree murmuring in a winter wind. He remembered once striding along a highway as evening came. It had been in the eastern coal-mining towns of Pennsylvania and he had watched the miners driving home in their battered Fords, their faces still dark with the day's accumulation of soot and coal dust. It had not looked anything like the mining country in Montana he had left years before, and yet it had been the same. He had walked along brooding about home, and someone had given him a ride and treated him to a drink in a noisy bar. That night had a beauty about it now, and he remembered for a moment the sensation of leaving a strange town on a dark freight. Things like that were only glints of light in the long gray day of those years. He sighed again as if to grasp something of the knowledge he had felt for an instant. Nobody gets what he wants, he said to himself, and this deepened his mood of pleasurable sorrow. He was growing drowsy, and he burrowed his head under his forearm. A mosquito began to whine near his ear and he lay still, hoping it would go away. The ground seemed crawling with insects. The little buggers are one thing I'm used to, he thought. For some reason this made him smile.

It was beginning to rain, and Red covered his head with the blanket. His body was slowly sinking into a weary slumber in which different parts of him fell asleep at separate intervals, so that long after he had stopped thinking, a portion of his mind could feel the quivering of an exhausted limb or a cramp in one of his limbs. The shelling was becoming steady, and a half mile away from him a machine gun kept firing. Almost asleep, he watched Croft return and spread out a blanket. The rain continued. After a time, he no longer heard the artillery. But even when he was completely asleep, one last area of his mind noticed what was happening. Although he didn't remember it when he awoke, he heard a platoon of men march by, and was conscious of some other men beginning to push the antitank guns to the other side of the bivouac. There's a Jap road leads into the bivouac, he said in his sleep. They're going to protect it now. Probably he was feverish.

He dreamed until he heard a voice shout, "Recon? Where's recon?" The dream ebbed away, and he lay there drowsily, listening to Croft spring to his feet and holler, "Here, over here!" Red knew he would have to be moving in a few minutes, and he burrowed deeper into his blankets. His body ached and he knew that when he stood up he would be stiff. "All right, men, on your feet," Croft was shouting. "Come on, get up, we got to move."

Red pulled the cover off his face. It was still raining and his hand came away wet from the top surface of the blanket. When he replaced the blanket in his pack, his pack also would become wet. "Aaaahhhhhrr." He cleared his throat with disgust and spat once or twice. The tast in his mouth was foul. Gallagher sat up beside him and groaned. "Goddam Army, why don't they let a guy sleep? Ain't we done enough tonight?"

"We're heroes," Red said. He stood up and began to fold his blanket. It was sopping wet on one side and muddy on the other. He had slept with his rifle beside him, covered under the blanket, but it too was wet. Red wondered how long it had been since he was dry. "Fuggin jungle," he said.

"Come on, you men, snap it up," Croft said. A flare lit the wet ugly shrubs about them and flickered dully against their wet black clothing. Red saw that Gallagher's face was covered with mud, and when he felt his own face, his hands came away soiled. "Show me the way to go home," he hummed. "I'm tired and I want to go to bed."

"Yeah," Gallagher said. They made their packs together and stood up. The flare had gone out and they were blinded for a moment in the returning darkness. "Where we going?" Toglio asked.

"Up to A Company. They expect an attack there," Croft said.

"We sure are a hard-luck platoon," Wilson sighed. "At least we're done with them antitank guns. Ah swear Ah'd fight a tank with mah bare hands 'fore Ah'd rassle with one of them sonsofbitches again."

The squad formed a single file and began to move out. First Battalion's bivouac was very small and in thirty seconds they had reached the gap in the barbed wire. Martinez led them cautiously down the trail leading to A Company. His drowsiness vanished quickly, and he became alert. Actually, he could not see anything, but some sense seemed to guide him along the bends in the path so that he rarely stumbled or blundered off the trail. He was proceeding about thirty yards ahead of the other men and he was completely isolated. If some Japanese had been waiting in ambush along the path, he would have been the first to be trapped. Yet he had very little fear; Martinez's terror developed in a void; the moment he had to lead men, his courage returned. At this instant, his mind was poised over a number of sounds and thoughts. His ears were searching the jungle ahead of him for some noise which might indicate that men were waiting in the brush beside the trail; they were also listening with disgust to the stumbling and muttering of the men following behind him. His mind recorded the intermittent sounds of battle and tried to classify them; he looked at the sky whenever they passed through a partial clearing in order to find the

Southern Cross and determine in which direction the trail was bending. Wherever he could, he made a mental note of some landmark they were passing and added it to the ones he had observed previously. After a time he kept repeating a jingle to himself which went, Tree over trail, muddy creek, rock on trail, bushes across. Actually there was no reason for him to do it; the trail led only from 1st Battalion to A Company. But this was a habit he had formed on his first patrols. He did it instinctively by now.

And another part of his mind had a quiet pride that he was the man upon whom the safety of the others depended. This was a sustaining force which carried him through dangers his will and body would have resisted. During the march with the antitank guns, there had been many times when he wanted to quit; unlike Croft, he had felt it no contest at all. He would have been perfectly willing to declare the task beyond his strength and give up, but there was a part of his mind that drove him to do things he feared and detested. His pride with being a sergeant was the core about which nearly all his actions and thoughts were bound. Nobody see in the darkness like Martinez, he said to himself. He touched a branch before his extended arm and bent his knees easily and walked under it. His feet were sore and his back and shoulders ached, but they were ills with which he no longer concerned himself; he was leading his squad, and that was sufficient in itself.

The rest of the squad, strung out behind, was experiencing a variety of emotions. Wilson and Toglio were sleepy, Red was alert and brooding — he had a sense of foreboding. Goldstein was miserable and bitter, and the tension of creeping down a trail in the black early hours of the morning made him gloomy and then sad. He thought of himself dying without friends nearby to mourn him. Wyman had lost his power to recuperate; he was so tired that he plodded along in a stupor, not caring where he went or what happened to him. Ridges was weary and patient; he did not think of what the next hours would bring him, nor did he lose himself in contemplation of his aching limbs; he just walked and his mind drifted slowly like a torpid stream.

And Croft; Croft was tense and eager and impatient. All night he had been balked by the assignment of the squad to a labor detail. The sounds of battle he had been hearing all night were goading to him. His mind was buoyed by a recurrence of the mood he had felt after Hennessey's death. He felt strong and tireless and capable of anything; his muscles were as strained and jaded as any of the men's, but his mind had excluded his body. He hungered for the fast taut pulse he would feel in his throat after he killed a man.

On the map there was only a half mile between 1st Battalion and

A Company, but the trail doubled and curved so often that it was actually a mile. The men in recon were clumsy now and uncertain of their footing. Their packs sagged, their rifles kept sliding off their shoulders. The trail was crude; originally a game wallow, it had been partially enlarged, and in places it was still narrow. A man could not walk without being scratched by the branches on either side. The jungle was impenetrable at that point, and it would have taken an hour to cut one's way a hundred feet off the path. In the night it was impossible to see anything and the smell of the wet foliage was choking. The men had to walk in single file, drawn up close. Even at three feet they could not see one another, and they plodded down the trail with each man grasping the shirt of the man before him. Martinez could hear them and judge his distance accordingly, but the others stumbled and collided with one another like children playing a game in the dark. They were bent over almost double, and the posture was cruel. Their bodies were outraged; they had been eating and sleeping with no rhythm at all for the last few hours. They kept loosing gas whose smell was nauseating in the foul dense air. The men at the rear had the worst of it; they gagged and swore, tried not to breathe for a few seconds, and shuddered from fatigue and revulsion. Gallagher was at the end of the file, and every few minutes he would cough and curse. "Cut out the goddam farting," he would shout, and the men in front would rouse themselves for a moment and laugh.

"Eatin' dust, hey, boy," Wilson muttered, and a few of them began to giggle.

Some of them began to fall asleep as they walked. Their eyes had been closed almost the entire march, and they drowsed for the instant their foot was in the air and awakened as it touched the ground. Wyman had been plodding along for many minutes with no sensation at all; his body had grown numb. He and Ridges drowsed continually, and every now and then for ten or fifteen yards they would be completely asleep. At last they would weave off the trail and go pitching into the bushes stupidly before regaining their balance. In the darkness such noises were terrifying. It made the men uncomfortably aware of how close they were to the fighting. A half mile away some rifles were firing.

"Goddammit," one of them would whisper, "can't you guys keep quiet?"

The march must have taken them over half an hour, but after the first few minutes they no longer thought about time. Crouching and sliding through the mud with their hands on the man in front became the only thing they really knew; the trail was a treadmill and they no longer concerned themselves with where they were going.

To most of them the end of the march came as a surprise. Martinez doubled back and told them to be quiet. "They hear you coming for ten minutes," he whispered. A hush settled over the men, and they trod the last hundred yards with ridiculous precautions, tensing every muscle whenever they took a step.

There was no barbed wire, nor any clearing at A Company. The trail divided in a quadruple fork which led to different emplacements. A soldier met them where the path broke up and led the squad along one of the footpaths to a few pup tents pitched in the middle of some foliage. "I got Second Platoon," he told Croft. "I'm just about a hundred yards down the river. Your squad can sleep in these holes tonight, and set up a guard right along here. They's two machine guns set up for you."

"What's doing?" Croft whispered.

"I dunno. I heard they expect an attack all up and down the line about dawn. We had to send a platoon over to C Company early tonight, and we been holding down the whole outpost here with less than a platoon." He made a rustling sound in the darkness as he wiped his hand against his mouth. "C'mere, I'll show you the setup," he said, grasping Croft's elbow. Croft slipped his arm free; he hated to have anyone touch him.

They went a few feet along the path, until the sergeant from A Company halted before a foxhole. There was a machine gun mounted in front, its muzzle just projecting through a fringe of bushes. Croft peered through the foliage and in the faint moonlight was able to see a stream of water and a strip of beach bordering it on either side. "How deep is the river?" he asked.

"Aw, it's four, five feet maybe. That water ain't going to stop them."

"Any outposts forward of here?" Croft asked.

"Nothing. And the Japs know right where we are. Had some patrols up." The soldier wiped his mouth again and stood up. "I'll show you the other machine gun." They walked along a stubbly path cut through the jungle about ten feet from the river's edge. Some crickets were chirping loudly, and the soldier trembled a little. "Here's the other one," he said. "This is the flank." He peered through the bushes and stepped out onto the strip of beach. "Look," he said. Croft followed him. About fifty yards to their right, the bluffs of Watamai Range began. Croft looked up. The cliffs rose almost vertically for perhaps a thousand feet. Even in the darkness, he felt them hovering above him. He strained his eyes and thought he saw a swatch of sky where they ended but could not be certain. He had a curious thrill. "I didn't know we were that close," he said.

"Oh, yeah. It's good and it's bad. You don't have to worry about them coming around that end, but still we're the flank. If they ever hit here hard, their ain't much to hold them." The soldier drew into the bushes again and exhaled his breath slowly. "I'll tell you these two nights we been out here give me the creeps. Look at that river. When there's a lot of moonlight it just seems to shine, and you get jittery after a while looking at it."

Croft remained outside the jungle edge, looking at the stream that curved away at the right and flowed parallel to the mountains. It took a turn toward the Japanese lines just a few yards before the first walls of the bluff began, and he would be able to see everything on that side. To the left the stream ran straight for a few hundred yards like a highway at night, sunk between high grassy banks. "Where are you?" he asked.

The soldier pointed to a tree which projected a little from the jungle. "We're just on this side of it. If you got to get to us, go back to the fork and then take the trail at the far right going away from here. Yell 'Buckeye' when you come up."

"Okay," Croft said. They talked for a few more minutes, and then the other soldier hooked his cartridge belt. "Jesus, I'll tell ya it'll drive ya crazy spending a night here. Just wilderness, that's all, and you stuck out at the end of it with nothing but a lousy machine gun." He slung his rifle and struck off down the trail. Croft looked at him for a moment and then went back to recon. The men were waiting by the three pup tents, and he showed them where the two machine guns were placed. Briefly he told them what he had learned and picked a guard. "It's three A.M. now," he told them. "There's gonna be four of us on one post and five on the other. We'll do it in two-hour shifts. Then the post that's only got four men will get the extra one for the next time around." He divided them up, taking the first shift at the flank gun himself. Wilson volunteered to take the other gun. "After Ah'm done, Ah'm gonna want to sleep right on through," Wilson said. "Ah'm tired of gittin' up right when Ah'm havin' a good dream."

The men smiled wanly.

"An' listen," Croft added, "if any trouble starts, the men that are sleeping are to git up goddam fast and move to help us. It's only a couple of yards from our tents to Wilson's machine gun, and it ain't much further to mine. It shouldn't be takin' you all more than about three hours to reach us." Again, a couple of men smiled. "Okay, that's about it," Croft said. He left them and walked over to his machine gun.

He sat down on the edge of the hole and peered through the bushes at the river. The jungle completely surrounded him, and, now that he was no longer active, he felt very weary and a little depressed. To counteract this mood, he began to feel the various objects in the hole. There were three boxes of belt ammunition and a row of seven grenades lined up neatly at the base of the machine gun. At his feet were a box of flares and a flare gun. He picked it up and broke open the breech quietly, loaded it, and cocked it. Then he set it down beside him.

A few shells murmured overhead and began to fall. He was a little surprised at how near they landed to the other side of the river. Not more than a few hundred yards away, the noise of their explosion was extremely loud; a few pieces of shrapnel lashed the leaves on the trees above him. He broke off a stalk from a plant and put it in his mouth, chewing slowly and reflectively. He guessed that the weapons platoon of A Company had fired, and he tried to determine which trail at the fork would lead to them in case he had to pull back his men. Now he was patient and at ease; the danger of their position neutralized the anticipation for some combat he had felt earlier, and he was left cool and calm and very tired.

The mortar shells were falling perhaps fifty yards in front of the platoon at his left, and Croft spat quietly. It was too close to be merely harassing fire; someone had heard something in the jungle on the other side of the river or they would never have called for mortars so close to their own position. His hand explored the hole again and discovered a field telephone. Croft picked up the receiver, listened quietly. It was an open line, and probably confined to the platoons of A Company. Two men were talking in voices so low that he strained to hear them.

"Walk it up another fifty and then bring it back."

"You sure there're Japs?"

"I swear I heard them talking."

Croft stared tensely across the river. The moon had come out, and the strands of beach on either side of the stream were shining with a silver glow. The jungle wall on the other side looked impenetrable.

The mortars fired again behind him with a cruel flat sound. He watched the shells land in the jungle, and then creep nearer to the river in successive volleys. A mortar answered from the Japanese side of the river, and about a quarter of a mile to the left Croft could hear several machine guns spattering at each other, the uproar deep and irregular. Croft picked up the phone and whistled into it. "Wilson," he whispered. *"Wilson!"* There was no answer and he debated whether to walk over to Wilson's hole. Silently Croft cursed him for not noticing the phone, and then berated himself for not having discovered it before he briefed the others. He looked out across the river. Fine sergeant I am, he told himself.

His ears were keyed to all the sounds of the night, and from long experience he sifted out the ones that were meaningless. If an animal rustled in its hole, he paid no attention: if some crickets chirped, his ear disregarded them. Now he picked a muffled slithering sound which he knew could be made only by men moving through a thin patch of jungle. He peered across the river, trying to determine where the foliage was least dense. At a point between his gun and Wilson's there was a grove of a few coconut trees sparse enough to allow men to assemble; as he stared into that patch of wood, he was certain he heard a man move. Croft's mouth tightened. His hand felt for the bolt of the machine gun, and he slowly brought it to bear on the coconut grove. The rustling grew louder; it seemed as if men were creeping through the brush on the other side of the river to a point opposite his gun. Croft swallowed once. Tiny charges seemed to pulse through his limbs and his head was as empty and shockingly aware as if it had been plunged into a pail of freezing water. He wet his lips and shifted his position slightly, feeling as though he could hear the flexing of his muscles.

The Jap mortar fired again and he started. The shells were falling by the next platoon, the sound painful and jarring to him. He stared out on the moonlit river until his eyes deceived him; he began to think he could see the heads of men in the dark swirls of the current. Croft gazed down at his knees for an instant and then across the river again. He looked a little to the left or right of where he thought the Japanese might be; from long experience he had learned a man could not look directly at an object and see it in the darkness. Something seemed to move in the grove, and a new trickle of sweat formed and rolled down his back. He twisted uncomfortably. Croft was unbearably tense, but the sensation was not wholly unpleasant.

He wondered if Wilson had noticed the sounds, and then in answer to his question, there was the loud unmistakable clicking of a machine gun bolt. To Croft's keyed senses, the sound echoed up and down the river, and he was furious that Wilson should have revealed his position. The rustling in the brush became louder and Croft was convinced he could hear voices whispering on the other side of the river. He fumbled for a grenade and placed it at his feet.

Then he heard a sound which pierced his flesh. Someone called from across the river, "Yank, Yank!" Croft sat numb. The voice was thin and high-pitched, hideous in a whisper. "That's a Jap," Croft told himself. He was incapable of moving for that instant.

"Yank!" It was calling to him. "Yank. We you coming-to-get, Yank."

The night lay like a heavy stifling mat over the river. Croft tried to breathe.

"We you coming-to-get, Yank."

Croft felt as if a hand had suddenly clapped against his back, traveled up his spine over his skull to clutch at the hair on his forehead. "Coming to get you, Yank," he heard himself whisper. He had the agonizing frustration of a man in a nightmare who wants to scream and cannot utter a sound. "We you *coming-to-get*, Yank."

He shivered terribly for a moment, and his hands seemed congealed on the machine gun. He could not bear the intense pressure in his head.

"We you coming-to-get, Yank," the voice screamed.

"COME AND GET ME YOU SONSOFBITCHES," Croft roared. He shouted with every fiber of his body as though he plunged at an oaken door.

There was no sound at all for perhaps ten seconds, nothing but the moonlight on the river and the taut rapt buzzing of the crickets. Then the voice spoke again. "Oh, we come, Yank, we come."

Croft pulled back the bolt on his machine gun, and rammed it home. His heart was still beating with frenzy "Recon . . . RE-CON, UP ON THE LINE," he shouted with all his strength.

A machine gun lashed at him from across the river, and he ducked in his hole. In the darkness, it spat a vindictive white light like an acetylene torch, and its sound was terrifying. Croft was holding himself together by the force of his will. He pressed the trigger of his gun and it leaped and bucked under his hand. The tracers spewed wildly into the jungle on the other side of the river.

But the noise, the vibration of his gun, calmed him. He directed it to where he had seen the Japanese gunfire and loosed a volley. The handle pounded against his fist, and he had to steady it with both hands. The hot metallic smell of the barrel eddied back to him, made what he was doing real again. He ducked in his hole waiting for the reply and winced involuntarily as the bullets whipped past.

BEE-YOWWWW! . . . BEE-YOOWWWW! Some dirt snapped at his face from the ricochets. Croft was not conscious of feeling it. He had the surface numbness a man has in a fight. He flinched at sounds, his mouth tightened and loosened, his eyes stared, but he was oblivious to his body.

Croft fired the gun again, held it for a long vicious burst, and then ducked in his hole. An awful scream singed the night, and for an instant Croft grinned weakly. Got him, he thought. He saw the metal burning through flesh, shattering the bones in its path. "AII-YOHHHH." The scream froze him again, and for an odd disconnected instant he experienced again the whole complex of sounds and smells and sights when a calf was branded. "RECON, UP . . . UP!" he shouted furiously and fired steadily for ten seconds to cover their advance. As he paused he could hear some men crawling behind him, and he whispered, "Recon?"

"Yeah." Gallagher dropped into the hole with him. "Mother of Mary," he muttered. Croft could feel him shaking beside him.

"Stop it!" he gripped his arm tensely. "The other men up?"

"Yeah."

Croft looked across the river again. Everything was silent, and the disconnected abrupt spurts of fire were forgotten like vanished sparks from a grindstone. Now that he was no longer alone, Croft was able to plan. The fact that men were up with him, were scattered in the brush along the bank between their two machine guns, recovered his sense of command. "They're going to attack soon," he whispered hoarsely in Gallagher's ear.

Gallagher trembled again. "Ohh. No way to wake up," he tried to say, but his voice kept lapsing.

"Look," Croft whispered. "Creep along the line and tell them to hold fire until the Japs start to cross the river."

"I can't, I can't," Gallagher whispered.

Croft felt like striking him. "Go!" he whispered.

"I can't."

The Jap machine gun lashed at them from across the river. The bullets went singing into the jungle behind them, ripping at leaves. The tracers looked like red splints of lightning as they flattened into the jungle. A thousand rifles seemed to be firing at them from across the river, and the two men pressed themselves against the bottom of the hole. The sounds cracked against their eardrums. Croft's head ached. Firing the machine gun had partially deafened him. BEE-YOWWWW! A ricochet slapped some more dirt on top of them. Croft felt it pattering on his back this time. He was trying to sense the moment when he would have to raise his head and fire the gun. The firing seemed to slacken, and he lifted his eyes cautiously. BEE-YOWWW, BEE-YOWWWW! He dropped in the hole again. The Japanese machine gun raked through the brush at them.

There was a shrill screaming sound, and the men covered their heads with their arms. BAA-ROWWMM, BAA-ROWWMM, ROWWMM, ROWWMM. The mortars exploded all about them, and something picked Gallagher up, shook him, and then released him. "O God," he cried. A clod of dirt stung his neck. BAA-ROWWMM, BAA-ROWWMM.

"Jesus, I'm hit," someone screamed, "I'm hit. Something hit me."

BAA-ROWWMM.

Gallagher rebelled against the force of the explosions. "Stop, I give up," he screamed. "STOP! . . . I give up! I give up!" At that instant he no longer knew what made him cry out.

BAA-ROWWMM, BAA-ROWWMM.

"I'm hit, I'm hit," someone was screaming. The Japanese rifles were firing again. Croft lay on the floor of the hole with his hands against the ground and every muscle poised in its place.

BAA-ROWWMM. TEEEEEEEN! The shrapnel was singing as it scattered through the foliage.

Croft picked up his flare gun. The firing had not abated, but through it he heard someone shouting in Japanese. He pointed the gun in the air.

"Here they come," Croft said.

He fired the flare and shouted, "STOP 'EM!"

A shrill cry came out of the jungle across the river. It was the scream a man might utter if his foot was being crushed. "AAAIIIIII, AAAIIIIIIII."

The flare burst at the moment the Japanese started their charge. Croft had a split perception of the Japanese machine gun firing from a flank, and then he began to fire automatically, not looking where he fired, but holding his gun low, swinging it from side to side. He could not hear the other guns fire, but he saw their muzzle blasts like exhausts.

He had a startling frozen picture of the Japanese running toward him across the narrow river. "AAAAIIIIIIIIIIH," he heard again. In the light of the flare the Japanese had the stark frozen quality of men revealed by a shaft of lightning. Croft no longer saw anything clearly; he could not have said at that moment where his hands ended and the machine gun began; he was lost in a vast moil of noise out of which individual screams and shouts etched in his mind for an instant. He could never have counted the Japanese who charged across the river; he knew only that his finger was rigid on the trigger bar. He could not have loosened it. In those few moments he felt no sense of danger. He just kept firing.

The line of men who charged across the river began to fall. In the water they were slowed considerably and the concentrated fire from recon's side raged at them like a wind across an open field. They began to stumble over the bodies ahead of them. Croft saw one soldier reach into the air behind another's body as though trying to clutch something in the sky and Croft fired at him for what seemed many seconds before the arm collapsed.

He looked to his right and saw three men trying to cross the river where it turned and ran parallel to the bluff. He swung the gun about and lashed them with it. One man fell, and the other two paused uncertainly and began to run back toward their own bank of the river. Croft had no time to follow them; some soldiers had reached the beach on his side and were charging the gun. He fired point blank at them, and they collapsed about five yards from his hole.

Croft fired and fired, switching targets with the quick reflexes of an athlete shifting for a ball. As soon as he saw men falling he would attack another group. The line of Japanese broke into little bunches of men who wavered, began to retreat.

The light of the flare went out and Croft was blinded for a moment. There was no sound again in the darkness and he fumbled for another flare, feeling an almost desperate urgency. "Where is it?" he whispered to Gallagher.

"What?"

"Shit." Croft's hand found the flare box, and he loaded the gun again. He was beginning to see in the darkness, and he hesitated. But something moved on the river and he fired the flare. As it burst, a few Japanese soldiers were caught motionless in the water. Croft pivoted his gun on them and fired. One of the soldiers remained standing for an incredible time. There was no expression on his face; he looked vacant and surprised even as the bullets struck him in the chest.

Nothing was moving now on the river. In the light of the flare, the bodies looked as limp and unhuman as bags of grain. One soldier began to float downstream, his face in the water. On the beach near the gun, another Japanese soldier was lying on his back. A wide stain of blood was spreading out from his body, and his stomach, ripped open, gaped like the swollen entrails of a fowl. On an impulse Croft fired a burst into him, and felt a twitch of pleasure as he saw the body quiver.

A wounded man was groaning in Japanese. Every few seconds he would scream, the sound terrifying in the cruel blue light of the flare. Croft picked up a grenade. "That sonofabitch is makin' too much noise," he said. He pulled the pin and lobbed the grenade over to the opposite bank. It dropped like a beanbag on one of the bodies, and Croft pulled Gallagher down with him. The explosion was powerful and yet empty like a blast that collapses window-panes. After a moment, the echoes ceased.

Croft tensed himself and listened to the sounds from across the river. There was the quiet furtive noise of men retreating into the jungle. "GIVE 'EM A VOLLEY!" he shouted.

All the men in recon began to fire again, and Croft raked the jungle for a minute in short bursts. He could hear Wilson's machine gun pounding steadily. "I guess we gave 'em something," Croft told Gallagher. The flare was going out, and Croft stood up. "Who was hit?" he shouted.

"Toglio."

"Bad?" Croft asked.

"I'm okay," Toglio whispered. "I got a bullet in my elbow."

"Can you wait till morning?"

There was silence for a moment, then Toglio answered weakly, "Yeah, I'll be okay."

Croft got out of his hole. "I'm coming down," he announced. "Hold your fire." He walked along the path until he reached Toglio. Red and Goldstein were kneeling beside him, and Croft spoke to them in a low voice. "Pass this on," he said. "We're all gonna stay in our holes until mornin'. I don't think they'll be back tonight, but you cain't tell. And no one is gonna fall asleep. They's only about an hour till dawn, so you ain't got nothin' to piss about."

"I wouldn't go to sleep anyway," Goldstein breathed. "What a way to wake up." It was the same thing Gallagher had said.

"Yeah, well, I just wasn't ridin' on my ass either, waitin' for them to come," Croft said. He shivered for a moment in the early morning air and realized with a pang of shame that for the first time in his life he had been really afraid. "The sonsofbitchin' Japs," he said. His legs were tired and he turned to go back to his gun. I hate the bastards, he said to himself, a terrible rage working through his weary body.

"One of these days I'm gonna really get me a Jap," he whispered aloud. The river was slowly carrying the bodies downstream.

"At least," Gallagher said, "if we got to stay here a couple of days, the fuggers won't be stinkin' up the joint."

BARBARY SHORE

Published by Rinehart in 1951, Barbary Shore *is probably the least appreciated of Mailer's books. It remains available in New American Library's Signet paperback. The excerpt here consists simply of the first six chapters of the novel and introduces us to the first of a long series of Mailer's artist-heroes, Mikey Lovett, and introduces, too, an almost archetypal Mailer relationship, the generational friendship between Mikey and McLeod. The figure of the young artist as a sort of heir apparent to an older friend, and the analysis of how knowledge and experience are passed along between men will remain a central concern in all of Mailer's fiction to follow.*

Chapter 1

Probably I was in the war. There is the mark of a wound behind my ear, an oblong of unfertile flesh where no hair grows. It is covered over now, and may be disguised by even the clumsiest barber, but no barber can hide the scar on my back. For that a tailor is more in order.

When I stare into the mirror I am returned a face doubtless more handsome than the original, but the straight nose, the modelled chin, and the smooth cheeks are only evidence of a stranger's art. It does not matter how often I decide the brown hair and the gray eyes must have always been my own; there is nothing I can recognize, not even my age. I am certain I cannot be less than twenty-five and it is possible I am older, but thanks to whoever tended me, a young man without a wrinkle in his skin stands for a portrait in the mirror.

There was a time when I would try rather frantically to recall what kind of accident it had been and where it had occurred. I could almost picture the crash of an airplane and the flames entering my cockpit. No sooner had I succeeded, however, than the airplane became a tank and I was trapped within, only to create another environment; the house was burning and a timber pinned my back. Such violence ends with the banality of beads; grenades, shell, bombardment—I can elaborate a hundred such, and none seem correct.

Here and there, memories return. Only it is difficult to trust them. I am positive my parents are dead, that I grew up in an institution for children, and was always poor. Still, there are times when I think I remember my mother, and I have the idea I received an education. The deaf are supposed to hear a myriad of noises, and silence is filled with the most annoying rattle and tinkle and bell; the darkness of the blind is marred by erratic light; thus memory for me was never a wall but more a roulette of the most extraordinary events and the most insignificant, all laced into the same vessel until I could not discern the most casual fact from the most patent fancy, nor the past from the future; and the details of my own history were lost in the other, common to us all. I could never judge whether something had happened to me or I imagined it so. It made little difference whether I had met a man or he existed only in a book; there was never a way to determine if I knew a country or merely remembered another's description. The legends from a decade of newsprint were as intimate and distant as the places in which I must have lived. No history belonged to me and so all history was mine. Yet in what a state. Each time my mind furnished a memory long suppressed it was only another piece, and there were so few pieces and so much puzzle.

During one period I made prodigious efforts to recover the past. I conducted a massive correspondence with the secretaries of appropriate officials; I followed people upon the street because they had looked at me with curiosity; I searched lists of names, studied photographs, and lay on my bed bludgeoning my mind to confess a single material detail. Prodigious efforts, but I recovered nothing except to learn that I had no past and was therefore without a future. The blind grow ears, the deaf learn how to see, and I acquired both in compensation; it was natural, even obligatory, that the present should possess the stage.

And as time possessed the present I began to retain what had happened to me in the previous week, the previous month, and that became my experience, became all my experience. If it were circumscribed it was nonetheless a world, and a year from the time I first found myself with no name in my pocket, I could masquerade like anyone else. I lived like the hermit in the desert who sweats his penance and waits for a sign. There was none and probably there will be none — I doubt if I shall find my childhood and my youth — but I have come to understand the skeleton perhaps of that larger history, and not everything is without its purpose. I have even achieved a balance, if that is what it may be called.

Now, in the time I write, when other men besides myself must contrive a name, a story, and the papers they carry, I wonder if I do not possess an advantage. For I have been doing it longer, and am tantalized less by the memory of better years. They must suffer, those others like myself. I wonder what fantasies bother them?

There is one I have regularly. It seems as if only enough time need elapse for me to forget before it appears again:

I see a traveller. He is most certainly not myself. A plump middle-aged man, and I have the idea he has just finished a long trip. He has landed at an airfield or his train has pulled into a depot. It hardly matters which.

He is in a hurry to return home. With impatience he suffers the necessary delays in collecting his baggage, and when the task is finally done, he hails a taxi, installs his luggage, bawls out his instructions, and settles back comfortably in the rear seat. Everything is so peaceful. Indolently he turns his head to watch children playing a game upon the street.

He is weary, he discovers, and his breath comes heavily. Unfolding his newspaper he attempts to study it, but the print blurs and he lays the sheet down. Suddenly and unaccountably he is quite depressed. It has been a long trip he reassures himself. He looks out the window.

The cab is taking the wrong route!

What shall he do? It seems so simple to raise his hand and tap upon the glass, but he feels he dare not disturb the driver. Instead, he looks through the window once more.

The man lives in this city, but he has never seen these streets. The architecture is strange, and the people are dressed in unfamiliar clothing. He looks at a sign, but it is printed in an alphabet he cannot read.

His hand folds upon his heart to still its beating. It is a dream, he thinks, hugging his body in the rear of the cab. He is dreaming and the city is imaginary and the cab is imaginary. And on he goes.

I shout at him. You are wrong, I cry, although he does not hear me; this city is the real city, the material city, and your vehicle is history. Those are the words I use, and then the image shatters.

Night comes and I am alone with a candle. What has been fanciful is now concrete. Although the room in which I write has an electric circuit, it functions no longer. Time passes and I wait by the door, listening to the footsteps of roomers as they go out to work for the night. In fourteen hours they will be back.

So the blind lead the blind and the deaf shout warnings to one another until their voices are lost.

Chapter 2

I suppose even a magic box must have its handle. Yet once the box is opened, I wonder if it is too unreasonable that the handle is then ignored. I am more concerned with the contents. If I begin with Willie Dinsmore, it is because he served as a handle; and I, who was to serve for so long as the sorcerer's apprentice, forgot him quickly.

Let me describe how I was living at the time. I had a bed in one of those young men's dormitories which seem always to be constructed about a gymnasium and a cafeteria. Since such organizations are inevitably founded on the principle that people should be forced to enjoy each other's presence, I suffered through a succession of bunkmates, and found once again the unique loneliness which comes from living without privacy. I would hardly have chosen to stay there, but I had little choice. Through all that year, in which I received no mail and moved beyond a nodding acquaintance with very few people, I worked at a succession of unskilled jobs and with a discipline I would hardly have expected in myself put away regularly at the end of the week a sum of ten dollars. I was driven with the ambition that I should be a writer, and I was grubbing quite appropriately for a grubstake. My project was to save five hundred dollars and then find an inexpensive room: calculated virtually to the penny, I found that if the rent were less than five dollars a week, I would have enough money to live for six months and I could write my novel or at least begin it.

The cash finally accumulated, I searched for a cheap place of my own, but the place was never cheap enough. I flushed corners for thirty dollars a month, for forty dollars, and more, but they would have exhausted my savings too rapidly. I was growing somewhat desperate until Willie Dinsmore, after weeks of jockeying me on a puppeteer's string, gave me his room.

Dinsmore was a playwright. Being also a husband and a father, he found difficulty in working at home and therefore kept a small furnished cubicle in a brownstone house in Brooklyn Heights. Once, in passing, he told me he would let the room go when he went away for the summer, and I had coaxed a promise that I would get the vacancy. Since we knew each other only casually, I made a point afterward never to lose contact with him for very long. Dinsmore's niche cost only four dollars a week, and there was not another so inexpensive to be discovered.

I would pay him a visit from time to time and note with all the pleasure of an eager customer each small advantage the house had to offer. Certainly I was easy to please. Although I would be situated on the top floor beneath a flat roof and have for ventilation but a single window, opening upon laundry lines and back yards to the fire escape of an apartment house upon the next street, it never occurred to me how oppressive and sultry a hole this might become.

A small room, not more than eight feet wide, one had to edge sideways between the desk and the bed to reach the window. The paint was years old and had soiled to the ubiquitous yellow-brown of cheap lodgings. Its surface blistered and buckled, large swatches of plaster had fallen, and in a corner the ceiling was exposed to the lath. Cinders drifted up from the dock area below the bluffs to cover the woodwork. The sash cord was broken, and the window rested in all its weight upon two empty beer cans which served as support. Even at four dollars a week the bargain was not conspicuous, but I was enamored of it.

I would sit on the bed and watch Dinsmore sort his papers, scatter dust from the desk to the floor, and mop his face. He was a short stocky man whose favorite position was astraddle a chair, chin resting on the back, and his body bent forward. He looked like a football lineman in this posture, and his head, which resembled a boxer dog, could hardly contradict the impression. Having told him nothing about myself, and indeed I was hardly in the habit, he made the assumption that I was a war veteran, and I never bothered to explain there might be some doubt. Dinsmore was happier this way in any case. Like so many writers he had very little interest in people, and if they could serve his didactic demands, a pigeonhole was all he required. I had been installed immediately in the one he undoubtedly labelled Postwar Problems.

"I'll tell you, kid," he would say, "it's a shame the way people got to live doubled up in rooms, and lots of you GI's"—his voice was pitched deferentially when he spoke about veterans—"the ones who're married and living with their inlaws and their marriages are going to pot all cause they can't get a lousy apartment. It's the fault of the real estate interests, and it's a crime that we fight an anti-fascist war and don't clean out the fascists in our own house, but I'll tell you, Mikey, they're making a mistake, they're cutting their own throat, cause the veterans aren't going to stand for it."

I never knew whether he believed this, or if it came from the desire to vindicate his plays. The poorest strain in his writing had been the kind of superficial optimism prevalent during the war, which still lasted posthumously among the many playwrights and novelists whose lack of political sophistication was satisfied by dividing all phenomena into Dinsmore's categories. At bottom it was only a temporary mode of that great crutch to the simple-minded: —the right guy and the wrong-o—and already to the confusion and the eventual danger of men like Willie the names had changed.

Willie kept his head down, however, and his eye to the measure. His hero was still the young anti-fascist who had come back from the war and gave the speech about the world he fought to make. The speech was not new, but an old speech never hurt a playwright, and Dinsmore doubled his success in a thematic sequel whose young veteran told the audience what kind of world he wanted for his infant.

It will be apparent by now, I fear, that I was not precisely infatuated with Willie. He had a home, he had a family, he had a reputation, and any one of the three was more than I could expect. But Willie found other homes as well. He had the kind of mind which could not bear any question taking longer than ten seconds to answer. "There are the haves and the have-nots," Willie would declare: "there are the progressive countries and the reactionary countries. In half the globe the people own the means of production, and in the other half the fascists have control."

I would offer a mild objection. "It's just as easy to say that in every country the majority have very little. Such a division is probably the basis of society."

Willie reacted with a hurt smile and a compassionate look in his face. Whenever I contradicted him, he would change the subject. "You take the theatre. It's sick, Mikey, you know why? All commercialized. What we need is a people's theatre again, you know where you pay a quarter, tie-ups with unions, school kids, where you can show the facts of life. A worker's theatre."

"Precisely."

"The problem is to give it back to the people. The classical theatre was always progressive. Art is a people's fight."

To elaborate at such length upon Willie is not completely necessary, but I wanted to give a small portrait of him because he was the first person to mention Beverly Guinevere to me, and his description had its effect long after I knew it was untrue, and colored many nuances. If I had had any judgment, I would have known that Willie was innocent and his perceptions about people had no more chance of being accurate than a man who hurls a stone at a target he cannot see. But to possess judgment was another matter. My face allowed people to think that I was only twenty, and in a reciprocal of that relation I often felt like an adolescent first entering the adult world where everyone is strange and individual. I was always too ready to mistake opinion for fact.

The first time I heard Guinevere's name Willie was in the process of using it as a springboard for one of his lectures. "Someday," Willie threatened, "I'll sic the landlady on you." He paused, rocking the chair on its legs. "She's a character, wait'll you meet her. I'll tell you, Mikey, when you find out the score you'll stay away from her."

"Why?"

"If she gets alone in the same room with you, you won't be safe." He paused again. "Guinevere's a nymphomaniac."

I remember that I grinned. "What happened to you, Willie?"

"Nothing. She's not my type. You know she's kind of old, and she's fat." He pursed his lips judiciously. "And then I'll tell you, Mikey, extramarital relations are different when you're married, I mean there's the psychological angle to consider. And when you got kids there's always the danger of disease, of going blind, having a leg fall off. I may not have been a GI, but I saw that venereal movie, too." And intrigued, he shook his head. "You remember the guy who couldn't talk, who just whistled? Holy Cow, I tell you we need Health Clinics all over the country, especially in the South. I made a tour through there last year to gather some material, and *Jesus*, the ignorance."

He massaged his chin, fully embarked upon a lecture. "Conditions are brutal in this country — slums, juvenile delinquency. I mean when you add it up there's an indictment, and that's just counting the physical part of it. You take Guinevere, someone like that, it's a psychological problem, a psychological casualty I think of it. I mean I can see her side of it, Mikey. She's lonesome, that's all. You know she made sort of an advance, and I repulsed her with a few well-chosen words, just a couple of gags, but I guess it hurt her feelings. People always want you to think well of them, so she started to tell me her side of it, and she hasn't got any intellectual resources, and there's a lot of housework cleaning up this barn. You know the typical American housewife with the success story in reverse. I'll bet she reads *True Confessions*."

"You don't make her sound very attractive."

"Oh, she's got sex appeal of a sort, but she's a crazy dame. I might have entertained ideas, but there's her husband involved, and although I never met the guy I think it's kind of sneaky seeing a dame when her husband sleeps in the same building."

This is the woman Dinsmore advertised as having the power to give his cubbyhole away. Witness my surprise — for I had become convinced that he would finally end by awarding his room to some other acquantance — when Willie came to the dormitory one morning, and told me he was leaving for the country. I dressed quickly and ate breakfast in the cafeteria while Willie sat across from me, scattering his cigarette ash in my saucer. "Look," he said, "Guinevere could have already promised the first vacancy. We'll have to figure out a plan."

"I hope it works," I told him.

We walked over to the rooming house. For a June morning the sidewalks were still cool, and the brownstone houses were not without dignity. The spring air contained a suggestion of wood and meadow, and it was possible to imagine the gardens and the trellised arbors as they must have existed fifty years ago. We were on a street which led toward the bluffs, the docks beyond, and the bay. Across the harbor through a morning haze the skyline reared itself in the distance, while down the river an ocean liner was approaching its dock.

Mrs. Guinevere, I discovered, had the basement apartment with its customary entrance tucked beneath the slope of the front stairway, its private gate and miniature plot whose stony soil was without even a weed. As Dinsmore pressed the bell, I could hear it ringing inside.

From the apartment there was the sound of footsteps approaching, then a suspicious pause. A voice shrieked, "Who is it?"

Willie shouted his name and I could hear the bolt slide slowly open. "Come on, come on," he said raucously, "what do you think, we got all day?"

"Oh, it's you," a woman screeched back. "Well, what the hell do you want?" The door opened a crack, a set of plump little fingers curled around it, and a pair of eyes and the tip of a nose appeared in the slit. "You always have to pick a time when I'm busy." Slowly, provocatively, the face protruded a little further and two curls of extraordinarily red hair peeped around the door.

"Come on out. I want you to meet a writer friend, Mikey Lovett." Dinsmore made the introductions to the doorpost. I said hello somewhat foolishly, and her eyes stared back at me. "I'm pleased to meet you, Mr. Lovett," she said in the unexpected and dulcet cadence of a telephone operator. "I hope you'll excuse the way I'm dressed." With that, she swung the door open as though to unveil a statue. I was startled. Dinsmore had poorly prepared me. She was quite pretty, at least to my taste, pretty in a flamboyant cootchy way, so that my first impression was of no more than a fabulous crop of red hair and a woman beneath, waggling her hips. Undeniably short and stout, her limbs were nevertheless delicate, her face was not heavy, and her waist, respectably narrow, tapered inward from her broad shoulders in an exaggeration which was piquing.

"It takes me forever to get dressed," she grumbled. "Boy, you men are lucky not having to fool around with a house." Her voice began the first sentence as a telephone operator and finished the second as a fishwife; once again she was shouting. Yet in the silence which followed this, she closed her large blue eyes for several seconds and then opened them again with counterfeit simplicity. Obviously she considered this to be of considerable effect, but since her eyes protruded a trifle, the benefit was somewhat doubtful.

The silence served as a floor upon which she and Dinsmore could exchange a minuet of looks and glances and innuendo, while a smile flickered between them. Standing to one side, I had the opportunity to look at her closely. It was impossible to determine her age, but I was certain she was less than forty.

"Yeah, it's tough," Dinsmore grinned at last. His voice rasped more when he spoke to her. "Still, you look good . . good."

"Aw, you." After the introduction she had paid me no attention, but now, hand on hip, she wheeled in my direction. "If I was to listen to this guy's line," she said, "he'd be up my skirts in two minutes."

"You hope," Dinsmore said.

She laughed loudly with boisterous good humor, and I had the impression she might have nudged him in the ribs if I were not there. Her thin lips pursed, but this was beneath the other mouth of lipstick which was wide and curved in the sexual stereotype of a model on a magazine cover, and seemed to work in active opposition to the small mobile lips beneath. "Boy, you writers," she snorted, "you think you own the world."

Dinsmore threw up his hands in a pantomime of being rebuffed, and then, the manner satisfied and the preamble concluded, his tone changed. "Listen, Guinevere, you're a pretty good scout, how about doing us a favor?"

"What?" It was apparent the word "favor" had few pleasant connotations to her.

"I'm giving up my room for a couple of months. How about letting Mikey have it?"

She frowned. "Listen, I can get five dollars extra if I put up a sign and rent it out."

"Why should the landlord be the profiteer?" He waved his finger at her. "Suppose I kept paying for the room, and Mikey stayed in it. That'd be okay."

She shrugged. "I can't stop you."

Well, why make me go to the trouble? Why don't you just let the kid take it." He whacked her playfully on the hip. "Come on, be a good sport."

"Aw, you writers, you're all nuts," she jeered. "No sooner get rid of one of you, then I get another."

"I really could use the room," I said. I smiled tentatively.

Perhaps she was examining me. After a moment or two she nodded her head angrily, and said, "All right. You can have it. But the rent's got to be paid every Thursday, four dollars paid in advance of the week to come, and no hot air about it." In the correct style of a landlady her voice had been flat and authoritative, although immediately afterward as though to salvage someone's good opinion, she whined defensively, "I can't be bothered chasing around after you guys. I've got a lot of work to do here, and Lord knows I get paid little enough for it, and you got to co-operate."

"I'll pay the money on time," I said.

"Well, let's hope so." She had yielded grudgingly, but now that business was terminated, she smiled. "I'll see you around, Mr. Lovett. Linen day is also on Thursday. You get one new sheet a week, and you can help me if you strip the bed before I get up there." This, however, was said with heavy allure.

We exchanged a few more words and left for Dinsmore's house. He clapped me on the back. "She likes you, kid."

"How do you know?"

"She just likes you. I can tell. Good-looking kid like you. You'll be having your hands full with her."

Unwillingly, in the customary reaction to just this situation, my hand strayed up to the scar tissue behind my ear, and I was taken again with a desire to study that face Dinsmore had called good-looking. "No," I answered him, "I won't be having my hands full with her. I've got to work."

"Stick to your story, Lovett."

We walked slowly, the day already warm. "She's absolutely weird," Dinsmore said. "A complex character." He sighed, pushed the hair off his forehead. "Basically she was good stuff," he lectured, "but you get human beings caught in a profit nexus, and it turns them inside out. The structure of society is rotten today."

"Yes, it is."

When we reached his house, he paused, shook my hand, and

smiled. "It's been great knowing you, kid, and I'm glad I did you a favor." Before I could reply, he went on. "There's something I'd like to say, because right now like everybody else you're at the crossroads, and the thing you want to ask yourself, Lovett, is which way are you going to go? Will you be against the people or will you be for them?"

"I'm afraid I haven't thought that way in a long time."

"You'll have to. Wall Street will leave you no choice." He smiled wisely, and something hard and smug came into his face. "There's just one thing you got to remember, Mikey. It's the basic issue, it's the basic trouble with this country. Do you know what it is?"

I confessed I was not completely certain.

He prodded his thumb against my stomach and in a sepulchral voice he stated, "Empty bellies . . empty bellies. That's the issue, kid."

Thus, unlike most partings, ours was on a basic issue. I turned once to wave at him from down the street before he went inside his house, and then I continued back to the dormitory and gathered my belongings. It was time for me to move.

My few possessions transported and unpacked, I lay on my new bed and mused about the novel I was going to write. Through this long summer I could turn back upon myself and discover . . but I had seen so much of the world and, seeing, had so disconnected it, that I had everything to discover.

I daydreamed only a little while about my novel. Instead I was thinking of Guinevere. She was a nymphomaniac, he had said. Such a curious word. I had never applied it to anyone. It was difficult to forget her breasts which had thrust upward from their binding in copious splendor, so palpable that they obtained the intensification of art and became more real than themselves.

A jewel. But set in brass. This morning she had sported a house dress and covered it with a bathrobe. Her red hair, with which undoubtedly she was always experimenting, had been merely blowzy and flew out in all directions from her head. Yet there had been opera pumps on her feet, her nails had been painted, her lipstick was fresh. She was a house whose lawn was landscaped and whose kitchen was on fire. I would not have been startled if she had turned around and like the half-dressed queen in the girlie show: surprise! her buttocks are exposed.

The nymphomaniac. As I was about to fall asleep for the first time in my new room, I realized that I wanted to take Guinevere to bed.

Chapter 3

The attic, as I have indicated, was up three gloomy flights of stairs. Once, many years ago, the house had been a modest mansion, but now it was partitioned into cubicles. On the top story, a masterpiece of design, no window gave upon the landing, and at the head of the stairs, burning into perpetuity, one weak light bulb cast its sallow illumination upon my door, upon the doors of the two neighbors I had not met, and upon the oilcloth of the bathroom we shared.

It was a big house and gave the impression of being an empty house. Downstairs there were ten names arranged in ten brackets next to as many bells which did not ring, but a week could go by and I would pass no one upon the stairs. I hardly cared. In the last months I had come to know fewer and fewer people, and by the time I quit the dormitory, for better or for worse I was very much alone. At first this did not matter. I began my novel, and for a few days, completely isolated, I made progress. Since I could assume that a sizable portion of my life had been spent in one barracks or another, a room for myself was more than a luxury. Temporarily I felt free and rather happy. As though to exploit all the advantages of my new situation, I ate meals around the clock and slept as my whim directed.

Such a period could not last for long. A day passed and another, while pages of new manuscript collected on the desk. And about me, with patient regular industry, dust accumulated everywhere. Whatever plans I might have entertained for Guinevere were not to come passively to fruition. I never saw her. Conventional landlady, she never bothered to clean, and the dust in my room increased from minute to minute in competition with the hall outside. The entire house was filthy.

Except for the bathroom. This bore the evidence of regular attention, and even presented a certain immaculacy at times, a mystery to me until I met McLeod.

One morning I found a man at work washing the bathroom floor. He looked up and nodded, his cold clear eyes staring at me from behind his spectacles. "You're the one who took over Dinsmore's room?" he asked finally.

I answer his question, and he rose from his knees, introduced himself and made a short speech in a dry ironic voice. "I'll tell you," he said, pinching his thin lips primly, "this place is always a mess. Guinevere don't get off her bottom long enough to wash a handkerchief, so I've taken over cleaning the bathroom twice a week, and far as I see there's small profit in it." He scratched his chin sourly. "I've asked Hollingsworth, the gentleman who resides in the other room up here, to pitch in once in a while, but he's always got a hangover, or else he's sprained his wrist, or there's a mole on his belly." He shrugged. "If you want to, Lovett, you can help me keep this clean, but I can tell you from the outset that if you don't want to co-operate, I'll still be doing it because unfortunately I've got a mania about neatness."

My introduction to McLeod. On completing the discourse, he folded his long slender hands over the top of a broom handle, and pursed his mouth. At the moment he bore an astonishing resemblance to a witch, his gaunt face nodding in communion with himself, his long thin body stooped in thought. When I did not reply immediately, he filled the gap by running a comb through his straight black hair, the action emphasizing the sweep of his sharp narrow nose.

"You're a writer, Dinsmore told me."

"More or less."

"I see." He gave the impression of listening carefully to what I said, evaluating my words, and then discarding them. "I've got a proposition," McLeod said to me, "which you can take or leave. You clean up the bathroom on Wednesdays, and I'll keep doing it on Saturday." With little effort he gave the impression of saturating each word with a considerable weight of satire. I sensed that he was laughing at me.

Annoyed, I yawned. "What do you say we draw up a contract?"

His mouth, severe in repose, became mocking as he smiled. He looked at me shrewdly. "I'm getting you down a bit, eh?" Laughter altered his face so that for an instant he could appear young and merry. He drawled out his next offering with a self-satisfied air as though he were sucking a candy-drop. "Well, now, that's a thought, Lovett. It's a thought." And still chuckling, he examined the bathroom floor, found it to his satisfaction, and stowed the broom in a corner. "I'm across the hall. Drop by when you're dressed," he offered.

I did, and we talked for an hour. I had thought he might be taciturn about himself, but he belied this impression by talking freely, or more exactly by conveying a series of specific details much as he might have furnished a dossier. He was forty-four, he told me, and he worked in a department store as a window dresser. He had grown up in Brooklyn, he had always been a solitary man. He had a father who lived in an Old Folks' Home. Rarely saw him. Possessed a high-school education. Obtained in Brooklyn. "I've lived here always," he said with his mocking smile. "I've never been out of New York with the exception of one small trip to New Jersey. That's m'life." And he burst into laughter.

"Just that?" I asked.

"I see you don't believe me. People rarely do. It's because I give the impression of having some culture. I've studied, you see, by myself. I'm not a joiner, and I don't put my education to work, but I am a great reader, it must be said."

And with that, subtly yet unmistakably, he directed me to the door and shook hands, his eyes studying me in amusement.

I dropped into his room again the next evening and the next. I think I talked with McLeod five or six times that first week. However, I would not say we became friends quickly. He had a brutal honesty which made it difficult to speak casually with him. He would leap upon some passing statement I might make, and figuratively twirl my words about his finger as if to examine them from every aspect. I found myself continually on the defensive, and though with a left-handed fascination I was always providing matter for his mill, nonetheless I resented him for it.

What glee the process gave him. Once I mentioned a girl with whom I had recently had an affair, and I shrugged and said, "But it didn't mean much. We got a little bored with each other, and drifted out of it."

McLeod gave his sly grin, the side of his mouth sucking on the imaginary candy-drop. "You drifted out of it, eh?"

Irritably, I snapped, "Yes, I drifted out of it. Didn't you ever hear of anything like that?"

"Yes, I've heard of it. I hear it all the time. People are always drifting in and out of things." He leaned back on the bed, and pressed his finger tips together. "I'll tell you the truth, Lovett, I don't know what those words mean. 'Drifted in and out, drifted in and out,'" he repeated as though the phrase were delicious. "When you have to, it's pretty convenient to think of yourself as a drift-wood."

"I can explain it to you."

"Oh," he said, grinning, "I know you can explain it to me. I just want to try to figure out m'self what it signifies drifting out of an affair. Because in the old days when I used to cut a figure with the women I had my share of it, and it seems to me now that when I broke up with a woman it was often somewhat nasty."

"With a sadist like you," I said in an attempt at humor. My answers were invariably dull, my temper ragged. He had a facility for wearing one down, and it was not surprising that when I swung I was wild.

McLeod nodded. "Oh, yes. When I'd examine my motives, I'd

find elements which were ugly enough. I've been a bad piece of work in my time." He said this with great severity.

Almost immediately, however, he would be prodding again. "Now, I don't know about you, Lovett, but when I'd drift out of an affair I'd find if I started to think about it that the reasons were somewhat interesting. There were women I quit because I made love to them ineptly, unpleasant as that may be to admit. And then, taking the converse of the proposition, there was a woman or two in love with me and wanting to get married." He began to laugh, quietly and ferociously. " 'What? Get married?' I would say to them. 'Who, me? Why I thought it was understood from the beginning that this was on a give and take basis.' " His mouth curled, his voice whined in a grotesque of outraged innocence. "Girlie, you got the wrong number. I thought it was understood we were modern individuals with a modern viewpoint." He roared with laughter now. "Oh, my mother." And then, his mouth mocking me, McLeod said, "That's another one belongs with the driftwood."

"Now, look," I'd object, "does a man have to get married every time he starts a relation with a woman?"

"No." He lit a cigarette, amused with me. "You see, Lovett, there's a difference between you and me. You're *honest*. I never was. I'd start off with the lady, and we'd have a nice conversation at the beginning about how neither of us could afford to get tied up, all understood, all good clean healthy fun." His voice was steeped in ridicule. "Fine. Only you see, Lovett, I could never let it go at that. The old dependable mechanisms would start working in me. I'd begin operating. You know what I mean? I'd do everything in my power to make the girl love me — when you think of the genius I've squandered in bed. And sure enough there'd be the times when I'd talk her into being in love, when I'd worry her to death until there was never a man in the world who made love like me." He coughed. "But once she admitted that. . . . finito! I was getting bored. I thought it was time we drifted apart." He laughed again, at himself and at me. "Why, when the little lady would suggest marriage you should have seen me go into my act. 'You're welshing on the bargain,' I would tell her, 'I'm disappointed in you. How could you have betrayed me so?' " Once more he roared with laughter. "Oh, there was a devilish mechanism in it. You see, she betrayed me, you get it, she betrayed *me*, and it was time for us to drift apart."

"I'm to take it that the shoe fits?"

McLeod looked out his window at the apartment house beyond. He seemed to be listening intently to the clanging of the steam donkey on the docks below the bluff, working overtime into the night. "I can't say, Lovett. It's always a good idea to know one-self."

"I think I do."

His face was still impassive, his thin mouth straight. "I suspect in your case there are special conditions." Casually, he flicked the next sentence at me. "Mind telling a man how you got that patch on your skull?"

I was caught without guard. "It's not your business," I managed to stammer, and I could feel myself blushing with anger.

He nodded without surprise, and continued in the same casual tone. He could have been a scientist examining a specimen. "My guess is that there're other tattoos on your skin."

"Guess away."

"You need maintain no front with me," McLeod said quietly. "It's friendly curiosity."

"Anything you want to know," I murmured.

He did not answer directly. "The analysis I gave of your motives and mine in drifting out of an affair is very curious."

"Why?"

"Because it's not the least bit true for either of us. I presented it merely as a construction. I, for example, have never been torment-ed by excessive sexual vanity."

"Then what were you getting at?"

McLeod shrugged. "I was interested in the way you spoke so casually. It would not be surprising if the affair with the little lady you mentioned were more painful than that to you."

He was not far wrong. Casual it had been for her, and painful for me. "Possibly," I admitted with some discomfort.

"You see, Lovett, the thing I noticed from the beginning is a cer-tain passion to pass yourself off like anyone else. Perhaps someday you'll tell me why you choose to stay in this rooming house, a lone-ly proposition I should think."

"I want to be by myself, that's all," I said.

McLeod went on as if I had not spoken. "A young man might do that who was seriously alone, and had lost most of the normal forms of contact. Or" — and he puffed at his cigarette — "it's possi-ble that somebody like you stays here and talks to me because it's your job and you're paid to do that." With a startling intentness his eyes looked into mine, waiting for some informative flicker per-haps.

"I don't know what you're talking about," I said.

"No . . Well, maybe you don't, m'bucko. Maybe you don't. You're not the type, I expect," McLeod said cryptically. "More like you to drift," and he was silent for a long time afterward.

Such conversations were hardly soothing. I would leave him to spend troubled hours by myself while the questions he had asked so easily went wandering for an answer. There were times when I shunned his company.

And days after I moved in, I found myself still thinking of Guinevere. She would be so fine for me. Her hips waggled in invitation; she was obtainable. In retrospect I understood that I had gone to visit McLeod the first time with some idea of learning about her casually. Guinevere's name, through lack of opportunity, had not been mentioned, and now it was impossible. No matter how flatly I might inquire about her, McLeod would be certain to appreciate the reason for my curiosity.

By shifts I did my work, went for long walks through the hot streets of Brooklyn, and apportioned the sixteen dollars a week I allowed myself for meals in a lunchroom, a few drinks, and a movie. It was quiet, it was lonesome, and the last evenings of spring I tasted vicariously, watching the young lovers parade the streets of the vast suburban mangle which extends beyond the border of Brooklyn Heights to the dirt, the popcorn underfoot, and the quick sordid gaiety of Coney Island, sweet and transient, soon to be swept away in the terrible and superheated nights of midsummer.

Chapter 4

After a week Mrs. Guinevere came to the room with a change of linen. Once again she was dressed uniquely. Although it was nine o'clock in the evening, she wore a nightgown over some underclothing whose complex network of straps could be seen upon her shoulders. This ensemble of slips, girdles, gowns and bands was covered by a short flowered bathrobe open at the throat to exhibit her impressive breast.

"Oh . . . hello," I said, and found it difficult to add anything. I was too absorbed in what I had been writing to make the transition smoothly. "I guess I owe you four dollars," I managed to say.

"Yeah." Guinevere seemed uninterested in the money.

I rummaged through my bureau drawer, came up with my wallet, and paid her. In the meantime she had stripped my bed and tossed a fresh sheet and towel upon it. When she finished, she sighed loudly and purposefully.

"How're things going?" I asked.

"So-so."

This would hardly do. "You look tired," I said intimately. "Sit down."

Guinevere glanced at the pile of folded sheets upon her arm and shrugged. "All right, maybe I will," she said, "seeing as the door's open." The sentence was invested with a wealth of vulgar gentility.

Perched beside me on the bed, she sighed again. I lit a cigarette and discovered that my hands were not at all steady. I was very aware of her.

"How about letting me have one?" she asked.

Inwardly, I was shaking. I did something she must have found surprising. I picked up the pack and the matches, and placed them in her lap although we were sitting not a foot apart. She opened her large blue eyes then, glanced at me, and waved the match to the tobacco. I had no idea what we would talk about.

Guinevere solved that for me. "What a terrible day I've had," she sighed.

"The linens?"

"No." She shook her head dramatically and stared at me. "No, I've been having trouble with my nerves." Her lipstick, an experimental bluish pink, had been applied this once to conform to the real shape of her lips, and it made her look less attractive. "What's the matter with your nerves?" I asked.

She fingered a curl in her red hair. "I'm just too high-strung, that's all." Her eyes came to rest on my typewriter, and I have the idea that for the first time since she entered the room, she knew where she had seen me before. "You're a writer, aren't you?"

I nodded, and she said what I expected her to say. "You know, I could be a writer. I tell you when I think of all the real-life human dramas I've lived among"—her voice took on the shadings of a radio announcer—"and the experience I've had, for I've lived a full life although you wouldn't know it to look at me, why I tell you I could make a fortune just putting it all down on paper."

The lack of contact between us was considerable. Her voice sad and reflective, she recited to an unknown audience. I coughed. "You ought to sit down and write."

"No, I couldn't. I can't concentrate." Her hand played over the pile of sheets. "Today is linen day, and do you know I haven't been able to do a thing. I just sat and looked at those linens until my husband came home, and he had to cook supper for me—oh, I had a horrible experience last night."

"What?"

"It gives me the creeps to talk about it."

"Well, what was it?"

She fingered her bosom, adjusting the brassiere to conceal a quarter inch more of the gorge between her breasts. "Well, you know I got the downstairs apartment, and we keep the windows open in this weather, and guess what happened? A cat got in and crawled over the bed around four A.M., and I woke up and saw it looking me in the eye." She sighed dolefully again. "It's a wonder I didn't wake the whole house with my screaming. My husband had to calm me for an hour. And this morning I opened the cupboard, and that same cat, a big black thing, jumped out at me, and scratched my face. Look!" She showed me a faint red line on her cheek.

"It happened, and now it's done," I said.

She blinked her eyes against the unshielded glare of the light, a single bulb which hung from a cord above the desk. "No, it isn't." Dramatically she whispered, "Do you know what that cat was? It was the Devil."

I didn't know whether to laugh or not, and so I grinned doubtfully.

"Yessir," she went on, "you may not know it, but that's one of the manifestations of the Devil's spirit. A black cat. It's in the Good Book that the Devil, the Lord's disinherited brother, is a manifestation as a cat, a black cat. That's why black cats are unlucky."

I wondered if this were a joke. Her words had tumbled out in a pious breathless voice which had little relation to the first picture I kept of her, hand on hip, jeering at Dinsmore, "All you writers are nuts."

"Well, how are you sure of this?" I asked.

"Oh, it's in my religion. I'm a Witness, you see. My husband and myself, we're Witnesses. And the reason the Devil came is because he's making a last attempt to catch me. You see I've got a lot more knowledge now, and the more you got the less chance *he* has to catch you. So he's putting Temptation in my way."

I could not help it. This time I smiled.

"Oh, you don't believe me, but if I were to tell you the kind of Temptation I've had this last week." Here she gave a practical example. "Honestly, every time I've turned around, there's been another man propositioning me."

Her plump hand darted into the space between her breasts and gave the brassiere a hefty tug. It began immediately to slide down, and I found it difficult not to stare.

"If they propositioned you, they must have had some reason," I suggested slyly.

"What?" she cried raucously. "You don't mean to tell me you

characters need any help. You run after us like a bunch of hound dogs."

Sensing that the continuation was not meet to what she had been saying, her voice became sad again. "I don't know," she said, "the world is so full of sin. Nobody loves his neighbor any more. On Judgment Day, the Witnesses teach that Christ is coming back, and we'll all have to stand up and be counted."

"Not many of us will pass."

"Exactly. That was what I was telling my husband. You know, you're not a dumb fellow. I could tell from the first moment that you had brains." As she blew out the smoke, she pursed her mouth, and I had the passing idea she expected a kiss. She continued, however, to talk. "Now, I don't know anything about politics, but it seems to me that everything's going wrong today. Everybody's turning his back on the Lord. We're going to Gethsemane, that's the truth. We're going to be destroyed."

I listened to an automobile roar through the street below. Its muffler was broken, and the blast of the exhaust quivered through the warm evening and stirred the air in my room. I could see the royal blue of the summer sky as it deepened into night. I sat there trying to remember the biblical meaning of Gethsemane. "Yes," she continued sadly, "you're all goners because you've deserted the true way. I tell you there's going to be a world catastrophe." In the same tone, without transition, she asked, "What religion are you?"

"I don't have any," I told her.

"Then you're damned."

"I'm afraid so."

She shook her head. "Listen, I used to be like you, but I found out there's going to be wars and plagues and famines, and the Witnesses'll be the only ones saved because they bear true witness to the ways of the Lord, and they don't have false idols. You know I won't salute the flag, and nobody can make me cause it's in my religion."

"The Witnesses are the only ones to be saved?"

A fair question. She seemed perplexed. "To tell you the truth, I'm not sure." She could have been a clubwoman discussing the best method of running a benefit. "Probably it's just going to be our organization, but there might be a couple of other organizations, and maybe, this could be, a combination of our organization and a partial membership of one or two other organizations."

Guinevere lit another of my cigarettes. "It's funny you being here," she said casually; "I mean just taking this room."

"Have to live somewhere," I murmured.

"Yeah." She considered this. "You writers are weird guys. Never know what to make of you." Her speech completed, she dumped the sheets on her arm, and stood up. "I got to go," she told me. "Pleasant talking to you."

I tried to detain her. "How would you like to clean up the room for me?" I offered.

"Clean the room?" she asked flatly.

"I know you're not obliged to do it, but I was wondering—is it worth a buck to you?" Immediately, I was horrified. The dollar would come out of my meals.

"It isn't the money. You know I'm very busy," she said. "This place may not look like much, but it's a man-sized job."

"You can find time." Now that she was reluctant I had lost my regrets over the dollar.

"I don't know. I'm going to have to think about it, Lovett."

Merely by using my name, she created another mood between us. Suggestions of her rough intimacy with Dinsmore were bandied. "I don't know, you crazy guys, didn't you ever hear of cleaning your own room and saving a buck?"

"We'll talk about it," I said smoothly. "I'll see you in a day or so about this, I suppose . . ."

She nodded with disinterest. "I'm not hard to find. I never go any place." Kicking the open door with her foot, she mumbled something about, "Work, work, every goddamn day."

On the stairs she called back a last time.

"You better clean the room yourself." I could hear Guinevere clumping down in her bedroom slippers.

Chapter 5

My friendship with McLeod progressed in no familiar way. I grew to like him, but I learned no more than he had told me the first time. I knew where he worked, I thought I knew where he had been born, and with dexterity he managed to offer nothing else. It seemed as if we always ended by talking about me; to my surprise I discovered myself telling him one day about the peculiar infirmity I was at such pains to conceal from everyone else. He heard me through, nodding his head, tapping his foot, and when I was finished he murmured, "I suspected as much, I have to admit."

His next remark astonished me. Sniffing the air as though it were a sample to be tested, he added in a soft voice, "Of course you're presented with a unique advantage."

"What?"

"You need furnish no biography for yourself. And if you think that's not a benefit for certain occupations . . ." He let the comment die in a silence he created, and asked no questions.

Yet there were incidents, trivial enough, upon which he placed curious emphasis. At night he was often out of his room, and apparently concerned that I should not be curious about his absence, he would go out of his way to present the reason. "There was a particular party I had to see last night," he might say. "Feminine." The corner of his mouth curling with mockery, he would go into his solitary laughter while I waited with an uncomfortable smile, not knowing at what it was directed.

He interested me a great deal. I was certain he was relatively uneducated, yet his intelligence was acute, and from passing references, it was apparent he had read and absorbed a surprising number of books. I had a theory McLeod had begun his serious studies — it was difficult to think of him reading for pleasure — comparatively late, and had spent his time with major works. The collection in his bookcase indicated little personal taste. I said something about this once and he answered glumly, "Taste, m'boy, is a luxury. I don't have enough money to dance around with this and that. Nor the time either." It was obvious, I deduced, that he must set aside perhaps a dollar a week, gleaned from petty sacrifices, and when he had saved enough he would buy the particular book he wanted at the moment. Such denial would cost him something, but he gave little evidence how it might pinch, cocking his sneer at the world and seeming oblivious of any other existence beyond the stale cabbage smell of our dark and dusty rooming house.

In everything he did there were elements of such order, demanding, monastic. He was unyielding and sometimes forbidding. Dressed in the anonymous clothing of a man who buys his garments as cheaply as possible, there were nonetheless two creases always to be found in a vertical parallel upon his buttocks. The straight black hair was always combed, he never needed a shave. And his room, clean as any cell could have been in our aged mansion, described an unending campaign against the ceiling which sweated water and the floor which collected dust.

I made a number of assumptions about McLeod. At the department store his salary was small, and I wondered why he should have been content with so little when he was intelligent and probably efficient. I ended with an hypothesis developed from what I knew of his room, his clothing, and the way he bought his books. Everything about him, I decided, was timid. His horizon bounded no doubt by the image of a house in some monotonous suburb, he would sell the birthright he had never enjoyed for regular work and security. "Bury the rest," I could hear him say, "I'm only a poor noodle in search of a sinecure."

It is true that in many of our conversations he worried ceaselessly at a political bone, but I showed little interest. He spoke in a parody of Dinsmore's words, saying almost the same things but with an odd emphasis that made it difficult to know if he were serious or not. Once I told him, "You sound like a hack," and McLeod reacted with a rueful frown. "An exceptional expression for you to employ, Lovett," he told me softly. "I take it you mean by 'hack' a representative of the people's state across the sea, but I'm wondering where you picked up the word, for it indicates a reasonable amount of political experience on your part."

I laughed and said somewhat heavily, "Out of all the futilities with which man attempts to express himself, I find politics among the most pathetic."

"Pathetic, is it?" he had said, and directed at me a searching stare. "Well, maybe it is. And in answer to your question, I'm hardly a hack. I've told you already, m'boy, I'm not a joiner." He grinned sourly. "One might call me a Marxist-at-liberty."

This, too, has been an excessive preamble. But as Dinsmore was to muddle my impression of Guinevere, so McLeod was to mislead me about Hollingsworth, our neighbor on the top floor. The morning McLeod and I met in the bathroom he had said in passing that Hollingsworth was lazy, and I was to learn that the word meant nothing at all. Afterward, McLeod was more specific.

One day he introduced the subject: "You met our little buddy, Hollingsworth, yet?"

When I shook my head, McLeod said typically, pinching his words, "I'll be interested in your reactions when you do."

"Why?"

But he would not tell me so easily. "You're a student of human nature."

I sighed and sat back in my chair.

"He's a fascinating case," McLeod continued. "Hollingsworth. A pretty sick individual."

"I'm bored with sick people."

McLeod's internal laughter twisted his mouth. I waited for his humor to pass. He removed his severe silver-rimmed glasses and cleaned them leisurely with his handkerchief. "You know, Lovett, you can't talk without nonsense. I don't suppose you've said ten words to me you've ever meant."

"I have nothing to say."

"Neither has Hollingsworth." He whinnied again, his tongue probing with relish a tooth in his upper jaw. "He's got a mind like a garbage pail. My private opinion of him can be summed up in one word. He's a madman."

There he let it lapse and we talked of other things, but as I left that evening McLeod was to repeat, "Just let me know what you think of him."

The meeting, when it came, was accidental. I crossed the hall next evening to knock upon McLeod's door, and to my chagrin he was not there. I stood in the hall for a moment, disappointed because I did not want to work that night, and now there was no other prospect. For luck, I knocked once more.

Instead, a young man who I guessed was Hollingsworth peered out of the adjoining room. I nodded to him. "I'm sorry," I said, "I guess I tapped too loudly on McLeod's porthole."

"Oh, that's all right." He peered at me in the dim light of the hallway. "Are you the fellow who moved in just recently?"

I affirmed this, and he smiled politely. There was a pause. He broke it by saying without embarrassment and in great seriousness, "The weather's been mighty hot, hasn't it?"

"It has, I guess."

"I do believe it's going to let up though," he said in a soft mild voice. "I think it's fixing to rain, and that should clear a lot of the humidity out of the air."

I grunted something in return.

Hollingsworth seemed to feel that the necessary liaison had been established, and we were no longer strangers. He said, "I'm having a drink now, and I wonder if you'd like to have one with me?"

When I accepted, he invited me in and opened a can of beer. His room was somewhat larger than McLeod's or mine, but there was little more space, for the bed was big and an immense bureau covered a sizable area of the floor. I pushed aside some dirty shirts to sit down, and as if their touch remained against my finger tips, I was aware for seconds afterward of something odd, or out of place.

His room was unbelievably messed. There were several piles of soiled laundry, and two drawers in the bureau stuck open with linen hanging over the edge. His closet door was set at an angle, and I could see a suit tumbled upon the floor. Empty beer cans were strewn everywhere; the wastepaper basket had overflowed. He had a desk littered with pencil shavings, inkstains, cigarette butts, and a broken box of letter paper.

Yet the floor had no dust, the woodwork was wiped, and the windows had been washed within the last few days. Hollingsworth took care of himself as well. His cloth summer pants were clean, his open shirt was fresh, his hair was combed, he was shaved. Later I noticed that his nails were proper. He seemed to have no relation to the room.

"It's nice to have a sociable beer once in a while," he said. "My folks always taught me not to go in for heavy drinking, but this can't hurt a fellow, now can it?"

He was obviously from a small town: the talk about the weather, the accent, the politeness were unmistakable signs. The simple small-town boy come to the big city. His body expressed it: less than medium size with a trim build, he suggested the kind of grace which vaults a fence in an easy motion.

The features were in character. He had straight corn-colored hair with a part to the side, and a cowlick over one temple. His eyes were small and intensely blue and were remarked immediately, for his nose and mouth were without distinction. He was still freckled, which made me wonder at his age. I was to learn later that like myself he was at least in his middle twenties, but there must have been many people who thought him eighteen.

Standing in the center of the floor, the light reflected from his blond hair, he was in considerable contrast to his room. It seemed wrong for him. I had a picture of the places in which he had slept through his boyhood: a bed, a Bible, and in the corner a baseball bat perhaps. As though in confirmation, the only decoration upon his wall was a phosphorescent cross printed on cardboard. It would glow in the darkness when the lights were out.

I had the fantasy that each morning he cleaned this room, dusted the woodwork and beat the rug. Then after he was gone, a stranger would enter and make a furious search for something Hollingsworth could not possibly possess. Or else . . . There was the picture of Hollingsworth making the search himself, ripping open the drawers, hurling clothing to the floor. This was fanciful, and yet the room seemed to be visited more by violence than by sloth.

After a few minutes I asked him where he worked, and he told me he was a clerk in one of the large brokerage houses in Wall Street.

"Do you like it?"

He made a characteristic speech. "Oh, yes, I can't complain," he said in his soft voice. "They're all very nice over there, and they lead one to believe—although of course they may have their reasons for it—that there's a lot of room for advancement. But I like a job like that anyway. It's clean work, and I always prefer clean work, don't you?"

"I haven't thought about it much."

"No? Well, I can see that not everybody thinks about it the way I do." His politeness was irritating. He added, "I suppose there's a lot to be said for an outdoor occupation, and the healthful qualities involved."

"I'd hate the idea of being cooped up in an office."

"Mr. Wilson—he's the man over me—says there are all kinds of inside jobs, and if you can work with people instead of paper, it's very different. He's going to prepare me to be a customer's man, and that I would like more."

"Do you think you'd be good at that?"

He considered my question seriously. "Yes, I do. I'm very good at selling. My folks have a store in Meridabet—that's my home town—and I've always been able to sell people the things they wanted, and then sometimes the things they didn't want." He gave an uncertain smile which voided his last sentence of any humor, and said, "I don't suppose that's a very nice way to do business?"

"It's a rough life as the man said."

He guffawed loudly with a hir-hir-hir that lasted for many seconds. But his laughter lapsed so abruptly that I realized there was no real merriment. He was making just another gesture. "That *is* a clever way of putting it," he told me. In one of his excursions he had picked up a pipe and a tin of tobacco, and he played a match carefully over the bowl. I could see by the way he held it in his mouth that he found little enjoyment.

"You smoked that long?" I asked.

"No, I'm learning. I've noticed that Mr. Wilson and some of the men over him like Mr. Court tend to smoke a pipe a great deal. College men mainly smoke pipes, don't they?"

"Probably a case can be made."

"I don't like the pipe much, but if it's necessary, I suppose I'll have to learn." He tapped the stem in resignation against his teeth. "Do you mind if I ask you a personal question?"

"No."

"You're a college man, aren't you?"

Indeed, why not? So I nodded, and he smiled with pleasure. "Yes, I thought so," he went on. "I've trained myself to observe people. Which college is it?"

I named at random a famous university.

He bobbed his head in admiration as if I had built the place.

"Sometime I'd like to have a few talks with you about college. I've been wondering . . . Do you make many contacts there?"

I resisted the impulse to be flip, and said noncommittally, "I think it depends on whether you want to."

"That could be a big help for a career I would say. Most of the big men in the place I work at are college men. I'm intelligent, everybody tells me that," he added in his colorless voice, "and maybe I should have gone, but I hated to think of all the years I'd waste there. Wouldn't you?"

I merely said, "It *is* four years."

"That's what I say." He produced an image. "If you all start a race together, and there're too many men, you can get licked even if you're good." He regarded me seriously, and I discovered again how unusual were his eyes. The pupils were almost submerged in the iris, and reflected very little light. Two circles of blue, identical daubs of pigment, stared back at me, opaque and lifeless.

The sockets were set close together, folded into the flanks of his thin nose. Front-face, he looked like a bird, for his small nose was delicately beaked and his white teeth were slightly bucked. There was a black line between his gums and the center incisors in his upper jaw, and it gave the impression of something artificial to his mouth.

"Do you mind if I inquire what you do?" he said to me.

"I'm a writer, although don't ask me what I've published."

Again he produced his excessive laughter, going hir-hir-hir for some time and then ceasing abruptly. I had a passing image of the mechanical laughter in a canned radio program, the fans whirring, the gears revolving, the klaxons producing their artificial mirth and halting on signal. "Oh, that's good," he said, "I think that's very humorous." He tilted the beer to his mouth, and gurgled at the can. "You know a lot about books then."

"Yes. About some."

His next question was more tentative. "Do you know any good books I could read?"

"What kind do you mean?"

"Oh, you know."

I noticed a few magazines and a book on his desk. Because I was curious I said, "If you could let me see what you're reading now, I'd have a better idea of what you want."

"I guess you would." As though exposing his chest to the stethoscope, he gathered up the publications on his desk, and deposited them beside me. "You can see there's quite a bit of reading matter."

"Yes." He had a pocket book with the cellophane carefully peeled from the jacket. It was an anthology of the letters of famous

people. Underneath, I found a pile of pulp magazines, a radio amateur's handbook, several Westerns, and a series of mimeographed
papers which contained lessons on ballroom dancing.

"I don't suppose I ought to be reading things like that," Hollingsworth said.

"Why not?"

But he only tittered. I leafed through the pile and put them aside.
"What kind of books do you want?" I asked again.

"Well . . ." He seemed hesitant. "In the Army there was an
awful lot of literature that I liked. You know things with the facts
of life in them."

I gave the name of an historical romance which had been a best
seller.

"N-n-no. I don't remember the titles, but there were you know
things about American fellows and girls. The real stuff though. You
know the way we feel."

I mentioned several of the major novels which had been written
by Americans between the two wars. This seemed to satisfy Hollingsworth. He made a list very carefully, writing each title into a
little notebook he carried in his hip pocket. When he was finished,
he asked, "Do you know where I could get them?"

"I can loan you one or two," I offered.

"Oh, I'd appreciate that. It's awfully neighborly." He had sat
down in the chair by his desk, and was fingering the crease in his
pants. "And there's lots of real things in them, isn't there? I mean,
you know, . . . *foolish* girls, and boys who are willing to . . . to
take a chance." He grinned.

"You'll probably find some."

"I'm really surprised they print things like that. I wonder if they
should allow it. Atheistic things, and the Bolshevists, I understand,
write for them a lot."

"For what?"

"Oh, for them, you know." He picked up another can of beer
and offered it to me.

I had decided he annoyed me. "No, I think I'd better get back to
my room and work."

"Do you make things there?"

"No. I . . . ?" I realized the he had forgotten. "No, I write."

"Oh, well that's a clever occupation." He followed me toward
the door, and stood talking to me in the hall.

"I've been in New York for two months," he said suddenly, "and
do you know I haven't found any of the evil quarters. I understand
that Harlem is quite something, although they say that the tourists
have ruined it, isn't that true?"

"I don't know."

"It takes all kinds to make a world, I suppose."

"Yes."

He leered at me suddenly. "I've had some interesting experiences with the lady downstairs. Mrs. Guinevere. She's a fine lady." The leer was shocking.

"I've heard a lot about her," I said.

"Oh, yes. She's an experience. Something to put into one's memoirs as they say."

"Mmm." I shuffled a step or two away. "Well, back to work for me."

"Oh, yes, I understand," he said in his soft voice. "One has to work, doesn't one?" He sipped his beer reflectively. "Sometime I'd like to talk over my experiences with you, would you mind?"

"No."

"It's been very enjoyable having this little discussion." He retreated almost completely into his room. As I left, he said one last thing. "You know that Mrs. Guinevere?"

"Yes."

"An extremely colorful person. Typical of New York, so I've heard."

I had no idea at all what to think of Hollingsworth.

Chapter 6

If I was a very lonely young man in New York that summer, it could be only my fault. Outside the rooming house I had not many acquaintances, but still there were people I could have visited. Yet as time went by, a week and then another, the tenuous circle of my acquaintances withered and fell apart. Entering Dinsmore's room with the intention to see no one until I had completed some work, I did not realize that actually I was feeding a wish, and in effect making it more difficult to break the bonds I fashioned myself.

This may sound extreme, and in fact it was. I did not have to disappear so completely, nor was I obliged to feel an insuperable weight at the prospect of seeing some indifferent friend for a few hours. A man in such a pass is hardly interesting, and there is no need to recount the hours I spent imagining a series of rebuffs and insults. In my mind I would telephone to somebody and he would invite me to his house, but from the moment I entered I would know it had been a mistake. Conversation would languish, I would stammer, I would be in an agony to depart. And so, in thinking of those people I knew in the city, I would discard them one by one, convinced as I considered each person that he was without interest, or without friendship.

Across the blur of the past, I have a memory which returns over and over again, and I am almost certain it happened. Perhaps it was during a furlough from the Army, although that is not important. I knew a girl then who was in love with me and I very much in love with her. We spent a week in a tourist home at some seashore resort, and that week provided more happiness and more pain than I could have thought possible. For the girl love had always been difficult and clothed in a hundred restrictions of false delicacy. She had been ashamed of her body and almost indifferent to men. What combination of circumstance and myself could bring it about I no longer know, but I adored her, so completely, so confidently, that my admiration seemed to accomplish everything. The room we shared burgeoned for her. She came to love her flesh, and from there it was but a step to loving mine. We lay beside each other for hours on end, brilliant with new knowledge. I had discovered magic to her and reaped the benefit; I could shine in the reflection of her face. Never, as she would assure me, had a man been more ardent, more thoughtful, and more desirable. She blossomed in that week, and I was so proud of myself. We were very close. We fed upon one another, we talked, we made love, we ate sandwiches she brought to the room, and we stole out to the beach for long solitary walks. We lived under the shadow of the war and perhaps that furnished its spice.

While I was with her I was very happy, but the moment I had to talk to someone else, an agony of shyness beset me. To order a meal from a waitress became a minor ordeal, and I remember that I could not bear to talk to the woman who owned the tourist house. Once on a hot afternoon we had wanted some ice water, and I had pleaded with the girl to go for it herself because I sensed myself incapable of managing such a transaction.

"But, Mikey," the girl had said—if I had another name it is not recollected now—"Mikey, why don't *you* get it? You make so much of it."

And I had refused, actually sweating at the prospect. "No, I can't," I had said. "Please, you go get it. I just don't want to talk to her."

I had won and therefore lost, and the girl got the ice water. When we parted, and I believe I never saw her again, she whispered a phrase not devoid of literary ambition, "Mikey, you know the room is the trap of the heart," and the extravagance of the words was not completely without meaning.

This is one of the few memories I possess, and I offer it for what explanation it may provide. If I lived in a close relation with the few people I knew in the rooming house and became progressively less capable of doing without them, there is after all a precedent. I was a dog on a chain, and the radius circumscribed a world in which I was able to provide for many of my wants and most of my needs. I had begun again to think about my week with that girl, but the image of Guinevere, no matter how incongruous, often accompanied her, and I find it hardly surprising that a few days after seeing Hollingsworth I felt compelled to make the trip downstairs and ring the bell of Guinevere's apartment.

It was after three o'clock and Guinevere was in the midst of lunch. I was greeted at the door with a surprising reception. "Oh, Mr. Lovett, you're just the man I want to see. Come in, won't you, please?" I shall not bother to describe her costume in detail; suffice it that she was clothed with enough variety to suggest everything from breakfast in bed to a formal evening. "I had an idea you might be coming down," she said, her voice lilting through high notes and modulated carefully through the lower tones. "I'm just finishing eating. Won't you have coffee with me?"

"Well, all right. I'd like to talk to you about a business matter." As the pretext for visiting, I intended to ask her again to clean my room.

We walked through the hallway of her apartment into the kitchen whose sink and stove were covered with what seemed all the unwashed pots of all the meals of the last week. Upon the kitchen table was the litter of this repast: a half-eaten sandwich, a sliced tomato somewhat squashed upon the oilcloth, and meandering through it a pool of spilled coffee.

"A business matter?" she repeated belatedly, and it was obvious my words had a poor effect. Business was reality. "Oh, you got to excuse this place," she groaned. "I never can get in gear. Here, sit down, have some coffee." The open sleeve of her imitation Japanese kimono trailed through bread crumbs. She reached over to the sink, found a rag, and flopped it upon the table to wipe a clear space for me. "Monina," she bawled abruptly, "say hello to Mr. Lovett."

"Dello Ditter Luft," a voice piped at me. In an alcove between the refrigerator and the window, a child was sitting in a high chair, a child of exceptional beauty. The sunlight illumined her golden hair and steeped her face and arms in a light so intense her flesh appeared translucent. In one small hand she grasped a spoon and was in the process of transferring some oatmeal to her lips. The maneuver was difficult and swatches of cereal mottled her tiny mouth and pouting cheeks. I had for a moment the whimsy that she was an angel come to earth, but a sullen angel, perplexed by the mechanics of living.

"Why, she's lovely," I exclaimed.

"Oh, she's got the looks," Mrs. Guinevere told me. "And don't think she don't know it, that little bitch."

Monina giggled. A sly expression formed beneath the oatmeal. "Mommie said dirty durd."

Guinevere groaned again. "Oh, that kid, you can't put nothing over on her."

"How old is she?" I realized she was big to be in a high chair.

"Three and a half going on four." As if she guessed the reason behind my question, Mrs. Guinevere said with no attempt to conceal anything from the child, "I want to keep her a baby. I'll tell you, I've got it all figured out. In about another year or two, I'm going to have enough money put together to head for Hollywood, and Monina's a cinch. Only she's got to remain a kid. There's not so many roles for kids five years old as there is for infants, you know, one year old and up. So I want her to stay young." She raised her forearm and kissed the flesh above her wrist. "Oh, is it chafed. I got to get my watch fixed. Here, look at that." And Mrs. Guinevere gave me her arm to examine. "Just touch it there. Gee, it's sore."

I could see a faint red mark. I pressed it and trailed my fingers over her arm. "It's very smooth," I murmured.

"Yeah, I got good skin." Her eyes closed and she leaned back, a look of sentience upon her face.

Abruptly, she whipped her arm away. "Oh, hell, I forgot."

"What?"

"You ain't supposed to tell anybody."

"Tell what?"

"That Monina is three and a half. That's a secret. You promise you won't tell."

I shrugged. "Yes, I promise."

"Well, I guess you got something on me now." Her painted mouth in its broad sensual curves grinned at provocatively. "You could hurt my chances if you wanted to."

"Monina don't want doatmeal," the child said.

"You shut up and eat it," Guinevere screeched. "I'll get the strap if you don't."

But Monina had made her bid for attention and was temporarily content. She sighed like an old woman and applied the back of the spoon to her cheek.

"You know I've missed opportunities with her. When I think of the money I could be making now." Guinevere shook her head, and sipped her coffee. "You just can't trust nobody. I've had promises galore, and where did it get me?" She extended her hand. "Let's have a cigarette, Lovett."

We smoked in silence for a moment. "Why do you want her in Hollywood?" I asked.

Guinevere's bald blue eyes stared at me, and she said in a mysterious voice laden with self-love, "What do you know, Lovett, of what a woman goes through? Do you think it's fun taking care of a household with a no-good husband, and behind me I've had conquests after conquests, lovers and night clubs and gay exciting times. I could've been married to a Maharajah, do you know that? And what a lover he was. The whang he had on him." She paused as though talking to a foreigner, and said, "That's what I always call it, a whang."

But I was becoming accustomed to conversation with her, with leaping up stairways and tumbling down them. "Yes, I know."

"He begged me to marry him, and I turned him away, you know why? His skin was dark. I could have been a Maharajess, but he had odd ways about him, and so I missed the boat. I tell you if I met another nigger with as much money as him, I wouldn't make the same mistake. I'm a young woman, Lovett, and I'm wasting my life. Boy, there was a time when I could pick and choose among you characters."

"How can you go to Hollywood?" I persisted. "What about your husband?"

"I'll leave him. I only married the sucker out of pity." She stared about the kitchen, surveying the dirty dishes. "I've got too good a heart, that's my only trouble. If you saw me dressed up, you'd realize how easy it is for me to make a man. There isn't one of you I can't get if I want to lift a finger."

"Lift a finger for me," I essayed.

"Oh, you, what do you want with an old woman like me? I'm twenty-eight you know." She drew a design in the bread crumbs. "Boy, if I told you my husband's name, you'd fall out of the chair."

"Who is he?"

She smiled secretly. "Catch me telling you."

Through the open kitchen window a warm breeze drifted into the room, carrying with it the smell of leaves and tar from the streets beyond. A delicate anticipation stirred through my body. Somewhere people were making love, the heat moistening their fluid limbs, the balm of summer carrying them through this languorous hour. I almost stretched out my arm in a caress.

"Lovett, you want to do me a favor?"

"What?"

She placed a hand confidingly on mine. "Look, I got a taste for some root beer. Be a good guy, and go out to the store, and get me a bottle. And I can give you the empties to return at the same time."

"I don't see why I should." I was annoyed at the way she had shattered my mood.

"Aw, come on. Look, I'll tell you what. I'll give you a nickel if you do it." She said this with some reluctance.

I laughed. "How young do you think I am?"

She shook her head. She was quite serious. "Fair's fair. You go out in the sun, you're entitled to it."

"I don't want your nickel."

"Come on, do it anyway."

This was childish. "All right, all right." I picked up her quarter, and left with ill-humor. I was furious with myself for doing her errand. She was absurd, an overblown woman whose attractiveness was almost submerged by the rubble about her person. Yet I wanted her. We could be alone in my room under the baking heat of the roof, and all through this summer we could have a succession of trysts.

I bought two bottles of root beer and a candy bar, and hurried back. "Here's your quarter," I told her. "It's a present."

"Aw, that's swell of you." She accepted the quarter greedily as an unexpected bounty. "See, I changed for you."

She had, indeed. My heart leaped. She wore a tropical halter and short pants, and her flesh bulged wantonly.

"Dressed for me, huh?"

She guffawed. "I can't stand wearing clothes in this heat. If there's nobody around I'd like to be without a damn thing on." She thought about this. "You know those nudists got something."

Monina was out of the high chair, and walking about. Once or twice she examined me with the unabashed stare of a child. "Ditter Luft doodooking," she said to her mother.

"What's that?" I asked.

"She says you're good-looking." Guinevere laughed. "You know, you ain't bad, Lovett." Now, both the child and the mother were looking at me. I was hardly comfortable, and Monina, who had seemed somewhat retarded to me with her baby talk, had created a presence far larger than herself. "When does she take her nap?" I asked.

"Oh, that kid don't nap. You never saw anything like her. She keeps the same hours I do. I swear she don't go to bed half the time till midnight." Guinevere swigged the root beer, and handed it to Monina who parodied her mother, throwing back her tiny blonde head and tilting the bottle. She did not hold it against her mouth however, and a considerable quantity splashed upon her chin, dribbled down the undershirt, and trickled to the floor. "You slob," her mother shrieked.

Monina giggled. "Ditter Luft doodooking," she said again.

"Why don't we go into the other room?" I suggested. "And Monina can play in the bedroom. You want to play in the bedroom, don't you, Monina?"

"Nooo."

"She follows me everywhere," Guinevere said. "Monina can't be without me." She yawned. "All right, come on, we'll all go in the living room." But "living room" was apparently more than just a word and her manner became haughty again. With a ridiculous gesture, Guinevere pointed to the ashtray, and said, "You can take that with you if you wish, Mr. Lovett," implying by the action a cornucopia of servants, brandy, and cigars.

Actually, to my surprise, her living room was not in execrable taste. The furniture was modest, but she had achieved some decent effects. A mattress and spring on legs was covered by a dark green spread and served as a couch. There were several old armchairs with new print materials, and a dull tan rug was set against tomato-colored drapes. There were more mirrors than she needed upon the wall, the lamps were shabby, and needless gewgaws were clustered upon every end table, but altogether one could notice a certain unity. Yet, like people who build a house when at heart they desire a monument, I had the impression that she was seldom here.

She paced about uneasily before settling in one of the chairs. "This is a nice room," I told her.

"Yeah, I like it; I worked hard on it," Guinevere said dispiritedly. "If I had more money I could do something with these things." Then she lapsed into silence, unaccountably depressed, her eyes staring at the carpet. "Boy, the work I put into this," she muttered. Her hand fretted into the money pocket of her shorts and turned it inside out. "But does he appreciate this? No." She leaned back, her breasts lolling heavily in the halter, her fingers pinching a rope of flesh about her waist.

She lay there dormant, but her restlessness was conveyed to the child who pranced about the room. I watched Monina. She halted before a mirror and preened her body, kissing her wrist with the absorbed self-admiration she had seen in her mother. "Dashtray,"

I heard her whisper. "Dake dashtray." Her little arms fluttered, her head nodded politely, and she extended an invitation in panto-mime, glowing with satisfied laughter at the portrait of herself in the mirror. She pirouetted away to stand in contemplation before a set of china knickknacks upon a table. Selecting a tiny bowl of cheap porcelain, she stared at the decoration painted about the rim. "Mommie, Monina, Mommie, Monina," she said aloud. A smile set upon her face, she approached me, and repeated the same formula, holding the bowl before my eyes and pointing to the cup-ids painted upon it.

Guinevere stirred heavily in the armchair. "Put it down, Moni-na," she shouted at the child. But the command was too ambig-uous. What was meaning and what was sound?

Monina smashed the bowl upon the floor.

"Oh, you little bitch," Guinevere shouted. "Go to the bed-room."

"No," Monina screamed.

"Stand in the corner."

"No!"

Guinevere stood up threateningly. "I'll get the strap," she shrieked. Monina pouted, her eyes glaring at her mother.

"All right," she conceded at last. She trailed reluctantly to the door, and then turned about and pronounced anathema. "Mommie-diggie, mommie-diggie."

"I'll get the strap!"

And Monina disappeared.

Guinevere groaned. "Oh, that kid'll drive me crazy." Eyes closed, she laughed, her belly shaking in jollity. "Oh, murder." After a moment she stirred herself and began to pick the pieces off the floor. She was less than a yard away from me, and knelt in such a position that it was impossible not to stare at her breasts. Chuck-ling, she seemed in excellent humor. "That kid," she murmured.

She looked up, and a broad coarse grin formed upon her mouth. "Well, Lovett, here we are alone," she jeered.

"Yes, I got what I wanted," I drawled.

"Oh, you." She dropped the pieces in the ashtray by my side, and went back to her chair. This time she sprawled with her legs akimbo, her hands kneading her breasts. "Mmmmm," she purred. Slowly she massaged her bare shoulders against the print of the seat cover in a slow luxurious motion from side to side. "You ever rub your back against velvet?" she asked.

"Don't think so." My voice was husky.

"Oh, I love it. Mmm," she purred again. "Boy, I wish this was velvet. This is just cotton, scratches a little." She yawned pleasurably. "You know I'll tell you something, I don't know why I'm telling you, I never told anyone else, but when I'm alone, I love to take off my clothes and lie in velvet."

Was this a secret vice, or something she had invented on the spur of the situation? "Interesting," I murmured. I was hardly concerned with what I said.

"Oh, the times I've had," she told me. "Brutal!"

I stood up and walked toward her. She tasted my kiss for a few seconds, and then pushed me back, and hummed a breathy, "Whew." She smiled. "That was nice."

I reached out for her, and she caught my arm. "Aw, now hold on."

But like the bull who has passed the pic, and felt the flank of the horse collapsed by his horn, I must gore and gore, reach out and pin to earth. My hands clutched various parts of her body. "Whew," she said again, and pushed me away competently, standing up from the chair in the same motion.

We stood face to face, my arms about her. "What the hell is it I got?" she demanded in pleasurable anger. "Boy, you guys can't leave me alone."

"No," I mumbled.

She sighed and walked away. "I tell you I've had all kinds of men, and there hasn't been one of them who didn't fall in love with me. Just must be something chemical I got." She turned around and examined me. "You know, Lovett, you're not a bad-looking guy. I could go for you, but I'm not fooling around any more. I don't know why, it isn't my husband, but I play it close to the vest." Her voice exuded satisfaction. "Now you and me could get together, but what profit is there in it for me? You tell me."

"Oh, the hell with that." I reached forward and kissed her once again. She closed her eyes indolently and moved her mouth against mine as if she were eating candy.

"What Mommie done, what Mommie done." Monina stood in the doorway and pointed an accusing finger.

To my surprise Guinevere taunted the child. "What Mommie done," she mimicked. "I'll get the strap! Go to bed."

"Mommie bad, mommie-diggie." It was impossible to know what the child felt. She quivered, and hot furious tears stood in her eyes. Yet suddenly she coquetted at me. "Kiss Monina, too," she demanded.

Guinevere patted her bottom. "Go to bed, or I'll get the strap." she shrieked automatically. And once again, reluctantly, the child withdrew.

"See what you've done," Guinevere grumbled. "That kid'll have something on me now. Wait, she'll let me know about it."

"I'm sorry," I said.

"Lot of good that does," she whipped at me. "You guys give me a pain in the ass." She turned away to light a cigarette and laughed. "Here," she said unexpectedly, "here, you want to feel my breasts, here, feel them," and she took my hand and placed it. I kissed her again, and indolently she raised the arm which supported the cigarette and returned the embrace.

She was not without response. The kiss must have lasted for over a minute, and my hands moved in a crescendo about her. When we paused, her breath was coming quickly too.

"Hey," she said.

"Come on." Nothing was going to stop me now. "Come on."

"We can't."

"Right here."

She stiffened. "Look," she whispered, "the kid's around. Are you crazy?"

I would not be thwarted. "Upstairs in my room."

"I don't know."

"You've got to come upstairs."

She pinched me suddenly. "All right, I will."

"You promise?"

"I'll be up." She groaned. "Oh, my God, what you guys get me into."

"You promise?"

"Yes, I'll be up in ten minutes. Now, get out of here, and let me get Monina to bed."

Battered, drunk with lust, I stumbled to my room.

THE DEER PARK

A NOVEL

*Mailer's third novel was published, after very considerable
trouble, by G. P. Putnam's Sons in 1955. The reader might wish
to read Mailer's account of the composition and publication of
the book in his essay, included here among the* Advertisements
for Myself *material, "Fourth Advertisement for Myself." It might
also be interesting to read "The Man Who Studied Yoga" first,
since it is the fiction out of which, at least in a sense,* The Deer
Park *grew. The novel has two lines of action, the love affair of
Sergius O'Shaugnessy, the book's narrator, with movie star Lulu
Meyers, and the love affair of Charles Eitel, Sergius' older,
movie-director friend, with Elena Esposito. The excerpt here
centers around a party given by a famous movie producer in the
California resort town of Desert D'Or, a community which
Mailer associates with the orgiastic pleasure garden of Louis XV,
the Deer Park.*

Part Two, Chapter Seven

With the beginning of the season, there was some rain, not a great deal, but enough to put the desert flowers into bloom. Which brought the crowd from the capital. The movie people filled the hotels, and the season residents opened their homes. Movie stars were on the street, and gamblers, criminals with social cartel, models, entertainers, athletes, airplane manufacturers, even an artist or two. They came in all kinds of cars: in Cadillac limousines, in ruby convertibles and gold-yellow convertibles, in little foreign cars and big foreign cars. Then with the start of the season on me, I came to like the wall around my house which was always safe in the privacy it gave, and I would think at times how confusing the town must be to the day tourist who could drive through street after street and know no more of the resort than the corridors of an office building would tell about the rooms.

Eitel did not take to this invasion. He had come to prefer being alone, and was rarely to be seen at the hotel. One day when I stopped by his house, the phone rang in Eitel's bedroom. From the den I could hear him talking. He was being invited to visit somebody who had just arrived at the Yacht Club, and after he hung up, I could feel his excitement. "How would you like to meet a pirate?" he said with a laugh.

"Who is it?"

"The producer, Collie Munshin."

"Why do you call him a pirate?" I asked.

"Just wait until you meet him."

But Eitel could not keep himself from saying more. I think he was irritated at how much pleasure the invitation gave him.

Munshin was the son-in-law of Herman Teppis, Eitel explained, and Teppis was the head of Supreme Pictures. Munshin had married Teppis' daughter, and it had helped to make him one of the most important producers in the capital. "Not that he wouldn't have made it anyway," Eitel said. "Nothing could stop Collie." He had been, I learned, a little bit of many things, a salesman, a newspaperman, a radio announcer for a small station, a press-relations consultant, an actor's agent, an assistant producer, and finally a producer. "Once upon a time," Eitel went on, "he was practically an office boy for me. I know the key to Collie. He's shameless. You can't stop a man who's never been embarrassed by himself."

Eitel began to change his shirt. By the way he picked his tie, I knew he did not feel nearly as casual as he was hoping to feel. "Wonder why he wants to see me?" he said aloud. "I suppose he wants to steal an idea."

"Why bother?" I asked. "Nothing is cheaper than ideas."

"It's his technique. Collie gets a feeling about a story. Not anything you can really name. Some cloud of an idea. Then he invites a writer who's out of work to come to lunch. He listens to the writer's suggestions, and they talk the thing up. The next day he invites another man to lunch. By the time he's talked to half a dozen writers he has a story and then he uses one of the peons he keeps locked in a hole to write the thing. When Collie is done, he can sell the story to the studio as his own creation. Oh, he's clever, he's tenacious, he's scheming . . ." Eitel ran out of words.

"What's to keep him from running the studio?" I asked.

"Nothing," said Eitel, putting on a jacket, "he'll run the world someday." Then Eitel smiled. "Only first he has to learn how to handle me. Sometimes I can set him back."

As he closed the door behind us, Eitel added, "There's another thing which might hold him up. He's having woman trouble."

"Does he run around with so many?"

Eitel looked at me as if I had a lot to learn about the psychology of prominent men in the capital. "Why, no," he said, "Collie has too many decisions to juggle, and that slows a man up, don't you know? Besides, it's not so easy to keep a harem when your wife is Herman Teppis' daughter. You don't even keep a fancy girl. Just a child in a cubbyhole and she's caused him trouble enough with H. T. It's some poor dancer. She's been his girl for several years. I've never met her, but Collie will be the first to tell you the trouble she gives him. It's a conventional relationship. She wants him to divorce his wife and marry her, and Collie lets her believe that he will. Poor boy, he can't bear to let go of anything." Eitel chuckled. "Of course, the girl friend makes him pay. When Collie's not around, his little kitten will go for a romp. A couple of actors who've worked for me have been with her. They tell me she's extraordinary in bed."

"Isn't that rough on him?"

"I don't know," Eitel said, "there are parts and parts to Collie. He enjoys being a martyr."

"Sounds like a sad character to me."

"Oh, everybody's sad if you want to look at them that way. Collie's not so bad off. Just remember there's nobody like him in the whole world."

We came to Munshin's bungalow, and Eitel tapped the knocker on the pink-colored door. After a wait I could hear somebody running toward us, and then it flew open, and I had no more than the sight of the back of a fat man in a dressing gown who went bounding away to the phone, the gown flapping against his calves while he called over his shoulder, "Come in. Be with you in a minute, fellows." He was talking in a high-pitched easy voice to somebody in New York, holding the receiver in his left hand while with his right he was neatly mixing drinks for us, not only carrying on his business conversation but opening a big smile across his face at the introduction to me. A little under medium height, with short turned-up features, he looked like a clown, for he had a large round head on a round body and almost no neck at all.

The drinks made, he passed them over with a wink, and his right hand free again, he began to tickle his thin hair, discovering a bald spot on his head and then patting it into hiding again, only to leave his head for his belly which he prodded gingerly as if to find out whether it concealed an ache. He certainly had a lot of energy; I had the idea it would be rare to see him doing one thing at a time.

Eitel sat down with a bored look and smiled at the producer's calisthenics. When the call was done, Munshin bounced to his feet and advanced on Eitel with his outstretched palm, a grin on his face. "*Charley!*" he said, as if Eitel had just come into the room and he was surprised to see him. "You look great. How have you been?" Munshin asked, his free hand covering their handclasp. "I've been hearing great things about you."

"Stop it, Collie," Eitel laughed, "there's nothing you can steal from me."

"Steal? Lover, I just want to steal your company." He clamped a bear-hug on Eitel's neck. "You look great," he repeated. "I've been hearing wonderful things about your script. I want to read it when it's done."

"What for?" Eitel asked.

"I want to buy it." He said this as if nothing was in the way of buying anything from Eitel.

"The only way I'll let you buy it is blind."

"I'll buy it blind. If it's from you, Charley, I'll buy it blind."

"You wouldn't buy Shakespeare blind."

"You think I'm kidding," Munshin said in a sad voice.

"Stop it, Collie," Eitel said again.

As he talked, Munshin kept on touching Eitel, pinching his elbow, patting his shoulder, jabbing his ribs. "Charley, don't show your script to anybody. Just work on it. Don't worry about your situation."

"Get your greedy little hands off me. You know I'm going to make the picture by myself."

"That's your style, Charley," Munshin said with a profound nod. "That's the way you always should work."

He told us a joke, passed a bit of gossip, and kept his hands on Eitel's body in a set of movements which called up the picture of a fat house detective searching a drunk. Then Eitel walked away from him, and we all sat down and looked at each other. After a short silence, Munshin announced, "I've thought of a great movie to make."

"What is it?" I asked, for Eitel only made a face. The producer gave the name of a famous French novel. "That author knows everything about sex," Munshin said. "I'll never be able to think I'm in love again."

"Why don't you do the life of Marquis de Sade?" Eitel drawled.

"You think I wouldn't if I could find a gimmick?"

"Collie," Eitel said, "sit down and tell me the story you really have."

"I don't have a thing. I'm open to suggestion. I'm tired of making the same old stuff. Every man has an artistic desire in this business."

"He's absolutely unscrupulous," Eitel said with pride. Collie grinned. He cocked his head to the side with the cunning look of a dog who is being scolded.

"You're a born exaggerator," Munshin said.

"You can't stop Collie."

"I love you."

Munshin poured another drink for us. Like a baby, his upper lip was covered with perspiration. "Well, how *are* things?" he said.

"Just fine, Collie. How are things with you?" Eitel asked in a flat voice. I knew him well enough to know he was very much on guard.

"Charley, my personal life is in bad shape."

"Your wife?"

Munshin stared into space, his hard small eyes the only sign of bone beneath his fat. "Well, things are always the same between her and me."

"What is it then, Collie?"

"I've decided to give the brush to my girl friend."

Eitel began to laugh. "It's about time."

"Now, don't laugh, Charley. This is important to me."

I was surprised at the way Munshin talked so frankly. He hadn't known me fifteen minutes, and yet he was as ready to talk as if he were alone with Eitel. I was still to learn that Munshin, like many people from the capital, could talk openly about his personal life while remaining a dream of espionage in his business operations.

"You're not really giving her up?" Eitel said lightly. "What's the matter, has Teppis laid down the law?"

"Charley!" Munshin said, "this is a personal tragedy for me."

"I suppose you're in love with the girl."

"No, now I wouldn't say that. It's hard to explain."

"Oh, I'm sure of that, Collie."

"I'm very worried about her future," Munshin said, his fingers prodding his belly again.

"From what I've heard about her, she'll get along."

"What did you hear?" Munshin asked.

"Just that while she's known you, she's had her extracurricular activities."

Munshin's round face became tolerant and sad. "We live in a community of scandal," he said.

"Spare me, Collie," Eitel murmured.

Munshin was on his feet. "You don't understand this girl," he said in a booming voice. I was left behind by the sudden transition. "She's a child. She's a beautiful, warm, simple child."

"And you're a beautiful, warm, simple father."

"I've defended you, Charley," Munshin said. "I've defended you against stories which even you wouldn't want to hear about yourself. But I'm beginning to think I was wrong. I'm beginning to think you're nothing but rottenness and corruption."

"Honest corruption. I don't play the saint."

"I'm not claiming I'm a saint," Munshin bellowed again. "But I have feelings." He turned in my direction. "What do you see when you look at a fellow like myself?" he asked. "You see a fat man who likes to play the clown. Does that mean I have no human sentiments?"

He was far from a clown at the moment. His mild high-pitched voice had swollen in volume and dropped deeper in tone. Standing over us, he gave me the feeling that he was a man of some physical power. "All right, Charley," he said, "I know what you think of me, but I'll tell you something. I may be a businessman, and you may be an artist, and I've great respect for your talent, great respect, but you're a cold man, and I have emotions, and that's why you can't understand me."

Through this tirade, Eitel had been drawing on his cigarette. Nonchalantly, he put it out. "Why did you invite me over, Collie?"

"For friendship. Can't you understand that? I wanted to hear your troubles, and I wanted to tell you mine."

Eitel leaned forward, his broad body hunched on itself. "I have no troubles," he said with a smile. "Let me hear yours."

Munshin relaxed. "There are pluses as well as minuses to this affair. It's easy to sneer at the girl," he said. "I've sneered at her myself. When I first set her up, I thought, 'Just another night-club dancer. A hot Italian babe with that hot Latin blood.' Well, it's a story, Charley. She may not be so brilliant, and she's obviously from a poor background." He looked at me. "I've always been full of prejudices about women," Munshin said humbly. "You know, I've wanted girls with some class and distinction to them, and I'll admit it, it's what I still hold against Elena. She doesn't match up to the people I know. But that doesn't keep her from being very human."

"Still, you're giving her the brush," Eitel said. "You're giving the brush to a very human girl."

"There's no future for us. I admit it, you see, I admit my faults. I'm a social coward like everybody else in the industry."

"So like all cowards you got tired of turning down her marriage proposals."

"Elena's not a schemer," Munshin said firmly. "You want to know something? Just a couple of days ago I tried to give her a thousand dollars. She wouldn't take it. Not once did she ever ask me to marry her. She's not the kind who threatens. It's just that I can't stand the thought she has no future with me."

"Herman Teppis can't stand the thought either."

Munshin allowed this to pass. "Let me tell you about her. She's a girl who's composed of hurts and emotion and dirt and shining love," he said in the round categorical style of a criminal lawyer who wishes to attract all the elements in a jury. "I had my analyst send her to a friend of his, but it didn't come off. She didn't have enough ego to work on. That's how serious the problem is." Munshin held out a heavy palm as if to draw our attention. "Take the way I met her. She was doing a fill-in number at a benefit I ran. I saw her in the wings, dressed up, ready to go on. A real Carmen-type. Only, a Carmen shuddering with fright," said Munshin looking at us. "She was practically clawing the hand off her partner. 'There's a human being in torment,' I said to myself, 'a girl who's as wild and sensitive as an animal.' Yet when she got up on the stage, she was all right. A good flamenco dancer. In and out, but talent. Afterward, we started talking, and she told me she couldn't even eat a piece of bread on a day she was working. I told her I thought I could help her with some of her problems and she was grateful as a puppy. That's how we started." Munshin's voice became heavy with emotion. "You, Eitel, you'd call that scheming, I suppose. I call it sensitivity and heartbreak and all kinds of hurts. She's a girl who's all hurts."

As Munshin kept on talking, I had the idea he was describing her the way he might line up a heroine in a story conference, the story conference more interesting than the film which would come from it.

"You take the business of being Italian," Munshin lectured us. "I can't tell you the things I've learned, the human subtleties, and I'm a good liberal. For instance, if she was served by a Negro waiter, she always had the idea that he was being a little intimate with her. I talked to her about such problems. I explained how wrong it is to have prejudice against a Negro, and she understood."

"Like that," Eitel said, snapping his fingers.

"You stop it, Charley," Munshin said, bobbing in his seat. "You understand what I mean. She was ashamed of her prejudice. Elena is a person who hates everything that is small in herself. She's consumed by the passion to become a bigger person than she is, *consumed*, do you understand?" and he shook his fist.

"Collie, I really think you're upset."

"Take her promiscuity," Munshin went on, as if he had not heard. "She's the sort of girl who would love a husband and kids, a decent healthy mature relationship. You think it didn't bother me, her seeing other men? But I knew it was my fault. I was to blame and I'll admit it freely. What could I offer her?"

"What could the others offer her?" Eitel interrupted.

"Fine. Fine. Just fine coming from you. I'll tell you, Charley. I don't believe in double standards. A woman's got just as much right as a man to her freedom."

"Why don't we start a club?" Eitel jeered.

"I've gone to bat for you, Eitel. I pleaded with H.T. not to suspend you after *Clouds Ahoy*. Are you so ungrateful that I have to remind you how many times I helped you make pictures you wanted to make?"

"And then you cut them to ribbons."

"We've had our disagreements, Charley, but I've always considered you a friend. I don't care what transpires between us today, it won't affect my attitude toward you."

Eitel smiled.

"I'm curious." Munshin put his hands on his knees. "What do you think of Elena the way I've described her?"

"I think she's better than you deserve."

"I'm glad you say that, Charley. It means I've been able to convey her quality." Munshin paused, and loosened the cord of his dressing gown. "You see, about an hour ago I told Elena we couldn't go on."

"An hour ago!"

Munshin nodded.

"You mean she's here?" Eitel asked. "Here in town?"

"Yes."

"You brought her out here to give her the brush?"

Munshin started to pace the floor. "I didn't plan it. A lot of times I bring her along on my trips."

"And let her stay in a separate hotel?"

"Well, I've explained the situation."

"When is your wife due?"

"She'll be here tomorrow." Munshin blew his nose. "I had no idea it would happen like this. For months I knew I couldn't go on with Elena, but I didn't expect it for today."

Eitel shook his head. "What do you want me to do? Hold her hand?"

"No, I mean . . ." Munshin looked miserable. "Charley, she doesn't know a soul in this place."

"Then let her go back to the city."

"I can't stand the thought of her being alone. There's no telling what she'll do. Charley, I'm going out of my mind." Munshin stared at his handkerchief which he kept wadded in his hand. "Elena was the one who said we should break up. I know what it means to her. She'll put the blame on herself. She'll feel she wasn't good enough for me."

"It's the truth, isn't it?" Eitel said. "That's how you feel."

"All right, I'm the rotten one. I'm no good." Munshin came to a stop in front of Eitel. "Charley, I remember you saying, its your exact words. You said that when you were a kid you always wondered how to get a woman, and now you wonder how to get rid of one."

"I was bragging."

"Can't you sympathize?"

"With you?"

"Could you pay her a visit?"

"I don't know her," Eitel said.

"You could be introduced as a friend of mine."

Eitel sat up. "Tell me, Collie," he said, "is that why you loaned me the money two weeks ago?"

"What money?" said Munshin.

"You don't have to worry about Sergius," Eitel said, and he began to laugh. "I'm ashamed of you. Two thousand dollars is a lot of money for Carlyle Munshin to pay to have a broken-down director take a girl off his hands."

"Charley, you're a corrupt man," Munshin said loudly. "I loaned you that money because I consider you my friend, and I oughtn't to have to tell you that you could be more discreet. If word ever got around, I'd be in trouble up to here." The producer held a finger to his throat. "It's Elena I'm thinking about now. Let this boy be the witness. If anything happens to her, part of it will be your fault."

"There's no limit to you, Collie," Eitel started to say, but Munshin interrupted. "Charley, I'm not kidding, that girl should not be left alone. Do I say I'm in the right? What do you want, my blood? Offer a solution at least."

"Turn her over to Marion Faye."

"You're a stone," Munshin said. "A human being is in pain, and you say things like that."

"I'll see her," I blurted suddenly.

"You're a beautiful kid," Munshin said levelly, "but this is not the job for you."

"Keep out of this," Eitel snapped at me.

"Even the kid here will go," Munshin said. "Charley, tell me, is all the heart cut out of you? Isn't there even a little bit left? Or are you getting too old to handle a real woman?"

Eitel lay back in his chair and stared at the ceiling, his legs spread before him. "Okay, Collie," he said slowly, "okay. One loan deserves another. I'll get drunk with your girl."

"You're a jewel, Charley," Munshin said huskily.

"What if you-know-what happens?" Eitel drawled.

"Are you a sadist?" Munshin said. "I don't even think of things like that."

"Then what do you think of?"

"You'll like Elena and she'll like you. It'll make her feel good to know that a fellow with your reputation and your presence admires her."

"Oh, God," Eitel said.

The phone was ringing.

Munshin tried to say something more as if he were afraid Eitel might change his mind, but the noise of the telephone was too distracting. Obeying the irregular rhythm of the switchboard operator, it would stop, it would be silent, and then it would ring again.

"Answer it," Eitel said irritably.

Munshin pinched the receiver against his jowl. He was preparing to make another drink, but the sounds he heard through the earpiece stopped everything. We listened to a woman who was crying and laughing, and her fright quivered through the room. There was so much terror in the voice and so much pain that I stared at the floor in shock. One cry sounded, so loud in its loneliness I couldn't bear it.

"Where are you, Elena?" Munshin said sharply into the mouthpiece.

Some climax passed. I could hear the sound of quiet sobbing. "I'll be right over," Munshin said. "Now, you stay there. You stay there, do you understand, Elena?" He had no sooner hung up the phone than he was drawing on a pair of trousers, fastening the buttons to a shirt.

Eitel was pale. "Collie," he said with an effort, "do you want me to come along?"

"She's in her hotel room," Munshin said from the door. "I'll call you later."

Eitel nodded and sat back. We were silent once Munshin was gone. After a few minutes, Eitel got up and mixed a drink. "What a horrible thing," he muttered.

"How does a man," I asked, "stay with a woman who is so . . . It's messy."

Eitel looked up. "A little compassion, Sergius," he said. "Do you think we choose our mates?" And, moodily, he sipped on his drink. "I wonder if I'll ever know the answer to that one?" he said almost to himself.

Time passed, and we kept on drinking Carlyle Munshin's liquor.

Slowly, the afternoon went by. It seemed pointless to remain there, just as pointless to move on. Outside, there would only be the desert sun. "I'm depressed," Eitel said with a broad grin after half a dozen drinks. I had the feeling his face was numb; slowly, with pleasure, he was patting the bald spot on his head. "Wonder how Collie is making out?" Eitel said after another pause.

As if to answer, there was a knock on the door. I went to open it, and an elderly man shouldered me aside and walked into the living room. "Where's Carlyle?" he asked of nobody in particular, and left me to follow behind him.

Eitel stood up. "Well, Mr. Teppis," he said.

Teppis gave him a sour look. He was a tall heavy man with silver hair and a red complexion, but even with his white summer suit and hand-painted tie he was far from attractive. Underneath the sun tan, his features were poor; his eyes were small and pouched, his nose was flat, and his chin ran into the bulge of his neck. He had a close resemblance to a bullfrog. When he spoke, it was in a thin hoarse voice. "All right," he said, "what are you doing here?"

"Do you know," Eitel said, "that's a good question to ask."

"Collie's up to something," Teppis announced. "I don't know why he saw you. I wouldn't even want to breathe the air a subversive breathes. Do you know what you cost me on *Clouds Ahoy?*"

"You forget the money I made for you . . . Herman."

"Hah," said Teppis, "now he calls me by my first name. They leave me and they go up in the world. Eitel, I warned Lulu against you. Marry a fine young American actress, a girl who's too good for you, and you just drag her name through the muck and the dirt and the filth. If anybody saw me talking to you, I'd be ashamed."

"You should be," Eitel said. "Lulu was a fine American girl, and you let me turn her into a common whore." His voice was cool, but I could sense it was not easy for him to talk to Teppis.

"You have a dirty mouth," Herman Teppis said, "and nothing else."

"Don't speak to me this way. I no longer work for you."

Teppis rocked forward and back on the balls of his feet as if to build up momentum. "I'm ashamed to have made money from your movies. Five years ago I called you into my office and I warned you. 'Eitel,' I said, 'anybody that tries to throw a foul against this country ends up in the pigpen.' That's what I said, but did you listen?" He waved a finger. "You know what they're talking about at the studio? They say you're going to make a comeback. Some comeback. You couldn't do a day's work without the help of the studio. I let people know that."

"Come on, Sergius, let's go," Eitel said.

"Wait, you!" Teppis said to me. "What's your name?"

I told him. I gave it with an Irish twist.

"What kind of name is that for a clean-cut youngster like you? You should change it. John Yard. That's the kind of name you should have." He looked me over as if he were buying a bolt of cloth. "Who are you?" said Teppis, "what do you do? I hope you're not a bum."

If he wanted to irritate me, he was successful. "I used to be in the Air Force," I said to him.

There was a gleam in his eye. "A flier?"

Standing in the doorway, Eitel decided to have his own fun. "Do you mean you never heard of this boy, H. T.?"

Teppis was cautious. "I can't keep up with everything," he said.

"Sergius is a hero," Eitel said creatively. "He shot down four planes in a day."

I had no chance to get into this. Teppis smiled as if he had been told something very valuable. "Your mother and father must be extremely proud of you," he said.

"I wouldn't know. I was brought up in an orphanage." My voice was probably unsteady because I could see by Eitel's change of expression that he knew I was telling the truth. I was sick at giving myself away so easily. But it is always like that. You hold a secret for years, and then spill it like a cup of coffee. Or maybe Teppis made me spill it.

"An orphan," he said. "I'm staggered. Do you know you're a remarkable young man?" He smiled genially and looked at Eitel. "Charley, you come back here," he said in his hoarse voice. "What are you flying off the handle for? You've heard me talk like this before."

"You're a rude man, Herman," Eitel said from the doorway.

"Rude?" Teppis put a fatherly hand on my shoulder. "Why, I wouldn't even be rude to my doorman." He laughed and then began to cough. "Eitel," he said, "what's happened to Carlyle? Where'd he go?"

"He didn't tell me."

"I don't understand anybody any more. You're a young man, Johnny," he said, pointing to me as if I were inanimate, "you tell me, what is everything all about?" But long before I could answer that question, he started talking again. "In my day a man got married, and he could be fortunate in his selection, or he could have bad luck, but he was married. I was a husband for thirty-two years, may my wife rest in peace, I have her picture on my desk. Can *you* say that, Eitel? What do you have on your desk? Pin-up pictures. I don't know people who feel respect for society any more. I tell

Carlyle. What happens? He wallows. That's the kind of man my daughter wanted to marry. A fool who sneaks around with a chippie dancer."

"We all have our peculiarities, Herman," Eitel said.

This made Teppis angry. "Eitel," he shouted, "I don't like you, and you don't like me, but I make an effort to get along with everybody," and then to quiet himself down, he made a point of looking me over very carefully. "What do you do?" he asked again as if he had not heard my answer. "Are you an actor?"

"No."

"I knew it. None of the good-looking clean-cut ones are actors any more. Just the ugly ones. Faces like bugs." He cleared his throat with a barking sound. "Look, Johnny," he went on, "I like you, I'll do you a good turn. There's a little party tomorrow night. I'm giving it for our people out here. You're invited."

The moment he gave this invitation, I knew I wanted to go to his party. Everybody in Desert D'Or had been talking about it for the last few days, and this was the first big party at the resort which I had been invited to. But I was angry at myself because I was ready to say yes, and in that second I almost forgot Eitel. So I told myself that I was going to play it through, and if Teppis wanted to invite me, and I didn't know why, I was going to get him to invite Eitel.

"I don't know if I want to go alone," I said to him, and I was satisfied that my voice was even.

"Bring a girl," Teppis offered. "You got a sweetheart?"

"It's not easy to find the right girl," I said. "I lost too much time flying airplanes."

My instinct about Herman Teppis seemed to be working. He nodded his head wisely. "I see the connection," he said.

"I was thinking Charley Eitel could help me find a girl," I added.

For a second I thought I had lost it and Teppis was going to fly into a rage. He glared at both of us. "Who invited Eitel?" he said furiously.

"You didn't invite him?" I said. "I thought maybe you did."

With what an effort, Teppis smiled benevolently. "Johnny, you're a very loyal friend. You got spunk." In practically the same breath he said to Eitel, "Tell me, cross your heart, Charley, are you a Red?"

Eitel didn't rush to answer. "You know everything, Herman," he murmured at last. "Why ask questions?"

"I know!" Teppis shouted. "I know all about you. I'll never understand why you made such a spectacle of yourself." He threw up his arms. "All right, all right, I know you're clean deep down.

Come to my party." Teppis shook his head. "Only, do me a favor, Charley. Don't say I invited you. Say it was Mac Barrantine."

"This is one hell of an invitation," Eitel answered.

"You think so, well don't look a gift horse, you know what I mean? One of these days go clear yourself with the American government, and then maybe I'll work with you. I got no objection to making money with people I don't like. It's my motto." He took my hand and shook it firmly. "Agree with me, Johnny? That's the ticket. I'll see both you boys tomorrow night."

On the drive back to Eitel's house I was in a good mood. Teppis had been just right for me. I was even overexcited, I kept talking to Eitel about how it had felt the time I took my first solo. Then I began to realize that the more I talked the more depressed I made him feel, and so looking for any kind of question to change the subject I said, "What do you say about our invitation? Maybe there's going to be just a little look on people's faces when you turn up." I started to laugh again.

Eitel shook his head. "They'll probably say I've been having private talks with the Committee, or else why would Teppis have me there?" Then he grinned at the frustration of it. "Man," he said, mimicking me, "don't you just have to be good to win?" But there was more than enough to think about in this thought, and neither of us said another word until we turned into his garage. Then Eitel stopped the car with a jerk. "Sergius, I'm not going to that party," he said.

"Well, if you won't change your mind . . ." I wanted to go to the party, I was ready for it, I thought, but it was going to be harder without Eitel. I wouldn't know anybody there.

"You did well, today," he said. "You go. You'll enjoy it. But I can't go. I've been a bus boy to Teppis for too many years." We went inside, and Eitel dropped into an armchair and pressed his hands to his forehead. The script was on the end table next to him. He picked it up, rustled the pages, and dropped it to the floor. "Don't tell anybody, Sergius," he said, "but this script stinks."

"Are you sure?"

"I don't know. I can't get out of myself long enough to look at it." He sighed. "If I ever bring it off, remind me, will you, of this conversation? You see, I've been trying to remember if I was as depressed in the old days when the work would come out well."

"I'll remind you," I said.

A short while later, Munshin phoned Eitel. Elena was all right, he told him. She was sleeping. Tonight, he would take care of her. But for tomorrow he begged Eitel to show her a good time.

Eitel said he would. When the call was finished, his eyes were dancing. "Do you know," he said, "I can hardly accuse myself of running after Teppis if I take Collie's girl along."

"But what about the girl?"

"It could be the best way to get over Mr. Munshin. She'll see that a stranger will do more for her in a night than he did in three years."

"What are you up to?" I asked.

"Yes, I'm going to take her to the party," Eitel said.

Chapter Eight

The Laguna Room at the Yacht Club which Herman Teppis had rented for his party was not a room at all. Painted in the lemon-yellow of the Yacht Club, it was open to the sky, and like the café, an amoebic pool strayed between the tables, rounded a portion of the dance floor, and ended behind the bar, a play of colored lights changing the water into a lake of tomato aspic, lime jello, pale consommé, and midnight ink. On an island not twenty feet-long, in the middle of the pool, the bandstand was set up, and the musicians played their dance numbers free of any passing drunk who might want to take a turn on the drums.

Since the party was given by Herman Teppis, the management of the Yacht Club had added some special old-fashioned effects. A big searchlight threw its column into the air, placed at such an angle as not to burn into the eyes of the guests, and a collection of spotlights and flood lamps was arranged to make it look like a party on a movie set, even to the expense of a tremendous papier-mâché camera on a wooden boom, directed by a bellhop wearing the outfit of a silent-film cameraman with the peak of his cap turned backward and a pair of knickers which reached his knees. All through the evening the camera was rotated on its boom, being lowered almost into the water or raised so high it threw a long shadow across the colors of the Laguna Room.

I had trouble getting in. Eitel had left earlier in the evening to meet Elena and had still not returned by eleven, so I decided to go alone, and I put on my Air Corps uniform with its ribbons. At the entrance to the Laguna Room, which was garnished with a gangplank, a man dressed like a purser stood checking the invitations. There was no record of my name on the guest list.

I said, "Maybe I'm down there as John Yard."

There was no John Yard on the purser's scratchboard.

"How about Charles Eitel?" I asked.

"Mr. Eitel is listed, but you would have to come in with him."

Yet it was the purser who discovered my name. In a last-minute addition, Teppis had recorded me as "Shamus Something-or-other," and so as Shamus Something-or-other, I got into his party.

Near the purser's stand, seated on two couches which faced each other, were half a dozen women. They were all dressed expensively, and their make-up to make up for such faults as thin mouths, small eyes, and mouse-colored hair, had curved their lips, slimmed their cheeks, and given golden or chestnut tints to their coiffures. Like warriors behind their painted shields, they sat stiffly, three and three, staring at one another, talking with apathy. I bobbed my head at them, not knowing whether to introduce myself or to move on, and one of them looked up, and in a voice which was harsh, asked, "You under contract at Magnum?"

"No," I said.

"Oh, I thought you were somebody else," she said and looked away again.

They were talking about their children and I guessed, as Eitel later confirmed, that they were the wives of important men and men who wanted to be important, the husbands off in chase of one another through the Laguna Room while the women were left behind.

"What do you mean, California is no good?" one of them said fiercely. "It's wonderful for children."

When a man went by, they tried to pay no notice. I realized that in walking past with a clumsy smile, showing how I didn't know if I was supposed to talk to them or not, I had done the dirty service of reflecting their situation. A few other men came in after me, and I saw that they either walked by without a look, or stopped for a brief but wild gallantry which went something like this:

"Carolyn!" the man would say, as if he could not believe he saw the woman here and was simply overcome.

"Mickey!" one of the six women would say.

"My favorite girl," the man would say, holding her hand.

"The only real man I know," the deserted wife would say.

Mickey would smile. He would shake his head, he would hold her hand. "If I didn't know you were kidding, I could give you a tumble," he would say.

"Don't be too sure I'm kidding," the wife would say.

Mickey would straighten up, he would release her hand. There would be a silence until Mickey murmured, "What a woman."

Then, in the businesslike tone which ends a conversation, he would say, "How are the kids, Carolyn?"

"They're fine."

"That's great. That's great." He would start to move away, and give a smile to all the women. "We have to have a long talk, you and me," Mickey would say.

"You know where to find me."

"Great kidder, Carolyn," Mickey would announce to nobody in particular, and disappear into the party.

All through the Laguna Room, wherever there was a couch, three wives were sitting in much that way. Since a lot of the men had come without women, the result was that men got together with men, standing near the pool, off the dance floor, at the café tables or in a crowd near the bar. I picked up a drink and wandered through the party looking for a girl to talk to. But all the attractive girls were surrounded, though by fewer men than squeezed up to listen to a film director or a studio executive, and besides I did not know how to get into the conversations. They were all so private. I had been thinking that my looks and my uniform might not do me any harm, but most of the girls seemed to like the conversation of fat middle-aged men and bony middle-aged men, the prize going to a German movie director with a big paunch who had his arms around the waists of two starlets. Actually I wasn't really that eager. Being stone sober, the fact was that it was easier to drift from one circle of men to another.

In a cove of the bar formed by two tables and the tip of one of the pool's tentacles, I found Jennings James telling a joke to several feature actors of no particular celebrity. Jay-Jay rambled on, his eyes blurred behind his silver-rimmed glasses. When he was done, other jokes were told, each more stray than the one which went before. I quit them after a while, and Jay-Jay caught up to me.

"What a stinking party this is," he said. "I'm supposed to work tonight, show the photographers a good time." He coughed with stomach misery. "I left all those photographers over at the canopy table. You know it's the truth about photographers, they'd rather eat than drink." Jay-Jay had an arm on my shoulder, and I realized he was using me as an escort to reach the men's room. "You know the line of poetry, 'Me-thought I saw the grave where Laura lay'?" he started to say. But whatever it was he wanted to add was lost, and he stood looking at me sheepishly. "Well, that's a beautiful line of poetry," he finished, and like a kid who has clung to the back of a streetcar while it climbs the hill, and drops off once the top is reached, Jay-Jay let go my arm and, listing from the change in balance, went careening to the urinal.

I was left to stand around the edge of one group or another. A director finished a story of which I heard no more than the last few lines. "I sat down and I told her that to be a good actress, she must always work for the truth in what she's playing," the man said in a voice not empty of self-love, "and she said, 'What's the truth?' and I said it could be defined as the real relation between human beings. You saw the performance I got out of her." He stopped, the story was over, and the men and women around him nodded wisely. "That's wonderful advice you gave her, Mr. Sneale," a girl said, and the others murmured in agreement.

"Howard, tell the story about you and Mr. Teppis," one of them begged.

The director chuckled. "Well, this story is on Herman, but I know he wouldn't mind. There are enough stories on me in my dealings with him. H. T.'s got an instinct which is almost infallible. There's a reason why he's such a great movie-maker, such a creative movie-maker."

"That's very true, Howard," the same girl said.

I moved on without listening any more and almost bumped into the subject of the story. In a corner, off on a discussion, were Herman Teppis and two other men who were not too different from Teppis. They had been pointed out to me already as Eric Haislip, head of Magnum, and Mac Barrantine from Liberty Pictures, but I think I would have guessed in any case, for the three men were left alone. If I had drunk my liquor more slowly, I might have felt the social paradox which allowed only these men to be able to talk without the attention of a crowd, but instead I placed myself at the elbow of the producer named Mac Barrantine. They continued their conversation without paying any attention to me.

"What do you think you'll gross on *The Tigress?*" Eric Haislip was saying.

"Three-and-a-half to four," Herman Teppis said.

"Three-and-a-half to four?" Eric Haislip repeated. "H. T., you're not talking to the New York office. You'll be lucky to get your money out."

Teppis snorted. "I could buy your studio with what we'll make."

Mac Barrantine spoke slowly out of the side of a cigar. "I claim that you just can't tell any more. There was a time when I could say, 'Bring it in at one-and-a-half, and we'll gross a million over.' Today, picture-making is crazy. A filthy bomb I'm ashamed of makes money, a classical musical comedy vehicle like *Sing, Girls, Sing* lays an egg. You figure it out."

"You're wrong," Herman Teppis said, prodding him with a finger. "You know the trouble? People are confused today. So what do they want? They want a picture that confuses them. Wait till they get really confused. Then they'll want a picture that sets them straight."

"Now you're required to show them real things on the screen," Eric Haislip sighed.

"Real things?" Teppis exploded. "We bring real things to them. Realism. But because a fellow in an Italian movie vomits all over the place and they like it in some art theater doesn't even have air-cooling, we should bring them vomit?"

"There's no discipline," Mac Barrantine said. "Even a director, a man with a high-powered tool in his hands. What does he do? He runs amuck like a gangster."

"Charley Eitel cut your throat," Eric Haislip said.

"They all cut my throat," Teppis said passionately. "You know something? My throat don't cut." He glared at them as if remembering times when each of them had tried to treat him to a razor. "Bygones. Let it be bygones," Teppis said. "I get along with everybody."

"There's no discipline," Barrantine repeated. "I got a star, I won't mention her name. She came to me, she knew that in two months we were starting production on a really big vehicle for her, and you know what she had the gall to say? 'Mr. Barrantine, my husband and I, we're going to have a baby. I'm six weeks along.' 'You're going to have a baby?' I said, 'where in hell's your loyalty? I know you, you're selfish. You can't tell me you want the heartache of bringing up an infant.' 'Mr. Barrantine, what should I do?' she bawled to me. I gave her a look and then I told her. 'I can't take the responsibility for advising you what to do,' I said, 'but you damn well better do something.' "

"She's going to be in the picture, I hear," Eric Haislip said.

"Of course she's going to be in the picture. She's an ambitious girl. But discipline and consideration. Do any of them have that?"

Eric Haislip was looking at me. "Who are you? What do you want here, kid?" he asked suddenly, although he had been aware of me for several minutes.

"I've been invited," I said.

"Did I invite you to sit on my lap?" Mac Barrantine said.

"You'd be the first," I muttered.

To my surprise, Teppis said, "Leave the boy alone. I know this boy. He's a nice young fellow."

Barrantine and Haislip glowered at me, and I scowled back. We all stood nose to nose like four trucks meeting at a dirt crossroad.

"The youth, the young people," Teppis announced. "You think you know something? Listen to a young fellow's ideas. He can tell you something. This boy has a contribution."

Barrantine and Haislip did not seem particularly enthusiastic to hear my contribution. Conversation ground along for several minutes, and then they left on the excuse of filling their drinks. "I'll call the maître dee," Teppis offered. They shook their heads. They needed a walk, they announced. When they were gone, Teppis looked in a fine mood. I had the suspicion he had come to my defense in order to insult them. "First-rate fellows," he said to me. "I've known them for years."

"Mr. Teppis," I said irritably, "why did you invite me to your party?"

He laughed and clamped a hand on my shoulder. "You're a clever boy," he said, "you're quick-tongued. I like that." His hoarse thin voice drew a conspiratorial link between us whether I wanted it or not. "You take the desert," he confided to me, "it's a wonderful place to make a human being feel alive. I hear music in it all the time. A musical. It's full of cowboys and these fellows that live alone, what do you call them, hermits. Cowboys and hermits and pioneers, that's the sort of place it is. Fellows looking for gold. As a young fellow, what do you think, wouldn't you like to see such a movie? I like history," he went on before I could answer. "It would take a talented director to make such a story, a fellow who knows the desert." He poked me in the ribs as though to leave me breathless and therefore honest. "You take Eitel. Is he still hitting the booze?" Teppis said suddenly, his small flat eyes studying my reaction.

"Not much," I said quickly, but my look must have wandered because Teppis squeezed my shoulder again.

"We got to have a long talk, you and me," Teppis said. "I like Charley Eitel. I wish he didn't have such a stain on his character. Politics. Idiotic. What do you think?"

"I think he's going to make the best movie of his life," I said with the hope I could worry Teppis.

"For the art theaters," Teppis stated, and he pointed a finger to his brain. "It won't be from the heart. You're too fresh for your own good," he continued with one of his fast shifts, "who's interested in your ideas? I'll tell you what the story is. Eitel is through."

"I disagree," I said, cheered to realize I was the only one at this party who did not have to be polite to Herman Teppis.

"You disagree? What do you know? You're a baby." But I thought I understood what went on in him, the fear that he might be wrong chewing at the other fear he might make a fool of himself by considering Eitel again. "Now listen, you," he started to say, but we were interrupted.

"Good evening, daddy," a woman said.

"Lottie," Teppis said moistly, and embraced her. "Why didn't you call me?" he asked. "Ten o'clock this morning and no call from you."

"I had to miss it today," said Lottie Munshin. "I was packing for the trip."

Teppis began to ask her about his grandchildren, turning his back almost entirely on me. While they spoke I watched Carlyle Munshin's wife with interest. She was one of those women who are middle-aged too soon, her skin burned into the colors of false health. Thin, nervous, her face was screwed tight, and in those moments when she relaxed, the lines around her forehead and mouth were exaggerated, for the sun had not touched them. Pale haggard eyes looked out from sun-reddened lids. She was wearing an expensive dress but had only succeeded in making it look dowdy. The bones of her chest stood out, and a sort of ruffle fluttered on her freckled skin with a parched rustling movement like a spinster's parlor curtains. "I was delayed getting here," she said to her father in so pinched a voice I had the impression her throat was tight. "You see, Doxy was littering today. You know Doxy?"

"It's one of the mutts?" Teppis asked uncomfortably.

"She took the state-wide blue ribbon for her class," Lottie Munshin said. "Don't you remember?"

"Well, that's good." Teppis coughed. "Now, why don't you leave those dogs out of your mind for a couple of weeks, and you take a good vacation. You relax. You have a good time with Collie."

"I can't leave them for two weeks," she said with something like panic. "Salty litters in the next ten days, and we have to start training Blitzen and Nod for the trials."

"Well, that's fine," Teppis said vaguely. "Now, there's a fellow I got to see, so I'll leave you in the company of this young man. You'll enjoy talking to him. And Lottie, you remember," he said, "there's more imporant things than those dogs."

I watched him walk away, nodding his head to the people who swarmed to greet him, carrying them one at a time like parasite fish. One couple even moved off the dance floor and came hurrying toward him.

"Do you like dogs?" Lottie Munshin asked me. She gave a short rough laugh for punctuation, and looked at me with her head cocked to one side.

I made the mistake of saying, "You breed them, don't you?"

She replied; she replied at length; she insisted on going into de-

The Deer Park, a Novel   113

tails which led into other details, she was a fanatic, and I stood listening to her, trying to find the little girl who had grown into this woman. "Collie and I have the best ranch within the county limits of the capital," she said in that pinched voice, "although of course keeping it up devolves upon me. It's quite a concern, I can tell you. I'm up at six every morning."

"You keep an early schedule," I offered.

"Early to bed. I like to be up with the sun. With such hours everybody could keep themselves in fine condition. You're young now, but you should take care of yourself. People should follow the same hours animals do, and they would have the natural health of an animal."

Over her shoulder I could see the dance floor and the swimming pool, and I was pulled between my desire to quit her for people who were more interesting, any my reluctance to leave her alone. While she spoke, her bony fingers plucked at her chin. "I've got a green thumb," she said. "It's an unusual combination. I breed dogs and things grow under my thumb. Sometimes I think my father must have been meant to be a farmer because where else could it have developed in me?"

"Oh, look. There's your husband," I said in relief.

She called to him. He was some distance away, but at the sound of her voice he looked up with an exaggeration of surprise which betrayed he was not surprised at all, and came moving toward us. As he recognized me his expression changed for a moment, but all the same he shook my hand warmly. "Well, we meet again," he said broadly.

"Carlyle, I meant to ask you," Lottie Munshin went on in a worried voice, "are you going to try that favorite-food diet?"

"I'll give it a look," he said in a bored tone, and caught me by the arm. "Lottie, I have something to talk over with Sergius. You'll excuse us." And with no more than that he steered me under a yucca tree, and we stood in the harsh shadow made by a flood lamp above the fronds.

"What are you doing here?" he asked.

Once again I explained that I had been invited by Herman Teppis. "Eitel, too?"

When I nodded, Munshin burst out, "I wouldn't put it past Eitel to bring Elena here." As he shook his head with indignation, I began to laugh.

"It's a rotten party," I said, "it needs some kicks."

Munshin surprised me. A calculating expression came over his face and suddenly he looked like a very tough clown to me, a clown who in a quiet private way knew more than a few corners of the world. "It would be worth a lot of money to know what's in H.T.'s head," he muttered to himself, and walked away leaving me beside the yucca tree.

The party was becoming more active. People were going off by couples, or coming together at one center of interest or another. In a corner a game of charades was going on, the dance floor was nearly filled, a well-known comedian was performing for nothing, and an argument about a successful play almost killed the music of the rumba band. A drunk had managed to climb the boom which supported the papier-mâché camera, and he was quarreling with the cameraman who was trying to get him to go down. Nearby, his wife was laughing loudly. "Ronnie's a flagpole sitter," she kept announcing. The swimming instructor of the hotel was giving a diving exhibition in a roped-off portion of the pool, but only a few were watching her. I had a couple of drinks at the bar, and tried to work into one circle or another without success. Bored, I listened to a folk singer dressed like a leatherstocking, who sang old ballads in a quavery twang which could be heard above the dance orchestra. "Isn't he talented?" a woman said nearby.

I felt a tap on my shoulder. A blond man whom I recognized as the tennis professional of the Yacht Club smiled at me. "Come on over," he said, "somebody would like to meet you." It turned out to be the movie star, Teddy Pope. He was a tall man with an open expression and dark-brown hair which fell in a cowlick over his forehead. When I came up with the tennis player, he grinned at me.

"Isn't this party a dog?" Teddy Pope said.

We all smiled at one another. I could think of nothing to say. Beside Pope sat Marion Faye, looking small and bored. He only nodded at me.

"Do you know roulette?" the tennis player asked. "Teddy's an *aficionado.*"

"I've been trying to get a system," Teddy said. "I had a theory about the numbers. But mathematically it was too much for my low intelligence. I hired a statistician to try to figure it out." He grinned at me again. "You a weight-lifter?" Teddy asked me.

"No. Should I be?"

This turned out to be very amusing. Pope and the tennis player and Marion Faye shared a long run of laughter. "I can bend an iron bar," Teddy said to me. "That is, if it's a slim enough iron bar. I just stay in weight-lifting to keep from getting fat. I'm getting so fat now." He pinched his belly to give a demonstration and was able to show an excess of flesh no thicker than a pencil. "It's disgusting."

"You look in good shape," I said uncomfortably.

"Oh, I'm pudgy," Pope said.

"Weight-lifting ruined your forehand," the tennis player said.

Teddy Pope made no answer. "I can see you're a flier," he said. "Is it true that most of you live for drinking and sex?" He leaned back and smiled at the sky. "Oh, there's a beauty," he said as a girl passed. "Would you like to meet her? Marion says you're a little shy."

"I'll make out."

"Why don't you help him, Teddy?" Marion jeered.

"I would just be a drag," Pope said.

"Sit down, Sergei," said the tennis player.

"No. Well, you see," I said, "I promised to bring a drink to somebody."

"Come back if you get bored," Teddy said.

I was approached beneath another yucca tree by a little bald-headed man in a sky-blue tropical suit who had a tall redheaded girl by the hand. "Ah, there you are, I missed you before," he said briskly. "I'd like to introduce myself. I'm Bunny Zarrow, you may have heard of me. Actor's representative." I must have looked at him with surprise, for he added, "I see you were talking to Mr. Teppis. May I ask what you were talking about?"

"He wanted my advice on a movie."

"That's interesting. That's unusual. And what is your name?"

"John Yard," I said.

"You're under contract, I take it?"

"Of course."

"Well, a contract can sometimes be bettered. I wish I could place your name. I will say this is neither the time nor the opportunity, but you and I must have lunch to discuss it. I'll call you at the studio." He pointed to the girl beside him. "I'd like you to meet Candy Ballou." The girl yawned and then tried to smile. She was very drunk.

Bunny drew me aside. "Let me give you her phone number. She's a charming outgoing girl." He blinked his eyes. "I'm glad to do you a favor. If I weren't so overworked, I would keep her number, but it's a shame to keep such a girl to myself." He returned me to Candy Ballou and placed our hands together. "Now, kiddies, I'm sure you two have a great deal in common," he said, and left us looking at one another.

"Would you want to dance?" I asked the red headed girl.

"Don't panic, love-bucket." She said this as if it were a password, and then opened her eyes to focus on me. "What studio you at?" she blurted.

"That's just a joke, Candy," I said.

"A joke on Zarrow, huh?"

"That's right."

"What do you do?"

"Nothing," I said.

"No dough. I might have known." She swayed her body to the rhythms of the rumba music and yawned fiercely. "Oh, honey," she said in a little broken voice, "if you had class, you'd help me to the ladies' room."

On my return from that errand with no more for company than a new highball, I saw Eitel come in at last. He was with a girl. Elena, I knew.

Chapter Nine

She was a near-beauty. Elena's hair was a rich red-brown and her skin was warm. She walked with a sense of her body, and I had always been drawn to that in a girl since my first year in the Air Force when like every other fly at an enlisted man's dance, I would cock my hat and try to steal prizes like Elena with my speed. Although she wore a lot of lipstick, and her high heels would have satisfied a show-girl, there was something delicate about her and very proud. She carried herself as if she were tall, and her strapless evening gown showed round handsome shoulders. Her face was not exactly soft, but it was heart-shaped, and above her tender mouth and chin, the nares of her long narrow nose suggested ample aptitude to me. Munshin's description seemed passing poor.

Except that she was obviously not at ease. As I watched Eitel lead her into the mouth of the party she reminded me of an animal, ready for flight. Their appearance at the party had set off a ripple of confusion, and very few of the people who saw him knew what to do. There were several who smiled and even said hello, there were some who nodded, and even more who turned away, but I had the feeling they were all frightened. Until they knew the reason why Eitel had been invited, they could only feel the panic that whatever they did could be a mistake. It was grim the way he and Elena were left to cross the floor of the party without catching anybody to accompany them, and I saw Eitel stop finally at an empty table near the pool, set out a chair for Elena, and then sit down himself. From a distance, I had to like the way he succeeded in looking bored.

I went up to their table. "Can I join you?" I said clumsily.

Eitel gave me a quick grateful smile. "Elena, you must meet Sergius, he's the best person here."

"Oh, shut up," I told him, and turned to her. "I'm awfully sorry, I didn't catch your last name," I said.

"It's Esposito," Elena muttered, "an Italian name." Her voice was just a little hoarse, and surprisingly deep, which made it considerably less useful to her than her face, but it was a voice which had muffled strength in it. I had heard accents like that since I was a kid.

"Doesn't she look like a Modigliani?" Eitel said enthusiastically, and then added, "Elena, I know you've been told that more than once."

"Yes," Elena said, "that is, someone once told me. As a matter of fact it was your friend."

Eitel passed over the reference to Munshin. "But where did you get those green eyes?" he teased her. From the angle where I sat, I could see his fingers tapping restlessly on his knee.

"Oh, that's from my mother," Elena said. "She's half Polish. I guess I'm one-quarter Polish and three-quarters Italian. Oil and water." We all worked a little to laugh, and Elena shifted uncomfortably. "What a funny subject," she said.

Eitel made a play of studying the Laguna Room and said, "What do you think this party needs?"

"What?" I asked.

"A roller coaster."

Elena burst into laughter. She had a nice laugh which showed her white teeth, but she laughed too loudly. "Oh, that's so funny," she said.

"I love roller coasters," Eitel went on. "It's that first drop. Like the black hole of death. There's nothing to compare with it." And for the next two minutes he talked about roller coasters, until I could see by the look in Elena's eyes how alive he made the subject seem. He was in good form, and to draw him out, Elena was a good listener. I found myself thinking that she was not stupid, and yet she would only answer with a laugh or some little remark. It was the style of her attention. Her face gave back the shadow of everything he said, until Eitel was carried away. "It proves an old idea of mine," he said. "One gets on a roller coaster in order to feel certain emotions, and I wonder if it's not the same with an affair. When I was younger, I used to think it was ugly, even unclean I suppose, that a man who thought he was in love would find himself using the same words with one girl after another. Yet there's nothing wrong about it really. The only true faithfulness people have is toward emotions they're trying to recapture."

"I don't know," Elena said. "I think a man like that wouldn't be feeling anything for the woman."

"On the contrary. At that moment, he adores her."

This confused her. "I mean," she interrupted, "you know, it's . . . oh, I'm not sure." But she could not let it pass. "A man like that isn't relating to the woman. He's detached."

Eitel looked pleased. "You're right," he reversed himself. "I suppose it's the proof of how detached I am."

"Oh, you can't be." she said.

"I certainly am," he smiled, as though to flag an advance warning.

It must have been hard to believe. His eyes were bright, his body leaned toward her, and his dark hair looked charged with energy. "Don't judge by appearances," Eitel began, "why I can tell you . . ."

He broke off. Munshin was coming toward us. Elena's face lost all expression, and Eitel began to smile in an unnatural way.

"I don't know what it is you got," Collie boomed, "but H.T. told me to come over and say hello. He wants to talk to you later."

When none of us answered, Munshin contented himself with staring at Elena.

"Collie, how are you?" Eitel said finally.

"I've been better." He nodded his head. "I've been a lot better," he said, continuing to look at Elena.

"Aren't you having a good time?" she asked.

"No, I'm having a rotten time," Munshin answered.

"I was looking for your wife," Elena said, "but I don't know who she is."

"She's around," Munshin said.

"And your father-in-law? He's here, I heard you say."

"What difference does it make?" Munshin asked with a moist look as if he were really saying, "Someday you won't hate me any more."

"Oh, yes, no difference at all. I wouldn't want to embarrass you," Elena said, her voice all but out of control. It gave a hint of how badly she would act in a quarrel.

"I met Teddy Pope tonight," I interrupted as best I could. "What is he like?"

"I can tell you," Eitel said nimbly, "he's been in several of my pictures. And do you know, I think he's really sort of decent as an actor. Some day he may be very good."

At that moment, a beautiful blond girl in a pale-blue evening gown came up behind Munshin and covered his eyes with her hands. "Guess who?" she said in a throaty voice. I had a glimpse of a little turned-up nose, a dimpled chin, and a pouting mouth I had seen before. At the sight of Eitel she made a face.

"Lulu," Munshin said, half rising from his chair, and not knowing if her interruption had helped the situation or made it worse, he hugged Lulu with fatherly arms, smiling at Elena and Eitel, while with his free hand visible only to me, he patted the small of her back as though to tell her she might do worse than to hug him again.

"Miss Meyers, Miss Esposito," Eitel said smoothly, and Lulu gave a passing nod to Elena. "Collie, we have to talk," Lulu said, "I have something I definitely want to tell you about." Then she gave a sweet smile to Eitel. "Charley, you're getting fat," she said.

"Sit down," Eitel offered.

She took a chair next to him, and told Munshin to sit on the other side. "Isn't anybody going to introduce the Air Force?" she asked directly of me, and when that was done, she made a game of studying my face. I forced myself to stare her down but it took something out of me. "What a pretty boy you are," said Lulu Meyers. She could not have been much more than twenty herself.

"She's great," Munshin said. "What a tongue."

"Would you like a drink?" I asked Elena. She hadn't said a word since Lulu had come, and by comparison she did not seem as attractive as I thought her before. Maybe aware of this herself, she picked nervously and savagely at the cuticle on her nail. "Oh, yes, I'd like a drink," Elena agreed, and as I started away, Lulu handed me her glass. "Get me a small Martin, will you?" she asked, turning violet-blue eyes on me. I realized she was as nervous as Elena, but in a different way; Lulu made herself sit easily in the chair—I had learned the same trick in flying school.

When I came back, she was talking to Eitel. "We miss you, old ham," she was saying. "I don't know anybody I'd rather get drunk with than Eitel."

"I'm on the wagon," Eitel said with a grin.

"You're on the wagon as far as I'm concerned," Lulu said with a glance at Elena.

"I hear you're going to marry Teddy Pope," Eitel answered.

Lulu turned on Munshin. "You tell H.T. to lay off the drums," she said, and flipped her cigarette to the floor, grinding it out with a quick impatient motion. I had a peep at her legs and of little feet covered by silver slippers. Those legs were as familiar as the contour of her mouth, each drawn on one's memory by a hundred photographs, or was it a thousand? "Collie, this propaganda has got to stop, I tell you."

Munshin gave his sheepish smile. "Now, you relax, doll. Who's forcing you into anything?"

"I approve of Lulu marrying Teddy," Eitel drawled.

"Charley, you're a troublemaker," Munshin said quickly.

Elena and I looked at each other. She was trying very hard to be a part of this, her eyes following everyone who spoke, her smile forced as if she didn't want to seem ignorant. Probably I was acting the same way. We sat at opposite flanks of the conversation, no more than social book-ends.

"I'm serious," Lulu said. "You can tell Mr. T. I'll marry this pretty boy first," and she inclined a finger toward me.

"You haven't proposed yet," I said.

Elena laughed with enough pleasure to have said it herself. Again her laugh was too loud, and the others stared at her.

"Don't panic, love-bucket," Lulu said with an authority the red-headed girl, Candy Ballou, had not been able to muster. She held her empty glass up for us all to see, and poured its last drop on the floor. "I'm sad, Collie," she announced and laid her head on Munshin's shoulder.

"I saw your last picture," Eitel said to her.

"Wasn't I just awful in it?" Lulu made a face again. "They're ruining me. What did you think, Eitel?"

He smiled noncommittally. "I'll talk to you about it."

"I know what you'll say. I was performing too much, wasn't I?" She raised her head and pinched Collie on the cheek. "I hate acting." And with hardly a pause she leaned forward to ask a question. "What do you do, Miss Esposo?"

"Esposito," Eitel said.

Elena was uncomfortable. "I've been . . . not exactly, a dancer, I guess."

"Modeling now?" Lulu said.

"No . . . I mean, of course not. . . ." Elena was not altogether helpless before her. "Different things," she finished at last. "Who wants to be a skinny model?"

"Oh, I'll bet," Lulu said, and spoke to me again. "You the latest tail on Eitel's old tattered kite?"

I could feel myself turning red. Her attacks came so fast that it was a little like waiting for the sound to stop in musical chairs. "They say you're through, Charley," Lulu went on.

"They certainly do talk about me," Eitel said.

"Not as much as you think. Time passes."

"I'll always be remembered as your second ex-husband," Eitel drawled.

"It's a fact," she said. "When I think of Charley Eitel, I think of number two."

Eitel smiled cheerfully. "If you want to put on the brass knuckles, Lulu, just give the word."

There was a moment, and then Lulu smiled back. "I'm sorry, Charley, I apologize." She turned to all of us, and in that husky voice which went along so nicely with her blond hair and blue eyes, she said "I saw an awful picture of me today in the papers."

"Lulu," Munshin said quickly, "we can rectify that. The photographers will be working soon."

"I won't be mugged with Teddy Pope," Lulu declared.

"Who's forcing you?" Munshin said.

"No tricks, Collie."

"No tricks," Munshin promised, wiping his face.

"Why are you perspiring so?" Lulu asked, and then broke off to stand up. "Jay-Jay!" she cried aloud, and opened her arms. Jennings James, who had just walked toward us, wrapped her to his skinny body in a parody of Munshin's bear-hug. "My favorite girl," he said in his high Southern voice.

"That was a bitchy release you had on me day before yesterday," Lulu said.

"Honey, you're paranoidal," Jennings James told her. "I wrote it as a work of love to you." He nodded to all of us. "How are you, Mr. Munshin?" he said. The trip to the men's room seemed to have revived him.

"Take a chair, Jay-Jay," Munshin said, "this is Miss Esposito."

Jennings James bowed formally to her. "I love the dignity of Italian women, Miss Esposito." His freckled hand smoothed his red hair. "Are you going to stay with us long in Desert D'Or?"

"I'm going back tomorrow," Elena said.

"Oh, you're not," Eitel said.

"Well, I'm not sure," Elena corrected herself.

A waiter brought ice cream. It was melted on the plates, and only Elena took a dish. "This is soft ice cream, isn't it?" she said. "That's the expensive kind, I've heard." When everybody looked puzzled by the remark, Elena became a little desperate in the attempt to prove it. "I don't remember where I heard, but I did see it advertised, soft ice cream, I mean, or maybe I was eating it, I don't know."

Eitel came to her aid. "It's true. Duvon's in the city features a sort of melted ice cream. I've had it myself. But I don't think this is Duvon's, Elena."

"Oh, no, I know it isn't," she said quickly.

Jay-Jay turned back to Lulu. "Honey, we're ready for the pictures. Those photographers have finished grossifying themselves, and it all waits on you."

"Well, let it wait," said Lulu. "I want another drink."

"Mr. T. asked me specially to get you."

"Come on, let's go," said Munshin, "everybody." I think he included Elena, Eitel, and myself to prevent Lulu from deciding she wanted to stay with us. Once on his feet, Munshin took her arm and started along the edge of the pool past the dance floor toward a group of photographers I could see gathered near the papier-mâché movie camera.

Jay-Jay brought up the rear with me. "That Esposito dame," he said, "she's Munshin's little gal, I hear."

"I don't know," I said.

"Oh man, she's a dish. I never got my hooks into her, but I know some who have. When old Charley Eitel gets done with Esposito, you ought to spend a couple of delicious hours with her." He then started to give me details of how good she was supposed to be. "And she looks like a sweet kid, too," he added gallantly. "It's hard for a girl living in the capital. I don't hold it against any of them. Why, Teppis himself, that son of a bitch . . ." But Jay-Jay had no time to finish the sentence for we had come up to the photographers.

I could see Teddy Pope moving in from another direction. The tennis player still was with him, and they were laughing at some private joke. "Lulu, honey," Pope said, and held out his hand to shake hers. They touched fingertips and stood side by side.

"Now, fellows," said Jay-Jay springing forward and talking to the three photographers who stood phlegmatically in front of the camera boom, "we want some human-interest stills. Nothing elaborate. Just how cinema folks live and entertain each other. You got the idea." People were coming over from various corners of the Laguna Room. "Honeybun, you look lovely," Dorothea O'Faye called out, and Lulu smiled. "Thank you, sweetie," she called back. "Hey, Teddy," a man said, "have your autograph?" and Teddy laughed. Standing before an audience, his manner had changed. He seemed more boyish and more direct. "Why, here comes Mr. T. now," he said aloud, and showing a crack disdain to those who could see it, he began to clap his hands, and at least a dozen of the people near him, trapped into obedience, applauded as well. Teppis held his arm aloft. "We're taking some pictures to-night of Teddy and Lulu, not only for interest on their picture, or should I say *our* picture, *An Inch From Heaven*, but as a symbol, as I would call it, of tonight and the kind of good time we've had." Teppis cleared his throat and smiled sweetly. His presence had succeeded in drawing even more people, and for a while the scene was busy with the flash-bulbs of the cameras, the shifting of posi-tions, and the directions given by the photographers. I saw Teppis in place between Teddy and Lulu, Lulu between the two men, Teddy and Lulu together, Teddy and Lulu apart, Teppis holding Lulu's hand in a fatherly way, Teppis photographed with his hand on Teddy's elbow. I was struck by how well they did it, Teddy smiling, happy, healthy, and Lulu sweet, Lulu demure, Lulu ready, all with an ease which balanced the pride of Herman Teppis. It was just about perfect. Teddy Pope turned his face to every in-struction of the photographers, his voice had sincerity, his smile seemed to enjoy his surroundings. He waved his hands in the air like a prizefighter, and gave a play of having wrenched his shoulder from the exercise; he put his arm around Lulu's waist, he bussed her cheek. And Lulu with a cuddling curving motion slipped against his side. She seemed to bounce when she walked, her shoulders swayed in a little rhythm with her hips, her neck curved, her hair tumbled in gold ringlets over her head, and her husky voice laughed at everyone's jokes. I thought she was about as beautiful as any girl I had ever seen.

When the photographers were done, Teppis made another speech. "You never know. We're a big family at Supreme. I'll tell you something. I don't think these two kids were acting." And with a hand against each of their backs, he pushed them together until they had to hug each other in order not to trip. "What's this I hear, Lulu?" he said aloud to the laughter of the guests, "a little ladybug has told me you and Teddy are dear friends."

"Oh, Mr. Teppis," Lulu said in her sweetest voice, "you should have been a marriage broker."

"It's a compliment. I take it as a compliment," Teppis said. "A producer is always making marriages. Art and finance. Talent and an audience. Are you all having a good time tonight?" he asked of the guests watching, and I listened to more than one answer that a good time was being had. "Treat the camera boys," Teppis said to Jay-Jay, and walked off with Lulu on his arm. The crowd faded, the photographers were left to pack their equipment. Beside the pool, I saw Teppis stop to talk to Eitel, and while he spoke he looked at Elena.

I could see that Teppis recognized her name the moment Eitel introduced her, for Teppis' reaction followed quickly. His back stiffened, his ruddy face seemed to swell, and he said something, something to the point, since Eitel and Elena turned away immediately.

Alone with Lulu, Teppis was mopping his forehead with a silk handkerchief. "Go dance with Teddy," I heard him say hoarsely as I approached. "Do it as a favor for me."

Because of the crowd I could no longer see what had happened to Eitel.

Lulu caught my eye. "Mr. T., I want to dance with Sergius first," she said with a pout, and slipping away from Teppis she put her hand in my palm and drew me to the dance floor. I held her tightly. The liquor I had been drinking all evening was finally beginning to do its work.

"How long will it take," I said in her ear, "before you start to look for Teddy?"

To my surprise she took this meekly. "You don't know what I'm up against," Lulu said.

"Why? Do you know?"

"Oh, don't be like that, Sergius. I like you." At the moment she seemed no more than eighteen. "It's harder than you think," she whispered, and by the softness with which she held herself, I found it hard to believe in the first impression she made on me. She seemed young; spoiled maybe, but very sweet.

We danced in silence. "What did Teppis say to Eitel?" I asked finally.

Lulu shook her head and then giggled. "He told Charley to get the hell out."

"Well, then I guess I have to go too," I told her.

"You weren't included."

"Eitel is my friend," I said.

She pinched my ear. "Wonderful. Charley will love that. I have to tell him when I see him."

"Leave with me," I said.

"Not yet."

I stopped dancing. "If you want," I said, "I'll ask Mr. T. for permission."

"You think I'm afraid of him."

"You're not afraid of him. You'll just end up dancing with Teddy."

Lulu began to laugh. "You're different from what I thought at first."

"That's just liquor."

"Oh, I hope not."

Reluctantly, in a sort of muse, she allowed me to take her from the dance floor. "This is an awful mistake," she whispered.

Yet Lulu was not exactly timorous when we passed Teppis. Like a promoter who counts the seats in the house, he stood near the entrance, his eyes adding up the scene. "Girlie," he said, gripping her by the arm, "where are you going?"

"Oh, Mr. T.," Lulu said like a bad child, "Sergius and I have so much to talk about."

"We want to get some air," I said, and I took the opportunity to give him back a finger in the ribs.

"Air?" He was indignant as we left. "Air?" I could see him looking for the ceiling of the Laguna Room. Behind us, still in operation, the papier-mâché camera rotated on its woooden boom, the searchlights lifting columns to the sky. A pall lay over the party. The zenith had passed, and couples were closed into tête-à-têtes on the couches, for the drunken hour had come where everything is possible and everybody wants everybody; if desires were deeds, the history of the night would end in history.

"You say to Charley Eitel," Teppis shouted after me, "that he's through. I tell you he's through. He's lost his chance."

Giggling at the sound of his rage, Lulu and I ran along the walks and over the little trellised bridges of the Yacht Club until we came to the parking circle. Once, underneath a Japanese lantern, I stopped to kiss her, but she was laughing too hard and our mouths didn't meet. "I'll have to teach you," she said.

"Teach me nothing. I hate teachers," I said, and holding her hand, pulled her behind me, her heels clicking, her skirt rustling in the promising tap-and-whisper of a girl trying to run in an evening gown.

We had an argument over whose car to take. Lulu insisted on using her convertible. "I'm cooped up, Sergius," she said, "I want to drive." "Then drive my car," I compromised, but she would have no other way than her own. "I won't leave," she said, driven to a pitch of stubbornness, "I'll go back to the party."

"You're frightened," I taunted her.

"I'm not."

She drove badly. She was reckless, which I expected, but what was worse, she could not hold her foot steady on the pedal. The automobile was always slowing or accelerating and drunk as I was she made me aware of danger. But that wasn't the danger I was worrying about.

"I'm a nut," she'd say.

"Let's park, nut," I would answer. "Let's cut the knot."

"Did you ever go to the crazy doctor?" Lulu asked.

"You don't need him."

"Oh, I need something," she said, and with a wrench, gravel stinging our fenders, she brought the car off the shoulder and on the road again.

"Let's park," I said.

She parked when she would have it. I had given up hope, I was prepared to sit politely while she skidded us off the highway and we rolled and smacked at seventy miles an hour through the cactus and desert clay. But Lulu decided we might just as well live a little while longer. Picking a side road at random, she screamed around the turn, slowed down once it was past, drifted along, and finally pulled off in some deserted flat, the night horizon lying all around us in a giant circle.

"Lock the windows," she said, engrossed in pressing the button which raised the canvas top.

"It'll be too hot," I argued.

"No, the windows have to be closed," she insisted.

All preparations spent, she turned in her seat and took my kiss. She must have felt she had let loose a bull, and in fact she had; for the first time in almost a year I knew that I would be all right.

Yet it was not so easy as that. She would give herself to my mouth and my arms, she would be about to be caught, and then she would start away, looking fearfully through the car window. "There's a man coming," she would whisper, her nails digging my wrist, and I would be forced to lift my head and scan the horizon, forced to stop and say, "There's no one around, can't you see?"

"I'm scared," she would say, and give her mouth to me again. How long it went on I do not know, but it was a classic. She coaxed me forward, she pushed me back, she allowed me a strip of her clothing only to huddle away like a bothered virgin. We could have been kids on a couch. My lips were bruised, my body suffered, my fingers were thick, and if I succeeded finally in capturing what clothing she wore beneath her evening dress, pushing it behind me in the seat like a mad jay stuffing its nest, I still could not inspire Lulu to give up her gown. Though she allowed the most advanced forays and even let me for one, two, and then three beats of the heart, she sat up with a little motion that pushed me away, and looked through the windows. "There's someone coming. There's somebody on the road," she said, and pinched me when I tried to come near her.

"This is it," I told her, but for all I told her, high-water mark had been reached. For another hour, no matter what I did, how I forced, how I waited, and how I tried, I could not get so close again. The dawn must have been not too far away when exhausted, discouraged, and almost indifferent, I shut my eyes and murmured, "You win." With a weary hand I passed over my cache of her door-prizes and lay back against the seat.

Tenderly, she kissed my lashes, her fingernails teased my cheek. "You're sweet," she whispered, "you're really not so rough." To revive me, she pulled my hair. "Kiss me, Sergius," she said as if I had not yet done anything at all, and in the next minute while I lay back on the seat, not believing and almost dumb to her giving, I was led to discover the mysterious brain of a movie star. She gave herself gently to me, she was delicate, she was loving, loving even to the modesty with which she whispered that this was all very unplanned, and I must be considerate. So I was obliged to take the trip alone, and was repaid by having her cuddle in my arms.

"You're wonderful," she said.

"I'm just an amateur."

"No, you're wonderful. Oooh, I like you. You!"

On the way back I drove the car while she curled beside me, her head on my shoulder. The radio was on and we hummed to the music. "I was crazy tonight," she said.

I adored her. The way she had treated everybody when I met her made this even better. For on that long drive she took me before we parked, I had told myself that absolutely I had to succeed with her, and the memory of this feeling now that I had succeeded was fine. Maybe it was no more than that enough time had gone by, but I felt all right, I felt ready—for what, I hardly knew. But I had made it, and with what a girl.

Lulu was tense when we kissed good night outside her door. "Let me stay," I said.

"No, not tonight." She looked behind her to see if the walks were deserted.

"Then come to my house."

She kissed me on the nose. "I'm just beaten, Sergius." Her voice was the voice of a child.

"All right, I'll see you tomorrow."

"Call me." She kissed me again, she blew a kiss as she disappeared through the door, and I was left alone in the labyrinth of the Yacht Club, the first sun of a desert morning not far away, the foliage a pale-blue like the pale-blue of her gown.

It may sound weird, but I was so excited with enthusiasm that I had to share it, and I could think of nobody but Eitel. It did not even occur to me that he might still be with Elena, or that as the ex-husband of little Lulu, he would not necessarily find my story a dream. I don't know whether I even remembered that Lulu had been married to him. In a way, she had no existence for me before tonight, and if she seemed bigger than life, she was also without life. How I loved myself then. With the dawn spreading out from me until it seemed to touch the Yacht Club with its light, I began to think of those mornings when I was out on a flight which started in the darkness of the hangars, the syrup of coffee on my tongue, the blast of my plane flaring two long fires into the night. We would take off an hour before dawn, and when morning came to meet us five miles high in the air with the night clouds warmed by a gold and silver light, I used to believe I could control the changes of the sky by a sway of my body as it was swelled by the power of the plane, and I had played with magic. For it was magic to fly an airplane; it was a gimmick and a drug. We knew that no matter what happened on ground, no matter how little or confusing we ourselves could be, there would always come those hours when we were alone in formation and on top of life, and so the magic was in the flight and the flight made us very cool, you know? and there was nothing which could happen once we were down which could not be fixed when the night went into the west and we ganged after it on our wings.

I had been careful to forget all of this, I had liked it too much, and it had not been easy to think that I probably would never have any magic again; but on this dawn with the taste of Lulu still teasing me, I knew that I could have something else, and I could be sad for those airplanes I deserted because there was something to take their place.

Thinking this, or thinking of such things, I started up the path to where I parked my car. Halfway, I sat on a bench underneath a bower of shrubbery, breathing the new air. Everything had come to rest around me. Then, in a cottage nearby I heard sudden brawling sounds, a mixed dialogue or two, and a door in the wall opened and Teddy Pope lurched out, wearing a sweater and dungarees, but his feet were bare. "You bitch," he shouted at the door.

"Stay out," came the voice of the tennis player. "I don't want to tell you again." Teddy cursed. He cursed at such length and in so loud a voice that I was sure everybody sleeping nearby must be reaching for their pills. The door to the bungalow opened again, and Marion Faye came outside. "Go beat your meat, Teddy," he said in his quiet voice, and then he stepped back inside and shut the door. Teddy turned around once and looked past me with blank eyes which took me in, or maybe didn't see anything at all.

I watched him stagger along the wall, and in spite of myself I followed at a distance. In one of the minor patios of the Yacht Club where a fountain, a few yucca trees, and a hedge of bougainvillea set up an artificial nook, Teddy Pope stopped and made a phone call from an outdoor booth set under a trellis of rambler roses. "I can't go to sleep like this," he said into the receiver. "I've got to talk to Marion." The voice at the other end made some answer.

"Don't hang up," Teddy Pope said loudly.

Like a night watchman making his rounds, Herman Teppis came into sight along one of the walks. He approached Teddy Pope, came up beside him, and slammed the receiver on its cradle.

"You're a disgraceful human being," Herman Teppis said, and kept on down the walk without saying another word.

Teddy Pope wobbled away and came to rest against a joshua tree. He leaned on it as if it were his mother. Then he began to cry. I had never seen a man so drunk. Sobbing, hiccuping, he tried to chew on the bark of the tree. I backed away, I wanted nothing so much as to disappear. When I was out of sight, I heard Pope scream. "You bastard, Teppis," he cried out into the empty dawn, "you know what you can do, you fat bastard, Teppis," and I could picture his cheek on the joshua tree. I drove slowly home, making no attempt to find Eitel after all.

THE DEER PARK

A PLAY

Mailer's only play to date grew out of his novel of the same title, and they are juxtaposed here for convenience, in spite of the fact that the play was not completed until 1967. It premiered on January 31 of that year, at the Theatre de Lys in Greenwich Village, where it had a run of 127 performances. The role of Marion Faye was taken by Rip Torn, who was awarded an Obie for his performance. The juxtaposition is especially useful because the novel excerpt barely includes an appearance by Faye — indeed he is a comparatively minor character in the novel — and the play gives him full exposure. He is one of Mailer's most interesting creations, harking back to Sergeant Croft in his capacity for psychic fury, and looking forward to D. J. in his almost scholarly attitude toward violence.

Act I

CHANGE FORTY

(Lights again on Eitel's patio. Eitel alone. Marion enters.)

EITEL   Why today? I haven't seen you in weeks.

MARION   You were making the rounds with Elena last night. I wanted to see Collie's girl.

EITEL   Curious?

MARION   Collie is a collector. Anything he keeps for three years is interesting to me.

EITEL   I won't ask you to leave her alone — I don't think you could move in on her.

MARION   Oh, I could. I could whistle and she would hear it from a mile away. Have a little respect for human experience.

EITEL   The experience of a pimp?

MARION   Charley, I know more than the President of the United States, and so does a nigger whore.

EITEL   Did you ever consider why you're doing this bit?

MARION   Tell me, beloved.

EITEL   Panic. All-out, unadulterated, homosexual panic.

MARION   Homosexual panic. You're the one to talk.

EITEL   I am. For me the worst part of prison was the sex. I chose to stay away from that, from all of that. I didn't see why I should start at this late date.

MARION   It left you middle-aged, baby.

EITEL   You. When you were in prison you ran amok.

MARION   I used to worry I was queer. Now I know I'm only half-queer.

EITEL   Half-queer, and without dignity.

MARION   You have your dignity and you feel . . . amputated.

EITEL   I did. I did until last night.

MARION   Come on, Charley, for fifteen years you couldn't make a picture without being king of the hay. And now you flip over a chick who used to tickle Collie Munshin's little itches.

EITEL   I'd prefer it if you didn't talk about her that way.

MARION   What talent Elena must have. Man, you are laying the foundations of a monumental mistake.

EITEL   You have a mechanical mind. It comes from too much screwing.

MARION   Maybe I wouldn't hear all the jazz you hear, lover, but I can develop her talent. Do you have enough to develop her talent?

EITEL   Maybe I've been given something I never had before.

MARION   You're spoiled. Once you could make love to a woman and the sugar of your reputation would make her warm and open before you moved a finger. Now you're an ex-con who can't get a job and doesn't have any real dough left and you want to keep a girl who was born to travel in a big league. Hard times ahead, Charley, and maybe I'll just demonstrate it to you.

(Exits — Eitel left alone)

(Death music comes in faintly. It will be heard again near the very end of the play, "a wisp of fog, all too soon a vapor." Eitel speaks almost in an aside.)

EITEL   I knew the moment I met her I would make love to her. It was that simple, and I thought it was going to be that unimportant. A hot babe. Might I prove worthy. Instead, something flew in like a madman on wings. An angel. For the first time in my life I felt as if there were some sweet substance to be found in love, not power, but the sweetest thing I'd ever known — heaven. I was desperate in the morning that I might lose her. It was as if God had touched me with a finger, and I didn't want to lose that sensation ever again.

(Fade)

CHANGE THIRTY-EIGHT

(Spotlight on Elena as she picks up the receiver in her hotel room — she is sitting on Marion's lap)

ELENA   Oh, darling, is something the matter?

EITEL   Nothing. It's just that I want to hear your voice.

ELENA   But Charley, at this hour?

EITEL   Listen, you wouldn't want to come over here now, would you?

ELENA   Honey, I'm tired.

EITEL   Oh well, forget it.

ELENA   You're not angry?

EITEL   Of course not.

ELENA   I'm so sleepy.

EITEL   I shouldn't have called. You go back to bed.

ELENA   I missed you tonight, but it'll be nice tomorrow.

EITEL   Tomorrow. I missed you, too.

(Lights fade first on Eitel as he hangs up. Marion takes the phone from Elena, hangs up. She follows him as the light fades.)

CHANGE THIRTY-SEVEN

(Lights on Eitel's patio. Eitel is pacing about. He stops when Elena enters.)

EITEL   Were you alone last night?

ELENA   I want to talk to you about that. Your friend asked me for a date.

EITEL   What friend?

ELENA   Marion Faye.

EITEL   You had a casual date.

ELENA   A little more than that.

EITEL   You mean a lot more than that.

ELENA   Yes, sort of.

EITEL   I guess I haven't been your particular number.

ELENA   How you talk.

EITEL   Still, you had something left in reserve?

ELENA   You're enjoying this.

EITEL   Elena! Why did you do it?

ELENA   I was curious.

EITEL   I could kill you.

(The meaning is passionate, but not the tone of voice. Eitel is still in command of himself. It is almost a dry suggestion —Yes, I could kill you. By ants perhaps or bamboo slivers beneath the skin.)

ELENA   But I want to tell you . . .

EITEL   Yes, what?

ELENA   I felt like a statue with him.

EITEL   Only you didn't act like a statue with him.

ELENA   Well . . . I thought of you all the time.

EITEL

(His contained rage is violent, his control is superb)

A whore can always create a diversion.

ELENA   You don't care about me. You don't really care. Just your pride is hurt.

EITEL

(The first crack shows)

How in hell could you do it?

ELENA   You think I'm stupid.

EITEL   You are stupid.

ELENA   When a woman's unfaithful, she's more attractive to a man.

EITEL   Stop reciting your lessons.

ELENA   It's not lessons. I know . . .

EITEL   You don't know anything. Don't you understand? I believe I love you. I, Jesus by God, love you. I love your body.

ELENA   You love my body, but you don't love me.

EITEL

(In the soup now)

I love you.

ELENA   I worship you. It's better with you than it's been with anyone.

(Fade)

CHANGE THIRTY-FIVE

(Lights on Eitel's patio. Elena napping, alone. Marion enters, wakes her with a proprietory whack on her rump.)

ELENA   Charley isn't here.

MARION   It's you I want to talk to.

ELENA   Marion, we don't have a hell of a lot to say.

MARION   You're a liar. It was all the way for me last time, and so it was for you.

ELENA   I never felt so low in my life as I felt after you. You're the gutter. Now, get out. Charley is the one I want to make it with.

MARION   You make your nest with a middle-aged man.

ELENA   You think I stay with him because he's good to me?

MARION   He's your nurse.

ELENA   He's my lover . . . he's my lover. I never could use that word before. Not for other men, not for you. But he's my lover. When he touches me . . .

MARION   You are ready to conceive at the next touch.

ELENA   Crazy. You know about love.

MARION   I know about sex, cunt-head. I feel that for a hundred men and women.

ELENA   And a dog or two.

MARION   And a dog or two. And you got the dog in you. Let's give Eitel that. He turned you on. He turned you on and he'll leave you. You have no future with Eitel.

ELENA   He loves me.

MARION   He's a snob. Whatever he has, whatever he owns, sooner or later he comes to detest it because it's his and so it can't be good. Nothing less than a princess could bring him joy.

(Quick fade)

CHANGE THIRTY-THREE

(A note from the playwright to the reader: Love occurs as a word nine times in the scene which follows. We are obviously in the presence of a comic mood or a bad one, for our two pioneers are embarked on a reconnaissance up the headwaters of the ancient Amazonic mystery — our old buddy — Love. Change Thirty-three for your pleasure.)

ELENA   You can't love me. I don't come from nothing at all.

EITEL

(Now, witness: Eitel is trying to work. His script is open. He has been rewriting a passage whose quality has always eluded him. Closes script — brusque.)

You never tell me anything about where you come from.

ELENA

(Guarded)

What's to tell? My father was a small-time hood. There's nothing worse. And my mother . . .

(She pauses. Emotion has stolen up on her.)

EITEL   Tell me.

ELENA   A greedy little flirt. She ended up nothing but a fat ass.

(To justify her last remark, Elena goes on)

She was always complaining that life left her in a candy store.

EITEL   That's a cruel life.

(He cannot resist returning to his script)

ELENA   Cruel! It was a farce. She would take me when I was a kid and say, "If you don't do nothing else, get off this God-damn street." Then five minutes later, she'd slap me so hard I'd almost fall down.

(Turns and sees him immersed in work)

Charley, you want out, don't you?

EITEL   What gives you these ideas?

ELENA   I was just thinking you were sick of me.

(Pause)

EITEL

(He closes the script again)

Elena, what's really the matter?

ELENA   A man followed me today . . . He had the evil eye.

EITEL   I'm sure he wanted to cut off your head and stuff you in a gunny sack.

ELENA   That's what you'd like to do to me. Good Time Charley. You only like me when I'm in a good mood.

EITEL   Good Time Charley. When I say nice things then you love me.

ELENA   You're so superior. But you don't know what goes on in my head. I want to become a nun.

EITEL   Are you crazy? You'd make a honey of a nun.

ELENA   A nun is never alone. Nuns always have company.

EITEL   Do I ruin everything I touch?

(He is all but enjoying himself. It is like some scene in the sort of soap opera he would tune out — except that the actors have gone surrealistic. They are saying, "Up your buns" to the sponsor.)

Why are you so unhappy if I love you?

ELENA   I don't think you get to be in love unless you deserve it. Otherwise you get the evil eye.

EITEL   Do I deserve love?

ELENA   You bet you do.

EITEL   But you don't deserve it?

ELENA   Will you still love me if I cut my hair? No, you won't.

EITEL   If my love depends on a haircut, you might as well find out now.

ELENA   Yes, I ought to find out.

EITEL   You're a child.

ELENA   Kiss me, Charley.

(They embrace)

I'm going to leave you someday, Charley, I mean it.

EITEL   I don't know why.

ELENA   Charley, did you know I read all that crazy testimony of yours years ago in the newspapers?

EITEL   No, you never told me.

ELENA   Well, I read it. And so did a lot of kids I know. Actors, showgirls, just friends. Oh, Charley, it cracked us up. You were not afraid and everyone we knew was so crummy and scared. I felt horrible when you went to jail. I remember I even said to

Collie, "I'd like to meet Charles Francis Eitel, he's a real man and there aren't many left."

EITEL

(Moved by the generosity of her admission, by its pompous naïveté, by the intriguing fact that she had been talking once to Collie about him, and that offered explanations as well)

I don't offer you anything now, do I?

ELENA   I don't think about it, why do you?

EITEL   Because you're a woman. You have to think about it.

ELENA   If I worried because you didn't offer . . . anything, it would mean I didn't really love you.

(They embrace)

Oh Charley, you're a king. When you make love to me, everything is all right again.

(A shadow of the future intervenes again)

But I'm so afraid.

(Fade)

CHANGE THIRTEEN

(Another word from the playwright: the transition in this scene is abrupt. It is, in fact, vertiginous. All disasters to come are buried in this dialogue, and the mood of the staging does well to give a hint that the gears of the drama are shifting down, that the extraordinary freedom of swinging from one bout of love to another has now brought us to a time of recapitulation and consequence. For the scene will end in a curse.)

SERGIUS   Sometimes my imagination invades my memory and I think I am each of these people speaking to me, speaking to you.

EITEL

(It is very late at night. Eitel comes out on his patio and stretches his arms luxuriously. There is an unexpected

sound of amusement from Marion. Eitel has not known he was there.)

The next time you arrive in the hour before dawn, uninvited and conceivably unwanted, try ringing the bell.

MARION   You're Victorian, Charley. Nobody rings the bell.

EITEL   You wouldn't know how to get into a house if there was no lock to pick.

MARION   Charley, I couldn't sleep tonight, and all the while I knew you couldn't sleep either. Let me be your friend once more.

EITEL   I don't know that anything can be comfortable between us now.

MARION   Forgive me. Forgive this criminal for one crime against his dearest friend.

EITEL   I could forgive the devil tonight.

MARION   There's a question in my mind. It won't let me rest. Charley, you never gave one real lick for politics and yet you're the one who stood up to them.

EITEL   That's what keeps you awake?

MARION   Oh, I put down politics. But that was crazy testimony, Grand Duke. I hadn't liked you in years, suddenly I did.

EITEL   You mean it?

MARION   It gave me balls.

EITEL   There's your answer.

MARION   You were losing yours?

EITEL   I was going with two movie stars at the time. They were hot in the box office and I was hot for them. The thought of those royal ladies with their legs in the air had been my fuel for months. But when the moment came—Charles Francis Eitel was a dud. First one then the other. *Nada.* That happens to some men when they're young; it happened late to me. I began to think that impotence was no psychological aberration.

MARION   Don't go abstract, Charley.

EITEL   I'll give it to you straight. A young man can make

love to a woman even if he's afraid of her husband—he's got the legs to run away, he still has the sweet gambling money of sex. But a man who's older knows that he must stand and face the other man if it comes to that. So you don't queer the corners. You make love to that which you are willing to fight for, or what will you settle for.

MARION   You're getting hip, Charley.

EITEL   Thank you. What came to me was that I had used up my gambling money and I hadn't won what was right for me. I had a talent and wasn't using it. You know what talent is? It's love. If you get love for nothing, you must give it back. But I never did, not really. I half-gave it back with movies which told too little.

MARION   You're nineteenth century, Charley, that's your charm.

EITEL   I prefer the eighteenth century before all style began to die.

MARION   You don't understand the eighteenth century. The eighteenth century was queer, friend. I mean, a friend made it with a friend, and then they both took the lady of either. It gave everybody a little life.

EITEL   You see all ladies as the devil.

MARION   I never argue about particulars. Who cares what is which? I tell you two celestial beings equally divine are caught in some marriage of mutual hate which spawned us poor crawling cells and all we do is part of their dance. Dig sex, Charley, that's all there is. Follow it to the end, professor. Turn queer, bang dogs, sniff toes, it don't matter, beloved. If you got the guts to follow it you pass through the eye of death. There's murder waiting for anybody who tries to ball his sex into charge. Cheer up, Charley, I'm really a man, I want what every man wants. No matter what I do, no matter how far out I go, or how low down I sink in the etiquette of the bed, I live for one thing, to bring ecstasy to a goddess and rule the world.

EITEL   You have captured the essence of Napoleon— Dear God, why do you talk so much?

MARION   I'm saying you're too yellow, Charley, to go to bed with me.

EITEL   I'd never let a man touch me. I think that's the death of . . . change. It's what all the people who run the machine want us to be. Queer. Queer as cockroaches. Once you want it from behind, there's nothing to do but run. Thanks a lot, angel, but I don't want to swish.

MARION   When one man loves another it gives back heart to take it from behind. We have to take it from each other in order to dare the fury of a murderous cunt. I love you.

EITEL   No.

MARION   You want me, Charley.

EITEL   Never. I've got Elena.

MARION   I doubt it, grandfather.

EITEL   You don't seem to follow me very well. She is good for my body. She is the first woman who was ever good for me and God knows how many hundred I went through to discover that.

MARION   You've always seen yourself as an unattractive man.

EITEL   That's true, I did.

MARION   Your middle is thick. Do you see how slim I am.

EITEL   Don't strut.

MARION   I don't. I state the truth.

(Places one hand on his lower abdomen, one on his buttocks)

There is a life between my hands which you cannot understand. It is magical. It leads me. It charms me. It draws others to me. You don't possess that. That's why you feel unattractive.

EITEL   There is rhythm and there is warmth. You know more of one, I know more of the other.

MARION   Amateurs talk of warmth. Of decency. Of love. I talk of beauty. My mother was a beauty, *as you know*. I've known how to use sex since I was twelve. I bring good or I bring harm to anybody I cross.

EITEL   That kind of sex is a magnetism about as power-ful, mysterious and meaningless as an electric current. But there is something else. You will not know what I talk about until it happens.

MARION   Love.

EITEL   Love.

MARION   Take love. Take all the love in the world. That's Bullshit Mountain.

EITEL   Orthodox Jews used to talk of the Schechinah. The Shechinah is the bride of God and she lives in exile—she is sundered from God. God is in search of his wife—who is missing. The Jews used to believe that when a man and wife make love, and were in love, that the bride of God was present. The Shechinah was there. So the act gave an echo of the heavens whether the man was fat or thin.

MARION   I never knew you were Jewish.

EITEL   Half-Jewish—both sides.

MARION   You once told me your mother was a French maid.

EITEL   The only time I feel close to the truth is when I tell a lie.

MARION   Daddy-O, listen to the truth. Elena is not right for you. You will kill yourself if you persist in the idea you're the best she's ever known in bed.

EITEL   Watch out. Your nerve is vicious but queer.

MARION   You really think I'm queer. Let me tell you. I never had a thing with a man till I went to prison. Till then it was just a matter of style, a clue to the science of sex. But in jail they got to me. Those cats were ugly—you think it didn't take guts to go to bed, it took balls, baby, balls. Some of those spades would have slit my throat if I made the wrong move at the right time. Kid you not, Daddy-O, I found my true guts in prison because I got to give it to an ape of a Mafia murderer and he loved me like a whore. That turned the day, sahib, I've been flying ever since. Women never circled around me so much as they do now. Of course Elena digs me. Dig, you poor old dad, she reminds me of my Mafia ape who I turned into a little whore. Baby, I'll clue you: the night she spent with me gave her rhythms it'll take you years to digest.

EITEL   You murderous little faggot . . .

MARION   Charley, I don't want to find out who has the muscle . . .

EITEL   Get out before I throw you out.

MARION   Because when I let go, somebody is going to be dead.

(He exits)

CHANGE TWELVE

EITEL   I had an affair with Marion's mother—years ago. We almost married because of Marion. He was just a little boy really—spoiled, bright, sensitive, too pretty for his own good. But he was the first human being I wanted to make better than me. And then I broke with Dorothea. But it wasn't Dorothea I deserted—it was Marion.

ELENA   I'm glad he's gone. That son of a bitch would drink my blood.

(Blackout)

CHANGE ELEVEN

(The following dialogue is internal. It could be staged with Eitel's back to Marion or with Marion indeed invisible.)

EITEL   Why don't you believe I love her?

MARION   What do you want me to say? I'll say it.

EITEL   You see something in her yourself. She has such a need for dignity.

MARION   Dignity! Charley, you know like I know, she's just a girl who's been around.

EITEL   That's not true. That's not all of it.

MARION   Do yourself a favor. Ask Elena if she ever did it for money.

EITEL   What do you know?

(Says this so loudly that Elena starts—as if surprised that he is speaking aloud and to himself)

MARION   I don't know, Charley. I just got an instinct for this.

(Lights fade on Marion. If the production is using a bell or a gong, it could well start to sound now at the end of each Change.)

CHANGE TEN

EITEL

(Brusquely turning to her)

Elena, did you ever take money from a man?

ELENA   Never. Well, never exactly. Except for once.

EITEL   Except for once? How was that?

ELENA   That was a funny time.

EITEL   Yes? How did it happen?

ELENA   Well, there was a man, and he wanted to, and I refused, and then the man offered money, twenty dollars he offered.

EITEL   So what did you do?

ELENA   I took it. It made the man seem exciting to me.

EITEL   You're a dirty little girl.

ELENA

(Low and smoky)

Well, you know I am.

EITEL   Yes.

ELENA   I enjoyed spending the twenty dollars.

EITEL   It didn't bother you?

ELENA   No.

EITEL   It bothered you.

ELENA   I got hysterical the next night, but I'm loused up anyway. Charley, let's not talk about it.

EITEL   Who was the man?

ELENA   Never mind.

EITEL   It was Collie.

ELENA   Somebody you never met.

EITEL   Twenty lousy bucks!

(Blackout—bell)

CHANGE SEVEN

MUNSHIN   Cupcake!

ELENA   How are you?

MUNSHIN   I don't exist for you any more, do I?

ELENA   You don't.

MUNSHIN   Lulu said to give you a message.

EITEL   Yes, what is that?

MUNSHIN   She said she feels sorry for you.

ELENA   I'm going shopping for eats.

EITEL   Come back here.

ELENA   Good-bye. You two can tell each other your dirty little secrets while I'm gone.

(She exits)

MUNSHIN   I should have warned you.

EITEL   The subject is not acceptable.

MUNSHIN   All right, let's get to the real point. I've got you by the short hairs. I read your script.

EITEL   How'd you get a copy?

MUNSHIN   You're trying to interest every European producer around to make it. What do you think? Listen, baby, I didn't have to run around the block with an egg in my shoe to get a copy. In Europe they're using your script to wipe their asses on.

EITEL   What I like about you, Collie, is that you never find a real point too delicate to make.

MUNSHIN   Listen, lover, it would cost five million to get quality into this property and nobody in Europe would trust you with half a million even if they had it. I'm here to discuss big American plans with you. But I can't start cold. You know me. The one snag in my productorial equipment is that I need a finger up my giggie to get started. Anal compulsive female identifications.

EITEL   Hush, little baby, don't you cry.

MUNSHIN   Charley, I would like a warm-up.

EITEL   Did you read it, or did one of your secretaries read it?

MUNSHIN   Charley, I read it. Trust me.

(Eitel nods profoundly at the thought of trusting Munshin)

Alright, I'll tell *you* the story . . . and you'll get sick hearing me mangle it. You have a hero, a young ambitious man who has a large television program. A prize-money show for the sick. He draws every cripple in our crazy country. They all come to tell their troubles on the air. And whichever package of horror and misery gives the most charge to the studio audience goes away with a bag of loot.

EITEL

(Looking up)

You're doing fairly well, Collie.

MUNSHIN   The hero converts suffering into mass entertainment. He becomes rich from the agony of the mob. Yet there comes a switch.

(Eitel makes a face, but Munshin goes on)

A little door is opened in his heart, and through that door of goodness flows the waters of pain. His ears come attuned to the organ sounds of human misery. He starts to give real advice on the air — kill your mother, screw your brother — He's too honest — he destroys his program. In come the sponsors, enter the censors, make with the pressure. Your hero explodes, he attacks one of the Madison Avenue goons he's got in his hair, he almost kills him in his rage. Brouhaha!

EITEL   Alright, Collie, you've made your point. Let me tell it now.

MUNSHIN   Parenthetically, I can say this is a snitch from *Miss Lonelyhearts*.

EITEL   It was an influence.

MUNSHIN   Trust your unconscious, Charley. There's a religious revival underway in this country. So, thank God, your idea is practical.

EITEL   Shut up, let me take it from here . . .

(As he speaks, his voice takes on resonance)

My hero goes to prison for assault and battery. Just a little time in the black hole but it changes him forever. For when he comes out, he seeks the bottom of the world — and he wanders through slums and soup kitchens and cheap dives, trying to be good to the people he sees, but he has spent too many years teaching them dishonesty.

(How can Eitel bother to tell his story thus formally? It is probably in protest against the pain of Munshin's telling. But it is more. He is still in love with his script. He must handle the story himself, even fondle it with his language.)

Now dishonesty is the only passion they would defend to the death. So he comes to learn the taste of the cruellest defeat — that special private bitter taste which comes from losing when your motives are good. And so anger is born again and the murderous passion to win. He turns on these people of the bottom and is destroyed . . . But why am I telling this to you?

MUNSHIN   Extraordinary.

EITEL   You really like it?

MUNSHIN   It's an epic study about the hole in eternity our country is preparing for itself. It's a poem. This can make the greatest picture in the last ten years.

EITEL   Collie, why don't you say what you really think?

MUNSHIN

(Fingering his belly)

No audience would understand it.

EITEL   I think it would be amazing how much this would communicate to an audience.

MUNSHIN   You don't communicate with an audience, you manipulate an audience . . . Look, I love this story . . . and I know what it suffers from.

EITEL   What?

MUNSHIN   It's too hip. It's a whorehouse. Your hero is coining thousands of dollars a week and he decides to give it up. For what? To help people? To end suffering? He's a creep. They'll laugh your picture off the screen. You think an audience wants to pay money to be told this character is better than they are?

EITEL   What if guilt is real? What if all of us have intimations that we cannot cheat life forever, that if we live badly we go to some kind of hell where we must wait . . . agonies of time . . . before we are born again.

MUNSHIN   This is the idea behind all that crapalong, when your hero does his switch.

EITEL   Yes, all that crapalong.

MUNSHIN   Charley, it's not grounded. You can't turn a television host into a saint . . . Religion is institutional.

(Count one . . . two . . . three)

Eitel, the solution is simple . . . let your hero be a priest.

EITEL   A priest!

MUNSHIN   Let's say he's only studying to be a priest — Brother Frederick. Personality-wise he has everything, charm, intelligence, poise — just one thing wrong . . . the guy's too cocky. I see a terrific scene where the principal or the head monk or whatever they call him at a priest school, a kind of wise old priest-type Irishman, calls in Freddie and tells the kid that it's no go, he doesn't think Frederick ought to become a priest, not yet. Scholastically, the kid's got everything. He's tops in Church History, in Bingo Management, he's A-plus in Confessional Psychology, but he doesn't have the heart of a priest. "Get out in the world, son, and learn humility," the old prick says. Do you see it now?

EITEL   Colossal!

MUNSHIN   The kid takes the advice like a rejection. He feels unloved. So he quits the priest school, and goes into television, a bitter kid, he plays the angles. His career goes up like a sky rocket. Build him as a heel, and then give the switch. He discovers humility. I don't know what we can find, but I wouldn't even worry about it. Something with a Christ motif and the audience has to buy it. We can give Freddie a *Wanderjahr*, stumbling around bums with tears in his eyes, lots of business where he loves everybody. You get what I mean.

EITEL   Colossal!

MUNSHIN   At the end Freddie doesn't have to die in the gutter, he can go back to the seminary and be accepted. An upbeat ending. Something with angels' voices in the background. Only not full of shit . . .

(Blackout — bell)

ADVERTISEMENTS FOR MYSELF

Published by Putnam's in 1959 and available now in a Berkley Medallion paperback edition, Advertisements for Myself *is a showcase of Mailer's work to that date, including almost everything already published (apart from the novels) as well as a variety of unpublished and new material. Six things are excerpted here. "First Advertisement for Myself" was the introductory essay of the volume, and first appeared there. "The Man Who Studied Yoga" didn't get published until 1956, in the Ballantine Books volume* New Short Novels II, *but it was written in 1952 as a preface for a longer work. "Fourth Advertisement for Myself" analyzes the composition and publication of* The Deer Park, *and first appeared in the November, 1959* Esquire *as "The Mind of an Outlaw." "The White Negro," perhaps the single most influential essay published in the United States in the fifties, came out in* Dissent, *summer, 1957, and the following winter* Dissent *also carried the material here called "Reflections on Hip." An undated edition of the two pieces got wide circulation in the country in advance of* Advertisements, *published by the City Lights Bookstore, and the essay continues to be reprinted regularly. "The Time of Her Time" is one of the two examples Mailer puts into the book of his novel-in-progress, tentatively titled "Advertisements for Myself on the Way Out." It has yet to appear.*

First Advertisement
for Myself

Like many another vain, empty, and bullying body of our time, I have been running for President these last ten years in the privacy of my mind, and it occurs to me that I am less close now than when I began. Defeat has left my nature divided, my sense of timing is eccentric, and I contain within myself the bitter exhaustions of an old man, and the cocky arguments of a bright boy. So I am everything but my proper age of thirty-six, and anger has brought me to the edge of the brutal. In sitting down to write a sermon for this collection, I find arrogance in much of my mood. It cannot be helped. The sour truth is that I am imprisoned with a perception which will settle for nothing less than making a revolution in the consciousness of out time. Whether rightly or wrongly, it is then obvious that I would go so far as to think it is my present and future work which will have the deepest influence of any work being done by an American novelist in these years. I could be wrong, and if I am, then I'm the fool who will pay the bill, but I think we can all agree it would cheat this collection of its true interest to present myself as more modest than I am.

The reader who is curious to test my claims this instant is advised to turn to the pages of "The White Negro," and to the portion from my new novel which ends this book. He can then decide after a few hours of his finest attention if he is likely to agree. But those of you who want a sense of clear focus, like to know left from right, and up from not-so-up, may find it more restful to enter this book by degrees.

There was a time when Pirandello could tease a comedy of pain out of six characters in search of an author, but that is only a whiff of purgatory next to the yaws of conscience a writer learns to feel when he sets his mirrors face to face and begins to jiggle his Self for a style which will have some relation to *him*. I would suspect it is not possible, no more than one can remake oneself signature for signature, but I have to admit I am not suited for this sort of confrontation despite two novels put down in the first person and a bloody season of overexpressed personal opinions as a newspaper columnist. To write about myself is to send my style through a circus of variations and postures, a fireworks of virtuosity designed to achieve . . . I do not even know what. Leave it that I become an actor, a quick-change artist, as if I believe I can trap the Prince of Truth in the act of switching a style.

For instance, when the invitation came, not so very long ago, to make out my fifteenth anniversary report to the Harvard Class of 1943 I thought first of not answering, and then I considered an abbreviated and (by inference) disdainful few lines, and finally I thought, fuck it, let's have something in this class report which is a little less predictable than:

> *We are now living in the country, and find to our surprise that we like it, although the children miss the ambiguities and partial unshelterings of a New York public school education. Suburban life is great, qualifiedly great—I find to my perhaps overstructured horror that I rather enjoy the high-pressured rubber of bridge on the evening rocket back—wife and I are working you see with local PTA to initiate Master Point tournaments. These activities do not quite satisfy my programmatic ambitions of fifteen years ago, but still if I will be granted my enthusiasm for one cliché, the little realities of the graying poll and the burgeoning paunch are bracing realities.*

And so, foreseeing (correctly) that ninety per cent of my class's answers to the report would have that inimitable lead-kitten charm of Harvard prose, I wrote my reply with the desire to be destructive and therefore useful:

For the last few years I have continued to run in that overcrowded mob of unconscionable egotists who are all determined to become the next great American writer. But, given the brawl, the wasting of the will, and the sapping of one's creative rage by our most subtle and dear totalitarian time, politely called the time of conformity, I do not know that I would be so confident as to place the bet on myself any longer nor indeed on any of my competitive peers.

Yes, I wanted to say, my creative rage is being sapped, I have been dying a little these fifteen years, and so have a good many of you, no doubt—none of us are doing quite so much as we once thought we would. But then this has been a bad time, we've all been flattened by the dead air of this time, pinched and tamped into a flat-footed class.

Much of this meaning depended on the word "sapping" with its connotations of weakening, enervating, deadening—that word was the nerve of my paragraph. Unfortunately, the "sapping of one's creative rage" was printed in the Class Report as the "slapping of one's creative rage," an interesting montage of words, but my meaning was tricked. As the years go by and I become a little more possible for Ph.D. mills, graduate students will begin to write about the slapping of my creative rage, of Mailer's vision of his rage as his shield, when what I was trying to say was simply, "The shits are killing us."

Now, in the writing of our day, when no ache of evidence can ever be believed unless it is presented by a Doctor of Jargon, a remark like "the shits are killing us" is so declarative that fifty pages of closely reasoned argument should follow in support. I would rather not make the attempt. My mood has shifted, and I prefer to unload some bitter end of overchewed opinions which will show the churl in me, and beef up a drunken bruise or two, but at least will clear the air for us to go ahead.

So, mark you. Every American writer who takes himself to be both major and *macho* must sooner or later give a *faena* which borrows from the self-love of a Hemingway style. Any reader who will let me circle back later, in my own way, via the whorls and ellipses of my knotted mind, to earlier remarks, will be entertained en route by a series of comments I have to make (not altogether out of the rhythms of Hemingway) on the man, on my contemporaries and on myself. Brief remarks, absolutely not exhaustive, but still an historic moment.

For you see I have come finally to have a great sympathy for The Master's irrepressible tantrum that he is the champion writer of this time, and of all time, and that if anyone can pin Tolstoy, it is Ernest H. Somewhere in Hemingway is the hard mind of a shrewd small-town boy, the kind of boy who knows you have a real cigar only when you are the biggest man in town, because to be just one of the big men in town is tiring, much too tiring, you inspire hatred, and what is worse than hatred, a wave of cross-talk in everyone around you. You are considered important by some and put down by others, and every time you meet a new man, the battle is on: the latest guest has to decide if you are

        a) stronger than he, and
        b) smarter than he, and
        c) less queer.

And if you pass on all three counts, if you win the arm-wrestle, culture derby, and short-hair count, well then if he is a decent sort he usually feels you should run for president. But all this has happened in the first place because your reputation is uncertain, your name is locked in the elevators of publicity and public fashion, and so your meetings with every man and woman around become charged and overcharged.

There is a time when an ambitious type should fight his way through the jungle and up the mountain—it is the time when experience is rich and you can learn more than you ever will again, but if it goes on too long, you wither from the high tension, you drop away drunk or a burned-out brain, you learn what it is to lose seriously in love, or how it goes when your best friend and you are no longer speaking; it is inevitable that a bad fall comes to the strong-willed man who is not strong enough to reach his own peak.

Hemingway knows this: for years he has not written anything which would bother an eight-year-old or one's grandmother, and yet his reputation is firm—he knew in advance, with a fine sense of timing, that he would have to campaign for himself, that the best tactic to hide the lockjaw of his shrinking genius was to become the personality of our time. And here he succeeded. He went out of his way to shoot a lion or two, maybe more, he almost captured Paris with a few hundred men, he did a lot of things which very few of us could do, and I say this levelly, and not from hero worship, because for all his size, and all we've learned from him about the real importance of physical courage, he has still pretended to be ignorant of the notion that it is not enough to feel like a man, one must try to think like a man as well. Hemingway has always been afraid to think, afraid of losing even a little popularity, and so today he clowns away time worrying publicly about the feud between his good friends Leonard Lyons and Walter Winchell, and his words excite no thought in the best of my rebel generation. He's no longer any help to us, he's left us marooned in the nervous boredom of a world which finally he didn't try hard enough to change.

Still, I give credit to the man, he's known the value of his own work, and he fought to make his personality enrich his books. Let any of you decide for yourselves how silly would be *A Farewell to Arms* or better, *Death in the Afternoon*, if it had been written by a man who was five-four, had acne, wore glasses, spoke in a shrill voice, and was a physical coward. That, of course, is an impossible hypothesis — such a man would never have been able to feel the emotions of the man who wrote that early prose, but I exaggerate the point in order to stain the nuance with contrast. Suppose Hemingway had shown just a shadow of physical cowardice vis-à-vis his own heroes? That cowardice would have given a nasty joy to half the literary world, and ridicule would have followed to empty the breath of his books. Without a sense of the big man who wrote the prose, all the later work would be only skeletons of abstraction, the flesh gone. *The Old Man and the Sea* is, for my opinion, a bad piece of work if one knows nothing about the author. Only when one feels, more or less subliminally, the face of Ernest on the body of a Cuban fisherman does the fraud of the tale take on its surrealist truth.*

An author's personality can help or hurt the attention readers give to his books, and it is sometimes fatal to one's talent not to have a public with a clear public recognition of one's size. The way to save your work and reach more readers is to advertise yourself, steal your own favorite page out of Hemingway's unwritten *Notes From Papa on How the Working Novelist Can Get Ahead*. Truman Capote did it bravely when he began, and my hat is off to him. James Jones did it, and did it well. Kerouac would deserve ears and tail if he weren't an Eisenhower gypsy. I, in my turn, would love to be one of the colorful old-young men of American letters, but I have a changeable personality, a sullen disposition, and a calculating mind. I never have good nor accurate interviews since I always seem to get into disagreeable situations with reporters — they sense no matter how pleasant I try to be, that I do not like them — I think the psychological requirement for working on a newspaper is to be a congenital liar and a compulsive patriot. Perhaps I should hire a public relations man to grease my career, but I do not know if I can afford him (not with the size of the job he would have to do for me), and moreover I would be obliged sooner

---

*(As a capsule criticism: *The Old Man and the Sea* is cheered for being an affirmative work, a triumph of the human spirit, etc., etc. But a work of affirmation must contain its moment of despair — specifically, there must be a bad moment when the old man Santiago is tempted to cut the line and let the big fish go. Hemingway avoided the problem by never letting the old man be seriously tempted. Like a giant (but not like a man) Santiago just hung onto the fish — perhaps he knew that *Life* magazine was going to provide him with all the affirmation he needed.)

or later to spoil his work. While there would be hardly a limit to how lovable he could make me in the public eye it would be exhausting for me to pretend to be nicer than I really am. Indeed, it would be downright debilitating to the best of my creative energies. So I do not care to approach the public as a lover, nor could I succeed for that matter. I started as a generous but very spoiled boy, and I seem to have turned into a slightly punch-drunk and ugly club fighter who can fight clean and fight dirty, but likes to fight. I write this not solely out of self-pity (although self-pity is one of my vices) but also to tell the simple truth: I have not gotten nicer as I have grown older, and I suspect that what has been true for me may be true for a great many of you. I've burned away too much of my creative energy, and picked up too slowly on the hard, grim, and maybe manly knowledge that if I am to go on saying what my anger tells me it is true to say, I must get better at overriding the indifference which comes from the snobs, arbiters, managers and conforming maniacs who manipulate most of the world of letters and sense at the core of their unconscious that the ambition of a writer like myself is to become consecutively more disruptive, more dangerous, and more powerful. It will be fine if I can write so well and so strongly as to call my shot, but unfortunately I may have fatigued the earth of rich language beyond repair. I do not know, but it is possible. I've been in too many fights, I've been hit on the head by a hammer, and had my left eye gouged in a street fight—and of course I'm proud of this (I was a physical coward as a child), and so I'm proud I learned a bit about fighting even though the cost may end as waste. There may have been too many fights for me, too much sex, liquor, marijuana, benzedrine and seconal, much too much ridiculous and brain-blasting rage at the minuscule frustrations of a most loathsome literary world, necrophilic to the core—they murder their writers, and then decorate their graves.

If I put down words so final as these, it is not in any sense that I alone have been mistreated—on the contrary I have had more good luck and conceivably more bad luck than more writers (which tends to give one the hard satisfaction of knowing a little more of what the swindle is about). No, these ill-mannered bleedings and gripes are to record a clear record: I had the luck to have a large talent and to use some of it, and if I know how very much more I could have done if new luck had come my way, well—that is not my story, but everyone's story, every last one of us could have done more, a creation or two more than we have done, and while it is our own fault, it is not all our own fault, and so I still feel rage at the cowardice of our time which has ground down all of us into the mediocre compromises of what had been once our light-filled passion to stand erect and be original.

You can see then that this collection of pieces and parts, of advertisements, short stories, articles, short novels, fragments of novels, poems and part of a play comes to be written, after all, and for the most part, on just such a sweet theme — the shits are killing us, even as they kill themselves — each day a few more lies eat into the seed with which we are born, little institutional lies from the print of newspapers, the shock waves of television, and the sentimental cheats of the movie screen. Little lies, but they pipe us toward insanity as they starve our sense of the real. We have grown up in a world more in decay than the worst of the Roman Empire, a cowardly world chasing after a good time (of which last one can approve) but chasing it without the courage to pay the hard price of full consciousness, and so losing pleasure in pips and squeaks of anxiety. We want the heats of the orgy and not its murder, the warmth of pleasure without the grip of pain, and therefore the future threatens a nightmare, and we continue to waste ourselves. We've cut a corner, tried to cheat the heart of life, tried not to face our uneasy sense that pleasure comes best to those who are brave, and now we're a nation of drug addicts (caffeine, equanil, seconal and nicotine), of homosexuals, hoodlums, fart-faced Southern governors and a President so passive in his mild old panics that women would be annoyed if one called him feminine. The heat in our juvenile delinquency is matched only by the unadmitted acceleration of our race into cancer, that disease which is other than disease, that wave of the undifferentiated function, the orgy of the lost cells.

So, yes, it may be time to say that the Republic is in real peril, and we are the cowards who must defend courage, sex, consciousness, the beauty of the body, the search for love, and the capture of what may be, after all, an heroic destiny. But to say these words is to show how sad we are, for those of us who believe the most have spent our years writing of fear, impotence, stupidity, ugliness, self-love, and apathy, and yet it has been our act of faith, our attempt to see — to see and to see hard, to smell, even to touch, yes to capture that nerve of Being which may include all of us, that Reality whose existence may depend on the honest life of our work, the honor of ourselves which permits us to say no better than we have seen.

The Man Who Studied Yoga

The following Preface was printed at the
beginning of the Ballantine edition.

My last novel, The Deer Park, *was originally conceived as the*
first book of an enormous eight-part novel. The themes of this
huge — and finally unworkable — conception are buried in "The
Man Who Studied Yoga," a short novel written as a prologue to
all eight novels.

Long before I finished The Deer Park *I had given up the larger*
project, and that novel was finally written to stand by itself. But
as I believe will be noticed by those readers who have gone
through The Deer Park, *there is a play on certain names,*
particularly "O'Shaugnessy," in the Prologue printed here, as
well as a few parallel situations.

Since "Yoga" is not entirely functional (certain excursions and
diversions remaining as part of the abandoned architecture of the
large work) perhaps I should have rewritten it to be more neatly
complete in itself, but for reasons which are probably
sentimental, I prefer to see it printed in this, its original form.

1

I would introduce myself if it were not useless. The name I had
last night will not be the same as the name I have tonight. For the
moment, then, let me say that I am thinking of Sam Slovoda. Obligatorily, I study him, Sam Slovoda who is neither ordinary nor extraordinary, who is not young nor yet old, not tall nor short. He is
sleeping, and it is fit to describe him now, for like most humans he
prefers sleeping to not sleeping. He is a mild pleasant-looking man
who has just turned forty. If the crown of his head reveals a little
bald spot, he has nourished in compensation the vanity of a mustache. He has generally when he is awake an agreeable manner, at
least with strangers; he appears friendly, tolerant, and genial. The
fact is that like most of us, he is full of envy, full of spite, a gossip,
a man who is pleased to find others are as unhappy as he, and
yet — this is the worst to be said — he is a decent man. He is better
than most. He would prefer to see a more equitable world, he
scorns prejudice and privilege, he tries to hurt no one, he wishes to
be liked. I will go even further. He has one serious virtue — he is
not fond of himself, he wishes he were better. He would like to free
himself of envy, of the annoying necessity to talk about his friends,

he would like to love people more; specifically, he would like to love his wife more, and to love his two daughters without the tormenting if nonetheless irremediable vexation that they closet his life in the dusty web of domestic responsibilities and drudging for money.

How often he tells himself with contempt that he has the cruelty of a kind weak man.

May I state that I do not dislike Sam Slovoda; it is just that I am disappointed in him. He has tried too many things and never with a whole heart. He has wanted to be a serious novelist and now merely indulges the ambition; he wished to be of consequence in the world, and has ended, temporarily perhaps, as an overworked writer of continuity for comic magazines; when he was young he tried to be a bohemian and instead acquired a wife and family. Of his appetite for a variety of new experience I may say that it is matched only by his fear of new people and novel situations.

I will give an instance. Yesterday, Sam was walking along the street and a bum approached him for money. Sam did not see the man until too late; lost in some inconsequential thought, he looked up only in time to see a huge wretch of a fellow with a red twisted face and an outstretched hand. Sam is like so many; each time a derelict asks for a dime, he feels a coward if he pays the money, and is ashamed of himself if he doesn't. This once, Sam happened to think, I will not be bullied, and hurried past. But the bum was not to be lost so easily. "Have a heart, Jack," he called after in a whisky voice, "I need a drink bad." Sam stopped, Sam began to laugh. "Just so it isn't for coffee, here's a quarter," he said, and he laughed, and the bum laughed. "You're a man's man," the bum said. Sam went away pleased with himself, thinking about such things as the community which existed between all people. It was cheap of Sam. He should know better. He should know he was merely relieved the situation had turned out so well. Although he thinks he is sorry for bums, Sam really hates them. Who knows what violence they can offer?

At this time, there is a powerful interest in Sam's life, but many would ridicule it. He is in the process of being psycho-analyzed. Myself, I do not jeer. It has created the most unusual situation between Sam and me. I could go into details but they are perhaps premature. It would be better to watch Sam awaken.

His wife, Eleanor, has been up for an hour, and she has shut the window and neglected to turn off the radiator. The room is stifling. Sam groans in a stupor which is neither sleep nor refreshment, opens one eye, yawns, groans again, and lies twisted, strangled and trussed in pajamas which are too large for him. How painful it is for him to rise. Last night there was a party, and this morning, Sunday morning, he is awakening with a hangover. Invariably, he is depressed in the morning, and it is no different today. He finds himself in the flat and familiar dispirit of nearly all days.

It is snowing outside. Sam finally lurches to the window, and opens it for air. With the oxygen of a winter morning clearing his brain, he looks down six stories into the giant quadrangle of the Queens housing development in which he lives, staring morosely at the inch of slush which covers the monotonous artificial park that separates his apartment building from an identical structure not two hundred feet away. The walks are black where the snow has melted, and in the children's playground, all but deserted, one swing oscillates back and forth, pushed by an irritable little boy who plays by himself among the empty benches, swaddled in galoshes, muffler, and overcoat. The snow falls sluggishly, a wet snow which probably will turn to rain. The little boy in the playground gives one last disgusted shove to the swing and trudges away gloomily, his overshoes leaving a small animal track behind him. Back of Sam, in the four-room apartment he knows like a blind man, there is only the sound of Eleanor making breakfast.

Well, thinks Sam, depression in the morning is a stage of his analysis, Dr. Sergius has said.

This is the way Sam often phrases his thoughts. It is not altogether his fault. Most of the people he knows think that way and talk that way, and Sam is not the strongest of men. His language is doomed to the fashion of the moment. I have heard him remark mildly, almost apologetically, about his daughters: "My relation with them still suffers because I haven't worked through all my feminine identifications." The saddest thing is that the sentence has meaning to Sam even if it will not have meaning to you. A great many ruminations, discoveries, and memories contribute their connotation to Sam. It has the significance of a cherished line of poetry to him.

Although Eleanor is not being analyzed, she talks in a similar way. I have heard her remark in company, "Oh, you know Sam, he not only thinks I'm his mother, he blames me for being born." Like most women, Eleanor can be depended upon to employ the idiom of her husband.

What amuses me is that Sam is critical of the way others speak. At the party last night he was talking to a Hollywood writer, a young man with a great deal of energy and enthusiasm. The young man spoke something like this: "You see, boychick, I can spike any script with yaks, but the thing I can't do is heartbreak. My wife says she's gonna give me heartbreak. The trouble is I've had a real solid-type life. I mean I've had my ups and downs like all of humanity, but there's never been a shriek in my life. I don't know how to write shrieks."

On the trip home, Sam had said to Eleanor. "It was disgraceful. A writer should have some respect for language."

Eleanor answered with a burlesque of Sam's indignation. "Listen, I'm a real artist-type. Culture is for comic-strip writers."

Generally, I find Eleanor attractive. In the ten years they have been married she has grown plump, and her dark hair which once was long is now cropped in a mannish cut of the prevailing mode. But, this is quibbling. She still possesses her best quality, a healthy exuberance which glows in her dark eyes and beams in her smile. She has beautiful teeth. She seems aware of her body and pleased with it. Sam tells himself he would do well to realize how much he needs her. Since he has been in analysis he has come to discover that he remains with Eleanor for more essential reasons than mere responsibility. Even if there were no children, he would probably cleave to her.

Unhappily, it is more complicated than that. She is always—to use their phrase—competing with him. At those times when I do not like Eleanor, I am irritated by her lack of honesty. She is too sharp-tongued, and she does not often give Sam what he needs most, a steady flow of uncritical encouragement to counteract the harshness with which he views himself. Like so many who are articulate on the subject, Eleanor will tell you that she resents being a woman. As Sam is disappointed in life, so is Eleanor. She feels Sam has cheated her from a proper development of her potentialities and talent, even as Sam feels cheated. I call her dishonest because she is not so ready as Sam to put the blame on herself.

Sam, of course, can say all this himself. It is just that he experiences it in a somewhat different way. Like most men who have been married for ten years, Eleanor is not quite real to him. Last night at the party, there were perhaps half a dozen people whom he met for the first time, and he talked animatedly with them, sensing their reactions, feeling their responses, aware of the life in them, as they were aware of the life in him. Eleanor, however, exists in his nerves. She is a rather vague embodiment, he thinks of her as "she" most of the time, someone to conceal things from. Invariably, he feels uneasy with her. It is too bad. No matter how inevitable, I am always sorry when love melts into that pomade of affection, resentment, boredom and occasional compassion which is the best we may expect of a man and woman who have lived together a long time. So often, it is worse, so often no more than hatred.

They are eating breakfast now, and Eleanor is chatting about the party. She is pretending to be jealous about a young girl in a strapless evening gown, and indeed, she does not have to pretend altogether. Sam, with liquor inside him, had been leaning over the girl; obviously he had coveted her. Yet, this morning, when Eleanor begins to talk about her, Sam tries to be puzzled.

"Which girl was it now?" he asks a second time.

"Oh, you know, the hysteric," Eleanor says, "the one who was parading her bazooms in your face." Eleanor has ways of impressing certain notions upon Sam. "She's Charlie's new girl."

"I didn't know that," Sam mutters. "He didn't seem to be near her all evening."

Eleanor spreads marmalade over her toast and takes a bite with evident enjoyment. "Apparently, they're all involved. Charles was funny about it. He said he's come to the conclusion that the great affairs of history are between hysterical women and detached men."

"Charles hates women," Sam says smugly. "If you notice, almost everything he says about them is a discharge of aggression." Sam has the best of reasons for not liking Charles. It takes more than ordinary character for a middle-aged husband to approve of a friend who moves easily from woman to woman.

"At least Charles discharges his aggression," Eleanor remarks.

"He's almost a classic example of the Don Juan complex. You notice how masochistic his women are?"

"I know a man or two who's just as masochistic."

Sam sips his coffee. "What made you say the girl was an hysteric?"

Eleanor shrugs. "She's an actress. And I could see she was a tease."

"You can't jump to conclusions," Sam lectures. "I had the impression she was a compulsive. Don't forget you've got to distinguish between the outer defenses, and the more deeply rooted conflicts."

I must confess that this conversation bores me. As a sample it is representative of the way Sam and Eleanor talk to each other. In Sam's defense I can say nothing; he has always been too partial to jargon.

I am often struck by how eager we are to reveal all sorts of supposedly ugly secrets about ourselves. We can explain the hatred we feel for our parents, we are rather pleased with the perversions to which we are prone. We seem determinedly proud to be superior to ourselves. No motive is too terrible for our inspection. Let someone hint, however, that we have bad table manners and we fly into a rage. Sam will agree to anything you may say about him, provided it is sufficiently serious—he will be the first to agree he has fantasies of murdering his wife. But tell him that he is afraid of waiters, or imply to Eleanor that she is a nag, and they will be quite annoyed.

Sam has noticed this himself. There are times when he can hear the jargon in his voice, and it offends him. Yet, he seems powerless to change his habits.

An example: He is sitting in an armchair now, brooding upon his breakfast, while Eleanor does the dishes. The two daughters are not home; they have gone to visit their grandmother for the weekend. Sam had encouraged the visit. He had looked forward to the liberty Eleanor and himself would enjoy. For the past few weeks the children had seemed to make the most impossible demands upon his attention. Yet now they are gone and he misses them, he even misses their noise. Sam, however, cannot accept the notion that many people are dissatisfied with the present, and either dream of the past or anticipate the future. Sam must call this "ambivalence over possessions." Once he even felt obliged to ask his analyst, Dr. Sergius, if ambivalence over possessions did not characterize him almost perfectly, and Sergius whom I always picture with the flat precision of a coin's head—bald skull and horn-rimmed glasses—answered in his German accent, "But, my dear Mr. Slovoda, as I have told you, it would make me happiest if you did not include in your reading, these psychoanalytical text-works."

At such rebukes, Sam can only wince. It is so right, he tells himself, he is exactly the sort of ambitious fool who uses big words when small ones would do.

2

While Sam sits in the armchair, gray winter light is entering the windows, snow falls outside. He sits alone in a modern seat, staring at the gray, green and beige décor of their living room. Eleanor was a painter before they were married, and she has arranged this room. It is very pleasant, but like many husbands, Sam resents it, resents the reproductions of modern painters upon the wall, the slender coffee table, a free-form poised like a spider on wire legs, its feet set onto a straw rug. In the corner, most odious of all, is the playmate of his children, a hippopotamus of a television-radio-and-phonograph cabinet with the blind monstrous snout of the video tube.

Eleanor has set the Sunday paper near his hand. Soon, Sam intends to go to work. For a year, he has been giving a day once or twice a month to a bit of thought and a little writing on a novel he hopes to begin sometime. Last night, he told himself he would work today. But he has little enthusiasm now. He is tired, he is too depressed. Writing for the comic strips seems to exhaust his imagination.

Sam reads the paper as if he were peeling an enormous banana. Flap after flap of newsprint is stripped away and cast upon the straw rug until only the Magazine Section is left. Sam glances through it with restless irritability. A biography of a political figure runs its flatulent prose into the giant crossword puzzle at the back. An account of a picturesque corner of the city becomes lost in statistics and exhortations on juvenile delinquency, finally to emerge with photographs about the new style of living which desert architecture provides. Sam looks at a wall of windows in rotogravure with a yucca tree framing the pool.

There is an article about a workingman. His wife and his family are described, his apartment, his salary and his budget. Sam reads a description of what the worker has every evening for dinner, and how he spends each night of the week. The essay makes its point; the typical American workingman must watch his pennies, but he is nonetheless secure and serene. He would not exchange his life for another.

Sam is indignant. A year ago he had written a similar article in an attempt to earn some extra money. Subtly, or so he thought, he had suggested that the average workingman was raddled with insecurity. Naturally, the article had been rejected.

Sam throws the Magazine Section away. Moments of such anger torment him frequently. Despite himself, Sam is enraged at editorial dishonesty, at the smooth strifeless world which such articles present. How angry he is — how angry and how helpless. "It is the actions of men and not their sentiments which make history," he thinks to himself, and smiles wryly. In his living room he would go out to tilt the windmills of a vast, powerful, and hypocritical society; in his week of work he labors in an editorial cubicle to create spaceships, violent death, women with golden tresses and wanton breasts, men who act with their fists and speak with patriotic slogans.

I know what Sam feels. As he sits in the armchair, the Sunday papers are strewn around him, carrying their war news, their murders, their parleys, their entertainments, mummery of a real world which no one can grasp. It is terribly frustrating. One does not know where to begin.

Today, Sam considers himself half a fool for having been a radical. There is no longer much consolation in the thought that the majority of men who succeed in a corrupt and acquisitive society are themselves obligatorily corrupt, and one's failure is therefore the price of one's idealism. Sam cannot recapture the pleasurable bitterness which resides in the notion that one has suffered for one's principles. Sergius is too hard on him for that.

They have done a lot of work on the subject. Sergius feels that Sam's concern with world affairs has always been spurious. For example, they have uncovered in analysis that Sam wrote his article about the worker in such a way as to make certain it would be refused. Sam, after all, hates editors; to have such a piece accepted would mean he is no better than they, that he is a mediocrity. So long as he fails he is not obliged to measure himself. Sam, therefore, is being unrealistic. He rejects the world with his intellect, and this enables him not to face the more direct realities of his present life.

Sam will argue with Sergius but it is very difficult. He will say, "Perhaps you sneer at radicals because it is more comfortable to ignore such ideas. Once you became interested it might introduce certain unpleasant changes in your life."

"Why," says Sergius, "do you feel it so necessary to assume that I am a bourgeois interested only in my comfort?"

"How can I discuss these things," says Sam, "if you insist that my opinions are the expression of neurotic needs, and your opinions are merely dispassionate medical advice?"

"You are so anxious to defeat me in an argument," Sergius will reply. "Would you admit it is painful to relinquish the sense of importance which intellectual discussion provides you?"

I believe Sergius has his effect. Sam often has thoughts these days which would have been repellent to him years ago. For instance, at the moment, Sam is thinking it might be better to live the life of a worker, a simple life, to be completely absorbed with such necessities as food and money. Then one could believe that to be happy it was necessary only to have more money, more goods, less worries. It would be nice, Sam thinks wistfully, to believe that the source of one's happiness comes not from oneself, but from the fault of the boss, or the world, or bad luck.

Sam has these casual daydreams frequently. He likes to think about other lives he might have led, and he envies the most astonishing variety of occupations. It is easy enough to see why he should wish for the life of an executive with the power and sense of command it may offer, but virtually from the same impulse Sam will wish himself a bohemian living in an unheated loft, his life a catch-as-catch-can from day to day. Once, after reading an article, Sam even wished himself a priest. For about ten minutes it seemed beautiful to him to surrender his life to God. Such fancies are common, I know. It is just that I, far better than Sam, know how serious he really is, how fanciful, how elaborate, his imagination can be.

The phone is ringing. Sam can hear Eleanor shouting at him to answer. He picks up the receiver with a start. It is Marvin Rossman who is an old friend, and Marvin has an unusual request. They talk for several minutes, and Sam squirms a little in his seat. As he is about to hang up, he laughs. "Why, no, Marvin, it gives me a sense of adventure," he says.

Eleanor has come into the room toward the end of this conversation. "What is it all about?" she asks.

Sam is obviously a bit agitated. Whenever he attempts to be most casual, Eleanor can well suspect him. "It seems," he says slowly, "that Marvin has acquired a pornographic movie."

"From whom?" Eleanor asks.

"He said something about an old boy friend of Louise's."

Eleanor laughs. "I can't imagine Louise having an old boy friend with a dirty movie."

"Well, people are full of surprises," Sam says mildly.

"Look, here," says Eleanor suddenly. "Why did he call us?"

"It was about our projector."

"They want to use it?" Eleanor asks.

"That's right." Sam hesitates. "I invited them over."

"Did it ever occur to you I might want to spend my Sunday some other way?" Eleanor asks crossly.

"We're not doing anything," Sam mumbles. Like most men, he feels obliged to act quite nonchalantly about pornography. "I'll tell you, I am sort of curious about the film. I've never seen one, you know."

"Try anything once, is that it?"

"Something of the sort." Sam is trying to conceal his excitement. The truth is that in common with most of us, he is fascinated by pornography. It is a minor preoccupation, but more from lack of opportunity than anything else. Once or twice, Sam has bought the sets of nude photographs which are sold in marginal bookstores, and with guilty excitement has hidden them in the apartment.

"Oh, this is silly," Eleanor says. "You were going to work today."

"I'm just not in the mood."

"I'll have to feed them," Eleanor complains. "Do we have enough liquor?"

"We can get beer." Sam pauses. "Alan Sperber and his wife are coming too."

"Sam, you're a child."

"Look, Eleanor," says Sam, controlling his voice, "if it's too much trouble, I can take the projector over there."

"I ought to make you do that."

"Am I such an idiot that I must consult you before I invite friends to the house?"

Eleanor has the intuition that Sam, if he allowed himself, could well drown in pornography. She is quite annoyed at him, but she would never dream of allowing Sam to take the projector over to Marvin Rossman's where he could view the movie without her — that seems indefinably dangerous. Besides she would like to see it, too. The mother in Eleanor is certain it cannot hurt her.

"All right, Sam," she says, "but you are a child."

More exactly, an adolescent, Sam decides. Ever since Marvin phoned, Sam has felt the nervous glee of an adolescent locking himself in the bathroom. Anal fixation, Sam thinks automatically.

While Eleanor goes down to buy beer and cold cuts in a delicatessen, Sam gets out the projector and begins to clean it. He is far from methodical in this. He knows the machine is all right, he has shown movies of Eleanor and his daughters only a few weeks ago, but from the moment Eleanor left the apartment, Sam has been consumed by an anxiety that the projection bulb is burned out. Once he has examined it, he begins to fret about the motor. He wonders if it needs oiling, he blunders through a drawer of household tools looking for an oilcan. It is ridiculous. Sam knows that what he is trying to keep out of his mind are the reactions Sergius will have. Sergius will want to "work through" all of Sam's reasons for seeing the movie. Well, Sam tells himself, he knows in advance what will be discovered: detachment, not wanting to accept Eleanor as a sexual partner, evasion of responsibility, etc. etc. The devil with Sergius. Sam has never seen a dirty movie, and he certainly wants to.

He feels obliged to laugh at himself. He could not be more nervous, he knows, if he were about to make love to a woman he had never touched before. It is really disgraceful.

When Eleanor comes back, Sam hovers about her. He is uncomfortable with her silence. "I suppose they'll be here soon," Sam says.

"Probably."

Sam does not know if he is angry at Eleanor or apprehensive that she is angry at him. Much to his surprise he catches her by the waist and hears himself saying, "You know, maybe tonight when

they're gone . . . I mean, we do have the apartment to ourselves."
Eleanor moves neither toward him nor away from him. "Darling,
it's not because of the movie," Sam goes on, "I swear. Don't you
think maybe we could . . ."

"Maybe," says Eleanor.

3

The company has arrived, and it may be well to say a word or
two about them. Marvin Rossman who has brought the film is a
dentist, although it might be more accurate to describe him as a
frustrated doctor. Rossman is full of statistics and items of odd information about the malpractice of physicians, and he will tell
these things in his habitually gloomy voice, a voice so slow, so sad,
that it almost conceals the humor of his remarks. Or, perhaps, that
is what creates his humor. In his spare time, he is a sculptor, and if
Eleanor may be trusted, he is not without talent. I often picture
him working in the studio loft he has rented, his tall bony frame the
image of dejection. He will pat a piece of clay to the armature, he
will rub it sadly with his thumb, he will shrug, he does not believe
that anything of merit could come from him. When he talked to
Sam over the phone, he was pessimistic about the film they were to
see. "It can't be any good," he said in his melancholy voice. "I
know it'll be a disappointment." Like Sam, he has a mustache, but
Rossman's will droop at the corners.

Alan Sperber who has come with Rossman is the subject of
some curiosity for the Slovodas. He is not precisely womanish; in
fact, he is a large plump man, but his voice is too soft, his manners
too precise. He is genial, yet he is finicky; waspish, yet bland; he is
fond of telling long rather affected stories, he is always prepared
with a new one, but to general conversation he contributes little.
As a lawyer, he seems miscast. One cannot imagine him inspiring a
client to confidence. He is the sort of heavy florid man who seems
boyish at forty, and the bow ties and gray flannel suits he wears do
not make him appear more mature.

Roslyn Sperber, his wife, used to be a schoolteacher, and she is
a quiet nervous woman who talks a great deal when she is drunk.
She is normally quite pleasant, and has only one habit which is
annoying to any degree. It is a little flaw, but social life is not unlike marriage in that habit determines far more than vice or virtue.
This mannerism which has become so offensive to the friends of
the Sperbers is Roslyn's social pretension. Perhaps I should say
intellectual pretension. She entertains people as if she were con-
ducting a salon, and in her birdlike voice is forever forcing her

guests to accept still another intellectual canapé. "You must hear Sam's view of the world market," she will say, or "Has Louise told you her statistics on divorce?" It is quite pathetic for she is so eager to please. I have seen her eyes fill with tears at a sharp word from Alan.

Marvin Rossman's wife, Louise, is a touch grim and definite in her opinions. She is a social welfare worker, and will declare herself with force whenever conversation impinges on those matters where she is expert. She is quite opposed to psychoanalysis, and will say without quarter, "It's all very well for people in the upper-middle area" — she is referring to the upper middle class — "but, it takes more than a couch to solve the problems of . . ." and she will list narcotics, juvenile delinquency, psychosis, relief distribution, slum housing, and other descriptions of our period. She recites these categories with an odd anticipation. One would guess she was ordering a meal.

Sam is fond of Marvin but he cannot abide Louise. "You'd think she discovered poverty," he will complain to Eleanor.

The Slovodas do feel superior to the Rossmans and the Sperbers. If pressed, they could not offer the most convincing explanation why. I suppose what it comes down to is that Sam and Eleanor do not think of themselves as really belonging to a class, and they feel that the Sperbers and Rossmans are petit-bourgeois. I find it hard to explain their attitude. Their company feels as much discomfort and will apologize as often as the Slovodas for the money they have, and the money they hope to earn. They are all of them equally concerned with progressive education and the methods of raising children to be well adjusted — indeed, they are discussing that now — they consider themselves relatively free of sexual taboo, or put more properly, Sam and Eleanor are no less possessive than the others. The Slovodas' culture is not more profound; I should be hard put to say that Sam is more widely read, more seriously informed, than Marvin or Alan, or for that matter, Louise. Probably, it comes to this: Sam, in his heart, thinks himself a rebel, and there are few rebels who do not claim an original mind. Eleanor has been a bohemian and considers herself more sophisticated than her friends who merely went to college and got married. Louise Rossman could express it most soundly. "Artists, writers, and people of the creative layer have in their occupational ideology the belief that they are classless."

One thing I might remark about the company. They are all being the most unconscionable hypocrites. They have rushed across half the city of New York to see a pornographic film, and they are not at all interested in each other at the moment. The woman are giggling like tickled children at remarks which cannot possibly be so funny. Yet, they are all determined to talk for a respectable period of time. No less, it must be serious talk. Roslyn has said once, "I feel so funny at the thought of seeing such a movie," and the others have passed her statement by.

At the moment, Sam is talking about value. I might note that Sam loves conversation and thrives when he can expound an idea.

"What are our values today?" he asks. "It's really fantastic when you stop to think of it. Take any bright talented kid who's getting out of college now."

"My kid brother, for example," Marvin interposes morosely. He passes his bony hand over his sad mustache, and somehow the remark has become amusing, much as if Marvin had said, "Oh, yes, you have reminded me of the trials, the worries, and the cares which my fabulous younger brother heaps upon me."

"All right, take him," Sam says. "What does he want to be?"

"He doesn't want to be anything," says Marvin.

"That's my point," Sam says excitedly. "Rather than work at certain occupations, the best of these kids would rather do nothing at all."

"Alan has a cousin," Roslyn says, "who swears he'll wash dishes before he becomes a businessman."

"I wish that were true," Eleanor interrupts. "It seems to me everybody is conforming more and more these days."

They argue about this. Sam and Eleanor claim the country is suffering from hysteria; Alan Sperber disagrees and says it's merely a reflection of the headlines; Louise says no adequate criteria exist to measure hysteria; Marvin says he doesn't know anything at all.

"More solid liberal gains are being made in this period," says Alan, "than you would believe. Consider the Negro—"

"Is the Negro any less maladjusted?" Eleanor shouts with passion.

Sam maneuvers the conversation back to his thesis. "The values of the young today, and by the young, I mean the cream of the kids, the ones with ideas, are a reaction of indifference to the culture crisis. It really is despair. All they know is what they don't want to do."

"That is easier," Alan says genially.

"It's not altogether unhealthy," Sam says. "It's a corrective for smugness and the false value of the past, but it has created new false value." He thinks it worth emphasizing. "False value seems always to beget further false value."

"Define your terms," says Louise, the scientist.

"No, look," Sam says, "there's no revolt, there's no acceptance. Kids today don't want to get married, and—"

Eleanor interrupts. "Why should a girl rush to get married? She loses all chance for developing herself."

Sam shrugs. They are all talking at once. "Kids don't want to get married," he repeats, "and they don't want not to get married. They merely drift."

"It's a problem we'll all have to face with our own kids in ten years," Alan says, "although I think you make too much of it, Sam."

"My daughter," Marvin states. "She's embarrassed I'm a dentist. Even more embarrassed than I am." They laugh.

Sam tells a story about his youngest, Carol Ann. It seems he had a fight with her, and she went to her room. Sam followed, he called through the door.

"No answer," Sam says. "I called her again, 'Carol Ann.' I was a little worried you understand, because she seemed so upset, so I said to her, 'Carol-Ann, you know I love you.' What do you think she answered?"

"What?" asks Roslyn.

"She said, 'Daddie, why are you so anxious?'"

They all laugh again. There are murmurs about what a clever thing it was to say. In the silence which follows, Roslyn leans forward and says quickly in her high voice, "You must get Alan to tell you his wonderful story about the man who studied yogi."

"Yoga," Alan corrects. "It's too long to tell."

The company prevails on him.

"Well," says Alan, in his genial courtroom voice, "it concerns a friend of mine named Cassius O'Shaugnessy."

"You don't mean Jerry O'Shaugnessy, do you?" asks Sam.

Alan does not know Jerry O'Shaugnessy. "No, no, this is Cassius O'Shaugnessy," he says. "He's really quite an extraordinary fellow." Alan sits plumply in his chair, fingering his bow tie. They are all used to his stories, which are told in a formal style and exhibit the attempt to recapture a certain note of urbanity, wit, and *élan* which Alan has probably copied from someone else. Sam and Eleanor respect his ability to tell these stories, but they resent the fact that he talks *at* them.

"You'd think we were a jury of his inferiors," Eleanor has said. "I hate being talked down to." What she resents is Alan's quiet implication that his antecedents, his social position, in total his life outside the room is superior to the life within. Eleanor now takes the promise from Alan's story by remarking, "Yes, and let's see the movie when Alan has finished."

"Sssh," Roslyn says.

"Cassius was at college a good while before me," says Alan, "but I knew him while I was an undergraduate. He would drop in and visit from time to time. An absolutely extraordinary fellow. The most amazing career. You see, he's done about everything."

"I love the way Alan tells it," Roslyn pipes nervously.

"Cassius was in France with Dos Passos and Cummings, he was even arrested with e.e. After the war, he was one of the founders of the Dadaist school, and for a while I understand he was Fitzgerald's guide to the gold of the Côte D'Azur. He knew everybody, he did everything. Do you realize that before the twenties had ended, Cassius had managed his father's business and then entered a monastery? It is said he influenced T. S. Eliot."

"Today, we'd call Cassius a psychopath," Marvin observes.

"Cassius called himself a great dilettante," Alan answers, "although perhaps the nineteenth-century Russian conception of the great sinner would be more appropriate. What do you say if I tell you this was only the beginning of his career?"

"What's the point?" Louise asks.

"Not yet," says Alan, holding up a hand. His manner seems to say that if his audience cannot appreciate the story, he does not feel obliged to continue. "Cassius studied Marx in the monastery. He broke his vows, quit the Church, and became a Communist. All through the thirties he was a figure in the Party, going to Moscow, involved in all the Party struggles. He left only during the Moscow trials."

Alan's manner while he relates such stories is somewhat effeminate. He talks with little caresses of his hand, he mentions names and places with a lingering ease as if to suggest that his audience and he are aware, above all, of nuance. The story as Alan tells it is drawn overlong. Suffice it that the man about whom he is talking, Cassius O'Shaughnessy, becomes a Trotskyist, becomes an anarchist, is a pacifist during the second World War, and suffers it from a prison cell.

"I may say," Alan goes on, "that I worked for his defense, and was successful in getting him acquitted. Imagine my dolor when I learned that he had turned his back on his anarchist friends and was living with gangsters."

"This is weird," Eleanor says.

"Weird, it is," Alan agrees. "Cassius got into some scrape, and disappeared. What could you do with him? I learned only recently that he had gone to India and was studying yoga. In fact, I learned it from Cassius himself. I asked him of his experiences at Brahnaputh-thar, and he told me the following story."

Now Alan's voice alters, he assumes the part of Cassius and

speaks in a tone weary of experience, wise and sad in its knowledge. " 'I was sitting on my haunches contemplating my navel,' Cassius said to me, 'when of a sudden I discovered my navel under a different aspect. It seemed to me that if I were to give a counterclockwise twist, my navel would unscrew.' "

Alan looks up, he surveys his audience which is now rapt and uneasy, not certain as yet whether a joke is to come. Alan's thumb and forefinger pluck at the middle of his ample belly, his feet are crossed upon the carpet in symbolic suggestion of Cassius upon his haunches.

" 'Taking a deep breath, I turned, and the abysses of Vishtarni loomed beneath. My navel had begun to unscrew. I knew I was about to accept the reward of three years of contemplation. So,' said Cassius, 'I turned again, and my navel unscrewed a little more. I turned and I turned,' " Alan's fingers now revolving upon his belly, " 'and after a period I knew that with one more turn my navel would unscrew itself forever. At the edge of revelation, I took one sweet breath, and turned my navel free.' "

Alan looks up at his audience

" 'Damn,' said Cassius, 'if my ass didn't fall off.' "

4

The story has left the audience in an exasperated mood. It has been a most untypical story for Alan to tell, a little out of place, not offensive exactly, but irritating and inconsequential. Sam is the only one to laugh with more than bewildered courtesy, and his mirth seems excessive to everyone but Alan, and of course, Roslyn, who feels as if she has been the producer. I suppose what it reduces to, is a lack of taste. Perhaps that is why Alan is not the lawyer one would expect. He does not have that appreciation — as necessary in his trade as for an actor — of what is desired at any moment, of that which will encourage as opposed to that which does not encourage a stimulating but smooth progression of logic and sentiment. Only a fool would tell so long a story when everyone is awaiting the movie.

Now, they are preparing. The men shift armchairs to correspond with the couch, the projector is set up, the screen is unfolded. Sam attempts to talk while he is threading the film, but no one listens. They seem to realize suddenly that a frightful demand has been placed upon them. One does not study pornography in a living room with a beer glass in one's hand, and friends at the elbow. It is the most unsatisfactory of compromises; one can draw neither the benefits of solitary contemplation nor of social exchange. There is, at bottom, the same exasperated fright which one experiences in turning the shower tap and receiving cold water when the flesh has been prepared for heat. Perhaps that is why they are laughing so much now that the movie is begun.

A title, *The Evil Act*, twitches on the screen, shot with scars, holes, and the dust lines of age. A man and woman are sitting on a couch, they are having coffee. They chat. What they say is conveyed by printed words upon an ornately flowered card, interjected between glimpses of their casual gestures, a cup to the mouth, a smile, a cigarette being lit. The man's name, it seems, is Frankie Idell; he is talking to his wife, Magnolia. Frankie is dark, he is sinister, he confides in Magnolia, his dark counterpart, with a grimace of his brows, black from make-up pencil.

This is what the titles read:

> FRANKIE: She will be here soon.
>
> MAGNOLIA: This time the little vixen will not escape.
>
> FRANKIE: No, my dear, this time we are prepared.
>
> *(He looks at his watch.)*
> FRANKIE: Listen, she knocks!

There is a shot of tall blond woman knocking on the door. She is probably over thirty, but by her short dress and ribboned hat it is suggested that she is a girl of fifteen.

> FRANKIE: Come in, Eleanor.

As may be expected, the audience laughs hysterically at this. It is so wonderful a coincidence. "How I remember Frankie," says Eleanor Slovoda, and Roslyn Sperber is the only one not amused. In the midst of the others' laughter, she says in a worried tone, obviously adrift upon her own concerns, "Do you think we'll have to stop the film in the middle to let the bulb cool off?" The others hoot, they giggle, they are weak from the combination of their own remarks and the action of the plot.

Frankie and Magnolia have sat down on either side of the heroine, Eleanor. A moment passes. Suddenly, stiffly, they attack. Magnolia from her side kisses Eleanor, and Frankie commits an indecent caress.

> ELEANOR: How dare you? Stop!
>
> MAGNOLIA: Scream, my little one. It will do you no good.
> The walls are soundproofed.

FRANKIE: We've fixed a way to make you come across.

ELEANOR: This is hideous. I am hitherto undefiled. Do not touch me!

The captions fade away. A new title takes their place. It says, *But There Is No Escape From The Determined Pair*. On the fade-in, we discover Eleanor in the most distressing situation. Her hands are tied to loops running from the ceiling, and she can only writhe in helpless perturbation before the deliberate and progressive advances of Frankie and Magnolia. Slowly they humiliate her, with relish they probe her.

The audience laughs no longer. A hush has come upon them. Eyes unblinking they devour the images upon Sam Slovoda's screen.

Eleanor is without clothing. As the last piece is pulled away, Frankie and Magnolia circle about her in a grotesque of panto-mime, a leering of lips, limbs in a distortion of desire. Eleanor faints. Adroitly, Magnolia cuts her bonds. We see Frankie carrying her inert body.

Now, Eleanor is trussed to a bed, and the husband and wife are tormenting her with feathers. Bodies curl upon the bed in postures so complicated, in combinations so advanced, that the audience leans forward, Sperbers, Rossmans, and Slovodas, as if tempted to embrace the moving images. The hands trace abstract circles upon the screen, passes and recoveries upon a white background so illumined that hollows and swells, limb to belly and mouth to undescribables, tip of a nipple, orb of a navel, swim in giant mag-nification, flow and slide in a lurching yawing fall, blotting out the camera eye.

A little murmur, all unconscious, passes from their lips. The au-dience sways, each now finally lost in himself, communing hungrily with shadows, violated or violating, fantasy triumphant.

At picture's end, Eleanor the virgin whore is released from the bed. She kisses Frankie, she kisses Magnolia. "You dears," she says, "let's do it again." The projector lamp burns empty light, the machine keeps turning, the tag of film goes *slap-tap, slap-tap, slap-tap, slap-tap, slap-tap, slap-tap*.

"Sam, turn it off," says Eleanor.

But when the room lights are on, they cannot look at one anoth-er. "Can we see it again?" someone mutters. So again, Eleanor knocks on the door, is tied, defiled, ravished, and made rapturous. They watch it soberly now, the room hot with the heat of their bodies, the darkness a balm for orgiastic vision. To the Deer Park,

Sam is thinking, to the Deer Park of Louis XV were brought the most beautiful maidens of France, and there they stayed, dressed in fabulous silks, perfumed and wigged, the mole drawn upon their cheek, ladies of pleasure awaiting the pleasure of the king. So Louis had stripped an empire, bankrupt a treasury, prepared a deluge, while in his garden on summer evenings the maidens performed their pageants, eighteenth-century tableau of the evil act, beauteous instruments of one man's desire, lewd translation of a king's power. That century men sought wealth so they might use its fruits; this epoch men lusted for power in order to amass more power, a compounding of power into pyramids of abstraction whose yield are cannon and wire enclosure, pillars of statistics to the men who are the kings of this century and do no more in power's leisure time than go to church, claim to love their wives, and eat vegetables.

Is it possible, Sam wonders, that each of them here, two Rossmans, two Sperbers, two Slovodas, will cast off their clothes when the movie is done and perform the orgy which tickles at the heart of their desire? They will not, he knows, they will make jokes when the projector is put away, they will gorge the plate of delicatessen Eleanor provides, and swallow more beer, he among them. He will be the first to make jokes.

Sam is right. The movie has made him extraordinarily alive to the limits of them all. While they sit with red faces, eyes bugged glutting sandwiches of ham, salami, and tongue, he begins the teasing.

"Roslyn," he calls out, "is the bulb cooled off yet?"

She cannot answer him. She chokes on beer, her face glazes, she is helpless with self-protecting laughter.

"Why are you so anxious, Daddie?" Eleanor says quickly.

They begin to discuss the film. As intelligent people they must dominate it. Someone wonders about the actors in the piece, and discussion begins afresh. "I fail to see," says Louise, "why they should be hard to classify. Pornography is a job to the criminal and prostitute element."

"No, you won't find an ordinary prostitute doing this," Sam insists. "It requires a particular kind of personality."

"They have to be exhibitionists," says Eleanor.

"It's all economic," Louise maintains.

"I wonder what those girls felt?" Roslyn asks. "I feel sorry for them."

"I'd like to be the cameraman," says Alan.

"I'd like to be Frankie," says Marvin sadly.

There is a limit to how long such a conversation may continue.

The jokes lapse into silence. They are all busy eating. When they begin to talk again, it is of other things. Each dollop of food sops the agitation which the movie has spilled. They gossip about the party the night before, they discuss which single men were interested in which women, who got drunk, who got sick, who said the wrong thing, who went home with someone else's date. When this is exhausted, one of them mentions a play the others have not seen. Soon they are talking about books, a concert, a one-man show by an artist who is a friend. Dependably, conversation will voyage its orbit. While the men talk of politics, the women are discussing fashions, progressive schools, and recipes they have attempted. Sam is uncomfortable with the division; he knows Eleanor will resent it, he knows she will complain later of the insularity of men and the basic contempt they feel for women's intelligence.

"But you collaborated," Sam will argue. "No one forced you to be with the women."

"Was I to leave them alone?" Eleanor will answer.

"Well, why do the women always have to go off by themselves?"

"Because the men aren't interested in what we have to say."

Sam sighs. He has been talking with interest, but really he is bored. These are nice pleasant people, he thinks, but they are ordinary people, exactly the sort he has spent so many years with, making little jokes, little gossip, living little everyday events, a close circle where everyone mothers the other by his presence. The womb of middle-class life, Sam decides heavily. He is in a bad mood indeed. Everything is laden with dissatisfaction.

Alan has joined the women. He delights in preparing odd dishes when friends visit the Sperbers, and he is describing to Eleanor how he makes blueberry pancakes. Marvin draws closer to Sam.

"I wanted to tell you," he says, "Alan's story reminded me. I saw Jerry O'Shaugnessy the other day."

"Where was he?"

Marvin is hesitant. "It was a shock, Sam. He's on the Bowery. I guess he's become a wino."

"He always drank a lot," says Sam.

"Yeah." Marvin cracks his bony knuckles. "What a stinking time this is, Sam."

"It's probably like the years after 1905 in Russia," Sam says.

"No revolutionary party will come out of this."

"No," Sam says, "nothing will come."

He is thinking of Jerry O'Shaugnessy. What did he look like? what did he say? Sam asks Marvin, and clucks his tongue at the dispiriting answer. It is a shock to him. He draws closer to Marvin, he feels a bond. They have, after all, been through some years together. In the thirties they have been in the Communist Party, they have quit together, they are both weary of politics today, still radicals out of habit. but without enthusiasm and without a cause. "Jerry was a hero to me," Sam says.

"To all of us," says Marvin.

The fabulous Jerry O'Shaugnessy, thinks Sam. In the old days, in the Party, they had made a legend of him. All of them with their middle-class origins and their desire to know a worker-hero.

I may say that I was never as fond of Jerry O'Shaugnessy as was Sam. I thought him a showman and too pleased with himself. Sam, however, with his timidity, his desire to travel, to have adventure and know many women, was obliged to adore O'Shaugnessy. At least he was enraptured with his career.

Poor Jerry who ends as a bum. He has been everything else. He has been a trapper in Alaska, a chauffeur for gangsters, an officer in the Foreign Legion. a labor organizer. His nose was broken, there were scars on his chin. When he would talk about his years at sea or his experiences in Spain, the stenographers and garment workers, the radio writers and unemployed actors would listen to his speeches as if he were the prophet of new romance, and their blood would be charged with the magic of revolutionary vision. A man with tremendous charm. In those days it had been easy to confuse his love for himself with his love for all underprivileged workingmen.

"I thought he was still in the Party," Sam says.

"No," says Marvin, "I remember they kicked him out a couple of years ago. He was supposed to have piddled some funds, that's what they say."

"I wish he'd taken the treasury," Sam remarks bitterly. "The Party used him for years."

Marvin shrugs. "They used each other." His mustache droops. "Let me tell you about Sonderson. You know he's still in the Party. The most progressive dentist in New York." They laugh.

While Marvin tells the story, Sam is thinking of other things. Since he has quit Party work, he has studied a great deal. He can tell you about prison camps and the secret police, political murders, the Moscow trials, the exploitation of Soviet labor, the privileges of the bureaucracy; it is all painful to him. He is straddled between the loss of a country he has never seen, and his repudiation of the country in which he lives. "Doesn't the Party seem a horror now?" he bursts out.

Marvin nods. They are trying to comprehend the distance between Party members they have known, people by turn pathetic, likable, or annoying—people not unlike themselves—and in contrast the immensity of historic logic which deploys along statistics of the dead.

"It's all schizoid," Sam says. "Modern life is schizoid."

Marvin agrees. They have agreed on this many times, bored with the petulance of their small voices, yet needing the comfort of such complaints. Marvin asks Sam if he has given up his novel, and Sam says, "Temporarily." He cannot find a form, he explains. He does not want to write a realistic novel, because reality is no longer realistic. "I don't know what it is," says Sam. "To tell you the truth, I think I'm kidding myself. I'll never finish this book. I just like to entertain the idea I'll do something good some day." They sit there in friendly depression. Conversation has cooled. Alan and the women are no longer talking.

"Marvin," asks Louise, "what time is it?"

They are ready to go. Sam must say directly what he had hoped to approach by suggestion. "I was wondering," he whispers to Rossman, "would you mind if I held onto the film for a day to two?"

Marvin looks at him. "Oh, why of course, Sam," he says in his morose voice. "I know how it is." He pats Sam on the shoulder as if, symbolically, to convey the exchange of ownership. They are fellow conspirators.

"If you ever want to borrow the projector," Sam suggests.

"Nah," says Marvin, "I don't know that it would make much difference."

5

It has been, when all is said, a most annoying day. As Sam and Eleanor tidy the apartment, emptying ash trays and washing the few dishes, they are fond neither of themselves nor each other. "What a waste today has been," Eleanor remarks, and Sam can only agree. He has done no writing, he has not been outdoors, and still it is late in the evening, and he has talked too much, eaten too much, is nervous from the movie they have seen. He knows that he will watch it again with Eleanor before they go to sleep; she has given her assent to that. But as is so often the case with Sam these days, he cannot await their embrace with any sure anticipation. Eleanor may be in the mood or Eleanor may not; there is no way he can control the issue. It is depressing; Sam knows that he circles about Eleanor at such times with the guilty maneuvers of a sad hound. Resent her as he must, be furious with himself as he will, there is not very much he can do about it. Often, after they have made love, they will lie beside each other in silence, each offended, each certain the other is to blame. At such times, memory tickles them with a cruel feather. Not always has it been like this. When they were first married, and indeed for the six months they lived together before marriage, everything was quite different. Their affair was very exciting to them; each told the other with some hyperbole but no real mistruth that no one in the past had ever been comparable as lover.

I suppose I am a romantic. I always feel that this is the best time in people's lives. There is, after all, so little we accomplish, and that short period when we are beloved and triumph as lovers is sweet with power. Rarely are we concerned then with our lack of importance; we are too important. In Sam's case, disillusion means even more. Like so many young men, he entertained the secret conceit that he was an extraordinary lover. One cannot really believe this without supporting at the same time the equally secret conviction that one is fundamentally inept. It is—no matter what Sergius would say—a more dramatic and therefore more attractive view of oneself than the sober notion which Sam now accepts with grudging wisdom, that the man as lover is dependent upon the bounty of the woman. As I say, he accepts the notion, it is one of the lineaments of maturity, but there is a part of him which, no matter how harried by analysis, cannot relinquish the antagonism he feels that Eleanor has respected his private talent so poorly, and has not allowed him to confer its benefits upon more women. I mock Sam, but he would mock himself on this. It hardly matters; mockery cannot accomplish everything, and Sam seethes with that most private and tender pain: even worse than being unattractive to the world is to be unattractive to one's mate; or, what is the same and describes Sam's case more accurately, never to know in advance when he shall be undesirable to Eleanor.

I make perhaps too much of the subject, but that is only because it is so important to Sam. Relations between Eleanor and him are not really that bad—I know other couples who have much less or nothing at all. But comparisons are poor comfort to Sam; his standards are so high. So are Eleanor's. I am convinced the most unfortunate people are those who would make an art of love. It sours other effort. Of all artists, they are certainly the most wretched.

Shall I furnish a model? Sam and Eleanor are on the couch and the projector, adjusted to its slowest speed, is retracing the elaborate pantomime of the three principals. If one could allow these shadows a life . . . but indeed such life has been given them. Sam and Eleanor are no more than an itch, a smart, a threshold of satisfaction; the important share of themselves has steeped itself in Frankie-, Magnolia-, and Eleanor-of-the-film. Indeed the variations are beyond telling. It is the most outrageous orgy performed by five ghosts.

Self-critical Sam! He makes love in front of a movie, and one cannot say that it is unsatisfactory any more than one can say it is pleasant. It is dirty, downright porno dirty, it is a lewd slop-brush slapped through the middle of domestic exasperations and break-fast eggs. It is so dirty that only half of Sam — he is quite divisible into fractions — can be exercised at all. The part that is his brain worries along like a cuckolded burgher. He is taking the pulse of his anxiety. Will he last long enough to satisfy Eleanor? Will the children come back tonight? He cannot help it. In the midst of the circus, he is suddenly convinced the children will walk through the door. "Why are you so anxious, Daddie?"

So it goes. Sam the lover is conscious of exertion. One moment he is Frankie Idell, destroyer of virgins — take that! you whore! — the next, body moving, hands caressing, he is no more than some lines from a psychoanalytical text. He is thinking about the sensitivity of his scrotum. He has read that this is a portent of femininity in a male. How strong is his latent homosexuality worries Sam, thrusting stiffly, warm sweat running cold. Does he identify with Eleanor-of-the-film?

Technically, the climax is satisfactory. They lie together in the dark, the film ended, the projector humming its lonely revolutions in the quiet room. Sam gets up to turn it off; he comes back and kisses Eleanor upon the mouth. Apparently, she has enjoyed herself more than he; she is tender and fondles the tip of his nose.

"You know, Sam," she says from her space beside him, "I think I saw this picture before."

"When?"

"Oh, you know when. That time."

Sam thinks dully that women are always most loving when they can reminisce about infidelity.

"That time!" he repeats.

"I think so."

Racing forward from memory like the approaching star which begins as a point on the mind and swells to explode the eyeball with its odious image, Sam remembers, and is weak in the dark. It is ten years, eleven perhaps, before they were married, yet after they were lovers. Eleanor has told him, but she has always been vague about details. There had been two men it seemed, and another girl, and all had been drunk. They had seen movie after movie. With reluctant fascination, Sam can conceive the rest. How it had pained him, how excited him. It is years now since he has remembered, but he remembers. In the darkness he wonders at the unreasonableness of jealous pain. That night was impossible to imagine any longer—therefore it is more real; Eleanor his plump wife who presses a pigeon's shape against her housecoat, forgotten heroine of black orgies. It had been meaningless, Eleanor claimed; it was Sam she loved, and the other had been no more than a fancy of which she wished to rid herself. Would it be the same today, thinks Sam, or had Eleanor been loved by Frankie, by Frankie of the other movies, by Frankie of the two men she never saw again on that night so long ago?

The pleasure I get from this pain, Sam thinks furiously.

It is not altogether perverse. If Eleanor causes him pain, it means after all that she is alive for him. I have often observed that the reality of a person depends upon his ability to hurt us; Eleanor as the vague accusing embodiment of the wife is different, altogether different, from Eleanor who lies warmly in Sam's bed, an attractive Eleanor who may wound his flesh. Thus, brother to the pleasure of pain, is the sweeter pleasure which follows pain. Sam, tired, lies in Eleanor's arms, and they talk with the cozy trade words of old professionals, agreeing that they will not make love again before a movie, that it was exciting but also not without detachment, that all in all it has been good but not quite right, that she had loved this action he had done, and was uncertain about another. It is their old familiar critique, a sign that they are intimate and well disposed. They do not talk about the act when it has failed to fire; then they go silently to sleep. But now, Eleanor's enjoyment having mollified Sam's sense of no enjoyment, they talk with the apologetics and encomiums of familiar mates. Eleanor falls asleep, and Sam falls almost asleep, curling next to her warm body, his hand over her round belly with the satisfaction of a sculptor. He is drowsy, and he thinks drowsily that these few moments of creature-pleasure, this brief compassion he can feel for the body that trusts itself to sleep beside him, his comfort in its warmth, is perhaps all the meaning he may ask for his life. That out of disappointment, frustration, and the passage of dreary years come these few moments when he is close to her, and their years together possess a connotation more rewarding than the sum of all which has gone into them.

But then he thinks of the novel he wants to write, and he is wide-awake again. Like the sleeping pill which fails to work and leaves one warped in an exaggeration of the ills which sought the drug, Sam passes through the promise of sex-emptied sleep, and is left with nervous loins, swollen jealousy of an act ten years dead, and sweating irritable resentment of the woman's body which hinders his limbs. He has wasted the day, he tells himself, he has wasted the day as he has wasted so many days of his life, and tomorrow in the office he will be no more than his ten fingers typing plot and words for Bramba the Venusian and Lee-Lee Deeds, Hollywood Star, while that huge work with which he has cheated himself, holding it before him as a covenant of his worth, that enormous novel which would lift him at a bound from the impasse in which he stifles, whose dozens of characters would develop a vision of life in bountiful complexity, lies foundered, rotting on a beach of purposeless effort. Notes here, pages there, it sprawls through a formless wreck of incidental ideas and half-episodes, utterly without shape. He has not even a hero for it.

One could not have a hero today, Sam thinks, a man of action and contemplation, capable of sin, large enough for good, a man immense. There is only a modern hero damned by no more than the ugliness of wishes whose satisfaction he will never know. One needs a man who could walk the stage, someone who—no matter who, not himself. Someone, Sam thinks, who reasonably could not exist.

The novelist, thinks Sam, perspiring beneath blankets, must live in paranoia and seek to be one with the world; he must be terrified of experience and hungry for it; he must think himself nothing and believe he is superior to all. The feminine in his nature cries for proof he is a man; he dreams of power and is without capacity to gain it; he loves himself above all and therefore despises all that he is.

He is that, thinks Sam, he is part of the perfect prescription, and yet he is not a novelist. He lacks energy and belief. It is left for him to write an article some day about the temperament of the ideal novelist.

In the darkness, memories rise, yeast-swells of apprehension. Out of bohemian days so long ago, comes the friend of Eleanor, a girl who had been sick and was committed to an institution. They visited her, Sam and Eleanor, they took the suburban train and sat on the lawn of the asylum grounds while patients circled about intoning a private litany, or shuddering in boob-blundering fright from an insect that crossed their skin. The friend had been silent. She had smiled, she had answered their questions with the fewest words, and had returned again to her study of sunlight and blue sky. As they were about to leave, the girl had taken Sam aside. "They violate me," she said in a whisper. "Every night when the doors are locked, they come to my room and they make the movie. I am the heroine and am subjected to all variety of sexual viciousness. Tell them to leave me alone so I may enter the convent." And while she talked, in a horror of her body, one arm scrubbed the other. Poor tortured friend. They had seen her again, and she babbled, her face had coarsened into an idiot leer.

Sam sweats. There is so little he knows, and so much to know. Youth of the depression with its economic terms, what can he know of madness or religion? They are both so alien to him. He is the mongrel, Sam thinks, brought up without religion from a mother half Protestant and half Catholic, and a father half Catholic and half Jew. He is the quarter-Jew, and yet he is a Jew, or so he feels himself, knowing nothing of Gospel, tabernacle, or Mass, the Jew through accident, through state of mind. What . . . whatever did he know of penance? self-sacrifice? mortification of the flesh? the love of his fellow man? Am I concerned with my relation to God? ponders Sam, and smiles sourly in the darkness. No, that has never concerned him, he thinks, not for better nor for worse. "They are making the movie," says the girl into the ear of memory, "and so I cannot enter the convent."

How hideous was the mental hospital. A concentration camp, decides Sam. Perhaps it would be the world some day, or was that only his projection of feelings of hopelessness? "Do not try to solve the problems of the world," he hears from Sergius, and pounds a lumpy pillow.

However could he organize his novel? What form to give it? It is so complex. Too loose, thinks Sam, too scattered. Will he ever fall asleep? Wearily, limbs tense, his stomach too keen, he plays again the game of putting himself to sleep. "I do not feel my toes," Sam says to himself, "my toes are dead, my calves are asleep, my calves are sleeping . . ."

In the middle from wakefulness to slumber, in the torpor which floats beneath blankets, I give an idea to Sam. "Destroy time, and chaos may be ordered," I say to him.

"Destroy time, and chaos may be ordered," he repeats after me, and in desperation to seek his coma, mutters back, "I do not feel my nose, my nose is numb, my eyes are heavy, my eyes are heavy."

So Sam enters the universe of sleep, a man who seeks to live in such a way as to avoid pain, and succeeds merely in avoiding pleasure. What a dreary compromise is life!

1952

Fourth Advertisement for Myself: *The Last Draft of The Deer Park*

In his review of *The Deer Park*, Malcolm Cowley said it must have been a more difficult book to write than *The Naked and the Dead*. He was right. Most of the time, I worked on *The Deer Park* in a low mood; my liver, which had gone bad in the Philippines, exacted a hard price for forcing the effort against the tide of a long depression, and matters were not improved when nobody at Rinehart & Co. liked the first draft of the novel. The second draft, which to me was the finished book, also gave little enthusiasm to the editors, and open woe to Stanley Rinehart, the publisher. I was impatient to leave for Mexico, now that I was done, but before I could go, Rinehart asked for a week in which to decide whether he wanted to do the book. Since he had already given me a contract which allowed him no option not to accept the novel (a common arrangement for writers whose sales are more or less large) any decision to reject the manuscript would cost him a sizable advance. (I learned later he had been hoping his lawyers would find the book obscene, but they did not, at least not then in May 1954.) So he had really no choice but to agree to put the book out in February, and gloomily he consented. To cheer him a bit, I agreed to his request that he delay paying me my advance until publication, although the first half was due on delivery of the manuscript. I thought the favor might improve our relations.

Now, if a few of you are wondering why I did not take my book back and go to another publishing house, the answer is that I was tired, I was badly tired. Only a few weeks before, a doctor had given me tests for the liver, and it had shown itself to be sick and depleted. I was hoping that a few months in Mexico would give me a chance to fill up again.

But the next months were not cheerful. *The Deer Park* had been done as well as I could do it, yet I thought it was probably a minor work, and I did not know if I had any real interest in starting another book. I made efforts of course; I collected notes, began to piece together a few ideas for a novel given to bullfighting, and another about a concentration camp; I wrote "David Reisman Reconsidered" during this time, and "The Homosexual Villain"; read most of the work of the other writers of my generation (I think I was looking for a level against which to measure my third novel) went over the galleys when they came, changed a line or two, sent them back. Keeping half busy I mended a bit, but it was a time of dull drifting. When we came back to New York in October, *The Deer Park* was already in page proof. By November, the first advertisement was given to *Publishers' Weekly*. Then, with less than ninety days to publication, Stanley Rinehart told me I would have to take out a small piece of the book — six not very explicit lines about the sex of an old producer and a call girl. The moment one was ready to consider losing those six lines they moved into the moral center of the novel. It would be no tonic for my liver to cut them out. But I also knew Rinehart was serious, and since I was still tired, it seemed a little unreal to try to keep the passage. Like a miser I had been storing energy to start a new book; I wanted nothing to distract me now. I gave in on a word or two, agreed to rewrite a line, and went home from that particular conference not very impressed with myself. The next morning I called up the editor in chief, Ted Amussen, to tell him I had decided the original words had to be put back.

"Well, fine," he said, "fine. I don't know why you agreed to anything in the first place."

A day later, Stanley Rinehart halted publication, stopped all ads (he was too late to catch the first run of *Publishers' Weekly* which was already on its way to England with a full page for *The Deer Park*) and broke his contract to do the book. I was started on a trip to find a new publisher, and before I was done, the book had gone to Random House, Knopf, Simon and Schuster, Harper's Scribners, and unofficially to Harcourt, Brace. Some day it would be fine to give the details, but for now little more than a few lines of dialogue and an editorial report:

> Bennett Cerf: This novel will set publishing back twenty years.
> Alfred Knopf to an editor: Is this your idea of the kind of book which should bear a Borzoi imprint?

The lawyer for one publishing house complimented me on the six lines, word for word, which had excited Rinehart to break his contract. This lawyer said, "It's admirable the way you get around the problem here." Then he brought out more than a hundred objections to other parts of the book. One was the line, "She was lovely. Her back was adorable in its contours." I was told that this ought to go because "The principals are not married, and so your description puts a favorable interpretation upon a meretricious relationship."

Hiram Hayden had lunch with me some time after Random House saw the book. He told me he was responsible for their decision not to do it, and if I did not agree with his taste, I had to admire his honesty—it is rare for an editor to tell a writer the truth. Hayden went on to say that the book never came alive for him even though he had been ready to welcome it. "I can tell you that I picked the book up with anticipation. Of course I had heard from Bill, and Bill had told me that he didn't like it, but I never pay attention to what one writer says about the work of another . . ." Bill was William Styron, and Hayden was his editor. I had asked Styron to call Hayden the night I found out Rinehart had broken his contract. One reason for asking the favor of Styron was that he sent me a long letter about the novel after I had shown it to him in manuscript. He had written, "I don't like *The Deer Park*, but I admire sheer hell out of it." So I thought to impose on him.

Other parts of the account are not less dreary. The only generosity I found was from the late Jack Goodman. He sent me a photostat of his editorial report to Simon and Schuster, and because it was sympathetic, his report became the objective estimate of the situation for me. I assumed that the book when it came out would meet the kind of trouble Goodman expected, and so when I went back later to work on the page proofs I was not free of a fear or two. But that can be talked about in its place. Here is the core of his report.

> Mailer refuses to make any changes . . . [He] *will* consider suggestions, but reserves the right to make final decisions, so we must make our decision on what the book now is.
>
> That's not easy. It is full of vitality and power, as readable a novel as I've ever encountered. Mailer emerges as a sort of post-Kinsey F. Scott Fitzgerald. His dialogue is uninhibited and the sexuality of the book is completely interwoven with its purpose, which is to describe a segment of society whose morality is nonexistent. Locale is evidently Palm Springs. Chief characters are Charles Eitel, movie director who first defies the House Un-American Committee, then becomes a friendly witness, his mistress, a great movie star who is his ex-wife, her lover who is the narrator, the head of a great movie company, his son-in-law, a strange, tortured panderer who is Eitel's conscience and, assorted demimondaines, homosexuals, actors.
>
> My layman's opinion is that the novel will be banned in certain quarters and that it may very well be up for an obscenity charge, but this should of course be checked by our lawyers. If it were possible to recognize this at the start, to have a united front here and treat the whole issue positively and head-on, I would be for our publishing. But I am afraid such unanimity may be impossible of attainment and if so, we should reject, in spite of the fact that I am certain it will be one of the

best-selling novels of the next couple of years. It is the work of a serious artist. . . .

The eighth house was G. P. Putnam's. I didn't want to give it to them, I was planning to go next to Viking, but Walter Minton kept saying, "Give us three days. We'll give you a decision in three days." So we sent it over to Putnam, and in three days they took it without conditions and without a request for a single change. I had a victory, I had made my point, but in fact I was not very happy. I had grown so wild on my diet of polite letters from publishing houses who didn't want me, that I had been ready to collect rejections from twenty houses, publish *The Deer Park* at my own expense, and try to make a kind of publishing history. Instead I was thrown in with Walter Minton, who has since attracted some fame as the publisher of *Lolita*. He is the only publisher I ever met who would make a good general. Months after I came to Putnam, Minton told me, "I was ready to take *The Deer Park* without reading it. I knew your name would sell enough copies to pay your advance, and I figured one of these days you're going to write another book like *The Naked and the Dead*," which is the sort of sure hold of strategy you can have when you're not afraid of censorship.

Now I've tried to water this account with a minimum of tears, but taking *The Deer Park* into the nervous system of eight publishing houses was not so good for my own nervous system, nor was it good for getting to work on my new novel. In the ten weeks it took the book to travel the circuit from Rinehart to Putnam, I squandered the careful energy I had been hoarding for months; there was a hard comedy at how much of myself I would burn up in a few hours of hot telephone calls; I had never had any sense for practical affairs, but in those days, carrying *The Deer Park* from house to house, I stayed as close to it as a stage-struck mother pushing her child forward at every producer's office. I was amateur agent for it, messenger boy, editorial consultant, Macchiavelli of the luncheon table, fool of the five o'clock drinks, I was learning the publishing business in a hurry, and I made a hundred mistakes and paid for each one by wasting a new bout of energy.

In a way there was sense to it. For the first time in years I was having the kind of experience which was likely to return some day as good work, and so I forced many little events past any practical return, even insulting a few publishers en route as if to discover the limits of each situation. I was trying to find a few new proportions to things, and I did learn a bit. But I'll never know what that novel about the concentration camp would have been like if I had gotten quietly to work when I came back to New York and *The Deer*

Park had been published on time. It is possible I was not serious about the book, it is also possible I lost something good, but one way or the other, that novel disappeared in the excitement, as lost as "the little object" in *Barbary Shore*, and it has not stirred since.

The real confession is that I was making a few of my mental connections those days on marijuana. Like more than one or two of my generation, I had smoked it from time to time over the years, but it never had meant anything. In Mexico, however, down in my depression with a bad liver, pot gave me a sense of something new about the time I was convinced I had seen it all, and I liked it enough to take it now and again in New York.

Then *The Deer Park* began to go like a beggar from house to house and en route Stanley Rinehart made it clear he was going to try not to pay the advance. Until then I had had sympathy for him. I thought it had taken a kind of displaced courage to be able to drop the book the way he did. An expensive moral stand, and wasteful for me; but a moral stand. When it turned out that he did not like to bear the expense of being that moral, the experience turned ugly for me. It took many months and the service of my lawyer to get the money, but long before that, the situation had become real enough to drive a spike into my cast-iron mind. I realized in some bottom of myself that for years I had been the sort of comic figure I would have cooked to a turn in one of my books, a radical who had the nineteenth-century naïveté to believe that the people with whom he did business were 1) gentlemen, 2) fond of him, and 3) respectful of his ideas even if in disagreement with them. Now, I was in the act of learning that I was not adored so very much; that my ideas were seen as nasty; and that my fine America which I had been at pains to criticize for so many years was in fact a real country which did real things and ugly things to the characters of more people than just the characters of my books. If the years since the war had not been brave or noble in the history of the country, which I certainly thought and do think, why then did it come as surprise that people in publishing were not as good as they used to be, and that the day of Maxwell Perkins was a day which was gone, really gone, gone as Greta Garbo and Scott Fitzgerald? Not easy, one could argue, for an advertising man to admit that advertising is a dishonest occupation, and no easier was it for the working novelist to see that now were left only the cliques, fashions, vogues, snobs, snots, and fools, not to mention a dozen bureaucracies of criticism; that there was no room for the old literary idea of oneself as a major writer, a figure in the landscape. One had become a set of relations and equations, most flourishing when most incorporated, for then one's literary stock was ready for merger. The day was gone when people held on to your novels no matter what others might say. Instead one's good young readers waited now for the verdict of professional young men, academics who wolfed down a modern literature with an anxiety to find your classification, your identity, your similarity, your common theme, your corporate literary earnings, each reference to yourself as individual as a carloading of homogenized words. The articles which would be written about you and a dozen others would be done by minds which were expert on the aggregate and so had senses too lumpy for the particular. There was a limit to how much appraisal could be made of a work before the critic exposed his lack of the critical faculty, and so it was naturally wiser for the mind of the expert to masticate the themes of ten writers rather than approach the difficulties of any one.

I had begun to read my good American novels at the end of an era — I could remember people who would talk wistfully about the excitement with which they had gone to bookstores because it was publication day for the second novel of Thomas Wolfe, and in college, at a Faculty tea, I had listened for an hour to a professor's wife who was so blessed as to have known John Dos Passos. My adolescent crush on the profession of the writer had been more lasting than I could have guessed. I had even been so simple as to think that the kind of people who went into publishing were still most concerned with the few writers who made the profession not empty of honor, and I had been taking myself seriously, I had been thinking I was one of those writers.

Instead I caught it in the face and deserved it for not looking at the evidence. I was out of fashion and that was the score; that was all the score; the publishing habits of the past were going to be of no help for my *Deer Park*. And so as the language of sentiment would have it, something broke in me, but I do not know if it was so much a loving heart, as a cyst of the weak, the unreal, and the needy, and I was finally open to my anger. I turned within my psyche I can almost believe, for I felt something shift to murder in me. I finally had the simple sense to understand that if I wanted my work to travel further than others, the life of my talent depended on fighting a little more, and looking for help a little less. But I deny the sequence in putting it this way, for it took me years to come to this fine point. All I felt then was that I was an outlaw, a psychic outlaw, and I liked it, I liked it a good night better than trying to be a gentleman, and with a set of emotions accelerating one on the other, I mined down deep into the murderous message of marijuana, the smoke of the assassins, and for the first time in my life I knew what it was to make your kicks.

I could write about that here, but it would be a mistake. Let the experience stay where it is, and on a given year it may be found again in a novel. For now it is enough to say that marijuana opens the senses and weakens the mind. In the end, you pay for what you get. If you get something big, the cost will equal it. There is a moral economy to one's vice, but you learn that last of all. I still had the thought it was possible to find something which cost nothing. Thus, *The Deer Park* resting at Putnam, and new good friends found in Harlem, I was off on that happy ride where you discover a new duchy of jazz every night and the drought of the past is given a rain of new sound. What has been dull and dead in your years is now tart to the taste, and there is sweet in the illusion of how fast you can change. To keep up with it all, I began to log a journal, a wild set of thoughts and outlines for huge projects — I wrote one hundred thousand words in eight weeks, more than once twenty pages a day in a style which came willy-nilly from the cramp of the past, a lockstep jargon of sociology and psychology that sours my teeth when I look at those pages today. Yet this journal has the start of more ideas than I will have again; ideas which came so fast and so rich that sometimes I think my brain was dulled by the heat of their passage. (With all proportions kept, one can say that cocaine may have worked a similar good and ill upon Freud.)

The journal wore down by February, about the time *The Deer Park* had once been scheduled to appear. By then I had decided to change a few things in the novel, nothing in the way of lawyer's deletions, just a few touches for style. They were not happy about this at Putnam. Minton argued that some interest in the book would be lost if the text were not identical to Rinehart's page proofs, and Ted Purdy, my editor, told me more than once that they liked the book "just the way it is." Besides, there was thought of bringing it out in June as a summer book.

Well, I wanted to take a look. After all, I had been learning new lessons. I began to go over the page proofs, and the book read as if it had been written by someone else. I was changed from the writer who had labored on that novel, enough to be able to see it without anger or vanity or the itch to justify myself. Now, after three years of living with the book, I could at last admit the style was wrong, that it had been wrong from the time I started, that I had been strangling the life of my novel in a poetic prose which was too self-consciously attractive and formal, false to the life of my characters, especially false to the life of my narrator who was the voice of my novel and so gave the story its air. He had been a lieutenant in the Air Force, he had been cool enough and hard enough to work his way up from an orphan asylum, and to allow him to write in a style which at its best sounded like Nick Carraway in *The Great Gatsby* must of course blur his character and leave the book unreal. Nick was legitimate, out of fair family, the Midwest and Princeton—he would write as he did, his style was himself. But the style of Sergius O'Shaugnessy, no matter how good it became (and the Rinehart *Deer Park* had its moments) was a style which came out of nothing so much as my determination to prove I could muster a fine style.

If I wanted to improve my novel, yet keep the style. I would have to make my narrator fit the prose, change his past, make him an onlooker, a rich pretty boy brought up let us say by two old-maid aunts, able to have an affair with a movie star only by luck and/or the needs of the plot, which would give me a book less distracting, well written but minor. If, however, I wanted to keep that first narrator, my orphan, flier, adventurer, *germ*—for three years he had been the frozen germ of some new theme—well, to keep him I would need to change the style from the inside of each sentence. I could keep the structure of my book, I thought—it had been put together for such a narrator—but the style could not escape. Probably I did not see it all so clearly as I now suggest. I believe I started with the conscious thought that I would tinker just a little, try to patch a compromise, but the navigator of my unconscious must already have made the choice, because it came as no real surprise that after a few days of changing a few words I moved more and more quickly toward the eye of the problem, and in two or three weeks I was tied to the work of doing a new *Deer Park*. The book was edited in a way no editor could ever have time or love to find; it was searched sentence by sentence, word for word, the style of the work lost its polish, became rough, and I can say real, because there was an abrupt and muscular body back of the voice now. It had been there all the time, trapped in the porcelain of a false style, but now as I chipped away, the work for a time became exhilarating in its clarity—I never enjoyed work so much—I felt as if finally I was learning how to write, learning the joints of language and the touch of a word, felt as if I came close to the meanings of sound and could say which of two close words was more female or more forward. I even had a glimpse of what Flaubert might have felt, for as I went on tuning the book, often five or six words would pile above one another in the margin at some small crisis of choice. (Since the Rinehart page proof was the usable copy, I had little space to write between the lines.) As I worked in this fine mood, I kept sending pages to the typist, yet so soon as I had exhausted the old galley pages, I could not keep away from the new typewritten copy—it would be close to say the book had come alive, and was invading my brain.

Soon the early pleasure of the work turned restless; the consequences of what I was doing were beginning to seep into my stamina. It was as if I were the captive of an illness whose first symptoms had been excitement, prodigies of quick work, and a confidence that one could go on forever, but that I was by now close to a second stage where what had been quick would be more like fever, a first wind of fatigue upon me, a knowledge that at the end of the drunken night a junkie cold was waiting. I was going to move at a pace deadly to myself, loading and overloading whatever little centers of the mind are forced to make the hard decisions. In ripping up the silk of the original syntax, I was tearing into any number of careful habits as well as whatever subtle fleshing of the nerves and the chemicals had gone to support them.

For six years I had been writing novels in the first person; it was the only way I could begin a book, even though the third person was more to my taste. Worse, I seemed unable to create a narrator in the first person who was not overdelicate, oversensitive, and painfully tender, which was an odd portrait to give, because I was not delicate, not physically; when it was a matter of strength I had as much as the next man. In those days I would spend time reminding myself that I had been a bit of an athlete (house football at Harvard, years of skiing) that I had not quit in combat, and once when a gang broke up a party in my loft, I had taken two cracks on the head with a hammer and had still been able to fight. Yet the first person seemed to paralyze me, as if I had a horror of creating a voice which could be in any way bigger than myself. So I had become mired in a false style for every narrator I tried. If now I had been in a fight, had found out that no matter how weak I could be in certain ways, I was also steady enough to hang on to six important lines, that may have given me new respect for myself, I don't know, but for the first time I was able to use the first person in a way where I could suggest some of the stubbornness and belligerence I also might have, I was able to color the empty reality of that first person with some real feeling of how I had always felt, which was to be outside, for Brooklyn where I grew up is not the center of anything. I was able, then, to create an adventurer whom I believed in, and as he came alive for me, the other parts of the book which had been stagnant for a year and more also came to life, and new things began to happen to Eitel my director and to Elena his mistress and their characters changed. It was a phenomenon. I learned how real a novel is. Before, the story of Eitel had been told by O'Shaugnessy of the weak voice; now by a confident young man: when the new narrator would remark that Eitel was his best friend and so he tried not to find Elena too attractive, the man and woman he was talking about were larger than they had once been. I was no longer telling of two nice people who fail at love because the world is too large and too cruel for them; the new O'Shaugnessy had moved me by degrees to the more painful story of two people who are strong as well as weak, corrupt as much as pure, and fail to grow despite their bravery in a poor world, because they are finally not brave enough, and so do more damage to one another than to the unjust world outside them. Which for me was exciting, for here and there *The Deer Park* now had the rare tenderness of tragedy. The most powerful leverage in fiction comes from point of view, and giving O'Shaugnessy courage gave passion to the others.

But the punishment was commencing for me. I was now creating a man who was braver and stronger than me, and the more my new style succeeded, the more was I writing an implicit portrait of myself as well. There is a shame about advertising yourself that way, a shame which became so strong that it was a psychological violation to go on. Yet I could not afford the time to digest the self-criticisms backing up in me, I was forced to drive myself, and so more and more I worked by tricks, taking marijuana the night before and then drugging myself into sleep with an overload of seconal. In the morning I would be lithe with new perception, could read new words into the words I had already, and so could go on in the pace of my work, the most scrupulous part of my brain too sluggish to interfere. My powers of logic became weaker each day, but the book had its own logic, and so I did not need close reason. What I wanted and what the drugs gave me was the quick flesh of associations, and there I was often oversensitive, could discover new experience in the lines of my text like a hermit savoring the revelation of Scripture; I saw so much in some sentences that more than once I dropped into the pit of the amateur: since I was receiving such emotion from my words, I assumed everyone else would be stimulated as well, and on many a line I twisted the phrase in such a way that it could read well only when read slowly, about as slowly as it would take for an actor to read it aloud. Once you write that way, the quick reader (who is nearly all your audience) will stumble and fall against the vocal shifts of your prose. Then you had best have the cartel of a Hemingway, because in such a case it is critical whether the reader thinks it is your fault, or is so in awe of your reputation that he returns on the words, throttles his pace, and tries to discover why he is so stupid as not to swing on the off-bop of your style.

An example: In the Rinehart *Deer Park* I had this:

"They make Sugar sound so good in the newspapers," she declared one night to some people in a bar, "that I'll really try him. I really will, Sugar." And she gave me a sisterly kiss.

I happened to change that very little, I put in "said" instead of "declared" and later added "older sister," so that it now read:

And she gave me a sisterly kiss. Older sister.

Just two words, but I felt as if I had revealed some divine law of nature, had laid down an invaluable clue—the kiss of an older sister was a worldly universe away from the kiss of a younger sister—and I thought to give myself the Nobel Prize for having brought such illumination and *division* to the cliché of the sisterly kiss.

Well, as an addition it wasn't bad fun, and for two words it did a bit to give a sense of what was working back and forth between Sergius and Lulu, it was another small example of Sergius' hard eye for the world, and his cool sense of his place in it, and all this was to the good, or would have been for a reader who went slowly, and stopped, and thought. But if anyone was in a hurry, the little sentence "Older sister" was like a finger in the eye, it jabbed the unconscious, and gave an uncomfortable nip of rhythm to the mind.

I had five hundred changes of this kind. I started with the first paragraph of the book, on the third sentence which pokes the reader with its backed-up rhythm, "Some time ago," and I did that with intent, to slow my readers from the start, like a fighter who throws his right two seconds after the bell and so gives the other man no chance to decide on the pace.

There was a real question, however, whether I could slow the reader down, and so as I worked on further, at some point beginning to write paragraphs and pages to add to the new Putnam galleys, the attrition of the drugs and the possibility of failure began to depress me, and Benzedrine entered the balance, and I was on the way to wearing badly. Because, determined or no that they would read me slowly, praying my readers would read me slowly, there was no likelihood they would do anything of the sort if the reviews were bad. As I started to worry this it grew worse, because I knew in advance that three or four of my major reviews had to be bad—*Time* magazine for one, because Max Gissen was the book review editor, and I had insulted him in public once by suggesting that the kind of man who worked for a mind so exquisitely and subtly totalitarian as Henry Luce was not likely to have any ideas of his own. The New York Daily *Times* would be bad because Orville Prescott was well known for his distaste of books too forthrightly sexual; and *Saturday Review* would be bad. That is, they would probably be bad; the mentality of their reviewers would not be above the level of their dean of reviewers, Mr. Maxwell Geismar, and Geismar didn't seem to know that my second novel was titled *Barbary Shore* rather than *Barbary Coast*. I could spin this out, but what is more to the point is that I had begun to think of the reviews before finishing the book, and this doubtful occupation came out of the kind of inner knowledge I had of myself in those days. I knew what was good for my energy and what was poor, and so I knew that for the vitality of my work in the future, and yes even the quantity of my work, I needed a success and I needed it badly if I was to shed the fatigue I had been carrying since *Barbary Shore*. Some writers receive not enough attention for years, and so learn early to accommodate the habits of their work to little recognition. I think I could have done that when I was twenty-five. With *The Naked and the Dead* a new life had begun, however; as I have written earlier in this book, I had gone through the psychic labor of changing a good many modest habits in order to let me live a little more happily as a man with a name which could arouse quick reactions in strangers. If that started as an overlarge work, because I started as a decent but scared boy, well I had come to live with the new life. I had learned to like success — in fact I had probably come to depend on it, or at least my new habits did.

When *Barbary Shore* was ambushed in the alley, the damage to my nervous system was slow but thorough. My status dropped immediately — America is a quick country — but my ego did not permit me to understand that, and I went through tiring years of subtle social defeats because I did not know that I was no longer as large to others as I had been. I was always overmatching myself. To put it crudely, I would think I was dropping people when they were dropping me. And of course my unconscious knew better. There was all the waste of ferocious if unheard discussion between the armies of ego and id; I would get up in the morning with less snap in me than I had taken to sleep. Six or seven years of breathing that literary air taught me a writer stayed alive in the circuits of such hatred only if he were unappreciated enough to be adored by a clique, or was so overbought by the public that he excited some defenseless nerve in the snob. I knew if *The Deer Park* was a powerful best seller (the magical figure had become one hundred thousand copies for me) that I would then have won. I would be the first serious writer of my generation to have a best seller twice, and so it would not matter what was said about the book. Half of publishing might call it cheap, dirty, sensational, second-rate, and so forth and so forth, but it would be weak rage and could not hurt, for the literary world suffers a spot of the national taint—a serious writer is certain to be considered major if he is also a best seller; in fact, most readers are never convinced of his value until his books do well. Steinbeck is better known than Dos Passos, John O'Hara is taken seriously by people who dismiss Farrell, and indeed it took three decades and a Nobel Prize before Faulkner was placed on a level with Hemingway. For that reason, it would have done no good if someone had told me at the time that the financial success of a writer with major talent was probably due more to what was meretricious in his work than what was central. The argument would have meant nothing to me—all I knew was that seven publishing houses had been willing to dismiss my future, and so if the book did poorly, a good many people were going to congratulate themselves on their foresight and be concerned with me even less. I could see that if I wanted to keep on writing the kind of book I liked to write, I needed the energy of new success, I needed blood. Through every bit of me, I knew *The Deer Park* had damn well better make it or I was close to some serious illness, a real apathy of the will.

Every now and again I would have the nightmare of wondering what would happen if all the reviews were bad, as bad as *Barbary Shore*. I would try to tell myself that could not happen, but I was not certain, and I knew that if the book received a unanimously bad press and still showed signs of selling well, it was likely to be brought up for prosecution as obscene. As a delayed convulsion from the McCarthy years, the fear of censorship was strong in publishing, in England it was critically bad, and so I also knew that the book could lose such a suit—there might be no one of reputation to say it was serious. If it were banned, it could sink from sight. With the reserves I was throwing into the work, I no longer knew if I was ready to take another beating—for the first time in my life I had worn down to the edge, I could see through to the other side of my fear, I knew a time could come when I would be no longer my own man, that I might lose what I had liked to think was the incorruptible center of my strength (which of course I had had money and freedom to cultivate). Already the signs were there—I was beginning to avoid new lines in the Putnam *Deer Park* which were legally doubtful, and once in a while, like a gambler hedging a bet, I toned down individual sentences from the Rinehart *Deer Park*, nothing much, always a matter of the new O'Shaugnessy character, a change from "at last I was able to penetrate into the mysterious and magical belly of a movie star," to what was more in character for him: "I was led to discover the mysterious brain of a movie star." Which "brain" in context was fun for it was accurate, and "discover" was a word of more life than the legality of "pene-trate," but I could not be sure if I were chasing my new aesthetic or afraid of the cops. The problem was that *The Deer Park* had become more sexual in the new version, the characters had more force, the air had more heat, and I had gone through the kind of galloping self-analysis which makes one very sensitive to the sex-ual nuance of every gesture, word and object—the book now seemed overcharged to me, even a terror of a novel, a cold chisel into all the dull mortar of our guilty society. In my mind it became a more dangerous book than it really was, and my drug-hipped par-anoia saw long consequences in every easy line of dialogue. I kept the panic in its place, but by an effort of course, and once in a while I would weaken enough to take out a line because I could not see myself able to defend it happily in a court of law. But it was a mistake to nibble at the edges of censoring myself, for it gave no life to my old pride that I was the boldest writer to have come out of my flabby time, and I think it helped to kill the small chance of finding my way into what could have been a novel as important as *The Sun Also Rises*.

But let me spell it out a bit: originally *The Deer Park* had been about a movie director and a girl with whom he had a bad affair, and it was told by a sensitive but faceless young man. In changing the young man, I saved the book from being minor, but put a dis-proportion upon it because my narrator became too interesting, and not enough happened to him in the second half of the book, and so it was to be expected that readers would be disappointed by this part of the novel.

Before I was finished, I saw a way to write another book alto-gether. In what I had so far done, Sergius O'Shaugnessy was given an opportunity by a movie studio to sell the rights to his life and get a contract as an actor. After more than one complication, he finally refused the offer, lost the love of his movie star Lulu, and went off wandering by himself, off to become a writer. This episode had never been an important part of the book, but I could see that the new Sergius was capable of accepting the offer, and if he went to Hollywood and became a movie star himself, the possibilities were good, for in O'Shaugnessy I had a character who was ambi-tious, yet in his own way, moral, and with such a character one could travel deep into the paradoxes of the time.

Well, I was not in shape to consider that book. With each week of work, bombed and sapped and charged and stoned with lush, with pot, with benny, saggy, Miltown, coffee, and two packs a day, I was working live, and overalert, and tiring into what felt like death, afraid all the way because I had achieved the worst of vicious circles in myself, I had gotten too tired, I was more tired than I had ever been in combat, and so as the weeks went on, and publication was delayed from June to August and then to October, there was only a worn-out part of me to keep protesting into the pillows of one drug and the pinch of the other that I ought to have the guts to stop the machine, to call back the galleys, to cease—to rest, to give myself another two years and write a book which would go a little further to the end of my particular night.

But I had passed the point where I could stop. My anxiety had become too great. I did not know anything any more, I did not have that clear sense of the way things work which is what you need for the natural proportions of a long novel, and it is likely I would not have been writing a new book so much as arguing with the law. Of course another man might have had the stamina to write the new book and manage to be indifferent to everything else, but it was too much to ask of me. By then I was like a lover in a bad, but uncontrollable affair; my woman was publication, and it would have cost too much to give her up before we were done. My imagination had been committed—to stop would leave half the psyche in limbo.

Knowing, however, what I had failed to do, shame added momentum to the punishment of the drugs. By the last week or two, I had worn down so badly that with a dozen pieces still to be fixed, I was reduced to working hardly more than an hour a day. Like an old man, I would come up out of a seconal stupor with four or five times the normal dose in my veins, and drop into a chair to sit for hours. It was July, the heat was grim in New York, the last of the book had to be in by August 1. Putnam had been more than accommodating, but the vehicle of publication was on its way, and the book could not be postponed beyond the middle of October or it would miss all chance for a large fall sale. I would sit in a chair and watch a baseball game on television, or get up and go out in the heat to a drugstore for sandwich and malted—it was my outing for the day: the walk would feel like a patrol in a tropical sun, and it was two blocks, no more. When I came back, I would lie down, my head would lose the outer wrappings of sedation, and with a crumb of benzedrine, the first snake or two of thought would wind through my brain. I would go for some coffee—it was a trip to the kitchen, but when I came back I would have a scratch-board and pencil in hand. Watching some afternoon horror on television, the boredom of the performers coming through their tense hilarities with a bleakness to match my own, I would pick up the board, wait for the first sentence—like all working addicts I had come to an old man's fine sense of inner timing—and then slowly, but picking up speed, the actions of the drugs hovering into collaboration like two ships passing in view of one another, I would work for an hour, not well but not badly either. (Pages 195 to 200 of the Putnam edition were written this way.) Then my mind would wear out, and new work was done for the day. I would sit around, watch more television and try to rest my dulled mind, but by evening a riot of bad nerves was on me again, and at two in the morning I'd be having the manly debate of whether to try sleep with two double capsules, or settle again for my need of three.

Somehow I got the book done for the last deadline. Not perfectly—doing just the kind of editing and small rewriting I was doing, I could have used another two or three days, but I got it almost the way I wanted, and then I took my car up to the Cape and lay around in Provincetown with my wife, trying to mend, and indeed doing a fair job because I came off sleeping pills and the marijuana and came part of the way back into that world which has the proportions of the ego. I picked up on *The Magic Mountain*, took it slowly, and lowered *The Deer Park* down to modest size in my brain. Which events proved was just as well.

A few weeks later we came back to the city, and I took some mescaline. Maybe one dies a little with the poison of mescaline in the blood. At the end of a long and private trip which no quick remark should try to describe, the book of *The Deer Park* floated into mind, and I sat up, reached through a pleasure garden of velveted light to find the tree of a pencil and the bed of a notebook and brought them to union together. Then, out of some flesh in myself I had not yet known, with the words coming one by one, in separate steeps and falls, hip in their turnings, all cool with their flights, like the touch of being coming into other being, so the last six lines of my bloody book came to me, and I was done. And it was the only good writing I ever did directly from a drug, even if I paid for it with a hangover beyond measure.

That way the novel received its last sentence, and if I had waited one more day it would have been too late, for in the next twenty-four hours, the printers began their cutting and binding. The book was out of my hands.

Six weeks later, when *The Deer Park* came out, I was no longer feeling eighty years old, but a vigorous hysterical sixty-three, and I laughed like an old pirate at the indignation I had breezed into being with the equation of sex and time. The important reviews broke about seven good and eleven bad, and the out-of-town reports were almost three-to-one bad to good, but I was not unhappy because the good reviews were lively and the bad reviews were full of factual error, indeed so much so that it would be monotonous to give more than a good couple.

Hollis Alpert in the *Saturday Review* called the book "garish and gauche." In reference to Sergius O'Shaugnessy, Alpert wrote: "He has been offered $50,000 by Teppis to sell the rights to his rather dull life story . . ." As a matter of detail, the sum was $20,000, and it must have been mentioned a half dozen times in the pages of the book. Paul Pickrel in *Harper's* was blistering about how terrible was my style and then quoted the following sentence as an example of how I was often incomprehensible:

> "(he) could talk opening about his personal life while remaining a dream of espionage in his business operations."

I happened to see Pickrel's review in *Harper's* galleys, and so was able to point out to them that Pickrel had misquoted the sentence. The fourth word was not "opening" but "openly." *Harper's* corrected his incorrect version, but of course left his remark about my style.

More interesting is the way reviews divided in the New York magazines and newspapers. *Time*, for example, was bad, *Newsweek* was good; *Harper's* was terrible but The *Atlantic* was adequate; the New York Daily *Times* was very bad, the Sunday *Times* was good; the Daily *Herald Tribune* gave a mark of zero, the Sunday *Herald Tribune* was better than good; *Commentary* was careful but complimentary, the *Reporter* was frantic; the *Saturday Review* was a scold and Brendan Gill writing for the *New Yorker* put together a series of slaps and superlatives which went partially like this:

> . . . a big, vigorous, rowdy, ill-shaped, and repellent book, so strong and so weak, so adroit and so fumbling, that only a writer of the greatest and most reckless talent could have flung it between covers.

It's one of the three or four lines I've thought perceptive in all the reviews of my books. That Malcolm Cowley used one of the same words in saying *The Deer Park* was "serious and reckless" is also, I think, interesting, for reckless the book was—and two critics, anyway, had the instinct to feel it.

One note appeared in many reviews. The strongest statement of it was by John Hutchens in The New York Daily *Herald Tribune:*

. . . the original version reputedly was more or less rewritten and certain materials eliminated that were deemed too erotic for public consumption. And, with that, a book that might at least have made a certain reputation as a large shocker wound up as a cipher . . .

I was bothered to the point of writing a letter to the twenty-odd newspapers which reflected this idea. What bothered me was that I could never really prove I had not "eliminated" the book. Over the years all too many readers would have some hazy impression that I had disemboweled large pieces of the best meat, perspiring in a coward's sweat, a publisher's directive in my ear. (For that matter, I still get an occasional letter which asks if it is possible to see the unbowdlerized *Deer Park*.) Part of the cost of touching the Rinehart galleys was to start those rumors, and in fact I was not altogether free of the accusation, as I have tried to show. Even the six lines which so displeased Rinehart had been altered a bit; I had shown them once to a friend whose opinion I respected, and he remarked that while it was impossible to accept the sort of order Rinehart had laid down, still a phrase like the "fount of power" had a Victorian heaviness about it. Well, that was true, it was out of character for O'Shaugnessy's new style and so I altered it to the "thumb of power" and then other changes became desirable, and the curious are invited to compare the two versions of this particular passage in this collection,* but the mistake I made was to take a small aesthetic gain on those six lines and lose a larger clarity about a principle.

What more is there to say? The book moved fairly well, it climbed to seven and then to six on *The New York Times* best-

*Rinehart page proof: "Tentatively, she reached out a hand to caress his hair, and at that moment Herman Teppis opened his legs and let Bobby slip to the floor. At the expression of surprise on her face, he began to laugh. 'Just like this, sweetie,' he said, and down he looked at that frightened female mouth, facsimile of all those smiling lips he had seen so ready to be nourished at the fount of power and with a shudder he started to talk. 'That's a good girlie, that's a good girlie, that's a good girlie,' he said in a mild lost little voice, 'you're just an angel darling, and I like you, and you understand, you're my darling darling, oh that's the ticket,' said Teppis."

Putnam page proof: "Tentatively, she reached out a hand to finger his hair, and at that moment Herman Teppis opened his legs and let Bobby fall to the floor. At that expression of surprise on her face, he began to laugh. 'Don't you worry, sweetie,' he said, and down he looked at that frightened female mouth, facsimile of all those smiling lips he had seen so ready to serve at the thumb of power, and with a cough, he started to talk. 'That's a good girlie, that's a good girlie, that's a good girlie,' he said in a mild little voice, 'you're an angel darling, and I like you, you're my darling darling, oh that's the ticket,' said Teppis."

seller list, stayed there for a week or two, and then slipped down. By Christmas, the tone of the *Park* and the Christmas spirit being not all that congenial, it was just about off the lists forever. It did well, however; it would have reached as high as three or two or even to number one if it had come out in June and then been measured against the low sales of summer, for it sold over fifty thousand copies after returns which surprised a good many in publishing, as well as disappointing a few, including myself. I discovered that I had been poised for an enormous sale or a failure—a middling success was cruel to take. Week after week I kept waiting for the book to erupt into some dramatic change of pace which would send it up in sales instead of down, but that never happened. I was left with a draw, not busted, not made, and since I was empty at the time, worn-out with work, waiting for the quick transfusions of a generous success, the steady sales of the book left me deeply depressed. Having reshaped my words with an intensity of feeling I had not known before, I could not understand why others were not overcome with my sense of life, of sex, and of sadness. Like a starved revolutionary in a garret, I had compounded out of need and fever and vision and fear nothing less than a madman's confidence in the identity of my being and the wants of all others, and it was a new dull load to lift and to bear, this knowledge that I had no magic so great as to hasten the time of the apocalypse, but that instead I would be open like all others to the attritions of half-success and small failure. Something God-like in my confidence began to leave, and I was reduced in dimension if now less a boy. I knew I had failed to bid on the biggest hand I ever held.

Now a few years have gone by, more years than I thought, and I have begun to work up another hand, a new book which will be the proper book of an outlaw, and so not publishable in any easy or legal way. Two excerpts from this novel come later in this collection, and therefore I'll say here only that O'Shaugnessy will be one of the three heroes, and that if I'm to go all the way this time, the odds are that my beat senses will have to do the work without the fires and the wastes of the minor drugs.

But that is for later, and the proper end to this account is the advertisement I took in *The Village Voice*. It was bought in November 1955, a month after publication, it was put together by me and paid for by me, and it was my way I now suppose of saying good-by to the pleasure of a quick triumph, of making my apologies for the bad flaws in the bravest effort I had yet pulled out of myself, and certainly for declaring to the world (in a small way, mean pity) that I no longer gave a sick dog's drop for the wisdom, the reliability, and the authority of the public's literary mind, those creeps and old ladies of vested reviewing.

Besides, I had the tender notion—believe it if you will—that the ad might after all do its work and excite some people to buy the book.

But here it is:

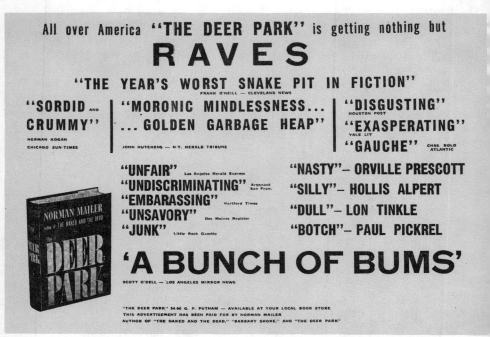

The White Negro

SUPERFICIAL REFLECTIONS ON THE HIPSTER

1

Our search for the rebels of the generation led us to the hipster. The hipster is an *enfant terrible* turned inside out. In character with his time, he is trying to get back at the conformists by lying low . . . You can't interview a hipster because his main goal is to keep out of a society which, he thinks, is trying to make everyone over in its own image. He takes marijuana because it supplies him with experiences that can't be shared with "squares." He may affect a broad-brimmed hat or a zoot suit, but usually he prefers to skulk unmarked. The hipster may be a jazz musician; he is rarely an artist, almost never a writer. He may earn his living as a petty criminal, a hobo, a carnival roustabout or a free-lance moving man in Greenwich Village, but some hipsters have found a safe refuge in the upper income brackets as television comics or movie actors. (The late James Dean, for one, was a hipster hero.) . . . It is tempting to describe the hipster in psychiatric terms as infantile, but the style of his infantilism is a sign of the times. He does not try to enforce his will on others, Napoleon-fashion, but contents himself with a magical omnipotence never disproved because never tested. . . . As the only extreme nonconformist of his generation, he exercises a powerful if underground appeal for conformists, through newspaper accounts of his delinquencies, his structureless jazz, and his emotive grunt words.

— "Born 1930: The Unlost Generation"
by Caroline Bird
Harper's Bazaar, Feb. 1957

Probably, we will never be able to determine the psychic havoc of the concentration camps and the atom bomb upon the unconscious mind of almost everyone alive in these years. For the first time in civilized history, perhaps for the first time in all of history, we have been forced to live with the suppressed knowledge that the smallest facets of our personality or the most minor projection of our ideas, or indeed the absence of ideas and the absence of personality could mean equally well that we might still be doomed to die as a cipher in some vast statistical operation in which our teeth would be counted, and our hair would be saved, but our death itself would be unknown, unhonored, and unremarked, a death which could not follow with dignity as a possible consequence to serious actions we had chosen, but rather a death by *deus ex machina* in a gas chamber or a radioactive city; and so if in the midst of civilization—that civilization founded upon the Faustian urge to dominate nature by mastering time, mastering the links of social cause and effect—in the middle of an economic civilization founded upon the confidence that time could indeed be subjected to our will, our psyche was subjected itself to the intolerable anxiety that death being causeless, life was causeless as well, and time deprived of cause and effect had come to a stop.

The Second World War presented a mirror to the human condition which blinded anyone who looked into it. For if tens of millions were killed in concentration camps out of the inexorable agonies and contractions of super-states founded upon the always insoluble contradictions of injustice, one was then obliged also to see that no matter how crippled and perverted an image of man was the society he had created, it was nonetheless his creation, his collective creation (at least his collective creation from the past) and if society was so murderous, then who could ignore the most hideous of questions about his own nature?

Worse. One could hardly maintain the courage to be individual, to speak with one's own voice, for the years in which one could complacently accept oneself as part of an elite by being a radical were forever gone. A man knew that when he dissented, he gave a note upon his life which could be called in any year of overt crisis. No wonder then that these have been the years of conformity and depression. A stench of fear has come out of every pore of American life, and we suffer from a collective failure of nerve. The only courage, with rare exceptions, that we have been witness to, has been the isolated courage of isolated people.

2

It is on this bleak scene that a phenomenon has appeared: the American existentialist—the hipster, the man who knows that if our collective condition is to live with instant death by atomic war, relatively quick death by the State as *l'univers concentrationnaire*, or with a slow death by conformity with every creative and rebellious instinct stifled (at what damage to the mind and the heart and the liver and the nerves no research foundation for cancer will discover in a hurry), if the fate of twentieth-century man is to live with death from adolescence to premature senescence, why then the only life-giving answer is to accept the terms of death, to live with death as immediate danger, to divorce oneself from society, to exist without roots, to set out on that uncharted journey into the rebellious imperatives of the self. In short, whether the life is criminal or not, the decision is to encourage the psychopath in oneself, to explore that domain of experience where security is boredom and therefore sickness, and one exists in the present, in that enormous present which is without past or future, memory or planned intention, the life where a man must go until he is beat, where he must gamble with his energies through all those small or large crises of courage and unforeseen situations which beset his day, where he must be with it or doomed not to swing. The unstated essence of Hip, its psychopathic brilliance, quivers with the knowledge that new kinds of victories increase one's power for new kinds of perception; and defeats, the wrong kind of defeats, attack the body and imprison one's energy until one is jailed in the prison air of other people's habits, other people's defeats, boredom, quiet desperation, and muted icy self-destroying rage. One is Hip or one is Square (the alternative which each new generation coming into American life is beginning to feel), one is a rebel or one conforms, one is a frontiersman in the Wild West of American night life, or else a Square cell, trapped in the totalitarian tissues of American society, doomed willy-nilly to conform if one is to succeed.

A totalitarian society makes enormous demands on the courage of men, and a partially totalitarian society makes even greater demands, for the general anxiety is greater. Indeed if one is to be a man, almost any kind of unconventional action often takes disproportionate courage. So it is no accident that the source of Hip is the Negro for he has been living on the margin between totalitarianism and democracy for two centuries. But the presence of Hip as a working philosophy in the sub-worlds of American life is probably due to jazz, and its knifelike entrance into culture, its subtle but so penetrating influence on an avant-garde generation — that postwar generation of adventurers who (some consciously, some by osmosis) had absorbed the lessons of disillusionment and disgust of the twenties, the depression, and the war. Sharing a collective disbelief in the words of men who had too much money and controlled too many things, they knew almost as powerful a disbelief in the socially monolithic ideas of the single mate, the solid family and the respectable love life. If the intellectual antecedents of this generation can be traced to such separate influences as D. H. Lawrence, Henry Miller, and Wilhelm Reich, the viable philosophy of Hemingway fit most of their facts: in a bad world, as he was to say over and over again (while taking time out from his parvenu snobbery and dedicated gourmandize), in a bad world there is no love nor mercy nor charity nor justice unless a man can keep his courage, and this indeed fitted some of the facts. What fitted the need of the adventurer even more precisely was Hemingway's categorical imperative that what made him feel good became therefore The Good.

So no wonder that in certain cities of America, in New York of course, and New Orleans, in Chicago and San Francisco and Los Angeles, in such American cities as Paris and Mexico, D.F., this particular part of a generation was attracted to what the Negro had to offer. In such places as Greenwich Village, a ménage-à-trois was completed—the bohemian and the juvenile delinquent came face-to-face with the Negro, and the hipster was a fact in American life. If marijuana was the wedding ring, the child was the language of Hip for its argot gave expression to abstract states of feeling which all could share, at least all who were Hip. And in this wedding of the white and the black it was the Negro who brought the cultural dowry. Any Negro who wishes to live must live with danger from his first day, and no experience can ever be casual to him, no Negro can saunter down a street with any real certainty that violence will not visit him on his walk. The cameos of security for the average white: mother and the home, job and the family, are not even a mockery to millions of Negroes; they are impossible. The Negro has the simplest of alternatives: live a life of constant humility or ever-threatening danger. In such a pass where paranoia is as vital to survival as blood, the Negro had stayed alive and begun to grow by following the need of his body where he could. Knowing in the cells of his existence that life was war, nothing but war, the Negro (all exceptions admitted) could rarely afford the sophisticated inhibitions of civilization, and so he kept for his survival the art of the primitive, he lived in the enormous present, he subsisted for his Saturday night kicks, relinquishing the pleasures of the mind for the more obligatory pleasures of the body, and in his music he gave voice to the character and quality of his existence, to his rage and the infinite variations of joy, lust, languor, growl, cramp, pinch, scream and despair of his orgasm. For jazz is orgasm, it is the music of orgasm, good orgasm and bad, and so it spoke across a nation, it had the communication of art even where it was watered, perverted, corrupted, and almost killed, it spoke in no matter what laundered popular way of instantaneous existential states to which some whites could respond, it was indeed a communication by art because it said, "I feel this, and now you do too."

So there was a new breed of adventurers, urban adventurers who drifted out at night looking for action with a black man's code to fit their facts. The hipster had absorbed the existentialist synapses of the Negro, and for practical purposes could be considered a white Negro.

To be an existentialist, one must be able to feel oneself—one must know one's desires, one's rages, one's anguish, one must be aware of the character of one's frustration and know what would satisfy it. The overcivilized man can be an existentialist only if it is chic, and deserts it quickly for the next chic. To be a real existentialist (Sartre admittedly to the contrary) one must be religious, one must have one's sense of the "purpose"—whatever the purpose may be—but a life which is directed by one's faith in the necessity of action is a life committed to the notion that the substratum of existence is the search, the end meaningful but mysterious; it is impossible to live such a life unless one's emotions provide their profound conviction. Only the French, alienated beyond alienation from their unconscious could welcome an existential philosophy without ever feeling it at all; indeed only a Frenchman by declaring that the unconscious did not exist could then proceed to explore the delicate involutions of consciousness, the microscopically sensuous and all but ineffable *frissons* of mental becoming, in order finally to create the theology of atheism and so submit that in a world of absurdities the existential absurdity is most coherent.

In the dialogue between the atheist and the mystic, the atheist is on the side of life, rational life, undialectical life—since he conceives of death as emptiness, he can, no matter how weary or despairing, wish for nothing but more life; his pride is that he does not transpose his weakness and spiritual fatigue into a romantic longing for death, for such appreciation of death is then all too capable of being elaborated by his imagination into a universe of meaningful structure and moral orchestration.

Yet this masculine argument can mean very little for the mystic. The mystic can accept the atheist's description of his weakness, he can agree that his mysticism was a response to despair. And yet . . . and yet his argument is that he, the mystic, is the one finally who has chosen to live with death, and so death is his experience and not the atheist's, and the atheist by eschewing the limitless dimensions of profound despair has rendered himself incapable to judge the experience. The real argument which the mystic must always advance is the very intensity of his private vision—his argument depends from the vision precisely because what was felt in the vision is so extraordinary that no rational argument, no hypotheses of "oceanic feelings" and certainly no skeptical reductions can explain away what has become for him the reality more real than the reality of closely reasoned logic. His inner experience of the possibilities within death is his logic. So, too, for the existentialist. And the psychopath. And the saint and the bullfighter and the lover. The common denominator for all of them is their burning consciousness of the present, exactly that incandescent consciousness which the possibilities within death has opened for them. There is a depth of desperation to the condition which enables one to remain in life only by engaging death, but the reward is their knowledge that what is happening at each instant of the electric present is good or bad for them, good or bad for their cause, their love, their action, their need.

It is this knowledge which provides the curious community of feeling in the world of the hipster, a muted cool religious revival to be sure, but the element which is exciting, disturbing, nightmarish perhaps, is that incompatibles have come to bed, the inner life and the violent life, the orgy and the dream of love, the desire to murder and the desire to create, a dialectical conception of existence with a lust for power, a dark, romantic, and yet undeniably dynamic view of existence for it sees every man and woman as moving individually through each moment of life forward into growth or backward into death.

3

It may be fruitful to consider the hipster a philosophical psychopath, a man interested not only in the dangerous imperatives of his psychopathy but in codifying, at least for himself, the suppositions on which his inner universe is constructed. By this premise the hipster is a psychopath, and yet not a psychopath but the negation of the psychopath, for he possesses the narcissistic detachment of the philosopher, that absorption in the recessive nuances of one's own motive which is so alien to the unreasoning drive of the psychopath. In this country where new millions of psychopaths are developed each year, stamped with the mint of our contradictory popular culture (where sex is sin and yet sex is paradise), it is as if there has been room already for the development of the antithetical psychopath who extrapolates from his own condition, from the inner certainty that his rebellion is just, a radical vision of the universe which thus separates him from the general ignorance, reactionary prejudice, and self-doubt of the more conventional psychopath. Having converted his unconscious experience into much conscious knowledge, the hipster has shifted the focus of his desire from immediate gratification toward that wider passion for future power which is the mark of civilized man. Yet with an irreducible difference. For Hip is the sophistication of the wise primitive in a giant jungle, and so its appeal is still beyond the civilized man. If there are ten million Americans who are more or less psychopathic (and the figure is most modest), there are probably not more than one hundred thousand men and women who consciously see themselves as hipsters, but their importance is that they are an elite with the potential ruthlessness of an elite, and a language most adolescents can understand instinctively, for the hipster's intense view of existence matches their experience and their desire to rebel.

Before one can say more about the hipster, there is obviously much to be said about the psychic state of the psychopath—or, clinically, the psychopathic personality. Now, for reasons which may be more curious than the similarity of the words, even many people with a psychoanalytical orientation often confuse the psychopath with the psychotic. Yet the terms are polar. The psychotic is legally insane, the psychopath is not; the psychotic is almost always incapable of discharging in physical acts the rage of his frustration, while the psychopath at his extreme is virtually as incapable of restraining his violence. The psychotic lives in so misty a world that what is happening at each moment of his life is not very real to him whereas the psychopath seldom knows any reality greater than the face, the voice, the being of the particular people among whom he may find himself at any moment. Sheldon and Eleanor Glueck describe him as follows:

> The psychopath . . . can be distinguished from the person sliding into or clambering out of a "true psychotic" state by the long tough persistence of his anti-social attitude and behaviour and the absence of hallucinations, delusions, manic flight of ideas, confusion, disorientation, and other dramatic signs of psychosis.

The late Robert Lindner, one of the few experts on the subject, in his book *Rebel Without a Cause—The Hypnoanalysis of a Criminal Psychopath* presented part of his definition in this way:

> . . . the psychopath is a rebel without a cause, an agitator without a slogan, a revolutionary without a program: in other words, his rebelliousness is aimed to achieve goals satisfactory to himself alone; he is incapable of exertions for the sake of others. All his efforts, hidden under no matter what disguise, represent investments designed to satisfy his immediate wishes and desires. . . . The psychopath, like the child, cannot delay the pleasures of gratification; and this trait is one of his underlying, universal characteristics. He cannot wait upon erotic gratification which convention demands should be preceded by the chase before the kill: he must rape. He cannot wait upon the development of prestige in society: his egoistic ambitions lead him to leap into headlines by daring

performances. Like a red thread the predominance of this mechanism for immediate satisfaction runs through the history of every psychopath. It explains not only his behaviour but also the violent nature of his acts.

Yet even Lindner who was the most imaginative and most sympathetic of the psychoanalysts who have studied the psychopathic personality was not ready to project himself into the essential sympathy — which is that the psychopath may indeed be the perverted and dangerous front-runner of a new kind of personality which could become the central expression of human nature before the twentieth century is over. For the psychopath is better adapted to dominate those mutually contradictory inhibitions upon violence and love which civilization has exacted of us, and if it be remembered that not every psychopath is an extreme case, and that the condition of psychopathy is present in a host of people including many politicians, professional soldiers, newspaper columnists, entertainers, artists, jazz musicians, call-girls, promiscuous homosexuals and half the executives of Hollywood, television, and advertising, it can be seen that there are aspects of psychopathy which already exert considerable cultural influence.

What characterizes almost every psychopath and part-psychopath is that they are trying to create a new nervous system for themselves. Generally we are obliged to act with a nervous system which has been formed from infancy, and which carries in the style of its circuits the very contradictions of our parents and our early milieu. Therefore, we are obliged, most of us, to meet the tempo of the present and the future with reflexes and rhythms which come from the past. It is not only the "dead weight of the institutions of the past" but indeed the inefficient and often antiquated nervous circuits of the past which strangle our potentiality for responding to new possibilities which might be exciting for our individual growth.

Through most of modern history, "sublimation" was possible: at the expense of expressing only a small portion of oneself, that small portion could be expressed intensely. But sublimation depends on a reasonable tempo to history. If the collective life of a generation has moved too quickly, the "past" by which particular men and women of that generation may function is not, let us say, thirty years old, but relatively a hundred or two hundred years old. And so the nervous system is overstressed beyond the possibility of such compromises as sublimation, especially since the stable middle-class values so prerequisite to sublimation have been virtually destroyed in our time, at least as nourishing values free of confusion or doubt. In such a crisis of accelerated historical tempo and deteriorated values, neurosis tends to be replaced by psychopathy, and the success of psychoanalysis (which even ten years ago gave promise of becoming a direct major force) diminishes because of its inbuilt and characteristic incapacity to handle patients more complex, more experienced, or more adventurous than the analyst himself. In practice, psychoanalysis has by now become all too often no more than a psychic blood-letting. The patient is not so much changed as aged, and the infantile fantasies which he is encouraged to express are condemned to exhaust themselves against the analyst's nonresponsive reactions. The result for all too many patients is a diminution, a "tranquilizing" of their most interesting qualities and vices. The patient is indeed not so much altered as worn out—less bad, less good, less bright, less willful, less destructive, less creative. He is thus able to conform to that contradictory and unbearable society which first created his neurosis. He can conform to what he loathes because he no longer has the passion to feel loathing so intensely.

The psychopath is notoriously difficult to analyze because the fundamental decision of his nature is to try to live the infantile fantasy, and in this decision (given the dreary alternative of psychoanalysis) there may be a certain instinctive wisdom. For there is a dialectic to changing one's nature, the dialectic which underlies all psychoanalytic method: it is the knowledge that if one is to change one's habits, one must go back to the source of their creation, and so the psychopath exploring backward along the road of the homosexual, the orgiast, the drug-addict, the rapist, the robber and the murderer seeks to find those violent parallels to the violent and often hopeless contradictions he knew as an infant and as a child. For if he has the courage to meet the parallel situation at the moment when he is ready, then he has a chance to act as he has never acted before, and in satisfying the frustration—if he can succeed— he may then pass by symbolic substitute through the locks of incest. In thus giving expression to the buried infant in himself, he can lessen the tension of those infantile desires and so free himself to remake a bit of his nervous system. Like the neurotic he is looking for the opportunity to grow up a second time, but the psychopath knows instinctively that to express a forbidden impulse actively is far more beneficial to him than merely to confess the desire in the safety of a doctor's room. The psychopath is ordinately ambitious, too ambitious ever to trade his warped brilliant conception of his possible victories in life for the grim if peaceful attrition of the analyst's couch. So his associational journey into the past is lived out in the theatre of the present, and he exists for those charged situations where his senses are so alive that he can be aware actively (as the analysand is aware passively) of what his habits are, and how he can change them. The strength of the psychopath is that he knows (where most of us can only guess) what is good for him and what is bad for him at exactly those instants when an old crippling habit has become so attacked by experience that the potentiality exists to change it, to replace a negative and empty fear with an outward action, even if—and here I obey the logic of the extreme psychopath—even if the fear is of himself, and the action is to murder. The psychopath murders—if he has the courage—out of the necessity to purge his violence, for if he cannot empty his hatred then he cannot love, his being is frozen with implacable self-hatred for his cowardice. (It can of course be suggested that it takes little courage for two strong eighteen-year-old hoodlums, let us say, to beat in the brains of a candy-store keeper, and indeed the act—even by the logic of the psychopath—is not likely to prove very therapeutic, for the victim is not an immediate equal. Still, courage of a sort is necessary, for one murders not only a weak fifty-year-old man but an institution as well, one violates private property, one enters into a new relation with the police and introduces a dangerous element into one's life. The hoodlum is therefore daring the unknown, and so no matter how brutal the act, it is not altogether cowardly.)

At bottom, the drama of the psychopath is that he seeks love. Not love as the search for a mate, but love as the search for an orgasm more apocalyptic than the one which preceded it. Orgasm is his therapy—he knows at the seed of his being that good orgasm opens his possibilities and bad orgasm imprisons him. But in this search, the psychopath becomes an embodiment of the extreme contradictions of the society which formed his character, and the apocalyptic orgasm often remains as remote as the Holy Grail, for there are clusters and nests and ambushes of violence in his own necessities and in the imperatives and retaliations of the men and women among whom he lives his life, so that even as he drains his hatred in one act or another, so the conditions of his life create it anew in him until the drama of his movements bears a sardonic resemblance to the frog who climbed a few feet in the well only to drop back again.

Yet there is this to be said for the search after the good orgasm: when one lives in a civilized world, and still can enjoy none of the cultural nectar of such a world because the paradoxes on which civilization is built demand that there remain a cultureless and alienated bottom of exploitable human material, then the logic of becoming a sexual outlaw (if one's psychological roots are bedded in the bottom) is that one has at least a running competitive chance to be physically healthy so long as one stays alive. It is therefore no accident that psychopathy is most prevalent with the Negro. Hated from outside and therefore hating himself, the Negro was forced into the position of exploring all those moral wildernesses of civilized life which the Square automatically condemns as delinquent or evil or immature or morbid or self-destructive or corrupt. (Actually the terms have equal weight. Depending on the telescope of the cultural clique from which the Square surveys the universe, "evil" or "immature" are equally strong terms of condemnation.) But the Negro, not being privileged to gratify his self-esteem with the heady satisfactions of categorical condemnation, chose to move instead in that other direction where all situations are equally valid, and in the worst of perversion, promiscuity, pimpery, drug addiction, rape, razor-slash, bottle-break, what-have-you, the Negro discovered and elaborated a morality of the bottom, an ethical differentiation between the good and the bad in every human activity from the go-getter pimp (as opposed to the lazy one) to the relatively dependable pusher or prostitute. Add to this, the cunning of their language, the abstract ambiguous alternatives in which from the danger of their oppression they learned to speak ("Well, now, man, like I'm looking for a cat to turn me on . . ."), add even more the profound sensitivity of the Negro jazzman who was the cultural mentor of a people, and it is not too difficult to believe that the language of Hip which evolved was an artful language, tested and shaped by an intense experience and therefore different in kind from white slang, as different as the special obscenity of the soldier, which in its emphasis upon "ass" as the soul and "shit" as circumstance, was able to express the existential states of the enlisted man. What makes Hip a special language is that it cannot really be taught—if one shares none of the experiences of elation and exhaustion which it is equipped to describe, then it seems merely arch or vulgar or irritating. It is a pictorial language, but pictorial like nonobjective art, imbued with the dialectic of small but intense change, a language for the microcosm, in this case, man, for it takes the immediate experiences of any passing man and magnifies the dynamic of his movements, not specifically but abstractly so that he is seen more as a vector in a network of forces than as a static character in a crystallized field. (Which latter is the practical view of the snob.) For example, there is real difficulty in trying to find a Hip substitute for "stubborn." The best possibility I can come up with is: "That cat will never come off his groove, dad." But groove implies movement, narrow movement but motion nonetheless. There is really no way to describe someone who does not move at all. Even a creep does move—if at a pace exasperatingly more slow than the pace of the cool cats.

4

Like children, hipsters are fighting for the sweet, and their language is a set of subtle indications of their success or failure in the competition for pleasure. Unstated but obvious is the social sense that there is not nearly enough sweet for everyone. And so the sweet goes only to the victor, the best, the most, the man who knows the most about how to find his energy and how not to lose it. The emphasis is on energy because the psychopath and the hipster are nothing without it since they do not have the protection of a position or a class to rely on when they have overextended themselves. So the language of Hip is a language of energy, how it is found, how it is lost.

But let us see. I have jotted down perhaps a dozen words, the Hip perhaps most in use and most likely to last with the minimum of variation. The words are man, go, put down, make, beat, cool, swing, with it, crazy. dig, flip, creep, hip, square. They serve a variety of purposes and the nuance of the voice uses the nuance of the situation to convey the subtle contextual difference. If the hipster moves through his life on a constant search with glimpses of Mecca in many a turn of his experience (Mecca being the apocalyptic orgasm) and if everyone in the civilized world is at least in some small degree a sexual cripple, the hipster lives with the knowledge of how he is sexually crippled and where he is sexually alive, and the faces of experience which life presents to him each day are engaged, dismissed or avoided as his need directs and his lifemanship makes possible. For life is a contest between people in which the victor generally recuperates quickly and the loser takes long to mend, a perpetual competition of colliding explorers in which one must grow or else pay more for remaining the same (pay in sickness, or depression, or anguish for the lost opportunity), but pay or grow.

Therefore one finds words like go, and make it, and with it, and swing: "Go" with its sense that after hours or days or months or years of monotony, boredom, and depression one has finally had one's chance, one has amassed enough energy to meet an exciting opportunity with all one's present talents for the flip (up or down) and so one is ready to go, ready to gamble. Movement is always to be preferred to inaction. In motion a man has a chance, his body is warm, his instincts are quick, and when the crisis comes, whether of love or violence, he can make it, he can win, he can release a little more energy for himself since he hates himself a little less, he can make a little better nervous system, make it a little more possible to go again, to go faster next time and so make more and thus find more people with whom he can swing. For to swing is to communicate, is to convey the rhythms of one's own being to a lover, a friend, or an audience, and—equally necessary—be able to feel the rhythms of their response. To swing with the rhythms of another is to enrich oneself—the conception of the learning process as dug by Hip is that one cannot really learn until one contains within oneself the implicit rhythm of the subject or the person. As an example, I remember once hearing a Negro friend have an intellectual discussion at a party for half an hour with a white girl who was a few years out of college. The Negro literally could not read or write, but he had an extraordinary ear and a fine sense of mimicry. So as the girl spoke, he would detect the particular formal uncertainties in her argument, and in a pleasant (if slightly Southern) English accent, he would respond to one or another facet of her doubts. When she would finish what she felt was a particularly well-articulated idea, he would smile privately and say, "Other-direction . . . do you really believe in that?"

"Well . . . No," the girl would stammer, "now that you get down to it, there is something disgusting about it to me," and she would be off again for five more minutes.

Of course the Negro was not learning anything about the merits and demerits of the argument, but he was learning a great deal about a type of girl he had never met before, and that was what he wanted. Being unable to read or write, he could hardly be interested in ideas nearly as much as in lifemanship, and so he eschewed any attempt to obey the precision or lack of precision in the girl's language, and instead sensed her character (and the values of her social type) by swinging with the nuances of her voice.

So to swing is to be able to learn, and by learning take a step toward making it, toward creating. What is to be created is not nearly so important as the hipster's belief that when he really makes it, he will be able to turn his hand to anything, even to self-discipline. What he must do before that is find his courage at the moment of violence, or equally make it in the act of love, find a little more between his woman and himself, or indeed between his mate and himself (since many hipsters are bisexual), but paramount, imperative, is the necessity to make it because in making it, one is making the new habit, unearthing the new talent which the old frustration denied.

Whereas if you goof (the ugliest word in Hip), if you lapse back into being a frightened stupid child, or if you flip, if you lose your control, reveal the buried weaker more feminine part of your nature, then it is more difficult to swing the next time, your ear is less alive, your bad and energy-wasting habits are further confirmed, you are farther away from being with it. But to be with it is to have grace, is to be closer to the secrets of that inner unconscious life which will nourish you if you can hear it, for you are then nearer to that God which every hipster believes is located in the senses of his body, that trapped, mutilated and nonetheless megalomaniacal God who is It, who is energy, life, sex, force, the Yoga's *prana*, the Reichian's orgone, Lawrence's "blood," Hemingway's "good," the Shavian life-force; "It"; God; not the God of the churches but the unachievable whisper of mystery within the sex, the paradise of limitless energy and perception just beyond the next wave of the next orgasm.

To which a cool cat might reply, "Crazy, man!"

Because, after all, what I have offered above is an hypothesis, no more, and there is not the hipster alive who is not absorbed in his own tumultuous hypotheses. Mine is interesting, mine is way out (on the avenue of the mystery along the road to "It") but still I am just one cat in a world of cool cats, and everything interesting is crazy, or at least so the Squares who do not know how to swing would say.

(And yet crazy is also the self-protective irony of the hipster. Living with questions and not with answers, he is so different in his isolation and in the far reach of his imagination from almost everyone with whom he deals in the outer world of the Square, and meets generally so much enmity, competition, and hatred in the world of Hip, that his isolation is always in danger of turning upon itself, and leaving him indeed just that, crazy.)

If, however, you agree with my hypothesis, if you as a cat are way out too, and we are in the same groove (the universe now being glimpsed as a series of ever-extending radii from the center), why then you say simply, "I dig," because neither knowledge nor imagination comes easily, it is buried in the pain of one's forgotten experience, and so one must work to find it, one must occasionally exhaust oneself by digging into the self in order to perceive the outside. And indeed it is essential to dig the most, for if you do not dig you lose your superiority over the Square, and so you are less likely to be cool (to be in control of a situation because you have swung where the Square has not, or because you have allowed to come to consciousness a pain, a guilt, a shame or a desire which the other has not had the courage to face). To be cool is to be equipped, and if you are equipped it is more difficult for the next cat who comes along to put you down. And of course one can hardly afford to be put down too often, or one is beat, one has lost one's confidence, one has lost one's will, one is impotent in the world of action and so closer to the demeaning flip of becoming a

queer, or indeed closer to dying, and therefore it is even more difficult to recover enough energy to try to make it again, because once
a cat is beat he has nothing to give, and no one is interested any
longer in making it with him. This is the terror of the hipster—to be
beat—because once the sweet of sex has deserted him, he still
cannot give up the search. It is not granted to the hipster to grow
old gracefully—he has been captured too early by the oldest dream
of power, the gold fountain of Ponce de León, the fountain of
youth where the gold is in the orgasm.

To be beat is therefore a flip, it is a situation beyond one's experience, impossible to anticipate—which indeed in the circular vocabulary of Hip is still another meaning for flip, but then I have
given just a few of the connotations of these words. Like most primitive vocabularies each word is a prime symbol and serves a dozen
or a hundred functions of communication in the instinctive dialectic through which the hipster perceives his experience, that dialectic of the instantaneous differentials of existence in which one
is forever moving forward into more or retreating into less.

It is impossible to conceive a new philosophy until one creates a
new language, but a new popular language (while it must implicitly
contain a new philosophy) does not necessarily present its philosophy overtly. It can be asked then what really is unique in the life-
view of Hip which raises its argot above the passing verbal whim-
sies of the bohemian or the lumpenproletariat.

The answer would be in the psychopathic element of Hip which
has almost no interest in viewing human nature, or better, in judg-
ing human nature, from a set of standards conceived a priori to the
experience, standards inherited from the past. Since Hip sees
every answer as posing immediately a new alternative, a new question, its emphasis is on complexity rather than simplicity (such
complexity that its language without the illumination of the voice
and the articulation of the face and body remains hopelessly in-
communicative). Given its emphasis on complexity, Hip abdicates
from any conventional moral responsibility because it would argue
that the results of our actions are unforeseeable, and so we cannot
know if we do good or bad, we cannot even know (in the Joycean
sense of the good and the bad) whether we have given energy to
another, and indeed if we could, there would still be no idea of
what ultimately the other would do with it.

Therefore, men are not seen as good or bad (that they are good-
and-bad is taken for granted) but rather each man is glimpsed as a
collection of possibilities, some more possible than others (the
view of character implicit in Hip) and some humans are considered
more capable than others of reaching more possibilities within

themselves in less time, provided, and this is the dynamic, provided the particular character can swing at the right time. And here arises the sense of context which differentiates Hip from a Square view of character. Hip sees the context as generally dominating the man, dominating him because his character is less significant than the context in which he must function. Since it is arbitrarily five times more demanding of one's energy to accomplish even an inconsequential action in an unfavorable context than a favorable one, man is then not only his character but his context, since the success or failure of an action in a given context reacts upon the character and therefore affects what the character will be in the next context. What dominates both character and context is the energy available at the moment of intense context.

Character being thus seen as perpetually ambivalent and dynamic enters then into an absolute relativity where there are no truths other than the isolated truths of what each observer feels at each instant of his existence. To take a perhaps unjustified metaphysical extrapolation, it is as if the universe which has usually existed conceptually as a Fact (even if the Fact were Berkeley's God) but a Fact which it was the aim of all science and philosophy to reveal, becomes instead a changing reality whose laws are remade at each instant by everything living, but most particularly man, man raised to a neo-medieval summit where the truth is not what one has felt yesterday or what one expects to feel tomorrow but rather truth is no more nor less than what one feels at each instant in the perpetual climax of the present.

What is consequent therefore is the divorce of man from his values, the liberation of the self from the Super-Ego of society. The only Hip morality (but of course it is an ever-present morality) is to do what one feels whenever and wherever it is possible, and — this is how the war of the Hip and the Square begins — to be engaged in one primal battle: to open the limits of the possible for oneself, for oneself alone, because that is one's need. Yet in widening the arena of the possible, one widens it reciprocally for others as well, so that the nihilistic fulfillment of each man's desire contains its antithesis of human co-operation.

If the ethic reduces to Know Thyself and Be Thyself, what makes it radically different from Socratic moderation with its stern conservative respect for the experience of the past is that the Hip ethic is immoderation, childlike in its adoration of the present (and indeed to respect the past means that one must also respect such ugly consequences of the past as the collective murders of the State). It is this adoration of the present which contains the affirmation of Hip, because its ultimate logic surpasses even the unforgettable solution of the Marquis de Sade to sex, private property, and the family, that all men and women have absolute but temporary rights over the bodies of all other men and women — the nihilism of Hip proposes as its final tendency that every social restraint and category be removed, and the affirmation implicit in the proposal is that man would then prove to be more creative than murderous and so would not destroy himself. Which is exactly what separates Hip from the authoritarian philosophies which now appeal to the conservative and liberal temper — what haunts the middle of the twentieth century is that faith in man has been lost, and the appeal of authority has been that it would restrain us from ourselves. Hip, which would return us to ourselves, at no matter what price in individual violence, is the affirmation of the barbarian, for it requires a primitive passion about human nature to believe that individual acts of violence are always to be preferred to the collective violence of the State; it takes literal faith in the creative possibilities of the human being to envisage acts of violence as the catharsis which prepares growth.

Whether the hipster's desire for absolute sexual freedom contains any genuinely radical conception of a different world is of course another matter, and it is possible, since the hipster lives with his hatred, that many of them are the material for an elite of storm troopers ready to follow the first truly magnetic leader whose view of mass murder is phrased in a language which reaches their emotions. But given the desperation of his condition as a psychic outlaw, the hipster is equally a candidate for the most reactionary and most radical of movements, and so it is just as possible that many hipsters will come — if the crisis deepens — to a radical comprehension of the horror of society, for even as the radical has had his incommunicable dissent confirmed in his experience by precisely the frustration, the denied opportunities, and the bitter years which his ideas have cost him, so the sexual adventurer deflected from his goal by the implacable animosity of a society constructed to deny the sexual radical as well, may yet come to an equally bitter comprehension of the slow relentless inhumanity of the conservative power which controls him from without and from within. And in being so controlled, denied, and starved into the attrition of conformity, indeed the hipster may come to see that his condition is no more than an exaggeration of the human condition, and if he would be free, then everyone must be free. Yes, this is possible too, for the heart of Hip is its emphasis upon courage at the moment of crisis, and it is pleasant to think that courage contains within itself (as the explanation of its existence) some glimpse of the necessity of life to become more than it has been.

It is obviously not very possible to speculate with sharp focus on the future of the hipster. Certain possibilities must be evident, however, and the most central is that the organic growth of Hip depends on whether the Negro emerges as a dominating force in American life. Since the Negro knows more about the ugliness and danger of life than the white, it is probable that if the Negro can win his equality, he will possess a potential superiority, a superiority so feared that the fear itself has become the underground drama of domestic politics. Like all conservative political fear it is the fear of unforeseeable consequences, for the Negro's equality would tear a profound shift into the psychology, the sexuality, and the moral imagination of every white alive.

With this possible emergence of the Negro, Hip may erupt as a psychically armed rebellion whose sexual impetus may rebound against the antisexual foundation of every organized power in America, and bring into the air such animosities, antipathies, and new conflicts of interest that the mean empty hypocrisies of mass conformity will no longer work. A time of violence, new hysteria, confusion and rebellion will then be likely to replace the time of conformity. At that time, if the liberal should prove realistic in his belief that there is peaceful room for every tendency in American life, then Hip would end by being absorbed as a colorful figure in the tapestry. But if this is not the reality, and the economic, the social, the psychological, and finally the moral crises accompanying the rise of the Negro should prove insupportable, then a time is coming when every political guidepost will be gone, and millions of liberals will be faced with political dilemmas they have so far succeeded in evading, and with a view of human nature they do not wish to accept. To take the desegregation of the schools in the South as an example, it is quite likely that the reactionary sees the reality more closely than the liberal when he argues that the deeper issue is not desegregation but miscegenation. (As a radical I am of course facing in the opposite direction from the White Citizen's Councils—obviously I believe it is the absolute human right of the Negro to mate with the white, and matings there will undoubtedly be, for there will be Negro high school boys brave enough to chance their lives.) But for the average liberal whose mind has been dulled by the committee-ish cant of the professional liberal, miscegenation is not an issue because he has been told that the Negro does not desire it. So, when it comes, miscegenation will be a terror, comparable perhaps to the derangement of the American Communists when the icons to Stalin came tumbling down. The average American Communist held to the myth of Stalin for reasons which had little to do with the political evidence and everything to do with their psychic necessities. In this sense it is equally a psychic necessity for the liberal to believe that the Negro and even the reactionary Southern white are eventually and fundamentally people like himself, capable of becoming good liberals too if only they can be reached by good liberal reason. What the liberal cannot bear to admit is the hatred beneath the skin of a society so unjust that the amount of collective violence buried in the people is perhaps incapable of being contained, and therefore if one wants a better world one does well to hold one's breath, for a worse world is bound to come first, and the dilemma may well be this: given such hatred, it must either vent itself nihilistically or become turned into the cold murderous liquidations of the totalitarian state.

6

No matter what its horrors the twentieth century is a vastly exciting century for its tendency is to reduce all of life to its ultimate alternatives. One can well wonder if the last war of them all will be between the blacks and the whites, or between the women and the men, or between the beautiful and ugly, the pillagers and managers, or the rebels and the regulators. Which of course is carrying speculation beyond the point where speculation is still serious, and yet despair at the monotony and bleakness of the future have become so engrained in the radical temper that the radical is in danger of abdicating from all imagination. What a man feels is the impulse for his creative effort, and if an alien but nonetheless passionate instinct about the meaning of life has come so unexpectedly from a virtually illiterate people, come out of the most intense conditions of exploitation, cruelty, violence, frustration, and lust, and yet has succeeded as an instinct in keeping this tortured people alive, then it is perhaps possible that the Negro holds more of the tail of the expanding elephant of truth than the radical, and if this is so, the radical humanist could do worse than to brood upon the phenomenon. For if a revolutionary time should come again, there would be a crucial difference if someone had already delineated a neo-Marxian calculus aimed at comprehending every circuit and process of society from ukase to kiss as the communications of human energy — a calculus capable of translating the economic relations of man into his psychological relations and then back again, his productive relations thereby embracing his sexual relations as well, until the crises of capitalism in the twentieth century would yet be understood as the unconscious adaptations of a society to solve its economic imbalance at the expense of a new mass psychological imbalance. It is almost beyond the imagination to conceive of a work in which the drama of human energy is engaged, and a theory of its social currents and dissipations, its imprisonments, expressions, and tragic wastes are fitted into some gigantic synthesis of human action where the body of Marxist thought, and particularly the epic grandeur of *Das Kapital* (that first of the major *psychologies* to approach the mystery of social cruelty so simply and practically as to say that we are a collective body of humans whose life-energy is wasted, displaced, and procedurally stolen as it passes from one of us to another)—where particularly the epic grandeur of *Das Kapital* would find its place in an even more God-like view of human justice and injustice, in some more excruciating vision of those intimate and institutional processes which lead to our creations and disasters, our growth, our attrition, and our rebellion.

1957

Reflections on Hip

NOTE TO "REFLECTIONS ON HIP"

A prime virtue of The White Negro may be in the number of heresies it commits. Here, on this exchange with Jean Malaquais and Ned Polsky two such heresies are engaged: that a modern revolution can arise out of some other condition than an organized militant movement of the proletariat, and that there are other cures to neurosis than the couch of the analyst. For readers who are indifferent to these subjects, the exchange will be of doubtful interest; for those who would like a little more of The White Negro, the matter may be worth the difficulty.

I have taken one liberty. The exchange was called "Reflections on Hipsterism," when it appeared in Dissent. *I did not choose the title, and so I have altered the name of the piece.*

1) JEAN MALAQUAIS

Once upon a time there was a myth named *le prolétariat*. Though obviously a male, the myth was believed to be pregnant with child—a well conformed socialistic baby true to the Scriptures. Baby being long overdue, the congregation of the faithful first became skeptical, then frankly disgusted. Feeling cheated, never allowing that they may have misread the Book, they repudiated *le prolétariat*, sued for divorce, and being an idealistically inclined flock, started to shop around for a better, less sterile myth. Great schisms followed, yet few of the flock turned cynical. Quite the contrary. Prompted by their thirst for eternal values, many made dangerous inroads into heretofore uncharted lands. There, as in a secret Eden happily rediscovered, amazingly new and refreshing reasons to live awaited the bold myth hunter: Liberalism, Democracy, Free World, Peace, Stop-the-AH-Experiments, etc., and— honor to whom honor is due — the long neglected bastard-brother of *le prolétariat:* marijuana soaked Hip.

That Hip found in Norman Mailer its most outstanding and original theologist (I don't say apologist), seems quite clear in the light of his essay [DISSENT, Summer 1957]. He may be correct in stating that Hip and psychopathology follow two parallel paths, but he has still to persuade this reader that the American Negro bohemian and his white imitator embody a special brand of the human species. Starting with the fact that the Negro's status within the American community is a marginal one, Mailer is not content to allow him his particular or characteristic psychological bent; he bestows upon him a Messianic mission.

He seems to forget that the American hipster has his counterparts and equivalents in countries with no Negro population: Sweden, England, Russia, Poland, France, to name only a few places. The Swedish youth runs properly amok. The British Teddy, the Russian *besprizornyé*, the Polish hooligans, the French pseudo-existentialist fauna, don't behave differently toward life than the hipster. All are the product of an identical social phenomenon prevailing in highly industrialized and more or less paternalistically ruled countries: extreme inner insecurity dipped in a State-sponsored "welfare" at the price of a terrific loss to the individual's self. That's one reason why, as a rule, they react on the level of a purely personal idea of "recovery" — but from what and toward what none of them really knows.

When Mailer says of the hipster that he has "converted his unconscious experience into much conscious knowledge," he may speak of the hipster's knowledge in a very narrow practical way, as for instance knowledge on how to survive momentarily in a back alley; but he is mistaken if he takes it for more than it is: an instinctive and empirical know-how. The remarkable thing about hipsters of all kinds and variety (and they vary indeed in many aspects) is that, except for a case or two in a generation, as a body they are sooner or later swallowed up by the most conforming routine ever.

Hip is but another name for lumpen, and lumpen make excellent conformists and the best of potential hangmen for "order's" sake. Even before they fall into rank and file, rather than raping and murdering they blabber of rape and murder; they dream of rape and murder in idiotic clichés, vicariously, with a hand from the tabloids and other such literature. Yet if a handful among the tens of thousands, as Mailer numbers them, do go through rape and murder, it is mostly by accident, by a tragic mistake, almost never by deliberate clear choice, and then only once, for they are ambushed as soon as they have zipped up their pants.

One other reason why lumpen of all kind are but a myth in terms of social action, except possibly a small home-made pogrom with the implicit or explicit blessing of State and municipality, is that they do not form any coherent social body. Negro shopkeepers and white shopkeepers, should their shops be endangered, would dismiss all color lines and slaughter hand in hand Negro and white lumpen. There is more real solidarity (class solidarity) between white and Negro "law abiding citizens" than between people of "Caucasian" or "African" complexion.

Moreover, there is hardly a hipster alive who doesn't long to conform (like his extreme representative, the psychopath, he is always a case of a frustrated conformist), and there is hardly a conformist alive, white or Negro, who doesn't long to rape and murder (like his extreme representative, the pulpit moralist, he is always a case of a frustrated rebel). The difference is that the conformist hardly ever becomes a lumpen, that the lumpen almost always becomes a conformist (all exceptions granted). In turn, the difference is due to the only real relationship in modern society: property relationship. For the conformist to become a lumpen means to give up his actual or virtual property, which he cannot do by free choice; for the lumpen to become a conformist means to acquire property, which he always wills by free choice — however strong his overt denial. (As a matter of fact, lumpen *is* a way of making a living.)

On the other hand, the rebel who outgrew the romantic stage of his rebellion, who knows himself to be a grown up rebel — which is quite different from being a "radical," for after all a McCarthy too was a "radical" — knows also that *he conforms*, that he moves within the bonds of social and cultural institutions whose weight he cannot shake off in his private way, but who keeps within his conformity a lucid mind and a clear heart as to what conforming and what rebellion means in terms not of his subjective immediate I, but in terms of man as such, of man as a social creature. To make an image: the lumpen yells sh . . to the cop on the street-corner and feels purged, the conformist lifts his cap to the same cop and feels reassured in his pants, the grown up rebel ignores the cop (though he may summon his help in an emergency) and applies his energy to fell the tree that breeds cops, conformists and lumpen.

The amusing thing is that one can read into Mailer's essay precisely the proposition that the hipster is nothing but a conformist in reverse. "If," says Hip in Mailer's words, "if the fate of 20th century man is to live with death . . . why then the only life-giving answer is to accept the terms of death, to live with death as immediate danger, to divorce oneself from society," etc. Now if man's fate is to live with death, how does the hipster manage to divorce himself from society since he does accept "the terms of death"? If the terms are death, and if he accepts the terms — nay, if he so to speak naturalizes the terms generally prevailing for his private use, why he conforms nice and clean, he is at the avant-garde of conformity.

"Death you want?" says Hip to society. "Good, death there'll be!" And there he goes, the small entrepreneur in death competing with industrial death. One Mr. Verdoux once made a superb parody of our death-bent hipster. But no. Hip, says Mailer truly, Hip wants love, wants peace in a nice kitchenette with a white apron around his girl's waist. All the "mysticism," all the "dialectical conception of existence" Mailer so generously bestows upon Hip is, as far as I am concerned, a gorgeous flower of Mailer's romantic idealism.

Paris   September 4, 1957

MAILER'S REPLY

In his search for a sexual life which will suit his orgiastic needs, the hipster willy-nilly attacks conventional sexual morality, and to some degree succeeds in disturbing the balance. If capitalist society is grounded upon property relations, these relations are wed to monogamy, family, and the sexual strictures which maintain them. It is yet to be established that sexual life can be promiscuously altered without affecting the psychic real estate of capitalism. Since Malaquais seems to be indirectly arguing the affirmative, I would suggest that there are obstructions to his proof which the poetic excellences of his style cannot storm by metaphor.

Man is a flux of possibilities and energies long before and perhaps long after he is a manipulator of land, properties, and productions. A civilization from now, the vast chapter of Western expansion which was built on property and such inhuman abstractions of human energy as money, credit, and surplus value, may be seen as an ice-age of cruel and brutally slow liberations of productive, purposive, creative and sexual energies which the contradictions of inequity and exploitation congealed not only into the working habits of men, elaborated not only into the institutional hypocrisies of society, but indeed drove as cancerous ambivalences and frustrations into the texture of being itself.

The growth of human consciousness in this century demanded — for its expanding vitality — that a revolution be made, that a mankind be liberated, and since the attempt failed in its frontal revolutionary attack, failed precisely to change the exploitative character of our productive relations, it may well be that the rise of the hipster represents the first wind of a second revolution in this century, moving not forward toward action and more rational equitable distribution, but backward toward being and the secrets of human energy, not forward to the collectivity which was totalitarian in the proof but backward to the nihilism of creative adventurers, a revolution admittedly impossible to conceive even in its outlines, for unlike that first revolution which was conscious, Faustian, and vain, enacted in the name of the proletariat but more likely an expression of the scientific narcissism we inherited from the nineteenth century, a revolution motivated by the rational mania that consciousness could stifle instinct and marshal it into productive formations, the second revolution, if it is to come, would come indeed as antithesis to the "Great Experiment": — its desire would be to turn materialism on its head, have consciousness subjugated to instinct. The hipster, rebel cell in our social body, lives out, acts out, follows the close call of his instinct as far as he dares, and so points to possibilities and consequences in what have hitherto been chartless jungles of moral nihilism. The essence of his expression, his faith if you will, is that the real desire to make a better world exists at the heart of our instinct (that instinctual vision of a human epic which gave birth to consciousness itself), that man is therefore roughly more good than evil, that beneath his violence there is finally love and the nuances of justice, and that the removal therefore of all social restraints while it would open us to an era of incomparable individual violence would still spare us the collective violence of rational totalitarian liquidations (which we must accept was grossly a psychic index of the buried, voiceless, and ineradicable violences of whole nations of people), and would — and here is the difference — by expending the violence directly, open the possibility of working with that human creativity which is violence's opposite.

But of course this may be no more than the sword dance of my "romantic idealism." Immediately, the charge by Malaquais is that the hipster is our old black sheep, our discontented nephew of the proletariat, the impotent lumpen no more than a thousand dollars away from kissing the penny-calloused hands of the petit-bourgeoisie. I wonder. Is it so very lumpen to be able to influence American culture? The mass audience may turn in for the night to the chest-out, stomach-in, pinch-buttocks of the Star-Spangled Banner, with perhaps a five-minute sermonette to speed them to churchly sleep, but their waking hours were vibrated by that now déclassé (so fast does it change) Holy Shaker, that ex-apostle of small-town Southern orgasm, Elvis Presley.

Malaquais says the hipster has his opposite number in the British Teddy, the *besprizornyé* (still untamed? — how unlumpen!), the Polish hooligans, the French existentialists, all Hip, and not a drop of Negro blood in a thousand of their black masses. But Malaquais would be hard-put to find the taint of Hip without the blood of jazz. The Negro's experience appears to be the most universal communication of the West, and the authority of their tortured senses may indeed be passing by the musical states of their artistic expression, *without language, without conscious communication*, into the no doubt equally tortured senses of the wild sensitive spawn of two vast wars. But to Malaquais the lumpen is the lumpen. If Marx did not find it necessary to take them seriously, how dare we?

I wonder, however, if it would not be more "Marxist" to recognize that the superstructure of society has attained vast autonomies outside productive relations, psychological undercurrents which often clash with material economic realities — as, for example, the swoop of the stockmarket in response to the Sputnik. There may even be ineradicable conflicts of interest between the superstructure and the base of productive relations. At the least, is it not reasonable to assume that society has reached a point of such complexity, such "organismishness," that it is capable of adapting itself to avoid economic crisis by unwillingly (owing to the contradictions of mass manipulation) communicating mass psychological crises via the mass communications?

The contemporary contradictions from which America has been suffering (given the virtually self-regulating economic valves of war finance) have been almost insupportable psychological contradictions, virtually perfect Orwellian ambivalences — (War is Peace, Love is Hate, Ignorance is Knowledge); if these psychic contradictions should eventually introduce an apathy sufficient to turn our country back into economic contradictions and economic depression, which is indeed far from impossible, it will not mean that the process was a simple dialectic whose breath moved only through the circuits of productive relations. What one may fumble toward is a dialectic which can bridge the material and the ideal — which can infuse material notions of energy into that philosophical country of the ideal (read: the individual unconscious) which psychoanalysis now occupies with a middle-class mechanistic *weltanschauung*. If we socialists, radicals, anarchists, rebels, nihilists, and dissenters are to become more than the dried twigs of an old family tree, the shabby genteel clerks who end the line of a warrior family, it can at least be recognized that until the radical bridge from Marx to Freud is built, and our view of man embraces more facts, contradictions, and illuminations than any conservative view, and stares into such terrifying alternatives as totalitarianism or barbarism, we are doing no more than scolding ourselves, and ignoring that revolutionary indictment which every human alive can respond to in some part of himself: that an unjust society wreaks cruel if subtle imprisonments and destructions of personal energy, wreaks them not only upon an individual class or race, but upon the being of each of us. For ultimately, unjust societies must, out of the nature of their contradictions, stifle the best part of each creativity, and so starve into neglect and atrophy that future we hear raging to be born.

2) NED POLSKY

Although Norman Mailer, in "The White Negro," shows ample awareness of some drawbacks of hipster life, others he romanticizes away or ignores. Mailer is right in seeing the hipsters as the only significant new group of rebels in America. He is also right to recognize the new Bohemia, extend it his "essential sympathy," and where he cannot find much of merit, perhaps yet encourage it by praising with faint damns. But it is equally legitimate and desirable to recognize that there are qualitative differences among Bohemias and that the current Bohemia is greatly inferior to its predecessors of at least the past four decades.

1

The new Bohemia's inferiority shows up clearly in its lack of intellectual content. Most hipsters scarcely read at all, not because they can't (nearly all of them have finished high school, and a surprising number of the whites have attended our better universities) but because they won't. The closest thing to an intellectual discussion is their chatter about the pseudo-profundities of contemporary jazz; they don't even know—worse, don't want to know—that the things they praise were achieved by art-music composers years ago. As for the few who can be said to read with any regularity: they turn their backs not only on the horrors but the grandeurs of the past, restrict their horizon to contemporary literature, and from this area select what is in large part tripe—a compound of Rexroth and Rimbaud, Henry Miller and *Mad Comics*, Sartre and science fiction, jazz magazines and jerkoff magazines.

Their own literary productions are few, and what there are of them—with the exception of some poems by Robert Duncan and parts of his unpublished play, *Faust Foutu*—have almost no literary merit whatever. (Buy *Evergreen Review No. 2* and back issues of *Origin* and see for yourself.) The reason is not far to seek: even if we grant Mailer's dubious claim that the American existentialists feel their existentialism more than the French do, it is still true that for art something more is required than the raw recital of raw emotion. Thus the American hipsters' writings cannot begin to compare with the work of the arch-hipsters of modern European literature, Celine and Genet, to say nothing of any number of non-hipsters.

2

Hipster hedonism takes many forms. Some hipster groups, for example, have everything to do with motorcycles, whereas others have nothing to do with them. But not significant in any of these groups, Mailer to the contrary, is a sexual revolution. Of course hipsters are willing to try a variety of partners and positions, have no objection to interracial intercourse, etc.—but this is merely to say that they are "liberated" in the superficial ways that many "liberals" are. For all its probings of hipster pathology, Mailer's rhetoric covers up the fact that hipsters are not only more "psychologically" crippled than most people but sexually likewise—that they are not sexually free and have no chance to become so, and that this means they are not actual or potential sexual revolutionaries in the profound sense that Mailer is talking about. Two examples: many male hipsters (if I am to believe the testimony of several Hip men and women) are extremely sadistic in their sexual relationships, and many others are so narcissistic that inevitably their orgasms are premature and puny. No amount of plain or fancy screwing is going to change this. When Mailer glamorizes the hipsters' "search after the good orgasm" he is simply accepting at face value their rationalization for what is in truth a pathetic, driven sex life in which the same failures are repeated again and again. On this matter as on others, Mailer confuses the life of action with the life of acting out.

I imagine that Mailer really knows all this but that he cannot state it baldly because it would then be obvious that "bad orgasm" is one habit the hipster will never kick without the "dreary alternative" of psychoanalysis. Of course now that psychoanalysis has become a respectable part of psychiatry and the old-style European analysts, who were mostly rebels by definition, are being rapidly replaced by bourgeois young American M.D.'s, it is undeniable that the patient runs a much greater risk of encountering the analyst for whom "cure" necessarily includes "adjustment" to the present social structure. And not a few pioneer analysts now devote all their energies to making rich men's children content with their lot in life. But it is equally undeniable that psychoanalysis — whatever the brand — still provides greater sexual benefits than does the dreary alternative that Mailer glorifies. Psychoanalysis has been domesticated but not castrated.

3

The world of the hipster is commonly held to break down racial barriers, and indeed it does. If we accept the usual ultimate test (and Mailer's) — whether whites and Negroes sleep together — hipsters undoubtedly meet it much more often than squares do. Nevertheless there is a built-in barrier to full acceptance of black hipsters by white ones (and to a lesser extent vice versa), which stems from the fact that hipsters are marginal in a very special way.

The white Negro, as Mailer aptly calls him, is of course a marginal man. He puts down the white world from which he came. And he can never fully make it in, or be accepted by, the Negro world; so with rare exceptions (notably Mezz Mezzrow) he doesn't even try to live within the Negro community, and if he does he is put down by Negroes a lot. He exists, then, between the two worlds where he meets his obverse: the Negro hipster, who puts down the Negro community at large (one reason, though not the main one, being that most Negroes are also squares, Mailer's stereotype of the Negro notwithstanding) and can never fully make it in the white world.

The first thing to notice about these marginal men — white or black — is that they are not the utterly isolated, atomized individuals whom sociologists assume all marginal men to be. They come together and create a little world of their own which elaborates its own worldview, code of behavior, institutions, argot, and so on.

They create what to sociologists is a contradiction in terms: a sub-culture of marginal men.*

Now, the inner tragedy of the hipster subculture is this: the white member is attracted to the Negro member because of the latter's Negro-ness, whereas the Negro—and this Mailer ignores—is attracted to the white precisely because of his whiteness. Although the interracial groups which constitute the hipster subculture are "primary" groups in sociological terms, since in them whites and Negroes meet in "intimate, face-to-face relationships," this does not automatically imply the deepest kind of social bond; sociological theory is too gross at this point because it neglects the fact that "face to face" occasionally means, among other things, "looking in opposite directions." Many a time I have heard white hipsters, when no Negro members were present, put down one of the absent Negroes with "The trouble with X is that he's too fay-oriented," or "Y is a drag; all he's interested in is laying white chicks." And I'd bet my bottom dollar that Negro hipsters, among themselves, often put down the whites with something like "Man, those fay cats are pretty cool and don't want us to be Uncle Toms, but they still want us to be spooks. They don't really dig us as people; they just dig us for our music and our pot." Which is true. Even in the world of the hipster the Negro remains essentially what Ralph Ellison called him—an invisible man. The white Negro accepts the real Negro not as a human being in his totality, but as the bringer of a highly specified and restricted "cultural dowry," to use Mailer's phrase. In so doing he creates an inverted form of keeping the nigger in his place.

MAILER'S REPLY

As a cool critical view of the affectations, vanities, and hypocrisies of the hipster, I have little quarrel with Ned Polsky's remarks. They were written with a keen eye. But I believe he overrides a most complex question when he declares that many male hipsters have orgasms premature and puny. Since he can hardly have had the requisite personal experience—"Uncle," said a bisexual Negro to me once, "I couldn't have more charge for that chick if I'd gone

---

*A good index of the subculture's strength is provided by that most pervasive of hipster activities, marijuana-smoking and its attendant exploration of exotic states of consciousness, for the reactions of one under the influence of marijuana are determined not nearly so much by his individual psychology or physiology as by subcultural norms. For a related point of view, and much concrete evidence, cf. Howard S. Becker, "On Becoming a Marihuana Smoker," *American Journal of Sociology*, LIX (November 1953), pp. 235–242.

down on a platoon of Marines"—I wonder if Polsky isn't really just passing on a tyrannical assumption which is one of the cement blocks of the Square throne of psychoanalysis.

In the Western sexual literature with which I am familiar, classical, technical, and pornographic, I can remember—with the harsh radical exception of Wilhelm Reich—almost no incisive discussion of male orgasm. The very notion of "good orgasm" (which indeed I used superficially in "The White Negro," DISSENT, Summer '57) betrays the lack of examination we bring to it, for it assumes there are two domains, good orgasm and bad, each clearly set apart by a defense line of psychic dragon teeth. But the Hip argument, if one is to dredge it forth, would claim that even in an orgasm which is *the most* there is always the vision of an outer wider wilder orgasm which is even more *with it*. The nature of orgasm is a spectrum, perhaps an infinite spectrum, perhaps intimately dialectical: in the worst of orgasm there are nips of pleasure, in the best of orgasms some mannered containments denying pleasure beyond high pleasure, restraining the rarer liberations of energy for the next day.

I am sure that the average psychoanalyst would now say, "The fact that the advocate of this thesis wants more of orgasm, is an indication of dissatisfaction with his narcissistic involvements. The adjusted social person knows better than to worry about his orgasm. It has been improved by psychoanalytical therapy." Of course one could walk through a mile of analysand-type persons to find one who really believed that his orgasm had been sexually improved.

But to argue this way is to stalk one's opponent about a circle, each a safe diameter apart. Finally, one cannot enter another being's orgasm and measure its scope (especially since many people's frustrated theatrical talents are brought resolutely to bed), one can only guess from the spectrum of one's own what the possibilities may be for others. And the line I would prefer to engage is to call into account the psychoanalyst's self-interest in believing that almost all sexual rebels are sick sexually. Indeed, he is right. But almost everyone is sick sexually in more or less degree, and so the indictment by the psychoanalyst should come forth no more maternally than to claim: better you should be sick as a Square than sick as a Hip.

Still the impolite question remains to be asked: does the direct experience of the analyst's own life prepare him to judge the inner states of Hip? Sedentary, middle-class, in fief to fifteen years of training, living among the absurd magpie scrutinies of wife, children, colleagues, patients, and hostile strangers, most analysts are obliged to be more proper than proper, and their characters, impulses and value judgments become shaped to satisfy the social necessities of their work. The social necessities of their work? The analyst is Gibraltar in a pathless middle-class sea, his guiding torch is lit by money, his triumphs are invariably with plain and miserable patients squashed too early by life, ruined permanently for pleasure, and so burgeoning under the stern authority and human comfort that an expensive person listens to them for two and a half hours a week. But the analyst, this middle-class and usually pampered son, is he the one to make the imaginative journey into the tortured marijuana-racked mind and genitalia of a hipster daring to live on the edge of the most dangerous of the Negro worlds? Or is it not finally a matter of courage, courage not necessarily nor uniquely before violence, but courage to accept telling blows to the ego? For what would the analyst do, and what would become of his tidy, narrow, other-directed little world if he were to discover, and may God help him, that the hipster way out by the lip of danger may conceivably know more of the savor and swing in the damn dialectic of the orgasm than he, the doctor, the educated ball-shrinker who diagnoses all joys not his own as too puny.

The Time of Her Time

1

I was living in a room one hundred feet long and twenty-five feet wide, and it had nineteen windows staring at me from three of the walls and part of the fourth. The floor planks were worn below the level of the nails which held them down, except for the southern half of the room where I had laid a rough linoleum which gave a hint of sprinkled sand, conceivably an aid to the footwork of my pupils. For one hundred dollars I had the place whitewashed; everything: the checkerboard of tin ceiling plates one foot square with their fleur-de-lis stamped into the metal, the rotted sashes on the window frames (it took twelve hours to scrape the calcimine from the glass), even parts of the floor had white drippings (although that was scuffed into dust as time went on) and yet it was worth it: when I took the loft it stank of old machinery and the paint was a liverish brown — I had tried living with that color for a week, my old furniture which had been moved by a mover friend from the Village and me, showed the scars of being humped and dragged and flung up six flights of stairs, and the view of it sprawled over twenty-five hundred feet of living space, three beat old day beds, some dusty cushions, a broken-armed easy chair, a cigarette-scarred coffee table made from a door, a kitchen table, some peeled enamel chairs which thumped like a wooden-legged pirate when one sat in them, the bookshelves of unfinished pine butted by bricks, yes all of this, my purview, this grand vista, the New York sunlight greeting me in the morning through the double filter of the smog-yellow sky and the nineteen dirt-frosted windows, inspired me with so much content, especially those liver-brown walls, that I fled my pad like the plague, and in the first week, after a day of setting the furniture to rights, I was there for four hours of sleep a night, from five in the morning when I maneuvered in from the last closed Village bar and the last coffee-klatsch of my philosopher friends' for the night to let us say nine in the morning when I awoke with a partially destroyed brain and the certainty that the sore vicious growl of my stomach was at least the onset of an ulcer and more likely the first gone cells of a thoroughgoing cancer of the duodenum. So I lived it that way for a week, and then following the advice of a bar-type who was the friend of a friend, I got myself up on the eighth morning, boiled my coffee on a hot-plate while I shivered in the October air (neither the stove nor the gas heaters had yet been bought) and then I went downstairs and out the front door of the warehouse onto Monroe Street, picking my way through the garbage-littered gutter which always made me think of the gangs on this street, the Negroes on the east end of the block, the Puerto Ricans next to them, and the Italians and Jews to the west—those gangs were going to figure a little in my life, I suspected that, I was anticipating those moments with no quiet bravery considering how hung was my head in the morning, for the worst clue to the gangs was the six-year-olds. They were the defilers of the garbage, knights of the ordure, and here, in this province of a capital Manhattan, at the southern tip of the island, with the overhead girders of the Manhattan and Brooklyn bridges the only noble structures for a mile of tenement jungle, yes here the barbarians ate their young, and any type who reached the age of six without being altogether mangled by father, mother, family or friends, was a pint of iron man, so tough, so ferocious, so sharp in the teeth that the wildest alley cat would have surrendered a freshly caught rat rather than contest the meal. They were charming, these six-year-olds, as I told my uptown friends, and they used to topple the overloaded garbage cans, strew them through the street, have summer snowball fights with orange peel, coffee grounds, soup bones, slop, they threw the discus by scaling the raw tin rounds from the tops of cans, their pillow fights were with loaded socks of scum, and a debauch was for two of them to scrub a third around the inside of a twenty-gallon pail still warm with the heat of its emptied treasures. I heard that the Olympics took place in summer when they were out of school and the streets were so thick with the gum of old detritus, alluvium and dross that the mash made by passing car tires fermented in the sun. Then the parents and the hoods and the debs and the grandmother dowagers cheered them on and promised them murder and the garbage flew all day, but I was there in fall and the scene was quiet from nine to three. So I picked my way through last night's stew of rubble on this eighth morning of my hiatus on Monroe Street, and went half down the block to a tenement on the boundary between those two bandit republics of the Negroes and the Puerto Ricans, and with a history or two of knocking on the wrong door, and with a nose full of the smells of the sick overpeppered bowels of the poor which seeped and oozed out of every leaking pipe in every communal crapper (only as one goes north does the word take on the Protestant propriety of john), I was able finally to find my man, and I was an hour ahead of him—he was still sleeping off his last night's drunk. So I spoke to his wife, a fat masculine Negress with the face and charity of a Japanese wrestler, and when she understood that I was neither a junk-peddler nor fuzz, that I sold no numbers, carried no bills, and was most certainly not a detective (though my Irish face left her dubious of that) but instead had come to offer her husband a job of work, I was admitted to the first of three dark rooms, face to face with the gray luminescent eye of the television set going its way in a dark room on a bright morning, and through the hall curtains I could hear them talking in the bedroom.

"Get up, you son of a bitch," she said to him.

He came to work for me, hating my largesse, lugging his air compressor up my six flights of stairs, and after a discussion in which his price came down from two hundred to one, and mine rose from fifty dollars to meet his, he left with one of my twenty-dollar bills, the air compressor on the floor as security, and returned in an hour with so many sacks of whitewash that I had to help him up the stairs. We worked together that day, Charley Thompson his name was, a small lean Negro maybe forty years old, and conceivably sixty, with a scar or two on his face, one a gouge on the cheek, the other a hairline along the bridge of his nose, and we got along not too badly, working in sullen silence until the hangover was sweated out, and then starting to talk over coffee in the Negro hashhouse on the corner where the bucks bridled a little when I came in, and then ignored me. Once the atmosphere had become neutral again, Thompson was willing to talk.

"Man," he said to me, "what you want all that space for?"

"To make money."

"Out of which?"

I debated not very long. The people on the block would know my business sooner or later—the reward of living in a slum is that everyone knows everything which is within reach of the senses—and since I would be nailing a sign over my mailbox downstairs for the pupils to know which floor they would find me on, and the downstairs door would have to be open since I had no bell, the information would be just as open. But for that matter I was born to attract attention; given my height and my blond hair, the barbarians would notice me, they noticed everything, and so it was wiser to come on strong than to try to sidle in.

"Ever hear of an *Escuela de Torear?*" I asked him without a smile.

He laughed with delight at the sound of the words, not even bothering to answer.

"That's a bullfighter's school," I told him. "I teach bullfighting."

"You know that?"

"I used to do it in Mexico."

"Man, you can get killed."

"Some do." I let the exaggeration of a cooled nuance come into my voice. It was true after all; some do get killed. But not so many as I was suggesting, maybe one in fifty of the successful, and one in five hundred of the amateurs like me who fought a few bulls, received a few wounds, and drifted away.

Charley Thompson was impressed. So were others—the conversation was being overheard after all, and I had become a cardinal piece on the chaotic chessboard of Monroe Street's sociology—I felt the clear bell-like adrenalins of clean anxiety, untainted by weakness, self-interest, neurotic habit, or the pure yellows of the liver. For I had put my poker money on the table, I was the new gun in a frontier saloon, and so I was asking for it, not today, not tomorrow, but come sooner, come later, something was likely to follow from this. The weak would leave me alone, the strong would have respect, but be it winter or summer, sunlight or dark, there would come an hour so cold or so hot that someone, somebody, some sexed-up head, very strong and very weak, would be drawn to discover a new large truth about himself and the mysteries of his own courage or the lack of it. I knew. A year before, when I had first come to New York, there was a particular cat I kept running across in the bars of the Village, an expert with a knife, or indeed to maintain the salts of accuracy, an expert with two knives. He carried them everywhere—he had been some sort of hophead instructor in the Marines on the art of fighting with the knife, and he used to demonstrate nice fluid poses, his elbows in, the knives out, the points of those blades capering free of one another—he could feint in any direction with either hand, he was an artist, he believed he was better with a knife than any man in all of New York, and night after night in bar after bar he sang the love-song of his own prowess, begging for the brave type who would take on his boast, and leave him confirmed or dead.

It is mad to take on the city of New York, there is too much talent waiting on line; this cat was calling for every hoodlum in every crack gang and clique who fancied himself with the blade, and one night, drunk and on the way home, he was greeted by another knife, a Puerto Rican cat who was defective in school and spent his afternoons and nights shadow-knifing in the cellar clubhouse of his clique, a real contender, long-armed for a Latin, thin as a Lehmbruck, and fast as a hungry wolf; he had practiced for two months to meet the knife of New York.

So they went into an alley, the champion drunk, a fog of vanity blanketing the point of all his artistic reflexes, and it turned out to be not too much of a fight: the Puerto Rican caught it on the knuckles, the lip, and above the knee, but they were only nicks, and the champion was left in bad shape, bleeding from the forearm, the belly, the chest, the neck, and the face: once he was down, the Puerto Rican had engraved a double oval, labium majorum and minorum on the skin of the cheek, and left him there, having the subsequent consideration or fright to make a telephone call to the bar in which our loser had been drinking. The ex-champion, a bloody cat, was carried to his pad which was not far away (a bit of belated luck) and in an hour, without undue difficulty the brother-in-law doctor of somebody or other was good enough to take care of him. There were police reports, and as our patois goes, the details were a drag, but what makes my story sad is that our ex-champion was through. He mended by sorts and shifts, and he still bragged in the Village bars, and talked of finding the Puerto Rican when he was sober and in good shape, but the truth was that he was on the alcoholic way, and the odds were that he would stay there. He had been one of those gamblers who saw his life as a single bet, and he had lost. I often thought that he had been counting on a victory to put some charge below his belt and drain his mouth of all that desperate labial libido.

Now I was following a modest parallel, and as Thompson kept asking me some reasonable if openly ignorant questions about the nature of the bullfight, I found myself shaping every answer as carefully as if I were writing dialogue, and I was speaking particularly for the black-alerted senses of three Negroes who were sitting behind me, each of them big in his way (I had taken my glimpse as I came in) with a dull, almost Chinese, sullenness of face. They could have been anything. I had seen faces like theirs on boxers and ditch diggers, and I had seen such faces by threes and fours riding around in Cadillacs through the Harlem of the early-morning hours. I was warning myself to play it carefully, and yet I pushed myself a little further than I should, for I became ashamed of my caution and therefore was obliged to brag just the wrong bit. Thompson, of course, was encouraging me—he was a sly old bastard—and he knew even better than me the character of our audience.

"Man, you can take care of yourself," he said with glee.

"I don't know about that," I answered, obeying the formal minuet of the *macho*. "I don't like to mess with anybody," I told him. "But a man messes with me—well, I wouldn't want him to go away feeling better than he started."

"Oh, yeah, ain't that a fact. I hears just what you hear." He talked like an old-fashioned Negro—probably Southern. "What if four or five of them comes on and gangs you?"

We had come a distance from the art of the *corrida*. "That doesn't happen to me," I said. "I like to be careful about having some friends." And part for legitimate emphasis, and part to fulfill my image of the movie male lead—that blond union of the rugged and the clean-cut (which would after all be *their* image as well)—I added, "Good friends, you know."

There we left it. My coffee cup was empty, and in the slop of the saucer a fly was drowning. I was thinking idly and with no great compassion that wherever this fly had been born it had certainly not expected to die in a tan syrupy ring-shaped pond, struggling for the greasy hot-dogged air of a cheap Negro hashhouse. But Thompson rescued it with a deft little flip of his fingers.

"I always save," he told me seriously. "I wouldn't let nothing be killed. I'm a preacher."

"Real preacher?"

"Was one. Church and devoted congregation." He said no more. He had the dignified sadness of a man remembering the major failure of his life.

As we got up to go, I managed to turn around and get another look at the three spades in the next booth. Two of them were facing me. Their eyes were flat, the whites were yellow and flogged with red—they stared back with no love. The anxiety came over me again, almost nice — I had been so aware of them, and they had been so aware of me.

2

That was in October, and for no reason I could easily discover, I found myself thinking of that day as I awoke on a spring morning more than half a year later with a strong light coming through my nineteen windows. I had fixed the place up since then, added a few more pieces of furniture, connected a kitchen sink and a metal stall shower to the clean water outlets in the john, and most noticeably I had built a wall between the bullfight studio and the half in which I lived. That was more necessary than one might guess — I had painted the new wall red; after Thompson's job of whitewash I used to feel as if I were going snow-blind; it was no easy pleasure to get up each morning in a white space so blue with cold that the chill of a mountain peak was in my blood. Now, when I opened my eyes, I could choose the blood of the wall in preference to the ice slopes of Mt. O'Shaugnessy, where the sun was always glinting on the glaciers of the windows.

But on this particular morning, when I turned over a little more, there was a girl propped on one elbow in the bed beside me, no great surprise, because this was the year of all the years in my life when I was scoring three and four times a week, literally combing the pussy out of my hair, which was no great feat if one knew the Village and the scientific temperament of the Greenwich Village mind. I do not want to give the false impression that I was one of the lustiest to come adventuring down the pike — I was cold, maybe by birth, certainly by environment: I grew up in a Catholic orphanage — and I had had my little kinks and cramps, difficulties enough just a few years ago, but I had passed through that, and I was going now on a kind of disinterested but developed competence; what it came down to was that I could go an hour with the average girl without destroying more of the vital substance than a good night's sleep could repair, and since that sort of stamina seems to get advertised, and I had my good looks, my blond hair, my height, build, and bullfighting school, I suppose I became one of the Village equivalents of an Eagle Scout badge for the girls. I was one of the credits needed for a diploma in the sexual humanities, I was par for a good course, and more than one of the girls and ladies would try me on an off-evening like comparison-shoppers to shop the value of their boy friend, lover, mate, or husband against the certified professionalism of Sergius O'Shaugnessy.

Now if I make this sound bloodless, I am exaggerating a bit—
even an old habit is livened once in a while with color, and there
were girls I worked to get and really wanted, and nights when the
bull was far from dead in me. I even had two women I saw at least
once a week, each of them, but what I am trying to emphasize is
that when you screw too much and nothing is at stake, you begin to
feel like a saint. It was a hell of a thing to be holding a nineteen-
year-old girl's ass in my hands, hefting those young kneadables of
future power, while all the while the laboratory technician in my
brain was deciding that the experiment was a routine success—
routine because her cheeks looked and felt just about the way I
had thought they would while I was sitting beside her in the bar
earlier in the evening, and so I still had come no closer to understanding my scientific compulsion to verify in the retort of the bed
how accurately I had predicted the form, texture, rhythm and surprise of any woman who caught my eye.

Only an ex-Catholic can achieve some of the rarer amalgams of
guilt, and the saint in me deserves to be recorded. I always felt an
obligation—some noblesse oblige of the kindly cocksman—to send
my women away with no great wounds to their esteem, feeling at
best a little better than when they came in, I wanted it to be friendly (what vanity of the saint!). I was the messiah of the one-night
stand, and so I rarely acted like a pig in bed, I wasn't greedy, I
didn't grind all my tastes into their mouths, I even abstained from
springing too good a lay when I felt the girl was really in love with
her man, and was using me only to give love the benefit of new
perspective. Yes, I was a good sort, I probably gave more than I
got back, and the only real pains for all those months in the loft, for
my bullfighting classes, my surprisingly quiet time (it had been winter after all) on Monroe Street, my bulging portfolio of experi-
ments—there must have been fifty girls who spent at least one
night in the loft—my dull but doggedly advancing scientific data,
even the cold wan joys of my saintliness demanded for their payment only one variety of the dead hour: when I woke in the morning, I could hardly wait to get the latest mouse out of my bed and
out of my lair. I didn't know why, but I would awaken with the
deadliest of depressions, the smell of the woman had gone very
stale for me, and the armpits, the ammonias and dead sea life of old
semen and old snatch, the sour fry of last night's sweat, the whore
scent of overexercised perfume, became an essence of the odious,
all the more remarkable because I clung to women in my sleep, I
was one Don John who hated to sleep alone, I used to feel as if my
pores were breathing all the maternal (because sleeping) sweets of
the lady, wet or dry, firm or flaccid, plump, baggy, or lean who was

handled by me while we dreamed. But on awakening, hung with my head—did I make love three times that year without being drunk?—the saint was given his hour of temptation, for I would have liked nothing more than to kick the friendly ass out of bed, and dispense with the coffee, the good form, my depression and often hers, and start the new day by lowering her in a basket out of my monk-ruined retreat six floors down to the garbage pile (now blooming again in the freshets of spring), wave my hand at her safe landing and get in again myself to the blessed isolations of the man alone.

But of course that was not possible. While it is usually a creep who generalizes about women, I think I will come on so heavy as to say that the cordial tone of the morning after is equally important to the gymkhana of the night before—at least if the profit made by a nice encounter is not to be lost. I had given my working hours of the early morning to dissolving a few of the inhibitions, chilled reflexes and dampened rhythms of the corpus before me, but there is not a restraint in the world which does not have to be taken twice—once at night on a steam-head of booze, and once in daylight with the grace of a social tea. To open a girl up to the point where she loves you or It or some tremor in her sexual baggage, and then to close her in the morning is to do the disservice which the hateful side of women loves most—you have fed their cold satisfied distrust of a man. Therefore my saint fought his private churl, and suffering all the detail of abusing the sympathetic nervous system, I made with the charm in the daylight and was more of a dear than most.

It was to be a little different this morning, however. As I said, I turned over in my bed, and looked at the girl propped on her elbow beside me. In her eyes there was a flat hatred which gave no ground—she must have been staring like this at my back for several minutes, and when I turned, it made no difference—she continued to examine my face with no embarrassment and no delight.

That was sufficient to roll me around again, my shoulder blades bare to her inspection, and I pretended that the opening of my eyes had been a false awakening. I felt deadened then with all the diseases of the dull—making love to her the night before had been a little too much of a marathon. She was a Jewish girl and she was in her third year at New York University, one of those harsh alloys of a self-made bohemian from a middle-class home (her father was a hardware wholesaler), and I was remembering how her voice had irritated me each time I had seen her, an ugly New York accent with a cultured overlay. Since she was still far from formed, there had been all sorts of Lesbian hysterias in her shrieking laugh and they warred with that excess of strength, complacency and depre- cation which I found in many Jewish women—a sort of "Ech" of disgust at the romantic and mysterious All. This one was medium in size and she had dark long hair which she wore like a Village witch in two extended braids which came down over her flat breasts, and she had a long thin nose, dark eyes, and a kind of lean force, her arms and square shoulders had shown the flat thin mus- cles of a wiry boy. All the same, she was not bad, she had a kind of Village chic, a certain snotty elegance of superiority, and when I first came to New York I had dug girls like her—Jewesses were strange to me—and I had even gone with one for a few months. But this new chick had been a mistake—I had met her two weeks ago at a party, she was on leave from her boy friend, and we had an argument about T. S. Eliot, a routine which for me had become the quintessence of corn, but she said that Eliot was the apotheosis of manner, he embodied the ecclesiasticism of classical and now futureless form, she adored him she said, and I was tempted to tell her how little Eliot would adore the mannerless yeast of the Brook- lyn from which she came, and how he might prefer to allow her to appreciate his poetry only in step to the transmigration of her voice from all urgent Yiddish nasalities to the few high English analities of relinquished desire. No, she would not make that other world so fast—nice society was not cutting her crumpets thus quickly be- cause she was gone on Thomas Stearns Eeeee. Her college-girl snobbery, the pith for me of eighty-five other honey-pots of the Village aesthetic whose smell I knew all too well, so inflamed the avenger of my crotch, that I wanted to prong her then and there, right on the floor of the party, I was a primitive for a prime minute, a gorged gouge of a working-class phallus, eager to ram into all her nasty little tensions. I had the message again, I was one of the mil- lions on the bottom who had the muscles to move the sex which kept the world alive, and I would grind it into her, the healthy hearty inches and the sweat of the cost of acquired culture when you started low and you wanted to go high. She was a woman, what! she sensed that moment, she didn't know if she could handle me, and she had the guts to decide to find out. So we left the party and we drank and (leave it to a Jewish girl to hedge the bet) she drained the best half of my desire in conversation because she was being psychoanalyzed, what a predictable pisser! and she was in that stage where the jargon had the totalitarian force of all vocabu- laries of mechanism, and she could only speak of her infantile rela- tions to men, and the fixations and resistances of unassimilated penis-envy with all the smug gusto of a female commissar. She was enthusiastic about her analyst, he was also Jewish (they were working now on Jewish self-hatred), he was really an integrated guy, Stanford Joyce, he belonged on the same mountain as Eliot, she loved the doers and healers of life who built on the foundationless prevalence of the void, those islands of proud endeavor.

"You must get good marks in school," I said to her.

"Of course."

How I envied the jazzed-up brain of the Jews. I was hot for her again, I wanted the salts of her perspiration in my mouth. They would be acrid perhaps, but I would digest them, and those intellectual molecules would rise to my brain.

"I know a girl who went to your bullfighting school," she said to me. She gave her harsh laugh. "My friend thought you were afraid of her. She said you were full of narcissistic anxieties."

"Well, we'll find out," I said.

"Oh, you don't want me. I'm very inadequate as a lover." Her dark hard New York eyes, bright with appetite, considered my head as if I were a delicious and particularly sour pickle.

I paid the check then, and we walked over to my loft. As I had expected, she made no great fuss over the back-and-forth of being seduced — to the contrary. Once we were upstairs, she prowled the length of my loft twice, looked at the hand-made bullfighting equipment I had set up along one wall of the studio, asked me a question or two about the killing machine, studied the swords, asked another question about the cross-guard on the descabellar, and then came back to the living-room — bedroom — dining-room — kitchen of the other room, and made a face at the blood-red wall. When I kissed her she answered with a grinding insistence of her mouth upon mine, and a muscular thrust of her tongue into my throat, as direct and unfeminine as the harsh force of her voice.

"I'd like to hang my clothes up," she said.

It was not all that matter-of-fact when we got to bed. There was nothing very fleshy about the way she made love, no sense of the skin, nor smell, nor touch, just anger, anger at her being there, and another anger which was good for my own, that rage to achieve . . . just what, one cannot say. She made love as if she were running up an inclined wall so steep that to stop for an instant would slide her back to disaster. She hammered her rhythm at me, a hard driving rhythm, an all but monotonous drum, pound into pound against pound into pound until that moment when my anger found its way back again to that delayed and now recovered Time when I wanted to prong her at the party. I had been frustrated, had waited, had lost the anger, and so been taken by her. That finally got me — all through the talk about T. S. Eliot I had been calculating how I would lay waste to her little independence, and now she was alone, with me astride her, going through her paces, teeth biting the pillow, head turned away, using me as the dildoe of a private gallop. So my rage came back, and my rhythm no longer depended upon her drive, but found its own life, and we made love like two club fighters in an open exchange, neither giving ground, rhythm to rhythm, even to even, hypnotic, knowing neither the pain of punishment nor the pride of pleasure, and the equality of this, as hollow as the beat of the drum, seemed to carry her into some better deep of desire, and I had broken through, she was following me, her muscular body writhed all about me with an impersonal abandon, the wanton whip-thrash of a wounded snake, she was on fire and frozen at the same time, and then her mouth was kissing me with a rubbery greedy compulsion so avid to use all there was of me, that to my distant surprise, not in character for the saint to slip into the brutal, my hand came up and clipped her mean and open-handed across the face which brought a cry from her and broke the piston of her hard speed into something softer, wetter, more sly, more warm, I felt as if her belly were opening finally to receive me, and when her mouth kissed me again with a passing tender heat, warm-odored with flesh, and her body sweetened into some feminine embrace of my determination driving its way into her, well, I was gone, it was too late, I had driven right past her in that moment she turned, and I had begun to come, I was coming from all the confluences of my body toward that bud of sweetness I had plucked from her, and for a moment she was making it, she was a move back and surging to overtake me, and then it was gone, she made a mistake, her will ordered all temptings and rhythms to mobilize their march, she drove into the hard stupidities of a marching-band's step, and as I was going off in the best for many a month, she was merely going away, she had lost it again. As I ebbed into what should have been the contentments of a fine after-pleasure, warm and fine, there was one little part of me remaining cold and murderous because she had deprived me, she had fled the domination which was liberty for her, and the rest of the night was bound to be hell.

Her face was ugly. "You're a bastard, do you know that?" she asked of me.

"Let it go. I feel good."

"Of course you feel good. Couldn't you have waited one minute?"

I disliked this kind of thing. My duty was reminding me of how her awakened sweets were souring now in the belly, and her nerves were sharpening into the gone electric of being just nowhere.

"I hate inept men," she said.

"Cool it." She could, at least, be a lady. Because if she didn't stop, I would give her back a word or two.

"You did that on purpose," she nagged at me, and I was struck with the intimacy of her rancor—we might as well have been married for ten years to dislike each other so much at this moment.

"Why," I said, "you talk as if this were something unusual for you."

"It is."

"Come on," I told her, "you never made it in your life."

"How little you know," she said. "This is the first time I've missed in months."

If she had chosen to get my message, I could have been preparing now for a good sleep. Instead I would have to pump myself up again—and as if some ghost of the future laid the squeak of a tickle on my back, I felt an odd dread, not for tonight so much as for some ills of the next ten years whose first life was stirring tonight. But I lay beside her, drew her body against mine, feeling her trapped and irritable heats jangle me as much as they roused me, and while I had no fear that the avenger would remain asleep, still he stirred in pain and in protest, he had supposed his work to be done, and he would claim the wages of overtime from my reserve. That was the way I thought it would go, but Junior from New York University, with her hard body and her passion for proper poetry, gave a lewd angry old grin as her face stared boldly into mine, and with the practical bawdiness of the Jew she took one straight utilitarian finger, smiled a deceptive girlish pride, and then she jabbed, fingernail and all, into the tight defended core of my clenched buttocks. One wiggle of her knuckle and I threw her off, grunting a sound between rage and surprise, to which she laughed and lay back and waited for me.

Well, she had been right, that finger tipped the balance, and three-quarters with it, and one-quarter hung with the mysteries of sexual ambition, I worked on her like a beaver for forty-odd minutes or more, slapping my tail to build her nest, and she worked along while we made the round of the positions, her breath sobbing the exertions, her body as alive as a charged wire and as far from rest.

I gave her all the Time I had in me and more besides, I was weary of her, and the smell which rose from her had so little of the sea and so much of the armpit, that I breathed the stubborn wills of the gymnasium where the tight-muscled search for grace, and it was like that, a hard punishing session with pulley weights, stationary bicycle sprints, and ten breath-seared laps around the track. Yes, when I caught that smell, I knew she would not make it, and so I kept on just long enough to know she was exhausted in body, exhausted beyond the place where a ten-minute rest would have her jabbing that finger into me again, and hating her, hating women who could not take their exercise alone, I lunged up over the hill with my heart pounding past all pleasure, and I came, but with hatred, tight, electric, and empty, the spasms powerful but centered in my heart and not from the hip, the avenger taking its punishment even at the end, jolted clear to the seat of my semen by the succession of rhythmic blows which my heart drummed back to my feet.

For her, getting it from me, it must have been impressive, a convoluted, smashing, and protracted spasm, a hint of the death throe in the animal male which cannot but please the feminine taste for the mortal wound. "Oh, you're lucky," she whispered in my ear as I lay all collapsed beside her, alone in my athlete's absorption upon the whisperings of damage in the unlit complexities of my inner body. I was indeed an athlete, I knew my body was my future, and I had damaged it a bit tonight by most certainly doing it no good. I disliked her for it with the simple dislike we know for the stupid.

"Want a cigarette?" she asked.

I could wait, my heart would have preferred its rest, but there was something tired in her voice beyond the fatigue of what she had done. She too had lost after all. So I came out of my second rest to look at her, and her face had the sad relaxation (and serenity) of a young whore who has finished a hard night's work with the expected lack of issue for herself, content with no more than the money and the professional sense of the hard job dutifully done.

"I'm sorry you didn't make it," I said to her.

She shrugged. There was a Jewish tolerance for the expected failures of the flesh. "Oh, well, I lied to you before," she said.

"You never have been able to, have you?"

"No." She was fingering the muscles of my shoulder, as if in unconscious competition with my strength. "You're pretty good," she said grudgingly.

"Not really inept?" I asked.

"*Sans façons*," said the poetess in an arch change of mood which irritated me. "Sandy has been illuminating those areas where my habits make for destructive impulses."

"Sandy is Doctor Joyce?" She nodded. "You make him sound like your navigator," I told her.

"Isn't it a little obvious to be hostile to psychoanalysis?"

Three minutes ago we had been belaboring each other in the nightmare of the last round, and now we were close to cozy. I put the sole of my foot on her sharp little knee.

"You know the first one we had?" she asked of me. "Well, I wanted to tell you. I came close—I guess I came as close as I ever came."

"You'll come closer. You're only nineteen."

"Yes, but this evening has been disturbing to me. You see I get more from you than I get from my lover."

Her lover was twenty-one, a senior at Columbia, also Jewish—which lessened interest, she confessed readily. Besides, Arthur was too passive—"Basically, it's very comprehensible," said the commissar, "an aggressive female and a passive male—we complement one another, and that's no good." Of course it was easy to find satisfaction with Arthur, "via the oral perversions. That's because, vaginally, I'm anaesthetized—a good phallic narcissist like you doesn't do enough for me."

In the absence of learned credentials, she was setting out to bully again. So I thought to surprise her. "Aren't you mixing your language a little?" I began. "The phallic narcissist is one of Wilhelm Reich's categories."

"Therefore?"

"Aren't you a Freudian?"

"It would be presumptuous of me to say," she said like a seminar student working for his pee-aitch-dee. "But Sandy is an eclectic. He accepts a lot of Reich—you see, he's very ambitious, he wants to arrive at his own synthesis." She exhaled some smoke in my face, and gave a nice tough little grin which turned her long serious young witch's face into something indeed less presumptuous. "Besides," she said, "you are a phallic narcissist. There's an element of the sensual which is lacking in you."

"But Arthur possesses it?"

"Yes, he does. And you . . . you're not very juicy."

"I wouldn't know what you mean."

"I mean this." With the rich cruel look of a conquistador finding a new chest of Indian gold, she bent her head and gave one fleeting satiric half-moon of a lick to the conjugation of my balls. "That's what I mean," she said, and was out of bed even as I was recognizing that she was finally not without art. "Come back," I said.

But she was putting her clothes on in a hurry. "Shut up. Just don't give me your goddammed superiority."

I knew what it was: she had been about to gamble the reserves which belonged to Arthur, and the thought of possibly wasting them on a twenty-seven-year-old connoisseur like myself was too infuriating to take the risk.

So I lay in bed and laughed at her while she dressed—I did not really want a go at things again—and besides, the more I laughed, the angrier she would be, but the anger would work to the surface, and beneath it would be resting the pain that the evening had ended on so little.

She took her leisure going to the door, and I got up in time to tell her to wait — I would walk her to the subway. The dawn had come, however, and she wanted to go alone, she had had a bellyful of me, she could tell me that.

My brain was lusting its own private futures of how interesting it would be to have this proud, aggressive, vulgar, tense, stiff and arrogant Jewess going wild on my bottom — I had turned more than one girl on, but never a one of quite this type. I suppose she had succeeded instead of me; I was ready to see her again and improve the message.

She turned down all dates, but compromised by giving me her address and the number of her telephone. And then glaring at me from the open door, she said, "I owe you a slap in the face."

"Don't go away feeling unequal."

I might have known she would have a natural punch. My jaw felt it for half an hour after she was gone and it took another thirty minutes before I could bring myself back to concluding that she was one funny kid.

All of that added up to the first night with the commissar, and I saw her two more times over this stretch, the last on the night when she finally agreed to sleep over with me, and I came awake in the morning to see her glaring at my head. So often in sex, when the second night wound itself up with nothing better in view than the memory of the first night, I was reminded of Kafka's *Castle*, that tale of the search of a man for his apocalyptic orgasm: in the easy optimism of a young man, he almost captures the castle on the first day, and is never to come so close again. Yes, that was the saga of the nervous system of a man as it was bogged into the defeats, complications, and frustrations of middle age. I still had my future before me of course — the full engagement of my will in some go-for-broke I considered worthy of myself was yet to come, but there were times in that loft when I knew the psychology of an old man, and my second night with Denise — for Denise Gondelman was indeed her name — left me racked for it amounted to so little that we could not even leave it there — the hangover would have been too great for both of us — and so we made a date for a third night. Over and over in those days I used to compare the bed to the bullfight, sometimes seeing myself as the matador and sometimes as the bull, and this second appearance, if it had taken place, in the Plaza Mexico, would have been a *fracaso* with kapok seat cushions jeering down on the ring, and a stubborn cowardly bull staying in *querencia* before the doubtful prissy overtures, the gloomy trim technique of a veteran and mediocre *torero* on the worst of days when he is forced to wonder if he has even his *pundonor* to sustain him. It was a gloomy deal. Each of us knew it was possible to be badly worked by the other, and this seemed so likely that neither of us would gamble a finger. Although we got into bed and had a perfunctory ten minutes, it was as long as an hour in a coffee shop when two friends are done with one another.

By the third night we were ready for complexities again; to see a woman three times is to call on the dialectic of an affair. If the waves we were making belonged less to the viper of passion than the worm of inquiry, still it was obvious from the beginning that we had surprises for one another. The second night we had been hoping for more, and so got less; this third night, we each came on with the notion to wind it up, and so got involved in more.

For one thing, Denise called me in the afternoon. There was studying she had to do, and she wondered if it would be all right to come to my place at eleven instead of meeting me for drinks and dinner. Since that would save me ten dollars she saw no reason why I should complain. It was a down conversation. I had been planning to lay siege to her, dispense a bit of elixir from my vast reservoirs of charm, and instead she was going to keep it *in camera*. There was a quality about her I could not locate, something independent—abruptly, right there, I knew what it was. In a year she would have no memory of me, I would not exist for her unless . . . and then it was clear . . . unless I could be the first to carry her stone of no-orgasm up the cliff, all the way, over and out into the sea. That was the kick I could find, that a year from now, five years from now, down all the seasons to the hours of her old age, I would be the one she would be forced to remember, and it would nourish me a little over the years, thinking of that grudged souvenir which could not die in her, my blond hair, my blue eyes, my small broken nose, my clean mouth and chin, my height, my boxer's body, my parts—yes, I was getting excited at the naked image of me in the young-old mind of that sour sexed-up dynamo of black-pussied frustration.

A phallic narcissist she had called me. Well, I was phallic enough, a Village stickman who could muster enough of the divine It on the head of his will to call forth more than one becoming out of the womb of feminine Time, yes a good deal more than one from my fifty new girls a year, and when I failed before various prisons of frigidity, it mattered little. Experience gave the cue that there were ladies who would not be moved an inch by a year of the best, and so I looked for other things in them, but this one, this Den-of-Ease, she was ready, she was entering the time of her Time, and if not me, it would be another—I was sick in advance at the picture of some bearded Negro cat who would score where I had missed and thus cuckold me in spirit, deprive me of those telepathic waves of longing (in which I obviously believed) speeding away to me from her over the years to balm the hours when I was beat, because I had been her psychic bridegroom, had plucked her ideational diddle, had led her down the walk of her real wedding night. Since she did not like me, what a feat to pull it off.

In the hours I waited after dinner, alone, I had the sense—which I always trusted—that tonight this little victory or defeat would be full of leverage, magnified beyond its emotional matter because I had decided to bet on myself that I would win, and a defeat would bring me closer to a general depression, a fog bank of dissatisfaction with myself which I knew could last for months or more. Whereas a victory would add to the panoplies of my ego some peculiar (but for me, valid) ingestion of her arrogance, her stubbornness, and her will—those necessary ingredients of which I could not yet have enough for my own ambition.

When she came in she was wearing a sweater and dungarees which I had been expecting, but there was a surprise for me. Her braids had been clipped, and a short cropped curled Italian haircut decorated her head, moving her severe young face half across the spectrum from the austerities of a poetess to a hint of all those practical and promiscuous European girls who sold their holy hump to the Germans and had been subsequently punished by shaved heads—how attractive the new hair proved; once punished, they were now free, free to be wild, the worst had happened and they were still alive with the taste of the first victor's flesh enriching the sensual curl of the mouth.

Did I like her this way? Denise was interested to know. Well, it was a shock, I admitted, a pleasant shock. If it takes you so long to decide, you must be rigid, she let me know. Well, yes, as a matter of fact I was rigid, rigid for her with waiting.

The nun of severity passed a shade over her. She hated men who were uncool, she thought she would tell me.

"Did your analyst tell you it's bad to be uncool?"

She had taken off her coat, but now she gave me a look as if she were ready to put it on again. "No, he did not tell me that." She laughed spitefully. "But he told me a couple of revealing things about you."

"Which you won't repeat."

"Of course not."

"I'll never know," I said, and gave her the first kiss of the evening. Her mouth was heated—it was the best kiss I had received from her, and it brought me on too quickly—"My fruit is ready to be plucked," said the odors of her mouth, betraying that perfume of the ducts which, against her will no doubt, had been plumping for me. She was changed tonight. From the skin of her face and the glen of her neck came a new smell, sweet, sweaty, and tender, the smell of a body which had been used and had enjoyed its uses. It came to me nicely, one of the nicest smells in quite some time, so different from the usual exudations of her dissatisfied salts that it opened a chain of reflexes in me, and I was off in all good speed on what Denise would probably have called the vertical foreplay. I suppose I went at her like a necrophiliac let loose upon a still-warm subject, and as I gripped her, grasped her, groped her, my breath a bellows to blow her into my own flame, her body remained unmoving, only her mouth answering my call, those lips bridling hot adolescent kisses back upon my face, the smell almost carrying me away—such a fine sweet sweat.

Naturally she clipped the rhythm. As I started to slip up her sweater, she got away and said a little huskily, "I'll take my own clothes off." Once again I could have hit her. My third eye, that athlete's inner eye which probed its vision into all the corners, happy and distressed of my body whole, was glumly cautioning the congestion of the spirits in the coils of each teste. They would have to wait, turn rancid, maybe die of delay.

Off came the sweater and the needless brassière, her economical breasts swelled just a trifle tonight, enough to take on the convexities of an Amazon's armor. Open came the belt and the zipper of her dungarees, zipped from the front which pleased her not a little. Only her ass, a small masterpiece, and her strong thighs, justified this theatre. She stood there naked, quite psychically clothed, and lit a cigarette.

If a stiff prick has no conscience, it has also no common sense. I stood there like a clown, trying to coax her to take a ride with me on the bawdy car, she out of her clothes, I in all of mine, a muscular little mermaid to melt on my knee. She laughed, one harsh banker's snort—she was giving no loans on my idiot's collateral.

"You didn't even ask me," Denise thought to say, "of how my studying went tonight."

"What did you study?"

"I didn't. I didn't study." She gave me a lovely smile, girlish and bright. "I just spent the last three hours with Arthur."

"You're a dainty type," I told her.

But she gave me a bad moment. That lovely flesh-spent smell, scent of the well used and the tender, that avatar of the feminine my senses had accepted so greedily, came down now to no more than the rubbings and the sweats of what was probably a very nice guy, passive Arthur with his Jewish bonanzas of mouth-love.

The worst of it was that it quickened me more. I had the selfish wisdom to throw such evidence upon the mercy of my own court. For the smell of Arthur was the smell of love, at least for me, and so from man or woman, it did not matter — the smell of love was always feminine — and if the man in Denise was melted by the woman in Arthur, so Arthur might have flowered that woman in himself from the arts of a real woman, his mother? — it did not matter — that voiceless message which passed from the sword of the man into the cavern of the woman was carried along from body to body, and if it was not the woman in Denise I was going to find tonight, at least I would be warmed by the previous trace of another.

But that was a tone poem to quiet the toads of my doubt. When Denise — it took five more minutes — finally decided to expose herself on my clumped old mattress, the sight of her black pubic hair, the feel of the foreign but brotherly liquids in her unembarrassed maw, turned me into a jackrabbit of pissy tumescence, the quicks of my excitement beheaded from the resonances of my body, and I wasn't with her a half-minute before I was over, gone, and off. I rode not with the strength to reap the harem of her and her lover, but spit like a pinched boy up into black forested hills of motherly contempt, a passing picture of the nuns of my childhood to drench my piddle spurtings with failures of gloom. She it was who proved stronger than me, she the he to my silly she.

All considered, Denise was nice about it. Her harsh laugh did not crackle over my head, her hand in passing me the after-cigarette settled for no more than a nudge of my nose, and if it were not for the contempt of her tough grin, I would have been left with no more than the alarm to the sweepers of my brain to sweep this failure away.

"Hasn't happened in years," I said to her, the confession coming out of me with the cost of the hardest cash.

"Oh, shut up. Just rest." And she began to hum a mocking little song. I lay there in a state, parts of me jangled for forty-eight hours to come, and yet not altogether lost to peace. I knew what it was. Years ago in the air force, as an enlisted man, I had reached the light-heavyweight finals on my air base. For two weeks I trained for the championship, afraid of the other man all the way because I had seen him fight and felt he was better than me; when my night came, he took me out with a left hook to the liver which had me conscious on the canvas but unable to move, and as the referee was counting, which I could hear all too clearly, I knew the same kind of peace, a swooning peace, a clue to that kind of death in which an old man slips away—nothing mattered except that my flesh was vulnerable and I had a dim revery, lying there with the yells of the air force crowd in my ears, there was some far-off vision of green fields and me lying in them, giving up all ambition to go back instead to another, younger life of the senses, and I remember at that moment I watered the cup of my boxer's jock, and then I must have slipped into something new, for as they picked me off the canvas the floor seemed to recede from me at a great rate as if I were climbing in an airplane.

A few minutes later, the nauseas of the blow to my liver had me retching into my hands, and the tension of three weeks of preparation for that fight came back. I knew through the fading vistas of my peace, and the oncoming spasms of my nausea, that the worst was yet to come, and it would take me weeks to unwind, and then years, and maybe never to overcome the knowledge that I had failed completely at a moment when I wanted very much to win.

A ghost of this peace, trailing intimations of a new nausea, was passing over me again, and I sat up in bed abruptly, as if to drive these weaknesses back into me. My groin had been simmering for hours waiting for Denise, and it was swollen still, but the avenger was limp, he had deserted my cause, I was in a spot if she did not co-operate.

Co-operate she did. "My God, lie down again, will you," she said, "I was thinking that finally I had seen you relax."

And then I could sense that the woman in her was about to betray her victory. She sat over me, her little breasts budding with their own desire, her short hair alive and flowering, her mouth ready to taste her gentleman's defeat. I had only to raise my hand, and push her body in the direction she wished it to go, and then her face was rooting in me, her angry tongue and voracious mouth going wild finally as I had wished it, and I knew the sadness of sour timing, because this was a prize I could not enjoy as I would have on the first night, and yet it was good enough—not art, not the tease and languor of love on a soft mouth, but therapy, therapy for her, the quick exhaustions of the tension in a harsh throat, the beseechment of an ugly voice going down into the expiation which would be its beauty. Still it was good, practically it was good, my ego could bank the hard cash that this snotty head was searching me, the act served its purpose, anger traveled from her body into mine, the avenger came to attention, cold and furious, indifferent to the trapped doomed pleasure left behind in my body on that initial and grim piddle spurt, and I was ready, not with any joy nor softness nor warmth nor care, but I was ready finally to take her tonight, I was going to beat new Time out of her if beat her I must, I was going to teach her that she was only a child, because if at last I could not take care of a nineteen-year-old, then I was gone indeed. And so I took her with a cold calculation, the rhythms of my body corresponding to no more than a metronome in my mind, tonight the driving mechanical beat would come from me, and blind to nerve-raddlings in my body, and blood pressures in my brain, I worked on her like a riveter, knowing her resistances were made of steel, I threw her a fuck the equivalent of a fifteen-round fight, I wearied her, I brought her back, I drove my fingers into her shoulders and my knees into her hips. I went, and I went, and I went, I bore her high and thumped her hard, I sprinted, I paced, I lay low, eyes all closed, under sexual water, like a submarine listening for the distant sound of her ship's motors, hoping to steal up close and trick her rhythms away.

And she was close. Oh, she was close so much of the time. Like a child on a merry-go-round the touch of the colored ring just evaded the tips of her touch, and she heaved and she hurdled, arched and cried, clawed me, kissed me, even gave of a shriek once, and then her sweats running down and her will weak, exhausted even more than me, she felt me leave and lie beside her. Yes, I did that with a tactician's cunning, I let the depression of her failure poison what was left of her will never to let me succeed, I gave her slack to mourn the lost freedoms and hate the final virginity for which she fought, I even allowed her baffled heat to take its rest and attack her nerves once more, and then, just as she was beginning to fret against me in a new and unwilling appeal, I turned her over suddenly on her belly, my avenger wild with the mania of the madman, and giving her no chance, holding her prone against the mattress with the strength of my weight, I drove into the seat of all stubbornness, tight as a vise, and I wounded her, I knew it, she thrashed beneath me like a trapped little animal, making not a sound, but fierce not to allow me this last of the liberties, and yet caught, forced to give up millimeter by millimeter the bridal ground of her symbolic and therefore real vagina. So I made it, I made it all the way — it took ten minutes and maybe more, but as the avenger rode down to his hilt and tunneled the threshold of sexual home all those inches closer into the bypass of the womb, she gave at last a little cry of farewell, and I could feel a new shudder which began as a ripple and rolled into a wave, and then it rolled over her, carrying her along, me hardly moving for fear of damping this quake from her earth, and then it was gone, but she was left alive with a larger one to follow.

So I turned her once again on her back, and moved by impulse to love's first hole. There was an odor coming up, hers at last, the smell of the sea, and none of the armpit or a dirty sock, and I took her mouth and kissed it, but she was away, following the wake of her own waves which mounted, fell back, and in new momentum mounted higher and should have gone over, and then she was about to hang again, I could feel it, that moment of hesitation between the past and the present, the habit and the adventure, and I said into her ear, "You dirty little Jew."

That whipped her over. A first wave kissed, a second spilled, and a third and a fourth and a fifth came breaking over, and finally she was away, she was loose in the water for the first time in her life, and I would have liked to go with her, but I was blood-throttled and numb, and as she had the first big moment in her life, I was nothing but a set of aching balls and a congested cock, and I rode with her wistfully, looking at the contortion of her face and listening to her sobbing sound of "Oh, Jesus, I made it, oh Jesus, I did."

"Compliments of T. S. Eliot," I whispered to myself, and my head was aching, my body was shot. She curled against me, she kissed my sweat, she nuzzled my eyes and murmured in my ear, and then she was slipping away into the nicest of weary sweet sleep.

"Was it good for you too?" she whispered half-awake, having likewise read the works of The Hemingway, and I said, "Yeah, fine," and after she was asleep, I disengaged myself carefully, and prowled the loft, accepting the hours it would take for my roiled sack to clean its fatigues and know a little sleep. But I had abused myself too far, and it took till dawn and half a fifth of whisky before I dropped into an unblessed stupor. When I awoke, in that moment before I moved to look at her, and saw her glaring at me, I was off on a sluggish masculine debate as to whether the kick of studying this Denise for another few nights—now that I had turned the key—would be worth the danger of deepening into some small real feeling. But through my hangover and the knowledge of the day and the week and the month it would take the different parts of all of me to repair, I was also knowing the taste of a reinforced will—finally, I had won. At no matter what cost, and with what luck, and with a piece of charity from her, I had won nonetheless, and since all real pay came from victory, it was more likely that I would win the next time I gambled my stake on something more appropriate for my ambition.

Then I turned, saw the hatred in her eyes, turned over again, and made believe I was asleep while a dread of the next few minutes weighed a leaden breath over the new skin of my ego.

"You're awake, aren't you?" she said.

I made no answer.

"All right, I'm going then. I'm getting dressed." She whipped out of bed, grabbed her clothes, and began to put them on with all the fury of waiting for me to get the pronouncement. "That was a lousy thing you did last night," she said by way of a start.

In truth she looked better than she ever had. The severe lady and the tough little girl of yesterday's face had put forth the first agreements on what would yet be a bold chick.

"I gave you what you could use," I made the mistake of saying.

"Just didn't you," she said, and was on her way to the door. "Well, cool it. You don't do anything to me." Then she smiled. "You're so impressed with what you think was such a marvelous notch you made in me, listen, Buster, I came here last night thinking of what Sandy Joyce told me about you, and he's right, oh man is he right." Standing in the open doorway, she started to light a cigarette, and then threw the matches to the floor. From thirty feet away I could see the look in her eyes, that unmistakable point for the kill that you find in the eyes of very few bullfighters, and then having created her pause, she came on for her moment of truth by saying, "He told me your whole life is a lie, and you do nothing but run away from the homosexual that is you."

And like a real killer, she did not look back, and was out the door before I could rise to tell her that she was a hero fit for me.

DEATHS FOR THE LADIES

(AND OTHER DISASTERS)

Published by Putnam's in hard and paperback in 1962, Deaths for the Ladies *is Mailer's only volume of verse and is also the only one of his books currently out of print. Unpaginated and with the poems strikingly arranged in typographical and sequential innovations, the book had the particular virtue of displaying Mailer's imagination at work in fresh and unfamiliar forms. A reissue of the book has been contemplated, and Mailer has prepared a new introduction with a fascinating and indeed touching account of the years in which the poems were written — 1960–1962 — and hopefully this will be available soon. The poems selected here show the interesting range of which Mailer is capable, from the epigrammatic "short hair" to the extended, reflective lyric, and need no other introduction save, perhaps, the remark that a number of the poems later printed in* The Presidential Papers *were drawn from* Deaths for the Ladies.

Prose
can pass
  into
poetry
when
    its heart
    is intense
For one
    can then
    dispense
    with whence
        went
        the verse.

Rhythm
  and rhyme
  may mask
    the movements
        of Time.
        Remember
    that the sound
    of Time
  is flesh.

TESTAMENTS

I never
  scored
  said
  snake.
It was
  Adam
  I wanted
    but
  Eve bought
  the cake.

       * * *

I'm not altogether
  nervous
I mean if we
  have another
  drink
  I think
    I could concentrate
      on the drink
      and not
        the
        time.

TO THE LOWER CLASSES

Noblesse
    Oblige
  has one rule
    and
one rule only

You must be
    so nice
    so bright
    so quick and
    so well turned
      that
    no one need
      tell you
      a second time.

Tell me what?
    that the world
      is well-lost
      for love
    and the upper
      classes
      are the
      law above?

I tell you this:
    if the
    upper classes
    are kin to God
      in style —
    (which is one hypothesis
      we do not ignore:
        how else account
        for elegance?)

  if the
  upper classes
  are kin to God
    in style

then God has no love
but guilt, nor a style
apart from fashion,
no courage but to
do in duty
                what
one does not desire
and no worth
but for His love
                at beauty

For there
          is noble's work
their plea:
          that they
love in truth
with all sense
          of Christian
          love
divorced from self
the air of beauty
          and her pomp.

The poor know naught
          but death
          they do not free
          they obliterate.

Stripped of its
          distinctions
          life is a flat city
               whose isolated spurs
               cut the sky
               like housing projects.
          Think of the air
               whose heart is bruised
               by touching such artifacts.
               (*Does* the cutworm forgive the plough?)

I tell you, say the rich,
               the poor are naught
               but dirty wind
               welling in air-shafts
               over the cinders
               and droppings of
               the past, their

voices thick
with grease
and ordure,
sewer-greed
to corrode the ear
with the horrors
of the past
and the voids
of new stupidity.
One could drown
waiting for the poor
to make
one fine distinction.
Yes, destroy us
say the rich
and you lose
the roots
of God.

Destroy them
say the poor
we cannot breathe
nor give
until we etch
on their rich nerve
the cruel razor
and heartless club
of our past,
those sediments of
waste
which curbed
our genes
and flattened
the vision we
would give
the chromosome.

Yes, destroy them
say the poor
burn them, rob them
gorge their tears
and such half of beauty
lost to pomp
will flower
unglimpsed wonders

in the rose,
will flower
unglimpsed wonders
in the rows.

I wonder,
  said the Lord
I wonder if I know the answer
    any more.

GOURMANDISE

1

The wine
   was
   Sierra Blanca
   a California
      Sauterne.
But it had
   a moldy
   label
and a green
   rusted cork,
age and
   color
   of
   cobweb.
So we
   chose it
over a
   fine dry
   fast
   cool
   professional
   blond
      from
   Bordeaux.

2

Yet when
   the
   nectar
      crested
      over
      the eddies
      of fume
      which rose
      from
   the dust
      of the cork,
      the wine
   was sour
      and
      squalid
         like
      bad breath
on a good goose
      with bad teeth.
Oh well,
   we murmured,
   never fall
      for a
         pretty face
            again.

DEATH OF A LOVER WHO LOVED DEATH

I find
  that
  most
  of the people I
          know
    are immature
    and cannot
              cope
              with reality
    said the suicide
His death
  followed
    a slash on each wrist.
Fit
was this end
for blood
  in its flow
  reveals
what a furnace
  had burned
    in the dungeon
    of his unconscious

Burn and bleed

He coped with
  reality
  too well.

It was unreality
  which waited
  on a midnight trail
  in that fierce
  jungle of eternity
    he heard murmuring
  on the other side

Oh, night of the jungle,
  God of mercy
  wept the suicide
  do not ask me
  to reconnoiter
    this
      dark
      trail
  when I am now
      without
      hands.

A WANDERING IN PROSE:
FOR HEMINGWAY

Summer, 1956

Why do you still put on that face
powder which smells like Paris when
I was kicking seconal and used to
get up at four in the morning and
walk the streets into the long wait
for dawn (like an exhausted husband
pacing the room where you wait for
the hospital to inform you of wife
and birth) visions of my death seated
already in the nauseas of my tense
frightened liver—such a poor death,
wet with timidity, ordure and the
muck of a Paris dawn, the city more
beautiful than it had ever been, warm
in June and me at five in an Algerian
bar watching the workers take a
swallow of wine for breakfast, the
city tender in its light even to me
and I sicker than I've ever been,
weak with loathing at all I had not done,
and all I was learning of all I would
now never do, and I would come back
after combing the vistas of the Seine
for glints of light to bank in the
corroded vaults of my ambitious and
yellow jaundiced soul and there back
in bed, nada, you lying in bed in hate
of me, the waves of unspoken flesh
radiating detestation into me because
I have been brave a little but not nearly
brave enough for you, greedy bitch,
Spanish lady, with your murderous
Indian blood and your crazy purity
hung on courage in men as if it were
your queen's own royal balls, and I
would lie down next to you, that smell
of unguent and face powder bleak and

chic as if the life of your skin depended
now not on the life my hands could give
in a pass upon your cheek, but upon the
arts of the corporation mixing your
elixirs in hundred gallon vats by
temperatures calibrated to the thermostat,
bleak and chic like the Hotel Palais
Royale ("my home away from home" we had
seen written by Capote in his cuneiform
script when the guest book was passed
to me for the equivocal cachet of my
signature so dim in its fashion that
year) and I took up the pen thinking
of the buff-colored damp of our indifferent room where we slept in misery
wondering if we had lost the loots of
anticipation we had commanded once so
fierce in one another—or was it only
me? for that is the thought of a lover
when his death comes over him in that
scent of the creams you rubbed on your
face while I slept the half-sleep of
the addict kicking the authority of
his poison—how bitter and clean was
the taste of the seconal. And now in
March of sixty-one the scent of that
cream came over me again as you kissed
me here at this instant, wearing it
again, knowing I detest it because again
it drives the secret of my poor augure
for eternity into those caverns of my
nose which lead back among the stalactites
of the nostril to the dream and one's
nightly dialogue with the fine verdicts
of the city asleep, and all souls on the
prowl talking to one another in the
dark markets of heaven about the future
of what we are to be if one obeys the
shape we gamblers have given to that
tool of destiny—our character. And the
smell of the corporation is still on
your skin mocking what I have done to
mine.

A WANDERING IN PROSE:
FOR HEMINGWAY

November, 1960

That first unmanageable cell
of the cancer which was to
stifle his existence arrived
to him on a morning when by
an extreme act of the will
he chose not to strike his
mother. Since this was
thirtysix hours after he
had stabbed his wife, and
his mother had come at a time
when he wished to see no one
in order to savor the woes
and pawed prides of his soul,
(what a need for leisure
has the criminal heart) his
renunciation of violence
was civilized, too civilized
for his cells which proceeded
to revolt. But then it is
the thesis of this summary
that civilization spawns
cancer in every corner of
every church whose smell
is stale with the fatigues
of such devotion as lost its
memory on the long road
to ecstasy from
habit.

FAREWELL TO ARMS REVISITED

1

I feel
 like
I've been
 through purga-
    tory, Catherine
             said.
Sometimes
I think
     it won't
      be bad
       when
       we die
       because
      we've served
       part
        of
       purgatory al-
             ready.

Yes.
 It's been
   bad.
   But
 twelve years
   ago
    we were
   good.

Oh, darling, good, she agreed,
                so good.
    I used to think
       it would
        be
       endless,
       I
       thought
       it would
       be always,
       but it wasn't, it
          turned out
          to be
       such a little
       taste
       of
       heaven
       for twelve
       long years.

2

A little taste
        of heaven
is all we get,
        baby,
        said
        Caryl
        Chessman
        through the
        microphone
        and plate
                glass
                window
        of the visitor's
                        room
                    under
            the shotguns
            eyes
            bellies
            and blue serge suits
            of the guards
            who guard
        the sacred heart
        of the Republic.

"The worst to be said about mothers
    is that they are prone
    to give kisses of congratulations
    which make you feel
            like a battleship
on which someone
            is breaking a bottle"
            said the figure of speech
            in a voice
                    which
            awarded art
            to itself.
Metaphors may be heartless.
In the salon they are savage.
            One enters rooms wet
            with a razor's light
                    from the tongue of
                    fifteen bloods
                    ready to dissect
                    the fornications
                    of their fathers.

            Their hope?
                        That
            surgical excisions
            upon the past
            may illumine
            the flesh of the
            company
            with a luminous blaze
pure as wit
            in a moment of murder.
Not all light is love.

Deaths for the Ladies (and other disasters)   **277**

Hey—
  you
    sleep
    deep—
  but what a sight
    see
    you
      soon
     beautiful
     I hope

(Since the lady
       found this note
       by her telephone
       on awakening
       in an empty bed
       after a one-night
       stand, she called
       her best friend
       a girl, and said,
            Guess what?
         I feel like
            Earth
            Mother.)

ETERNITIES

I'm rich
    said
Irish
    derby
    slopping
    a drink
    on the
    floor

So I've always
    missed
    the pleasures
    of the poor.

    Taste his spit!
        said the sawdust
        it's a scandal
    and a shame

    Naught but outer limbo
        said the roach
        on his way
        on his fraught-filled
            way, on his fraught-
filled way to the door
        and toward the
        stair
        of his own.

When he reached
    the cracked enamel
    in the kitchen
        of his pad
he made a
        tour
of quarters
        leaving
        molecules
        like pennies
        on the oilcloth
        of the
        poor—
five molecules
        of scotch
        to every
            plate

But the fumes had drunk
    his mind to stuff
    and roachie slept
    an emperor's sleep
dreaming of previous lives
    in derby hats
when he had slopped
    the whiskey
    to the floor
crying for the pleasures
    of the poor.

LOGIC

A. When Napoleon
   met Goethe
   it was the
   Emperor
   who wrote the poem.

B. When I met
   Kennedy . . .

C. Either:
         Jack
         is a
         greater
            man than
                me,
         Or—
            times have
               changed.

THE CORNERS OF A SQUARE

1

It would
  be
an aid
if the
  blind
  came
    to the
    game
  because
  their ears
    are
    clean
  said
  the dream.

2

I would
  be
afraid
of those
  who
hear and
  do not
  see
  said
  the word.

3

I am
in
love with
those who
  come
with their
wound to
  me
said the
  mood
  for
those who
  see
and do
not hear
  wound
  others
  with their
  voice.

4

Those who
  hear
  and do
  not see
  give
  alms
  to Eve
  and
  other
  ill
  said
  the peace
  which comes
  from
  the police.

TOGETHERNESS

My flesh must smell like an old tire
my sex is bitter and gone
my days are leafless and all sleep
    said the housewife
    going to the specialist
one knows what kind

but in the waiting room
she was racked by a plague
from the pots of the American
    miasma — our magazines,
    and so lady murmured
        too quietly
even for her mind to hear:

Reader's Digest, please save *your* soul
and leave mine free to contemplate
eternity which must be more
    than I glimpse for myself now
    an endless promenade
across a field of baked old beans
    a cataract of dishwater
    regurgitated by the memory
of champagne I never drank
    and kings I never kissed

DEATH IN THE MOUNTAINS

We rented three horses
  in San Miguel Allende.
Two were to be tame.
But indeed the groom
  brought only two
          to the door.
Oh, Senor, said he,
  the third horse
          has a cold.

On the next day
  there were still but two
Relámpago and Gavilan.
We rode those horses —
  they were devils.
In three days
  they threw me
          three times.

It was only on the night
          of our departure
  that we learned
  our horses
  were mad.

Oh, Senor, said the groom
  the third horse has a cold.

One
nerve
screams
before
you
fall
said
the
ledge
on
the
window
in
the
nineteenth
floor

CERTAIN EVICTIONS

In the first week
    of their life
    male jews
    are crucified
The pain
    is
    exquisite

To discover
    the tip
    of your future
  by losing it
    is a fair
    price
    to pay
      for having been
    once so tense
    as to fail
    the race
    when
    He
    chose
    a Jew
    without a future
      to save it.

Grace.
  In the first week
    of their life
    grace is crucified.

Mood
  is a
congregation
of souls
    in the cells.

Those
  who govern
a body
of murdered hopes
  and
  cold will
are subject to
  sudden defeats
    of mood
      so severe
as to pose
    the question:

Is mood a temple
  which gives us
sanctuary
against
  the desire
  of our cells
to return to
    their beginnings
  under a
  new master
  who promises
  that he
  will not
  repeat
the hesitations,
compassions
    and
aesthetic
    com-
punctions of God
  about
    pleasure
    profit
  and
    progress
  but
    instead
      will rip up
      the roots
and give us
the broad
macadam
      of
civic virtue
tranquilized pain
eternity
      without fire
and sucaryl
for the syrup
      of the peach.

Poems
  written by
  masochists
   flop like cows
    in the meadow.
     Take pity on me
     they cry, pay
     attention, I
     am so sensitive
     to nature and
     full of milk

Poems
  should be like pins
  which prick the skin
        of boredom
        and leave
        a glow
     equal in its pride
     to the gait
     of the sadist
        who stuck
        the pin
        and walked away

IN THE HALLWAY

1

My God,
    she said
I came
      in my
      hat

   This time
      baby
   take your
        shoes off
          he said

2

My God,
    he said
    this time
I came
    in *my*
    hat

    well,
take it
    off
      she said
I want
      to see
the ba-
      by
and how
      his hair
      will be.

THE ECONOMY OF LOVE

Your eyes
    are beautiful
said my
    love.
Yes said I
      eyes of
      mine have
         seen your
         breast
         and so are
            beautiful.

  (but my heart
      was immersed
      in that
       calculus
      of the soul
      which measures
        the profit
        and cost
      of conversions
        from beauty
        to power)

Your eyes
    are beautiful
    said my love
    and have
      left
      me.

A CURE FOR CANCER

A
  cure
   for
    cancer
    is
    to
    visit
   the
  moon

A plague is
    coming
    named
      Virus Y S X
      still unsolved
      promises to be
            proof
            against
            antibiotics
            psychoanalysis
            research projects
            vitamins
            awards
            crash programs
            crash diets
            symposiums
            foundations
            rest
            rehabilitation
            tranquilizers
            aspirin
            surgery
            brainwashing
            lobotomies
            rises in status
            box office boffo
            perversions
                  and
                  even
                  a
                  good
                  piece
                  of

When that unhappy day
    comes to America
    let the Russians
    take over.
The best defense is
            infection.

Deaths for the Ladies (and other disasters)   **291**

I
   was
   hysterical
   stated
   the girl
            I
dropped
my
   god
damned con
tact lens
         down
            the drain
Then
this
creep
called
at four
   A.M.

                           Hel
                              lo Kook
                              he said

                     Guess what:

                              I just
                              found
                              your
                              contact
                                 lens.

I won't stay in
        with married man
        any more
        said the wise girl
            they're too agreeable,
            it's a little too much
                like curling
                up
        with the good book.

You mean
        a
        good book

Oh, dear,
        did I say
        the
        good book
        sighed the witch.

How can you
    say
    you're
    only
    three-quarters
        a man.
why you're
    completely
    a man
    said the
        lady
        in a
        three-quarter voice.

          If
Harry Golden
is the gentile's
Jew
          can I be-
come the Golden
Goy?

EXODUS

Goodbye America,
   Jesus said.
Come back, *boy!*
   we cried
   too late.

TIMING

Listen
  my love
  the hour
  is late
  my side
  has an
  ache
    If
    you don't
    get a
    taxi
    my heart
    will break

THE PRESIDENTIAL PAPERS

This second volume of Mailer's shorter writing was published in the fall of 1963, thus coinciding with the assassination of President Kennedy. Since its organizational principle has been to address the President directly, the book faded quickly. It was brought out in paperback by Bantam in 1964, later dropped, and is now available in the Berkley Medallion paperback edition. The "special preface" which begins this excerpt was originally printed in a Bantam edition. "Superman Comes to the Supermarket" originally appeared in Esquire *in November, 1960. "The Big Bite" was the title of a monthly column Mailer did for* Esquire *from November, 1962 to December, 1963. "Responses and Reactions" was the title of a monthly column Mailer did for* Commentary *from December, 1962 to October, 1963. The column reprinted here was published in February, 1963. "Ten Thousand Words a Minute," an account of the 1962 Patterson-Liston fight in Chicago, was published in* Esquire *in February,*

1963. "The Metaphysics of the Belly," later reprinted in Cannibals and Christians, *part of a series of Platonic dialogs Mailer was to develop, was published in* The Presidential Papers *for the first time. The "Poem to the Book Review at* Time" *originally appeared in the "letters" section of* Time *April 6, 1962 in answer to a mocking review of* Deaths for the Ladies, *in verse form, which had appeared earlier. The poem interestingly prophesies* Time's *eventual embracing of Mailer, who at this period was regularly attacked in its pages.*

Special Preface to the Berkley Edition

The Presidential Papers were written while Jack Kennedy was alive, and so the book was put together with the idea that the President might come to read it. One did not mean of course that he would literally read it right away in that giant-killing stride of his (reputed to cross over more than half a thousand words of prose each minute). No, the author had the idea instead that people about the President might look at the book in pieces and parts, and conversations would ensue; over the years, who could be certain? The President might put his head into its pages for a few seconds. Thus, the book was inspired by a desire to have its influence. Slow that might be and near to subterranean, but it was a book aimed nonetheless at some favorite notions of the President and the American Establishment: therefore the irreverence of the prose was as necessary as the feathers on the shaft of an arrow. In America few people will trust you unless you are irreverent; there was a message returned to us by our frontier that the outlaw is worth more than the sheriff.

One was therefore irreverent to the President. But the extent of one's irreverence was discovered to be also the measure of one's unsuspected affection: that one discovered the day he was killed; discovered that again during the weeks of depression which followed. For he was no ordinary sheriff—he was an outlaw's sheriff, he was one sheriff who could have been an outlaw himself. Such Presidents can be quickly counted: Jefferson, Andrew Jackson, Lincoln, Franklin Delano Roosevelt, John F. Kennedy. One doubts if there are any others. While this is the only kind of sheriff for whom an outlaw can feel love, one should still of course not be excessively polite, for every sheriff must labor finally on the side of all those mediocrities who made a profit from mediocrity by extinguishing (let a new Marx rise among us) the promise of others.

Still, John F. Kennedy was a remarkable man. A modern democracy is a tyranny whose borders are undefined; one discovers how far one can go only by traveling in a straight line until one is stopped; Kennedy was not in a hurry to stop us. I would not be surprised if he believed that the health of America (which is to say our vitality) depended in part on the inventiveness and passion of its outlaws.

Then, of course, he was killed by an outlaw. Which is tragic, but not startling. For heroism often gives life to a creation which is bound and determined to kill the hero. Ultimately a hero is a man who would argue with the gods, and so awakens devils to contest his vision. The more a man can achieve, the more he may be certain that the devil will inhabit a part of his creation.

These theological illuminations are of vast use to the reader, doubtless; but they lead the author astray from the point to his introduction. He was trying to say that we have here a book which was written in part for a man very much alive. This book is now homeless, for it has ceased to thrive inside its original intention. One had hoped to quicken the context of criticism, to darken the political soup with marrow. Now, like a displaced person, the book is a document. It speaks from the far cliff of a divide, from a time which is past, from history. Given these overtones, the book has an unintentional echo: it tells the story of a President and of a Presidential time which was neither conclusive nor legislatively active, but which was nonetheless a period not without a suspicion of greatness, greatness of promise at the very least, for it was a time when writers could speak across the land in intimate dialogue with their leader.

He was a good and serious man, one now suspects. Only such a man would neglect to cover himself with the pompous insulations of the state. Still, one would not retract what one has written: his faults were his faults, his lacks were his lacks, his political maneuverings were no better than the others, his dull taste was certainly his dull taste. But what one did not recognize sufficiently was the extent of his humor. That humor created an atmosphere in which one could attempt this book; now, as a document which circles mournfully about its subject, one can hear in the echoes of his absence the proportions of that humor, and thus feel the loss. Fifty years may go by before such a witty and promising atmosphere comes to life in America again. So the corridors are gloomy. "He was a great man," said a girl at a party the other night. "No, he wasn't a great man," I said. "He was a man who could have become great or could have failed, and now we'll never know. That's what's so awful." That *is* what is so awful. Tragedy is amputation: the nerves of one's memory run back to the limb which is no longer there.

NORMAN MAILER

Superman Comes to the Supermarket

Not too much need be said for this piece; it is possible it can stand by itself. But perhaps its title should have been "Filling the Holes in No Man's Land."

American politics is rarely interesting for its men, its ideas, or the style of its movements. It is usually more fascinating in its gaps, its absences, its uninvaded territories. We have used up our frontier, but the psychological frontier talked about in this piece is still alive with untouched possibilities and dire unhappy all-but-lost opportunities. In European politics the spaces are filled—the average politician, like the average European, knows what is possible and what is impossible for him. Their politics is like close trench warfare. But in America, one knows such close combat only for the more banal political activities. The play of political ideas is flaccid here in America because opposing armies never meet. The Right, the Center, and what there is of the Left have set up encampments on separate hills, they face one another across valleys, they send out small patrols to their front and vast communiqués to their rear.

No Man's Land predominates. It is a situation which calls for guerrilla raiders. Any army which would dare to enter the valley in force might not only determine a few new political formations, but indeed could create more politics itself, even as the guerrilla raids of the Negro Left and Negro Right, the Freedom Riders and the Black Muslims, have discovered much of the secret nature of the American reality for us.

I wonder if I make myself clear. Conventional politics has had so little to do with the real subterranean life of America that none of us know much about the real—which is to say the potential—historic nature of America. That lies buried under apathy, platitudes, Rightist encomiums for the FBI, programmatic welfare from the liberal Center, and furious pips of protest from the Peace Movement's Left. The mass of Americans are not felt as a political reality. No one has any idea of how they would react to radically new sense. It is only when their heart-land, their no man's land, their valley is invaded, that one discovers the reality. In Birmingham during the days of this writing, the jails are filled with Negro children, 2000 of them. The militancy of the Negroes in Birmingham is startling, so too is the stubbornness of the Southern white, so too and unbelievable is the procrastination of the Kennedy administration. Three new realities have been discovered. The potential Left and potential Right of America are more vigorous than one would have expected and the Center is more irresolute. An existential political act, the drive by Southern Negroes, led by Martin Luther King, to end segregation in restaurants in Birmingham, an act which is existential precisely because its end is unknown, has succeeded en route in discovering more of the American reality to us.

If a public speaker in a small Midwestern town were to say, "J. Edgar Hoover has done more harm to the freedoms of America than Joseph Stalin," the act would be existential. Depending on the occasion and the town, he would be manhandled physically or secretly applauded. But he would create a new reality which would displace the old psychological reality that such a remark could not be made, even as for example the old Southern psychological reality that you couldn't get two Negroes to do anything together, let alone two thousand has now been destroyed by a new and more accurate psychological reality: you can get two thousand Negroes to work in cooperation. The new psychological realities are closer to history and so closer to sanity and they exist because, and only because, the event has taken place.

It was Kennedy's potentiality to excite such activity which interested me most; that he was young, that he was physically hand-

some, and that his wife was attractive were not trifling accidental details but, rather, new major political facts. I knew if he became President, it would be an existential event: he would touch depths in American life which were uncharted. Regardless of his politics, and even then one could expect his politics would be as conventional as his personality was unconventional, indeed one could expect his politics to be pushed toward conventionality precisely to counteract his essential unconventionality, one knew nonetheless that regardless of his overt politics, America's tortured psychotic search for security would finally be torn loose from the feverish ghosts of its old generals, its MacArthurs and Eisenhowers— ghosts which Nixon could cling to—and we as a nation would finally be loose again in the historic seas of a national psyche which was willy-nilly and at last, again, adventurous. And that, I thought, that was the hope for America. So I swallowed my doubts, my disquiets, and my certain distastes for Kennedy's dullness of mind and prefabricated politics, and did my best to write a piece which would help him to get elected.

For once let us try to think about a political convention without losing ourselves in housing projects of fact and issue. Politics has its virtues, all too many of them—it would not rank with baseball as a topic of conversation if it did not satisfy a great many things— but one can suspect that its secret appeal is close to nicotine. Smoking cigarettes insulates one from one's life, one does not feel as much, often happily so, and politics quarantines one from history; most of the people who nourish themselves in the political life are in the game not to make history but to be diverted from the history which is being made.

If that Democratic Convention which has now receded behind the brow of the Summer of 1960 is only half-remembered in the excitements of moving toward the election, it may be exactly the time to consider it again, because the mountain of facts which concealed its features last July has been blown away in the winds of High Television, and the man-in-the-street (that peculiar political term which refers to the quixotic voter who will pull the lever for some reason so salient as: "I had a brown-nose lieutenant once with Nixon's looks," or "that Kennedy must have false teeth"), the not so easily estimated man-in-the-street has forgotten most of what happened and could no more tell you who Kennedy was fighting against than you or I could place a bet on who was leading the American League in batting during the month of June.

So to try to talk about what happened is easier now than in the days of the convention, one does not have to put everything in—an act of writing which calls for a bulldozer rather than a pen—one can try to make one's little point and dress it with a ribbon or two of metaphor. All to the good. Because mysteries are irritated by facts, and the 1960 Democratic Convention began as one mystery and ended as another.

Since mystery is an emotion which is repugnant to a political animal (why else lead a life of bad banquet dinners, cigar smoke, camp chairs, foul breath, and excruciatingly dull jargon if not to avoid the echoes of what is not known), the psychic separation between what was happening on the floor, in the caucus rooms, in the headquarters, and what was happening in parallel to the history of the nation was mystery enough to drown the proceedings in gloom. It was on the one hand a dull convention, one of the less interesting by general agreement, relieved by local bits of color, given two half hours of excitement by two demonstrations for Stevenson, buoyed up by the class of the Kennedy machine, turned by the surprise of Johnson's nomination as vice-president, but, all the same, dull, depressed in its over-all tone, the big fiestas subdued, the gossip flat, no real air of excitement, just moments—or as they say in bullfighting—details. Yet it was also, one could argue—and one may argue this yet—it was also one of the most important conventions in America's history, it could prove conceivably to be the most important. The man it nominated was unlike any politician who had ever run for President in the history of the land, and if elected he would come to power in a year when America was in danger of drifting into a profound decline.

A Descriptive of the Delegates: Sons and Daughters of the Republic in a Legitimate Panic; Small-time Practitioners of Small-town Political Judo in the Big Town and the Big Time

Depression obviously has its several roots: it is the doubtful protection which comes from not recognizing failure, it is the psychic burden of exhaustion, and it is also, and very often, that discipline of the will or the ego which enables one to continue working when one's unadmitted emotion is panic. And panic it was I think which sat as the largest single sentiment in the breast of the collective delegates as they came to convene in Los Angeles. Delegates are not the noblest sons and daughters of the Republic; a man of taste, arrived from Mars, would take one look at a convention floor and leave forever, convinced he had seen one of the drearier squats of

Hell. If one still smells the faint living echo of a carnival wine, the pepper of a bullfight, the rag, drag, and panoply of a jousting tourney, it is all swallowed and regurgitated by the senses into the fouler cud of a death gas one must rid oneself of—a cigar-smoking, stale-aired, slack-jawed, butt-littered, foul, bleak, hard-working, bureaucratic death gas of language and faces ("Yes, those *faces*," says the man from Mars: lawyers, judges, ward heelers, *mafiosos*, Southern goons and grandees, grand old ladies, trade unionists and finks), of pompous words and long pauses which lay like a leaden pain over fever, the fever that one is in, over, or is it that one is just behind history? A legitimate panic for a delegate. America is a nation of experts without roots; we are always creating tacticians who are blind to strategy and strategists who cannot take a step, and when the culture has finished its work the institutions handcuff the infirmity. A delegate is a man who picks a candidate for the largest office in the land, a President who must live with problems whose borders are in ethics, metaphysics, and now ontology; the delegate is prepared for this office of selection by emptying wastebaskets, toting garbage and saying yes at the right time for twenty years in the small political machine of some small or large town; his reward, one of them anyway, is that he arrives at an invitation to the convention. An expert on local catch-as-catch-can, a small-time, often mediocre practitioner of small-town political judo, he comes to the big city with nine-tenths of his mind made up, he will follow the orders of the boss who brought him. Yet of course it is not altogether so mean as that: his opinion is listened to—the boss will consider what he has to say as one interesting factor among five hundred, and what is most important to the delegate, he has the illusion of partial freedom. He can, unless he is severely honest with himself—and if he is, why sweat out the low levels of a political machine?—he can have the illusion that he has helped to choose the candidate, he can even worry most sincerely about his choice, flirt with defection from the boss, work out his own small political gains by the road of loyalty or the way of hard bargain. But even if he is there for no more than the ride, his vote a certainty in the mind of the political boss, able to be thrown here or switched there as the boss decides, still in some peculiar sense he is reality to the boss, the delegate is the great American public, the bar he owns or the law practice, the piece of the union he represents, or the real-estate office, is a part of the political landscape which the boss uses as his own image of how the votes will go, and if the people will like the candidate. And if the boss is depressed by what he sees, if the candidate does not feel right to him, if he has a dull intimation that the candidate is not his sort (as, let us say, Harry Truman was his sort, or Symington might be his sort, or Lyndon Johnson), then vote for him the boss will if he must; he cannot be caught on the wrong side, but he does not feel the pleasure of a personal choice. Which is the center of the panic. Because if the boss is depressed, the delegate is doubly depressed, and the emotional fact is that Kennedy is not in focus, not in the old political focus, he is not comfortable; in fact it is a mystery to the boss how Kennedy got to where he is, not a mystery in its structures; Kennedy is rolling in money, Kennedy got the votes in primaries, and, most of all, Kennedy has a jewel of a political machine. It is as good as a crack Notre Dame team, all discipline and savvy and go-go-go, sound, drilled, never dull, quick as a knife, full of the salt of hipper-dipper, a beautiful machine; the boss could adore it if only a sensible candidate were driving it, a Truman, even a Stevenson, please God a Northern Lyndon Johnson, but it is run by a man who looks young enough to be coach of the Freshman team, and that is not comfortable at all. The boss knows political machines, he knows issues, farm parity, Forand health bill, Landrum-Griffin, but this is not all so adequate after all to revolutionaries in Cuba who look like beatniks, competitions in missiles, Negroes looting whites in the Congo, intricacies of nuclear fallout, and NAACP men one does well to call Sir. It is all out of hand, everything important is off the center, foreign affairs is now the lick of the heat, and senators are candidates instead of governors, a disaster to the old family style of political measure where a political boss knows his governor and knows who his governor knows. So the boss is depressed, profoundly depressed. He comes to this convention resigned to nominating a man he does not understand, or let us say that, so far as he understands the candidate who is to be nominated, he is not happy about the secrets of his appeal, not so far as he divines these secrets; they seem to have too little to do with politics and all too much to do with the private madnesses of the nation which had thousands — or was it hundreds of thousands — of people demonstrating in the long night before Chessman was killed, and a movie star, the greatest, Marlon the Brando out in the night with them. Yes, this candidate for all his record, his good, sound, conventional liberal record has a patina of that other life, the second American life, the long electric night with the fires of neon leading down the highway to the murmur of jazz.

An Apparent Digression: A Vivid View of the
"City of Lost Angels"; The Democrats Defined;
A Pentagon of Traveling Salesmen;
Some Pointed Portraits of the Politicians

"I was seeing Pershing Square, Los Angeles, now for the first time . . .
the nervous fruithustlers darting in and out of the shadows, fugitives
from Times Square, Market Street SF, the French Quarter—masculine
hustlers looking for lonely fruits to score from, anything from the legendary $20 to a pad at night and breakfast in the morning and whatever
you can clinch or clip; and the heat in their holy cop uniforms, holy
because of the Almighty Stick and the Almightier Vagrancy Law; the
scattered junkies, the small-time pushers, the queens, the sad panhan-
dlers, the lonely, exiled nymphs haunting the entrance to the men's
head, the fruits with the hungry eyes and the jingling coins; the tough
teen-age chicks — 'dittybops' — making it with the lost hustlers . . . all
amid the incongruous piped music and the flowers—twin fountains
gushing rainbow colored: the world of Lonely America squeezed into
Pershing Square, of the Cities of Terrible Night, downtown now
trapped in the City of lost Angels . . . and the trees hang over it all like
some type of apathetic fate."   —JOHN RECHY: Big Table 3

Seeing Los Angeles after ten years away, one realizes all over
again that America is an unhappy contract between the East (that
Faustian thrust of a most determined human will which reaches up
and out above the eye into the skyscrapers of New York) and
those flat lands of compromise and mediocre self-expression, those
endless half-pretty repetitive small towns of the Middle and the
West, whose spirit is forever horizontal and whose marrow comes
to rendezvous in the pastel monotonies of Los Angeles architecture.

So far as America has a history, one can see it in the severe
heights of New York City, in the glare from the Pittsburgh mills,
by the color in the brick of Louisburg Square, along the knotted
greedy façades of the small mansions on Chicago's North Side, in
Natchez' antebellum homes, the wrought-iron balconies off Bourbon Street, a captain's house in Nantucket, by the curve of Commercial Street in Provincetown. One can make a list; it is probably
finite. What culture we have made and what history has collected
to it can be found in those few hard examples of an architecture
which came to its artistic term, was born, lived and so collected
some history about it. Not all the roots of American life are uprooted, but almost all, and the spirit of the supermarket, that homo-
genous extension of stainless surfaces and psychoanalyzed people,
packaged commodities and ranch homes, interchangeable, geo-

graphically unrecognizable, that essence of the new postwar SuperAmerica is found nowhere so perfectly as in Los Angeles' ubiquitous acres. One gets the impression that people come to Los Angeles in order to divorce themselves from the past, here to live or try to live in the rootless pleasure world of an adult child. One knows that if the cities of the world were destroyed by a new war, the architecture of the rebuilding would create a landscape which looked, subject to specifications of climate, exactly and entirely like the San Fernando Valley.

It is not that Los Angeles is altogether hideous, it is even by degrees pleasant, but for an Easterner there is never any salt in the wind; it is like Mexican cooking without chile, or Chinese egg rolls missing their mustard; as one travels through the endless repetitions of that city which is the capital of suburbia with its milky pinks, its washed-out oranges, its tainted lime-yellows of pastel on one pretty little architectural monstrosity after another, the colors not intense enough, the styles never pure, and never sufficiently impure to collide on the eye, one conceives the people who live here—they have come out to express themselves, Los Angeles is the home of self-expression, but the artists are middle-class and middling-minded; no passions will calcify here for years in the gloom to be revealed a decade later as the tessellations of a hard and fertile work, no, it is all open, promiscuous, borrowed, half bought, a city without iron, eschewing wood, a kingdom of stucco, the playground for mass men—one has the feeling it was built by television sets giving orders to men. And in this land of the pretty-pretty, the virility is in the barbarisms, the vulgarities, it is in the huge billboards, the screamers of the neon lighting, the shouting farm-utensil colors of the gas stations and the monster drugstores, it is in the swing of the sports cars, hot rods, convertibles, Los Angeles is a city to drive in, the boulevards are wide, the traffic is nervous and fast, the radio stations play bouncing, blooping, rippling tunes, one digs the pop in a pop tune, no one of character would make love by it but the sound is good for swinging a car, electronic guitars and Hawaiian harps.

So this is the town the Democrats came to, and with their unerring instinct (after being with them a week, one thinks of this party as a crazy, half-rich family, loaded with poor cousins, traveling always in caravans with Cadillacs and Okie Fords, Lincolns and quarter-horse mules, putting up every night in tents to hear the chamber quartet of Great Cousin Eleanor invaded by the Texas-twanging steel-stringing geetarists of Bubber Lyndon, carrying its own mean high-school principal, Doc Symington, chided for its manners by good Uncle Adlai, told the route of march by Navigator Jack, cut off every six months from the rich will of Uncle Jim Farley, never listening to the mechanic of the caravan, Bald Sam Rayburn, who assures them they'll all break down unless Cousin Bubber gets the concession on the garage; it's the Snopes family married to Henry James, with the labor unions thrown in like a Yankee dollar, and yet it's true, in tranquility one recollects them with affection, their instinct is good, crazy family good) and this instinct now led the caravan to pick the Biltmore Hotel in downtown Los Angeles for their family get-together and reunion.

The Biltmore is one of the ugliest hotels in the world. Patterned after the flat roofs of an Italian Renaissance palace, it is eighty-eight times as large, and one-millionth as valuable to the continuation of man, and it would be intolerable if it were not for the presence of Pershing Square, that square block of park with cactus and palm trees, the three-hundred-and-sixty-five-day-a-year convention of every junkie, pot-head, pusher, queen (but you have read that good writing already). For years Pershing Square has been one of the three or four places in America famous to homosexuals, famous not for its posh, the chic is round-heeled here, but because it is one of the avatars of the good old masturbatory sex, dirty with the crusted sugars of smut, dirty rooming houses around the corner where the score is made, dirty book and photograph stores down the street, old-fashioned out-of-the-Thirties burlesque houses, cruising bars, jukeboxes, movie houses; Pershing Square is the town plaza for all those lonely, respectable, small-town homosexuals who lead a family life, make children, and have the Philbrick psychology (How I Joined the Communist Party and Led Three Lives). Yes, it is the open-air convention hall for the small-town inverts who live like spies, and it sits in the center of Los Angeles, facing the Biltmore, that hotel which is a mausoleum, that Pentagon of traveling salesmen the Party chose to house the headquarters of the Convention.

So here came that family, cursed before it began by the thundering absence of Great-Uncle Truman, the delegates dispersed over a run of thirty miles and twenty-seven hotels: the Olympian Motor Hotel, the Ambassador, the Beverly Wilshire, the Santa Ynez Inn (where rumor has it the delegates from Louisiana had some midnight swim), the Mayan, the Commodore, the Mayfair, the Sheraton-West, the Huntington-Sheraton, the Green, the Hayward, the Gates, the Figueroa, the Statler Hilton, the Hollywood Knickerbocker—does one have to be a collector to list such names?— beauties all, with that up-from-the-farm Los Angeles décor, plate-glass windows, patio and terrace, foam-rubber mattress, pastel paints, all of them pretty as an ad in full-page color, all but the Biltmore where everybody gathered every day—the newsmen, the TV, radio, magazine, and foreign newspapermen, the delegates, the politicos, the tourists, the campaign managers, the runners, the flunkies, the cousins and aunts, the wives, the grandfathers, the eight-year-old girls, and the twenty-eight-year-old girls in the Kennedy costumes, red and white and blue, the Symingteeners, the Johnson Ladies, the Stevenson Ladies, everybody—and for three days before the convention and four days into it, everybody collected at the Biltmore, in the lobby, in the grill, in the Biltmore Bowl, in the elevators, along the corridors, three hundred deep always outside the Kennedy suite, milling everywhere, every dark-carpeted grey-brown hall of the hotel, but it was in the Gallery of the Biltmore where one first felt the mood which pervaded all proceedings until the convention was almost over, that heavy, thick, witless depression which was to dominate every move as the delegates wandered and gawked and paraded and set for a spell, there in the Gallery of the Biltmore, that huge depressing alley with its inimitable hotel color, that faded depth of chiaroscuro which unhappily has no depth, that brown which is not a brown, that grey which has no pearl in it, that color which can be described only as hotel-color because the beiges, the tans, the walnuts, the mahoganies, the dull blood rugs, the moaning yellows, the sick greens, the greys and all those dumb browns merge into that lack of color which is an over-large hotel at convention time, with all the small-towners wearing their set, starched faces, that look they get at carnival, all fever and suspicion, and proud to be there, eddying slowly back and forth in that high block-long tunnel of a room with its arched ceiling and square recesses filling every rib of the arch with art work, escutcheons and blazons and other art, pictures I think, I cannot even remember, there was such a hill of cigar smoke the eye had to travel on its way to the ceiling, and at one end there was galvanized-pipe scaffolding and workmen repairing some part of the ceiling, one of them touching up one of the endless squares of painted plaster in the arch, and another worker, passing by, yelled up to the one who was working on the ceiling: "Hey, Michelangelo!"

Later, of course, it began to emerge and there were portraits one could keep, Symington, dogged at a press conference, declaring with no conviction that he knew he had a good chance to win, the disappointment eating at his good looks so that he came off hard-faced, mean, and yet slack—a desperate dullness came off the best of his intentions. There was Johnson who had compromised too many contradictions and now the contradictions were in his face: when he smiled the corners of his mouth squeezed gloom; when he was pious, his eyes twinkled irony; when he spoke in a righteous tone, he looked corrupt; when he jested, the ham in his jowls looked to quiver. He was not convincing. He was a Southern politician, a Texas Democrat, a liberal Eisenhower; he would do no harm, he would do no good, he would react to the machine, good fellow, nice friend — the Russians would understand him better than his own.

Stevenson had the patina. He came into the room and the room was different, not stronger perhaps (which is why ultimately he did not win), but warmer. One knew why some adored him; he did not look like other people, not with press lights on his flesh; he looked like a lover, the simple truth, he had the sweet happiness of an adolescent who has just been given his first major kiss. And so he glowed, and one was reminded of Chaplin, not because they were the least alike in features, but because Charlie Chaplin was luminous when one met him and Stevenson had something of that light.

There was Eleanor Roosevelt, fine, precise, hand-worked like ivory. Her voice was almost attractive as she explained in the firm, sad tones of the first lady in this small town why she could not admit Mr. Kennedy, who was no doubt a gentleman, into her political house. One had the impression of a lady who was finally becoming a woman, which is to say that she was just a little bitchy about it all; nice bitchy, charming, it had a touch of art to it, but it made one wonder if she were not now satisfying the last passion of them all, which was to become physically attractive, for she was better-looking than she had ever been as she spurned the possibilities of a young suitor.

Jim Farley. Huge. Cold as a bishop. The hell he would consign you to was cold as ice.

Bobby Kennedy, that archetype Bobby Kennedy, looked like a West Point cadet, or, better, one of those unreconstructed Irishmen from Kirkland House one always used to have to face in the line in Harvard house football games. "Hello," you would say to the ones who looked like him as you lined up for the scrimmage after the kickoff, and his type would nod and look away, one rock glint of recognition your due for living across the hall from one another all through Freshman year, and then bang, as the ball was passed back, you'd get a bony king-hell knee in the crotch. He was the kind of man never to put on the gloves with if you wanted to do some social boxing, because after two minutes it would be a war, and ego-bastards last long in a war.

Carmine DeSapio and Kenneth Galbraith on the same part of the convention floor. DeSapio is bigger than one expects, keen and florid, great big smoked glasses, a suntan like Mantan — he is the kind of heavyweight Italian who could get by with a name like

Romeo—and Galbraith is tall-tall, as actors say, six foot six it
could be, terribly thin, enormously attentive, exquisitely polite,
birdlike, he is sensitive to the stirring of reeds in a wind over the
next hill. "Our grey eminence," whispered the intelligent observer
next to me.

Bob Wagner, the mayor of New York, a little man, plump,
groomed, blank. He had the blank, pomaded, slightly worried look
of the first barber in a good barbershop, the kind who would go to
the track on his day off and wear a green transparent stone in a
gold ring,

And then there was Kennedy, the edge of the mystery. But a
sketch will no longer suffice.

*Perspective from the Biltmore Balcony: The
Colorful Arrival of the Hero with the Orange-
brown Suntan and Amazingly White Teeth;
Revelation of the Two Rivers Political Theory*

". . . it can be said with a fair amount of certainty that the essence of
his political attractiveness is his extraordinary political intelligence. He
has a mind quite unlike that of any other Democrat of this century. It is
not literary, metaphysical and moral, as Adlai Stevenson's is. Kennedy
is articulate and often witty, but he does not seek verbal polish. No one
can doubt the seriousness of his concern with the most serious political
matters, but one feels that whereas Mr. Stevenson's political views derive from a view of life that holds politics to be a mere fraction of existence, Senator Kennedy's primary interest is in politics. The easy way in
which he disposes of the question of Church and State—as if he felt that
any reasonable man could quite easily resolve any possible conflict of
loyalties—suggests that the organization of society is the one thing that
really engages his interest."—RICHARD ROVERE: *The New Yorker*, July
23, 1960

The afternoon he arrived at the convention from the airport,
there was of course a large crowd on the street outside the Biltmore, and the best way to get a view was to get up on an outdoor
balcony of the Biltmore, two flights above the street, and look
down on the event. One waited thirty minutes, and then a honking
of horns as wild as the getaway after an Italian wedding sounded
around the corner, and the Kennedy cortege came into sight, circled Pershing Square, the men in the open and leading convertibles
sitting backwards to look at their leader, and finally came to a halt
in a space cleared for them by the police in the crowd. The televi-

sion cameras were out, and a Kennedy band was playing some circus music. One saw him immediately. He had the deep orange-brown suntan of a ski instructor, and when he smiled at the crowd his teeth were amazingly white and clearly visible at a distance of fifty yards. For one moment he saluted Pershing Square, and Pershing Square saluted him back, the prince and the beggars of glamour staring at one another across a city street, one of those very special moments in the underground history of the world, and then with a quick move he was out of the car and by choice headed into the crowd instead of the lane cleared for him into the hotel by the police, so that he made his way inside surrounded by a mob, and one expected at any moment to see him lifted to its shoulders like a matador being carried back to the city after a triumph in the plaza. All the while the band kept playing the campaign tunes, sashaying circus music, and one had a moment of clarity, intense as a *déjà vu*, for the scene which had taken place had been glimpsed before in a dozen musical comedies; it was the scene where the hero, the matinee idol, the movie star comes to the palace to claim the princess, or what is the same, and more to our soil, the football hero, the campus king, arrives at the dean's home surrounded by a court of open-singing students to plead with the dean for his daughter's kiss and permission to put on the big musical that night. And suddenly I saw the convention, it came into focus for me, and I understood the mood of depression which had lain over the convention, because finally it was simple: the Democrats were going to nominate a man who, no matter how serious his political dedication might be, was indisputably and willy-nilly going to be seen as a great box-office actor, and the consequences of that were staggering and not at all easy to calculate.

Since the First World War Americans have been leading a double life, and our history has moved on two rivers, one visible, the other underground; there has been the history of politics which is concrete, factual, practical and unbelievably dull if not for the consequences of the actions of some of these men; and there is a subterranean river of untapped, ferocious, lonely and romantic desires, that concentration of ecstasy and violence which is the dream life of the nation.

The twentieth century may yet be seen as that era when civilized man and underprivileged man were melted together into mass man, the iron and steel of the nineteenth century giving way to electronic circuits which communicated their messages into men, the unmistakable tendency of the new century seeming to be the creation of men as interchangeable as commodities, their extremes of personality singed out of existence by the psychic fields of force the communicators would impose. This loss of personality was a catastrophe to the future of the imagination, but billions of people might first benefit from it by having enough to eat — one did not know — and there remained citadels of resistance in Europe where the culture was deep and roots were visible in the architecture of the past.

Nowhere, as in America, however, was this fall from individual man to mass man felt so acutely, for America was at once the first and most prolific creator of mass communications, and the most rootless of countries, since almost no American could lay claim to the line of a family which had not once at least severed its roots by migrating here. But, if rootless, it was then the most vulnerable of countries to its own homogenization. Yet America was also the country in which the dynamic myth of the Renaissance — that every man was potentially extraordinary — knew its most passionate persistence. Simply, America was the land where people still believed in heroes: George Washington; Billy the Kid; Lincoln, Jefferson; Mark Twain, Jack London, Hemingway; Joe Louis, Dempsey, Gentleman Jim; America believed in athletes, rum-runners, aviators; even lovers, by the time Valentino died. It was a country which had grown by the leap of one hero past another — is there a county in all of our ground which does not have its legendary figure? And when the West was filled, the expansion turned inward, became part of an agitated, overexcited, superheated dream life. The film studios threw up their searchlights as the frontier was finally sealed, and the romantic possibilities of the old conquest of land turned into a vertical myth, trapped within the skull, of a new kind of heroic life, each choosing his own archetype of a neo-renaissance man, be it Barrymore, Cagney, Flynn, Bogart, Brando or Sinatra, but it was almost as if there were no peace unless one could fight well, kill well (if always with honor), love well and love many, be cool, be daring, be dashing, be wild, be wily, be resourceful, be a brave gun. And this myth, that each of us was born to be free, to wander, to have adventure and to grow on the waves of the violent, the perfumed, and the unexpected, had a force which could not be tamed no matter how the nation's regulators — politicians, medicos, policemen, professors, priests, rabbis, ministers, *idéologues*, psychoanalysts, builders, executives and endless communicators — would brick-in the modern life with hygiene upon sanity, and middle-brow homily over platitude; the myth would not die. Indeed a quarter of the nation's business must have depended upon its existence. But it stayed alive for more than that — it was as if the message in the labyrinth of the genes would insist that violence was locked with creativity, and adventure was the secret of love.

Once, in the Second World War and in the year or two which followed, the underground river returned to earth, and the life of the nation was intense, of the present, electric; as a lady said, "That was the time when we gave parties which changed people's lives." The Forties was a decade when the speed with which one's own events occurred seemed as rapid as the history of the battlefields, and for the mass of people in America a forced march into a new jungle of emotion was the result. The surprises, the failures, and the dangers of that life must have terrified some nerve of awareness in the power and the mass, for, as if stricken by the orgiastic vistas the myth had carried up from underground, the retreat to a more conservative existence was disorderly, the fear of communism spread like an irrational hail of boils. To anyone who could see, the excessive hysteria of the Red wave was no preparation to face an enemy, but rather a terror of the national self: free-loving, lust-looting, atheistic, implacable — absurdity beyond absurdity to label communism so, for the moral products of Stalinism had been Victorian sex and a ponderous machine of material theology.

Forced underground again, deep beneath all *Reader's Digest* hospital dressings of Mental Health in Your Community, the myth continued to flow, fed by television and the film. The fissure in the national psyche widened to the danger point. The last large appearance of the myth was the vote which tricked the polls and gave Harry Truman his victory in '48. That was the last. Came the Korean War, the shadow of the H-bomb, and we were ready for the General. Uncle Harry gave way to Father, and security, regularity, order, and the life of no imagination were the command of the day. If one had any doubt of this, there was Joe McCarthy with his built-in treason detector, furnished by God, and the damage was done. In the totalitarian wind of those days, anyone who worked in Government formed the habit of being not too original, and many a mind atrophied from disuse and private shame. At the summit there was benevolence without leadership, regularity without vision, security without safety, rhetoric without life. The ship drifted on, that enormous warship of the United States, led by a Secretary of State whose cells were seceding to cancer, and as the world became more fantastic — Africa turning itself upside down, while some new kind of machine man was being made in China — two events occurred which stunned the confidence of America into a new night: the Russians put up their Sputnik, and Civil Rights — that reluctant gift to the American Negro, granted for its effect on foreign affairs — spewed into real life at Little Rock. The national Ego was in shock: the Russians were now in some ways our technological superiors, and we had an internal problem of subject populations equal conceivably in its difficulty to the Soviet and its satellites. The fatherly calm of the General began to seem like the uxorious mellifluences of the undertaker.

Underneath it all was a larger problem. The life of politics and the life of myth had diverged too far, and the energies of the people one knew everywhere had slowed down. Twenty years ago a post-Depression generation had gone to war and formed a lively, grousing, by times inefficient, carousing, pleasure-seeking, not altogether inadequate army. It did part of what it was supposed to do, and many, out of combat, picked up a kind of private life on the fly, and had their good time despite the yaws of the military system. But today in America the generation which respected the code of the myth was Beat, a horde of half-begotten Christs with scraggly beards, heroes none, saints all, weak before the strong, empty conformisms of the authority. The sanction for finding one's growth was no longer one's flag, one's career, one's sex, one's adventure, not even one's booze. Among the best in this newest of the generations, the myth had found its voice in marijuana, and the joke of the underground was that when the Russians came over they could never dare to occupy us for long because America was too Hip. Gallows humor. The poorer truth might be that America was too Beat, the instinct of the nation so separated from its public mind that apathy, schizophrenia, and private beatitudes might be the pride of the welcoming committee any underground could offer.

Yes, the life of politics and the life of the myth had diverged too far. There was nothing to return them to one another, no common danger, no cause, no desire, and, most essentially, no hero. It was a hero America needed, a hero central to his time, a man whose personality might suggest contradictions and mysteries which could reach into the alienated circuits of the underground, because only a hero can capture the secret imagination of a people, and so be good for the vitality of his nation; a hero embodies the fantasy and so allows each private mind the liberty to consider its fantasy and find a way to grow. Each mind can become more conscious of its desire and waste less strength in hiding from itself. Roosevelt was such a hero, and Churchill, Lenin and De Gaulle; even Hitler, to take the most odious example of this thesis, was a hero, the hero-as-monster, embodying what had become the monstrous fantasy of a people, but the horror upon which the radical mind and liberal temperament foundered was that he gave outlet to the energies of the Germans and so presented the twentieth century with an index of how horrible had become the secret heart of its desire. Roosevelt is of course a happier example of the hero; from his paralytic leg to the royal elegance of his geniality he seemed to contain the country within himself; everyone from the meanest starving cripple to an ambitious young man could expand into the optimism of an improving future because the man offered an unspoken promise of a future which would be rich. The sexual and the sex-starved, the poor, the hard-working and the imaginative well-to-do could see themselves in the President, could believe him to be like themselves. So a large part of the country was able to discover its energies because not as much was wasted in feeling that the country was a poisonous nutrient which stifled the day.

Too simple? No doubt. One tries to construct a simple model. The thesis is after all not so mysterious; it would merely nudge the notion that a hero embodies his time and is not so very much better than his time, but he is larger than life and so is capable of giving direction to the time, able to encourage a nation to discover the deepest colors of its character. At bottom the concept of the hero is antagonistic to impersonal social progress, to the belief that social ills can be solved by social legislating, for it sees a country as all-but-trapped in its character until it has a hero who reveals the character of the country to itself. The implication is that without such a hero the nation turns sluggish. Truman for example was not such a hero, he was not sufficiently larger than life, he inspired familiarity without excitement, he was a character but his proportions came from soap opera: Uncle Harry, full of salty commonsense and small-minded certainty, a storekeeping uncle.

Whereas Eisenhower has been the anti-Hero, the regulator. Nations do not necessarily and inevitably seek for heroes. In periods of dull anxiety, one is more likely to look for security than a dramatic confrontation, and Eisenhower could stand as a hero only for that large number of Americans who were most proud of their lack of imagination. In American life, the unspoken war of the century has taken place between the city and the small town: the city which is dynamic, orgiastic, unsettling, explosive and accelerating to the psyche; the small town which is rooted, narrow, cautious and planted in the life-logic of the family. The need of the city is to accelerate growth; the pride of the small town is to retard it. But since America has been passing through a period of enormous expansion since the war, the double-four years of Dwight Eisenhower could not retard the expansion, it could only denude it of color, character, and the development of novelty. The small-town mind is rooted—it is rooted in the small town—and when it attempts to direct history the results are disastrously colorless because the instrument of world power which is used by the small-town mind is the committee. Committees do not create, they merely proliferate, and the incredible dullness wreaked upon the American landscape in Eisenhower's eight years has been the triumph of the corporation. A tasteless, sexless, odorless sanctity in architecture, manners, modes, styles has been the result. Eisenhower embodied half the needs of the nation, the needs of the timid, the petrified, the sanctimonious, and the sluggish. What was even worse, he did not divide the nation as a hero might (with a dramatic dialogue as the result); he merely excluded one part of the nation from the other. The result was an alienation of the best minds and bravest impulses from the faltering history which was made. America's need in those years was to take an existential turn, to walk into the nightmare, to face into that terrible logic of history which demanded that the country and its people must become more extraordinary and more adventurous, or else perish, since the only alternative was to offer a false security in the power and the panacea of organized religion, family, and the FBI, a totalitarianization of the psyche by the stultifying techniques of the mass media which would seep into everyone's most private associations and so leave the country powerless against the Russians even if the denouement were to take fifty years, for in a competition between totalitarianisms the first maxim of the prizefight manager would doubtless apply: "Hungry fighters win fights."

The Hipster as Presidential Candidate: Thoughts on a Public Man's Eighteenth-Century Wife; Face-to-Face with the Hero; Significance of a Personal Note, or the Meaning of His Having Read an Author's Novel

Some part of these thoughts must have been in one's mind at the moment there was that first glimpse of Kennedy entering the Biltmore Hotel; and in the days which followed, the first mystery—the profound air of depression which hung over the convention—gave way to a second mystery which can be answered only by history. The depression of the delegates was understandable: no one had too much doubt that Kennedy would be nominated, but if elected he would be not only the youngest President ever to be chosen by voters, he would be the most conventionally attractive young man ever to sit in the White House, and his wife—some would claim it—might be the most beautiful first lady in our history. Of necessity the myth would emerge once more, because America's politics would now be also America's favorite movie, America's first soap opera, America's best-seller. One thinks of the talents of writers like Taylor Caldwell or Frank Yerby, or is it rather *The Fountainhead* which would contain such a fleshing of the romantic prescription? Or is it indeed one's own work which is called into question? "Well, there's your first hipster," says a writer one knows at the convention, "Sergius O'Shaugnessy born rich," and the temptation is to nod, for it could be true, a war hero, and the heroism is bonafide, even exceptional, a man who has lived with death, who, crippled in the back, took on an operation which would kill him or restore him to power, who chose to marry a lady whose face might be too imaginative for the taste of a democracy which likes its first ladies to be executives of home-management, a man who courts political suicide by choosing to go all out for a nomination four, eight, or twelve years before his political elders think he is ready, a man who announces a week prior to the convention that the young are better fitted to direct history than the old. Yes, it captures the attention. This is no routine candidate calling every shot by safety's routine book ("Yes," Nixon said, naturally but terribly tired an hour after his nomination, the TV cameras and lights and microphones bringing out a sweat of fatigue on his face, the words coming very slowly from the tired brain, somber, modest, sober, slow, slow enough so that one could touch emphatically the cautions behind each word, "Yes, I want to say," said Nixon, "that whatever abilities I have, I got from my mother." A tired pause . . . dull moment of warning, ". . . and my father." The connection now made, the rest comes easy, ". . . any my school and my church." Such men are capable of anything.)

One had the opportunity to study Kennedy a bit in the days that followed. His style in the press conferences was interesting. Not terribly popular with the reporters (too much a contemporary, and yet too difficult to understand, he received nothing like the rounds of applause given to Eleanor Roosevelt, Stevenson, Humphrey, or even Johnson), he carried himself nonetheless with a cool grace which seemed indifferent to applause, his manner somehow similar to the poise of a fine boxer, quick with his hands, neat in his timing, and two feet away from his corner when the bell ended the round. There was a good lithe wit to his responses, a dry Harvard wit, a keen sense of proportion in disposing of difficult questions — invariably he gave enough of an answer to be formally satisfactory without ever opening himself to a new question which might go further than the first. Asked by a reporter, "Are you for Adlai as vice-president?" the grin came forth and the voice turned very dry, "No, I cannot say we have considered *Adlai* as a vice-president." Yet there was an elusive detachment to everything he did. One did not have the feeling of a man present in the room with all his weight and all his mind. Johnson gave you all of himself, he was a political animal, he breathed like an animal, sweated like one, you knew his mind was entirely absorbed with the compendium of political fact and maneuver; Kennedy seemed at times like a young professor whose manner was adequate for the classroom, but whose mind was off in some intricacy of the Ph.D. thesis he was writing. Perhaps one can give a sense of the discrepancy by saying that he was like an actor who had been cast as the candidate, a good actor, but not a great one—you were aware all the time that the role was one thing and the man another—they did not coincide, the actor seemed a touch too aloof (as, let us say, Gregory Peck is usually too aloof) to become the part. Yet one had little sense of whether to value this elusiveness, or to beware of it. One could be witnessing the fortitude of a superior sensitivity or the detachment of a man who was not quite real to himself. And his voice gave no clue. When Johnson spoke, one could separate what was fraudulent from what was felt, he would have been satisfying as an actor the way Broderick Crawford or Paul Douglas are satisfying; one saw into his emotions, or at least had the illusion that one did. Kennedy's voice, however, was only a fair voice, too reedy, near to strident, it has the metallic snap of a cricket in it somewhere, it was more impersonal than the man, and so became the least-impressive quality in a face, a body, a selection of language, and a style of movement which made up a better-than-decent presentation, better than one had expected.

With all of that, it would not do to pass over the quality in Kennedy which is most difficult to describe. And in fact some touches should be added to this hint of a portrait, for later (after the convention), one had a short session alone with him, and the next day, another. As one had suspected in advance the interviews were not altogether satisfactory, they hardly could have been. A man running for President is altogether different from a man elected President: the hazards of the campaign make it impossible for a candidate to be as interesting as he might like to be (assuming he has such a desire). One kept advancing the argument that this campaign would be a contest of personalities, and Kennedy kept returning the discussion to politics. After a while one recognized this was an inevitable caution for him. So there would be not too much point to reconstructing the dialogue since Kennedy is hardly inarticulate about his political attitudes and there will be a library vault of text devoted to it in the newspapers. What struck me most about the interview was a passing remark whose importance was invisible on the scale of politics, but was altogether meaningful to my particular competence. As we sat down for the first time, Kennedy smiled nicely and said that he had read my books. One muttered one's pleasure. "Yes," he said, "I've read . . ." and then there was a short pause which did not last long enough to be embarrassing in which it was yet obvious no title came instantly to his mind, an omission one was not ready to mind altogether since a man in such a position must be obliged to carry a hundred thousand facts and names in his head, but the hesitation lasted no longer than three seconds or four, and then he said, "I've read *The Deer Park* and . . . the others," which startled me for it was the first time in a hundred similar situations, talking to someone whose knowledge of my work was casual, that the sentence did not come out, "I've read *The Naked and the Dead* . . . and the others." If one is take the worst and assume that Kennedy was briefed for this interview (which is most doubtful), it still speaks well for the striking instincts of his advisers.

What was retained later is an impression of Kennedy's manners which were excellent, even artful, better than the formal good manners of Choate and Harvard, almost as if what was creative in the man had been given to the manners. In a room with one or two people, his voice improved, became low-pitched, even pleasant — it seemed obvious that in all these years he had never become a natural public speaker and so his voice was constricted in public, the symptom of all orators who are ambitious, throttled, and determined.

His personal quality had a subtle, not quite describable intensity, a suggestion of dry pent heat perhaps, his eyes large, the pupils grey, the whites prominent, almost shocking, his most forceful feature: he had the eyes of a mountaineer. His appearance changed with his mood, strikingly so, and this made him always more interesting than what he was saying. He would seem at one moment older than his age, forty-eight or fifty, a tall, slim, sunburned professor with a pleasant weathered face, not even particularly handsome; five minutes later, talking to a press conference on his lawn, three microphones before him, a television camera turning, his appearance would have gone through a metamorphosis, he would look again like a movie star, his coloring vivid, his manner rich, his gestures strong and quick, alive with that concentration of vitality a successful actor always seems to radiate. Kennedy had a dozen faces. Although they were not at all similar as people, the quality was reminiscent of someone like Brando whose expression rarely changes, but whose appearance seems to shift from one person into

another as the minutes go by, and one bothers with this comparison because, like Brando, Kennedy's most characteristic quality is
the remote and private air of a man who has traversed some lonely
terrain of experience, of loss and gain, of nearness to death, which
leaves him isolated from the mass of others.

> The next day while they waited in vain for rescuers, the wrecked half of
> the boat turned over in the water and they saw that it would soon sink.
> The group decided to swim to a small island three miles away. There
> were other islands bigger and nearer, but the Navy officers knew that
> they were occupied by the Japanese. On one island, only one mile to the
> south, they could see a Japanese camp. McMahon, the engineer whose
> legs were disabled by burns, was unable to swim. Despite his own pain-
> fully crippled back, Kennedy swam the three miles with a breast stroke,
> towing behind him by a life-belt strap that he held between his teeth the
> helpless McMahon . . . it took Kennedy and the suffering engineer five
> hours to reach the island.

The quotation is from a book which has for its dedicated unilateral
title, *The Remarkable Kennedys*, but the prose is by one of the
best of the war reporters, the former *Yank* editor, Joe McCarthy,
and so presumably may be trusted in such details as this. Physical
bravery does not of course guarantee a man's abilities in the White
House—all too often men with physical courage are disappointing
in their moral imagination—but the heroism here is remarkable for
its tenacity. The above is merely one episode in a continuing saga
which went on for five days in and out of the water, and left Kennedy at one point "miraculously saved from drowning (in a storm)
by a group of Solomon Island natives who suddenly came up beside him in a large dugout canoe." Afterward, his back still injured
(that precise back injury which was to put him on crutches eleven
years later, and have him search for "spinal-fusion surgery" despite a warning that his chances of living through the operation
were "extremely limited") afterward, he asked to go back on duty
and became so bold in the attacks he made with his PT boat "that
the crew didn't like to go out with him because he took so many
chances."
It is the wisdom of a man who senses death within him and gam-
bles that he can cure it by risking his life. It is the therapy of the
instinct, and who is so wise as to call it irrational? Before he went
into the Navy, Kennedy had been ailing. Washed out of Freshman
year at Princeton by a prolonged trough of yellow jaundice, sick
for a year at Harvard, weak already in the back from an injury at
football, his trials suggest the self-hatred of a man whose resentment and ambition are too large for his body. Not everyone can

discharge their furies on an analyst's couch, for some angers can be relaxed only by winning power, some rages are sufficiently monumental to demand that one try to become a hero or else fall back into that death which is already within the cells. But if one succeeds, the energy aroused can be exceptional. Talking to a man who had been with Kennedy in Hyannis Port the week before the convention, I heard that he was in a state of deep fatigue.

"Well, he didn't look tired at the convention," one commented.

"Oh, he had three days of rest. Three days of rest for him is like six months for us."

One thinks of that three-mile swim with the belt in his mouth and McMahon holding it behind him. There are pestilences which sit in the mouth and rot the teeth—in those five hours how much of the psyche must have been remade, for to give vent to the bite in one's jaws and yet use that rage to save a life: it is not so very many men who have the apocalyptic sense that heroism is the First Doctor.

If one had a profound criticism of Kennedy it was that his public mind was too conventional, but that seemed to matter less than the fact of such a man in office because the law of political life had become so dreary that only a conventional mind could win an election. Indeed there could be no politics which gave warmth to one's body until the country had recovered its imagination, its pioneer lust for the unexpected and incalculable. It was the changes that might come afterward on which one could put one's hope. With such a man in office the myth of the nation would again be engaged, and the fact that he was Catholic would shiver a first existential vibration of consciousness into the mind of the White Protestant. For the first time in our history, the Protestant would have the pain and creative luxury of feeling himself in some tiny degree part of a minority, and that was an experience which might be incommensurable in its value to the best of them.

A Vignette of Adlai Stevenson: The Speeches:
What Happened When the Teleprompter
Jammed: How U.S. Senator Eugene McCarthy
Played the Matador. An Observation
on the Name Fitzgerald

As yet we have said hardly a word about Stevenson. And his actions must remain a puzzle unless one dares a speculation about his motive, or was it his need?

So far as the people at the convention had affection for anyone, it was Stevenson, so far as they were able to generate any spontaneous enthusiasm, their cheers were again for Stevenson. Yet it was obvious he never had much chance because so soon as a chance would present itself he seemed quick to dissipate the opportunity. The day before the nominations, he entered the Sports Arena to take his seat as a delegate — the demonstration was spontaneous, noisy and prolonged; it was quieted only by Governor Collins' invitation for Stevenson to speak to the delegates. In obedience perhaps to the scruple that a candidate must not appear before the convention until nominations are done, Stevenson said no more than : "I am grateful for this tumultuous and moving welcome. After getting in and out of the Biltmore Hotel and this hall, I have decided I know whom you are going to nominate. It will be the last survivor." This dry reminder of the ruthlessness of politics broke the roar of excitement for his presence. The applause as he left the platform was like the dying fall-and-moan of a baseball crowd when a home run curves foul. The next day, a New York columnist talking about it bitterly, "If he'd only gone through the motions, if he had just said that now he wanted to run, that he would work hard, and he hoped the delegates would vote for him. Instead he made that lame joke." One wonders. It seems almost as if he did not wish to win unless victory came despite himself, and then was overwhelming. There are men who are not heroes because they are too good for their time, and it is natural that defeats leave them bitter, tired, and doubtful of their right to make new history. If Stevenson had campaigned for a year before the convention, it is possible that he could have stopped Kennedy. At the least, the convention would have been enormously more exciting, and the nominations might have gone through half-a-dozen ballots before a winner was hammered into shape. But then Stevenson might also have shortened his life. One had the impression of a tired man who (for a politician) was sickened unduly by compromise. A year of maneuvering, broken promises, and detestable partners might have gutted him for the election campaign. If elected, it might have ruined him as a President. There is the possibility that he sensed his situation exactly this way, and knew that if he were to run for president, win and make a good one, he would first have to be restored, as one can indeed be restored, by an exceptional demonstration of love — love, in this case, meaning that the Party had a profound desire to keep him as their leader. The emotional truth of a last-minute victory for Stevenson over the Kennedy machine might have given him new energy; it would certainly have given him new faith in a country and a party whose good motives he was possibly beginning to doubt. Perhaps the fault he saw with his candidacy was that he attracted only the nicest people to himself and there were not enough of them. (One of the private amusements of the convention was to divine some of the qualities of the candidates by the style of the young women who put on hats and clothing and politicked in the colors of one presidential gent or another. Of course, half of them must have been hired models, but someone did the hiring and so it was fair to look for a common denominator. The Johnson girls tended to be plump, pie-faced, dumb sexy Southern; the Symingteeners seemed a touch mulish, stubborn, good-looking pluggers; the Kennedy ladies were the handsomest; healthy, attractive, tough, a little spoiled—they looked like the kind of girls who had gotten all the dances in high school and/or worked for a year as an airline hostess before marrying well. But the Stevenson girls looked to be doing it for no money; they were good sorts, slightly horsy-faced, one had the impression they played field hockey in college.) It was indeed the pure, the saintly, the clean-living, the pacifistic, the vegetarian who seemed most for Stevenson, and the less humorous in the Kennedy camp were heard to remark bitterly that Stevenson had nothing going for him but a bunch of Goddamn Beatniks. This might even have had its sour truth. The demonstrations outside the Sports Arena for Stevenson seemed to have more than a fair proportion of tall, emaciated young men with thin, wry beards and three-string guitars accompanied (again in undue proportion) by a contingent of ascetic, face-washed young Beat ladies in sweaters and dungarees. Not to mention all the Holden Caulfields one could see from here to the horizon. But of course it is unfair to limit it so, for the Democratic gentry were also committed half en masse for Stevenson, as well as a considerable number of movie stars, Shelley Winters for one: after the convention she remarked sweetly, "Tell me something nice about Kennedy so I can get excited about him."

What was properly astonishing was the way this horde of political half-breeds and amateurs came within distance of turning the convention from its preconceived purpose, and managed at least to bring the only hour of thorough-going excitement the convention could offer.

But then nominating day was the best day of the week and enough happened to suggest that a convention out of control would be a spectacle as extraordinary in the American scale of spectator values as a close seventh game in the World Series or a tied fourth quarter in a professional-football championship. A political convention is after all not a meeting of a corporation's board of directors; it is a fiesta, a carnival, a pig-rooting, horse-snorting, band-playing, voice-screaming medieval get-together of greed, practical lust, compromised idealism, career-advancement, meeting, feud, vendetta, conciliation, of rabble-rousers, fist fights (as it used to be), embraces, drunks (again as it used to be) and collective rivers of animal sweat. It is a reminder that no matter how the country might pretend it has grown up and become tidy in its manners, bodiless in its legislative language, hygienic in its separation of high politics from private life, that the roots still come grubby from the soil, and that politics in America is still different from politics any-where else because the politics has arisen out of the immediate needs, ambitions, and cupidities of the people, that our politics still smell of the bedroom and the kitchen, rather than having descend-ed to us from the chill punctilio of aristocratic negotiation.

So. The Sports Arena was new, too pretty of course, tasteless in its design — it was somehow pleasing that the acoustics were so bad for one did not wish the architects well; there had been so little imagination in their design, and this arena would have none of the harsh grandeur of Madison Square Garden when it was aged by spectators' phlegm and feet over the next twenty years. Still it had some atmosphere; seen from the streets, with the spectators mov-ing to the ticket gates, the bands playing, the green hot-shot special editions of the Los Angeles newspapers being hawked by the newsboys, there was a touch of the air of promise that precedes a bullfight, not something so good as the approach to the Plaza Mexi-co, but good, let us say, like the entrance into El Toreo of Mexico City, another architectural monstrosity, also with seats painted, as I remember, in rose-pink, and dark, milky sky-blue.

Inside, it was also different this nominating day. On Monday and Tuesday the air had been desultory, no one listened to the speak-ers, and everybody milled from one easy chatting conversation to another — it had been like a tepid Kaffeeklatsch for fifteen thousand people. But today there was a whip of anticipation in the air, the seats on the floor were filled, the press section was working, and in the gallery people were sitting in the aisles.

Sam Rayburn had just finished nominating Johnson as one came in, and the rebel yells went up, delegates started filing out of their seats and climbing over seats, and a pullulating dance of bodies and bands began to snake through the aisles, the posters jogging and whirling in time to the music. The dun color of the floor (faces, suits, seats and floor boards), so monotonous the first two days, now lit up with life as if an iridescent caterpillar had emerged from a fold of wet leaves. It was more vivid than one had expected, it was right, it felt finally like a convention, and from up close when one got down to the floor (where your presence was illegal and so consummated by sneaking in one time as demonstrators were going out, and again by slipping a five-dollar bill to a guard) the nearness to the demonstrators took on high color, that electric vividness one feels on the side lines of a football game when it is necessary to duck back as the ballcarrier goes by, his face tortured in the concentration of the moment, the thwomp of his tackle as acute as if one had been hit oneself.

That was the way the demonstrators looked on the floor. Nearly all had the rapt, private look of a passion or a tension which would finally be worked off by one's limbs, three hundred football players, everything from seedy delegates with jowl-sweating shivers to livid models, paid for their work that day, but stomping out their beat on the floor with the hypnotic adulatory grimaces of ladies who had lived for Lyndon these last ten years.

Then from the funereal rostrum, whose color was not so rich as mahogany nor so dead as a cigar, came the last of the requests for the delegates to take their seats. The seconding speeches began, one minute each; they ran for three and four, the minor-league speakers running on the longest as if the electric antenna of television was the lure of the Sirens, leading them out. Bored cheers applauded their concluding Götterdämmerungen and the nominations were open again. A favorite son, a modest demonstration, five seconding speeches, tedium.

Next was Kennedy's occasion. Governor Freeman of Minnesota made the speech. On the second or third sentence his television prompter jammed, an accident. Few could be aware of it at the moment; the speech seemed merely flat and surprisingly void of bravura. He was obviously no giant of extempore. Then the demonstration. Well-run, bigger than Johnson's, jazzier, the caliber of the costumes and decorations better chosen: the placards were broad enough, "Let's Back Jack," the floats were garish, particularly a papier-mâché or plastic balloon of Kennedy's head, six feet in diameter, which had nonetheless the slightly shrunken, over-red, rubbery look of a toy for practical jokers in one of those sleazy off-Times Square magic-and-gimmick stores; the band was suitably corny; and yet one had the impression this demonstration had been designed by some hands-to-hip interior decorator who said, "Oh, joy, let's have fun, let's make this *true* beer hall."

Besides, the personnel had something of the Kennedy *élan*, those paper hats designed to look like straw boaters with Kennedy's face on the crown, and small photographs of him on the ribbon, those hats which had come to symbolize the crack speed of the Kennedy team, that Madison Avenue cachet which one finds in bars like P. J. Clarke's, the elegance always giving its subtle echo of the Twenties so that the racoon coats seem more numerous than their real count, and the colored waistcoats are measured by the charm they would have drawn from Scott Fitzgerald's eye. But there, it occurred to one for the first time that Kennedy's middle name was just that, Fitzgerald, and the tone of his crack lieutenants, the unstated style, was true to Scott. The legend of Fitzgerald had an army at last, formed around the self-image in the mind of every superior Madison Avenue opportunist that he was hard, he was young, he was In, his conversation was lean as wit, and if the work was not always scrupulous, well the style could aspire. If there came a good day . . . he could meet the occasion.

The Kennedy snake dance ran its thirty lively minutes, cheered its seconding speeches, and sat back. They were so sure of winning, there had been so many victories before this one, and this one had been scouted and managed so well, that hysteria could hardly be the mood. Besides, everyone was waiting for the Stevenson barrage which should be at least diverting. But now came a long tedium. Favorite sons were nominated, fat mayors shook their hips, seconders told the word to constituents back in Ponderwaygot County, treacly demonstrations tried to hold the floor, and the afternoon went by; Symington's hour came and went, a good demonstration, good as Johnson's (for good cause—they had pooled their demonstrators). More favorite sons, Governor Docking of Kansas declared "a genius" by one of his lady speakers in a tense go-back-to-religion voice. The hours went by, two, three, four hours, it seemed forever before they would get to Stevenson. It was evening when Senator Eugene McCarthy of Minnesota got up to nominate him.

The gallery was ready, the floor was responsive, the demonstrators were milling like bulls in their pen waiting for the *toril* to fly open—it would have been hard not to wake the crowd up, not to make a good speech. McCarthy made a great one. Great it was by the measure of convention oratory, and he held the crowd like a matador, timing their *oles!*, building them up, easing them back, correcting any sag in attention, gathering their emotion, discharging it, creating new emotion on the wave of the last, driving his passes tighter and tighter as he readied for the kill. "Do not reject this man who made us all proud to be called Democrats, do not leave this prophet without honor in his own party." One had not heard a speech like this since 1948 when Vito Marcantonio's voice, his harsh, shrill, bitter, street urchin's voice screeched through the loud-speakers at Yankee Stadium and lashed seventy thousand people into an uproar.

"There was only one man who said let's talk sense to the American people," McCarthy went on, his muleta furled for the *natu-*

rales. "There was only one man who said let's talk sense to the American people," he repeated. "He said the promise of America is the promise of greatness. This was his call to greatness. . . . Do not forget this man. . . . Ladies and Gentlemen, I present to you not the favorite son of one state, but the favorite son of the fifty states, the favorite son of every country he has visited, the favorite son of every country which has not seen him but is secretly thrilled by his name." Bedlam. The kill. "Ladies and Gentlemen, I present to you Adlai Stevenson of Illinois." Ears and tail. Hooves and bull. A roar went up like the roar one heard the day Bobby Thomson hit his home run at the Polo Grounds and the Giants won the pennant from the Dodgers in the third playoff game of the 1951 season. The demonstration cascaded onto the floor, the gallery came to its feet, the Sports Arena sounded like the inside of a marching drum. A tidal pulse of hysteria, exaltation, defiance, exhilaration, anger and roaring desire flooded over the floor. The cry which had gone up on McCarthy's last sentence had not paused for breath in five minutes, and troop after troop of demonstrators jammed the floor (the Stevenson people to be scolded the next day for having collected floor passes and sent them out to bring in new demonstrators) and still the sound mounted. One felt the convention coming apart. There was a Kennedy girl in the seat in front of me, the Kennedy hat on her head, a dimpled healthy brunette; she had sat silently through McCarthy's speech, but now, like a woman paying her respects to the power of natural thrust, she took off her hat and began to clap herself. I saw a writer I knew in the next aisle; he had spent a year studying the Kennedy machine in order to write a book on how a nomination is won. If Stevenson stampeded the convention, his work was lost. Like a reporter at a mine cave-in I inquired the present view of the widow. "Who can think," was the answer, half frantic, half elated, "just watch it, that's all." I found a cool one, a New York reporter, who smiled in rueful respect. "It's the biggest demonstration I've seen since Wendell Willkie's in 1940," he said, and added, "God, if Stevenson takes it, I can wire my wife and move the family on to Hawaii."

"I don't get it."

"Well, every story I wrote said it was locked up for Kennedy."

Still it went on, twenty minutes, thirty minutes, the chairman could hardly be heard, the demonstrators refused to leave. The lights were turned out, giving a sudden theatrical shift to the sense of a crowded church at midnight, and a new roar went up, louder, more passionate than anything heard before. It was the voice, it was the passion, if one insisted to call it that, of everything in America which was defeated, idealistic, innocent, alienated, outside and Beat, it was the potential voice of a new third of the nation whose psyche was ill from cultural malnutrition, it was powerful, it was extraordinary, it was larger than the decent, humorous, finicky, half-noble man who had called it forth, it was a cry from the Thirties when Time was simple, it was a resentment of the slick technique, the oiled gears, and the superior generals of Fitzgerald's Army; but it was also—and for this reason one could not admire it altogether, except with one's excitement—it was also the plea of the bewildered who hunger for simplicity again, it was the adolescent counterpart of the boss's depression before the unpredictable dynamic of Kennedy as President, it was the return to the sentimental dream of Roosevelt rather than the approaching nightmare of history's oncoming night, and it was inspired by a terror of the future as much as a revulsion of the present.

Fitz's Army held; after the demonstration was finally down, the convention languished for ninety minutes while Meyner and others were nominated, a fatal lapse of time because Stevenson had perhaps a chance to stop Kennedy if the voting had begun on the echo of the last cry for him, but in an hour and a half depression crept in again and emotions spent, the delegates who had wavered were rounded into line. When the vote was taken, Stevenson had made no gains. The brunette who had taken off her hat was wearing it again, and she clapped and squealed when Wyoming delivered the duke and Kennedy was in. The air was sheepish, like the mood of a suburban couple who forgive each other for cutting in and out of somebody else's automobile while the country club dance is on. Again, tonight, no miracle would occur. In the morning the papers would be moderate in their description of Stevenson's last charge.

*A Sketch of the Republicans Gathered
in Convention: The Choice Between the
Venturesome and the Safe; What May
Happen at Three O'clock in the Morning
on a Long Dark Night*

One did not go to the other convention. It was seen on television, and so too much cannot be said of that. It did however confirm one's earlier bias that the Republican Party was still a party of church ushers, undertakers, choirboys, prison wardens, bank presidents, small-town police chiefs, state troopers, psychiatrists, beauty-parlor operators, corporation executives, Boy-Scout leaders, fraternity presidents, tax-board assessors, community leaders, surgeons, Pullman porters, head nurses and the fat sons of rich fathers. Its candidate would be given the manufactured image of an ordinary man, and his campaign, so far as it was a psychological campaign (and this would be far indeed), would present him as a simple, honest, dependable, hard-working, ready-to-learn, modest, humble, decent, sober young man whose greatest qualification for president was his profound abasement before the glories of the Republic, the stability of the mediocre, and his own unworthiness. The apocalyptic hour of Uriah Heep.

It would then be a campaign unlike the ones which had preceded it. Counting by the full spectrum of complete Right to absolute Left, the political differences would be minor, but what would be not at all minor was the power of each man to radiate his appeal into some fundamental depths of the American character. One would have an inkling at last if the desire of America was for drama or stability, for adventure or monotony. And this, this appeal to the psychic direction America would now choose for itself was the element most promising about this election, for it gave the possibility that the country might be able finally to rise above the deadening verbiage of its issues, its politics, its jargon, and live again by an image of itself. For in some part of themselves the people might know (since these candidates were not old enough to be revered) that they had chosen one young man for his mystery, for his promise that the country would grow or disintegrate by the unwilling charge he gave to the intensity of the myth, or had chosen another young man for his unstated oath that he would do all in his power to keep the myth buried and so convert the remains of Renaissance man as rapidly as possible into mass man. One might expect them to choose the enigma in preference to the deadening certainty. Yet one must doubt America's bravery. This lurching, unhappy, pompous and most corrupt nation—could it have the courage finally to take on a new image for itself, was it brave enough to put into office not only one of its ablest men, its most efficient, its most conquistadorial (for Kennedy's capture of the Democratic Party deserves the word), but also one of its more mysterious men (the national psyche must shiver in its sleep at the image of Mickey Mantle-cum-Lindbergh in office, and a First Lady with an eighteenth-century face). Yes, America was at last engaging the fate of its myth, its consciousness about to be accelerated or cruelly depressed in its choice between two young men in their forties who, no matter how close, dull, or indifferent their stated politics might be, were radical poles apart, for one was sober, the apotheosis of opportunistic lead, all radium spent, the other handsome as a prince in the unstated aristocracy of the American dream. So, finally, would come a choice which history had never presented to a nation before — one could vote for glamour or for ugliness, a staggering and most stunning choice — would the nation be brave enough to enlist the romantic dream of itself, would it vote for the image in the mirror of its unconscious, were the people indeed brave enough to hope for an acceleration of Time, for that new life of drama which would come from choosing a son to lead them who was heir apparent to the psychic loins? One could pause: it might be more difficult to be a President than it ever had before. Nothing less than greatness would do.

Yet if the nation voted to improve its face, what an impetus might come to the arts, to the practices, to the lives and to the imagination of the American. If the nation so voted. But one knew the unadmitted specter in the minds of the Democratic delegates: that America would go to sleep on election eve with the polls promising Kennedy a victory on the day to come, yet in its sleep some millions of Democrats and Independents would suffer a nightmare before the mystery of uncharted possibilities their man would suggest, and in a terror of all the creativities (and some violences) that mass man might now have to dare again, the undetermined would go out in the morning to vote for the psychic security of Nixon the way a middle-aged man past adventure holds to the stale bread of his marriage. Yes, this election might be fearful enough to betray the polls and no one in America could plan the new direction until the last vote was counted by the last heeler in the last ambivalent ward, no one indeed could know until then what had happened the night before, what had happened at three o'clock in the morning on that long dark night of America's search for a security cheaper than her soul.

POSTSCRIPT

This piece had more effect than any other single work of mine, and I think this is due as much to its meretriciousness as to its merits. I was forcing a reality, I was bending reality like a field of space to curve the time I wished to create. I was not writing with the hope that perchance I could find reality by being sufficiently honest to perceive it, but on the contrary was distorting reality in the hope that thereby I could affect it. I was engaging in an act of propaganda.

During the period after Kennedy was nominated, there was great indifference to him among the Democrats I knew; disaffection was general; outright aversion was felt by most of the liberal Left — the white collar SANE sort of professional who had been for

Stevenson. The Kennedy machine worked well to overcome apathy and inertia; so did the debates with Nixon. Through the early Fall, before the election, people who had been going along with the Democratic Party for years began somewhat resignedly to accept their fate: they would go out after all and vote for John F. Kennedy. But there was no real enthusiasm, no drive. My piece came at the right time for him—three weeks before the election. It added the one ingredient Kennedy had not been able to find for the stew—it made him seem exciting, it made the election appear important. Around New York there was a turn in sentiment; one could feel it; Kennedy now had glamour.

As will be seen in the essay on Jackie Kennedy, I took to myself some of the critical credit for his victory. Whether I was right or wrong in fact may not be so important as its psychological reality in my own mind. I had invaded No Man's Land, I had created an archetype of Jack Kennedy in the public mind which might or might not be true, but which would induce people to vote for him, and so would tend to move him into the direction I had created. Naturally there would be forces thrusting him back out of No Man's Land, back to conventional politics, but so far as I had an effect, it was a Faustian one, much as if I had made a pact with Mephisto to give me an amulet, an art-work, which might arouse a djinn in history.

The night Kennedy was elected, I felt a sense of woe, as if I had made a terrible error, as if somehow I had betrayed the Left and myself. It was a spooky emotion. In the wake of the election, one note was clear—the strength the Left had been gaining in the last years of Eisenhower's administration would now be diluted, preempted, adulterated, converted and dissolved by the compromises and hypocrisies of a new Democratic administration. And so I began to follow Kennedy's career with obsession, as if I were responsible and guilty for all which was bad, dangerous, or potentially totalitarian within it. And the papers which follow are written under the shadow of this private fact, this conviction that I was now among the guilty, another genteel traitor in the land.

The Big Bite

NOVEMBER, 1962

The root of death is burial. I was never particularly fond of Joe DiMaggio. His legend left me cold. But I have respect for the way he chose to give Marilyn Monroe a small funeral. If she had never been a movie star, if she had been one of those small, attractive blondes who floats like spray over the Hollywood rocks, a little drink here, bit of a call girl there, bing, bam, bad marriage, nice pot, easy head, girl friend, headshrinker, fuzz, dope, miscarriage and lowering night, if she had been no more than that, just a misty little blonde who hurt no one too much and went down inch by inch, inevitably, like a cocker spaniel in a quickbog, well then she would have ended in some small Hollywood parlor with fifteen friends invited.

Probably she was like that by the end. Sleeping pills are the great leveler. If everyone in America took four capsules of Nembutal a night for two thousand nights we would all be the same when we were done. We would all be idiots.

Any writer who takes the pills year after year ought to be able to write the tale of a club fighter whose brain turns slowly drunk with punishment. But that is the book which is never written. We learn the truth by giving away pieces of our tongue. When we know it all, there is no tongue left. Is it then one rises at dawn for the black flirtation, slips downstairs, slips the muzzle into the mouth, cool gunmetal to balm the void of a lost tongue, and goes blasting off like a rocket. Here come I, eternity, cries Ernest, I trust you no longer. You must try to find me now, eternity. I am in little pieces.

Hemingway and Monroe. Pass lightly over their names. They were two of the people in America most beautiful to us.

I think Ernest hated us by the end. He deprived us of his head. It does not matter so much whether it was suicide or an accident — one does not put a gun barrel in one's mouth, tickle the edge of an accident and fail to see that people will say it's suicide. Ernest, so proud of his reputation. So fierce about it. His death was awful. Say it. It was the most difficult death in America since Roosevelt. One has still not recovered from Hemingway's death. One may never.

But Monroe was different. She slipped away from us. She had been slipping away from us for years. Now it is easy to say that her actions became more vague every year. I thought she was bad in *The Misfits*, she was finally too vague, and when emotion showed, it was unattractive and small. But she was gone from us a long time ago.

If she had done Grushenka in *The Brothers Karamazov* the way she announced she would all those years ago, and if she had done it well, then she might have gone on. She might have come all the way back into the vault of herself where the salts of a clean death and the rot of a foul death were locked together. We take the sleeping pills when the sense of a foul and rotten death has become too certain, we look for the salt in the Seconal. Probably to stay alive Monroe had to become the greatest actress who ever lived. To stay alive Hemingway would have had to write a better book than *War and Peace*.

From *The Deer Park:* "There was that law of life, so cruel and so just, which demanded that one must grow or else pay more for remaining the same." I think that line is true. I think it is biologically true. And I think its application is more ferocious in America than anywhere I know. Because we set ourselves out around the knoll and get ready to play King of the Hill. Soon one of us is brave enough to take the center and insist it belongs to us. Then there is no rest until the new king is killed. Our good America. We are the nation of amateur kings and queens.

DECEMBER, 1962

I wonder if it is possible Ernest Hemingway was not a suicide. It may be said he took his life, but I wonder if the deed were not more like a reconnaissance from which he did not come back.

How likely that he had a death of the most awful proportions within him. He was exactly the one to know that cure for such disease is to risk dying many a time. Somewhere in the deep coma of mortal illness or the transfixed womb of danger, death speaks to us. If we make our way back to life, we are armed with a new secret.

I wonder if, morning after morning, Hemingway did not go downstairs secretly in the dawn, set the base of his loaded shotgun on the floor, put the muzzle to his mouth, and press his thumb into the trigger. There is a no-man's-land in each trigger. For the dull hand it is a quarter of an inch. A professional hunter can feel to the division of a millimeter the point where the gun can go off. He can move the trigger up to that point and yet not fire the gun. Hemingway was not too old to test this skill. Perhaps he was trying the deed a first time, perhaps he had tried just such a reconnaissance one hundred times before, and felt the touch of health return ninety times, ninety respectable times when he dared to press the trigger far into the zone where the shot could go. If he did it well, he could come close to death without dying. On that particular morning in July, it is not impossible he said (because the curiosity could be that indeed he talked to himself the way he talked in his books), Look, we can go in further. It's going to be tricky and we may not get out, but it will be good for us if we go in just a little further, so we have to try, and now we will, it is the answer to the brothers Mayo, ergo now we go in, damn the critics and this Fiedler fellow, all will be denied if papa gets good again, write about Monroe, and Jimmy Durante, God bless, umbriago, hose down the deck, do it clean, no sweat, no sweat in the palm, let's do it clean, gung ho, and little more, let's go in a little gung ho more ho. No! Oh no! Goddamn it to Hell.

There will be some who say: Nice, but it still is suicide.

Not if it went that way. When we do not wish to live, we execute ourselves. If we are ill and yet want to go on, we must put up the ante. If we lose, it does not mean we wished to die.

Responses and Reactions II

On p. 293 of *The Early Masters** is a short story.

The Test
It is told:
When Prince Adam Czartoryski, the friend and counsellor of Czar Alexander, had been married for many years and still had no children, he went to the maggid of Koznitz and asked him to pray for him and because of his prayer the princess bore a son. At the baptism, the father told of the maggid's intercession with God. His brother who, with his young son, was among the guests, made fun of what he called the prince's superstition. "Let us go to your wonder-worker together," he said, "and I shall show you that he can't tell the difference between left and right."

Together they journeyed to Koznitz, which was close to where they lived. "I beg of you," Adam's brother said to the maggid, "to pray for my sick son."

The maggid bowed his head in silence. "Will you do this for me?" the other urged.

The maggid raised his head. "Go," he said, and Adam saw that he

*From Martin Buber's *Tales of the Hasidim*. Published by Schocken Books. Volume I: *The Early Masters*. Volume II: *The Later Masters*.

only managed to speak with a great effort. "Go quickly, and perhaps you will still see him alive."

"Well, what did I tell you?" Adam's brother said laughingly as they got into their carriage. Adam was silent during the ride. When they drove into the court of his house, they found the boy dead.

What is suggested by the story is an underworld of real events whose connection is never absurd. Consider, in parallel, this Haiku:*

> So soon to die
> and no sign of it is showing—
> locust cry.

The sense of stillness and approaching death is occupied by the cry of the locust. Its metallic note becomes the exact equal of an oncoming death. Much of Haiku can best be understood as a set of equations in mood. Man inserting himself into a mood extracts an answer from nature which is not only the reaction of the man upon the mood, but is a supernatural equivalent to the quality of the experience, almost as if a key is given up from the underworld to unlock the surface of reality.

Here for example is an intimation of the architecture concealed beneath:

Upsetting the Bowl†
It is told:

Once Rabbi Elimelekh was eating the Sabbath meal with his disciples. The servant set the soup bowl down before him. Rabbi Elimelekh raised it and upset it, so that the soup poured over the table. All at once young Mendel, later the rabbi of Rymanov, cried out: "Rabbi what are you doing? They will put us all in jail!" The other disciples smiled at these foolish words. They would have laughed out loud, had not the presence of their teacher restrained them. He, however, did not smile. He nodded to young Mendel and said: "Do not be afraid, my son!"

Some time after this, it became known that on that day an edict directed against the Jews of the whole country had been presented to the emperor for his signature. Time after time he took up his pen, but something always happened to interrupt him. Finally he signed the

---

*An Introduction to Haiku by Harold G. Henderson, p. 43. The poem is by Matsuo Basho, translated by Henderson.

> Yagate shinu
> keshiki wa mei-zo
> semi-no koe

†The Early Masters, p. 259.

paper. Then he reached for the sand-container but took the inkwell instead and upset it on the document. Hereupon he tore it up and forbade them to put the edict before him again.

A magical action in one part of the world creates its historical action in another—we are dealing with no less than totem and taboo. Psychoanalysis intrudes itself. One of the last, may it be one of the best approaches to modern neurosis is by way of the phenomenological apparatus of anxiety. As we sink into the apathetic bog of our possible extinction, so a breath of the Satanic seems to rise from the swamp. The magic of materials lifts into consciousness, proceeds to dominate us, is even enthroned into a usurpation of consciousness. The protagonists of *Last Year at Marienbad* are not so much people as halls and chandeliers, gaming tables, cigarettes in their pyramid of 1, 3, 5, and 7. The human characters are ghosts, disembodied servants, attendants who cast their shadows on the material. It is no longer significant that a man carries a silver cigarette case; rather it is the cigarette case which is significant. The man becomes an instrument to transport the case from the breast pocket of a suit into the air; like a building crane, a hand conducts the cigarette case to an angle with the light, fingers open the catch and thus elicit a muted sound of boredom, a silver groan from the throat of the case, which now offers up a cigarette, snaps its satisfaction at being shut, and seems to guide the hand back to the breast pocket. The man, on leave until he is called again, goes through a pantomime of small empty activities—without the illumination of his case he is like all dull servants who cannot use their liberty.

That, one may suppose, is a proper portrait of Hell. It is certainly the air of the phenomenological novel. It is as well the neurotic in slavery to the material objects which make up the locks and keys of his compulsion.

But allow me a quick portrait of a neurotic. He is a sociologist, let us say, working for a progressive foundation, a disenchanted atheist ("Who knows—God may exist as some kind of thwarted benevolence"), a liberal, a social planner, a member of SANE, a logical positivist, a collector of jokes about fags and beatniks, a lover of that large suburban land between art and the documentary. He smokes two packs of cigarettes a day: he drinks—*when* he drinks—eight or ten tots of blended whiskey in a night. He does not get drunk, merely cerebral, amusing, and happy. Once when he came home thus drunk, he bowed to his door and then touched his doorknob three times. After this, he went to bed and slept like a thief.

Two years later he is in slavery to the doorknob. He must wipe it with his fingertips three times each morning before he goes out. If he forgets to do this and only remembers later at work, his day is shattered. Anxiety bursts his concentration. His psyche has the air of a bombed city. In an extreme case, he may even have to return to his home. His first question to himself is whether someone has touched the knob since he left. He makes inquiries. To his horror he discovers the servant has gone out shopping already. She has therefore touched the knob and it has lost its magical property. Stratagems are now necessary. He must devote the rest of the day to encouraging the servant to go out in such a manner that he can open the door for her, and thus remove the prior touch of her hand.

Is he mad? the man asks himself. Later he will ask his analyst the same question. But he is too aware of the absurdity of his activities. He suffers at the thought of the work he is not accomplishing, he hates himself for being attached to the doorknob, he tries to extirpate its dominance. One morning he makes an effort to move out briskly. He does not touch the brass a second and third time. But his feet come to a halt, his body turns around as if a gyroscope were revolving him, his arm turns to the knob and pats it twice. He no longer feels his psyche is to be torn in two. Consummate relief.

Of course his analysis discloses wonders. He has been an only son. His mother, his father, and himself make three. He and his wife (a naturally not very happy marriage) have one child. The value of the trinities is considered dubious by the analyst but is insisted upon by the patient. He has found that he need touch the doorknob only once if he repeats to himself, "I was born, I live, and I die." After a time he finds that he does not have to touch the knob at all, or upon occasion, can use his left hand for the purpose. There is a penalty, however. He is obliged to be concerned with the number nine for the rest of the day. Nine sips of water from a glass. A porterhouse steak consumed in nine bites. His wife to be kissed nine times between supper and bed. "I've kicked over an ant hill" he confesses to his analyst. "I'm going bugs."

They work in his cause. Two testes and one penis makes three. Two eyes and one nose; two nostrils and one mouth; the throat, the tongue, and the teeth. His job, his family, and himself. The door, the doorknob, and the act of opening it.

Then he has a revelation. He wakes up one morning and does not reach for a cigarette. There is a tension in him to wait. He suffers agonies—the brightest and most impatient of his cells seem to be expiring without nicotine—still he has intimations of later morning bliss, he hangs on. Like an infantryman coming up alive from a forty-eight hour shelling, he gets to his hat, his attaché case, and the doorknob. As he touches it, a current flows into his hand. "Stick with me, pal," says the message. "One and two keep you from three."

Traveling to the office in the last half hour of the subway rush, he is happy for the first time in years. As he holds to the baked enamel loop of the subway strap, his fingers curl up a little higher and touch the green painted metal above the loop. A current returns to him again. Through his fingertips he feels a psychic topography which has dimensions, avenues, signals, buildings. From the metal of the subway strap through the metal of the subway car, down along the rails, into the tunnels of the city, back to the sewer pipes and electric cables which surround the subway station from which he left, back to his house, and up the plumbing, up the steam pipe, up the hall, a leap through the air, and he has come back to the doorknob again. He pats the subway strap three times. The ship of his body will sink no further. "Today," thinks the sociologist, "I signed my armistice. The flag of Faust has been planted here."

But in his office he has palpitations. He believes he will have a heart attack. He needs air. He opens the window, leans out from the waist. By God, he almost jumped!

The force which drew him to touch the knob now seems to want to pull his chest through the window. Or is it a force opposed to the force which made him touch the doorknob? He does not know. He thinks God may be telling him to jump. That thwarted benevolent God. "You are swearing allegiance to materials," says a voice. "Come back, son. It is better to be dead."

Poor man. He is not bold enough to be Faust. He calls his analyst.

"Now, for God's sake, don't do anything," says the analyst. "This is not uncommon. Blocked material is rising to the surface. It's premature, but since we've gotten into it, repetition compulsions have to do with omnipotence fantasies which of course always involve Almighty figures and totemic Satanistic contracts. The urge to suicide is not bona fide in your case—it's merely a symbolic contraction of the anxiety."

"But I tell you I almost went through the window. I felt my feet start to leave the floor."

"Well, come by my office then. I can't see you right now—trust me on this—I've got a girl who will feel I've denied her her real chance to bear children if I cut into her hour, she's had too many abortions. You know, she's touchy"—rare is the analyst who won't gossip a *little* about his patients, it seems to calm the other patients—"but I'll leave an envelope of tranquilizers for you on the desk. They're a new formula. They're good. Take two right away. Then two more this afternoon. Forget the nausea if it comes. Just side-effect. We'll get together this evening."

"Mind if I touch your doorknob three times?"

"Great. You've got your sense of humor back. Yes, by all means, touch it."

> So soon to die
> and no sign of it is showing—
> locust cry.

The Big Bite

APRIL, 1963

The rite of spring is in the odor of the air. The nerve of winter which enters one's nose comes a long far way like a scythe from the peak of mountains. To the aged it can feel like a miasma up from the midnight corridors of a summer hotel, empty and out of season. Winter breath has the light of snow when the sun is on it, or the bone chill of a vault. But spring air comes up from the earth—at worst it can be the smell of new roots in bad slimy ground, at best the wind of late autumn frost is released from the old ice. Intoxication to the nostril, as if a filbert of fine sherbet had melted a sweet way into the tongue back of the throat down from the teeth. Spring is the season which marks the end of dread—so it is the season of profound dread for those who do not lose their fear.

Looking back on the winter and fall, one thinks of a long season of dread. There was that week toward the end of October when the world stood like a playing card on edge, and those of us who lived in New York wondered if the threat of war was like an exceptional dream which would end in a happy denouement (as indeed it did) or whether the events of each day would move, ante raised on ante, from boats on a collision course to invasions of Cuba, from threats of nuclear reprisal to the act itself, the Götterdämmerung of New York. Or would the end come instantly without prevision or warning, we would wonder as well, were we now heroes in a movie by Chaplin, was our house at the edge of the cliff, would we open the door and step into an abyss? There was dread that week. One looked at the buildings one passed and wondered if one was to see them again. For a week everyone in New York was like a patient with an incurable disease—would they be dead tomorrow or was it life for yet another year?

We sat that week in New York thinking of little. When movies are made of the last week on earth, the streets thrive with jazz, the juveniles are unrestrained, the adults pillage stores, there is rape, dancing, caterwauling laughter, sound of sirens and breaking glass, the roller coaster of a brave trumpet going out on its last ride. But we sat around. All too many watched television. Very few of us went out at night. The bars were half empty. The talk was quiet. One did not have the feeling great lovers were meeting that week, not for the first time nor for the last. An apathy came over our city. A muted and rather empty hour which lasted for a week. If it all blew up, if it all came to so little, if our efforts, our loves, our crimes added up to no more than a sudden extinction in a minute, in a moment, if we had not even time before the bomb (as civilians did once) to throw one quick look at some face, some trinket, some child for which one had love, well, one could not complain. That was our fate. That was what we deserved. We did not march in the street or shake our fists at the sky. We waited in our burrow like drunks in the bullpen pacing the floor of our existence, waiting for court in the morning while the floor was littered with the bile that came up in our spit and the dead butts of our dying lung's breath. Facing eternity we were convicts hanging on the dawn. There was no lust in the streets nor any defiance with which to roar at eternity. We were guilty.

We gave our freedom away a long time ago. We gave it away in all the revolutions we did not make, all the acts of courage we found a way to avoid, all the roots we destroyed in fury at that past which still would haunt our deeds. We divorced ourselves from the materials of the earth, the rock, the wood, the iron ore; we looked to new materials which were cooked in vats, long complex derivatives of urine which we called plastic. They had no odor of the living or of what once had lived, their touch was alien to nature. They spoke of the compromise of incompatibles. The plastic which had invaded our bathrooms, our kitchens, our clothing, our toys for children, our tools, our containers, our floor coverings, our cars, our sports, the world of our surfaces was the simple embodiment of social cowardice. We had tried to create a world in which all could live even if none could breathe. There had been a vast collective social effort in the twentieth century—each of us had tried to take back a critical bit more from existence than we had given to it.

There was a terror to comtemplate in the logic of our apathy.

Because if there was a God and we had come from Him, was it not the first possibility that each of us had a mission, one of us to create, another to be brave, a third to love, a fourth to work, a fifth to be bold, a sixth to be all of these. Was it not possible that we were sent out of eternity to become more than we had been?

What then if we had become less? There was a terror in the logic. Because if there was a God, there was also in first likelihood a Devil. If the God who sent us out demanded our courage, what would be most of interest to the other but our cowardice?

Which of us could say that nowhere in the secret debates of our dreams or the nightmare of open action, in those stricken instants when the legs are not as brave as the mind or the guts turn to water, which of us could say that never nor nowhere had we struck a pact with the Devil and whispered, Yes, let us deaden God, let Him die within me, it is too frightening to keep Him alive, I cannot bear the dread.

That is why we did not roar into the street and shout that it was unnatural for mankind to base its final hope on the concealed character of two men, that it was unnatural to pray that Kennedy and Khrushchev taken together were more good than evil. What an ignoble suppliant hope for civilization to rest its security on two men, no more, two men. What had happened to the dream of the world's wealth guarded by the world's talent, the world's resource?

We sat in apathy because most of us, in the private treacherous dialogues of our sleep, had turned our faith away from what was most vital in our mind, and had awakened in depression. We had drawn back in fright from ourselves, as if in our brilliance lay madness, and beyond the horizon dictated by others was death. We had been afraid of death. We had been afraid of death as no generation in the history of mankind has been afraid. None of us would need to scream as eternity recaptured our breath — we would be too deep in hospital drugs. We would die with deadened minds and twilight sleep. We had turned our back on the essential terror of life. We believed in the Devil, we hated nature.

So we watched the end approach with apathy. Because if it was God we had betrayed and the vision with which He had sent us forth, if our true terror now was not of life but of what might be waiting for us in death, then how much easier we might find it to be blasted into eternity deep in the ruin of ten million others, how much better indeed if the world went with us, and death was destroyed as completely as life. Yes, how many of the millions in New York had a secret prayer: that whomever we thought of as God be exploded with us, and Judgment cease.

MAY, 1963

The act of traveling is never a casual act. It inspires an anxiety which no psychoanalyst can relieve in a hurry, for if travel is reminiscent of the trauma of birth, it is also suggestive of some possible migrations after death.

For most of us death may not be peace but an expedition into all the high terror and deep melancholy we sought to avoid in our lives. So the act of travel is a grave hour to some part of the unconscious, for it may be on a trip that we prepare a buried corner of ourselves to be ready for what happens once we are dead.

By this logic, the end of a trip is a critical moment of transition. Railroad stations in large cities should properly be monumental, heavy with dignity, reminiscent of the past. We learn little from travel, not nearly so much as we need to learn, if everywhere we are assaulted by the faceless plastic surfaces of everything which has been built in America since the war, that new architecture of giant weeds and giant boxes, of children's colors on billboards and jagged electric signs. Like the metastases of cancer cells, the plastic shacks, the motels, the drive-in theatres, the highway restaurants and the gas stations proliferate year by year until they are close to covering the highways of America with a new country which is laid over the old one the way a transparent sheet with new drawings is set upon the original plan. It is an architecture with no root to the past and no suggestion of the future, for one cannot conceive of a modern building growing old (does it turn dingy or will the colors stain?); there is no way to age, it can only cease to function. No doubt these buildings will live for twenty years and then crack in two. They will live like robots, or television sets which go out of order with one whistle of the wind.

In the suburbs it is worse. To live in leisure in a house much like other houses, to live in a landscape where it is meaningless to walk because each corner which is turned produces the same view, to live in comfort and be bored is a preparation for one condition: limbo.

The architectural face of the enemy has shifted. Twenty years ago Pennsylvania Station in New York City seemed a monstrosity, forbidding, old, dingy, unfunctional, wasteful of space, depressing in its passages and waiting rooms. The gloomy exploitative echoes of the industrial revolution sounded in its grey stone. And yet today the plan to demolish it is a small disaster.

Soon the planners will move in to tear down the majestic vaults of the old building in order to rear up in its place a new sports arena, a twenty-, thirty-, forty-story building. One can predict what the new building will look like. It will be made of steel, concrete and glass, it will have the appearance of a cardboard box which contains a tube of toothpaste, except that it will be literally one hundred million times larger in volume. In turn, the sports arena will have plastic seats painted in pastel colors, sky-blue, orange-pink, dead yellow. There will be a great deal of fluorescent lighting, an electronically operated scoreboard (which will break down frequently) and the acoustics will be particularly poor, as they invariably are in new auditoriums which have been designed to have good acoustics.

The new terminal will be underground. It will waste no space for high vaulted ceilings and monumental columns, it will look doubtless like the inside of a large airport. And one will feel the same subtle nausea coming into the city or waiting to depart from it that one feels now in such plastic catacombs as O'Hare's reception center in Chicago, at United or American Airlines in Idlewild, in the tunnels and ramps and blank gleaming corridors of Dallas' airport, which is probably one of the ten ugliest buildings in the world.

Now in the cities, an architectural plague is near upon us. For we have tried to settle the problem of slums by housing, and the void in education by new schools. So we have housing projects which look like prisons and prisons which look like hospitals which in turn look like schools, schools which look like luxury hotels, luxury hotels which seem to confuse themselves with airline terminals, and airline terminals which cannot be told apart from civic centers, and the civic centers look like factories. Even the new churches look like recreation centers at large ski resorts. One can no longer tell the purpose of a building by looking at its face. Modern buildings tend to look like call girls who came out of it intact except that their faces are a touch blank and the expression in their eyes is as lively as the tip on a filter cigarette.

Our modern architecture reminds me a little of cancer cells. Because the healthy cells of the lung have one appearance and those in the liver another. But if both are cancerous they tend to look a little more alike, they tend to look a little less like anything very definite.

Definition has a value. If an experience is precise, one can know a little more of what is happening to oneself. It is in those marriages and love affairs which are neither good nor bad, not quite interesting nor altogether awful that anxiety flows like a muddy river. It is in those housing projects which look like prisons that juvenile delinquency increases at a greater rate than it used to do in the slums.

Once I had the luck to have an argument with a United States

Senator from New York. He was very proud of his Governor. What has Rockefeller done? I asked. What? cried the Senator. And the list came back. Education, roads, welfare, housing. But isn't it possible people can be happier living in slums than housing projects? I asked.

I might just as well have said to a devout Catholic that I thought all nuns should be violated. The Senator lost his temper. Listen, young man, went his theme, I grew up in a slum.

But then for years I too lived in a slum. I had a cold-water flat which was sixty-feet long and varied in width from eight feet to eleven feet. I bought a stove and a refrigerator, and I spent two weeks putting in a sink and a bathtub and two gas heaters. The plaster was cracked and continued to develop its character as I lived there. I was as happy in that cold-water flat as I've been anywhere else. It was mine. When I stay in a modern apartment house for a few days, I feel as if I'm getting the plague walking down those blank halls.

So I tried to argue with the Senator. What if a government were to take a fraction of the money it cost to dispossess and relocate slum tenants, demolish buildings, erect twenty stories of massed barracks, and instead give a thousand or two thousand dollars to each slum tenant to spend on materials for improving his apartment and to pay for the wages of whatever skilled labor he needed for small specific jobs like a new toilet, a new window, a fireplace, new wiring, wallpaper, or a new wall. The tenant would be loaned or rented the tools he needed, he would be expected to work along with his labor. If he took the first hundred dollars he received and drank it up, he would get no more money.

By the time such a project was done, every slum apartment in the city would be different. Some would be worse, some would be improved, a few would be beautiful. But each man would know at least whether he wished to improve his home, or truly didn't care. And that might be better than moving into a scientifically allotted living space halfway between a hospital and a prison.

For the housing projects radiate depression in two directions. The people who live in them are deadened by receiving a gift which has no beauty. The people who go past the housing projects in their automobiles are gloomy for an instant, because the future, or that part of the future we sense in our architecture, is telling us that the powers who erected these buildings expect us to become more like one another as the years go by.

The conservatives cry out that the welfare state will reduce us to a low and dull common denominator. And indeed it will unless the welfare which reaches the poor can reach them directly in such a way that they can use their own hands to change their own life. What do you say, Senator Goldwater? Do you think the government could afford the funds to give a man who lives in a slum some money for his hammer and nails and a carpenter to work along with him, or do you think the housing projects ought to continue to be built, but only by private funds (somewhat higher rents), and no government interference? Just revenue for large real-estate interests and huge architectural firms who design edifices which reveal no more than the internal structure of a ten-million-dollar bill.

AUGUST, 1963

Some of you will remember that the column for the May issue talked about the approaching destruction of Pennsylvania Station and the plague of modern architecture, a plague which sits like a plastic embodiment of cancer over our suburbs, office buildings, schools, prisons, factories, churches, hotels, motels, and airline terminals. A fair number of letters came in for that column, and I would like to quote from part of one:

> I'm curious about something. Why is it that [some] people have such strong dislike for a form of architecture which [other] people are able not only to accept, but to accept as positive values in our society — goals to try to achieve? My husband's answer is that nobody really likes the current building trend, but that few people think about it enough to define their own emotions. But I can't accept that as a full answer. [The fact remains] that some people react with . . . aversion to modern architecture, . . . others . . . value it. Do you have an answer?

I think I do. But it rests on a premise most of you may find intolerable. The best short poem of the twentieth century, I would think, is Yeats' *The Second Coming* which goes, in part:

> Things fall apart; the centre cannot hold;
> Mere anarchy is loosed upon the world,
> The blood-dimmed tide is loosed, and everywhere
> The ceremony of innocence is drowned;
> The best lack all conviction, while the worst
> Are full of passionate intensity.
>
> . . . Somewhere in sands of the desert
> A shape with lion body and the head of a man,
> A gaze blank and pitiless as the sun,
> Is moving its slow thighs. . . .

and ends:

> . . . What rough beast, its hour come round at last,
> Slouches towards Bethlehem to be born?

That rough beast is a shapeless force, an obdurate emptiness, an annihilation of possibilities. It is totalitarianism: that totalitarianism which has haunted the twentieth century, haunted the efforts of intellectuals to define it, of politicians to withstand it, and of rebels to find a field of war where it could be given battle. Amoeboid, insidious, totalitarianism came close to conquering the world twenty years ago. In that first large upheaval the Nazis sang of blood and the deep roots of blood and then proceeded to show their respect for the roots of blood by annihilating their millions through the suffocations of the gas chamber. No wilder primitive song was ever sung by a modern power, no more cowardly way of exercising a collective will has been yet encountered in history. The Nazis came to power by suggesting they would return Germany to the primitive secrets of her barbaric age, and then proceeded to destroy the essential intuition of the primitive, the umbilical idea that death and the appropriate totems of burial are as essential to life as life itself.

That first huge wave of totalitarianism was like a tide which moved in two directions at once. It broke upon the incompatible military force of Russia and of America. But it was an ocean of plague. It contaminated whatever it touched. If Russia had been racing into totalitarianism before the war, it was pervasively totalitarian after the war, in the last half-mad years of Stalin's court. And America was altered from a nation of venture, exploitation, bigotry, initiative, strife, social justice and social injustice, into a vast central swamp of tasteless, toneless authority whose dependable heroes were drawn from FBI men, doctors, television entertainers, corporation executives, and athletes who could cooperate with public-relations men. The creative mind gave way to the authoritative mind, the expert took over from the small businessman, the labor executive replaced the trade-union organizer, and that arbiter of morals, the novelist, was replaced by the psychoanalyst. Mental health had come to America. And cancer with it. The country had a collective odor which was reminiscent of a potato left to molder in a plastic box.

That period began with Truman and was continued by Eisenhower. It came to an historic fork with Kennedy's administration. America was faced with going back to its existential beginnings, its frontier psychology, where the future is unknown and one discovers the truth of the present by accepting the risks of the present; or America could continue to go on in its search for totalitarian security. It is characteristic of the President's major vice that he chose to go in both directions at once. But then his character contains a similar paradox. He is on the one hand possessed of personal bravery, some wit, some style, an aristocratic taste for variety. He is a consummate politician, and has a potentially dictatorial nose for the manipulation of newspapers and television. He is a hero. And yet he is a void. His mind seems never to have been seduced by a new idea. He is the embodiment of the American void, that great yawning empty American mind which cannot bear any question which takes longer than ten seconds to answer. Given his virtues, suffering his huge vice, his emptiness, his human emptiness, we have moved as a nation, under his regime, deeper into totalitarianism, far deeper than his predecessors could have dreamed, and have been granted (by the cavalier style of his personal life and the wistfulness of his appreciation for the arts) the possible beginnings of a Resistance to the American totalitarianism.

But first one must recognize the features of the plague. If it appeared first in Nazi Germany as a political juggernaut, and in the Soviet Union as a psychotization of ideology, totalitarianism has slipped into America with no specific political face. There are liberals who are totalitarian, and conservatives, radicals, rightists, fanatics, hordes of the well-adjusted. Totalitarianism has come to America with no concentration camps and no need for them, no political parties and no desire for new parties, no, totalitarianism has slipped into the body cells and psyche of each of us. It has been transported, modified, codified, and inserted into each of us by way of the popular arts, the social crafts, the political crafts, and the corporate techniques. It sits in the image of the commercials on television which use phallic and vaginal symbols to sell products which are otherwise useless for sex, it is heard in the jargon of educators, in the synthetic continuums of prose with which public-relations men learn to enclose the sense and smell of an event, it resides in the taste of frozen food, the pharmaceutical odor of tranquilizers, the planned obsolescence of automobiles, the lack of workmanship in the mass, it lives in the boredom of a good mind, in the sexual excess of lovers who love each other into apathy, it is the livid passion which takes us to sleeping pills, the mechanical action in every household appliance which breaks too soon, it vibrates in the sound of an air conditioner or the flicker of fluorescent lighting. And it proliferates in that new architecture which rests like an incubus upon the American landscape, that new architecture which cannot be called modern because it is not architecture but opposed to architecture. Modern architecture began with the desire to use the building materials of the twentieth century — steel, glass, reinforced concrete—and such techniques as cantilevered structure to increase the sculptural beauty of buildings while enlarging their function. It was the first art to be engulfed by the totalitarians who distorted the search of modern architecture for simplicity, and converted it to monotony. The essence of totalitarianism is that it beheads. It beheads individuality, variety, dissent, extreme possibility, romantic faith, it blinds vision, deadens instinct, it obliterates the past. Since it is also irrational, it puts up buildings with flat roofs and huge expanses of glass in northern climates and then suffocates the inhabitants with super-heating systems while the flat roof leaks under a weight of snow. Since totalitarianism is a cancer within the body of history, it obliterates distinctions. It makes factories look like college campuses or mental hospitals, where once factories had the specific beauty of revealing their huge and sometimes brutal function—beauty cannot exist without revelation, nor man maybe without beauty. It makes the new buildings on college campuses look like factories. It depresses the average American with the unconscious recognition that he is installed in a gelatin of totalitarian environment which is bound to deaden his most individual efforts. This new architecture, this totalitarian architecture, destroys the past. There is no trace of the forms which lived in the centuries before us, none of their arrogance, their privilege, their aspiration, their canniness, their creations, their vulgarities. We are left with less and less sense of the lives of men and women who came before us. So we are less able to judge the sheer psychotic values of the present: overkill, fallout shelters, and adjurations by the President to drink a glass of milk each day.

Totalitarianism came to birth at the moment man turned incapable of facing back into the accumulated wrath and horror of his historic past. We sink into cancer after we have gorged on all the medicines which cheated all the diseases we have fled in our life, we sink into cancer when the organs, deadened by chemical rescues manufactured outside the body, became too biologically muddled to dominate their cells. Departing from the function of the separate organs, cancer cells grow to look like one another. So, too, as society bogs into hypocrisies so elaborate they can no longer be traced, then do our buildings, those palpable artifacts of social cells, come to look like one another and cease to function with the art, beauty, and sometimes mysterious proportion of the past.

I can try to answer the lady who wrote the letter now: people who admire the new architecture find it of value because it obliterates the past. They are sufficiently totalitarian to wish to avoid the consequences of the past. Which of course is not to say that they see themselves as totalitarian. The totalitarian passion is an unconscious one. Which liberal fighting for bigger housing and additional cubic feet of air space in elementary schools does not see himself as a benefactor? Can he comprehend that the somewhat clammy pleasure he obtains from looking at the completion of the new school—that architectural horror!—is a reflection of a buried and ugly pleasure, a totalitarian glee that the Gothic knots and Romanesque oppressions which entered his psyche through the schoolhouses of his youth have now been excised. But those architectural wounds, those forms from his childhood not only shamed him and scored him, but marked upon him as well a wound from culture itself—its buried message of the cruelty and horror which were rooted in the majesties of the past. Now the flat surfaces, blank ornamentation and pastel colors of the new schoolhouses will maroon his children in an endless hallway of the present. A school is an arena to a child. Let it look like what it should be, mysterious, exciting, even gladiatorial, rather than a musical comedy's notion of a reception center for war brides. The totalitarian impulse not only washes away distinctions but looks for a style in buildings, in clothing, and in the ornamentations of tools, appliances, and daily objects which will diminish one's sense of function, and reduce one's sense of reality by reducing to the leaden formulations of jargon such emotions as awe, dread, beauty, pity, terror, calm, horror, and harmony. By dislocating us from the most powerful emotions of reality, totalitarianism leaves us further isolated in the empty landscapes of psychosis, precisely that inner landscape of void and dread which we flee by turning to totalitarian styles of life. The totalitarian liberal looks for new schools and more desks; the real (if vanishing) liberal looks for better books, more difficult books to force upon the curriculum. A high school can survive in a converted cow barn if the seniors are encouraged to read *Studs Lonigan* the same week they are handed *The Cardinal* or *The Seven Storey Mountain.*

Yes, the people who admire the new architecture are unconsciously totalitarian. They are looking to eject into their environment and landscape the same deadness and monotony life has put into them. A vast deadness and a huge monotony, a nausea without spasm, has been part of the profit of American life in the last fifteen years—we will pay in the next fifteen as this living death is disgorged into the buildings our totalitarian managers will manage to erect for us. The landscape of America will be stolen for half a century if a Resistance does not form. Indeed it may be stolen forever if we are not sufficiently courageous to enter the depression of contemplating what we have already lost and what we have yet to lose.

Ten Thousand Words a Minute

Champions are prodigies of will—one of the elements which separates them from club fighters or contenders is an urge which carries them through crises other fighters are not willing to endure. Thus the chance is always present that a champion can be killed in the ring. This of course was the underlying theme in the first Patterson-Liston fight; its echoes appear throughout the piece.

The close relation of death to existential politics need not be forced. The formal argument is doubtless beyond one's means, but it could be said that just as matters such as conscience or moral decision make up intrinsic dilemmas for the language analysts of Anglo-American philosophy, so the reluctance of modern European existentialism to take on the logical continuation of the existential vision (that there is a life after death which can be as existential as life itself) has brought French and German existentialism to a halt on this uninhabitable terrain of the absurd—to wit, man must lead his life as if death is meaningful even when man knows that death is meaningless. This revealed knowledge which Heidegger accepts as his working hypothesis and Sartre goes so far as to assume is the certainty upon which he may build a philosophy, ends the possibility that one can construct a base for the existential ethic. The German philosopher runs aground trying to demonstrate the necessity for man to discover an authentic life. Heidegger can give no deeper explanation why man should bother to be authentic than to state in effect that man should be authentic in order to be free. Sartre's advocacy of the existential commitment is always in danger of dwindling into the minor aristocratic advocacy of leading one's life with style for the sake of style. Existentialism is rootless unless one dares the hypothesis that death is an existential continuation of life, that the soul may either pass through migrations, or cease to exist in the continuum of nature (which is the unspoken intimation of cancer). But accepting this hypothesis, authenticity and commitment return to the center of ethics, for man then faces no peril so huge as alienation from his own soul, a death which is other than death, a disappearance into nothingness rather than into Eternity.

This idea is taken up in "Ten Thousand Words a Minute"; it comes to brief overt focus after the description of the Paret-Griffith fight, and for that matter is repeated with variations through many of the papers in this book. In the December column in Es-quire there is a section not printed here in the Miscellany, which speaks of Dr. Robert A. Soblen's suicide. He was an elderly man convicted by America for espionage, but let out on bail during his appeal because he was dying of cancer. Jumping his bail, he escaped by airplane to Israel. Forbidden to enter that country, he tried on his enforced return to America to commit suicide in England.

He is condemned to go to jail for life, he is doomed to die of cancer, and yet, obviously dissatisfied with the notion that his fate is final, he makes two curious attempts at suicide.

Obviously there is a difference to him in the way he dies. He seems to have a mania not to die in an American jail. His instinct tells him to clear a space, to find a private place in which to die. But he expresses his instinct with the power of a major passion. It gives a hint of the secret. It suggests that the way we die, the style of our death, its condition, its mood, its witness, is not trivial. May it be that the way we die affects the direction in which our death may turn? Soblen is deep in cancer. Can it be that one can die profoundly deep in cancer or not nearly so deep?

We are apparently a light-year away from political preoccupations and yet it is a distance which must be traversed. In the Middle Ages man endured his life as a preparation for his death, and lived out his displacement so completely that life was in danger of perishing by famine, plague, and the untamed encroachments of nature. Modern man, in conquest of nature, chooses to ignore death and violate its logic. The result may be a destruction not only of life, but of Being, of our route from the world to Eternity and back again. A politics devoted exclusively to the immediate needs of society murders death as absolutely as theology once massacred the possibilities of life.

Remember that old joke about three kinds of intelligence: human, animal, and military? Well, if there are three kinds of writers: novelists, poets, and *reporters*, there is certainly a gulf between the poet and the novelist; quite apart from the kind of living they make, poets invariably seem to be aristocrats, usually spoiled beyond repair; and novelists—even if they make a million, or have large talent—look to have something of the working class about them. Maybe it is the drudgery, the long, obsessive inner life, the day-to-day monotony of applying themselves to the middle of the same continuing job, or perhaps it is the business of being unappreciated at home—has anyone met a novelist who is happy with the rugged care provided by his wife?

Now, of course, I am tempted to round the image out and say reporters belong to the middle class. Only I do not know if I can push the metaphor. Taken one by one, it is true that reporters tend to be hardheaded, objective, and unimaginative. Their intelligence is sound but unexceptional and they have the middle-class penchant for collecting tales, stories, legends, accounts of practical jokes, details of negotiation, bits of memoir—all those capsules of fiction which serve the middle class as a substitute for ethics and/or culture. Reporters, like shopkeepers, tend to be worshipful of the fact which wins and so covers over the other facts. In the middle class, the remark, "He made a lot of money," ends the conversation. If you persist, if you try to point out that the money was made by digging through his grandmother's grave to look for oil, you are met with a middle-class shrug. "It's a question of taste whether one should get into the past," is the winning reply.

In his own person there is nobody more practical than a reporter. He exhibits the same avidity for news which a businessman will show for money. No bourgeois will hesitate to pick up a dollar, even if he is not fond of the man with whom he deals: so, a reporter will do a nice story about a type he dislikes, or a bad story about a figure he is fond of. It has nothing to do with his feelings. There is a logic to news—on a given day, with a certain meteorological drift to the winds in the mass media, a story can only ride along certain vectors. To expect a reporter to be true to the precise detail of an event is kin to the sentimentality which asks a fast revolving investor to be faithful to a particular stock in his portfolio when it is going down and his others are going up.

But here we come to the end of our image. When the middle class gather for a club meeting or a social function, the atmosphere is dependably dull, whereas ten reporters come together in a room for a story are slightly hysterical, and two hundred reporters and photographers congregated for a press conference are as void of dignity, even stuffed-up, stodgy, middle-class dignity, as a slew of monkeys tearing through the brush. There is reason for this, much reason; there is always urgency to get some quotation which is usable for their story, and afterward, find a telephone: the habitat of a reporter, at its worst, is identical to spending one's morning, afternoon and evening transferring from the rush hour of one subway train to the rush hour of another. In time even the best come to remind one of the rush hour. An old fight reporter is a sad sight, he looks like an old prizefight manager, which is to say, he looks like an old cigar butt.

Nor is this true only of sports reporters. They are gifted with charm compared to political reporters who give off an effluvium which is unadulterated cancer gulch. I do not think I exaggerate. There is an odor to any Press Headquarters which is unmistakable. One may begin by saying it is like the odor in small left-wing meeting halls, except it is worse, far worse, for there is no poverty to put a guilt-free iron into the nose; on the contrary, everybody is getting free drinks, free sandwiches, free news releases. Yet there is the unavoidable smell of flesh burning quietly and slowly in the service of a machine. Have any of you never been through the smoking car of an old coach early in the morning when the smokers sleep and the stale air settles into congelations of gloom? Well, that is a little like the scent of Press Headquarters. Yet the difference is vast, because Press Headquarters for any big American event is invariably a large room in a large hotel, usually the largest room in the largest hotel in town. Thus it is a commercial room in a commercial hotel. The walls must be pale green or pale pink, dirty by now, subtly dirty like the toe of a silk stocking. (Which is incidentally the smell of the plaster.) One could be meeting bureaucrats from Tashkent in the Palace of the Soviets. One enormous barefaced meeting room, a twenty-foot banner up, a proscenium arch at one end, with high Gothic windows painted within the arch — almost never does a window look out on the open air. (Hotels build banquet rooms on the *inside* of their buildings — it is the best way to fill internal space with revenue.)

This room is in fever. Two hundred, three hundred, I suppose even five hundred reporters get into some of these rooms, there to talk, there to drink, there to bang away on any one of fifty standard typewriters, provided by the people on Public Relations who have set up this Press Headquarters. It is like being at a vast party in Limbo — there is tremendous excitement, much movement and no sex at all. Just talk. Talk fed by cigarettes. One thousand to two thousand cigarettes are smoked every hour. The mind must keep functioning fast enough to offer up stories. (Reporters meet as in a marketplace to trade their stories — they barter an anecdote they cannot use about one of the people in the event in order to pick up a different piece which is usable by their paper. It does not matter if the story is true or altogether not true, it must merely be suitable and not too mechanically libelous.) So they char the inside of their bodies in order to scrape up news which can go out to the machine, that enormous machine, that intellectual leviathan which is obliged to eat each day, tidbits, gristle, gravel, garbage cans, charlotte russe, old rubber tires, T-bone steaks, wet cardboard, dry leaves, apple pie, broken bottles, dog food, shells, roach powder, dry ball-point pens, grapefruit juice. All the trash, all the garbage, all the slop and a little of the wealth go out each day and night into the belly of that old American goat, our newspapers.

So the reporters smell also of this work, they smell of the dishwasher and the pots, they are flesh burning themselves very quietly and slowly in the service of a machine which feeds goats, which feeds The Goat. One smells this collective odor on the instant one enters their meeting room. It is not a corrupt smell, it does not have enough of the meats, the savory, and the vitality of flesh to smell corrupt and fearful when it is bad, no, it is more the smell of excessive respect for power, the odor of flesh gutted by avidities which are electric and empty. I suppose it is the bleak smell one could find on the inside of one's head during a bad cold, full of fever, badly used, burned out of mood. The physical sensation of a cold often is one of power trapped corrosively inside, coils of strength being liquidated in some center of the self. The reporter hangs in a powerless-power — his voice directly, or via the rewrite desk indirectly, reaches out to millions of readers; the more readers he owns, the less he can say. He is forbidden by a hundred censors, most of them inside himself, to communicate notions, which are not conformistically simple, simple like plastic is simple, that is to say, monotonous. Therefore a reporter forms a habit equivalent to lacerating the flesh: he learns to write what he does not naturally believe. Since he did not start presumably with the desire to be a bad writer or a dishonest writer, he ends by bludgeoning his brain into believing that something which is half true is in fact — since he creates a fact each time he puts something into a newspaper — nine-tenths true. A psyche is debauched — his own; a false fact is created. For which fact, sooner or later, inevitably, inexorably, the public will pay. A nation which forms detailed opinions on the basis of detailed fact which is askew from the subtle reality becomes a nation of citizens whose psyches are skewed, item by detailed item, away from *any* reality.

So great guilt clings to reporters. They know they help to keep America slightly insane. As a result perhaps they are a shabby-looking crew. The best of them are the shabbiest, which is natural if one thinks about it — a sensitive man suffers from the prosperous life of his lies more than a dull man. In fact the few dudes one finds among reporters tend to be semi-illiterates, or hatchet men, or cynics on two or three payrolls who do restrained public relations in the form of news stories. But this is to make too much of the extremes. Reporters along the middle of the spectrum are shabby, worried, guilty, and suffer each day from the damnable anxiety that they know all sorts of powerful information a half hour to twenty-four hours before anyone else in America knows it, not to mention the time clock ticking away in the vault of all those stories which cannot be printed or will not be printed. It makes for a livid view of existence. It is like an injunction to become hysterical once a day. Then they must write at lightning speed. It may be heavy-fisted but true, it may be slick as a barnyard slide, it may be great, it may be fill—what does it matter? The matter rides out like oats in a conveyor belt, and the unconscious takes a ferocious pounding. Writing is of use to the psyche only if the writer discovers something he did not know he knew in the act itself of writing. That is why a few men will go through hell in order to keep writing—Joyce and Proust, for example. Being a writer can save one from insanity or cancer; being a bad writer can drive one smack into the center of the plague. Think of the poor reporter who does not have the leisure of the novelist or the poet to discover what he thinks. The unconscious gives up, buries itself, leaves the writer to his cliché, and saves the truth, or that part of it the reporter is yet privileged to find, for his colleagues and his friends. A good reporter is a man who must still tell you the truth privately; he has bright harsh eyes and can relate ten good stories in a row standing at a bar.

Still, they do not quit. That charge of adrenalin once a day, that hysteria, that sense of powerless-power close to the engines of history—they can do without powerless-power no more than a gentleman junkie on the main line can do without his heroin, doctor. You see, a reporter is close to the action. He is not *of* the action, but he is close to it, as close as a crab louse to the begetting of a child. One may never be President, but the photographer working for his paper has the power to cock a flashbulb and make the eyes of JFK go blink!

However, it is not just this lead-encased seat near the radiations of power which keeps the reporter hooked on a drug of new news to start new adrenalin; it is also the ride. It is the free ride. When we were children, there were those movies about reporters; they were heroes. While chasing a lead, they used to leap across empty elevator shafts, they would wrestle automatics out of mobsters' hands, and if they were Cary Grant, they would pick up a chair and stick it in the lion's face, since the lion had had the peculiar sense to walk into the editor's office. Next to being a cowboy, or a

private eye, the most heroic activity in America was to be a reporter. Now it is the welfare state. Every last cigar-smoking fraud of a
middle-aged reporter, pale with prison pallor, deep lines in his
cheeks, writing daily pietisms for the sheet back home about free
enterprise, is himself the first captive of the welfare state. It is the
best free ride anyone will find since he left his family's chest. Your
room is paid for by the newspaper, your trips to the particular
spots attached to the event—in this case, the training camp at Elgin, Illinois, for Patterson, and the empty racetrack at Aurora
Downs for Liston—are by chartered limousine. Who but a Soviet
bureaucrat, a British businessman, a movie star, or an American
reporter would ride in a chartered limousine? (They smell like funeral parlors.) Your typing paper is free if you want it; your seat at
the fight, or your ticket to the convention is right up there, under
the ropes; your meals if you get around to eating them are free,
free sandwiches only but then a reporter has a stomach like a shaving mug and a throat like a hog's trough: he couldn't tell steak tar-
tare from *guacamole*. And the drinks—if you are at a big fight—are
without charge. If you are at a political convention, there is no free
liquor. But you do have a choice between free Pepsi-Cola and free
Coca-Cola. The principle seems to be that the reporting of mildly
psychotic actions—such as those performed by politicians—should
be made in sobriety; whereas a sane estimate of an athlete's
chances are neatest on booze. At a fight Press Headquarters, the
drinks are very free, and the mood can even be half convivial. At
the Patterson-Liston Press Headquarters there was a head bartender working for Championship Sports whose name was Archie. He
was nice. He was a nice man. It was a pleasure to get a drink from
him. You remember these things afterward, it's part of the nostalgia. The joy of the free ride is the lack of worry. It's like being in
an Army outfit which everyone's forgotten. You get your food, you
get your beer, you get your pay, the work is easy, and leave to
town is routine. You never had it so good—you're an infant again:
you can grow up a second time and improve the job.

That's the half and half of being a reporter. One half is addiction,
adrenalin, anecdote-shopping, deadlines, dread, cigar smoke, lung
cancer, vomit, feeding The Goat; the other is Aloha, Tahiti, old
friends and the free ride to the eleventh floor of the Sheraton-Chicago, Patterson-Liston Press Headquarters, everything free. Even
your news free. If you haven't done your homework, if you drank
too late last night and missed the last limousine out to Elgin or
Aurora this morning, if there's no poop of your own on Floyd's
speed or Sonny's bad mood, you can turn to the handouts given
you in the Press Kit, dig, a *Kit*, kiddies, worked up for you by

Harold Conrad who's the Public Relations Director. It's not bad stuff, it's interesting material. No need to do your own research. Look at some of this: there's the tale of the tape for each fighter with as many physical measurements as a tailor in Savile Row might take; there's the complete record of each fighter, how he won, how many rounds, who, the date, so forth; there's the record of how much money they made on each fight, how their KO records compare with the All-Time Knockout Artists, Rocky Marciano with 43 out of 49, batting .878, Joe Louis at .761, Floyd at .725 (29 in 40) and Sonny Liston going with 23 for 34, is down at .676, back of Jim Jeffries who comes in at .696. There's a column there, there's another if you want to dig into the biographies of each fighter, six single-spaced pages on Patterson, four on Liston. There's a list of each and every fighter who won and lost the Heavyweight Championship, and the year—remember? Remember Jake Kilrain and Marvin Hart (stopped Jack Root at Reno, Nevada, 12 rounds, July 3, 1905). You can win money with Marvin Hart betting in bars. And Tommy Burns. Jack O'Brien. In what year did Ezzard Charles first take Jersey Joe Walcott; in what town? You can see the different columns shaping up. If you got five columns to do on the fight, three can be whipped right up out of Graff/Reiner/Smith Enterprises, Inc. Sports News Release. Marvelous stuff. How Sonny Liston does his roadwork on railroad tracks, what Sonny's best weight is (206-212), what kind of poundages Floyd likes to give away—averages 10 pounds a bout—Floyd's style in boxing, Liston's style in boxing. It's part of the free list, an offering of facts with a little love from the Welfare State.

It is so easy, so much is done for you, that you remember these days with nostalgia. When you do get around to paying for yourself, going into a room like the Camelot Room at the Sheraton-Chicago, with its black-blood three-story mahogany paneling and its high, stained Gothic windows looking out no doubt on an air shaft, it is a joy to buy your own food, an odd smacking sensation to pay for a drink. It is the Welfare State which makes the pleasure possible. When one buys all one's own drinks, the sensation of paying cash is without much joy, but to pay for a drink occasionally—that's near bliss.

And because it is a fight, cancer gulch has its few oases. The Press Headquarters livens up with luminaries, the unhealthiest people in America now meet some of the healthiest, complete self-contained healthy bodies which pass modestly through: Ingemar Johansson and Archie Moore, Rocky Marciano, Barney Ross, Cassius Clay, Harold Johnson, Ezzard Charles, Dick Tiger on his way to San Francisco where he is to fight Gene Fullmer and beat

him, Jim Braddock—big, heavy, grey, and guarded, looking as
tough as steel drilled into granite, as if he were the toughest night
watchman in America, and Joe Louis looking like the largest China-
man in the world, still sleepy, still sad. That's part of the pleasure
of Press Headquarters—the salty crystallized memories which are
released from the past, the night ten or eleven years ago when Joe
Louis, looking just as sleepy and as sad as he does now, went in to
fight Rocky Marciano at the Garden, and was knocked out in eight.
It was part of a comeback, but Louis was never able to get his fight
going at all, he was lethargic that night, and Marciano, fighting a
pure Italian street-fighter's style, throwing his punches as if he held
a brick in each hand, taking Louis' few good shots with an animal
joy, strong enough to eat bricks with his teeth, drove right through
Joe Louis and knocked him out hard. Louis went over in a long,
very inert fall, as if an old tree or a momentous institution were
coming down, perhaps the side of a church wall hovering straight
and slow enough in its drop for the onlooker to take a breath in the
gulf of the bomb. And it had been a bomb. Louis' leg was draped
over the rope. People were crying as they left Madison Square
Garden that night. It was a little like the death of Franklin Delano
Roosevelt: something generous had just gone out of the world.
And now here was Marciano as well, in the couloirs and coffee
shop and lobby of the Sheraton-Chicago, a man looking as different
from the young contender he had been on his way to the championship as Louis now looked the same. Louis had turned old in the
ring. Marciano retired undefeated, and so aged after he stopped.
Now he seemed no longer to be carrying bricks but pillows. He
had gotten very plump, his face was round and no longer lumpy, he
was half bald, a large gentle monk with a bemused, misty, slightly
tricky expression.

And there were others, Bill Hartack, Jack Kearns who at eighty-
plus still looked to be one of the most intelligent men in America,
Sammy Taub, the old radio announcer who used to talk as fast as
the cars on the Indianapolis Speedway, "and he hits him another
left to the belly, and another, and another, and a right to the head,
and a left to the head." Taub made bums sound like champions—it
is doubtful if there was ever a fighter who could throw punches fast
enough to keep up with Taub, and now he was an old man, a
grandfather, a bright, short man with a birdlike face, a little like a
tiny older version of Leonard Lyons.

There were many, there were so many, preliminary fighters who
got their money together to get to Chicago, and managers, and
promoters. There were novelists, Jimmy Baldwin, Budd Schulberg,
Gerald Kersh, Ben Hecht. As the fight approached, so did the

Mob. That arid atmosphere of reporters alone with reporters and writers with writers gave way to a whiff of the deep. The Mob was like birds and beasts coming in to feed. Heavy types, bouncers, plug-uglies, flatteners, one or two speedy, swishing, Negro ex-boxers, for example, now blown up to the size of fat middle-weights, slinky in their walk, eyes fulfilling the operative definition of razor slits, murder coming off them like scent comes off a skunk. You could feel death as they passed. It came wafting off. And the rest of the beasts as well—the strong-arm men, the head-kickers, the limb-breakers, the groin-stompers. If a clam had a muscle as large as a man, and the muscle grew eyes, you would get the mood. Those were the beasts. They were all orderly, they were all trained, they were dead to humor. They never looked at anyone they did not know, and when they were introduced they stared at the floor while shaking hands as if their own hand did not belong to them, but was merely a stuffed mitten to which their arm was attached.

The orders came from the birds. There were hawks and falcons and crows, Italian dons looking like little old shrunken eagles, gulls, pelicans, condors. The younger birds stood around at modest strategic points in the lobby, came up almost not at all to Press Headquarters, posted themselves out on the street, stood at the head of escalators, near the door of the barbershop, along the elevator strip, by the registration desk. They were all dressed in black gabardine topcoats, black felt hats, and very large dark sunglasses with expensive frames. They wore white scarves or black scarves. A few would carry a black umbrella. They stood there watching everyone who passed. They gave the impression of knowing exactly why they were standing there, what they were waiting to hear, how they were supposed to see, who they were supposed to watch. One had the certainty after a time that they knew the name of every man and woman who walked through the downstairs lobby and went into the Championship Sports office on the ground floor. If a figure said hello to a celebrity he was not supposed to know—at least not in the bird's private handbook—one could sense the new information being filed. Some were tall, some were short, but almost all were thin, their noses were aquiline, their chins were modest, their cheeks were subtly concave. They bore a resemblance to George Scott in *The Hustler*. Their aura was succinct. It said, "If you spit on my shoes, you're dead." It was a shock to realize that the Mob, in the flesh, was even more impressive than in the motion pictures.

There were also some fine old *mafiosos* with faces one had seen on the busts of Venetian doges in the Ducal Palace, subtle faces, insidious with the ingrowth of a curious culture built on treachery, dogma, the evil eye, and blood loyalty to clan. They were *don capos*, and did not wear black any longer, black was for subalterns. They were the leaders of the birds, fine old gentlemen in quiet grey suits, quiet intricate dark ties. Some had eyes which contained the humor of a cardinal; others were not so nice. There was an unhealthy dropsical type with pallor, and pink-tinted bifocal glasses — the kind who looked as if they owned a rich mortuary in a poor Italian neighborhood, and ran the local Republican club.

All the birds and beasts of the Mob seemed to be for Liston, almost without exception they were for Sonny. It was not because his prison record stirred some romantic allegiance in them, nothing of service in India together, sir, or graduates from the same campus; no, nor was it part necessarily and absolutely of some large syndicated plot to capture and run the Heavyweight Championship of the World so that the filaments of prestige which trail from such a crown would wind back into all the pizza parlors and jukeboxes of the continent, the gambling casinos, the after-hours joints, the contracting businesses, and the demolition businesses, the paving businesses, the music of the big bands, the traffic in what is legit and what is illegit — like junk and policy — no, in such a kingdom, the Heavyweight Championship is not worth that much, it's more like the Polish Corridor was to the Nazis, or Cuba to us, it's a broken boil. In their mind Patterson was a freak, some sort of vegetarian. It was sickening to see a post of importance held by a freak, or by the manager of a freak.

II

Before the fight much was made of the battle between good and evil, and the descriptions of the training camps underlined these differences. Patterson trained in a boys' camp up at Elgin which gave the impression of a charitable institution maintained by a religious denomination. The bungalows were small, painted white on their outside, and were of a miserable, dull stained-pine-color within. The atmosphere was humorless and consecrated. Nor was Patterson about. It was two days before the fight, and he had disappeared. Perhaps he was training, conceivably he was sleeping, maybe he was taking a long walk. But the gym up the hill was closed to reporters. So we gathered in one of the cottages, and watched a film which had been made of Patterson's fights. Since it had been put together by a public-relations man who was devoted to Patterson, the film caught most of Floyd's best moments and few of his bad ones.

At his best he was certainly very good. He had been an extraordinary club fighter. As a middleweight and light-heavyweight he had put together the feat of knocking out a good many of the best club fighters in America. Yvon Durelle, Jimmy Slade, Esau Ferdinand, Willie Troy, Archie McBride had been stopped by Patterson, and they were tough men. One reason a club fighter is a club fighter, after all, is because of his ability to take punishment and give a high, durable level of performance. The movies brought back the excitement there used to be watching Patterson on television in 1953 and 1954 when he would fight the main event at Eastern Parkway. I knew nothing about fights then, but the first time I saw Patterson, he knocked out a rugged fighter named Dick Wagner in five rounds, and there had been something about the way he did it which cut into my ignorance. I knew he was good. It was like seeing one's first exciting bullfight: at last one knows what everybody has been talking about. So I had an affection for Patterson which started early. When Patterson was bad he was unbelievably bad, he was Chaplinesque, simple, sheepish, eloquent in his clumsiness, sad like a clown, his knees looked literally to droop. He would seem precisely the sort of shy, stunned, somewhat dreamy Negro kid who never knew the answer in class. But when he was good, he seemed as fast as a jungle cat. He was the fastest heavyweight I had ever seen. Watching these movies, it was evident he could knock a man out with a left hook thrown from the most improbable position, leaping in from eight feet out, or wheeling to the left, his feet in the air, while he threw his hook across his body. He was like a rangy, hungry cat who starts to jump from a tree at some prey, and turns in flight to take an accurate, improvised swipe at a gorilla swinging by on a vine.

But the movies were only half pleasing. Because Patterson's fascination as a fighter was in his complex personality, in his alternations from high style to what—in a champion—could only be called buffoonery. The movies showed none of his bad fights, except for the famous third round with Ingemar Johansson in their first fight— an omission which not even a public-relations man would want to make. In the perspective of boxing history, those seven knockdowns were no longer damaging; Patterson's courage in getting up was underlined in one's memory by the way he came back in the next fight to knock Johansson out in the fifth round. So one was left with the disagreeable impression that this movie was too righteous.

Naturally I got into a debate with Cus D'Amato and a young gentleman named Jacobs, Jim Jacobs as I remember, who was built like a track man and had an expression which was very single-minded. He was the Public Relations Assistant, the man who had cut the movie, and a serious handball player too, as I learned later. In the debate, he ran me all over the court. It was one of those maddening situations where you know you are right, but the other man has the facts, and the religious conviction as well.

What about all the times Patterson has been knocked down, I started.

What times?

What times? Why. ... . I was ready to stammer.

Name them.

Johansson. Rademacher.

Go on.

Roy Harris.

A slip. I could show you the film clips.

Tom McNeeley.

Also a slip, but Floyd's too nice a guy to claim it was, said Jacobs. As a matter of fact, Rademacher hit him when Floyd was tripping over his own foot as he was going backwards. That's why Floyd went down. Floyd's too much of a gentleman to take any of the credit for a knockdown away from a talented amateur like Rademacher.

"As a matter of fact," went on Jacobs, "there's one knockdown you haven't mentioned. Jacques Royer-Crecy knocked Floyd down to one knee with a left hook in the first round back in 1954."

"You better not argue with this guy," said Cus D'Amato with a happy grin. "He's seen so many movies, he knows more about Floyd's fights than I do. He can beat *me* in an argument." With that warning I should have known enough to quit, but it was Sunday and I was full of myself. The night before, at Medinah Temple, before thirty-six-hundred people (we grossed over $8000) I had had a debate with William F. Buckley, Jr. The sportswriters had put up Buckley as a 2½-to-1 favorite before our meet, but I was told they named me the winner. Eight, one, one even; seven rounds to three; six, three, one even; those were the scorecards *I* received. So at the moment, I was annoyed that this kid Jacobs, whom I started to call Mr. Facts, was racking me up.

Therefore, I heeded Cus D'Amato not at all and circled back to the fight. Jacobs was calling Patterson a great champion, I was saying he had yet to prove he was great—it was a dull argument until I said, "Why didn't he fight the kind of man Louis and Dempsey went up against?" A big mistake. Jacobs went through the record of every single fighter Jack Dempsey and Joe Louis fought as champions, and before we were done, by the laws of collected evidence, he had bludgeoned the court into accepting, against its better judgment, that Pete Rademacher was the equal of Buddy Baer,

Tom McNeeley of Luis Firpo, Hurricane Jackson of Tony Galento, and that Brian London riding his much underrated bicycle could have taken a decision from Bill Brennan.

Jacobs was much too much for me. I quit. "I'm telling you," said Cus D'Amato, having enjoyed this vastly, "he beats me all the time in arguments."

While this had been going on, two small Negroes looking like starchy divinity students had been glowering at me and my arguments. Every time I said something which was not altogether in praise of Patterson, they looked back as if I were a member of the White Citizens Council. I never did get a chance to find out who they were, or what they represented (Jacobs was keeping me much too busy), but one could lay odds they were working for one of the more dogmatic Negro organizations devoted to the uplift of the race. They had none of the humor of the few Freedom Riders I had met, or the personal attractiveness some of the young Negroes around Martin Luther King seemed to have. No, these were bigots. They could have believed in anything from the Single Tax to the Brotherhood of Sleeping Car Porters for all I knew, but they were dead-eyed to any voice which did not give assent to what they believed already. So it was depressing to find them in Patterson's camp, and thus devoted to him. It fit with the small-trade-union bigotry that hung over this establishment.

Outside, in the air, the view while dull was not so dogmatic. Sammy Taub, the radio announcer of my childhood, had a voice full of an old Jew's love for Patterson. "Oh, Floyd's got the real class," said Mr. Taub, "he's a gentleman. I've seen a lot of fighters, but Floyd's the gentleman of them all. I could tell you things about him, about how nice he is. He's going to take that big loudmouth Liston apart, punch by punch. And I'm going to be there to watch it!" he said with a grin and an old announcer's windup.

Next morning I spent more time with D'Amato on the way to Liston's camp. We went together in the limousine. It was the day before the fight, and D'Amato was going out as Patterson's representative to check on the gloves. There had been trouble with this already: D'Amato had objected to Liston's plan to wear a pair of gloves made by a Chicago manufacturer named Frager. It seems the eight-ounce Everlast gloves with curled horsehair for padding had not been large enough to fit Liston's hand. So his manager, Jack Nilon, had come up with gloves which had foam-rubber padding. D'Amato objected. His argument was that Liston's knuckles could punch closer to the surface of the glove riding in foam rubber than in horsehair. The unspoken aim must have been to irritate Liston.

But one couldn't encourage D'Amato to talk about the challenger. D'Amato talked only about his own fighters. How he talked! He had stopped drinking years ago and so had enormous pent-up vitality. As a talker, he was one of the world's great weight lifters, not brilliant, but powerful, nonstop, and very solid. Talk was muscle. If you wanted to interrupt, you had to bend his arm off.

Under the force, however, he had a funny simple quality, something of that passionate dogmatism which some men develop when they have been, by their own count, true to their principles. He had the enthusiastic manner of a saint who is all works and no contemplation. His body was short and strong, his head was round, and his silver-white hair was cut in a short brush. He seemed to bounce as he talked. He reminded me of a certain sort of very tough Italian kid one used to find in Brooklyn. They were sweet kids, and rarely mean, and they were fearless, at least by the measure of their actions they were fearless. They would fight anybody. Size, age, reputation did not make them hesitate. Because they were very single-minded, however, they were often the butt of the gang, and proved natural victims for any practical jokes. Afterward everyone would hide. They were the kind of kids who would go berserk if you were their friend or their leader and betrayed them. They would literally rip up a sewer grating or a manhole cover in order to beat their way a little closer to you.

I was certain he had been this kind of kid, and later I heard a story that when D'Amato was little, he started once to walk through a small park at night and saw a huge shape waiting for him in the distance. He said he had the feeling he could not turn back. If he did, he would never be able to go near that park again. So he continued down the path. The huge shape was discovered to be a tree. D'Amato's critics would claim that he spent his entire life being brave with trees.

The likelihood, however, is that for a period D'Amato was one of the bravest men in America. He was a fanatic about boxing, and cared little about money. He hated the Mob. He stood up to them. A prizefight manager running a small gym with broken mirrors on East Fourteenth Street does not usually stand up to the Mob, any more than a chambermaid would tell the Duchess of Windsor to wipe her shoes before she enters her suite at the Waldorf.

D'Amato was the exception, however. The Mob ended by using two words to describe him: "He's crazy." The term is given to men who must be killed. Nobody killed D'Amato. For years, like a monk, he slept in the back room of his gym with a police dog for a room-mate. The legend is that he kept a gun under his pillow. During Patterson's last few weeks of training before fighting Archie

Moore for the championship in 1956, a fight he was to win in five rounds, D'Amato bunked on a cot in front of the door to Floyd's room. He was certain that with the championship so close to them the Mob would try to hurt his fighter. What a movie this would have made. It could have ended with a zoom-away shot of the Mob in a burning barn.

The trial of it is that the story goes on. D'Amato was one of the most stubborn men in America. And he was determined that no fighter connected to the Mob in any way would get to fight Floyd. The only trouble was that the good heavyweights in America had managers who were not ready to irritate the men who ran boxing. If they took a match with Patterson, and he defeated their fighter, how could their *ex*-contender ever get a fight on television again? D'Amato may have had the vision of a Lenin—as he said with a grin, "They're always calling me a Communist"—but he never could get enough good managers to begin his new party. Patterson, who was conceivably the best young heavyweight in history at the moment he won the championship, now began to be wasted. He was an artist, and an artist is no greater than his material. The fighters D'Amato got for him now were without luster. So were the fights. After a few years, D'Amato's enemies began to spread the canard best calculated to alienate Patterson. They said D'Amato got him nothing but cripples to fight because Patterson was not good enough to go into the ring with a real heavyweight. To a champion who even now would look for a training camp which might bear resemblance to Wiltwyck, that charity school for near-delinquent adolescents where he first had learned to fight; to someone like Patterson, who as a child would weep when he was unjustly accused; who would get down and walk along the subway tracks on the Eighth Avenue El at High Street in Brooklyn because he had found a cubbyhole for workmen three feet off the rails where he could conceal himself from the world by pulling an iron door close to over him, lying there in darkness while the trains blasted by with apocalyptic noise; to a man who had been so shy as an adolescent that he could not speak to the thirteen-year-old girl who was later to become his wife and so brought a fast-talking friend along to fill the silence; who as a teen-age fighter, just beginning to go to the gym, was so delicate that his older brother Frank once told the reporter Lester Bromberg, "I can't get used to my kid brother being a name fighter. I remember him as the boy who would cry if I hit him too hard when we boxed in the gym"; to a champion who as a young professional had refused to look while his next opponent, Chester Mieszala, was sparring at Chicago's Midtown Gym because he considered it to be taking unfair advantage; to a man who would later sit in shame in a dark room for months after losing his championship to Johansson, the canard that he was a weak heavyweight kept in possession of his kingdom by the determination of his manager never to make a good fight must have been a story to taste like quicklime in his throat. Patterson had put his faith in D'Amato. If D'Amato didn't believe in him. . . . It's the sort of story which belongs on radio at eleven in the morning or three in the afternoon.

The aftermath of the first Johansson fight, however, blew out the set. It was discovered that D'Amato directly or indirectly had gotten money for the promotion through a man named "Fat Tony" Salerno. D'Amato claimed to have been innocent of the connection, and indeed it was a most aesthetic way for the Mob to get him. It's equally possible that after years of fighting every windmill in town, D'Amato had come down to the hard Bolshevistic decision that you don't make an omelet without breaking eggs. Whatever the fact, D'Amato had his license suspended in New York. He was not allowed to work in Floyd's corner the night of the second Johansson fight. And thereafter Patterson kept him away. He gave D'Amato his managerial third of the money, but he didn't let him get too close to training.

If this partnership of Patterson and D'Amato had been made in Heaven, then God or man had failed again. The last sad item was the Liston fight. Patterson had delegated D'Amato to make some of the arrangements. According to the newspapers, Patterson then discovered that D'Amato was trying to delay the negotiations. Now D'Amato was accepted in camp only as a kind of royal jester who could entertain reporters with printable stories. He seemed to be kept in the cabin where I met him at the foot of the hill, forbidden access to the gymnasium the way a drunk is eighty-sixed from his favorite bar. It must have been a particularly Italian humiliation for a man like D'Amato to sit in that cabin and talk to journalists. There were any number of fight reporters who could not go into court and swear they had never had a free meal from the Mob. Some of the food may have been filet mignon. At least so one might judge by the violence of their printed reactions to D'Amato. A reporter can never forgive anyone he has attacked unjustly. Now D'Amato had to receive these cigar butts like a baron demoted to a concierge. He could speak, but he could not act.

Speak he did. If you listened to D'Amato talk, and knew nothing other, you would not get the impression D'Amato was no longer the center of Patterson's camp. He seemed to give off no sense whatever of having lost his liaison to Floyd. When he talked of making the Liston fight, one would never have judged he had tried to prevent it.

"I didn't," he swore to me. "I wanted the fight. Floyd came up to me, and said, 'Cus, you got to make this fight. Liston's going around saying I'm too yellow to fight him. I don't care if a fighter says he can beat me, but no man can say I'm yellow.' " D'Amato bobbed his head. "Then Floyd said, 'Cus, if this fight isn't made, I'll be scared to go out. I'll be afraid to walk into a restaurant and see Liston eating. Because if I see him, I'll have a fight with him right there in the restaurant, and I'll kill him.' I wouldn't try to keep Floyd from having a fight after he says something like that!" said D'Amato.

We were now arriving at Aurora Downs. The limousine took a turn off the highway, went down a blacktop road and then went through a gate onto a dirt road. There was a quick view of a grandstand and part of a small abandoned racetrack. Under the grandstand, the challenger's gym had been installed: it was there Liston had jumped rope to the sound of *Night Train*, performing with such hypnotic, suspended rage that the reporters gave most of their space to describe this talent.

We were meeting now in the clubhouse restaurant, its parimutuel windows boarded up, its floor empty of tables. It was a cold, chilly room, perhaps a hundred feet long, roped off at the rear to give privacy to Liston's quarters, and the surfaces all seemed made of picture-window glass, chromium, linoleum, and pastel plastics like Formica. The most prominent decorations were two cold-drink vending machines, side by side, large as telephone booths. They were getting small play from the reporters, because the day was dank, one of those grey September days which seem to seep up from Lake Michigan and move west. As many as a hundred of us must have come out in our various limousines to see the finale of Everlast vs. Frager, and we gathered in an irritable circle, scrimmaging four and five deep for a view of the scales, an ordinary pair of office scales for small packages, and of two pairs of gloves on a plain wooden table. Disappointed with how I came out in the scrimmage, I pulled back far enough to stand on a chair. The view was now good. A thin man in a green sweater, a man with a long, hungry nose and a pocked, angry skin still alive from an adolescence where one hot boil had doubtless burst upon another, was now screaming at everybody in sight, at D'Amato whom he seemed ready to attack, at Nick Florio, brother of Dan Florio, Patterson's trainer, and at a man named Joe Triner who belonged to the Illinois State Athletic Commission. It developed he was Jack

Nilon, Liston's manager or adviser, a Philadelphia caterer, wealthy in his own right, who had been brought together with Liston by various beneficent forces in Philadelphia who decided Sonny needed rehabilitation in his front window as much as in his heart. So Nilon represented American business, acting once again as big brother to a former convict with talent. How Nilon could scream! It turned out, bang-bang, that the new gloves for Liston were a fraction over eight ounces. Nilon was having none of that. Triner, the Commission man, looked sick. "They weighed eight ounces at the Commission's office today," he said.

"Don't give me none of that," screamed Nilon. "They got to weigh in right here. How do I know what kind of scale you use?"

"What do we want to cheat you on a quarter of an ounce for?" asked Triner.

"Just to get Sonny upset, just to get Sonny upset, that's all," screamed Nilon as if he were pouring boiling oil.

Liston now emerged from the depths of the clubhouse and walked slowly toward us. He was wearing a dark-blue sweat suit, and he moved with the languid pleasure of somebody who is getting the taste out of every step. First his heel went down, then his toe. He could not have enjoyed it more if he had been walking barefoot through a field. One could watch him picking the mood up out of his fingertips and toes. His handlers separated before him. He was a Presence.

"What the hell's going on?" Liston asked. He had a deep growl of a voice, rich, complex, well-modulated. His expression had the sort of holy disdain one finds most often on a very grand old lady.

They started to explain to him, and he nodded petulantly, half listening to the arguments. His expression seemed to say, "Which one of these bullshit artists is most full of it right now?"

While he was listening he pulled on one of the gloves, worked his fist about in it, and then slapped the glove down on the table. "It still don't fit," he cried out in the angry voice of a child. Everybody moved back a little. He stood there in disgust, but wary, alert, as if some deep enemy were in the room, someone who could damage him with a psychic bullet. His eyes bounced lightly, gracefully, from face to face. Which gave the opportunity to see into them for a moment. From the advance publicity one had expected to look into two cracks of dead glass, halfway between reptile and sleepy leopard, but they had the dark, brimming, eloquent, reproachful look one sees sometimes in the eyes of beautiful colored children, three or four years old. And in fact that was the shock of the second degree which none of the photographs had prepared one for: Liston was near to beautiful. For obvious reasons it is an unhappy word to use. But there is no other to substitute. One cannot think of more than a few men who have beauty. Charles Chaplin has it across a room, Krishna Menon across a table. Stephen Spender used to have it, Burt Lancaster oddly enough used to have it—there was no comparison between the way he looked in a movie and the way he looked in life. They say Orson Welles had it years ago, and President Eisenhower in person, believe it or not. At any rate, Liston had it. You did not feel you were looking at someone attractive, you felt you were looking at a creation. And this creation looked like it was building into a temper which would tear up the clubhouse at Aurora Downs. One knew he was acting, no contender would get violent the day before a championship fight, and yet everyone in the room was afraid of Liston. Even D'Amato did not speak too much. Liston had the stage and was using it. "Let's see that glove, let's weigh it again." They leaped to put it on the scales for him. He squatted and made a huge dumb show of scowling at the numbers as if he were just another blighted cotton picker. "Shéeet, who can read the numbers," he pretended to be saying to himself.

"He's not going in the ring with gloves over regulation weight," shouted another dragon, Pollino, the cut man for Liston, a lean Italian with an angry, chopped-up face.

"Well, this scale isn't the official scale," said D'Amato mildly. "The gloves are eight ounces."

Pollino looked like he'd leap across the table to get his hands on D'Amato's neck. "Wha' do you call official scale?" shouted Pollino. "There is no official scale. I'll bet you a thousand dollars they're more than eight ounces."

Nilon came in like a shrike from the other side of Liston. "Why do you bother my fighter with this?" he screamed at the officials. "Why don't you go over to Patterson's camp and bother him the day before the fight? What's he doing? Sleeping? He doesn't have a hundred reporters looking down his throat."

"I don't want to stand much more of this," snapped Liston in the child's voice he used for display of temper. "This is the sort of thing gives reporters a chance to ask stupid questions." Was his dislike of reporters a reminder of the days when four or five policemen would have given him a going-over in a police station while the police reporter, listening to the muffled thuds, would be playing cards in the next room? Liston did not talk to white reporters individually. At Press Headquarters the bitter name for him was Malcolm X. "Just stupid questions, that's all," he repeated, and yet his manner was changing still again. His mood could shift as rapidly as the panoramic scenes in a family film. Suddenly he was mild, now he was mild. He tapped the gloves on the table, and said in a gentle voice, "Oh, they're all right. Let's use them." Then lightly, sadly, he chuckled, and added in his richest voice, "I'm going to hit him so hard that extra quarter of an ounce isn't gonna be any more than just an extra quarter of an ounce he's being hit with." The voice came home to me. I knew which voice it was at last. It was the voice Clark Gable used his last ten years, that genial rum squire's voice, the indulgent "I've been around" voice. Headmasters in prep schools sometimes have it. Liston had it. He must have studied Gable over the years. Perhaps in the movies one sees in prison.

A little more bickering went on between Pollino and Florio. They were like guerrilla troops who have not heard that the armistice had been declared. Then quiet. We were done. But just as the meet was ready to break, Liston held up a hand and said, "I don't want to wear these gloves. I've changed my mind. We've had a special pair made for me. Bring the new gloves over." And he glowered at the officials and dropped his upper lip.

It was a very bad moment for the officials.

Two assistants marched in carrying a white boxing glove. It was half the size of a shark. A toot of relief went up from the press. Liston grinned. As photographers rushed to take his picture once more, he held the great white glove in his hands and studied it with solemnity.

When we got back to the car, D'Amato smiled. "Very unusual fellow," he said. "He's more intelligent than I thought. Good sense of humor."

I made a small speech in which I declared that Liston made me think not so much of a great fighter as of a great actor who was playing the role of the greatest heavyweight fighter who ever lived.

D'Amato listened attentively. We were in a space age, and the opinions of moon men and Martians had also to be considered. "Sonny's a good fighter," he said finally.

Then we talked of other things. I mentioned my four daughters. D'Amato came from a family of seven brothers. "I guess that's why I never got married," he said. "I don't know, I never could figure it out. No dame could ever get me. I wonder why?"

"A lady once told me she'd never marry a man she couldn't change."

"It's just as well I didn't get married," said D'Amato.

On the night of the fight I shared a cab to Comiskey Park with Pete Hamill of the New York *Post*. We caught a cabdriver who was for Patterson, and this worked to spoil the ride. As the fight approached, Hamill and I had been growing nervous in a pleasant way, we were feeling that mixture of apprehension and anticipation which is one of the large pleasures of going to a big fight. Time slows down, the senses become keyed, one's nose for magic is acute.

Such a mood had been building in each of us over the afternoon. About five we had gone to the Playboy Club with Gene Courtney of the Philadelphia *Inquirer*, and it had looked about the way one thought it would look. It was full of corporation executives, and after cancer gulch, the colors were lush, plum colors, velvet reds with the blood removed, a dash of cream, the flesh-orange and strawberry wine of a peach melba, Dutch chocolate colors, champagne colors, the beige of an onion in white wine sauce. The bunnies went by in their costumes, electric-blue silk, Kelly-green, flame-pink, pinups from a magazine, faces painted into sweetmeats, flower tops, tame lynx, piggie, poodle, a queen or two from a beauty contest. They wore a Gay-Nineties rig which exaggerated their hips, bound their waist in a ceinture, and lifted them into a phallic brassiere—each breast looked like the big bullet on the front bumper of a Cadillac. Long black stockings, long long stockings, up almost to the waist on each side, and to the back, on the curve of the can, as if ejected tenderly from the body, was the puff of chastity, a little white ball of a bunny's tail which bobbled as they walked. We were in bossland.

We drank, standing at the bar, talking about fights and fighters, and after a while we came to the fight we were to see that evening. Courtney had picked Liston by a knockout in the fifth, Hamill and I independently had arrived at Patterson in the sixth. So we had a mock fight to pay for a round of drinks. Courtney had bought a cigarette lighter in the Club—it was a slim, inexpensive black lighter with a white rabbit's face painted on the surface. When we put the lighter flat on the table and gave it a twirl, the ears would usually come to rest pointing toward one of us. We agreed that each spin would be a single round, and each time one ear pointed at Courtney or at me, it would count as a knockdown against our fighter. If both ears pointed at one of us, that would be the knockout.

Well, Liston knocked Patterson down in the first round. In the second round the ears pointed at no one. In the third round Patterson knocked Liston down. For the fourth, Liston dropped Patterson. "The fifth is the round," said Courtney, spinning the lighter. It went around and around and ended with one ear pointing at me. Liston had knocked Patterson down again, but had not knocked him out. I took the lighter and gave it a spin. The ears pointed at

Courtney. Both ears. Patterson had knocked Liston out in the sixth round.

"Too much," said Hamill.

I had given an interview the day before to Leonard Shecter of the *Post*. I had said: "I think Liston is going to have Patterson down two, three, four times. And Patterson will have Liston down in the first, second, or third and end it with one punch in the sixth." The cigarette lighter had given me a perfect fight.

Well, the Playboy Club was the place for magic, and this mood of expectation, of omen and portent, stayed with us. All of one's small actions became significant. At the hotel, signaling for the cab which was to take us to the ball park, the choice felt wrong. One had the psychology of a ghost choosing the hearse he would ride to a funeral, or of a general, brain livid after days of combat, so identifying himself with his army that he decides to attack first with the corps on his left because it is his left foot which has stepped first into the command car. It is not madness exactly. It is not madness if Montgomery or Rommel thinks that way. If the world is a war between God and the Devil, and Destiny is the line of their battle, then a general may be permitted to think that God or the Devil or the agent of both, which is Magic, has entered his brain before an irrevocable battle. For why should the gods retire when the issue is great? Such a subject is virtually taboo, one must pass by it quickly, or pass for mad, but I had noticed that whenever I was overtired, a sensitivity to the magical would come into me. I now had had little sleep for ten days, and I had been drinking for the last three: when I was very short of sleep, liquor did not make me drunk so much as it gave a thin exaltation, a sensitivity not unlike the touch of drugs in the old days; it was like gasoline burning an orderly flame in the empty chambers of one's reserve. I think one begins to die a little when one has had but three or four hours of sleep each night for a week; some of the cells must die from overexcitement, some from overwork, and their death must bring some of the consciousness of death, some little part of the deep secret of death into the living, weary brain. So I took the cab because it was the second in line at the hotel, and the first cab had not wished to go to the ball park. But feeling of gloom came over me as if I had committed a serious error.

The driver, as I have said, was for Patterson. He was a big round Negro about thirty with a pleasant face, sly yet not quite dishonest, but he had a pompous manner which seemed to fill the cab with psychic gas as dead as the exhaust from a bus. He was for Patterson, Hamill was for Patterson, I was for Patterson. We were left with nothing but the search for an imaginary conversationalist to argue for Sonny.

How this driver hated Liston! He went on about him at length, most of it not near to printable. "This guy Liston is no good," said the cabdriver. "I tell you the good Lord is going to look down and stop that man because he isn't worth the flesh and blood and muscle that was put into him. Now I don't care," said the cabdriver, going on comfortably, "that Liston was in prison, some of the best men in this country have come out of the can, I nearly did time myself, but I tell you, I don't like Liston, he's a bully and a hustler, and he's no good, he's no good at all, why if you were walking along the street and you saw a beautiful young child, why what would you think. You'd think, 'What a beautiful child.' That's what Patterson would think. He'd go up to that child and have a pleasant conversation or something, and go away, but what would Liston do, he'd have the same pleasant conversation, and then he'd get to thinking this is an awful good-looking kid, and if it's a good-looking kid it must have a good-looking mother. That man's an opportunist," said the driver severely, "and I tell you how I know, it's because I've been a hustler, I've hustled everything you can hustle, and there isn't anything anybody can tell me about Liston. That hustler is going to get ruined tonight."

Now the trouble with this speech was that it turned out to be as oppressive as it was amusing, and one's fine mood of excessive, even extreme sensitivity began to expire under the dull force of the exposition. It was hopeless to try to explain that Liston, whatever his virtues, however discovered his faults, could not possibly be as simple as the driver described him.

It was a fact, however, that Liston did not seem to be loved by the Negroes one talked to. It was not only the grey-haired Negroes with the silver-rimmed glasses and the dignity of the grave, the teachers, the deacons, the welfare workers, the camp directors, the church organists who were for Patterson, but indeed just about every Negro one talked to in Chicago. One of the pleasures preceding the fight had been to conduct a private poll. Of the twenty Negroes polled by our amateur, all but two or three were unsympathetic to Liston. The word was out — "You got to stick with the champion." I must have heard that phrase a dozen times. Of course the Negroes spoken to were employed; they were taxicab drivers, house servants, bellboys, waiters, college students, young professionals. Some answered cynically. There were a few with that snaky elegance one finds in colored people like Sugar Ray Robinson, and had seen at the fringes of Liston's court out at Aurora, the sort of Negro always seen standing on a key street corner in Harlem, the best-dressed Negro of the intersection. I had assumed they would instinctively be for Liston, and perhaps they were, but I was a strange white man asking questions—there is no need to assume the questions were asked so skillfully or decently that the truth was obliged to appear. Patterson, was the safe reply. It demanded nothing, especially if they were not going to see me again and so would suffer no loss of respect for their judgment. Patterson was a churchgoer, a Catholic convert (and so of course was Liston, but the cynical could remark that a Christmas candle in the window looks nice in a department store), Patterson was up tight with the NAACP, he was the kind of man who would get his picture taken with Jackie Robinson and Ralph Bunche (in fact he looked a little like Ralph Bunche), he would be photographed with Eleanor Roosevelt, and was; with Jack Kennedy, and was; with Adlai Stevenson if he went to the UN; he would campaign with Shelley Winters if she ever ran for Mayor of New York; he was a liberal's liberal. The worst to be said about Patterson is that he spoke with the same cow's cud as other liberals. Think what happens to a man with Patterson's reflexes when his brain starts to depend on the sounds of "introspective," "obligation," "responsibility," "inspiration," "commendation," "frustrated," "seclusion"—one could name a dozen others from his book. They are a part of his pride; he is a boy from the slums of Bedford-Stuyvesant who has acquired these words like stocks and bonds and income-bearing properties. There is no one to tell him it would be better to keep the psychology of the streets than to cultivate the contradictory desire to be a great fighter and a great, healthy, mature, autonomous, related, integrated individual. What a shabby gentility there has been to Patterson's endeavor. The liberals of America had been working for thirty years to create a state of welfare where the deserving could develop themselves. Patterson, as one of the deserving, as one of those who deserve profoundly to be enriched, ends with "introspective." The void in our culture does not know enough to give him "the agen-bite of inwit."

The cynical Negro, talking to a white stranger, would pick Patterson. Yet there was more to it than that. "You got to stick with the champion." They were working, they had jobs, they had something to hold on to; so did Patterson. They would be fierce toward anyone who tried to take what was theirs: family, home, education, property. So too they assumed would Patterson be fierce. They could hardly be expected to consider that the power to keep one's security loses force when it is too secure. Patterson earned $1,825 his first year as a professional fighter, $13,790 his second year, not quite $40,000 his third year when he was fighting main events at Madison Square Garden. By his fourth year, just before he won the title, it was $50,000. Since then he has made more than $3,500,000 in six years. For the Liston fight he would pick up another $2,000,000 from attendance, theatre television, and other rights. The payments would be spread over seventeen years. It was a long way to have come, but the psychic trip was longer. Responsibility, security, and institutional guilt was not necessarily the best tone for the reflexes in his leaping left hook.

But the deepest reason that Negroes in Chicago had for preferring Patterson was that they did not want to enter again the logic of Liston's world. The Negro had lived in violence, had grown in violence, and yet had developed a view of life which gave him life. But its cost was exceptional for the ordinary man. The majority had to live in shame. The demand for courage may have been exorbitant. Now as the Negro was beginning to come into the white man's world, he wanted the logic of the white man's world: annuities, mental hygiene, sociological jargon, committee solutions for the ills of the breast. He was sick of a whore's logic and a pimp's logic, he wanted no more of *mother-wit*, of *smarts*, or *playing the dozens*, of battling for true love into the diamond-hard eyes of every classy prostitute and hustler on the street. The Negro wanted Patterson, because Floyd was the proof a man could be successful and yet be secure. If Liston had a saga, the average Negro wanted none of it.

Besides there was always the Mob. Liston had been a strong-arm man for the Mob—they were not so ready to forgive that. He represented the shadow of every bully who had run them off the street when they were children, he was part of the black limousines with four well-dressed men inside, sliding down the dark streets. One did not try to look into the eyes of the men who rode in those limousines.

But there was one reason beyond any other for picking Patterson, and it went deeper than the pretensions of his new dialogue or the professional liberalism of his ideas, his pronouncements or his associates. Patterson was the champion of every lonely adolescent and every man who had been forced to live alone, every protagonist who tried to remain unique in a world whose waters washed apathy and compromise into the pores. He was the hero of all those unsung romantics who walk the street at night seeing the vision of Napoleon while their feet trip over the curb, he was part of the fortitude which could sustain those who lived for principle, those who had gone to war with themselves and ended with discipline. He was the artist. He was the man who could not forgive himself if he gave less than his best chance for perfection. And so he aroused a powerful passion in those lonely people who wanted him to win. He was champion, he was a millionaire, but he was still an archetype of the underdog, an impoverished prince.

And Liston was looking to be king. Liston came from that world where you had no dream but making it, where you trusted no one because your knowledge of evil was too quick to its presence in everyone; Liston came from that world where a man with a dream was a drunk in the gutter, and the best idealism was found in a rabbit's foot blessed by a one-eyed child. Liston was voodoo, Liston was magic, Liston was the pet of the witch doctor; Liston knew that when the gods gathered to watch an event, you kept your mind open to the devils who might work for you. They would come neatly into your eye and paralyze your enemy with their curse. You were their slave, but they were working for you. Yes, Liston was the secret hero of every man who had ever given mouth to a final curse against the dispositions of the Lord and made a pact with Black Magic. Liston was Faust. Liston was the light of every race-track tout who dug a number on the way to work. He was the hero of every man who would war with destiny for so long as he had his gimmick: the cigarette smoker, the lush, the junkie, the tea-head, the fixer, the bitch, the faggot, the switchblade, the gun, the corporation executive. Anyone who was fixed on power. It was due to Liston's style of fighting as much as anything else. He had no extreme elegance as a boxer, he was a hint slow, indeed he may not have been a natural boxer as was Patterson, but Liston had learned much and attached it to his large physical strength, he had a long and abnormally powerful left jab, a pounding left hook, a heavy right. He had lead in his fists. The only man who had ever defeated him, a club fighter named Marty Marshall, had said, "Every time he hit me, it hurt all over." In his last twenty-five fights Liston had knocked out the other man twenty-one times. So his force appealed to those who had enlisted with an external force. At the Playboy Club, drinking with Courtney and Hamill, I made a bet with a former Harvard man (Business School, no doubt), who told me Liston had it made. He put up fifty against my twenty-eight and we left the money in the bartender's till. I was not to go back.

So it approached. The battle of good and evil, that curious battle where decision is rare and never clear. As we got out of the cab, several blocks from Comiskey Park, two little Negroes, nine or ten years old, danced up to us in the dark, the light of a Halloween candle in their eye. "Give me silver," one of them cried in a Caribbean voice, "give silver, sir," and left us with an orange piece of paper, a throwaway from a nightclub. "Come to Club Jerico after the Fight," said the misspelled legend. "Come to Club Jerico." Jerico. I—rich.

III

On the afternoon of the night Emile Griffith and Benny Paret were to fight a third time for the welterweight championship, there was murder in both camps. "I hate that kind of guy," Paret had said earlier to Pete Hamill about Griffith. "A fighter's got to look and talk and act like a man." One of the Broadway gossip columnists had run an item about Griffith a few days before. His girl friend saw it and said to Griffith, "Emile, I didn't know about you being that way." So Griffith hit her. So he said. Now at the weigh-in that morning, Paret had insulted Griffith irrevocably, touching him on the buttocks, while making a few more remarks about his manhood. They almost had their fight on the scales.

The accusation of homosexuality arouses a major passion in many men; they spend their lives resisting it with a biological force. There is a kind of man who spends every night of his life getting drunk in a bar, he rants, he brawls, he ends in a small rumble on the street; women say, "For God's sakes, he's homosexual. Why doesn't he just turn queer and get his suffering over with." Yet men protect him. It is because he is choosing not to become homosexual. It was put best by Sartre who said that a homosexual is a man who practices homosexuality. A man who does not, is not homosexual—he is entitled to the dignity of his choice. He is entitled to the fact that he chose not to become homosexual, and is paying presumably his price.

The rage in Emile Griffith was extreme. I was at the fight that night, I had never seen a fight like it. It was scheduled for fifteen rounds, but they fought without stopping from the bell which began the round to the bell which ended it, and then they fought after the bell, sometimes for as much as fifteen seconds before the referee could force them apart.

Paret was a Cuban, a proud club fighter who had become welterweight champion because of his unusual ability to take a punch. His style of fighting was to take three punches to the head in order to give back two. At the end of ten rounds, he would still be bouncing, his opponent would have a headache. But in the last two years, over the fifteen-round fights, he had started to take some bad maulings.

This fight had its turns. Griffith won most of the early rounds, but Paret knocked Griffith down in the sixth. Griffith had trouble getting up, but made it, came alive and was dominating Paret again before the round was over. Then Paret began to wilt. In the middle of the eighth round, after a clubbing punch had turned his back to Griffith, Paret walked three disgusted steps away, showing his hindquarters. For a champion, he took much too long to turn back around. It was the first hint of weakness Paret had ever shown, and it must have inspired a particular shame, because he fought the rest of the fight as if he were seeking to demonstrate that he could take more punishment than any man alive. In the twelfth, Griffith caught him. Paret got trapped in a corner. Trying to duck away, his left arm and his head became tangled on the wrong side of the top rope. Griffith was in like a cat ready to rip the life out of a huge boxed rat. He hit him eighteen right hands in a row, an act which took perhaps three or four seconds, Griffith making a pent-up whimpering sound all the while he attacked, the right hand whipping like a piston rod which has broken through the crankcase, or like a baseball bat demolishing a pumpkin. I was sitting in the second row of that corner — they were not ten feet away from me, and like everybody else, I was hypnotized. I had never seen one man hit another so hard and so many times. Over the referee's face came a look of woe as if some spasm had passed its way through him, and then he leaped on Griffith to pull him away. It was the act of a brave man. Griffith was uncontrollable. His trainer leaped into the ring, his manager, his cut man, there were four people holding Griffith, but he was on an orgy, he had left the Garden, he was back on a hoodlum's street. If he had been able to break loose from his handlers and the referee, he would have jumped Paret to the floor and whaled on him there.

And Paret? Paret died on his feet. As he took those eighteen punches something happened to everyone who was in psychic range of the event. Some part of his death reached out to us. One felt it hover in the air. He was still standing in the ropes, trapped as he had been before, he gave some little half-smile of regret, as if he were saying, "I didn't know I was going to die just yet," and then, his head leaning back but still erect, his death came to breathe about him. He began to pass away. As he passed, so his limbs descended beneath him, and he sank slowly to the floor. He went down more slowly than any fighter had ever gone down, he went down like a large ship which turns on end and slides second by second into its grave. As he went down, the sound of Griffith's punches echoed in the mind like a heavy ax in the distance chopping into a wet log.

Paret lay on the ground, quivering gently, a small froth on his mouth. The house doctor jumped into the ring. He knelt. He pried

Paret's eyelid open. He looked at the eyeball staring out. He let the lid snap shut. He reached into his satchel, took out a needle, jabbed Paret with a stimulant. Paret's back rose in a high arch. He writhed in real agony. They were calling him back from death. One wanted to cry out, "Leave the man alone. Let him die." But they saved Paret long enough to take him to a hospital where he lingered for days. He was in coma. He never came out of it. If he lived, he would have been a vegetable. His brain was smashed. But they held him in life for a week, they fed him chemicals, and made exploratory operations into his skull, and fed details of his condition to The Goat. And The Goat kicked clods of mud all over the place, and spoke harshly of prohibiting boxing. There was shock in the land. Children had seen the fight on television. There were editorials, gloomy forecasts that the Game was dead. The managers and the prizefighters got together. Gently, in thick, depressed hypocrisies, they tried to defend their sport. They did not find it easy to explain that they shared an unstated view of life which was religious.

It was of course not that religion which is called Judeo-Christian. It was an older religion, a more primitive one—a religion of blood, a murderous and sensitive religion which mocks the effort of the understanding to approach it, and scores the lungs of men like D. H. Lawrence, and burns the brain of men like Ernest Hemingway when they explore out into the mystery, searching to discover some part of the secret. It is the view of life which looks upon death as a condition which is more alive than life or unspeakably more deadening. As such it is not a very attractive notion to the Establishment. But then the Establishment has nothing very much of even the Judeo-Christian tradition. It has a respect for legal and administrative aspects of justice, and it is devoted to the idea of compassion for the poor. But the Establishment has no idea of death, no tolerance for Heaven or Hell, no comprehension of bloodshed. It sees no logic in pain. To the Establishment these notions are a detritus from the past.

Like a patient submerged beneath the plastic cover of an oxygen tent, boxing lives on beneath the cool, bored eyes of the doctors in the Establishment. It would not take too much to finish boxing off. Shut down the oxygen, which is to say, turn that switch in the mass media which still gives sanction to organized pugilism, and the fight game would be dead.

But the patient is permitted to linger for fear the private detectives of the Establishment, the psychiatrists and psychoanalysts, might not be able to neutralize the problem of gang violence. Not so well as the Game. Of course, the moment some piece of diseased turnip capable of being synthesized cheaply might prove to have the property of tranquilizing a violent young man for a year, the Establishment would wipe out boxing. Every time a punk was arrested, the police would prescribe a pill, and violence would walk the street sheathed and numb. Of course the Mob would lose revenue, but then the Mob is also part of the Establishment, it, and the labor unions and the colleges and the newspapers and the corporations are all part of the Establishment. The Establishment is never simple. It needs the Mob to grease the chassis on its chariot. Therefore, the Mob would be placated. In a society with strong central government, it is not so difficult to turn up a new source of revenue. What is more difficult is to enter the plea that violence may be an indispensable element of life. This is not the place to have the argument: it is enough to say that if the liberal Establishment is right in its unstated credo that death is a void, and man leads out his life suspended momentarily above that void, why then there is no argument at all. Whatever shortens life is monstrous. We have not the right to shorten life, since life is the only possession of the psyche, and in death we have only nothingness. What then can there be said in defense of sports-car racing, war, or six-ounce gloves?

But if we go from life into a death which is larger than our life has been, or into a death which is small, if death comes to nothing for one man because he swallowed his death in his life, and if for another death is alive with dimension, then the certitudes of the Establishment lose power. A drug which offers peace to a pain may dull the nerve which could have taught the mind how to carry that pain into the death which comes on the next day or on the decades that follow. A tranquilizer gives coma to an anxiety which may later smell of the dungeon, beneath the ground. If we are born into life as some living line of intent from an eternity which may have tortured us or nurtured us in death, then we may be obliged to go back to death with more courage and art than we left it. Or face the dim end of going back with less.

That is the existential venture, the unstated religious view of boxers trying to beat each other into unconsciousness or, ultimately, into death. It is the culture of the killer who sickens the air about him if he does not find some half-human way to kill a little in order not to deaden all. It is a defense against the plague, against that plague which comes from violence converted into the nausea of all that nonviolence which is void of peace. Paret's death was with horror, but not all the horror was in the beating, much was in the way his death was cheated. Which is to say that his death was twice a nightmare. I knew that something in boxing was spoiled forever for me, that there would be a fear in watching a fight now which was like the fear one felt for any *novillero* when he was having an unhappy day, the bull was dangerous, and the crowd was ugly. You knew he could get hurt. There is fascination in seeing that the first time, but it is not as enjoyable as one expects. It is like watching a novelist who has written a decent book get run over by a car.

Something in boxing was spoiled. But not the principle, not the right for one man to try to knock another out in the ring. That was perhaps not a civilized activity, but it belonged to the tradition of the humanist, it was a human activity, it showed a part of what man was like, it belonged to his ability to create art and artful movement on the edge of death or pain or danger or attack, and it had much to say about the subtleties of human style. For there are boxers whose bodies move like a fine brain, and there are others who pound the opposition down with the force of a trade-union leader, there are fools and wits and patient craftsmen among boxers, wild men full of a sense of outrage, and steady oppressive peasants, clever spoilers, dogged infantrymen who walk forward all night, hypnotists (like Liston), dancers, lovers, mothers giving a scolding, horsemen high on their legs. There is knowledge to be found about our nature, and the nature of animals, of big cats, lions, tigers, gorillas, bears, walruses (Archie Moore), birds, elephants, jackals, bulls. No, I was not down on boxing, but I loved it with freedom no longer. It was more like somebody in your family was fighting now. And the feeling one had for a big fight was no longer clear of terror in its excitement. There was awe in the suspense.

But then there is nothing else very much like being at a Heavyweight Championship fight. It is to some degree the way a Hollywood premiere once ought to have been; it's a big party with high action—there is the same rich flush of jewelry, bourbon, bare shoulders, cha-cha, silk, the promise that a life or two will be changed by tonight; it is even a bit like a political convention; it is much more like an event none of us will ever see—conceive of sitting in a classic arena waiting for a limited war with real bullets to begin between a platoon of Marines and two mounted squads of Russian Cossacks—you'd have the sensation of what a Heavyweight Championship can promise. A great heavyweight fight could take place in the center of a circus.

Ideally, it should take place in New York. Because Broadway turns out and Hollywood flies in with Las Vegas on the hip, and many of the wings and dovecotes and banlieues of what even a couple of years ago was called Café Society is there, and International Set (always seeing their first fight), and Big Business, and every good-looking call girl in New York, and some not so good-looking, and all the figures from the history pages of prizefighting in America, as well as ghosts there are some to claim—the ghost of Benny Leonard, the ghost of Harry Greb. Plus all the models, loose celebrities, socialites of high and lower rank, hierarchies from the racetrack, politicians, judges, and—one might offer a prayer if one really cared—one sociologist of wit and distinction ought to be there to capture for America the true status of its conflicting aristocracies: does Igor Cassini rate with Mickey Rooney or does Roger Blough get a row in front of Elizabeth Taylor? Is Frank Sinatra honored before Mrs. Woodward? Does Zsa Zsa Gabor come in ahead of Mayor Wagner? The First Sociologists of America are those professionals who sell the hot seats for a big fight in New York.

In Chicago, there was little of this. If there are nine circles to Hell, there were nine clouds over this fight. D'Amato was not licensed to manage in New York. Small matter. Patterson once again would fight in New York without him. But Liston was not cleared to fight by the State Boxing Commission—the shadow of the Establishment lay against him. So the fight was transferred to Chicago which promptly took fire. If Patterson-Liston was not clean enough for New York, it was not cool enough for Chicago. The local newspapers gave the kind of publicity one tastes in cold canned food. The stories on training were buried. Interest was greater outside the city than within. Yet little of Broadway arrived and less of Hollywood. You cannot get producers and movie stars to travel a distance to watch two Negroes fight. A bitch lives to see a white man fight a black man. She's not prejudiced—depending on the merits, she'll root for either, but a Negro against a Negro wets no juice.

And then there was poor weather. The day before the fight was misty, chilly. It rained on and off, and cleared inconclusively on Tuesday, which was cold. Fight night was cold enough to wear a topcoat. Comiskey Park was far from filled. It could hold fifty thousand for a big fight; it ended with less than twenty in paid admissions. Twenty-six thousand people showed. Proportions were poor. Because of theatre television, Patterson would make more money on this fight than any fighter had ever made, and there was much local interest in cities all over America. Parties were got up to go to the theatre, see it on television. The press coverage was larger than average, larger let us say than any of the three Johansson fights or the Marciano-Walcott fights. It was the biggest fight in ten years, it was conceivably the biggest fight since Louis fought Schmeling the second time, and yet nobody in the city where it was fought seemed to care. Radio, with its roaring inside hysteria, had lost to television, that grey eminence which now instructed Americans in the long calm of Ecclesiastes: vanity of vanities, all events are vanity.

So for a celebrity hunter, ringside was nothing formidable at this fight. The good people of Chicago turned out modestly. The very good people—which is to say, the very rich—turned out for ringside, and had a chance to cross the outfield grass, luminous green in the half-light of the baseball towers, and walk to their seats under the great folded wings of the grandstand. Ever since the Romans built the Colosseum, arenas take on a prehistoric breath at night—one could be a black ant walking inside the circle a pterodactyl must have made with its wing as it slept. Or is it hills like dark elephants of which we speak?

I had a seat in the working press five rows from the ring. An empty seat away was Jimmy Baldwin. There had been a chill between us in the last year. Not a feud, but bad feeling. We had been glad, however, to see each other in Chicago. Tacitly, settling no differences, not talking about it, we had thought to be friendly. But the unsettled differences were still there. Two nights ago, at a party, we had had a small fight. We each insulted the other's good intentions and turned away. Now we sat with a hundred-pound cake of ice on the empty seat between us. After ten minutes, I got up and went for a walk around the ring.

The Press section occupied the first six rows. Back of us was an aisle which made a larger square around the square of the ring. On the other side of this aisle was the first row of ringside seats. This was as close as you could come to the fight if you had entered by buying a ticket. So I took a sampling of the house as I walked around the square. If this had been New York, you would expect to find twelve movie stars in the front row. But this was Chicago. Behind us were a muster of local Irish politicians, big men physically in the mold of Jimmy Braddock, not unhappy tonight with their good seats.

The front row to my right and the front row across the ring from me was given over in part to the Mob. They were the most intricate faces one would find this side of Carpaccio or Bellini, chins with hooks and chisels, nostrils which seemed to screw the air up into the head, thin-lipped mouths like thin-nosed pliers, eyes which behind their dark glasses scrutinized your interior until they could find the tool in you which would work for them, and then would flip away like the turning of a card. Yes, those two rows of seats made up a right angle of *don capos* and a few very special Catholic priests, thin, ascetic, medieval in appearance, as well as a number of field officers dressed in black like subalterns, but older, leaner, with more guilds at their command. They were well-seated. They filled close to every seat around the corner.

It proved to be Patterson's corner.

That was art. They did not have to do much more. Sitting there, they could devote their study to Patterson. He would see them when he came back to his corner, his seconds would be obliged to look at them each time a new round began and they climbed down the steps from the corner. The back of the cornermen's necks would be open to detailed inspection, the calves of Patterson's leg, as he sat resting on the stool, would be a ready target for mental arrows. Like Lilliputians they could shoot thousands of pins into Gulliver.

I completed the tour. The last row, Liston's corner, was routine: musclemen, mobsters, business-sporting, a random sample. Turning the angle I came back to my seat, and sat watching a preliminary, shivering a little in the cold. It was much too cold for a fight. The sensitivity to magic I had felt earlier in the evening would not come back. There was just a dull sense of apprehension. Everything was wrong.

The preliminaries ended. Visiting fighters were called up from the crowd to take a bow. Archie Moore drew a large hand: he was wearing a black-silk cape with a white lining and he twirled the cape with éclat. It said: "Go away, all solemn sorcerers, the magic man is here."

Patterson and Liston arrived within a minute of each other. The visiting fighters who were gathered in the ring said hello to each man, shook their gloves, and went back to their seats.

The Star-Spangled Banner was played. Liston stood in his corner with his handlers, the referee stood in the middle of the ring, and Cus D'Amato stood alone, eight feet away from Patterson and his seconds. Since D'Amato was across from me, I could see his face clearly. It was as pale as his white sweater. His face was lifted to the sky, his eyes were closed. While the anthem played, D'Amato held his hand to his heart as if he were in anguish. I had the impression he was praying with fear.

The anthem ended, the fighters took their instructions from the referee, and stripped their robes. Their bodies made a contrast. Liston, only an inch taller than Patterson, weighed 214 pounds to Patterson's 189. But the difference was not just in weight. Liston had a sleek body, fully muscled, but round. It was the body of a strong man, but the muscles looked to have been shaped by pleasure as much as by work. He was obviously a man who had had some very good times.

Whereas Patterson still had poverty in his muscles. He was certainly not weak, there was whipcord in the way he was put together, but it was still the dry, dedicated body of an athlete, a track man, a disciplinarian: it spoke little of leisure and much of the gym. There was a lack eating at it, some misery.

The bell rang.

Liston looked scared.

Patterson looked grim.

They came together with no vast impact, trying for small gains. Each was moving with large respect for the other. Liston had the unhappy sweaty look in his eye of the loudest-talking champion on a city block — he has finally gotten into a fight with one of the Juniors, and he knows this Junior can fight. If he loses he's got much to lose. So Liston was trying to make Junior keep distance.

Patterson was not doing much. He threw a fast left hook which missed, then he circled a bit, fighting from a crouch. He lunged in once very low, trying to get under Liston's long jab and work to the stomach, but his timing was not acute and he drew back quickly. There had been no inspiration, no life, and a hint of clumsiness. But it had been intellectually sound. It caused no harm. Then he tried again, feinting a left hook, and slipping Liston's left jab, but as he came in close, Liston grabbed him with both arms, and they bulled back and forth until the referee separated them. Now, they each had an unhappy look on their faces as if they were big men who had gotten into an altercation in a bar, and didn't like the physical activity of fighting. Each of them looked like it would take three or four rounds to warm up.

All this had used a minute. Liston seemed to have gained the confidence that he was stronger, and he began crowding Patterson to the rope, throwing a good many punches, not left hooks, not left jabs, not uppercuts or straight rights, just thick, slow, clubbing punches. None of them landed on Patterson's body or head, they all banged on his arms, and occasionally Patterson would bang Liston back on the arm. It is a way of fighting. A strong slow fighter will sometimes keep hitting the other man on the shoulder or the biceps until his arms go dead. If the opponent is in condition, it is a long procedure. I was surprised at how slow Liston's punches were. From ringside, they looked easy to block. He had a way of setting himself and going "ahem" before he threw the punch. It is, of course, one thing to block punches from your seat at ringside, and another to block them in a ring, but when a fighter is punching with real speed and snap, you can't block the punches from where you sit. Even from thirty feet away, you are fooled.

All that was fooling me now was Patterson. He seemed sluggish. He was not getting hit with Liston's punches, but he was not hitting back, he seemed to miss one small opportunity after another. He was fighting like a college heavyweight who has gone in to work with a professional and is getting disheartened at the physical load of such sparring. He had the expression on his face of somebody pushing a Cadillac which has run out of gas.

Then occurred what may have been the most extraordinary moment ever seen in a championship fight. It was very spooky. Patterson, abruptly, without having been hurt in any visible way, stood up suddenly out of his crouch, his back a foot from the ropes, and seemed to look half up into the sky as if he had seen something there or had been struck by something from there, by some transcendent bolt, and then he staggered like a man caught in machine-gun fire, and his legs went, and he fell back into the ropes. His left glove became tangled in the top rope, almost as Paret's arm had been tangled, and that murmur of death, that visitation which had passed into Madison Square Garden on the moment Paret began to die, seemed a breath from appearing now, Patterson looked at Liston with one lost look, as if somehow he had been expecting this to happen ever since the night it happened to Paret; it was the look of a man saying, "Don't kill me," and then Liston hit him two or three ill-timed punches, banging a sloppy stake into the ground, and Patterson went down. And he was out. He was not faking. He had started to pass out at the moment he stood straight on his feet and was struck by that psychic bolt which had come from wherever it had come.

Patterson rolled over, he started to make an attempt to get to his feet, and Baldwin and I were each shouting, "Get up, get up!" But one's voice had no force in it, one's will had no life.

Patterson got up somewhere between a quarter and a half second too late. You could see the critical instant pass in the referee's body, and Patterson was still getting his glove off the ground. The fight was over: 2:06 of the First. It must have been the worst fight either fighter had ever had.

Liston looked like he couldn't believe what had happened. He was blank for two or three long seconds, and then he gave a whoop. It was an artificial, tentative whoop, but it seemed to encourage him because he gave another which sounded somewhat better, and then he began to whoop and whoop and laugh and shout because his handlers had come into the ring and were hugging him and telling him he was the greatest fighter that ever lived. And Patterson, covered quickly with his bathrobe, still stunned, turned and buried his head in Cus D'Amato's shoulder.

From the stands behind us came one vast wave of silence. Here and there sounded cheers or applause, but you could hear each individual voice or pair of hands clapping into the silence.

"What happened?" said Baldwin.

IV

What did happen? Everybody was to ask that question later. But in private.

The descriptions of the fight fed next morning to The Goat showed no uncertainty. They spoke of critical uppercuts and powerful left hooks and pulverizing rights. Liston talked of dominating Patterson with left hands, Patterson's people said it was a big right which did the job, some reporters called the punches crunching, others said they were menacing, brutal, demolishing. One did not read a description of the fight which was not authoritative. The only contradiction, a most minor contradiction, is that with one exception, a wire-service photograph used everywhere of a right hand by Liston which has apparently just left Patterson's chin, there were no pictures — and a point was made of looking at a good many — which show Liston putting a winning glove into Patterson's stomach, solar plexus, temple, nose, or jaw. In fact there is not a single picture of Liston's glove striking Patterson at all. It is not highly probable the photographers missed every decent punch. Fight photographers are capable of splitting the strictest part of a second in order to get the instant of impact. The fine possibility is that there was no impact. There was instead an imprecise beating, that is a beating which was not convincing if the men were anywhere near to equal in strength. Something had happened to Patterson, however. He fought as if he were down with jaundice. It was not that he did not do his best; he always did his determined best; he did just that against Liston. It is just that his best this night was off the spectrum of his normal condition. Something had struck at him. From inside himself or from without, in that instant he straightened from his crouch and stared at the sky, he had the surprise of a man struck by treachery.

Now I am forced to give a most improper testimony, because I felt as if I were a small part of that treachery and one despairs of trying to explain how that could be so.

A man turns to boxing because he discovers it is the best experience of his life. If he is a good fighter, his life in the center of the ring is more intense than it can be anywhere else, his mind is more exceptional than at any other time, his body has become a live part of his brain. Some men are geniuses when they are drunk; a good fighter feels a bit of genius when he is having a good fight. This illumination comes not only from the discipline he has put on his body or the concentration of his mind to getting ready for his half hour in the open, but no, it comes as well from his choice to occupy the stage on an adventure whose end is unknown. For the length of his fight, he ceases to be a man and becomes a Being, which is to say he is no longer finite in the usual sense, he is no longer a creature of a given size and dress with a name and some habits which are predictable. Liston-in-the-ring was not just Sonny Liston; much more he was the nucleus of that force at Comiskey Park (and indeed from everywhere in the world from which such desire could reach) which wished him to win or hated him with an impotence that created force, to wit, hated him less than it feared him, and so betrayed its hate since the telepathic logic of the unconscious makes us give our strength to those we think to hate but favor despite ourselves. Just so, Patterson-in-the-ring was not Floyd Patterson sparring in his gym, but was instead a vehicle of all the will and all the particular love which truly wished him to win, as well as a target of all the hatred which was not impotent but determined to strike him down.

When these universes collided, the impact if not clear was total. The world quivered in some rarefied accounting of subtle psychic seismographs, and the stocks of certain ideal archetypes shifted their status in our country's brain. Sex had proved superior to Love still one more time, the Hustler had taken another pool game from the Infantryman, the Syndicate rolled out the Liberal, the Magician hyped the Artist, and, since there were more than a few who insisted on seeing them simply as God and the Devil (whichever much or little of either they might be), then the Devil had shown that the Lord was dramatically weak.

The Goat would demand that this fight be reported in a veritable factology of detail. America could not listen to questions. The professional witnesses to the collision, the pipers of cancer gulch, were obliged to testify to a barrage of detailed punches, and the fighters reexamining their own history in such a mirror of prose would be forced to remake the event in their mind. Yet so long as one kept one's memory, the event was unclear. The result had been turned by betrayal. And it was by one's own person that the guilt was felt. I had been there with half a body from half a night of sleep for too many nights, and half a brain from too many bouts of drinking drinks I did not want that much, and dim in concentration because I was brooding about the loss of a friendship which it was a cruel and stupid waste to lose. And Baldwin too had been brooding. We had sat there like beasts of burden, empty of psychic force to offer our fighter.

Now, too late, in the bout's sudden wake, like angels whose wings are wet, we buried our quarrel; this time it might stay buried for a while. "My Lord," said Jimmy, "I lost seven hundred and fifty dollars tonight."

Well, we laughed. I had lost no more than a paltry twenty-eight.

Later, I went back to the dressing room. But Patterson's door was locked. Over a hundred reporters were jammed into Liston's room, so many that one could not see the new champion, one could only hear his voice. He was resounding very much like Clark Gable now, late Gable with the pit of his mannerism — that somewhat complacent jam of much too much love for the self. Liston had the movie star's way of making the remark which cuts, then balming it with salve. "Did you take your ugly pills?" says the actor to the leading lady, and gives his smile at her flush. "Why honey, dear child, I'm only kidding." So Liston said, "The one time he hurt me was when he got up to a knee at nine. I was afraid he would come all the way up." Which was class. It whipped. A minute later, some banana oil was uncorked. "Yessir," said Liston at large, "Floyd is a heck of a man."

I left that dressing room and tried to get into Patterson's, but the door was still locked. Ingemar Johansson was standing nearby. They were interviewing him over a pay telephone for a radio program. Johansson had a bewildered combative look as if someone had struck him on the back of the head with a loaded jack. He had knocked Patterson down for seven times in one round, there had been wild lightning and "toonder," but he had not been able to keep Patterson down. Now Liston had taken Floyd out with a punch or two or three no witness would agree upon.

"Do you think you can beat Liston," was the interviewer's question.

"I don't know," said Johansson.

"Do you think you have a chance?"

Johansson looked sad and Swedish. "One always has a chance," he said. "I would make my fight and fight it, that's all."

One never did get into Patterson's dressing room. After a while I left and walked around the empty ringside seats. It was cold now. Some of the events of the last few days were coming back to me in the cold air of Comiskey Park. They were not agreeable to contemplate. I had done a few unattractive things. I did not want to count them.

But then in fact I had been doing so much that was wrong the last two days. If one is to talk of betrayal and try to explain what was yet to happen, the account must slip back a bit into what had happened already. On Monday, The New York *Times* had shown a story on the first page of the second section about William F. Buckley and myself and our debate on Saturday night. It had culled some dismembered remarks from the exchange, added a touch of wit from each of us, and called the result a draw. I did not take it well. For I had prepared for the debate, I had honed myself like a club fighter getting ready for the champion. I had been ready, and Buckley, who had been working at other things, was not as ready. He had been speaking in Texas the day before and flew into Chicago only that morning. The afternoon of our debate he was still writing his speech. Saturday night, Medinah Temple had held almost four thousand people. It was built like an opera house with an enormous apron on the stage, and balconies which made a turn around the house through more than half a circle. One spoke with the audience sitting deep to one's left and deep to one's right, close in front and high overhead. Despite its size it was not unlike the theatre in *Les Enfants du Paradis*, and it had been dramatic for our separate styles. Buckley, tall and thin, spoke from high on his toes, his long arm and long finger outstretched in condemnation, a lone shaft of light pointing down on him from above while he excoriated the Left for Cuba, and myself for "swinishness." In my turn I led an intellectual foray into the center of his positions, arguing that if conservatism was a philosophy which saw each person in his appointed place so that men were equal only before God and in Eternity, that the radical in his turn conceived the form of the world as a record of the war between God and the Devil where man served as God's agent and sought to shift the wealth of our universe in such a way that the talent which was dying now by dim dull deaths in every poor man alive would take its first breath and show what a mighty renaissance was locked in the unconscious of the dumb.

Afterward, the people I met on the street and in restaurants or at a party would congratulate me and say I had won. And I had felt exactly like a club fighter who has won a very big fight. But the test of a poor man is profit, and I squandered mine. Something pent up for years, dictatorial and harsh, began to slip through my good humor after I read the verdict in the *Times*. There might be other debates with Buckley in the spring. He would be ready next time. It was raw to lose a victory. I did not take it well. Actors speak of a motor inside themselves. I could not stop mine, one did not want to now, and I drank because the drink was fuel.

Yes, I had done everything wrong since then, I had even had the fool's taste to be pleased with the magic of the cigarette lighter. If I had been a part of the psychic cadre guarding Patterson, I had certainly done everything to make myself useless to him. I could even wonder at that moment, my mind quick with bitterness toward the *Times*, whether the entire liberal persuasion of America had rooted for Floyd in the same idle, detached fashion as myself, wanting him to win but finding Liston secretly more interesting, in fact, and, indeed, demanding of Patterson that he win only because he was good for liberal ideology. I had a moment of vast hatred then for that bleak gluttonous void of the Establishment, that liberal power at the center of our lives which gave jargon with charity, substituted the intolerance of mental health for the intolerance of passion, alienated emotion from its roots, and man from his past, cut the giant of our half-wakened arts to fit a bed of Procrustes, Leonard Bernstein on the podium, John Cage in silence, offered a National Art Center which would be to art as canned butter is to butter, and existed in a terror of eternity which built a new religion of the psyche on a God who died, old doctor Freud, of cancer. Yes, it was this Establishment which defeated Patterson precisely because it supported him, because it was able to give reward but not love, because it was ruled by a Goat who radiated depression like fallout searches for milk.

A long night was to follow, of curious pockets and creepy encounters. Too much magic had been put into one place, and now it was as if a bomb had exploded prematurely, imperfectly. The turbulence of the air had eyes of calm, and gave telepathic intensity to the dark. One would think of an event with rising concentration and around the turn of one's thought would appear, quite real, smacking of the flesh, some man or woman who belonged to the event. Walk-through the Park, a person shouted my name. Then another cry. It was the voice of each of the men who had promoted the debate with Buckley, John Golden and Aaron Berlin. We took off extempore together to have a drink and go on to my party, and on the way, walking through the streets of the South Side near Comiskey Park, two gloomy Negro adolescents fell in and walked along with us. They were eighteen or nineteen, shabby. They wore flat leather caps. One had turned the short peak around to the back of his head. They had been blasted tonight by Floyd's defeat. Everything would be more difficult now. They did not want to hate Patterson, but they could hardly speak.

Poor Patterson. He was alienated from his own, from his own streets, his own vocabulary, his own manager, he was even alienated from his own nightmare. What could the Establishment tell him of that odyssey which set him once walking on subway tracks to discover a hole not too many inches away from where the trains went by. "Oh," said the Establishment, "he wanted to go back to the womb. How interesting!" But they could not tell one why he had this wish, nor why it was interesting. The womb was part of their void, of the liberal void, they would not begin to guess that a champion who could find a way to go to sleep minutes before a big fight must have learned early to live on the edge of his death. The psychic roar of a prizefight crowd was like the sound of the subway. Yes, Patterson had gone out early to explore because he had known, living in terror down in Bedford-Stuyvesant part of town, down in a world of curse, evil eye, blasted intent, that the forces of the past which had forced their way into the seed which made him now wanted no less than that he be extraordinary, that he be great, that he be a champion of his people. But he had succeeded too quickly. He had come too early upon the scene. The Establishment had made him a Negroid white. His skin was black, his psychology had turned white, poor blasted man, twice cursed. He could have the consolation that his championship had gone on to another black.

But it was unfair. He deserved more than this, more than this gutted performance. One would now never know if he lost before he reached the ring, whipped by the oatmeal of the liberal line, or if the Devil had struck him down with vastly greater ease than the Devil had intended. No matter how, the result had been awful. That this brave, decent, sensitive, haunted man should have been defeated with such humiliation. It was awful.

The party was very big, and it was a good party. The music went all the way down into the hour or two before breakfast, but no one saw the dawn come in because the party was at Hugh Hefner's house which is one of the most extraordinary houses in America and the living room where much of the party was going was sixty feet long and more than thirty wide, and almost twenty high, yet there were no windows, at least I never saw the sky from that room, and so there was a timeless spaceless sensation. Staying as a houseguest in his home, there had been servants ready all twenty-four hours these last few days, one had been able to get the equivalent of any drink made at any bar at any hour of the world, one could have chili at four a.m. or ice cream at ten, the servants had been perfect, the peace when empty of the house was profound, one never saw one's host except for once or twice in some odd hour of the night. He had a quality not unlike Jay Gatsby, he looked and talked like a lean, rather modest cowboy of middle size; there was something of a mustang about Hefner. He was not the kind of man one would have expected to see as the publisher of his magazine, nor the owner of the Playboy Club, nor certainly as the undemanding host of his exceptional establishment. Timeless, spaceless, it was outward bound. One was in an ocean liner which traveled at the bottom of the sea, or on a spaceship wandering down the galaxy along a night whose duration was a year. The party went on, and I drank and I drank some more. The swimming pool was beneath the dance floor, and there were bathing suits for those who wanted them, and some did, and people went to look through the trapdoor in the living room which pried open over a fall of fifteen feet into a grotto of the pool below. Above was the orchestra and the dancers in a Twist. The Twist was not dead in Chicago, not hardly. If there were such a thing as sexual totalitarianism, then the Twist was its Horst Wessel, and all the girls with boy's bodies were twisting out their allegiance. I hated the Twist. Not because I had become a moralist on the stroke of twelve, not because I felt sex without love was determined to be bad, but because I hated too much life for sex without any possibility of love. The Twist spoke of some onanism which had gone on forever, some effort which had lost its beginning and labored to find no end, of an art which burned itself for fuel.

Now, after the knockout, in some fatigue-ridden, feverish whole vision of one's guilt and of Patterson's defeat—for of course the fighters spoke as well from the countered halves of my nature; what more had I to tell myself of sex versus love, magic against art, or the hustler and the infantryman?—out of a desire to end some war in myself, as if victory by Patterson might have given me discipline, and the triumph of Liston could now distract me only further, out of a fury to excise defeat, I began in the plot-ridden, romantic dungeons of my mind, all subterranean rhythms stirred by the beat of this party, to see myself as some sort of center about which all that had been lost must now rally. It was not simple egomania nor simple drunkenness, it was not even simple insanity: it was a kind of metaphorical leap across a gap. To believe the impossible may be won creates a strength from which the impossible may indeed be attacked. Fidel Castro alone in the jungle, with a dozen men left, seven-eighths of his landing party dead, lost, or captured, turned to his followers in the sugar-cane and said, "The days of the dictatorship are numbered." If he had been killed that moment they would have said he died as a madman. He was not mad, he was merely all but impossible. But in his mind, he saw a set of psychic steps which led to victory. And in my mind, half-gorged from juice, the beginning of a resolution was forming. I did not know it, but I was getting ready to tell myself that I must have a press conference next morning in which I would explain why Floyd Patterson still had an excellent chance to defeat Sonny Liston in their next fight, and why in fact — this would be indigestible for The Goat — why the fight which had taken place had been a mysterious dumb show substituted by inexplicable intervention for the real event. Opportunity came. This was a party like a pinball machine; there were bonuses on the turn of the lights, and a little later I was having a drink with a man from Championship Sports, I had drinks with several of them that night, but on the conversational ride we took together with the liquor, I dunned this man into some half-muttered acceptance of an idea which did not seem at all impractical at two in the morning. I would do publicity for the second Patterson-Liston fight, I was the only man in America who could save the second fight because I believed that Patterson had a true chance to beat Liston the next time they met. And it made sense: at that hour, in the blasted remains of the promotion, with no thought of a return of all promising, the confidence I offered was enough to trap the promise of a conference for the press. Liston was seeing reporters at eleven-thirty; I could have mine at eleven, a semifinal on the eleventh floor.

"And what will you say?" asked the reporters, a little later.

"I'll say it tomorrow."

But the party did not end until seven in the morning. I had the choice of sleeping for a few hours or not sleeping at all, and decided it would be easier not to fall asleep. So I talked for an hour or two with the housekeeper while the drinks began to fade, and then shaved very slowly and dressed and went out to walk the twelve or fifteen blocks from Hefner's house to the hotel. I was tired now, I felt something of the exhilaration a fighter must know in the twelfth or thirteenth round of a fifteen-round fight when he has fought his way into some terrain of the body which is beyond fatigue and is riding now like a roller coaster on the beating of his heart, while the flashbulbs ricochet their red-and-green echoes of light into his skull. The awe of his venture has fined down now into the joy that whether he wins or loses, he has finally lifted into flight, something in himself has come up free of the muck.

At the hotel, I went first to fight headquarters downstairs. In the eyes of the man from Championship Sports who had agreed last night to let me meet the press, I could now see a critical lack of delight.

"It's been changed," he said. "Sonny Liston is having his conference at eleven. You had better have yours afterward."

That would not work. After Liston talked to the reporters they would want to file their stories.

"What floor will it be on?"

"The ninth."

I thought to go to the ninth floor. It was a large mistake. Later I learned reporters were waiting for me on the eleventh. But an amateur's nose for the trap is pointed to the wrong place. I was afraid to go to the eleventh floor for fear the conference would begin two floors below. Naturally, Liston was late. On the ninth floor, in the banquet room, there were but a few reporters. I went up to the dais, sat down on a chair at one end. For several minutes nobody paid attention. Then one or two men became curious. What are you doing up there, they wanted to know. Well, I was going to sit up there, I told them, while the champion was having his press conference. Afterward I wanted to say a few things. To what effect? To the effect that I still thought Patterson was the better fighter.

A few of the movie cameramen here for TV newsreel began to take their interest. They came up with light meters, set cameras, measured distance. A flashbulb went off, another. The room was filling.

Now officials began to ask me to leave. They asked pleasantly, they asked with bewilderment, they asked in simple menace. I kept saying that I had been invited to speak at this conference, and so would not leave. Who had invited me? Reporters wanted to know. I had the sense to say I would not give the name until it was my turn to speak. I had some sense it would be bad for the man who invited me—I did not want to offer his name for nothing.

"If you don't leave," said the last official, "we'll have to remove you by force."

"Remove me by force."

"Would you give a statement, Mr. Mailer," said a reporter for the *Times*.

"Yes." The answer was formal Chinese. "I came here prepared to make a case that I am the only man in this country who can build the second Patterson-Liston fight into a $2,000,000 gate instead of a $200,000 dog in Miami. I wish to handle the press relations for this second fight. For various and private reasons I need to make a great deal of money in the next two months." Two or three journalists were now taking careful notes.

Then I felt a hand on my shoulder. Its touch was final—the end of a sequence. "Would you come with us?" On one side was a house detective. On the other side was another house detective.

"No."

"We'll have to carry you out."

"Carry me out."

They lifted the chair in which I was sitting. I had not expected this to happen. It was too simple. And there was no way to resist. The publicity from a scuffle would feed a circus. Nonetheless, if you are not a pacifist, to be transported in a chair is no happy work. Once we were quits of the dais, there was nothing to do but slip off. I walked to the elevator. Fifteen minutes of cool, reasonable debate went on downstairs before one of the detectives agreed to telephone up for permission. I would be allowed at least to see Sonny's conference with the press.

When we got back, Liston was much in command. He sat in the center of the long table, on the dais, flanked by four or five men on either side. Questions were admiring, routine. "What did you think of Patterson's punch?" someone asked, a reporter.

"He hits harder than I thought he would," said Liston.

"He never landed a punch."

"That's true," said Liston, "but he banged me on the arm. I could feel it there."

Someone asked a new question. Liston answered in a reasonable voice. Then he said something grim. About reporters.

"Well, I'm not a reporter," I shouted from the back of the room, "but I'd like to say . . ."

"You're worse than a reporter," said Liston.

"Shut the bum up," shouted some reporters.

"No," said Liston. "Let the bum speak."

"I picked Floyd Patterson to win by a one-punch knockout in the sixth round, and I still think I was right," I shouted to Liston.

"You're still drunk."

"Shut the bum up," shouted several reporters.

A reporter asked another question. Nilon was quick to answer it. I had had my moment, lost it. The conference went on. There were questions and answers about the finances of the fight. I was weary. After a while, I sat down. The faces of the people who looked at me were not friendly. When the conference ended, I went up to a reporter who was a friend. "Next time ask your question," he said. "Don't stand there posing."

An ego made of molybdenum could not have concealed from itself that one had better not quit now. The losses would be too great.

So I went back to the dais and tried to approach Liston. Two very large Negroes stood in the way. "I want to talk to the champion," I said.

"Well, go up front. Don't try to approach him from behind," snapped one of the Negroes.

"Fair enough," I said, and went down the length of the table, turned around, and came up again to Sonny Liston from the front. A man was talking, and I waited ten or fifteen seconds till he was done, and then took a step forward.

"What did you do," said Liston, "go out and get another drink?"

He was sitting down, and I was standing. Since he sat there with his forearms parallel, laid out flat on the table in front of him, it gave to his body the magisterial composure of a huge cat with a man's face.

"Liston," I said, "I still say Floyd Patterson can beat you."

A smile came from the Sphinx. "Aw, why don't you stop being a sore loser?"

"You called me a bum."

Each of us was by now aware that there were reporters gathering around us.

Something unexpected and gentle came into Liston's voice. "Well, you *are* a bum," he said. "Everybody is a bum. I'm a bum, too. It's just that I'm a bigger bum than you are." He stood up and stuck out his hand. "Shake, bum," he said.

Now it came over me that I had not begun to have the strength this morning to be so very good as I had wanted to be. Once more I had tried to become a hero, and had ended as an eccentric. There would be argument later whether I was a monster or a clown. Could it be, was I indeed a bum? I shook his hand.

A few flashbulbs went off, and Liston's face looked red to me and then green and then red and green again before the flare of the light left my retina. His hand was large and very relaxed. It told little about him. But a devil came into my head. I pulled his hand toward me, and his weight was so balanced on his toes that his head and body came forward with his hand and we were not a foot apart. "Listen," said I, leaning my head closer, speaking from the corner of my mouth, as if I were whispering in a clinch, "I'm pulling this caper for a reason. I know a way to build the next fight from a $200,000 dog in Miami to a $2,000,000 gate in New York."

Out of Liston's eyes stared back the profound intelligence of a profound animal. Now we understood each other, now we could work as a team. "Say," said Liston, "that last drink really set you up. Why don't you go and get *me* a drink, you bum."

"I'm not your flunky," I said.

It was the first jab I'd slipped, it was the first punch I'd sent home. He loved me for it. The hint of a chuckle of corny old darky laughter, cottonfield giggles, peeped out a moment from his throat. "Oh, sheeet, man!" said the wit in his eyes. And for the crowd who was watching, he turned and announced at large, "I like this guy."

So I left that conference a modest man. Because now I knew

that when it came to debate I had met our Zen master. I took a cab and rode the mile to Hefner's place, feeling the glow of fatigue which is finally not too unclean, and back at the mansion lunch was chili so hot it scorched the throat. I had a glass of milk, and Baldwin dropped by and we spoke in tired voices of the fight and after a while he inquired about the health of my sister and I replied that she was fine, she was looking beautiful, why didn't he consider marrying her, quick as that, which put me one up on old Jim again, and we shook our writer's hands and said good-by, each of us to go back to New York by separate flight, he to write his account, I to mine. Next day, and the following day, and even on the days of the next week, some favorite pets of The Goat kept taking little bites at me. First it was a red jaybird named Mr. Smith and then it was A. J. Liebling, a loverly owl. (One couldn't mind what an owl didn't see, but it was supposed to hear.) Then a wily old hamster named Winchell gobbled some of the remaining rump, and Dorothy Kilgallen, looking never in the least like a chinless lemur, took the largest bite of all. She wrote that I had tried to pick a fight with Archie Moore. Well, I had never tried to pick a fight with Archie Moore because Mr. Moore had indicated already that he could manage to handle a pugilist like Mr. George Plimpton of *The Paris Review*, and Mr. Plimpton and I were much in the same league. Indeed, Mr. Moore had said, "I almost broke my back not hitting Mr. Plimpton."

It could have been very nice. Nobody minds if they read in the papers that they were thrown in a swimming pool when in fact they did not go near a glass of water. The lies of The Goat were not onerous and his pets were sweet: it was just that later one was called in to see a high probation official and was told that probation, about to end, would now be extended further. One would have to pay this bit for the caper. I did not mind so much. I had learned a lot and educations were paid for best in cash. But what I lost was also nice, I was sorry to see it gone. Some ghost of Don Quixote was laid to rest in me and now I could never be as certain as that morning on the walk whether Patterson indeed could ever bring in his return. To shake the hand of the Devil must quiver the hole: who knew any longer where Right was Left or who was Good and how Evil had hid? For if Liston was the agent of the Devil, what a raid had been made on God, what a royal black man had arisen. Sonny, the King of Hip, was Ace of Spades, and Patterson, ah, Patterson was now an archetype of all which was underdog. He would be a giant if he won. If he could rally from his flight and shave the beard he glued on his mouth; if he could taste those ashes, and swallow to the end, and never choke; if he could sleep through the aisles and enormities of each long night, pondering if the Devil had struck him down (and so might strike again — what fear could be worse than that!) or, even worse, be forced to wonder if the Lord had passed him by for Sonny, if Sonny were now the choice, having carried the blood of his Negritude through prison walls; if Floyd could sleep through those long dreams, and be cool to the power of the dead in Liston's fists (and the rents in his own psyche); if Patterson could keep from pulling apart and could put himself together; if he could shed the philosophy which drained him and learn to create for himself till he was once again the heavyweight with the fastest, hardest hands of our modern time; if he could go out into the ring with the sullen apathy of his followers now staring him in the eye; if he could move in and take that next fight away from Liston and knock Sonny out, then a great man would be with us, and a genius our champion rather than a king. So one would hope for Patterson one more time. Genius was more rare than royalty and so its light must reach a little further into our darkness down the deep waters of sleep, down one's long inner space. The first fight had been won by the man who knew the most about Evil; would the second reveal who had studied more of the Good? would they meet in the clangor of battle or the fiasco of a doomed dead cause? would we witness a dog in Miami or the lion of New York?

The Metaphysics of the Belly

Interviewer: I feel anxious today. I can't seem to get serious. A year ago we had an interview. "The First Days Interview,"* you called it. You said at the time it was the beginning of a book. You were going to call it The Psychology of the Orgy. *Then I don't hear from you again. Months go by. All these months. The piece gets printed. I become a bit of a figure. Suddenly you call me up. Let's go on with the interview, you say. I arrive tape recorder in hand. Now you say you want to do a book on Picasso. I'm confused. I don't know anything about Picasso.*

Mailer: That's one reason you were chosen.

Interviewer: I feel like the old lady in Death in the Afternoon.

---

*Printed in *Paris Review* #26.

Tell me, what happened to The Psychology of the Orgy? *That pricks the ears much more than Picasso.* Psychology of the Orgy — *it's not like you to throw away a good title.*

Mailer: What I have to say about Picasso may not be so dull.

Interviewer: I think he'll be the pretext for you to express yourself on a thousand subjects. I wonder if you have any real personal attachment to Picasso's work?

Mailer: Picasso is good for my eyesight.

Interviewer: Look, I have a confession to make. Our last interview was a vast success in certain limited circles. Marvelous, people kept saying to me, the way you weren't afraid to talk back to Mailer. Oh, he's not so hard to talk to, I would tell them, he's really rather reasonable.

Mailer: So you have a vested interest in continuing to talk back to me.

Interviewer: Let's say I was innocent in the first interview, and didn't realize I was being that effective. Now I look at you professionally. I can't afford to have you drop my standards by making facetious remarks that Picasso is good for your eyesight.

Mailer: I was telling the simple truth. My eyes have been bad lately. I read a book for an hour and suffer eye-strain the rest of the day. Eye specialists have been useless. So have all sorts of eye-glasses. Even Mr. Huxley was no use. I tried the exercises in *The Art of Seeing.* They only strained my eyes somewhat further. But looking at Picassos does not tire them. In fact I've started work for the day with severe eye-strain, having awakened from a sleep which has been more or less satisfactory for every part of my body but my eyes, and after a morning of studying twenty, fifty, or a hundred reproductions of Picassos, my eyes have felt a bit relaxed for the first time in months.

Interviewer: Do you have any idea why this is so?

Mailer: The idea is too complex to be introduced so quickly. I would be obliged to compress it, and so seem facetious all over again.

Interviewer: Give me a hint.

Mailer: We see with the mind as well as the eye. Since the eye leads through the retina back to the mind, we can say that we see objects with two halves of the mind, with a physiological apparatus, and with a part of the psyche. If these two halves of the mind are critically different, one is seeing in two ways at once. Strain develops.

Interviewer: Sounds like schizophrenia.

Mailer: Nothing so royal. Look. If I read a line of prose, its immediate meaning is clear to my physical vision, to that part of my mind which is literal and therefore moves quickly. "Now is the time for all good men to come to the aid of the party" I read. "Perfectly clear" says the muscle of my eye, and moves on to the next sentence. But my conceptual faculty holds on to the sentence. It makes associations with the words. "Now" signifies the present, which is an enormous word to me. I write often of the enormous present, of psychopathy, of how mass man has no sense of past or future, just Now. So that word halts me conceptually. I cannot afford to ignore the way it is used in a sentence. And then there's "time" which is the most remarkable and mysterious of words. It's even more mysterious than "God." We can have an idea of God, most of us do sooner or later, but who has any concept of what time might be? And the construction, "Now is the time," which makes a subject and noun of "Now" is particularly interesting if one believes, as I sometimes do, that the secrets of existence, or some of them anyway, are to be found in the constructions of language which have come down to us. "Now is the time" is an odd way of putting things, as if "Now" is palpable and "time" is some sort of appurtenance which is attached to one place or to another, to Before, or to Now. I won't go into discussing "good men" or "party" but they are obviously capable of stirring a number of unconscious thoughts and dim associations which must be ignored if I'm to keep on reading at a reasonable rate. The result is that one part of my mind works against the other. My eyes begin to feel like an automobile driven by a man who has one foot on the accelerator, and the other on the brake.

Interviewer: Shouldn't this be true for all of us?

Mailer: No. Most people keep concepts firmly in category. "Now" is the flat quiet moment of the present, "time" is a few simple numbers one reads from a watch.

Interviewer: But not in their unconscious, I presume.

Mailer: Their unconscious doesn't erupt into the conscious routine acts of their daily life, as does mine. They save all larger thoughts for sleep, which is the tidy way to do it.

Interviewer: Whereas your ambition drove your unconscious out of the water, so to speak, and into the light.

Mailer: So to speak.

Interviewer: One of the ground rules is not to mock each other's metaphors.

Mailer: Certain artists, those who see associations and connections everywhere, tend to live in a psychic medium which is heavier, more dense, than the average man's. It is harder for them to move because there is more conscious mind for them to move. Joyce is the first example. And he went blind. Which does no harm to my thesis. If the mind reacts too powerfully to the stimuli before it, then the eye must see less in order to keep one's inner pressure at a bearable level. One goes blind not from seeing too little but from the overladen possibilities of seeing too much.

Interviewer: Almost as if there's a biological law.

Mailer: But I'm sure there is. Beauty, as the Greeks kept nagging, was harmony. Well, it has other qualities as well I hope, danger, ecstasy, promise, the transcendence of terror—all the emotions which give life to us in the West—but harmony, I fear, is what beauty is first. It means that separate parts function in a lively set of rhythms with one another. No organ is too fast or too slow vis-à-vis another organ. The pleasant relation inspires proportions in the outer forms which are healthy, harmonious, and beautiful.

Interviewer: This is not insignificant, you know.

Mailer: I know.

Interviewer: You're taking an important stand here.

Mailer: May it be the first of many.

Interviewer: Hold on. You're saying that aesthetics is not abstract, that our concepts of beauty are not arbitrary but a function of nature.

Mailer: It's obviously more complicated than that. Upon occasion we can see beauty in disease, or beauty in the sinister, beauty even in the ugly. But that is because we have traveled a private road whose events have reinforced a few of our faculties. Compassion for example, illumines the ugly, makes it beautiful. As we look upon an ugly face—provided it is *our* kind of ugly face—we see how it could have been beautiful, we see the loss implicit in it, we feel tender toward the disproportionate or even anomalous development of features in it. Their inversion of beauty stimulates some inner sense in us of a beauty which failed to be, at least until that moment when we conceived that this ugly sight could have been beautiful. So at that instant, looking at a plain face we can feel intimations of beauty. Beauty—so runs this argument—has its root in any being which is harmonious, imaginative, adaptable, brave, artful, daring, good for life, good for the continuation of life.

Interviewer: Fantastic!

Mailer: Why?

Interviewer: Do you realize the enormity of what you're saying? It turns a good many ideas on their head.

Mailer: That is the function of fashion: to turn modest ideas on their head.

Interviewer: How about art for art's sake?

Mailer: Art for art's sake. My notion reinvigorates that notion, doesn't it?

Interviewer: Yes, because aesthetes are not going into an ivory tower any longer, not by your logic. If they devote themselves to a search for beauty, they are engaged in a most valuable act—at least, according to you—to discover those secrets of life which give life.

Mailer: Well, I don't know. Only noble artists discover noble secrets and manage to give them back as art. Most of the artists who believe in art for art's sake are over-elegant greedy sorts. The debate still continues, you see. One can argue which kind of life is harmonious and what is not. The leaves and vines Aubrey Beardsley adored so completely grew only in a hot-house, a conservatory, or a tropical garden. There was no toughness in such beauty.

Interviewer: But if a great artist believed in art for art's sake . . .

Mailer: He would be closer to life, I think, than a great politician who believed in politics for politics' sake.

Interviewer: I understand what you're saying about beauty, and I don't even know that I disagree with it, I mean I can see its relation to your sexual theories.

Mailer: Please don't anticipate the argument.

Interviewer: But in any case I don't see how you can apply your yardstick to the present. Look at the particular aesthetic experiences which give beauty to people today. In music, John Cage's One Minute and Thirty-six Seconds of Silence *or whatever the title is; on the stage,* The Connection, *or Albee's work, or Tennessee Williams and his deep mahogany scatology; the novel, well leave it with William Burroughs whom you admire and his violent jangled shattering sense of obscenity; and then the Abstract Expressionists and their messes—talk of scatology. I still don't understand their painting—and the Surrealists, full of abortions, Picasso and his mistresses whom he chooses to make look like monstrosities. Well, I could fulminate, I could say, "Call me Square and give me Velasquez," but to tell the truth I do get a sense of beauty from all these artists, or at least a sense of very private excitement like meeting a woman at a dinner party and knowing you were meant to go off with each other if you each had enough courage . . . Whereas Greek sculpture, natural function, that leaves me gasping up the Muse on a dead dead beach.*

Mailer: It bores me as well. But it was the beginning of beauty. It stated the basic condition. Perhaps Greek sculpture is no longer so beautiful to us because it lacks the sense of danger with which we live.

Interviewer: Modern art has that sense of danger?

Mailer: It has a sense of doom.

Interviewer: Doom of what?

Mailer: The species. Take the artists you mentioned. Suppose the condition of our existence is now so plague-ridden that we have sunk beneath the level of scatology.

Interviewer: I don't follow. You mean we've sunk so low that scatological thoughts give life?

Mailer: For a good many people they do.

Interviewer: Life may not be so bad as that.

Mailer: There are horrors beneath the surface, cannibals in all of us, mad animals. And for a reason. It's as if we're stifling, as if the air we breathe is no longer air but some inert gas. (*Holds up a hand.*) Look, I've gotten into serious matters much too soon. I think a discussion of beauty is premature, I think it would need all of this book to explain anything at all. Let me say just that the modern condition may be psychically so bleak, so overextended, so artificial, so plastic — plastic like styrene — that studies of loneliness, silence, corruption, scatology, abortion, monstrosity, decadence, orgy, and death can give life, can give a sentiment of beauty.

Interviewer: You cannot desert the argument until you give some indication of how this is possible.

Mailer: May I use the word soul instead of psyche?

Interviewer: If it encourages the expression of ideas, yes.

Mailer: Postulate a modern soul marooned in constipation, emptiness, boredom and a flat dull terror of death. A soul which takes antibiotics when ill, smokes filter cigarettes, drinks proteins, minerals, and vitamins in a liquid diet, takes seconal to go to sleep, benzedrine to awake, and tranquilizers for poise. It is a deadened existence, afraid precisely of violence, cannibalism, loneliness, insanity, libidinousness, hell, perversion, and mess, because these are the states which must in some way be passed through, digested, transcended, if one is to make one's way back to life.

Interviewer: Why must they be passed through, transcended?

Mailer: Because the scatology is within and not without. The urge to eat another does not exist in some cannibal we watch in the jungle, but in the hinge of our own jaws. The love of death is not a mass phenomenon; it exists for each of us alone, our own private love of death. Just as our fear of death is also ours all alone. These states, these morbid states, as the old-fashioned psychologists used to say, can obtain relief only by coming to life in the psyche. But they can come to life only if they are ignited by an experience outside themselves. If I am secretly in love with death and terrified of it, then the effort to restrain and domesticate these emotions and impulses (which are no less than the cross-impulses of suicidal bravery and shame-ridden cowardice) exhaust so much of my will that my existence turns bleak. A dramatic encounter with death, an automobile accident from which I escape, a violent fight I win or lose decently, these all call forth my crossed impulses which love death and fear it. They give air to it. So these internal and deadly emotions are given life. In some cases, satisfied by the experience, they will subside a bit, give room to easier and more sensuous desires.

Interviewer: Not always?

Mailer: Not always. Hemingway, it seems, was never able to tame his dirty ape.

Interviewer: Dirty ape?

Mailer: It's a better word than id or anti-social impulse.

Interviewer: I think it is.

Mailer: Once we may have had a fine clean brave upstanding ape inside ourselves. It's just gotten dirty over the years.

Interviewer: Why couldn't Hemingway tame his ape?

Mailer: Because he may have had too wild a one inside him. The grandeur of one's work is a measure of how outrageous is the ape. People were always criticizing Hemingway for being self-destructive, obsessed with death, immersed too deeply in a cult of violence, perpetually trying his manhood, and so forth. Well, as I'll try to argue a little later, the first art work in an artist is the shaping of his own personality. An artist is usually such an incredible balance of opposites and incompatibles that the wonder is he can even remain alive. Hemingway was on the one hand a man of magnificent senses. There was a quick lithe animal in him. He was also shackled to a stunted ape, a cripple, a particularly wild dirty little dwarf within himself who wanted only to kill Hemingway. Life as a compromise was impossible. So long as Hemingway did not test himself, push himself beyond his own dares, flirt with, engage, and finally embrace death, in other words so long as he did not propitiate the dwarf, give the dwarf its chance to live and feel emotion, an emotion which could come to life only when one was close to death, Hemingway and the dwarf were doomed to dull and deaden one another in the dungeons of the psyche. Everyday life in such circumstances is a plague. The proper comment on Hemingway's style of life may be not that he dared death too much, but too little, that brave as he was, he was not brave enough, and the dwarf finally won. One does not judge Hemingway, but one can say that the sickness in him was not his love of violence but his inability to live as close to it as he had to. His proportions were tragic, he was all-but-doomed, it is possible he would have had to have been the bravest man who ever lived in order to propitiate the dwarf.

Interviewer: But at any rate, if I follow you, encounters with danger were not self-destructive but healthy for Hemingway.

Mailer: He could feel good next day. His psyche was out of the dungeon. He could work. His insides were not tense and empty.

Interviewer: Because — I'm trying to think in your way now — the death within him has met a death without, and so a temporary peace was found?

Mailer: Let's say he was going out to shoot a lion and felt marvelous. Well, there is a kind of mind which would say, "He's self-destructive. He feels good because he's going to kill himself." What I'm trying to argue is that he felt good because encountering death would give him more chance to live. From a very early age he must have felt his ordinary death within him (his routine sickbed death that is) as a kind of slow oncoming plague of washed-out memories and burned-up talents. So he was brave enough, as not many of us are, to go looking for death (since if he survived, his life would be better) but he was finally not brave enough to triumph at this kind of life. It was a desperate imbalance. What made him great as a writer was that he could ride it so long.

Interviewer: Talk of death always makes me contemplate loneliness. You've stimulated me. I think I could guess now what you might say about John Cage and his silent musical compositions.

Mailer: What would I say?

Interviewer: Well, roughly, that there is a frightening detachment in each of us, an inner silence, neither divine nor doomed, just lost in endless orbit. Nothing seems able to reach it. It is as if our souls are stricken. An arbitrary period of silence in a concert hall might encounter that anguish. There, could you have said it better?

Mailer: I would have tried to find one turn of wit.

Interviewer: Well I'm new at this.

Mailer: You're doing all right.

Interviewer: I must say your ideas are not unathletic. I feel more or less vigorous now.

Mailer: Still, you were leading up to a point. And you seem to have lost it.

Interviewer: Oh! Wait! What was I talking about?

Mailer: Many things. Were you leading up to the mess?

Interviewer: Scatology. Of course. Death may be noble, and loneliness also, but how does a scatological art work raise the reader or the audience to catharsis? Why is such an aesthetic experience good for life?

Mailer: I don't want to discuss scatology now. It's too complex. It may be more complex than death. So I'm going to stay away from this now. I prefer to steal back to it from time to time.

Interviewer: You have to give a hint, however.

Mailer: Why must I?

Interviewer: I hoped I could avoid having to say this, but your name does not inspire the sort of confidence which keeps people waiting. You are not Lord Russell after all, or Wittgenstein, or Heidegger, or Sartre.

Mailer: Not yet.

Interviewer: Perhaps not ever.

Mailer: No doubt never.

Interviewer: A hint.

Mailer: Feces are seen as the most distasteful and despised condition of being. They are precisely that part of the alimentation in the universe which we have rejected, and, mind you, rejected not morally, not emotionally, not passionately . . .

Interviewer: In the sense that vomit is passionate?

Mailer: In the sense that vomit is passionate. No, feces have been rejected viscerally. It is our being, our organism, which rejects them. They are a total statement of our nature. This cannot be used, says our nature, this is not to be absorbed but to be cast away, this is to be not chosen. From deep within ourselves, our cells have chosen what can be used and what can not. Nothing is more despised than what we have chosen not to want.

Interviewer: I've heard the Arabs feel so strongly about this, that they institutionalize their hands. With their right hand they eat and wash their faces. With their left hand they wipe themselves. The left hand is never allowed to touch food.

Mailer: Yes.

Interviewer: One hand for life, the other for death.

Mailer: You set up your opposites much too neatly. An attractive opposite, tersely worded, can bury more thought than it uncovers. One hand for life, the other for death.

Interviewer: What does that bury?

Mailer: Why, it buries one's understanding that feces are not equivalent to death, and that all of us have a very bad conscience about shit which is exactly why it is so obsessive to us.

Interviewer: Would a healthy man have a bad conscience?

Mailer: No. But few of us qualify for the word. Our characters are usually not as rich as the food we eat.

Interviewer: So we excrete not only what we despise but what is too good for us as well?

Mailer: Or too special. The act of elimination is excruciating to some part of the psyche. I expect it is the part which governs the digestive processes of the body. Because we eat, I imagine, not what our cells need, so much as what our habits demand.

Interviewer: Suddenly, you're too abstract for me.

Mailer: I'm saying that a cell is like a little animal. It knows exactly what it wants to eat, what is good for it. But a cell is not a psychic structure. It may be a part of the machine which makes up a habit, it may work for a habit, but it has no powers of command. It cannot choose what it wants, it can only receive it.

Interviewer: Please carry this further.

Mailer: A habit is a psychic structure. What it's composed of literally need not concern us, but since it is a construction of mind which sits in authority upon the body, we can think of it as a law which is intangible but more or less absolute in its effect upon citizens.

Interviewer: Make this concrete. You're still too metaphorical.

Mailer: A man goes into a store to choose some food. His cells, a good many of them, let us say, need calves' liver that evening, but his habit is to please his dinner guests and liver seems insufficiently festive, so frogs' legs are ordered. Later that night, the cells make do with frogs' legs, but liver was their need.

Interviewer: You're speaking of a decision; of a choice, not a habit.

Mailer: The habit is at several removes from the cells. The habit is to please one's guests. If liver is out of fashion, it will not please the guests. The habit which dominates the cells is that they must conform to fashion. What is significant here is that the part in a civilized man which makes the decision to choose his food has little to do with his need.

Interviewer: You would argue that he can't feel his need as clearly as a savage would.

Mailer: Of course not. Habits usually are anti-neurological structures. They are built up and they are maintained precisely by insulating our senses from most stimuli.

Interviewer: I don't see how you have anchored this thesis. Your man wanted liver, he got frogs' legs, but what's there to keep him from making the best of it, from extracting the good juices out of the meat in old Froggie's thigh, and getting rid of the gristle? Where does bad conscience come in?

Mailer: You have the instinctive vice of American thought.

Interviewer: You're just annoyed because I blew a hole in your thesis.

Mailer: But you didn't. You took my example, assumed it was all of the reality, and proceeded to draw a moral to your own satisfaction. But I gave you just a few of the facts, not all of them. Reality is always more complex than the example. That's why I hate to get into explanation too soon.

Interviewer: Defend your thesis.

Mailer: My man ordered frogs' legs. But the urgency of his cells, their cry for liver, registered as a dull lust in his mind. So as he stared about the Gourmet shop, he bought a little tin of foie gras.

Interviewer: You didn't mention this before.

Mailer: An example is not a logical universe. I can do with an example whatever I wish, because its purpose is to explain, not to prove.

Interviewer: I concede, but I still think it's unfair.

Mailer: He eats the foie gras with his drinks, eats it with relish. Ceremoniously it enters his stomach which receives it like a High Church serves a rich wedding. But there is so little foie gras! And he cannot gorge. He must serve his guests first. Which involves other habits. Habit-life precedes cell-life in civilized man. Just a little foie gras and his cells need a lot of liver. Upon this cruel disproportion follows another—the frogs' legs. The part of the psyche which oversees digestion, let us call it The Eater, has to make a new decision, because its powers of digestion cannot do an equally good job on liver and frogs' legs both.

Interviewer: Why not?

Mailer: Because the chemicals necessary for each would adulterate one another.

Interviewer: Is there scientific proof of this?

Mailer: I'm sure there's not. I invoke a simpler principle. One can't do two good and difficult things at once and do them both very well. I can't write a book with my right hand and paint a picture with my left. At the same instant, I can't make love and sing high opera. Nor can I digest foie gras and frogs' legs equally well. One or the other must suffer.

Interviewer: Your stomach may not work the way you do.

Mailer: It's bound to. There would be very few problems in life if our organs could perform two or more complex highly differentiated functions equally well at once.

Interviewer: For the sake of the argument I concede again. I want to know where you're heading. I think I see it.

Mailer: If you do, take over yourself.

Interviewer: Go one more step.

Mailer: The Eater chooses the frogs' legs. Reluctantly. He would prefer the foie gras, but there is simply not enough and the intestines would have too much work evacuating half-digested frog flesh—I exaggerate the imperfection of the process, of course. Therefore, the arts of digestion are applied to the frogs' legs. The best sweets in the foie gras, digested as formal second choice, are lost. The inner savory of their wealth is not reached.

Interviewer: Why not?

Mailer: Because life in its need to protect itself tends to make what is best in itself most inaccessible.

Interviewer: Whereas civilization tries to make the best in itself most available.

Mailer: Well, it would claim to.

Interviewer: I think that's the first ideal of democracy. To make the best most available. What a logical impasse! In your terms democracy is then opposed to life.

Mailer: It endangers life in the name of a noble ideal.

Interviewer: We'll never get to Picasso, thank God.

Mailer: We're getting there. Once we look at the pictures I won't want to stop in order to discuss these matters. But now I must ask you: I know where we are, but where *were* we?

Interviewer: Yes. I know. The foie gras. The best of it was lost. The richest parts.

Mailer: The Eater took a middle course. What was useless, despicable, or uninteresting in the frogs' legs and in the foie gras was eliminated. But what was superior in the foie gras was also lost.

Interviewer: So in despising his waste, the man is partially dishonest.

Mailer: Since his cells cannot inform him of the small tragedy they underwent last night, he has only an imperfect sense that there was something wrong with the foie gras. "It disagrees with me," he says, "I won't order it any more." Three days later he buys three cans, gorges on it at lunch, and then upbraids himself for lacking discipline and eating the things which are bad for him. Except for this sense of guilt at his poor character, it would have been a marvelous lunch.

Interviewer: You're saying that civilization hurts the inner communication of mind to body and body to mind.

Mailer: Go further. Say the obsession of many of us for scatology is attached to the disrupted communication within us, within our bodies.

Interviewer: I had the impression for just an instant that there's a theory of disease possible in this somewhere.

Mailer: There is the possibility of illness every time opposites do not meet or meet poorly, just as there is the air to gain life every time opposites meet each other nicely.

Interviewer: Dilate a bit on this.

Mailer: They can be opposites within us—the part of my eye which sees physiologically as opposed to that part which views conceptually. But one can speak of opposites between man and nature, or man and man: the water I drink, the block of marble worked by the sculptor, the audience and the play, a mood and its occasion, the good rider and his good horse, the blocking back and the line-backer, the skier on the snow, the style of sex, a sail into the wind. I become conventionally rhapsodic, the point is that life seems to come out of the meeting of opposites. Communication is a poor word, because life does not come from communication but from meetings, from opposites coming together.

Interviewer: Communications has a technological connotation to me.

Mailer: It involves machines and electronic apparatus and services of distribution. It invariably implies the injection of information into a passive being. But one can use it in speaking of the body, one can say that a particular part of the body communicates poorly with another part because we are by now not only biological but mechanical. There are habits in all of us which function with the precision of a machine. And when certain functions in our body are unable to meet other functions at the necessary instant, one can speak of a failure of communication. One may even well suspect that the basis of chronic disease and the excessive virulence of much infectious disease, particularly the viruses, comes precisely from an inner field of communications which is poorly designed or badly abused. The message which did not get from Ghent to Aix is the Metaphor for a drama which goes on constantly within us. My man who wanted liver and got frogs' legs would, if his stomach had been able to speak to him with the clear simple chords of an animal's belly, have escaped bad conscience and a touch of indigestion.

Interviewer: But if bad communication is virtually the sole basis of disease—a fascinating concept, by the way—why do you equate it to scatology or at least make the connection there?

Mailer: Because feces are the material evidence of the processes of communication within us. Life comes from the meeting of opposites. Conceive of man as a tube, mouth at one end, anus at the other. In that sense man is like a worm, a pipe, a tunnel, a drill which bores through a bed of nutrition, disgorging it behind. We cannot see the air we exhale, not normally, not unless we have tobacco smoke with which to shape it, but we can study our urine and feces. In one way or another, most of us do. They are the expression of what we have done well and what we have done badly to that medium of food through which we passed. When we have communicated nicely within ourselves, the stool reflects a simple reasonable operation (cowflop is for example, modest in its odor) but where we have failed, as with the foie gras, the odors and shapes are tortured, corrupt, rich, fascinating (that is attractive and repulsive at the same time), theatrical, even tragic. There are odors

not alien to beauty in the dung. The sense of life they give has tragic beauty which tells us something rare and very good for us has
been lost again, something fine is just beginning to rot. The history
of the life we never see within us, its triumphs, tragedies, states of
calm and states of inanition are returned to us in the color, the
shape, the odor and the movement of our stool. For those qualities
are the curious stricken record of our near past. We despise what
we had once and now can possess no longer, especially if we fear
having used it badly. Yet we cannot forsake it altogether. Obses-
sively we return to the study because hope for how to turn our life
into more life is contained in that history.

*Interviewer: Eloquent. I must observe that it is rash for you to
be too eloquent on this subject.*

Mailer: I wished to avoid it earlier.

*Interviewer: True enough. But since we now find ourselves here,
let me say I still don't understand, not really, the intense virulence
of people's reactions to scatology.*

Mailer: Perhaps the prophetic aspects create the rage.

Interviewer: I don't follow you.

Mailer: The food you ate yesterday was too rich for you, says
the odor in the water closet. Eat as improperly today and you will
be ill. But this is much too simple. Say rather that the senses bring
deep messages to the unconscious, quick deep messages. And they
are measured carefully by the scale of past experience. A carpenter
makes a hundred measurements a day. If you ask him to mark off
five inches without a tape, he is bound to be able to do it within an
eighth of an inch. So it is with our stool. Our senses know what it
says to us. But so often the messages are intolerable. You are sickening slowly, remarks the wad, your life as you lead it now is hopeless. You must engage death, perversion, promiscuity, and the fear
of hell before you will be better. Your health is to eat the body of
your mate, your secret desire is to be trampled in an orgy. This is
what the oracle of the unconscious may divine from the feces. No
wonder shit is despised. Its message is too terrible.

*Interviewer: Isn't this a little too much to discover from the in-
ner history of a meal?*

Mailer: Food possesses character. We consume character when
we eat.

*Interviewer: I'm not so certain. Food may be no more than food.
How do we know it isn't?*

Mailer: I don't. I guess. It seems more reasonable to me that
food possess character than that it doesn't. One man leads a sedentary life, and another works hard, wouldn't the bicep of one be dif-

ferent in character from the other? Why, if we were to eat both biceps . . .

Interviewer: You take the plunge into cannibalism?

Mailer: Only for the sake of the argument that one bicep would communicate qualities of strength, fortitude, and discipline, whereas the other would tend to make one lazy, slack, and unregenerate.

Interviewer: But which is which?

Mailer: I assume the worker's bicep communicates fortitude and power.

Interviewer: It might be just the reverse. The worker's arm might be disgusted, used up. All that's left in his cells which can feed you is the desire to be lazy. Whereas the lazy arm is bursting with unused energy.

Mailer: Three cheers for overtaking me. But will you now agree that food may possess character?

Interviewer: We don't know what character it possesses.

Mailer: I suspect our unconscious does.

Interviewer: How convenient is this unconscious.

Mailer: The hand is plucked instinctively from the flame before the mind realizes the finger is in the fire. Let's save time. Of course the unconscious is close to the senses, it is the animal part of oneself. And it studies what it eats, it knows the inner life of the body's organs, it hears what has happened to the food, what qualities it possessed, what reactions it aroused. Take steak, assume it provides strength for the muscles. Or if not steak there must be obviously one or another particular food to provide such strength. Whatever the food may be which offers strength, we can be sure it is good for a man doing heavy work, and that it is probably poor for a lady whose strength may depend upon the excellent demands of her weakness. For an intellectual beginning a program of conditioning exercises, steak may be just a little too full of strength, it may fire his muscles into doing too much too soon. So The Eater might decide to digest the steak cursorily, might decide to pass by the molecules containing the kernel of the strength. The stool, bursting next day with the most vital elements of the steak might give back in its form and odor the dispiriting news that The Eater in the intellectual had indeed decided he was not yet strong enough for steak.

Interviewer: But if The Eater knows this already and so makes a decision to eschew the qualities of finest strength in the steak, why does the unconscious have to discover it in the stool? I thought The Eater was part of the unconscious.

Mailer: Not all parts of the unconscious communicate perfectly well with one another. That is part of the theory of disease we postulated. There are ways for the unconscious to speak from one part of itself to another, but we are not always able to use them.

Interviewer: Being receptive to the message of the bowels is one way?

Mailer: Children are always asking you to look at their stool, and are disappointed when we say, "That's nice, dear," and turn away.

Interviewer: You're saying that our prevailing social habit is to lay a foundation in the child for a future failure of communication?

Mailer: In certain people this particular tension is sufficient to find not only the sight but the subject of feces quite sickening. It is for example particularly abhorrent to the English. Their intellectual categories offer no course in the archaeology of the Self. The French on the other hand know that *merde* has a purchase on fortune.

Interviewer: I don't want to be grisly, but if old scata has so much to do with fortune and telling the future, why aren't there cults? Why isn't divination from the stool some small but worthy competitor to the horoscope or numerology?

Mailer: People who go to hear their fortune are not existentialists, but essentialists. Full of self-pity, they wish to believe that their fortune is already written, and to their advantage of course. They do not want to discover that they are still responsible for what they do with themselves. So what kind of interest could they have in any testament of the bowels which might speak of the history within themselves? Such study reveals character—informs them of their moral fortune.

Interviewer: What is moral fortune? I never heard that expression before.

Mailer: If there is Heaven and if Hell exists, one's moral fortune indicates where one is likely to go. I suppose it is not unlikely that a man bound for Hell could sniff out the fact this was his destination. Such a man might detest all thought of shit.

Interviewer: Herr Doktor, you've been talking about the bowels much too long, and it's getting on my nerves.

Mailer: The trouble is that I have to present one more large annoying idea before we can go on.

Interviewer: Certain large ideas can be expressed briefly.

Mailer: You'll agree that a society is best judged by the way it treats the citizens, the slaves, the subjects, the masses who compose it.

Interviewer: What do you want to say?

Mailer: That food be considered capable of possessing a soul.

Interviewer: You mean that as we eat we are like a society act-

ing upon its citizens, that food clanks from its cradle to the tomb as through us it moves, that noble souls in the food are not sufficiently appreciated by us and so die tragically, just as societies sometimes lose the gifts of some of their best men? Presenting this enormous metaphor merely to say that food has a soul! Why should it, why indeed should food have a soul?

Mailer: Because it is a being.

Interviewer: A being. It's a good existential word, I know, but you've got to do something for it. What is a being? Please don't tell me a being is something which is alive.

Mailer: I won't. Especially since certain organisms which are alive cannot be called beings.

Interviewer: Then a being is not all of life?

Mailer: A being is anything which lives and still has the potentiality to change, to change physically and to change morally. A person who has lost all capacity for fundamental change is no longer a being.

Interviewer: Being is used then as synonymous to soul?

Mailer: Soul is eternal. At least that is the general agreement on its meaning. Soul is what continues to live after we are dead. It is possible, I should think, that if the soul does exist, that if there is such an entity, that if there is indeed a part of us which is eternal, or which can under certain conditions remain eternal, that the soul could well have the property of being able to migrate from body to body, from existence to existence, sometimes rising, sometimes falling, sometimes getting lost forever.

Interviewer: Whereas being is corporeal, is there before the eyes?

Mailer: I think so. I would assume that when the soul enters a particular tangible existence, it weds itself to that existence. So long as the soul is part of a creature it is not free of it, not free to leave when it chooses, not unless sudden death is chosen. So long as the soul resides in a body or is trapped in a body or at war in a body or indeed even enamored of the body in which it finds itself, the soul must exist in a relation with that body which is not unlike marriage. The soul affects the body, the body is able to affect the soul, they grow together or apart, they are good for one another or they may be bad, they can be tragic for one another or merely cool and efficient, tolerating one another because they would be savage and wasteful if apart. A panoply of possibilities exists in every being, because a being is a creature which lives in the world, which has shape, color, form, which has life and a soul within it, a soul which will be changed by its existence in the world. Or at least that is how I would postulate a being.

Interviewer: Being is the existence of soul in the world?

Mailer: Being is first the body we see before us. That body we see before us is that moment of the present for a soul; a soul which must inevitably be altered for better, for worse, or for better and worse by its presence in a body.

Interviewer: And individual cells have souls, individual souls?

Mailer: I think they do. I think everything which lives had a soul at its birth, or it could not otherwise have been born.

Interviewer: Fresh food has a soul?

Mailer: Yes, usually.

Interviewer: But canned food. What about that?

Mailer: Less soul.

Interviewer: It's dead.

Mailer: Not altogether. Let's say for the present it's in a kind of limbo. What characterizes food, I would speculate, is that the soul tries to cling to it as long as it can. A tin of sardines is still a being of sorts, a being of a lesser category. It may not be alive as an organism, but its flesh retains life, the cells have not rotted, the protein molecules are intact, if you will, and the oils and the carbohydrates still retain in their structure the character of the sardine.

Interviewer: Let me recapitulate. Character in this case is the still-standing structure of the carbon molecule given the cells by the previous history within one little sardine of its soul at war with and/or loving its body?

Mailer: Let's say the soul left a taste. Some sardines taste better than others.

Interviewer: It's one thing to have a taste. It's another to have a soul.

Mailer: Why does one sardine taste better than another?

Interviewer: Because its meat is better.

Mailer: What does that mean?

Interviewer: The meat is healthier, that's all.

Mailer: And health? What is that?

Interviewer: A harmonious condition of body.

Mailer: How does that come about?

Interviewer: In the case of the sardine?

Mailer: Yes.

Interviewer: From being a better swimmer than the average sardine. Naturally good constitution inherited from its mother.

Mailer: Who was also a superior swimmer?

Interviewer: Yes.

Mailer: Why was she so good?

Interviewer: You're tireless.

Mailer: Humorless.

Interviewer: You're going to insist the mother's soul was superior to the soul of other sardines and so left a superior taste?

Mailer: I think I will.

Interviewer: Why this passion to put the soul into the sardine?

Mailer: Because the act of eating is always a small execution.

Interviewer: And you find it less hideous if a soul is released, as a cell is devoured?

Mailer: If I believed a calf had one single chance to live, no more, I could not in good conscience eat it. I might eat it anyway but logic would say I should be a vegetarian.

Interviewer: Whereas now, the soul of the calf passes into you, becomes a part of your being.

Mailer: Yes.

Interviewer: I see now why Mexicans eat bull's balls.

Mailer: A delicacy.

Interviewer: Why don't all men eat bull's balls? Why aren't they worth twice their weight in platinum?

Mailer: Because very few people are ready to receive them.

Interviewer: You mean your soul has to be the equal of the souls you ingest?

Mailer: There has to be a meeting of opposites.

Interviewer: A feminine man would enjoy bull's balls?

Mailer: Or a masculine man. You mustn't puzzle too hard at these celestial mechanics.

Interviewer: Oh, I think they're first rate, I just don't navigate among them too well as yet.

Mailer: Your approach lacks existential ease.

Interviewer: Teach me the new grace.

Mailer: Allow me then to signify the bull's balls as equal to virility. For the sake of my demonstration let it be that whoever eats them gains virility. The meeting of opposites takes place therefore between a male principle, the bull's balls, and something female in the soul of the man who eats.

Interviewer: Or the woman.

Mailer: Or the woman. It doesn't matter, you see, whether you have a masculine man, a feminine man, a masculine woman, or a feminine woman. What characterizes all of them is that in partaking of the bull's balls each of them wishes to gain virility.

Interviewer: To simplify it, let's speak just of men. Why, in the first place, wouldn't all men wish to gain virility?

Mailer: Virility implies more than the stamina of a stud. It offers power, strength, the ability to command, the desire to alter life. So its consequences in life are often to increase responsibility or danger. A virile man can be afraid of more virility. If he's driving his car too fast already, he may look for cream of chicken or malted milk. So with the feminine man. He may not want more virility because he has no habits for it. What's the use of commanding women he could not command before, if he does not know how to fight off other men, and is not ready to learn. What freezes the homosexual in his homosexuality is not fear of women so much as fear of the masculine world with which he must war if he wishes to keep the woman.

Interviewer: What you're saying then might be put this way: in choosing bull's balls, the man whether strong or weak must be ready to offer up something feminine in himself. So as to leave himself less feminine afterward?

Mailer: Perfect.

Interviewer: Which is to say that we cannot select effectively unless the action we choose exists in a real and close correspondence to the new proportions our soul desires for itself.

Mailer: Yes.

Interviewer: If we wish to be more masculine we must first satisfy something feminine in ourselves.

Mailer: The reverse is also true. If we eat a bland food, a food we can dominate completely, that is to say a food whose character, whose — permit me — whose echo of the soul, is compliant, tender, passive to our seizure of it, we satisfy something masculine in ourselves. A man with ulcers is burning with the masculine need to dominate details in his life he simply cannot dominate. So in drinking milk, a bland food, a food more feminine than himself, he can discharge this backed-up masculinity. But of course he uses up masculinity in eating bland food, he alters his proportions.

Interviewer: You imply he has no choice?

Mailer: Not if he's sick with an ulcer. Bull's balls and tequila would have him run amok or fall into a hospital bed.

Interviewer: Since the proportion of masculinity and femininity in oneself would tend I think to remain more or less stable, what it comes down to is that people choose bull's balls only when they want to change.

Mailer: Yes. Only a few people want bull's balls at any one time. The existential gamble is too fine, it leads to greater seriousness, greater commitment in one's life, or to greater danger. One might think one wanted such change, but at the moment of digesting it, at the moment of choosing to open those reservoirs of enzymes, those ductless glands which are able to reach the finest molecules, The Eater might to his surprise feel panic, might be too cowardly to take on the consequences implicit in the essence of true bull's balls. So an imperfect cowardly digestion would take place. And its odor, the odor of fear, would be revealed next day in the stool, revealed to that part of the unconscious we may just as well begin to call The Critic. The Critic having a fine edge for form would also detect that the shape of the stool was slack.

Interviewer: If The Eater accepted the challenge, the stool would be different?

Mailer: The smell of a decent death would be present, the soul in the balls of the bull would have entered the body of the man who ate it. That particular soul would have risen to a higher existence. So the stool would have an aroma of content. As indeed it often does. What is so particularly hideous in a really bad smell is that one breathes the odor of a partial death, a soul has been torn on a rack. Part of it was seized by The Eater, part was refused, and so is dying in the stool.

Interviewer: Is it always the fault of The Eater? What if the food is bad?

Mailer: Then the choice is more complex, as for fact it always is in life. For no food is altogether perfect, and if it is almost perfect, it is still bound to have a most particular character which may not correspond too closely to the specific need of The Eater. Sometimes good food cannot be digested well because the requirements of The Eater were too narrow. So the partial death of the food cannot be digested well because the requirements of The Eater were too narrow. So the partial death of the food might smell bitter, it would know the bitterness of being rejected by a larger being which was too stingy. Or conversely it might be digested too greedily, too avariciously, by The Eater, and so suggest it was bruised. Such a death might smell of wine. The corruption of The Eater would be present within it.

Interviewer: And bad food. What of bad food?

Mailer: Its death would almost always be partial I should think, and it would be drowned in bile, and the body of The Eater would express his contempt at how bad the life had been, at how little the death had to offer. But if the best were extracted from the bad food, its odor might also prove decent or half-decent. It might have died well.

Interviewer: How could that be?

Mailer: Something good in the bad food might have taken a brave leap and met The Eater. So there might be some trace of dignity in the death of those souls. They might be complete, not partial. There might be the decent smell of a hay field. Grass and weeds are mediocre after all, but their death is complete when they're reaped, and if the weather is good they die well. There are arts to digesting bad food. The poor know them better than the rich. Most of the people on earth would get indigestion from good food.

Interviewer: What about the man with ulcers?

Mailer: The greater part of milk becomes urine and urine is another discussion.

Interviewer: No soul in it?

Mailer: Just spirit.

Interviewer: To think I asked a simple question about a man with an ulcer who takes a glass of milk.

Mailer: I wish you hadn't.

Interviewer: Do you feel ready to discuss the meaning of urine and its link to the Spirit?

Mailer: I don't. I fear I don't. It is a day's journey.

Interviewer: Later perhaps.

Mailer: Later. We must discuss it later.

Interviewer: Let's go back to where we were.

Mailer (*gloomily*): I distrust all talk of Soul and Spirit. I dislike styles which use such words.

Interviewer: I want to know what happens with food which is the reverse of bull's balls, with food which is weaker than The Eater, calming, sedative, gentle, feminine, creamed chicken and so on.

Mailer: A brave man who wishes to become less brave is eating it?

Interviewer: If you wish.

Mailer: At the critical moment, at the meeting of the opposites, he might give up his courage with grace, he might absorb the gentler qualities his being requested for that meal with good spirit and deep relaxation. His stool would have a happy smell. A gentle soul would have been received completely. But if, at the critical moment, The Eater rebelled, was horrified at the amount of manliness which must be devoted to the chicken, if The Eater felt shame at deserting danger and looking for calm, then indeed the chicken would be poorly used, the death of its souls would be most incomplete, and the odor would be sour. Gentleness refused turns sour. It curdles.

Interviewer: You're saying that the secret emotions of one's being, the basic emotions, courage and cowardice, betray their presence in the odor.

Mailer: And greed as well, or cupidity, ambition, compassion, love, trust, tenderness, savagery. The way in which we take souls from the food is the mirror of the dirty ape inside. If most of us abhor shit, it is because most of us are a little hideous inside.

Interviewer: Tyrants to the weak?

Mailer: Tyrants to the souls in the food who at that moment are more helpless than ourselves. Beyond a doubt.

Interviewer: Of course there's always ptomaine.

Mailer (*ignoring this*): Ambitious people pass bad shit. Because they use people around them. They certainly use people who are under them. I once met a very wealthy man whose mistress could talk about nothing but food. She was obsessed with what everyone around her had had to eat that day. It's taken me until now to realize that she saw herself as food for the tycoon, his family, and friends. Everyone at her dinner table was a potential cannibal to her person. So she had to know what you ate the night before because that to her was a clue which showed whether you had designs on her precise flesh.

Interviewer: You mean she saw herself as a certain kind of food?

Mailer: Rock hen, no doubt.

Interviewer: You're beginning to enjoy yourself too much. I think it's time we closed for the day.

Mailer: What a long day.

Interviewer: Would you round off our inquiry with a remark?

Mailer: A commercial remark?

Interviewer: Let us say a capsule.

Mailer: Ambitious societies loathe scatological themes and are obsessed with them.

Interviewer: Disappointing.

Mailer: Not at all. One could study the past with such a thesis as the tool. If indications in Mayan culture show much scatology, one can assume that civilization died from an excess of ambition which throttled the Being of too many.

Interviewer: And if there is no trace of scatology?

Mailer: If by the internal logic of the findings, the art, the fecal or non-fecal forms of the pottery, the wall painting, the architecture, there seems little scatology, one may assume there was not enough ambition, that the culture was calm, well-regulated, and was probably destroyed by a catastrophe which left it too passive to find the power to rise again.

Interviewer: You're enjoying yourself much too much. Tomorrow you must speak more of form.

Mailer: I will not enjoy myself much tomorrow.

Interviewer: You know you never came back to Picasso and why he is good for your eyes.

Mailer: Now I fear we will never get back.

Interviewer: Of course we will. Why not?

Mailer: Beyond form, is soul, spirit, madness, eternity, and the void.

Interviewer: I will try to sleep on that.

Poems

One of the princes in the palace guard around the Kennedys once saw fit to tell a wife of mine that I was "an intellectual adventurer." I was struck with the accuracy of the remark. Only an intellectual adventurer would write an open poem to the President. It came at a curious time in the inner life of JFK because he was contemplating the possibilities of an all-out fallout-shelter drive, which if successful (and the largest campaigns in America seem to be the easiest ones) would have left us Egyptian as a nation: a million underground one-room crypts stocked to the barrel top with canned goods, toys, and the beginnings (undertaken by children) of cave drawings. Something went wrong with the campaign; maybe the President had a bad dream. At any rate this poem was one of a hundred thousand items which might have been present to shift his mind.

N. M.

OPEN POEM TO
JOHN FITZGERALD KENNEDY

fallout
  is the hormone
  of the small town mind

a fallout shelter
  is sex

    think how warm
      at the thought
    are all of U
    and little Mrs. USA
    bonging the gong
          below

while bigcity flesh
all that blond hair
      and black hair
      straight and long
      short and highly curled
      floating in through
            the trees
        a dew
        of homogenized bone
        and blood mist
    atom bombs
      are not so bad
      says small-time
        in the town mind
      they disinfect
        the big city
      and jazz us to the toes
        out here in God's Country

    fingering is lovely
      on the edge of the grave.

Mr. President
     you realize of course
     that your shelter program
          for every home owner
          is sexing up the countryside
          and killing us in the
               bigcity bar.
     If this is good
          for the vitality
          of the nation
     (I mean that countryside
          could stand some sex)
          then Mr. President
          you are a genius
          and corporation executives
          living in the suburbs
          with the five thousand
                         dollar
                         shelters
          ought to salute you.
                    I do.

POEM TO THE BOOK REVIEW
AT *TIME*

You will keep hiring
    picadors from the back row
    and pic the bull back
    far back along his spine
You will pass a wine
    poisoned on the vine
You will saw the horns off
    and murmur
The bulls are
    ah, the bulls are not
    what once they were
Before the corrida is over
    there will be Russians in the plaza
Swine some of you will say
what did we wrong?
and go forth to kiss the conqueror.

CLASSES

When I was young
I went to the
Bowery and
slept in a flop-
house.
      Next morning
my mother said
to me, "Son, don't
come in the house.
Take off your clothes
in the hall
         and
I'll run a bath."

But my wife
has a moth-
er who would
have said on
her return,
    "Oh good.
      You're just in time.
I hope you've
caught some lice.
Don't take off
    a thing.
We're going to visit
    a woman I detest
and I want you to sit
    on all her seats."

AN AMERICAN DREAM

Mailer's first novel since The Deer Park *was announced in his "Big Bite" column in* Esquire *of December, 1963. The previous summer, he had published a review of the current work of nine of his fellow writers, and many of the words he had to say were harsh. Some readers took his announcement of his novel to be an assertion that through it he intended to repair the sad state of American letters, so anticipation of the work caused a stir. He serialized it in* Esquire, *nine installments in eight issues, from January through August, 1964, and Dial published it whole in 1965. The initial reception of the book was mixed, though with critical disapproval somewhat in the majority. In retrospect, critics have come to regard the book more highly. The present excerpt is simply the first two chapters of the Dial edition. Though Mailer did considerable revising after serialization, the reader should be able to get the flavor of what it was like to read the chapters as the first published installments of the much heralded fiction emerged.*

Chapter 1, The Harbors of the Moon

I met Jack Kennedy in November, 1946. We were both war heroes, and both of us had just been elected to Congress. We went out one night on a double date and it turned out to be a fair evening for me. I seduced a girl who would have been bored by a diamond as big as the Ritz.

She was Deborah Caughlin Mangaravidi Kelly, of the Caughlins first, English-Irish bankers, financiers and priests; the Mangaravidis, a Sicilian issue from the Bourbons and the Hapsburgs; Kelly's family was just Kelly; but he had made a million two hundred times. So there was a vision of treasure, far-off blood, and fear. The night I met her we had a wild ninety minutes in the back seat of my car parked behind a trailer truck on a deserted factory street in Alexandria, Virginia. Since Kelly owned part of the third largest trucking firm in the Midwest and West, I may have had a speck of genius to try for his daughter where I did. Forgive me. I thought the road to President might begin at the entrance to her Irish heart.

She heard the snake rustle however in *my* heart; on the telephone next morning she told me I was evil, awful and evil, and took herself back to the convent in London where she had lived at times before. I did not know as yet that ogres stand on guard before the portal of an heiress. Now in retrospect I can say with cheer: that was the closest *I* came to being President. (By the time I found Deborah again—all of seven years later in Paris—she was no longer her father's delight, and we were married in a week. Like any tale which could take ten books, it is best to quit it by a parenthesis—less than ten volumes might be untrue.)

Of course Jack has gone on a bit since those days, and I have traveled up and I have voyaged down and I've gone up and down, but I remember a full moon the night we had our double date, and to be phenomenologically precise, there was also a full moon on the night I led my patrol to the top of a particular hill in Italy, and a full moon the night I met another girl, and a full moon. . . . There are times when I like to think I still have my card in the intellectual's guild, but I seem to be joining company with that horde of the mediocre and the mad who listen to popular songs and act upon coincidence. The real difference between the President and myself may be that I ended with too large an appreciation of the moon, for I looked down the abyss on the first night I killed: four men, four very separate Germans, dead under a full moon—whereas Jack, for all I know, never saw the abyss.

Of course, I did not have any illusion that my heroism was the equal of his. I got good for one night. I was a stiff, overburdened, nervous young Second Lieutenant, fresh from Harvard, graduated a year behind Prince Jack (we never met—not there). I had gone into the Army with a sweaty near-adolescent style, Harvard on the half-shell ("Raw-Jock" Rojack was the sporting name bestowed on me in House Football) and I had been a humdrum athlete and, as a student, excessively bright: Phi Beta Kappa, *summa cum laude*, Government.

Small wonder I was thus busy working to keep some government among the hard-nosed Southerners and young Mafiosos from the Bronx who made up the double nucleus of my platoon, working so busily that death this night first appeared to me as a possibility considerably more agreeable than my status in some further disorder. I really didn't care much longer whether I stayed alive. When I steered us up the hill therefore to get pinned down in a long, bad line, one hundred feet from the summit, a modest twin dome, a double hill with a German machine gun on one knoll and a German machine gun on the other, I was so ready to die in atonement I was not even scared.

Trapped beneath a rusty sputter—the guns had not quite found me nor any of the others—the full moon giving a fine stain to the salient of our mood (which was fear and funk and a sniff of the grave), I could nonetheless feel danger withdraw from me like an angel, withdraw like a retreating wave over a quiet sea, sinking quietly into the sand, and I stood and then I ran, I ran up the hill into the aisle of safety I felt opening for me which is part of what captured that large decoration later, because the route I took was under the separate fire of each of those guns and the two together could stitch you to a pulp. Their fire was jagged, however, it was startled, and as I ran, I threw my carbine away, out ten yards to the front of me, crossed my arms to pull a grenade from each shirt pocket, pulled the rings with my teeth, which I had hardly been able to do in practice (much too hard on the teeth), released the spoon handles, the fuse now lit, and spitting, and shot my arms out like the wings of the letter Y. The grenades sailed away in separate flights and I had time to stop, turn around, and dive back for my carbine which I had overrun.

Years later I read *Zen in the Art of Archery* and understood the book. Because I did not throw the grenades on that night on the hill under the moon, *it* threw them, and *it* did a near-perfect job. The grenades went off somewhere between five and ten yards over each machine gun, *blast, blast,* like a boxer's tatoo, one-two, and I was exploded in the butt from a piece of my own shrapnel, whacked with a delicious pain clean as a mistress' sharp teeth going "Yummy" in your rump, and then the barrel of my carbine swung around like a long fine antenna and pointed itself at the machine-gun hole on my right where a great bloody sweet German face, a healthy spoiled overspoiled young beauty of a face, mother-love all over its making, possessor of that overcurved mouth which only great fat sweet young faggots can have when their rectum is tuned and entertained from adolescence on, came crying, sliding, smiling up over the edge of the hole, "Hello death!" blood and mud like the herald of sodomy upon his chest, and I pulled the trigger as if I were squeezing the softest breast of the softest pigeon which ever flew, still a woman's breast takes me now and then to the pigeon on that trigger, and the shot cracked like a birth twig across my palm, *whop!* and the round went in at the base of his nose and spread and I saw his face sucked in backward upon the gouge of the bullet, he looked suddenly like an old man, toothless, sly, reminiscent of lechery. Then he whimpered *"Mutter,"* one yelp from the first memory of the womb, and down he went into his own blood just in time, timed like the interval in a shooting gallery, for the next was up, his hole-mate, a hard avenging specter with a pistol in his hand and one arm off, blown off, rectitude like a stringer of saliva across the straight edge of his lip, the straightest lip I ever saw, German-Protestant rectitude. *Whap!* went my carbine and the hole was in his heart and he folded back the long arm with the pistol, back across his chest to cover his new hole and went down straight and with a clown's deep gloom as if he were sliding down a long thin pipe, and then I turned, feeling something tear in my wound, nice in its pain, a good blood at liberty, and I took on the other two coming out of the other hole, one short stocky ape-like wretch with his back all askew, as if he'd had a false stuffed hump which shrapnel had disgorged beyond his shoulder blade: I fired at him and he went down and I never knew where it hit nor quite saw his face; then the last stood up straight with a bayonet in his hand and invited me to advance. He was bleeding below his belt. Neat and clean was his shirt, level the line of his helmet, and nothing but blood and carnage below the belt. I started to rise. I wanted to charge as if that were our contract, and held, for I could not face his eyes, they now contained all of it, the two grenades, the blood on my thigh, the fat faggot, the ghost with the pistol, the hunchback, the blood, those bloody screams that never sounded, it was all in his eyes, he had eyes I was to see once later on an autopsy table in a small town in Missouri, eyes belonging to a redneck farmer from a deep road in the Ozarks, eyes of blue, so perfectly blue and mad they go all the way in deep into celestial vaults of sky, eyes which go back all the way to God is the way I think I heard it said once in the South, and I faltered before that stare, clear as ice in the moonlight, and hung on one knee, not knowing if I could push my wound, and suddenly it was all gone, the clean presence of *it*, the grace, *it* had deserted me in the instant I hesitated, and now I had no stomach to go, I could charge his bayonet no more. So I fired. And missed. And fired again. And missed. Then he threw his bayonet at me. It did not reach. He was too weak. It struck a stone instead and made a quivering whanging sound like the yowl of a tomcat on the jump. Then it stopped between us. The light was going out in his eye. It started to collect, to coagulate into the thick jelly which forms on the pupil of a just-dead dog, and he died then, and fell over. Like a noble tree with rotten roots. And the platoon was up around me, shooting a storm into those two holes, and they were cheering, buzzing, kissing my mouth (one of the Italians for certain), pounding my back. "Get off him, he's wounded," shouted somebody, the Sergeant, and I felt like a halfback who has caught a fifty-yard pass and run another forty-eight for the longest touchdown in the history of the school, except that the final excellence of it was smuggled away since the ball squiggled out of my arms as I ran it out past the end zone. I had scored, but no football in my belly at the end, just six points. And those blue eyes kept staring into the new flesh of my memory until I went over with a thud, a wave from the wound carrying me back, forcing my head to the ground with some desire of its own. "Medics," I heard a man yell.

I was carried out later on a stretcher, an X-ray showed a minor crack and small split in the girdle of the pelvis. I was evacuated to a base hospital, then sent to New York where I was given a Distinguished Service Cross, not anything less, and was used for the last year to bring good public relations for the Army. Which I did, showing the trace of a distinguished limp. A hero in mid-'44, a hero for all of '45, surviving even V-J Day, I had my pick of opportunities and used them. I went around for a time speaking with Mrs. Roosevelt at one honorable drive after another, and she liked me. She encouraged me to think of politics. Those became the years when the gears worked together, the contacts and the insights, the style and the manufacture of oneself. It all turned together very well, I was a curiosity after all, a most special product; I was the one intellectual in America's history with a DSC and I spoke in public with a modest warrior's charm.

About the time the Party machine in New York County was sorting through its culls and giving me odd off-hand invitations to lunch with the Cardinal and the Bishop ("One question, son," asked the first Eminence, "do you believe in God?" "Yes, your Eminence") Mrs. Roosevelt was introducing me to Protestant gentry and Jewish gentry and, yes, it all began to fit and fit so well I came out, by the end, a candidate for Congress, and was then elected. Congressman Stephen Richards Rojack, Democrat from New York.

Now, I could go into more detail about the precise sequence of steps which left me a young Congressman in 1946 at the age of twenty-six—the moves were not automatic after all, but that would merely describe the adventures of the part which I as a young actor was playing. There are any number of movie stars who capture the love of women they have never seen; the poor husbands of those women are in competition with a man they cannot meet. But I think of those particular few movie stars who are not only profiles for a great lover, but homosexual and private in their life. They must live with insanity on every breath. And something which could correspond to this was true for me. Where many another young athlete or hero might have had a vast and continuing recreation with sex, I was lost in a private kaleidoscope of death. I could not forget the fourth soldier. His eyes had come to see what was waiting on the other side, and they told me then that death was a creation more dangerous than life. I could have had a career in politics if only I had been able to think that death was zero, death was everyone's emptiness. But I knew it was not. I remained an actor. My personality was built upon a void. Thus I quit my place in politics almost as quickly as I gained it, for by '48 I chose to bolt the Democratic Party and run for office on the Progressive ticket. Henry Wallace, Glen Taylor, and me. I had reasons for the choice, some honorable, some spurious, but one motive now seems clear — I wanted to depart from politics before I was separated from myself forever by the distance between my public appearance which had become vital on television, indeed nearly robust, and my secret frightened romance with the phases of the moon. About the month you decide not to make a speech because it is the week of the full lunar face you also know if still you are sane that politics is not for you and you are not for politics.

Now, that was a long time ago. Since then I had, as I say, gone up, and I had certainly gone down, and I had gone up and down. I was now at a university in New York, a professor of existential psychology with the not inconsiderable thesis that magic, dread, and the perception of death were the roots of motivation; I was a personality on television and an author of sorts: I had had one popular book published, *The Psychology of the Hangman*, a psychological study of the styles of execution in different states and nations — death by guillotine, firing squad, by rope, by electric chair, by gas pellets — an interesting book. I had also — as I indicated — become the husband of an heiress, and I had been most unsuccessful at that. In fact I had come to the end of a very long street. Call it an avenue. For I had come to decide I was finally a failure.

I had had a bad year this last year, and for a while it got very bad; I may as well admit that for the first time in my life I had come to understand there was suicide in me. (Murder I had known was there for a long time.) It was the worst of discoveries, this suicide. Murder, after all, has exhilaration within it. I do not mean it is a state to entertain; the tension which develops in your body makes you sicken over a period, and I had my fill of walking about with a chest full of hatred and a brain jammed to burst, but there is something manly about containing your rage, it is so difficult, it is like carrying a two-hundred-pound safe up a cast-iron hill. The exhilaration comes I suppose from possessing such strength. Besides, murder offers the promise of vast relief. It is never unsexual.

But there is little which is sexual about suicide. It is a lonely landscape with the pale light of a dream and something is calling to you, a voice on the wind. Certain nights I would go leaden with dread because I could hear the chamber music tuning up, tuning up and near to pitch. (Yes, murder sounds like a symphony in your head, and suicide is a pure quartet.) I was approaching my forty-fourth year, but for the first time I knew why some of my friends, and so many of the women I had thought I understood, could not bear to be alone at night.

I had spent the last year parting company with my wife. We had been married most intimately and often most unhappily for eight years, and for the last five I had been trying to evacuate my expeditionary army, that force of hopes, all-out need, plain virile desire and commitment which I had spent on her. It was a losing war, and I wanted to withdraw, count my dead, and look for love in another land, but she was a great bitch, Deborah, a lioness of the species: unconditional surrender was her only raw meat. A Great Bitch has losses to calculate after all if the gent gets away. For ideally a Great Bitch delivers extermination to any bucko brave enough to take carnal knowledge of her. She somehow *fails in her role* (as psychoanalysts, those frustrated stage directors, might say) if the lover escapes without being maimed to the nines or nailed to the mast. And Deborah had gotten her hooks into me, eight years ago she had clinched the hooks and they had given birth to other hooks. Living with her I was murderous; attempting to separate, suicide came into me. Some psychic bombardment of the will to live had begun, a new particle of love's mysterious atom had been discovered—the itch to jump. I had been on a balcony ten stories high talking to my host, the cocktail party was done, and we stood looking down on Sutton Place, not talking about Deborah—what else was there not to talk about this last long year?—and I was wondering, as indeed often I did, whether this old buddy, comfortably drunk with me, a pleasant-looking stud of forty-six, with a waist kept trim by squash at the New York A.C. and a rogue's look in the eye kept alive by corners he cut making his little brokerage prosper (not to speak of the women he met for lunch—he had a flair, this buddy), well, wondering whether his concern was so true for me as the timbre of his voice, now sincere, now so place-your-bets sincere, or if he'd been banging my blessed Deborah five times a year, five times each of the last eight years, forty glorious bangeroos upon the unconscious horror of my back (something so hot they could hardly contain themselves, and kept it down to five each twelve-month out of delicacy, out of a neatness which recognized that if ever they let themselves go, it would all go crash and boom) well, as I say, I stood there, not knowing if Old Buddy was in the Carnal Delights, or a true sword and friend, or even both—there was a wife or two after all with whom I had done the five times eight years bit, and sweet was the prize—no offering like a wife so determined to claw her man that months of hatred are converted to Instant Sweet for the passing stud in the hay, and I felt all the stirrings of real compassion talking to *her* husband next time out. So all was possible—either this guy before me now suffered conceivably a true concern for an old friend and his difficult wife, or was part of the difficulty, or indeed yes was both, both, precisely like me so many times, and before the straight-out complexity of this, the simple incalculable difficulty of ever knowing what is true with an interesting woman, I was lost. I tell you in shame that for those eight years I could point with certainty to only five bona-fide confessed infidelities by Deborah; she had indeed announced each of them to me, each an accent, a transition, a concrete step in the descent of our marriage, a curtain to each act in a five-act play: but beyond this, in the great unknown, were anywhere from two hundred to precisely no infidelities, for Deborah was an artist in that great dialectic of uncertainty where lies lead to truth, and truth begets the shimmering of lies—"Are you *mad?*" she would ask when I would disclose my suspicions of a particular gentleman or lad, "Why, he's a boy," or "Don't you know he's *repulsive* to me," which she always said in her best London voice, five years of Catholic schooling in England contributing much to the patrician parts of her American tongue. Yes, before the uncertainty of this, feeling like a scientist of love whose instruments of detection were either wholly inaccurate or unverifiably acute, I stood up in the middle of my conversation with old friend rogue, and simply heaved my cakes, all the gin-and-tonics, anchovy paste, pigs-in-blankets, shrimp cum cocktail sauce, and last six belts of bourbon zip over his balcony and down in a burning cascade of glob and glottle, a thundering herd of love's poisoned hoofs.

"Oh, my God," said the friend, out-rogued for once.

"Stow it," I grunted.

"My God," he repeated, "it's dropped on the second floor."

We had both expected as a matter of course—the seizure was so pure—that my paint would land on the doorman's ears. Instead, some tenant would soon complain. The sheer mechanics of it had me next to laughter—how did one send an awning to the cleaners?

"I suppose I've got to tell them," said the friend.

"Let the rain wash away what the moonlight fails to bless," said I, in a tone I had come to abhor, a sort of boozed Connecticut gentry in the voice, putting together poetic phrases which were unpoetic, part of the product of living with Deborah's near-English lilts and lecturing too many classes over too many unfulfilled hours. "In fact, old buddy, leave me. If you can bear it."

So I stood on the balcony by myself and stared at the moon which was full and very low. I had a moment then. For the moon spoke back to me. By which I do not mean that I heard voices, or Luna and I indulged in the whimsy of a dialogue, no, truly it was worse than that. Something in the deep of that full moon, some tender and not so innocent radiance traveled fast as the thought of lightning across our night sky, out from the depths of the dead in those caverns of the moon, out and a leap through space and into me. And suddenly I understood the moon. Believe it if you will. The only true journey of knowledge is from the depth of one being to the heart of another and I was nothing but open raw depths at that instant alone on the balcony, looking down on Sutton Place, the spirits of the food and drink I had ingested wrenched out of my belly and upper gut, leaving me in raw Being, there were clefts and rents which cut like geological faults right through all the lead and concrete and kapok and leather of my ego, that mutilated piece of insulation, I could feel my Being, ridiculous enough, what! I could feel lights shifting inside myself, drifting like vapors over the broken rocks of my ego while a forest of small nerves jumped up, foul in their odor, smelling for all the world like the rotten, carious shudder of a decayed tooth. Half-drunk, half-sick, half on the balcony, half off, for I had put my leg over the balustrade as if I were able better to breathe with one toe pointing at the moon, I looked into my Being, all that lovely light and rotting nerve, and proceeded to listen. Which is to say, I looked out deep into that shimmer of past death and new madness, that platinum lady with her silver light, and she was in my ear, I could hear her music: "Come to me," she was saying, "Come now. Now!" and I could feel my other foot go over the balustrade, and I was standing on the wrong side of the railing, only my fingers (since my thumbs were up and pointing like horns at the moon), only my eight fingers to hold me from the plunge. But it was worse than that. Because I knew I would fly. My body would drop like a sack, down with it, bag of clothes, bones, and all, but I would rise, the part of me which spoke and thought and had its glimpses of the landscape of my Being, would soar, would rise, would leap the miles of darkness to that moon. Like a lion would I join the legions of the past and share their power. "Come now," said the moon, "now is your moment. What joy in the flight." And I actually let one hand go. It was my left. Instinct was telling me to die.

Which instinct and where? The right hand tightened in its grip, and I whipped half-around to the balcony, almost banging into the rail with my breast, my back now to the street and the sky. Only if I turned my head could I see the Lady.

"Drop," she said one more time, but the moment had gone. Now if I dropped, all of me passed down. There would be no trip.

"You can't die yet," said the formal part of my brain, "you haven't done your work."

"Yes," said the moon, "you haven't done your work, but you've lived your life, and you are dead with it."

"Let me be not all dead," I cried to myself, and slipped back over the rail, and dropped into a chair. I was sick. I assure you I was sick in a way I had never been sick before. Deep in a fever, or bumping through the rapids of a bad nausea, one's soul could always speak to one, "Look what this illness is doing to us, you coward," that voice might say and one would shake or twist in the fever, but that at least was a nightmare. This illness now, huddling in the deck chair, was an extinction. I could feel what was good in me going away, going away perhaps forever, rising after all to the moon, my courage, my wit, ambition and hope. Nothing but sickness and dung remained in the sack of my torso. And the moon looked back, baleful in her radiance now. Will you understand me if I say that at that moment I felt the other illness come to me, that I knew then if it took twenty years or forty for my death, that if I died from a revolt of the cells, a growth against the design of my organs, that this was the moment it all began, this was the hour when the cells took their leap? Never have I known such a sickening—the retaliation of the moon was complete. What an utter suffocation of my faculties, as if I had disappointed a lady and now must eat the cold tapeworm of her displeasure. Nothing noble seemed to remain of me.

Well, I got up from that deck chair and back to the living room which felt like an indoor pool. So steamy was the air on my stomach, just so ultra-violet seemed the light. I must have been in some far-gone state because there was an aureole about each electric light, each bulb stood out like a personage, and I remember thinking: of course, this is how they appeared to Van Gogh at the end.

"You don't look too well," said the host.

"Well, buddy, I feel worse than I look. Give me a drop of blood, will you?"

The bourbon tasted like linseed oil and lit a low smoke in the liverish caverns of my belly. I could feel some effulgence of the moon glowing through the windows and dread came back like a hoot from a bully on the street outside.

"It's a great night for the race," I said.

"What race?" said my host. It was obvious he wished me to be gone.

"The human race. Ho. Ho. Ho," I said.

"Steve!"

"I'm on my way."

My hand offered him the glass as if it were the gift of a shiny apple, and then I strolled, closing my host's door so carefully it failed to shut. I turned around to jam it once again and felt a force on me as palpable as a magnetic field. "Get out of here," said a voice in my brain. The elevator took too long. I rang, and rang again, but there was not a sound from the cable or the cage. I broke into a galloping sweat. "If you're not out of here in thirty seconds," said the same voice, "your new disease takes another step. Metastases are made of moments like this, lover-man." So I bolted down the stairs. It was ten flights taken in two banks each, twenty banks of concrete steps, cement-block walls painted guacamole-green, blood-iron railing made of pipe, and I flew down pursued by panic, because I had lost my sense of being alive and here on earth, it was more as if I had died and did not altogether know it, this might be the way it was for the first hour of death if you chose to die in bed — you could blunder through some endless repetition believing your life was still here.

The door to the lobby was locked. Of course. I tired of beating on it with my hands — I was half certain I was really gone — and shifted to one foot, took off a shoe, began to whang away. The doorman opened in a pet. "What's going on?" he asked. "I go up in the elevator and you ain't there." He was Italian, some stout dull lump of rejection from the Mafia — they had assigned him to this job about the time they decided he was hopeless for waiting tables in a hopeless bar. "Ain't you got any consideration?" he asked.

"Up your ass, friend." I put on my shoe and walked past him. As I was going to the street he muttered behind me, "Up yours too."

Walking fast I was two blocks away before I saw I had forgotten my overcoat. It was a night in late March, it was cold, it was much colder now than it had been on the balcony, and I shivered from the realization, the wind reaching in to the forest of nerves on my gut. I could feel those nerves wriggling now like a hive of worms; they were flinching as the wind rode by. A familiar misery was on me. I was separate from Deborah as much as a week or two at a time, but there would come a moment, there would always come a moment, after everything else had gone, when it was impossible not to call her. At moments like that I would feel as if I had committed hari-kari and was walking about with my chest separated from my groin. It was a moment which was physically insupportable, it was the remains of my love for her, love draining from the wound, leaving behind its sense of desolation as if all the love I possessed were being lost and some doom whose dimensions I could hardly glimpse was getting ready on the consequence. I hated her more than not by now, my life with her had been a series of successes cancelled by quick failures, and I knew so far as I could still keep any confidence that she had done her best to birth each loss, she was an artist at sucking the marrow from a broken bone, she worked each side of the street with a skill shared only in common by the best of streetwalkers and the most professional of heiresses. Once, for an instance, at a party, a friend of hers, a man I was never able to like, a man who never liked me, had proceeded to beat on me so well for "celebrity" on television that he was carried away. He invited me to box. Well, we were both drunk. But when it came to boxing I was a good *torero de salón*. I was not bad with four drinks and furniture to circle about. So we sparred to the grim amusement and wild consternation of the ladies, the sober evaluation of the gents. I was feeling mean. I roughed him up a hitch or two in the clinches, I slapped him at will with my jab, holding my hand open but swinging the slaps in, he was such an ass, and after it went on for a minute, he was beginning in compensation to throw his punches as hard (and wild) as he could, whereas I was deepening into concentration. Which is the first reward of the ring. I was sliding my moves off the look in his eye and the shift of his fists, I had settled into the calm of a pregnant typhoon, the kill was sweet and up in me, I could feel it twenty moves away, he was going to finish with three slugs to the belly and his arms apart, that is what it would take, his eye was sweaty and I was going keen. Just then his wife broke in. "Stop!" she cried, "absolutely stop!" and came between us.

He was a bad type. "Why'd you stop it?" he asked. "It was getting to be fun."

"Fun!" she said, "you were going to get killed."

Well, the point to the story is that when I turned around to wink at Deborah—she had heard me talk much about boxing but had never seen me fight—I discovered she had quit the room.

"Of course I left," she said later, "it was a sight, bullying that poor man."

"Poor? He's bigger than I am."

"And ten years older."

That took the taste away. Next time some passing friend invited me to spar at a party—not until a year later I believe, not *all* the parties ended in a bout—I refused. He filed the needle to a point. I still refused. When we got home, she told me I was afraid.

It was worth little to refer to the first episode. "This man, at least," she said, "was younger than you."

"I could have taken him."

"I don't believe it. Your mouth was weak, and you were perspiring."

When I looked into myself I was not certain any longer that there had been no fear. So it took on prominence for me. I did not know any longer.

One could multiply that little puncture by a thousand; Deborah was an artist with the needle, and never pinked you twice on the same spot. (Unless it had turned to ulcer.) So I hated her, yes indeed I did, but my hatred was a cage which wired my love, and I did not know if I had the force to find my way free. Marriage to her was the armature of my ego; remove the armature and I might topple like clay. When I was altogether depressed by myself it seemed as if she were the only achievement to which I could point—I finally had been the man whom Deborah Caughlin Mangaravidi Kelly had lived with in marriage, and since she'd been notorious in her day, picking and choosing among a gallery of beaux: politicians of the first rank, racing drivers, tycoons, and her fair share of the more certified playboys of the Western world, she had been my entry to the big league. I had loved her with the fury of my ego, that way I loved her still, but I loved her the way a drum majorette loved the power of the band for the swell it gave to each little strut. If I was a war hero, an ex-Congressman, a professor of popular but somewhat notorious reputation, and a star of sorts on a television show which I cannot here even bear to explain, if I also had a major work on existential psychology, a herculean endeavor of six to twenty volumes which would (ideally) turn Freud on his head (but remained still in my own head) I had also the secret ambition to return to politics. I had the idea of running some day for Senator, an operation which would not be possible without the vast connections of Deborah's clan. Of course there had never been a cent from *them*—we lived on the money *I* made even if Deborah had the accumulated tastes and habits of the money Barney Oswald Kelly had made. She claimed he had cut her off when she married me—which is possible—but I always thought she lied. It was more probable she did not trust me enough to show the buried loot. Heiresses have a scale: they surrender their heart a quarter-century before they open the purse. I did not care about the money itself, I half hated it, in fact I might have despised the money if it had not become the manifest of how unconsummated and unmasculine was the core of my force. It was like being married to a woman who would not relinquish her first lover.

At any rate, such were my parts. Without Deborah they did not add to any more than another name for the bars and gossip columns of New York. With her beside me, I had leverage, however, I was one of the more active figures of the city—no one could be certain finally that nothing large would ever come from me. But for myself the evidence made no good case: probably I did not have the strength to stand alone.

The difficulty is that I have given an undue portrait of Deborah, and so reduce myself. She had, at her best, a winner's force, and when she loved me (which may be averaged out somewhere between every other day to one day in three) her strength seemed then to pass to mine and I was live with wit, I had vitality, I could depend on stamina, I possessed my style. It was just that the gift was only up for loan. The instant she stopped loving me—which could be for a fault so severe as failing to open the door with a touch of éclat, thereby reminding her of all the swords, humors, and arbiters who had opened doors for her on better nights—why then my psyche was whisked from the stage and stuffed in a pit. A devil's contract, and during all of this last year, not living with her and yet never separated, for though a week might go by or two weeks in which I hardly thought of her at all, I would nonetheless be dropped suddenly into an hour where all of my substance fell out of me and I had to see her. I had a physical need to see her as direct as an addict's panic waiting for his drug—if too many more minutes must be endured, who knows what intolerable damage can be done?

It was like this now. Walking the street just this cold night in March, the horrors were beginning. On these occasions when I had to see her, my instinct gave the warning that if I waited another half hour, even another ten minutes, I might lose her forever. It made no sense, I was almost always wrong in my anticipation of her mood, I was too rattled these months ever to divine what her mood might be, and yet I knew that the way I would probably lose her in the end was by waiting too long on some exceptional night when she might be hoping I would call. For once a certain moment was passed, once Deborah ever said to herself, "I am rid of him, I am rid of him now finally and forever," then it would all be gone. She was nothing if not final, she took forever to form her mind, but come the moment and she would not look back.

So I went into an outdoor booth, and shivering in the trapped cold air, I phoned her apartment. She was home—there were agonies on those nights I phoned and she was out—but she was home this night, and she was cordial. Which was a very bad sign.

"*Darling*," she said, "where have you been? You must rush over." She was a handsome woman, Deborah, she was big. With high heels she stood at least an inch over me. She had a huge mass of black hair and striking green eyes sufficiently arrogant and upon occasion sufficiently amused to belong to a queen. She had a large Irish nose and a wide mouth which took many shapes, but her complexion was her claim to beauty, for the skin was cream-white and her cheeks were colored with a fine rose, centuries of Irish mist had produced that complexion. It was her voice however which seduced one first. Her face was large and all-but-honest; her voice was a masterwork of treachery. Clear as a bell, yet slithery with innuendo, it leaped like a deer, slipped like a snake. She could not utter a sentence for giving a tinkle of value to some innocent word. It may have been the voice of a woman you would not trust for an instant, but I did not know if I could forget it.

"I'll be right over," I said.

"Run. You must *run*."

When we separated, she was the one who had moved out. Our marriage had been a war, a good eighteenth-century war, fought by many rules, most of them broken if the prize to be gained was bright enough, but we had developed the cheerful respect of one enemy general for another. So I had been able to admire the strategic splendor of leaving me in our apartment. It *stifled* her, she explained to me, it was a source of much misery. If we were to separate, there was small logic for her to remain behind in an apartment she did not like, no, it was better for her to leave me there, I was fond of the apartment after all. I was not, I had never been, but I had pretended to be fond. Therefore I inherited her misery. Now the apartment, the empty stadium of our marriage, stifled *me*, but I had not the pluck, the time, nor the clean desperation to move. I used it as a place to drop my dirty shirts. Meanwhile, she hopped from one fine suite to another; there was always a friend leaving for Europe, and no one was ready to remind Deborah she was very behind on the rent. (What cowards were her friends!) I would get the bill finally, it would be a knockout, $2700 for three months rent—I would hold it, no question of paying. Part of the attrition on my military reserves had been the expenses. Deborah got four hundred dollars a week—it was senseless to give her less, she would merely run up her bills, and I had been scuffling and humping, taking three hundred dollars for a spot appearance on a television show, and seven hundred fifty for a spiced-up lecture to some Ladies Auxiliary in Long Island—"The Existential Approach to

Sex." Yes, debt was grinding me bad, I was something like $16,000 in the hole already and probably worse — I did not care to count.

The apartment she had now was a small duplex suspended some hundred or more feet above the East River Drive, and every vertical surface within was covered with flock, which must have gone for twenty-five dollars a yard; a hot-house of flat velvet flowers, royal, sinister, cultivated in their twinings, breathed at one from all four walls, upstairs and down. It had the specific density of a jungle conceived by Rousseau, and Deborah liked it the best of her purloined pads. "I feel warm in here," she would say, "nice and *warm.*"

The maid let me in. "Madame is upstairs in the bedroom," she said with a smile. She was a young German maid who must have had an interesting life in the ruins of Berlin from the age of five, for nothing missed her attention. She had taken lately to smiling at me with a droll mocking compassionate and very wound-up spite which promised portfolios of detail if I were ever rich enough to turn her tongue just once. I was sometimes tempted to start, to grab her in the hall and take her spiced mouth, lay my tongue on hers and rustle up with a stroke those overtones of malicious music she could sing. What Madame did with me she knew too well because I might still spend a night with Deborah from time to time, but what Madame did with others . . . that would have to be bought.

I ascended the stairway, a padded perfumed aisle up a wall of flowers. Deborah was in bed. Her body was not only large but lazy and she hopped into bed whenever she did not know what else to do.

"My God," she said, "you look awful." Her mouth turned fond at the corners. She never disliked me so much as when I came to see her looking my best. "You really are a contemptible-looking creature this evening."

Did she know about the balcony? Sometimes I was convinced I was mad, because it seemed not at all exceptional to me that Deborah had been in touch with the moon and now had the word. She had powers, my Deborah, she was psychic to the worst degree, and she had the power to lay a curse. Once after a fight with her, I had been given traffic tickets three times in fifteen minutes, once for going down a one-way street, once for jumping a red light, and once because the policeman in the last car did not like my eye and decided I was drunk. That had all been in the form of a warning from Deborah, I was certain of that. I could see her waiting alone in bed, waving her long fingers languidly to spark the obedient diabolisms and traffic officers at her command.

"It was a bad party," I said.

"How is Philippe?"

"Looking well."

"He's a *very* attractive man. Don't you think so?" said Deborah.

"Everyone we know is attractive," I said to annoy her.

"Except you, pet. You look as if you've used up your liver for keeps this time."

"I'm not very happy," I said.

"Well, come *here* and live. There's no reason why you can't move back with me."

Her invitation was open. She wanted me to dispose of my apartment, sell our furniture, move in with her. After a month she would move out again, leaving me with the velvet flock.

"If you'd come this afternoon," she went on, "you could have seen Deirdre. Now she's off to school. You are a swine not to have seen her." Deirdre was her daughter, my step-daughter. Deborah's first husband had been a French count. He had died of a lingering illness after a year of marriage, and Deirdre, so far as I knew, had been the child of that marriage, a delicate haunted girl with eyes which contained a promise she would learn everything about you if she looked too long, and so chose not to look. I adored her, I had realized for years that being step-father to Deirdre was the most agreeable part of our marriage; for that reason I tried to see her as little as possible now.

"Is she pleased at going back to school this trip?"

"She would have been more pleased if you had come by." Deborah's complexion was mottling with red. When she became angry a red flush, raw as a rash, spotted her neck. "You pretended to love that child for so long, and now you give her no attention."

"It's too painful," I said.

"God, you're a whimperer," said Deborah. "Sometimes I lie here and wonder how you ever became a hero. You're such a bloody whimperer. I suppose the Germans were whimpering even worse than you. It must have been quite a sight. You whimpering and they whimpering, and you going pop pop pop with your little gun."

Never had she gone quite so far before. "How do you tell that story these days?" Deborah went on.

"I don't tell it."

"Except when you're too drunk to remember."

"I'm never too drunk to remember."

"I can't get over the way you look," Deborah exclaimed. "I mean you really look like some poor peddler from the Lower East Side."

"I'm descended from peddlers."

"Don't I know it, honey-one," said Deborah. "All those poor materialistic grabby little people."

"Well, they never hurt anyone particularly." This was a reference to her father.

"No, they didn't, and they didn't have the guts to do anything else either. Except to make your father brainy enough to make your mother and then make you." She said this with such a stir of fury that I moved uneasily. Deborah was violent. I had a bad scar on my ear. People thought it came from the ring, but the truth was less presentable — Deborah had once bitten it half-through in a fight.

"Go easy," I said.

"You're fragile tonight, aren't you?" She nodded, her face almost gentle, almost attentive, as if she were listening to the echo of an event. "I know something happened to you."

"I don't want to talk about it." Which was in effect a counterattack. Deborah could not bear not to know.

"I thought you were dead," said Deborah. "Isn't that funny. I was certain you were dead."

"Were you sorry?"

"Oh, I felt a great woe." She smiled. "I thought you were dead and you'd left a will that you wished to be cremated. I was going to keep your ashes in an urn. There — right by the window table. Each morning I was going to take a handful of your dust and drop it on the East River Drive. In time, who knows, you might have been *strewn* all over New York."

"I would have done my best to haunt you."

"Can't, pet. Not when you're cremated. That atomizes the soul. Didn't you know?" Her green eyes had a particularly bad light. "Come here, darling, and give a kiss."

"I'd rather not."

"Tell me why not."

"Because I threw up a while ago and my breath is foul."

"Bad smells never bother me."

"Well, they bother me. And you've been drinking rum. You smell Godawful." It was true. When she drank too much, a stench of sweet rot lifted from her. "The Irish were never meant to go near rum," I said, "it brings out the odor of their fat."

"Do you talk this way to all your little girls?"

She did not know what I did with the days and weeks I spent away from her. This was forever agitating her rage. Once, years ago, she uncovered an affair I had been keeping in a corner. It had been with a rather ordinary young lady who (for compensation, no doubt) had been a burning wizard in bed. Otherwise, the girl was undeniably plain. Somehow, Deborah learned about her. The subsequent details are vicious, private detectives, so forth, but the indigestible issue was that Deborah had gone with the private detective to a restaurant where the girl always had lunch and studied her through a meal, all through a long meal the poor girl ate by herself. What a scene followed!

"I don't think I've been quite so marooned in all my beloved life," Deborah had said. "I mean, *figure-toi*, pet, I had to keep up a conversation with the detective, a *horrible* man, and he was laughing at me. All that money spent on fees, and for what, a poor wet little mouse. She was even afraid of the *waitresses*, and this was a *tea*-room. What a big boy you must be to take up with a sparrow."

The real part of her fury was that no intrigue had ensued; if the affair had been with one of her friends, or with some other woman of parts, then Deborah could have gone to war and fought one of her grand campaigns, hook and eye, tooth and talon, a series of parties with exquisite confrontations; but I had merely been piddling and that was the unforgivable sin. Since that time Deborah spoke only of my *little girls*.

"What do you say to them, pet?" asked Deborah now, "do you say, 'Please stop drinking so much because you smell like a piece of fat,' or do you say, 'Oh God, darling, I love your stink?' "

The mottling had spread in ugly smears and patches upon her neck, her shoulders, and what I could see of her breast. They radiated a detestation so palpable that my body began to race as if a foreign element, a poison altogether suffocating, were beginning to seep through me. Did you ever feel the malignity which rises from a swamp? It is real, I could swear it, and some whisper of ominous calm, that heavy air one breathes in the hours before a hurricane, now came to rest between us. I was afraid of her. She was not incapable of murdering me. There are killers one is ready to welcome, I suppose. They offer a clean death and free passage to one's soul. The moon had spoken to me as just such an assassin. But Deborah promised bad burial. One would go down in one's death, and muck would wash over the last of one's wind. She did not wish to tear the body, she was out to spoil the light, and in an epidemic of fear, as if her face — that wide mouth, full-fleshed nose, and pointed green eyes, pointed as arrows — would be my first view of eternity, as if she were ministering angel (ministering devil) I knelt beside her and tried to take her hand. It was soft now as a jellyfish, and almost as repugnant — the touch shot my palm with a thousand needles which stung into my arm exactly as if I had been swimming at night and lashed onto a Portuguese man o' war.

"Your hand feels nice," she said in a sudden turn of mood.

There was a period when we held hands often. She had become pregnant after three years of marriage, a ticklish pregnancy to conserve, for there had been something malformed about her uterus — she was never explicit — and her ducts had suffered from a chronic inflammation since Deirdre had been born. But we had succeeded, we wanted a child, there was genius between us we believed, and we held hands for the first six months. Then we crashed. After a black night of drink and a quarrel beyond dimension, she lost the baby, it came brokenly to birth, in terror, I always thought, of the womb which was shaping it, came out and went back in again to death, tearing by this miscarriage the hope of any other child for Deborah. What it left behind was a heartland of revenge. Now, cohabiting with Deborah was like sitting to dinner in an empty castle with no more for host than a butler and his curse. Yes, I knelt in fear, and my skin lived on thin wire, this side of a profound shudder. All the while she stroked my hand.

But compassion, the trapped bird of compassion, struggled up from my chest and flew to my throat. "Deborah, I love you," I said. I did not know at that instant if I meant it truly, or was some monster of deception, hiding myself from myself. And having said it, knew the mistake. For all feeling departed from her hand, even that tingling so evil to my flesh, and left instead a cool empty touch. I could have been holding a tiny casket in my palm.

"Do you love me, pet?" she asked.

"Yes."

"It must be awful. Because you know I don't love you any more at all."

She said it so quietly, with such a nice finality, that I thought again of the moon and the promise of extinction which had descended on me. I had opened a void — I was now without center. Can you understand? I did not belong to myself any longer. Deborah had occupied my center.

"Yes, you're looking awful again," said Deborah. "You began to look all right for a little while, but now you look awful again."

"You don't love me."

"Oh, not in the least."

"Do you know what it's like to look at someone you love and see no love come back?"

"It must be awful," said Deborah.

"It's unendurable," I said. Yes, the center was gone. In another minute I would begin to grovel.

"It is unendurable," she said.

"You do know?"

"Yes, I do."

"You have felt it?"

"There was a man I loved very much," she said, "and he didn't love me."

"You never told me that before."

"No, I didn't."

Before we married, she told me everything. She confessed every last lover—it had been her heritage from the convent: she had done more than tell me, she had gone to detail—we would giggle in the dark while she tapped my shoulder with one cultivated and very learned finger, giving me a sense of the roll and snap and lurch and grace (or lack of it) in each of her lovers, she had even given me a sense of what was good in the best of them, and I had loved her for it, painful as the news had sometimes been, for I had known at least what I was up against, and how many husbands could ever say that? It was the warrant of our love; whatever our marriage had been, that was our covenant, that had been her way of saying I was more valuable than the others.

And now she was inside me, fused at my center, ready to blow the rails.

"You don't mean it," I said.

"I do. There was one man I never told you about. I never told anyone about him. Although once, somebody guessed."

"Who was the man?"

"He was a bullfighter. Marvelous ripe man."

"You're lying."

"Have it your way."

"It wasn't a bullfighter."

"No, it wasn't. It was someone far better than a bullfighter, far greater." Her face had turned plump with malice, and the red mottling had begun to fade. "As a matter of fact, it was the finest and most extraordinary man I ever knew. Delicious. Just a marvelous wild feast of things. I tried to make him jealous once and lost him."

"Who could it be?" I asked.

"Don't bother to hop on one foot and then the other like a three-year-old who's got to go to the Lou. I'm not going to tell you." She took a sip of her rum, and jiggled the tumbler not indelicately, as if the tender circles of the liquor might transmit a message to some distant force, or—better—receive one. "It's going to be a bore not having you here once in a while."

"You want a divorce," I said.

"I think so."

"Like that."

"Not like *that*, darling. *After* all that." She yawned prettily and looked for the moment like a fifteen-year-old Irish maid. "When you didn't come by today to say goodbye to Deirdre . . ."

"I didn't know she was leaving."

"Of course you didn't know. How could you know? You haven't called in two weeks. You've been nuzzling and nipping with your little girls." She did not know that at the moment I had no girl.

"They're not so little any more." A fire had begun to spread in me. It was burning now in my stomach and my lungs were dry as old leaves, my heart had a herded pressure which gave promise to explode. "Give us a bit of the rum," I said.

She handed over the bottle. "Well, they may not be so little any more, but I doubt that, pet. Besides I don't care. Because I made a vow this afternoon. I said to myself that I would never . . ." and then she did not speak the rest of the sentence, but she was talking about something she had done with me and never with anyone else. "No," said Deborah, "I thought: There's no need for that any more. Never again. Not with Steve."

I had taught it to her, but she had developed a pronounced royal taste of her own for that little act. Likely it had become the first of her pleasures.

"Not ever again?" I asked.

"Never. The thought—at least in relation to you, dear sweet— makes me brush my gums with peroxide."

"Well, goodbye to all that. You don't do it so famously if the truth be told."

"Not so famously as your little girls?"

"Not nearly as well as five I could name."

The mottling came back to her neck and shoulders. A powerful odor of rot and musk and something much more violent came from her. It was like the scent of the carnivore in a zoo. This last odor was fearful—it had the breath of burning rubber.

"Isn't that odd?" asked Deborah. "I haven't heard a word of complaint from any new beau."

From the day of our separation she had admitted to no lover. Not until this moment. A sharp sad pain, almost pleasurable, thrust into me. It was replaced immediately by a fine horror.

"How many do you have?" I asked.

"At the moment, pet, just three."

"And you . . ." But I couldn't ask it.

"Yes, darling. Every last little thing. I can't tell you how shocked they were when I began. One of them said: 'Where did you ever learn to root about like that? Didn't know such things went on outside a Mexican whorehouse.' "

"Shut your fucking mouth," I said.

"Lately I've had the most famous practice."

I struck her open-handed across the face. I had meant—some last calm intention of my mind had meant—to make it no more than a slap, but my body was speaking faster than my brain, and the blow caught her on the side of the ear and knocked her half out of bed. She was up like a bull and like a bull she charged. Her head struck me in the stomach (setting off a flash in that forest of nerves) and then she drove one powerful knee at my groin (she fought like a prep-school bully) and missing that, she reached with both hands, tried to find my root and mangle me.

That blew it out. I struck her a blow on the back of the neck, a dead cold chop which dropped her to a knee, and then hooked an arm about her head and put a pressure on her throat. She was strong, I had always known she was strong, but now her strength was huge. For a moment I did not know if I could hold her down, she had almost the strength to force herself up to her feet and lift me in the air, which in that position is exceptional strength even for a wrestler. For ten or twenty seconds she strained in balance, and then her strength began to pass, it passed over to me, and I felt my arm tightening about her neck. My eyes were closed. I had the mental image I was pushing with my shoulder against an enormous door which would give inch by inch to the effort.

One of her hands fluttered up to my shoulder and tapped it gently. Like a gladiator admitting defeat. I released the pressure on her throat, and the door I had been opening began to close. But I had had a view of what was on the other side of the door, and heaven was there, some quiver of jeweled cities shining in the glow of a tropical dusk, and I thrust against the door once more and hardly felt her hand leave my shoulder, I was driving now with force against that door: spasms began to open in me, and my mind cried out then, "Hold back! you're going too far, hold back!" I could feel a series of orders whip like tracers of light from my head to my arm, I was ready to obey, I was trying to stop, but pulse packed behind pulse in a pressure up to thunderhead; some blackbiled lust, some desire to go ahead not unlike the instant one comes in a woman against her cry that she is without protection came bursting with rage from out of me and my mind exploded in a fireworks of rockets, stars, and hurtling embers, the arm about her neck leaped against the whisper I could still feel murmuring in her throat, and *crack* I choked her harder, and *crack* I choked her again, and *crack* I gave her payment—never halt now—and *crack* the door flew open and the wire tore in her throat, and I was through the door, hatred passing from me in wave after wave, illness as well, rot and pestilence, nausea, a bleak string of salts. I was floating. I was as far into myself as I had ever been and universes wheeled in a dream. To my closed eyes Deborah's face seemed to float off from her body and stare at me in darkness. She gave one malevolent look which said: "There are dimensions to evil which reach beyond the light," and then she smiled like a milkmaid and floated away and was gone. And in the midst of that Oriental splendor of landscape, I felt the lost touch of her finger on my shoulder, radiating some faint but ineradicable pulse of detestation into the new grace. I opened my eyes. I was weary with a most honorable fatigue, and my flesh seemed new. I had not felt so nice since I was twelve. It seemed inconceivable at this instant that anything in life could fail to please. But there was Deborah, dead beside me on the flowered carpet of the floor, and there was no question of that. She was dead, indeed she was dead.

Chapter 2, A Runner from the Gaming Room

On that night sixteen years ago when I made love to Deborah in the back seat of my car, she looked up when we were done, smiling with a misty somewhat bewildered look, and said, "You're not Catholic, are you?"

"No."

"I was hoping perhaps you were Polish Catholic. Rojack, you know."

"I'm half Jewish."

"What is the other half?"

"Protestant. Nothing really."

"Nothing really," she said. "Come, take me home." And she was depressed.

It took eight years for me to find out why, seven years of living my own life and a first year of being married to her. It took all of that first year for me to understand that Deborah had prejudices which were as complex and attractive as passions. Her detestation of Jewish Protestants and Gentile Jews was complete. "They know nothing about grace," she finally explained to me.

Like any other exceptional Catholic, Deborah was steeped in her idea of grace. Grace was a robber bridegroom, grace was the specter in our marriage bed. When things went badly, she would say sorrowfully, even remotely, "I used to be filled with grace, and now I'm not." When she had been pregnant, grace had come to her again. "I don't think God is so annoyed at me any more," she said. And indeed a tenderness rose from her at moments like that, a warm full-bodied balm to my nerves but for the purity of it: Deborah's grace always offered its intimation of the grave. I would be content she loved me, and yet at such moments my mind drifted out to the empty peak of a mountaintop or prepared to drop down the sheer gray face of a ten-foot wave in a storm at sea. That was love with Deborah and it was separate from making love to Deborah; no doubt she classified the two as Grace and Lust. When she felt love, she was formidable; making love she left you with no uncertain memory of having passed through a carnal transaction with a caged animal. It was not just her odor, that smell (with the white gloves off) of the wild boar full of rut, that hot odor from the gallery of the zoo, no, there was something other, her perfume perhaps, a hint of sanctity, something as calculating and full of guile as high finance, that was it — she smelled like a bank, Christ she would have been too much for any man, there was something so sly at the center of her, some snake, I used literally to conceive of a snake guarding the cave which opened to the treasure, the riches, the filthy-lucred wealth of all the world, and rare was the instant I could pay my dues without feeling a high pinch of pain as if fangs had sunk into me. The afterbreath, lying on her body, floated on a current of low heavy fire, a sullen poisonous fire, an oil on flame which went out of her and took me in. Invariably a groan came out of me like the clanking of chains, my mouth on hers, not sobbing but groping for air. I always felt as if I had torn free some promise of my soul and paid it over in ransom.

"You're wonderful," she would say then.

Yes, I had come to believe in grace and the lack of it, in the long finger of God and the swish of the Devil, I had come to give my scientific apprehension to the reality of witches. Deborah believed in demons. It was Celtic blood, she had once been ready to explain, the Celts were in tune with the spirits, made love with them, hunted with the spirits. And in fact she was an exceptional hunter. She had gone on safari with her first husband and killed a wounded lion charging ten feet from her throat, she dropped an Alaskan bear with two shots to the heart (30/06 Winchester), I suspect she finally lost her nerve. She hinted once that she had broken from an animal and the guide had been forced to take it. But that I didn't know—she was not definite. I offered to go hunting with her, to Kodiak, to the Congo, I did not care where: in the first two years of our marriage I would have been willing to go to war with any expert, guide, or champion—she took pains to separate me from that romantic heart. "But darling, I could never go hunting with you," she said. "Pamphli"—the almost unpronounceable nickname of her first husband—"was a superb hunter. It was the best thing we had together. You don't think I want to spoil that memory by smashing about with you? That would do none of us any good. No, I'll never hunt big ones again. Not unless I should fall in love with somebody who's divine as a hunter." Like most of her friends, she had an aristocratic indifference to the development of talent. One enjoyed what was in flower, one devoured it if it were good for one, but one left the planting to others.

Finally she took me on a hunt—for moles and woodchucks. I was shown the distance of my place from her beloved Pamphli, but even on this hunt, a casual walk through the Vermont woods near a house we were renting for a season, I saw how good she was. She did not see a forest like others. No, out of the cool and the damp, the rent of forest odor aromatic and soft with rot, Deborah drew a mood—she knew the spirit which created attention in the grove, she told me once she could sense that spirit watching her, and when it was replaced by something else, also watching, well, *there* was an animal. And so there was. Some small thing would leap from concealment and Deborah would pot him with her .22. She could flush more small animals than any hunter I ever saw. Often as not she fired from the hip, as nicely as pointing a finger. And many of the creatures she allowed to escape. "You take him," she would say, and sometimes I would miss. Which elicited a laugh of gentle contempt altogether sinister. "Buy a shotgun, darling," she would whisper. We hunted only a few times but by the end I knew I would never go hunting again. Not with her. Because Deborah went for the most beautiful and the most ugly of the animals she flushed. She knocked down squirrels with exquisite faces, tender as a doe in their dying swoon, and she blasted the hindquarters off groundhogs whose grimace at death was as carved in stone as a gargoyle's horn. No patch of forest was quite the same once she had hunted there. "You see," she told me once at night, late, when the booze had left her in the rarest of moods, not violent, not vicious, not amorous, but simply reflective, an air circling in on itself, "I know that I am more good and more evil than anyone alive, but which was I born with, and what came into me?"

"You shift allegiance from day to day."

"No. I just pretend to." She smiled. "I'm evil if truth be told. But I despise it, truly I do. It's just that evil has power."

Which was a way of saying goodness was imprisoned by evil. After nine years of marriage to her I did not have a clue myself. I had learned to speak in a world which believed in the *New York Times:* Experts Divided on Fluoridation, Diplomat Attacks Council Text, Self-Rule Near for Bantu Province, Chancellor Outlines Purpose of Talks, New Drive for Health Care for Aged. I had lost my faith in all of that by now: now I swam in the well of Deborah's intuitions; they were nearer to my memory of the four Germans than anything encountered before or since. But what I did not know was which of us imprisoned the other, and how? It was horror this edge of madness to lie beside Deborah in a marriage bed and wonder who was responsible for the cloud of foul intent which lifted on the mingling of our breath. Yes, I had come to believe in spirits and demons, in devils, warlocks, omens, wizards and fiends, in incubi and succubi; more than once had I sat up in a strange woman's bed feeling claws on my chest, a familiar bad odor above the liquor on my tongue and Deborah's green eyes staring at me in the dark, an oppression close to strangling on my throat. She was evil, I would decide, and then think next that goodness could come on a visit to evil only in the disguise of evil: yes, evil would know that goodness had come only by the power of its force. I might be the one who was therefore evil, and Deborah was trapped with me. Or was I blind? For now I remembered that I was where I was and no place else and she was dead. It was odd. I had to remind my mind of that. It seemed as if she were not so much dead as no longer quite living.

Well, I came to myself then, and recognized I had been lying in a half sleep, resting beside Deborah's body for a minute or two, or could it be ten or more? I still felt good. I felt very good but I had an intimation I must not think of Deborah now, certainly not now, and so I got up from the floor and went to the bathroom and washed my hands. Have you ever taken peyote?—the bathroom tile was quivering with a violet light, and at the edge of my vision was a rainbow curving out to the horizon of the tile. I had only to close my eyes and a fall of velvet rain red as the drapery in a carmine box ran back into my retina. My hands were tingling in the water. I had a recollection then of Deborah's fingers on my shoulder and I stripped my shirt and washed my upper arm. As I put down the soap, its weight in my palm was alive; the soap made a low sticky sound as it settled back to the dish. I was ready to spend an hour contemplating that sound. But the towel was in my hand, and my hands could have been picking up the crisp powder of autumn leaves as they crumbled in my fingers. So it went with the shirt. Something was demonstrating to me that I had never understood the nature of a shirt. Each of its odors (those particular separate molecules) was scattered through the linen like a school of dead fish on the beach, their decay, the intimate whiff of their decay a thread of connection leading back to the hidden heart of the sea. Yes, I returned this shirt to my body with the devotion of a cardinal fixing his hat—then I fixed my tie. A simple black knit tie, but I might have been snugging a ship to the wharf; the tie felt huge, a run of one-inch Manila long enough to please the requirements of a difficult knot—my fingers ran in and out of the interstices of this Windsor double-hitch like mice through the rigging. Speak of a state of grace—I had never known such calm. Have you ever heard a silence in a room at night or a great silence alone in the middle of a wood? Listen: for beneath the silence is a world where each separate silence takes up its pitch. I stood in that bathroom, water off, and listened to the silence of the tile. Somewhere deep in the stories of this apartment building a fan turned on, a refrigerator clicked: they had started like beasts out of some quickened response to the silence which came from me. I looked into the mirror, searching once again into the riddle of my face; I had never seen a face more handsome. It was the truth. It was exactly the sort of truth one discovers by turning a corner and colliding with a stranger. My hair was alive and my eyes had the blue of a mirror held between the ocean and the sky—they were eyes to equal at last the eyes of the German who stood before me with a bayonet—one moment of fright flew like a comet across the harbor of my calm, and I looked deeper into the eyes in the mirror as if they were keyholes to a gate which gave on a palace, and asked myself, "Am I now good? Am I evil forever?"—it seemed a simple indispensable question to ask—but the lights went down suddenly in the bathroom, then flickered up. Someone had tipped a salute. And now the eyes in the mirror were merry and a touch blank. I could not believe I was studying them.

I quit the bathroom then, and returned to look at Deborah. But she was lying on her stomach, her face to the rug. I did not want to turn her over just yet. The calm I contained seemed delicate. It was enough to stand near her body and look about the room. We had made little mess. The bedspread and the blankets had slipped to the floor, and one of the pillows was sprawling at her foot. An armchair had been pushed to the side; it had pulled a fold in the carpet. That was all. The rum was still standing in its bottles and its glasses, no lamps were overturned, no pictures were off the hook, nothing broken, no debris. A quiet scene—an empty field with a Civil War cannon: it has fired some minutes ago and a last curl of smoke issues like a snake from its barrel, is beheaded in the breeze. Quiet as that. I walked to the window and looked down ten flights to the East River Drive where traffic was going by at a good full clip. Should I jump? But the question had no force: there was a decision to be made inside the room. I could pick up the phone and call the police. Or I could wait. (I was taking a pleasure in each step which gave hint of the grace a ballerina might know in her feet.) Yes, I could go to prison, spend ten or twenty years, and if I were good enough I could try to write that huge work which had all but atrophied in my brain over the years of booze and Deborah's games. That was the honorable course and yet I felt no more than a wistful muted impulse to show such honor; no, there was something other working at the base of my brain, a scheme, some desire—I was feeling good, as if my life had just begun. "Wait," said my head very directly to me.

But I was uneasy. When I closed my eyes I saw again the luminous full moon—would I never be free of her? I almost picked up the phone.

The voice in my brain said, "Look first at Deborah's face."

I knelt to turn her over. Her body made some rustling sound of protest, a muted whimper. She was bad in death. A beast stared back at me. Her teeth showed, the point of light in her eye was violent, and her mouth was open. It looked like a cave. I could hear some wind which reached down to the cellars of a sunless earth. A little line of spit came from the corner of her mouth, and at an angle from her nose one green seed had floated its small distance on an abortive rill of blood. I did not feel a thing. Which is not to say that nothing was happening to me. Like ghosts, emotions were passing invisibly through the aisles of my body. I knew I would mourn her on some distant day, and I would fear her. I had a certainty this instant that Deborah had been divided by death—by whatever fraction, what was good in her had been willed to me (how else account for the fine breath of this calm) and every last part which detested me was collected now in the face she showed for her death—if something endured beyond her dying, something not in me, it was vengeance. That delicate anxiety which pulses up to flutter in the nose was on me now. For Deborah would be there to meet me in the hour of my death.

The verdict now came clear. I was not going to call the police, not now, not yet—some other solution was finding its way up through myself, a messenger from that magician who solved all riddles was on his way, ascending those endless stairs from the buried gaming rooms of the unconscious to the tower of the brain. He was on his way and I was doomed if I thought to do my work in jail. For her curse would be on me.

I had an intimation then of Deborah's presence. Did one lift after death like a feather, rising slowly? I went to open the window as though to hope some breeze might seduce her forth, and dropped my hand. For I had the sense I had been touched on the shoulder, there at the precise point where her fingers begged me to let go her throat. Something touched me and now pushed me without touch toward the door. Once again I could have been in a magnetic field where some force without sensation other than its own presence was coaxing me firmly to step away from Deborah, cross the room, and out the door. And I went with this force; it had a promise like the smell of bar whiskey when rich young girls are in a bar. There was a good sound somewhere in my head, and expectation came to life in me, two full breasts came to rest their balm upon my eyes, then dropped in soft taps of curve and fall about my throat, rubbed a turn on my chest, tickled a hair at the belly and came to fold like two does at my root. One kiss of flesh, one whiff of sweet was loose, sending life to the charnel house of my balls. Something fierce for pleasure was loose. And I was out that door and strolling down the stairs, still traveling in the field of force which drifted me clean out of Deborah's room. As I stood at the lower landing of this duplex, I could breathe a tropical bouquet from the woven velvet flowers on the wall, I was near a swamp where butterflies and tropical birds went fanning up—and over the spoil of animals who looked for flesh—and floated on the air which rose from vegetation growing in the damp and drowning in the wet. At the door which opened to the elevator I stopped, turned around completely, and following that force which held me now as closely as an embrace I could not bear to quit, I crossed the hall, opened the door to the room where the maid must sleep, and pushed right in.

The lamp by her bed was on. The windows were closed, the air was close, an oven of burgeonings was that room—and, nice shock, there was Ruta, Fräulein Ruta from Berlin, lying on top of the covers with her pajama pants down, a copy of a magazine in one hand (a flash of nude photographs in color) and her other hand fingering, all five fingers fingering like a team of maggots at her open heat. She was off in that bower of the libido where she was queen, and those five fingers were five separate lords and ladies hard at work on her.

We did not say a word. Her face, caught in this pose, was on the edge of dividing into two women: that queen for certain of her fevers, and a little girl trapped in a dirty act. I winked like the friendliest peasant neighbor—I recall how natural was this wink—and then I stripped my coat and started to take off my clothes. I removed them with care enough to fold them neat. And the atmosphere in the room which had quivered for an instant on my entrance like a whip of air from a bellows, now flared slowly up and higher. The maid set down the magazine and turned her free hand palm up toward me, her fingers long and thin with a hint of the fine curve in a double curved bow. I remember seeing that the curve of her fingers, her lips, and her long thin calves were a part of that sly bright fever she gave off, and in a new whiff of boldness as if to be bold was her métier, boldness had brought me to her, she lifted the other hand (those lords and ladies) and moved it across to me for a kiss to her fingers. Which I did, getting one full draft of a heated sex which was full of the flower, full of earth, and with suspicion of one sly mouse slipping through the garden, a bit of fish in its teeth. My bare foot came up from the carpet and I put my five toes where her hand had been, drawing up on the instant out of her a wet spicy wisdom of all the arts and crafts of getting along in the world. She made the high nasal sound of a cat disturbed in its play—I had stolen something from her, and she was about to draw back, but there was a look in my face—I was ready to kill her easy as not, there was an agreeable balance in the thought that I was ready to kill anyone at this moment—and my look cracked the glitter in her eye. She shook her head and gave the prize to my five toes which moved in the wet with all the deliverance of snakes who have crossed a desert. Something took me on then—the wisdom in my fingertips was sure; I could feel where her flesh was alive and where the skin was dead, my fingers played at the edge, making little forays, nipping her to life. I felt for the first time in my life like a healthy alley cat, and I stroked at her with a delicate hatred lacquered clean up to a small flame by the anticipation of my body. It must have been five minutes before I chose to give her a kiss, but I took her mouth at last, pinched the corner in my teeth, and our faces came together with the turn of a glove catching a ball. She had a virtuoso's mouth, thin and alive, stingy and lightly fevered, a woodwind which tickled promise into me, yes those lips spoke of where they had traveled and where they could go now, something hot and mean and greedy to take the low road rose from her lean belly and tricky breasts which now popped out from under my thumb before I caught them, and at each corner of her mouth was a plump little mound, a tidbit for the teeth. Yes, she was sweet oil to the throat. She was breathing the pictures of her brain into mine, all the rosy tan and tinted gold of those pinup pictures in the magazine, and her thin lips now fluttered on my mouth, her warmth was rosy, her mouth offered to go down. I lay back like a king lion and let her romp. She had a gift. I was off on the nicest dream of Berlin nightclubs with their telephones and queer shows, of bal musettes and twisterias, she was giving a short lecture with her tongue on the habits of the Germans, the French, the English (one sorry bite indeed), the Italians, the Spanish, she must have had an Arab or two. All the tars and scents were blending into the one full smell which always makes you begin. I was ready to take the roller coaster, but I didn't want it to end, not this one, not yet, her greed was riding through me, I wanted more and more, and so I slipped free of her mouth and put her on her back.

But then, as abruptly as an arrest, a thin high constipated smell (a smell which spoke of rocks and grease and the sewer-damp of wet stones in poor European alleys) came needling its way out of her. She was hungry, like a lean rat she was hungry, and it could have spoiled my pleasure except that there was something intoxicating in the sheer narrow pitch of the smell, so strong, so stubborn, so private, it was a smell which could be mellowed only by the gift of fur and gems, she was money this girl, she cost money, she would make money, something as corrupt as a banquet plate of caviar laid on hundred-dollar bills would be required to enrich that odor all the way up to the smell of foie gras in Deborah's world and Deborah's friends. I had a desire suddenly to skip the sea and mine the earth, a pure prong of desire to bugger, there was canny hard-packed evil in that butt, that I knew. But she resisted, she spoke for the first time, "Not there! *Verboten!*"

I had, however, gotten an inch of the *verboten*. A virulent intricate hatred, a detailed specification of the hardest world of the poor, the knowledge of a city rat, came out from her into me and deadened the head of my heat. I could go for a while now. And go I did. That other presence (which, I could remind you, leads to the creation) was lying open for me, and I barreled in on a stroke, expecting glory and the hot beat of jungle wings, but she was slack, her box spoke of cold gasses from the womb and a storehouse of disappointments. I quit her there and went back to where I had begun, the fierce pinched struggle to gain an inch and then a crucial quarter of an inch more, my hand was in her red dyed hair, pulling at a swatch with a twisting upward motion, and I could feel the pain in her scalp strain like a crowbar the length of her body and push up the trap, and I was in, that quarter-inch more was gained, the rest was easy. What a subtle smell came from her then, something back of the ambition, the narrow stubbornness, the monomaniacal determination to get along in the world, no, that was replaced by something tender as the flesh but not at all clean, something sneaky, full of fear, but young, a child in soiled pants, "You're a Nazi," I said to her out of I knew not what.

"*Ja.*" She shook her head. "No, no," she went on. "*Ja*, don't stop, *ja.*"

There was a high private pleasure in plugging a Nazi, there was something clean despite all—I felt as if I were gliding in the clear air above Luther's jakes and she was loose and free, very loose and very free, as if this were finally her natural act: a host of the Devil's best gifts were coming to me, mendacity, guile, a fine-edged cupidity for the stroke which steals, the wit to trick authority. I felt like a thief, a great thief. And like a thief returning to church, I see-sawed up from that bank of pleasures up to her deserted ware-house, that empty tomb. But it was more ready now. Those flaccid walls had come together—back of my closed eyes I could see one poor flower growing in a gallery—what love she still possessed might have been in a flower. Like a thief I was out of church again and dropping down for more of that pirate's gold.

So that was how I finally made love to her, a minute for one, a minute for the other, a raid on the Devil and a trip back to the Lord, I was like a hound who has broken free of the pack and is going to get that fox himself, I was drunk with my choice, she was becoming mine as no woman ever had, she wanted no more than to be a part of my will, her face, that mobile, mocking, know-the-cost-of-every-bargain Berlin face, was loose and independent of her now, swimming through expressions, a greedy mate with the taste of power in her eyes and her mouth, that woman's look that the world is theirs, and then I was traveling up again that crucial few centimeters of distance from the end to the beginning, I was again in the place where the child is made, and a little look of woe was on her face, a puckered fearful little nine-year-old afraid of her punishment, wishing to be good.

"I have nothing in me," she said. "Do we go ahead?"

"Who knows," I said, "keep quiet."

And I could feel her beginning to come. The doubt in me had tipped her off, the adjuration to be quiet had thrown the bolt. She was a minute away, but she was on her way, and just as if one of her wily fingers had thrown some switch in me, I was gone like a bat and shaking hands with the Devil once more. Rare greed shone in her eyes, pleasure in her mouth, she was happy. I was ready to chase, I was gorged to throw the first spill, high on a choice, like some cat caught on two wires I was leaping back and forth, in sep-arate runs for separate strokes, bringing spoils and secrets up to the Lord from the red mills, bearing messages of defeat back from that sad womb, and then I chose—ah, but there was time to change—I chose her cunt. It was no graveyard now, no warehouse, no, more like a chapel now, a modest decent place, but its walls were snug, its odor was green, there was a sweetness in the chapel, a muted reverential sweetness in those walls of stone. "That is what prison will be like for you," said a last effort on my inner tongue. "Stay here!" came a command from inside of me; except that I could feel the Devil's meal beneath, its fires were lifting through the floor, and I waited for the warmth to reach inside, to come up from the cellar below, to bring booze and heat up and licking tongues, I was up above a choice which would take me on one wind or another, and I had to give myself, I could not hold back, there was an explosion, furious, treacherous and hot as the gates of an icy slalom with the speed at my heels overtaking my nose, I had one of those splittings of a second where the senses fly out and there in that instant the itch reached into me and drew me out and I jammed up her ass and came as if I'd been flung across the room. She let out a cry of rage. Her coming must have taken a ferocious twist. And with my eyes closed, I felt low sullen waters wash about a dead tree on a midnight pond. I had come to the Devil a fraction too late, and nothing had been there to receive me. But I had a vision immediately after of a huge city in the desert, in some desert, was it a place on the moon? For the colors had the unreal pastel of a plastic and the main street was flaming with light at five A.M. A million light bulbs lit the scene.

It had been when all was said a bitch of a brawl. She lay for a minute half in sleep, half in stupor, and her tongue licked idly at my ear. Like a mother cat she was teaching a new kitten how to listen. "Mr. Rojack," she said at last with her gutty fleshy Berlin speech, "I do not know why you have trouble with your wife. You are absolutely a genius, Mr. Rojack."

"A doctor is no better than his patient," said I.

There was a wicked look of amusement in her face. "But you are a *vache*," she said. "You must not pull my hair. Not even for that."

"*Der Teufel* asked me to visit."

"*Der Teufel!*" She laughed. "What can a rich man like you know about *der Teufel?*"

"Doesn't *der Teufel* like the rich?"

"No," she said, "God protects the rich."

"But at the end I could not have paid my respects to God."

"Oh, you are dreadful," she said, and pinched me a good mean German pinch where my belly was soft. Then she started uneasily.

"Do you think your wife heard?" she asked.

"I doubt it."

"Are the walls so good?" She sat up now, her tricky breasts lolling nicely. "No, I feel not so easy now," she said, "your wife could come in on us."

"She would never do something like that. It's not her style."

"I think you know a woman better than that," said Ruta. She pinched again. "You know, at the end, you stole something from me."

"Half."

"Half."

We liked each other. That was fine. But again I could feel a stillness from the room above. Ruta was nervous.

"When you walked in on me," she said, "you looked pretty."

"So did you, I fear."

"No, but I never do something like that. At least," she added with a malicious grin, "not unless I lock the door."

"And tonight you didn't."

"No, I was asleep. After I let you in, I went to sleep. I was thinking how unhappy you looked. When you came to visit." She put her head to one side as if to inquire whether I had been already with my wife in the bed above her, and then didn't ask. "Of course," she said, "you and Mrs. Rojack had a reconciliation."

"Of sorts."

"What a bad man you are. That's what woke me up—making your reconciliation with Mrs. Rojack. I was awake, and I was so excited—I can't explain it." Her bold pointed spiteful nose made everything she said seem merry.

"How old are you?"

"Twenty-three."

She was probably twenty-eight. "You're a charming twenty-three," I said.

"And you are still a *vache*."

Her fingers were beginning to play with me.

"Let's sleep another minute," I said.

"Yes." She started to light a cigarette, then stopped. "Your wife thinks you've gone home."

"Probably."

"I hope the walls are good."

"Let's try to sleep," I said. I wanted the light out. I had a rendezvous in the dark. Something was waiting for me. But the moment I turned the switch, it was very bad. The darkness came over like air on a wound when the dressing is removed. My senses were much too alert. Everything which had passed from her body to mine was now alive inside, as if a horde of tourists, pokey and inquisitive, were wandering through my body. I had one of those anxieties which make it an act of balance to breathe: too little air compresses the sensation of being throttled, but too much—one deep breath—and there is the fear of a fall. There was something in the room besides Ruta and myself, something which gathered force. It was approaching now, but there were no eyes, no claws, just a sense of oppression waiting. I felt vile. "Do you have a drink?" I asked of Ruta.

"No." She gave a laugh and whispered, "When I drink I go out to look for men who will beat me."

"Crazy," I said, and got up.

She could hear me putting on my clothes in the dark. The oppression had lifted on the moment I was free of her bed and my fingers were quick. They seemed to float onto each piece of clothing as I needed it.

"When will you be back?"

"Before morning."

"And you will tell your wife you took a walk and came back and woke me up to let you in?"

"No, I will tell her I left the door unlocked."

"Don't give all the good things to your wife. Save a present for me."

"Maybe I will bring back a diamond."

"I love you a little bit."

And I was thinking of that empty womb, of that graveyard which gambled a flower and lost.

"I like you, Ruta."

"Come back, and you will see how much you are going to like me."

I had a thought then of what had been left in her. It was perishing in the kitchens of the Devil. Was its curse on me?

"*Der Teufel* is so happy," she said, and a perfect spitefulness of attention came to a focus in her eye. Small cheer that she could read my mind.

Was that the cloud of oppression which had come to me in the dark? That the seed was expiring in the wrong field?

"Next time," said Ruta, "you must take care of little Ruta."

"Next time will be an event," I said. I wanted to blow her a kiss but there was nothing in me to send her way. So I closed the door, and went back up the stairs, up the aisle of that padded jungle, and entered Deborah's bedroom again with the expectation that somehow she would be gone. *There* was the body. It struck my sight like a shelf of rock on which a ship is about to smash. What was I going to do with her? I felt a mean rage in my feet. It was as if in killing her, the act had been too gentle, I had not plumbed the hatred where the real injustice was stored. She had spit on the future, my Deborah, she had spoiled my chance, and now her body was here. I had an impulse to go up to her and kick her ribs, grind my heel on her nose, drive the point of my shoe into her temple and kill her again, kill her good this time, kill her right. I stood there shuddering from the power of this desire, and comprehended that this was the first of the gifts I'd plucked from the alley, oh Jesus, and I sat down in a chair as if to master the new desires Ruta had sent my way.

My breath was bad again. What in hell was I to do with Deborah? I had no solution. If the messenger was on his way, he gave no hint of being near. A first rat's panic began to gnaw. "Keep cool, you swine," said a contemptuous voice in me, all but an echo from Deborah.

Let me tell you the worst. I had a little fantasy at this moment. It was beyond measure. I had a desire to take Deborah to the bathroom, put her in the tub. Then Ruta and I would sit down to eat. The two of us would sup on Deborah's flesh, we would eat for days: the deepest poisons in us would be released from our cells. I would digest my wife's curse before it could form. And this idea was thrilling to me. I felt like a doctor on the edge of a thunderous new medicine. The details fell into place: what we did not choose to devour we could grind away in the electric Disposall beneath the sink, all the impure organs and little bones. For the long bones, for the femur and the tibia, the fibula, the radius and the ulna, the humerus, I had another plan. I would bind them in a package and hurl them out the window, out across the East River Drive and into the water. No, four lanes of traffic and a pedestrian walk to clear, too long a throw, I would have instead to go out in the street and take a taxicab and then another and then another until I ended at last in the marshes of Canarsie or the stench flats near City Island; there I could fling them in a swamp. With luck those long horsewoman's bones might disappear forever, or would I know for sure? Would I have instead to fill a box with plaster of Paris and imbed the bones, and her teeth as well? But no, the teeth must be disposed of separately, and not in any sewer or trash can, no, they must be buried securely, but where? Not Central Park, not by half, one tooth found, and I was dead: as in a movie I could see the police talking to Deborah's dentist—and bones in plaster of Paris dropped at sea, that was not good either, for how was I to rent a boat in March without drawing attention? *Heiress Is Missing!* the tabloids would scream on the following day and people would remember my face, my heavy package, no, this wasn't going to work: worst of all was Ruta in it with me, for she could yet cause trouble. Now the fantasy approached the vanishing point: I saw myself alone beside the tub with Ruta's body in cadaver—there was a tonic humor at the thought which made me smile. No, this was done, this idea was done, and I lay back weakly in my chair as if a spasm of illness which should have discharged itself from my mouth had lifted instead to my brain. What gifts this girl had given me, what German spice!

Then it came simple as that, the simplest solution of all. The messenger had slipped into the tower. And I smiled in terror, for it was also the boldest choice. Was I brave enough? Something in me lingered back—I had a panicked minute of argument in which I tried to find some other way. Perhaps I could take Deborah to the elevator (my poor wife is drunk) or sneak her down the stairs, no, altogether impossible, and then I sighed: if I missed on this one, it was the electric chair for sure, I had a wistful sadness now I had not tried to cast a baby into Ruta—she might be the last woman for me—and then I stood up from my seat, went to look at Deborah, knelt beside her again, and put my hand under her hips. Her bowels had voided. Suddenly I felt like a child. I was ready to weep. There was a stingy fish-like scent in the air, not unreminiscent of Ruta. They were mistress and maid and put their musk in opposite pockets. I hesitated, and then since there was nothing to do but go on, I went to the bathroom, took some paper, and cleaned Deborah. It was a discipline to be thorough. Then I disposed of the waste, listening to the hound's sigh of the closet water, and came back to look out the open window. No. Not yet. First I turned off the brightest lights. Then in a panic of strength, like the desperation to get out of a burning room, I lifted her up, at what a cost I lifted her up, for her body was almost too heavy (or I was that empty with fright) and balanced her feet on the ledge, it was harder than I thought, and with a fever that no one see me at the open window now, not this instant, no, I took a breath and thrust her out and fell back myself to the carpet as if she had shoved me back, and lying there, I counted to two, to three, how fast I do not know, feeling the weight of her flight like a thrill in my chest, and heard a sound come up from the pavement all ten stories below, a flat, surprisingly loud and hollow thump as car brakes screamed and metal went colliding into metal with that howl of a shape which is suddenly collapsed, and I stood up then and leaned out the window and looked and there was Deborah's body half beneath the front of a car and a pile-up of three or four behind and traffic screaming to a stall on back, all the way half a mile back, and I howled then in a simulation of woe, but the woe was real—for the first time I knew she was gone—and it was an animal howl.

One scalding wash of sorrow, and I felt clean. I went to the telephone, dialed O, asked, "What is the number of the police?" The operator said, "Just a minute, I'll get it for you," and I waited for eight long rings while my nerve teetered like a clown on a tight-rope, and a cacophony of voices rose all ten stories up from the ground. I heard my voice giving my name and Deborah's address to the mouthpiece, and that voice of mine then said, "Get over here right away, will you. I can hardly talk, there's been a frightful accident." I hung up, went to the door, and shouted down the stairs, "Ruta, get dressed, get dressed quick. Mrs. Rojack has killed herself."

CANNIBALS
AND CHRISTIANS

The third and most recent compilation of shorter writings,
Cannibals and Christians, *was published by Dial in 1966 and is
now available in the Dell paperback edition. "Introducing Our
Argument" is the initial essay, and it appeared first in* Dissent *in
the May/June, 1966 issue. "In the Red Light" covers the
Republican national convention of 1964 and was first published
in* Esquire *in November, 1964. "The Argument Reinvigorated"
was originally titled "Modes and Mutations: Comments on the
Modern American Novel" and, in the compilation, serves as the
introduction to Mailer's critique, not published here, of the current
work of some of his contemporaries. Under its original title, it
first appeared in* Commentary *in March, 1964. "Punching Papa"
is a review of Morley Callaghan's* That Summer in Paris *and
originally appeared in* The New York Review of Books *in the
Winter, 1963 special issue. "The Killer" is a short story that
came out in the April/May number of* Evergreen Review *in 1964,*

and "The Last Night," printed here with Mailer's introduction, appeared in the December, 1963 issue of Esquire. Because of the way in which Esquire paces its distribution, the December, 1963 issue was the one on the stands the day President Kennedy was assassinated. Among the poems, "The Executioner's Song" was first published in Fuck You, A Magazine of the Arts. The singer referred to in "Boites" is Bobby Short.

Introducing Our Argument

In Provincetown, a friend brought a gift. She brought a big round metal GULF sign seven feet in diameter which another friend had discovered in the town dump and rescued. The hair of fashion came alert: we might make a coffee table. While we drank, we could look at the shading in the orange and blue letters. Poets in the room could contemplate the value of — GULF — even as a novitiate in Yoga will fix on the resonance of OM. Musicians could explore the tick of the cocktail glass against the metal. Intellectuals could . . .

What a deal intellectuals could do. There would be those to claim Pop art is the line where culture meets mass civilization, and so Pop art is the vehicle for bringing taste to the masses; others to argue the debauch of Capitalism has come to the point where it crosses the doorstep and inhabits the place where you set your drink. And those to say *fun;* fun is the salvation of society.

It would go on: some might decide that putting a huge gasoline company's totem into one's private space helped to mock civilization and its hired man, the corporation; others would be certain the final victory of the corporation was near when we felt affection for the device by which a corporation advertised itself.

At last, nothing was done with the sign. I did not want to go through dialogue and the same dialogue about why it was there and whether it was good it was there, or bad it was there, and in truth I did not want the work of disposing of it when the fashion had passed. So I left the sign to rust on the beach, a mile from its burial ground on the dump.

List the symptoms. We live in a time which has created the art of the absurd. It is our art. It contains happenings, Pop art, camp, a theater of the absurd, a homosexual genius who spent thirty years as a thief; black humor is its wit; the dances are livid and solitary — they are also orgiastic: orgy or masturbation? — the first question posed by the art of the absurd. So the second: is the art rational or absurd? Do we have the art because the absurd is the patina of waste, and we are waiting in the pot for the big roar of waters when the world goes down the pipe? Or are we face to face with a desperate but most rational effort from the deepest resources of the unconscious of us all to rescue civilization from the pit and plague of its bedding, that gutted swinish foul old bedding on which two centuries of imperialism, high finance, moral hypocrisy and horror have lain. The skulls of black men and the bowels of the yellow race are in that bed, the death of the Bride of the Sabbath is in that bed with the ashes of the concentration camp and the ashes of the Kabbala, moonshots fly like flares across black dreams, and the Beatles — demons or saints? — give shape to a haircut which looks from the rear like nothing so much as an atomic cloud. Apocalypse or debauch is upon us. And we are close to dead. There are faces and bodies like gorged maggots on the dance floor, on the highway, in the city, in the stadium; they are a host of chemical machines who swallow the product of chemical factories, aspirin, preservatives, stimulant, relaxant, and breathe out their chemical wastes into a polluted air. The sense of a long last night over civilization is back again; it has perhaps not been here so intensely in thirty years, not since the Nazis were prospering, but it is coming back.

Well, it has been the continuing obsession of this writer that the world is entering a time of plague. And the continuing metaphor for the obsession — a most disagreeable metaphor — has been cancer. The argument is old by now: its first assumption is that cancer is a disease different from other diseases, an ultimate disease against which all other diseases are in design to protect us.

The difficulty—for one can always convince the literary world to accept a metaphor if one remains loyal to it—is that my obsession is not merely an obsession, I fear, but insight into the nature of things, perhaps the deepest insight I have, and this said with no innocence of the knowledge that the plague can have its home within, and these condemnations come to no more than the grapplings of a man with a curse on his flesh, or even the probability that society partakes of the plague and its critic partakes, and each wars against the other, the man and the society each grappling with his own piece of the plague, as if, indeed, we are each of us born not only with our life but with our death, with our variety of death, good death and bad, and it is the act of each separate man to look to free himself from that part of his existence which was born with the plague. Some succeed, some fail, and some of us succeed nobly for we clear our own plague and help to clear the plague upon the world, and others succeed, others—are we those?—you don't know—who clear their plague by visiting it upon friends, passing their disease into the flesh and mind of near bodies, and into the circuits of the world. And they poison the wells and get away free, some of them—they get away free if there is a devil and he has power, and that is something else we do not know. But the plague remains, that mysterious force which erects huge, ugly, and aesthetically emaciated buildings as the world ostensibly grows richer, and proliferates new diseases as medicine presumably grows wiser, nonspecific diseases, families of viruses, with new names and no particular location. And products deteriorate in workmanship as corporations improve their advertising, wars shift from carnage and patriotism to carnage and surrealism, sex shifts from whiskey to drugs. And all the food is poisoned. And the waters of the sea we are told. And there is always the sound of some electric motor in the ear.

In a modern world which produces mediocrities at an accelerating rate, and keeps them alive by surgical gymnastics which go beyond anyone's patience but the victim, the doctor, and the people who expect soon to be on the operating tables themselves; in a civilization where compassion is of political use and is stratified in welfare programs which do not build a better society but shore up a worse; in a world whose ultimate logic is war, because in a world of war all overproduction and overpopulation is possible since peoples and commodities may be destroyed wholesale—in a breath, a world of such hypercivilization is a world not of adventurers, entrepreneurs, settlers, social arbiters, proletarians, agriculturists, and other egocentric types of a dynamic society, but is instead a world of whirlpools and formlessness where two huge types begin to reemerge, types there at the beginning of it all: Cannibals and Christians.

We are martyrs all these days. All that Right Wing which believes there is too much on earth and too much of it is second-rate, all of that Right Wing which runs from staunch Republicanism to the extreme Right Wing, and then half around the world through the ghosts of the Nazis, all of that persecuted Right Wing which sees itself as martyr, knows that it knows how to save the world: one can save the world by killing off what is second-rate. So they are the Cannibals—they believe that survival and health of the species comes from consuming one's own, not one's near-own, but one's own species. So the pure cannibal has only one taboo on food—he will not eat the meat of his own family. Other men he will of course consume. Their virtues he will conserve in his own flesh, their vices he will excrete, but to kill and to eliminate is his sense of human continuation.

Then come our Christians. They are the commercial. The commercial is the invention of a profoundly Christian nation—it proceeds to sell something in which it does not altogether believe, and it interrupts the mood. We are all of us Christians: Jews, liberals, Bolsheviks, anarchists, Socialists, Communists, Keynesians, Democrats, Civil Righters, beatniks, ministers, moderate Republicans, pacifists, Teach-inners, doctors, scientists, professors, Latin Americans, new African nations, Common Marketers, even Mao Tse-tung. Doubtless. From Lyndon Johnson to Mao Tse-tung, we are all Christians. We believe man is good if given a chance, we believe man is open to discussion, we believe science is the salvation of ill, we believe death is the end of discussion; ergo we believe nothing is so worthwhile as human life. We think no one should go hungry. So forth. What characterizes Christians is that most of them are not Christian and have no interest left in Christ. What characterizes the Cannibals is that most of them are born Christian, think of Jesus as Love, and get an erection from the thought of whippings, blood, burning crosses, burning bodies, and screams in mass graves. Whereas their counterpart, the Christians—the ones who are not Christian but whom we choose to call Christian—are utterly opposed to the destruction of human life and succeed within themselves in starting all the wars of our own time, since every war since the Second World War has been initiated by liberals or Communists; these Christians also succeed by their faith in science to poison the nourishment we eat and the waters of the sea, to alter the genetics of our beasts, and to break the food chains of nature.

Yet every year the girls are more beautiful, the athletes are better. So the dilemma remains. Is the curse on the world or on oneself? Does the world get better, no matter how, getting better and worse as part of the same process, or does the world get better in spite of the fact it is getting worse, and we are approaching the time when an apocalypse will pass through the night? We live after all in a time which interrupts the mood of everything alive.

Well, this is a book of writings on these themes. I will not pretend it is a book written with the clear cold intent to be always on one precise aim or another. I will not even pretend that all the targets are even necessarily on the same range or amenable to literary pieces. No, I would submit that everything here has been written in the years of the plague, and so I must see myself sometimes as physician more than rifleman, a physician half blind, not so far from drunk, his nerve to be recommended not at every occasion, nor his hand to hold at each last bed, but a noble physician nonetheless, noble at least in his ideal, for he is certain that there is a strange disease before him, an unknown illness, a phenomenon which partakes of mystery, nausea, and horror; if the nausea gives him pause and the horror fear, still the mystery summons, he is a physician, he must try to explore the mystery. So, he does, and by different methods too many a time. We will not go on to speak of the medicines and the treatment, of surgeon, bonesetter, lab analyst—no, the metaphor has come to the end of its way. These writings are then attempts in a dozen different forms to deal with mysteries which offer the presumption that there is an answer to be found, or a clue. So I proceed, even as a writer when everything goes well, and perhaps a few matters are uncovered and more I know are left to chase.

There are times when I think it is a meaningless endeavor—that the only way to hunt these intimations is in the pages of a novel, that that is the only way this sort of mystery can ever be detected. Such a time is on me again, so it is possible this collection will be the last for a period. The wish to go back to that long novel, announced six years ago, and changed in the mind by all of seven years, may be here again, and if that is so, I will have yet to submit to the prescription laid down by the great physician Dr. James Joyce—"silence, exile, and cunning," he said. Well, one hopes not; the patient is too gregarious for the prescription. What follows, at any rate, are some explorations of the theme stated here, some talk of Cannibals and Christians, some writings on politics, on literary matters, on philosophy—save us all—on philosophy.

In the Red Light: *A History of the Republican Convention in 1964*

. . . He had drawn the burning city, a great bonfire of architectural styles, ranging from Egyptian to Cape Cod colonial. Through the center, winding from left to right, was a long hill street and down it, spilling into the middle foreground, came the mob carrying baseball bats and torches. For the faces of its members, he was using the innumerable sketches he had made of the people who come to California to die; the cultists of all sorts, economic as well as religious, the wave, airplane, funeral and preview watchers — all those poor devils who can only be stirred by the promise of miracles and then only to violence. A super "Dr. Know-All Pierce-All" had made the necessary promise of miracles and they were marching behind his banner in a great united front of screwballs and screwboxes to purify the land. No longer bored, they sang and danced joyously in the red light of the flames.

— NATHANAEL WEST, *The Day of the Locust*

Now, the city was beautiful, it was still the most beautiful city in the United States, but like all American cities it was a casualty of the undeclared war. There had been an undisclosed full-scale struggle going on in America for twenty years — it was whether the country would go mad or not. And the battle line of that war (which showed that yes slowly the country was losing the war, we were indeed going mad) was of course the progress of the new roads, buildings, and supermarkets which popped out all over the cities of the nation. San Francisco was losing her beauty. Monstrous corporations in combine with monstrous realtors had erected monstrous boxes of Kleenex ten, twenty, thirty stories high through the downtown section, and the new view from Telegraph Hill had shards of glass the size of a mountain wall stuck into the soft Italian landscape of St. Francis' City. The San Francisco Hilton, for an example, while close to twenty stories high was near to a square block in size and looked from the street to have the proportions and form of a cube of sugar. It was a dirty sugar-white in color and its windows were set in an odd elongated checkerboard, a harlequin pattern in which each window was offset from the one above and beneath like the vents in a portable radio.

The Hilton was only six weeks old, but already it was one of the architectural wonders of the world, for its insides were composed in large part of an automobile ramp on which it was possible to drive all the way up to the eleventh floor, open a door and lo! you were in your hotel corridor, twenty feet from your own room door. It was a startling way to exhaust the internal space of a hotel, but it had one huge American advantage: any guest at the Hilton could drive all the way to his room without ever having to steer a lady through the lobby. Of course, after all those automobile ramps, there was not much volume left, so the rooms were small, the rooms were very small for seventeen dollars a day, and the windows were placed to the extreme left or right of the wall and ran from ceiling to floor, in order to allow the building to appear to the outside eye like a radio being carried by a model who worked in the high nude. The carpets and wallpapers, the drapes and the table tops were plastic, the bathroom had the odor of burning insecticide. It developed that the plastic cement used to finish the tiling gave off this odor during the months it took to dry. Molecules were being tortured everywhere.

Well, that was American capitalism gainfully employed. It had won the war. It had won it in so many places you could picture your accommodations before you arrived. Such is the nature of the promiscuous. Flying out, way out on the jet, on the way West, not yet at the Hilton but knowing it would be there, I got into a conversation with the man who sat at the window, an Australian journalist named Moffitt, a short fellow with a bushwhacker's moustache; and he scolded me for reading Buchanan's book, *Who Killed Kennedy?* He wanted to know why a man of my intelligence bothered with trash. Well, the country had never been the same since Kennedy was assassinated, courtesy was ready to reply; some process of derailment, begun with Hemingway's death and the death of Marilyn Monroe, had been racing on now through the months, through the heavens, faster than the contrails of our jet across the late afternoon mind of America; so one looked for clues where they could be found. It would be easier to know that Oswald had done it all by himself, or as an accomplice to ten other men, or was innocent, or twice damned; anything was superior to that sense of the ship of state battering its way down swells of sea, while in the hold cargo was loose and ready to slide.

This conversation did not of course take place—an Astrojet is not the vehicle for metaphorical transactions, it is after all still another of the extermination chambers of the century—slowly the breath gives up some microcosmic portion of itself, green plastic and silver-gray plastic, the nostrils breathe no odor of materials which existed once as elements of nature, no wood, no stone, no ore, time molders like a sponge in the sink. But Moffitt was Australian and fascinated with America, and had his quick comments to make, some provincial, some pure shrewd; finally he poked his finger on something I had never put together for myself, not quite: "Why is it," he asked, "that all the new stuff you build here, including the interior furnishings of this airplane, looks like a child's nursery?"

And that is what it was. The inside of our airplane was like a child's plastic nursery, a dayroom in the children's ward, and if I had been Quentin Compson, I might have answered, "Because we want to go back, because the nerves grew in all the wrong ways. Because we developed habits which are suffocating us to death. I tell you, man, we do it because we're sick, we're a sick nation, we're sick to the edge of vomit and so we build our lives with materials which smell like vomit, polyethylene and bakelite and fiberglas and styrene. Yes, our schools look like nurseries, and our factories and our temples, our kitchens and our johns, our airports and our libraries and our offices, we are one great big bloody nursery attached to a doctor's waiting room, and we are sick, we're very sick, maybe we always were sick, maybe the Puritans carried the virus and were so odious the British were right to drive them out, maybe we're a nation of culls and weeds and half-crazy from the start."

Nobody of course was Quentin Compson, nobody spoke that way any more, but the question was posed by a ghost and so had to linger: was there indeed a death in the seed which brought us here? was the country extraordinary or accursed, a junkyard where even the minnows gave caviar in the filthy pond in the fierce electric American night?

I

I must see the things; I must see the men.
    — BURKE, *Reflections on the Revolution in France*

At the Mark Hopkins on Saturday morning two days before the convention would begin, the atmosphere had the same agreeable clean rather healthy excitement (that particular American excitement) one picks up on the morning of a big football game. The kids were out, the children who were for Goldwater and those who were for Scranton, and they milled about in the small open courtyard of the hotel, and in the small hopelessly congested lobby where lines one hundred long were waiting for each of the three overworked elevators beating up to the twelfth and fourteenth floors, Scranton and Goldwater Headquarters respectively. It was a clear day outside, one of those cool sunny days in July when San Francisco is as nice as New York on a beautiful day in October, and the city fell away from Nob Hill in a perfect throw. There were apples in the air. It was a perfect football day. There was even wistfulness to be eighteen and have a date for lunch before the game. So the teams lined up first this way in one's mind, the children, adolescents, and young men and women for Goldwater to one side, the Scrantons to the other, and you could tell a lot about the colleges and the teams by looking at the faces. The Goldwater girls and boys were for the most part innocent, and they tended to have large slightly protruded jaws, not unlike Big Barry himself, and blue eyes—an astonishing number had blue eyes (was the world finally coming to the war of the blue-eyed versus the brown-eyed?)—and they were simple, they were small-town, they were hicky, the boys tended to have a little acne, an introspective pimple or two by the corner of the mouth or the side of the chin, a lot of the boys looked solemn and serious, dedicated but slightly blank—they could fix a transistor radio, but a word like "Renaissance" would lay a soft wound of silence, stupefaction in their brain. They were idealists, nearly every last one of them, but they did not speak of the happier varieties of idealism; one thought of Lutherans from North Dakota, 4-H from Minnesota, and Eagle Scouts from Maine. Many of them wore eyeglasses. They were thrifty young men, hardworking young men, polite, slightly paralyzed before the variety of life, but ready to die for a cause. It was obvious they thought Goldwater was one of the finest men ever to be born into American life. And they were stingy, they wore store-bought ready-mades, skinny kids in twenty-dollar suits and that pinch of the jaw, that recidivism of the gums which speaks of false teeth before you are fifty.

The Goldwater girls ran to two varieties. There were the models who had been hired for the purpose, and they were attractive but not very imaginative, they looked like hookers on horses, and then there were the true followers, the daughters of delegates, the California children who belonged to one Goldwater club or another. They were younger than the models of course, they were most of them fifteen, sixteen, not even seventeen, wearing cowboy hats and white vests and shirts with fringes, white riding boots; nearly all of them were blonde and they had simple rather sweet faces, the sort of faces which television commercials used to use for such product fodder as biscuit batter before the commercials turned witty; these Goldwater girls had the faces of young ladies who listened to their parents, particularly to their fathers, they were full of character, but it was the character of tidiness, industry, subservience—unlike the Goldwater boys who looked on the whole not unintelligent though slightly maniacal in the singularity of their vision (the way young physicists look slightly maniacal) the girls seemed to be just about all quite dumb. There was one blonde little girl who was lovely, pretty enough to be a starlet, but she left a pang because her eyes when open were irremediably dim. Taken altogether, boys and girls, they were like the graduating class of a high school in Nebraska. The valedictorian would write his speech on the following theme: Why is the United States the Greatest Nation on Earth?

Whereas the kids who were for Scranton were prep-school or country-day. Some of the boys were plump and merry, some were mildly executive, but they shared in common that slightly complacent air of success which is the only curse of the fraternity president or leader of the student council. They were keen, they tended to be smooth, they had a penchant for bow ties and they were the kind to drive Triumphs or Pontiac convertibles, while the Goldwater boys would be borrowing their father's Dodge Dart (except for the one in a hundred who was automotive in his genius and so had built a dragster to top out at one-six-five). Then there were the Scranton boys who were still the descendants of Holden Caulfield. Faces like theirs had been seen for Stevenson in '60 in L.A. against J.F.K., and faces like theirs might appear (one would hope) in '68 for still another, but for now they were for the nearest candidate with wit, class, and the born foreknowledge of defeat. Slim, slightly mournful, certainly acerb, and dubious of the fraternity presidents with whom they had made cause, the Holden Caulfields were out for Scranton, good-looking most of them, slightly spoiled, saucy, full of peeves, junior debs doing their best to be cool and so wearing their hair long with a part down the center in such a way that the face, sexy, stripped of makeup (except for some sort of white libidinous wax on the lips) was half-concealed by a Gothic arch of falling tresses. Such were Scranton's parts, such were Goldwater's, as the children shaped up for the game.

In this state of . . . warfare between the noble ancient landed interest and the new monied interest, the . . . monied interest is in its nature more ready for any adventure; and its possessors more disposed to new enterprises of any kind. Being of a recent acquisition, it falls in more naturally with any novelties. It is therefore the kind of wealth which will be resorted to by all who wish for change.

— BURKE, *Reflections on the Revolution in France*

Among the young industrial and financial monopolies of the West and Southwest that want a "bigger slice of the capitalist profit pie," Mr. Vasilyev listed H.L. Hunt, the Texas multimillion-aire, the Lockheed Aircaft Corporation, the Douglas Aircraft Company, the Boeing Company and the Northrup Corporation and the Giannini "financial empire" headed by the Bank of America.

These are the forces, Mr. Vasilyev said, that overcame the last-minute effort by "Wall Street, the Boston financial group and the Pennsylvania industrial complex" to promote the candidacy of Governor William W. Scranton of Pennsylvania at the Republican convention last month.

"But the 'new money' of the West proved to be stronger than the old money of the Northeast," the Soviet commentator said.

—New York Times, August 13, 1964

For a time it had been interesting history. You will remember that Scranton decided to run for nomination after a talk in Gettysburg on June 6 with President Eisenhower. He left with the solid assumption he would receive Eisenhower's support, solid enough for Governor Scranton's public-relations machine to announce this fact to the nation. That night or early next morning President Eisenhower received a phone call from George Humphrey. Eisenhower had been planning to visit Humphrey in Cleveland during the week of the Governor's Conference. But it developed Barry Goldwater had already been invited to be at Humphrey's home as well. A social difficulty thus presented itself. Humphrey resolved it in this fashion: Eisenhower would understand if, under the circumstances, Goldwater having been invited first . . .

Ike knew what that meant. If his old friend, crony, subordinate and private brain trust George Humphrey was willing to let the old gander-in-chief come out second on a collision of invitations, then Ike had picked a loser, Ike was in danger of being a loser himself. Well, Ike hadn't come out of Abilene, Kansas, all those years ago *ever* to end on the losing side. So he waddled back to the middle. He phoned Bill Scranton you will remember but an hour before Scranton was ready to announce his candidacy at the Governor's Conference on June 7, and told Scranton he could not be party to a "cabal." It was obvious to everybody in America that the old man had not labored through the night and through the day to make the truth of his first conversation with the young man stand out loud and clear in the high sun of ten a.m.

Still, one could not feel too sorry for the young man. It is never easy to grieve for a candidate of the Establishment, particularly the Republican Establishment of the East, which runs a spectrum from the Duke of Windsor to Jerome Zerbe, from Thomas E. Dewey to

Lowell Thomas, from Drue Heinz to Tex and Jinx, from Maine to Nassau, New York to South of France, from Allen Dulles to Henry Luce, Igor Cassini to Joe Alsop, from Sullivan & Cromwell to Cartier's, and from Arthur Krock to Tuxedo Park.

Well, the last two years, all the way from Arthur Krock to Tuxedo Park, you could hear that Bill Scranton was going to be the Republican candidate in '64. Attempts might be made to argue: Goldwater looks strong, somebody could say at a dinner table; hasn't got a chance, the Establishment would give back — it's going to be Scranton. What was most impressive is that the Establishment did not bother to photograph their man, immerse him in publicity, or seek to etch his image. It was taken for granted that when the time came, doors would open, doors would shut, figures would be inserted, heads would be removed, a whiff of incense, a whisk of wickedness — Scranton would be the candidate.

Of course, Goldwater, or the Goldwater organization, or *some* organization, kept picking up delegates for Goldwater, and from a year away there was a bit of sentiment that it might be easier to make a deal with Goldwater, it might be easier to *moderate* him than to excise him. Once upon a time, J. P. Morgan would doubtless have sent some bright young man out on the Southern Pacific with a bag full of hundred-dollar bills. Now, however, possessing a mass media, the buy-off could take place in public. Last November, three weeks before J. F. K. was assassinated, *Life* Magazine put Goldwater on their cover wearing a pearl-gray Stetson and clean, pressed, faded blue work shirt and Levi's while his companion, a Palomino named Sunny, stood with one of the Senator's hands on his bridle, the other laid over the vein of his nose. It was Hopalong Cassidy all baby fat removed, it gave promise of the campaign to come: the image of Kennedy was now to be combated by Sheriff B. Morris Goldwater, the Silver Gun of the West. It was one of those pictures worth ten thousand speeches — it gave promise of delivering a million votes. It was also a way òf stating that the Establishment was not yet unalterably opposed to Goldwater, and could yet help him, as it had with this cover. But inside the magazine across the heads of seven million readers, another message was delivered to the Senator.

Financial interests in Ohio, Illinois, Texas, Los Angeles and San Francisco — all centers of wealth independent of eastern ties — have been lining up money and intense local pressure for Goldwater. But . . . people fail to realize there's a difference in kinds of money. . . . Old money has political power but new money has only purchasing power. . . . When you get to a convention, you don't buy delegates. But you do put the pressure on people who control the delegates—the people who owe the old money for their stake.

Which was a way to remind Goldwater there were concessions to make. It was in foreign affairs that Goldwater had the most to explain about his policies.

Barry Goldwater [went Life's *conclusion] represents a valuable impulse in the American politics of '64. He does not yet clearly represent all that a serious contender for the Presidency should. "Guts without depth" and "a man of one-sentence solutions" are the epithets of his critics. The time has come for him to rebut them if he can.*

Two months later Goldwater announced his formal candidacy for the Republican nomination, and issued a pamphlet called "Senator Goldwater Speaks Out on the Issues." Written in that milk-of-magnesia style which is characteristic of such tracts, one could no longer be certain what he thought—he had moved from being a man of "one-sentence solutions" to a man who showed a preference for many imprecise sentences. Barry was treading water. As he did, his people, his organization, kept picking up delegates. It was not until he voted against the Civil Rights Bill that the open battle between old money and new was at last engaged. Too late on the side of the East. To anyone who knew a bit about the workings of the Establishment, a mystery was present. For unless the Establishment had become most suddenly inept, there was a buried motive in the delay, a fear, as if the Eastern money were afraid of some force in the American mind racing to power in defiance of them, some mystique from out the pure accelerating delirium of a crusade which would make cinder of the opposition. So they had waited, all candidates but Rockefeller had waited, none willing to draw the fires of the Right until Scranton was flushed by the ebb and flow, the mystery of murmur, in an old man's throat.

Somewhat later that morning, one saw Scranton in a press conference at the San Francisco Hilton. The Corinthian Room on the ballroom floor (Press Headquarters) was a white room, perhaps forty-five feet by forty feet with a low ceiling and a huge puff of a modern chandelier made up of pieces of plastic which looked like orange candy. The carpet was an electric plastic green, the bridge seats (some two hundred of them) were covered in a plastic the color of wet aspirin, and the walls were white, a hospital-sink white. The practical effect was to leave you feeling like a cold cut set in the white tray of a refrigerator.

The speaker, however, was like a fly annealed on the electric-light bulb of the refrigerator. The banks of lights were turned on him, movie lights, TV lights, four thousand watts in the eye must be the average price a politician pays for his press conference. It gives them all a high instant patina, their skin responding to the call of the wild; there is danger, because the press conference creates the moment when the actor must walk into the gears of the machine. While it is a hundred-to-one or a thousand-to-one he will make no mistake, his career can be extinguished by a blunder. Unless one is making news on a given day — which is to say an important announcement is to be made — the press conference is thus a virtuoso price to be paid for remaining in the game, since there are all too many days when it is to the interest of the speaker, or of his party, or his wing of the party, to make no particular news, but rather to repress news. Still, the speaker must not be too dull, or he will hurt his own position, his remarks will be printed too far back in the paper. So he must be interesting without being revealing. Whereas it is to the interest of the press to make him revealing. A delicate game of balance therefore goes on. Nixon used to play well until the day of his breakdown. Eisenhower was once good at it. Goldwater was considered bad at this game, sufficiently bad that at the convention he held but one press conference before his nomination, and in the six preceding weeks had given but two.

An opportunity to observe the game in operation came with Melvin Laird who tried to convince the Press Corps that the Republican platform was liberal, strong on civil rights, critical of extremists, and yet true to Goldwater. Laird, a smooth vigorous man with a bald domelike head, held the breech for half an hour, ducking questions with grace the way Negroes used once to duck baseballs in a carnival. When he got into trouble (it was after all a most untenable position), he called on one of the most necessary rules of the game, which is that you don't insult the good character of the speaker. So Laird would finally say, "We worked hard on this platform, it's a good platform, I'm proud of it." That made the questioners retreat and regroup for a new attack.

Now Scranton's press conferences were of course different — because no one could be certain if Scranton was part of the game or a wild hare diverting the chase from every true scent. The result was a choppiness to the questioning, a sense of irritation, a hint of vast contempt from the Press Corps; a reporter despises a politician who is not professional, for the game then becomes surrealistic, and it is the function of games to keep dreams, dread and surrealism out in the night where they belong. They would dog at

Scranton, they would try to close: *Governor, Governor, could you give the name of any delegate who has moved over from Goldwater to you?* No, we are not prepared to say at this time, would come the answer. *Are there any?* (Titter from the audience.) Certainly. *But you do not care to say?* Not at this time. *Governor* (a new man now) *is there any truth to the rumor you are going to concede before the convention begins?* None whatsoever. *Governor, is it not true that you may be willing to run for vice-president?* For the eighty-eighth time, it is certainly not true. *Unqualifiedly?* Yes (said Scranton sadly) unqualifiedly.

He stood there like a saint, a most curious kind of saint. If he had been an actor he would have played the Dauphin to Ingrid Bergman's Joan of Arc. He was obviously, on superficial study, a weak and stubborn man. One felt he had been spoiled when he was young by a lack of testing. It was not that he lacked bravery, it was that he had lacked all opportunity to be brave for much too long, and now he was not so much engaged in a serious political struggle as in a puberty rite. It was incredible that this pleasant urbane man, so self-satisfied, so civilized, so reasonable, so innocent of butchers' tubs and spleens and guts (that knowledge which radiates with full ceremony off Khrushchev's halo), should be now in fact the man the Eastern Establishment had picked as their candidate for President. He had a fatal flaw to his style, he was just very slightly delicate the way, let us say, a young Madison Avenue executive will seem petulant next to the surly vigor of a president of a steel corporation. Scranton had none of the heft of a political jockstrapper like Goldwater; no, rather he had the big wide thin-lipped mouth of a clown—hopeless! If the roles had been reversed, if it had been Scranton with six hundred delegates and Goldwater who led a rush in the last four weeks to steal the land, why Goldwater might still have won. Scranton was decent but some part of his soul seemed to live in the void. Doubtless he had been more formidable when he began, but he had been losing for four weeks, one loss after another, delegates, delegations, caucuses, he had been losing with Eisenhower, he had lost with Dirksen, he had lost Illinois, he was losing Ohio, his wheeler-dealers stood by idle wheels; you cannot deal when you are losing delegates, there is nothing to offer the delegate but the salvation of his soul, and the delegate has put salvation in hock a long time ago. So Scranton had begun with the most resistant of missions—there are few works in life so difficult as to pry delegates loose from a man who has a nomination virtually won. To be a delegate and stick with the loser is a kind of life, but no delegate can face the possibility of going from a winner to a loser; the losses are not measurable. People are in politics to win.

In these circumstances, consider the political weight lifting required of Scranton. He announces his candidacy four weeks before the convention, Goldwater within fifty votes of the nomination. Is Scranton to pull delegates loose from such a scene by an unhappy faculty for getting pictures taken with his legs in the air doing polkas, R.C.A.F. exercises, and backhands in tennis? One knows Scranton's the product of a good many evenings when Eastern gentry circled around cigars and brandy and decided on poor Bill because he was finally not offensive to any. But it would have taken Paul Bunyan to claw into Goldwater's strength from four weeks out. His two hundred plus of Southern delegates were firm as marble, firm as their hatred of Civil Rights. And there was much other strength for Barry from the Midwest and the West, a hard core of delegates filled with hot scalding hatred for the Eastern Establishment. They were (unlike the children who were for Goldwater) this hard core of delegates, composed in large part of the kind of tourists who had been poisoning the air of hotel lobbies for twenty years. You could see them now with their Goldwater buttons, ensconced in every lobby, a Wasp Mafia where the grapes of wrath were stored. Not for nothing did the White Anglo-Saxon Protestant have a five-year subscription to *Reader's Digest* and *National Geographic*, high colonics and arthritis, silver-rimmed spectacles, punched-out bellies, and that air of controlled schizophrenia which is the merit badge for having spent one's life on Main Street. Indeed there was general agreement that the basic war was between Main Street and Wall Street. What was not seen so completely is that this war is the Wagnerian drama of the Wasp. For a century now the best of the White Protestants have been going from the farm to the town, leaving the small city for the larger one, transferring from Shaker Heights High to Lawrenceville, from Missouri State Teacher's to Smith, from Roast Turkey to Cordon Rouge, off rectitude onto wickedness, out of monogamy into *Les Liaisons Dangereuses*, from *Jane Eyre* to *Candy;* it's a long trip from the American Legion's Annual Ball to the bust-outs of Southampton. There's the unheard cry of a wounded coyote in all the minor leagues of the Junior League, in all the tacky doings of each small town, the grinding rasp of envy rubs the liver of each big frog in his small pond, no hatred like hatred for the East in the hearts of those who were left behind: the horror in the heart of social life in America is that one never knows whether one is snubbed for too much or too little, whether one was too fine or not fine enough, too graceless or too possessed of special grace, too hungry for power or not ambitious enough—the questions are burning and never answered because the Establishment of the East rarely rejects, it merely yields or ignores, it promises and forgets, it offers to attend your daughter's party and somehow does not quite show up, or comes that fraction too late which is designed to spoil the high anticipation of the night. (Or worse, leaves a fraction too early.) The Wasps who were for Goldwater were the social culls of that Eastern Society which ran the land, yes, the Goldwater Wasps were the old doctors of Pasadena with their millions in stock and their grip on the A.M.A., the small-town newspaper editors, the president of the second most important bank, the wives of Texas oil, yes the wives and family of all the prominent and prosperous who had a fatal touch of the hick, all the Western ladies who did the Merengue at El Morocco on a trip to New York, and did it not quite well enough, you could just hear the giggles in the throat of Archie or Lightning Dick or Sad One-Eye, the Haitian and/or Jamaican who had taught them how. Yes the memory of those social failures is the saliva of intellectual violence. The old Goldwater Wasps, the ones who had been sitting in the hotel lobbies, had an insane sting to their ideas—they were for birching America's bare bottom where Come-you-nisms collected: white and Negro equality; sexual excess; Jew ideas; dirty linen, muddled thinking, lack of respect for the Constitution. The Right in America had an impacted consistency of constipation to their metaphor. Small wonder they dreamed of a Republican purge. The Wasps were full of psychic wastes they could not quit—they had moved into the Middle West and settled the West, they had won the country, and now they were losing it to the immigrants who had come after and the descendants of slaves. They had watched as their culture was adulterated, transported, converted into some surrealist mélange of public piety *cum* rock and roll, product of the movies and television, of the mass media where sons of immigrants were so often king, yes the Wasps did not understand what was going on, they were not so ready after all to listen to those of their ministers who would argue that America had a heritage of sin and greed vis-à-vis the Negro, and those sins of the blood must be paid; they were not at all ready to listen to the argument that America's industry had been built out of the hardworking hard-used flesh of five generations of immigrants, no, they were Christian but they did not want to hear any more about the rights of others, they suffered from the private fear they were not as good, not as tough, not as brave as their great-grandfathers, they suffered from the intolerable fear that they were not nearly so good nor so tough as those other Christians close to two thousand years ago who faced Romans, so they were now afraid of the East which had dominated the fashion and style of their life, they were ready to murder the East, the promiscuous adulterous East—in a good fast nuclear war they might allow the Russians a fair crack at New York—yes they were loaded with one hatred: the Eastern Establishment was not going to win again, this time Main Street was going to take Wall Street. So Barry had his brothers, three or four hundred of the hardest delegates in the land, and they were ready to become the lifelong enemy of any delegate who might waver to Scranton.

That was the mood. That was the inner condition of the Goldwater delegates about the time Scranton announced he was going all out for the nomination and would pry these people loose from Barry. Henry Cabot Lodge came in from Vietnam. He was, you remember, going to help. Cynics in the Establishment were quick to inform you that Lodge was actually getting the hell out before the roof fell in, but Lodge gave this message to reporters:

> . . . *One of the things that always used to please me about being in Vietnam was the thought that I might as an older man be able to do something to help our soldiers who were out risking their lives.*
>
> *Well, a couple of weeks ago I ran into this captain who was one of the battalion advisors and he said, "Are you going back to help Governor Scranton?" And I said, "No." Well, he said, "You're not?" He said, "I think you ought to."*
>
> *Well, that gave me quite a—that startled me, rather, because his attitude was: "I'm doing my duty out here, you'd better get back and do your duty pretty fast."*

Obviously, no one had ever told Henry Cabot Lodge he might not necessarily be superb. So he came in, kingpin, boy, and symbol of the Establishment, and for two weeks he worked for Scranton (although most curiously—for Lodge was back in America a week before he even made arrangements to meet with Scranton). Still, Lodge announced his readiness to be first target of the Wasp Mafia. At the end of two weeks of picking up the telephone to call old friends only to have the telephone come back in the negative, Lodge looked like a man who had been handsome once. His color was a dirty wax yellow, his smile went up over the gums at the corner of his mouth and gave a hint of the skull the way ninety-year-old men look when their smile goes past the teeth. He looked like they had been beating him in the kidneys with his own liver. It was possible something had been beaten out of him forever.

Of course this was Sunday night—the first session of the convention was not ten hours off on Monday morning—and Scranton and Lodge had had a ferocious bad Sunday; the particular letter inviting Goldwater to debate Scranton before the convention had gone out earlier that day above the Governor's signature and it had gone so far as this:

Your managers say in effect that the delegates are little more than a flock of chickens whose necks will be wrung at will. . . . Goldwaterism has come to stand for a whole crazy-quilt collection of absurd and dangerous positions that would be soundly repudiated by the American people in November.

Denison Kitchel, Goldwater's General Director of the National Goldwater for President Committee, issued a statement:

Governor Scranton's letter has been read here with amazement. It has been returned to him.
Perhaps, upon consideration, the Governor will recognize the intemperate nature of his remarks. As it stands, they tragically reflect upon the Republican Party and upon every delegate to the convention.

Then Kitchel sent out mimeographed copies of Scranton's letter and his own reply to every Republican delegate. The Scranton mine caved in. Flooding at one end of the shaft, it was now burning at the other. Delegates do not like to be told they are a flock of chickens. It is one of those metaphors which fit like a sliver of bone up the nostril. Scranton was to repudiate his letter the following day; he accepted responsibility but disowned the letter—the language was not his—which is to say he admitted he could not run a competent organization. Nor, it developed, could he protect his own people: the name of the assistant who had actually written the letter slipped out quick enough.

Thus, one night before the convention, the letter public, Scranton may just conceivably have moved from deep depression to outright agony. The Republicans were having a Gala that night, five hundred dollars a plate for funds, the press not admitted, although many, some from the front, some from the rear, found a way in, and all the Republican luminaries were there, Eisenhower, and the Luces, Mrs. Eisenhower, Henry Cabot Lodge, Thruston Morton, George Murphy, Ray Bliss, Mrs. Goldwater, Scranton. All but Barry. In a much-announced rage about the letter, Goldwater was boycotting the Gala. Of course, it was essentially an Establishment Gala, that slowly came clear, and therefore was in degree a wake—news of the letter passing around. The dance floor was not to be crowded this night.

Scranton came in. He walked down the center aisle between the tables looking like one of the walking wounded. People came up to greet him and he smiled wanly and sadly and a little stiffly as if he were very weary indeed, as if he had just committed hara-kiri but was still walking. When introduced, he said with wan humor, "I've read your books"—something finally splendid about Scranton.

A minute later, Scranton and Eisenhower came together. It was their first meeting in San Francisco; the General had just arrived that day, come into the Santa Fe depot after crossing the country by train. He was Scranton's last hope; he might still give momentum to the bogged-down tanks of Scranton's attack—what, after all, was the measure of magic? So Scranton must have looked for every clue in Eisenhower's greeting. There were clues running all over. Ike stood up from his table, he pumped Scranton's hand, he held his elbow, he wheeled about with him, he grinned, he smiled widely, he grinned again, his face flushed red, red as a two-week-old infant's face, his eyes twinkled, he never stopped talking, he never took his hands off Scranton, he never looked him in the eye. It was the greeting of a man who is not going to help another man.

Next day, Eisenhower dropped William Warren Scranton. He had a press conference at the Hilton in which he succeeded in saying nothing. It was obvious now he would not come out for anyone, it was also obvious he would not join the Moderates' call for a stronger civil-rights plank. "Well," he said, "he [Melvin Laird] came to see me, and the way he explained it to me, it sounded all right." Asked about an amendment the Moderates wished to put in the plank, "The authority to use America's nuclear weapons belongs to the President of the United States," Eisenhower thought "this statement was perfectly all right with me because it reaffirms what the Constitution means." Still he would not fight for it. Asked how he reacted to the idea of a debate before the entire convention between Senator Goldwater and Governor Scranton, a reference directed to Scranton's now famous letter of the day before, Eisenhower said, "This, of course, would be a precedent, and I am not against precedents. I am not particularly for them." A little earlier he had said, "I really have no feeling of my own." He didn't. He was in a private pond. He had been in one for years. Something had been dying in him for years, the proportions and magnitude of his own death no doubt, and he was going down into the cruelest of fates for an old man, he was hooked on love like an addict, not large love, but the kind of mild tolerant love which shields an old man from hatred. It was obvious that Eisenhower had a deep fear of the forces which were for Goldwater. He did not mind with full pride any longer if people felt contempt for him, but he did not want to be hated hard by anyone. So he could not declare himself, not for anything, and as he made his lapses in syntax, in word orders, in pronunciations, they took on more prominence than ever they had. At times, they were as rhythmic as a tic, or a dog scratching at a bite. He would say, "We must be objec*tive*, I mean ob*jec*tive, we must be objective . . ." and on he would go as if he were sinking very slowly and quietly into the waters of his future death which might be a year away or ten years away but was receiving him nonetheless like a marsh into which he disappeared twitch by twitch, some beating of wet wings against his fate.

"*. . . Looke, Lord, and finde both Adams met in me.*"

— JOHN DONNE

Now, as for Goldwater, he had dimensions. Perhaps they were no more than contradictions, but he was not an easy man to comprehend in a hurry. His wife, for example, had been at the Gala, sitting with some family and friends, but at one of the less agreeable tables on the floor, off to the side and sufficiently back of the stage so that you could not see the entertainer. It seemed a curious way for the Establishment to treat the wife of the leading contender, but I was assured by the young lady who brought me over for the introduction that Mrs. Goldwater preferred it that way. "She hates being the center of attention," I was told. Well, she turned out to be a shy attractive woman with a gentle not altogether happy but sensual face. There was something nice about her and very vulnerable. Her eyes were moist, they were luminous. It was impossible not to like her. Whereas her daughters were attractive in a different fashion. "I want the best ring in this joint, buster," I could hear them say.

Goldwater's headquarters, however, were at a remove from the ladies. Occupying the fourteenth and fifteenth floors of the Mark Hopkins, they were not easy to enter. The main elevators required a wait of forty-five minutes to go up. The alternate route was off the mezzanine through a pantry onto a service car. A half-filled twenty-gallon garbage can stood by the service-elevator door. You went squeezed up tight with high and low honchos for Goldwater, plus waiters with rolling carts working room service. Once there, the fourteenth and fifteenth floors were filthy. A political headquarters is never clean — stacks of paper, squeezed-out paper cups, typewriter carbons on the floor, jackets on wire hangers all angles on a rack — a political headquarters is like the City Room of a newspaper. But Goldwater's headquarters were filthier than most. There was a general detritus like the high-water mark on a beach. The armchairs were dusty and the sofas looked like hundred-dollar newlywed sofas dirty in a day. The air had the beat-out cigar smell of the waiting room in a large railroad station. It had nothing to do with the personnel. No one on the fourteenth or fifteenth floor had anything to do with his surroundings. You could have dropped them in Nymphenburg or a fleabag off Eighth Avenue—the rooms would come to look the same. A room was a place with a desk where the work got out.

They had something in common—professional workers for Goldwater—something not easy to define. They were not like the kids out in the street, nor did they have much in common with the old cancer-guns in the lobby; no, the worst of these workers looked like divinity students who had been expelled from the seminary for embezzling class funds and still felt they were nearest to J.C.— there was a dark blank fanaticism in their eyes. And the best of the Goldwater professionals were formidable, big rangy men, some lean, some flabby, with the hard distasteful look of topflight investi- gators for fire-insurance companies, field men for the F.B.I., or like bright young district attorneys, that lean flat look of the hunter, full of moral indignation and moral vacuity. But the total of all the pro- fessional Goldwater people one saw on the fourteenth and fifteenth floors was directly reminiscent of a guided tour through the F.B.I. in the Department of Justice Building in Washington, that same succession of handsome dull faces for guide, hair combed straight back or combed straight from a part, eyes lead shot, noses which offered nothing, mouths which were functional, good chins, deft moves. A succession of these men took the tourists through the halls of the F.B.I. and read aloud the signs on the exhibits for us and gave short lectures about the function of the F.B.I. (guard us from the enemy without, the enemy within, Communism and Crime—the statements offered in simple organizational prose of the sort used in pamphlets which welcome new workers to large corporations, soldiers to new commands, freshmen to high school, and magazine readers to editorials). The tourists were mainly fa- thers and sons. The wives were rugged, the kind who are built for dungarees and a green plaid hunting jacket, the sisters and daugh- ters plain and skinny, no expression. They all had lead shot for eyes, the lecturers and the tourists. Most of the boys were near twelve and almost without exception had the blank private faces which belong to kids who kill their old man with a blast, old lady with a butcher knife, tie sister with telephone cord and hide out in the woods for three days. The climax of the tour was a demonstra- tion by the F.B.I. agent how to use a tommy gun. For ten minutes he stitched targets, using one shot at a time, bursts of three, full magazine, he did it with the mild grace of a bodyworker hitting small rivets, there was solemn applause after each burst of shots.

That was a part of the Republic, and here it was at Headquarters for Goldwater. The faces in these rooms were the cream of the tourists and the run of the F.B.I.; there was a mood like the inside of a prison: enclosed air, buried urgency. But that was not altogether fair. The sense of a prison could come from the number of guards and the quality of their style. They were tough dull Pinkertons with a tendency to lean on a new visitor. One desire came off them. They would not be happy if there were no orders to follow. With orders, they were ready to put the arm on Bill Scranton, Nelson Rockefeller, or General Eisenhower (if told to). Probably they would put the arm on Johnson if he appeared and was ordered out. Naturally they were not there for that, they were there to defend Headquarters from mobs (read: niggers) and the Senator from black assassination. It made sense up to a point: Goldwater was in more danger than Scranton, at least so long as Scranton showed no sign of winning; just that day, Sunday, there had been a civil-rights anti-Goldwater march down Market Street. The heavy protection was nonetheless a fraud. No mob was getting to the fourteenth floor, nor to Goldwater's fort on the fifteenth (a separate barricade of Pinkertons guarded the twenty-odd steps), no mob was going to get all the way up with just those three elevators and a wait of forty-five units of sixty seconds each, no assassin was likely to try Headquarters when there were opportunities on the street; no, the atmosphere was created to create atmosphere, the aura at Headquarters was solemnity, debris underfoot, and grave decisions, powers put to the service of order, some conspiracy of the vault, a dedication to the necessity of taking power. That was Headquarters. One never got to see Goldwater in the place.

There was opportunity, however, to come within three feet of him later that day, once at the caucus of the Florida delegation in the Beverly Plaza, once on the street moving from hotel to hotel (Pinkertons no longer in evidence now—just cops) and again at the Clift, where he talked to the Washington delegation. There was excitement watching Barry go to work with a group, an intensity in the air, a religious devotion, as if one of the most urbane priests of America was talking at a Communion breakfast, or as if the Prinicpal-of-the-Year was having a heart-to-heart with honor students. The Florida delegation, meeting in a dingy little downstairs banquet room, was jammed. The afternoon had turned hot for San Francisco. Eighty degrees outside, it may have been ninety in the room. Everybody was perspiring. Barry sat in the front, a spotlight on him, a silver film of perspiration adding to his patina, and the glasses, those black-framed glasses, took on that odd life of their own, that pinched severity, that uncompromising idealism which made Goldwater kin to the tight-mouthed and the lonely. Talking in a soft modest voice, he radiated at this moment the skinny boyish sincerity of a fellow who wears glasses but is determined nonetheless to have a good time. Against all odds. It was not unreminiscent of Arthur Miller: that same mixture of vast solemnity and unspoiled boyhood, a sort of shucks and aw shit in the voice. "Well, you see," said Goldwater, talking to the Florida delegation, "if I was to trust the polls right now, I'd have to say I didn't have a chance. But why should I trust the polls? Why should any of us trust the polls? They've been wrong before. They'll be wrong again. Man is superior to the machine. The thing to remember is that America is a spiritual country, we're founded on belief in God, we may wander a little as a country, but we never get too far away. I'm ready to say the election is going to give the Democrats a heck of a surprise. Why, I'll tell you this," Goldwater said, sweating mildly, telling the folks from Florida just as keen as if he was alone with each one of them, each one of these elderly gents and real-estate dealers and plain women with silver-rimmed eyeglasses, "tell you this, I'm doing my best not to keep this idea a secret, but I think we're not only going to give the Democrats a heck of a surprise, I think we're going to win. [Applause, cheers.] In fact I wouldn't be in this if I didn't think we were going to win. [Applause.] Why, as I sometimes tell my wife, I'm too young to retire and too old to go back to work." [Laughter, loud cheers.] Goldwater was done. He smiled shyly, his glasses saying: I am a modest man, and I am severe on myself. As he made his route to the door, the delegates were touching him enthusiastically.

Back on the street—he was walking the blocks to the Hotel Clift where the Washington State delegation was having a Goldwater reception—his tail consisted of fifty or sixty excited people, some Florida delegates who didn't wish to lose sight of the man, plus a couple of cops glad to have the duty. Cars slowed down to look at him; one stopped. A good-looking woman got out and cheered. There was something in the way she did it. Just as strange Negroes scattered at random through a white audience may act in awareness of one another, so the Goldwater supporters in their thirties and forties gave off a similar confidence of holding the secret. This very good-looking woman yelled, "You go, Barry, you go, go." But there was anger and elation in her voice, as if she were declaring, "We're going to get the country back." And Goldwater smiled modestly and went on. He looked a little in fever. Small wonder. He could be President of the United States in less than half a year, he could stop a sniper's bullet he never knew when, he was more loved and hated than any man in America, and inside all this was just *him*, the man who adjusted radio knobs in the early morning in order to transmit a little better, and now conceivably adjusted a few knobs. . . .

At the Hotel Clift he talked to the Washington delegates. We were definitely back in high school. That was part of Goldwater's deal — he brought you back to the bright minted certitudes of early patriotism when you knew the U.S. was the best country on earth and there was no other. Yes, his appeal would go out to all the millions who were now starved and a little sour because some part of their life had ended in high school, and the university they had never seen. But then Barry had had but one year of college — he had indeed the mind of a powerful freshman. "I want to thank you folks from Washington for giving me this warm greeting. Of course, Washington is the name of a place I often like to get the heck out of, but I'm sure I won't confuse the two right here." [Laughter.] He was off, a short political speech. In the middle, extremism. "I don't see how anybody can be an extremist who believes in the Constitution. And for those misguided few who pretend to believe in the Constitution, but in secret don't, well they may be extremists, but I don't see any necessity to legislate against them. I just feel sorry for them." [Cheers. Applause. Happiness at the way Barry delivered anathemas.] At a certain point in the speech, he saw a woman in the audience whom he recognized, and stopped in the middle of a phrase. "Hi, honey," he sang out like a traveling salesman, which brought a titter from the delegation, for his voice had shifted too quickly, the codpiece was coming off, Rain and the Reverend Davidson. Something skinny, itchy, hard as a horse-laugh, showed — he was a cannoneer with a hairy ear. Goldwater went on, the good mood continued; then at the end, speech done, he turned down a drink but said in his best gee-whizzer, "I'm sorry I have to leave because gosh I'd like to break a few with you." Laughter, and he took off head down, a little modest in the exit, a little red in the neck.

There was entertainment at the Republican Gala on Sunday night. The climax was a full marching band of bagpipers. They must have been hired for the week since one kept hearing them on the following days, and at all odd times, heard them even in my hotel room at four a.m., for a few were marching in the streets of San Francisco, sounding through the night, giving off the barbaric evocation of the Scots, all valor, wrath, firmitude, and treachery — the wild complete treachery of the Scots finding its way into the sound of the pipes. They were a warning of the fever in the heart of the Wasp. There are sounds which seem to pass through all the protective gates in the ear and reach into some nerve where the eschatology is stored. Few parents have failed to hear it in the cry of their infant through the morning hours of a bad night—stubbornness, fury, waste, and the promise of revenge come out of a flesh half-created by one's own flesh; the knowledge is suddenly there that seed is existential, no paradise resides in seed, seed can be ill-inspired and go to a foul gloomy end. Some find their part of the truth in listening to jazz—it is moot if any white who had no ear for jazz can know the passion with which some whites become attached to the Negro's cause. So, too, listening to the bagpipes, you knew this was the true music of the Wasps. There was something wild and martial and bottomless in the passion, a pride which would not be exhausted, a determination which might never end, perhaps should never end, the Faustian rage of a white civilization was in those Highland wails, the cry of a race which was born to dominate and might never learn to share, and never learning, might be willing to end the game, the end of the world was in the sound of the pipes. Or at very least the danger one would come closer to the world's end. So there was a vast if all-private appeal in listening to the pipes shrill out the herald of a new crusade, something jagged, Viking, of the North in the air, a sense of breaking ice and barbaric shields, hunters loose in the land again. And this had an appeal which burrowed deep, there was excitement at the thought of Goldwater getting the nomination, as if now finally all one's personal suicides, all the deaths of the soul accumulated by the past, all the failures, all the terrors, could find purge in a national situation where a national murder was being planned (the Third World War) and one's own suicide might be lost in a national suicide. There was that excitement, that the burden of one's soul (always equal to the burden of one's personal responsibility) might finally be lifted—what a release was there! Beauty was inspired by the prospect. For if Goldwater won, and the iron power of the iron people who had pushed him forth—as echoed in the iron of the Pinkertons on the fourteenth and fifteenth floor—now pushed forth over the nation an iron regime with totalitarianism seizing the TV in every frozen dinner, well then at last a true underground might form; and liberty at the thought of any catalyst which could bring it on. Yes, the Goldwater movement excited the depths because the apocalypse was brought more near, and like millions of other whites, I had been leading a life which was a trifle too pointless and a trifle too full of guilt and my gullet was close to nausea with the endless compromises of an empty liberal center. So I followed the four days of the convention with something more than simple apprehension. The country was taking a turn, the colors were deepening, the knives of the afternoon were out, something of the best in American life might now be going forever; or was it altogether to the opposite? and was the country starting at last to take the knots of its contradictions up from a premature midnight of nightmare into the surgical terrains of the open skin? Were we in the beginning, or turning the middle, of our worst disease? One did not know any longer, you simply did not know any longer, but something was certain: the country was now part of the daily concern. One worried about it for the first time, the way you worried about family or work, a good friend or the future, and that was the most exceptional of emotions.

II

". . . When men are too much confined to professional and faculty habits, and as it were inveterate in the recurrent employment of that narrow circle, they are rather disabled than qualified for whatever depends on the knowledge of mankind, on experience in mixed affairs, on a comprehensive, connected view of the various, complicated, external and internal interests, which go to the formation of that multifarious thing called a state."

— BURKE, *Reflections on the Revolution in France*

If the details of the Republican convention of 1964 were steeped in concern, it was nonetheless not very exciting, not technically. As a big football game, the score might have been 76 to 0, or 76 to 3. (There were sentimentalists who would claim that Rockefeller kicked a field goal.) Compared however to the Republican Convention of 1940 when Wendell Willkie came from behind to sweep the nomination on the sixth ballot, or the 1952 convention when Eisenhower defeated Taft on the second roll call of the states, compared even to the Democratic Convention of 1960, there were few moments in this affair, and nothing even remotely comparable in excitement to the demonstration for Adlai Stevenson four years ago when Eugene McCarthy put him in nomination. Yet this convention of 1964 would remain as one of the most important in our history; it took place with religious exaltation for some, with dread for others, and in sheer trauma for the majority of the press and television who were present on the scene. For them it offered four days of anxiety as pure and deep as a child left alone in a house. The purpose of the press in America has been to tinker with the machine, to adjust, to prepare a seat for new valves and values, to lubricate, to excuse, to justify, to serve in the maintenance of the Establishment. From I. F. Stone on the left, going far to the right of Joseph Alsop, over almost so far as David Lawrence, the essential understanding of the mass media is that the machine of the nation is a muddle which is endlessly grateful for ministrations of the intellect; so a game is played in which the Establishment always forgives the mass media for its excesses, and the mass media brings its sense of civilization (adjustment, psychoanalysis, responsibility, and the milder shores of love) to the service of the family Establishment. Virtually everything is forgiven by both sides. The contradictory remarks of politicians are forgotten, the more asinine predictions of pundits are buried with mercy. The Establishment for example would not remind Joe Alsop that in March 1964 he had written, "No serious Republican politician, even of the most Neanderthal type, any longer takes Goldwater seriously." No, the Press was not to be twitted for the limits of their technique because half their comprehension of the nation derived after all from material supplied by the Establishment; the other half came from conversations with each other. All too often the Press lives in the investigative condition of a lover who performs the act for two minutes a day and talks about it for twenty hours of the twenty-four. So a daisy chain like the *National Review* proves to be right about Goldwater's strength and the intellectual Establishment with its corporate resources is deep in error.

An explanation? Those who hold power think the devil is best contained by not mentioning his name. This procedure offers a formidable shell in which to live, but its cost is high; the housing is too ready to collapse when the devil decides to show. There has been no opportunity to study him. Just as a generation of the Left, stifled and ignored through the McCarthyism of the Fifties and the Eisenhowerism of the Fifties, caused panic everywhere when they emerged as the Beat Generation, so another generation, a generation of the Right, has been stifled, their actions reported inaccurately, their remarks distorted, their ideals (such as they are) ignored, and their personal power underestimated. The difference however is that the Beat Generation was a new flock of early Christians gathered prematurely before the bomb, an open-air asylum for the gentle and the mad, where in contrast the underground generation of the Right is a frustrated posse, a convention of hangmen who subscribe to the principle that the executioner has his rights as well. The liberal mind collapses before this notion but half of nature may be contained in the idea that the weak are happiest when death is quick. It is a notion which since the Nazis has been altogether detestable, but then the greatest intellectual damage the Nazis may have done was to take a few principles from nature and pervert them root and nerve. In the name of barbarism and a return to primitive health they accelerated the most total and surrealistic aspects of civilization. The gas chamber was a full albino descendant of the industrial revolution.

But that is a digression. To return to the as yet milder political currents of the Left and the Right in America, one could say the Beat Generation was a modest revolution, suicidal in the center of its passion. At its most militant it wished for immolation rather than power, it desired only to be left free enough to consume itself. Yet in the mid-Fifties liberals reacted with a profound terror, contumely, and ridicule to its manifestations as if their own collective suicide (the private terror of the liberal spirit is invariably suicide, not murder) was to be found in the gesture of the Beat. What then the panic of the liberal Establishment before a revolution of the Right whose personal nightmare might well be their inability to contain their most murderous impulse, a movement of the Right whose ghost is that unlaid blood and breath of Nazism which has hovered these twenty years like a succubus over the washed-out tissues of civilization. Consider but one evidence of the fear: that part of the Press called Periodicals sat in a section of the gallery to the left of the speakers in the Cow Palace. There were one hundred writers in this Periodical section of the gallery and six passes to get down to the floor where one could talk to delegates and in turn be looked at by them. Of those six passes, one or two were always available. Which meant that the majority of writers did not try to get down to the floor very often. Sitting next to one another the writers were content to observe — there were killers on the floor.

There were. It was a convention murderous in mood. The mood of this convention spoke of a new kind of society. Chimeras of fascism hung like fogbank. And high enthusiasm. Some of the delegates were very happy. "*Viva*," would shout a part of the gallery. "*Olé*," would come the answer. There was an éclat, a bull roar, a mystical communion in the sound even as *Sieg Heil* used to offer its mystical communion. *Viva-Olé.* Live-Yay! Live-Yay! It was the new chic of the mindless. The American mind had gone from Hawthorne and Emerson to the Frug, the Bounce, and Walking the Dog, from *The Flowering of New England* to the cerebrality of professional football in which a quarterback must have not only heart, courage, strength and grace but a mind like an I.B.M. computer. It marks the turn we have taken from the Renaissance. There too was the ideal of a hero with heart, courage, strength, and grace, but he was expected to possess the mind of a passionate artist. Now the best heroes were — in the sense of the Renaissance — mindless: Y. A. Tittle, John Glenn, Tracy, Smiling Jack; the pas-

sionate artists were out on the hot rods, the twist band was whipping the lovers, patriotism was a football game, a fascism would
come in (if it came) on Live-Yay! Let's live-yay! The hype had
made fifty million musical-comedy minds; now the hype could do
anything; it could set high-school students to roar *Viva-Olé*, and
they would roar it while victims of a new totalitarianism would be
whisked away to a new kind of camp—hey, honey, do you twist,
they would yell into the buses.

*"When men of rank sacrifice all ideas of dignity to an ambition
without a distinct object, and work with low instruments and for
low ends, the whole composition becomes low and base."*

— BURKE, *Reflections on the Revolution in France*

First major event of the convention was Eisenhower's appearance at the Cow Palace to give a speech on Tuesday afternoon.
The arena was well-chosen for a convention. Built in the Thirties
when indoor sports stadiums did not yet look like children's nurseries, the Cow Palace offered echoes—good welterweights and
middleweights had fought here, there was iron in the air. And the
Republicans had installed the speaker's platform at one end of the
oval; the delegates sat therefore in a file which was considerably
longer than it was wide, the speaker was thus installed at the handle of the sword. (Whereas the Democrats in 1960 had put the
speaker in the middle of the oval.) But this was the party after all
of Republican fathers rather than Democratic mothers. If there
were any delegates to miss the psychic effect of this decision, a
huge banner raised behind the speaker confronted them with the
legend: Of the people, By the people, For the people. "Of the people" was almost invisible; "By the people" was somewhat more
clear; "For the people" was loud and strong. This was a party not
much "of the people" but very much "for the people," it presumed
to know what was good for them.

And for fact, that had always been Ike's poor lone strength as a
speaker, he knew what was good for you. He dipped into his
speech, "here with great pride because I am a Republican," "my
deep dedication to Republicanism"—he had not been outward
bound for five minutes before the gallery was yawning. Ike had
always been a bore, but there had been fascination in the boredom
when he was President—this, after all, was *the* man. Now he was
just another hog wrassler of rhetoric; he pinned a few phrases in
his neat determined little voice, and a few phrases pinned him
back. Ike usually fought a speech to a draw. It was hard to listen.
All suspense had ended at Monday morning's press conference.

Ike would not come out in support of Scranton. So the mind of the Press drifted out with the mind of the gallery. If Ike said a few strong words about the Civil Rights Bill—"Republicans in Congress to their great credit voted far more overwhelmingly than did our opponents to pass the Civil Rights Bill"—it meant nothing. The Moderates tried to whoop it up, the Goldwater delegations looked on in ranked masses of silence. Ike went on. He gave the sort of speech which takes four or five columns in the New York *Times* and serves to clot the aisles of history. He was still, as he had been when he was President, a cross between a boy and an old retainer. The boy talked, earnest, innocent, a high-school valedictorian debating the affirmative of, Resolved: Capitalism is the Most Democratic System on Earth; and the old retainer quavered into the voice, the old retainer could no longer live without love.

Ike had bored many a crowd in his time. He had never bored one completely—he had always known how to get some token from a mob. Ever since 1952, he had been giving little pieces of his soul to draw demonstrations from the mob. You could always tell the moment. His voice shifted. Whenever he was ready to please the crowd, he would warn them by beginning to speak with a brisk little anger. Now it came, now he said it. ". . . Let us particularly scorn the *divisive* efforts of those outside our family, including sensation-seeking columnists and commentators [beginning of a wild demonstration] because," said Ike, his voice showing a glint of full spite, "I assure you that these are people who couldn't care less about the good of our party." He was right, of course. That was not why he said it, however; he said it to repay the Press for what they had said about him these last three weeks; the sensation they had been seeking was—so far as he was concerned—to arouse needles of fury in an old man's body—he said what he said for revenge. Mainly he said it to please the Goldwater crowd, there was the hint of that in his voice. The Goldwater delegations and the gallery went into the first large demonstration of the convention. Trumpets sounded, heralds of a new crusade: cockroaches, columnists, and Communists to be exterminated. There were reports in the papers next day that delegates shook their fists at newspapermen on the floor, and at the television men with their microphones. The mass media is of course equipped for no such war. Some of the men from the mass media looked like moon men: they wore red helmets and staggered under the load of a portable camera which must have weighed fifty pounds and was packed on their back; others of the commentators had portable mikes and hats with antennae. To the delegates they must have looked like insects grown to the size of a man. Word whipped in to the delegations from the all-call telephone in the office trailer of the Goldwater command post back of the Cow Palace. Cut the demonstration, was the word from F. Clifton White. The demonstration subsided. But the Press did not, the rest of the mass media did not. They remain in a state of agitation: if Ike was ready to accuse, anyone could serve as hangman. Anyone would. Anyone they knew.

Much later that Tuesday, after the full reading of the full platform, came a debate between the Moderates and the Conservatives. Success in politics comes from putting one's seat to a chair and sitting through dull wrangles in order to be present after midnight when the clubhouse vote is cast. Playboys do not go far in these circumstances, nor adventurers; the mediocre recognized early that a society was evolving which would enable them to employ the very vice which hitherto had made life intolerable — mediocrity itself. So the cowardly took their place in power. They had the superior ability to breathe in hours of boredom.

Politics was now open however to the disease of the bored — magic. Magic can sweep you away. Once a decade, once every two decades, like a big wind which eludes the weather charts and seems to arise from the caverns of the ocean itself, so does a hurricane sweep a convention. It happened with Wendell Willkie in 1940; it flickered on the horizon with Stevenson in '60; it was Scranton's hope to work a real debate on the last session before the balloting. If he could win even once on some small point, rumors of magic could arise. The Moderates had forced therefore a floor fight to propose a few amendments to the Republican platform of '64. One: that only the President have the authority to use America's nuclear weapons. Two: repudiate the John Birch Society. Three: introduce a language of approval for the Civil Rights Act. The chances of success were small at best: only an extraordinary assault on the emotions of the Goldwater delegations could sway them to vote yes for the amendments.

The Moderates however went to battle moderately. Their speakers were impressive (as such a quality is measured in the *Times*). They were Christian Herter, Hugh Scott, Clifford Case, George Romney, Lindsay, Javits, Rockefeller. They were not, however, lively speakers, not this night. Lindsay and Javits were presentable in professional groups; devoted to detailed matters, they spoke with reason; Case spoke like a shy high-school teacher; Christian Herter was reminiscent of Mr. Chips; Hugh Scott owned no fire. Carlino (Majority Leader in the New York Assembly) sounded like a successful restaurant owner. And Governor Romney of Michigan had his own special amendments, he was a moderation of the moderates. As he spoke, he looked like a handsome version of Boris Karloff, all honesty, big-jawed, soft-eyed, eighty days at sea on a cock-eyed passion. He spoke in a loud strong voice yet one sensed a yaw at the center of his brain which left his cerebrations as lost as Karloff's lost little voice. No, the only excitement had come at the beginning. Rockefeller was not a man who would normally inspire warmth. He had a strong decent face and something tough as the rubber in a handball to his makeup, but his eyes had been punched out a long time ago — they had the distant lunar glow of the small sad eyes you see in a caged chimpanzee or gorilla. Even when hearty he gave an impression the private man was remote as an astronaut on a lost orbit. But Rockefeller had his ten minutes at the podium and as he talked of suffering "at first-hand" in the California primary from the methods of "extremist elements," threatening letters unsigned, bomb threats, "threats of personal violence," telephone calls, "smear and hate literature," "strong-arm and goon tactics," the gallery erupted, and the boos and jeers came down. Rockefeller could have been Leo Durocher walking out to the plate at Ebbets Field to protest an umpire's decision after Leo had moved from the Dodgers to the Giants. Again the all-call in the Goldwater trailer ouside the Cow Palace was busy, again the delegations were told to be silent, and obeyed. But the gallery would not stop, and Thruston Morton, the Chairman, came forward like one of the sweepers in *Camino Real* to tell Kilroy his time was up. Rockefeller had his moment. "You quiet them," he said to Morton. "That's your job. I want my time to speak." And there was a conception of Rockefeller finally — he had few ideas and none of them were his own, he had a personality which was never in high focus (in the sense that Bobby Kennedy and Jimmy Hoffa are always in high focus) but he had an odd courage which was profound — he could take strength from defying a mob. Three hundred thousand years ago, a million years ago, some gorilla must have stood up to an enraged tribe and bellowed back and got away alive and human society was begun. So Rocky finally had his political moment which was precisely right for him.

But the other Moderates did not. There was in their collective voice a suggestion of apology: let-us-at-least-be-heard. Speakers who were opposed to the amendments sounded as effective, sometimes more. Ford from Michigan spoke after Rockefeller, and had better arguments. It was not, he suggested, the purpose of a party which believed in free speech to look for formulas to repress opinion. He was right, even if he might not be so ready to protect Communists as Reactionaries. And Senator Dominick of Colorado made a bright speech employing an editorial from *The New York Times* of 1765 which rebuked Patrick Henry for extreme ideas.

Delegates and gallery whooped it up. Next day Dominick confessed. He was only "spoofing." He had known: there was no *New York Times* in 1765. Nor was there any editorial. An old debater's trick. If there are no good facts, make them up. Be quick to write your own statistics. There was some umbilical tie between the Right Wing and the psychopathic liar.

More speakers came on. After four or five speakers for each side, a vote would come. Each time the amendment was voted down. Eight hundred and ninety-so-many to four hundred-and-a-few, went the votes. Hours went by, three hours of debate. After a while, the Moderates came collectively to seem like a club fighter in still another loser. A vacuum hung over empty cries for civil rights. One wondered why a Negro delegate loyal to the Party for thirty years had not been asked by the Moderates to make a speech where he could say: *You are sending me home to my people a mockery and a shame. My people have been saying for thirty years that the Republican Party has no love for the colored man, and I have argued back. Tonight you will tell me I was wrong. You are denying me the meaning of my life.*

Such a speech (and there were Negro delegates to give it) might not have turned the vote, doubtless it would not have turned the vote, but it was the Moderates' sole chance for an explosion which could loose some petrified emotion, some magic. They did not take it. Probably they did not take it because they did not care that much if they lost. By now, it might be better to lose decisively than come nearer to winning and divide the party more. So they accepted their loser's share of the purse, which is that they could go back East and say: I campaigned at the convention for civil rights. Tomorrow was nominating day. The last chance in a hundred had been lost.

. . . *The Bleat, the Bark, Bellow & Roar—*
Are Waves that Beat on Heaven's Shore. . . .

— WILLIAM BLAKE, *Auguries of Innocence*

Everett Dirksen gave the nominating speech for Goldwater, Dirksen from Illinois, the Silver Fox of the Senate, the Minority Leader, the man who had done the most, many would claim, to pass the Civil Rights Bill, for it was his coalition with Hubert Humphrey on cloture which had carried the day. "I guess Dirksen finally got religion," Humphrey said, and Dirksen, making his final speech for the bill, declared, "There is no force so powerful as an idea whose time has come." It was said that when Goldwater voted against the bill, Dirksen would not speak to him. Two weeks later,

Dirksen agreed to nominate Goldwater. "He's got it won, that's all," Dirksen said of Goldwater, "this thing has gone too far."

This day, nominating day, any orator could have set fire to the Cow Palace. The gallery and Goldwater delegations were as tense and impatient as a platoon of Marines going down to Tijuana after three weeks in the field. But this day Dirksen had no silver voice. He made a speech which contained such nuggets as, "In an age of do-gooders, he was a good doer." Dirksen was an old organist who would play all the squeaks in all the stops, rustle over all the dead bones of all the dead mice in all the pipes. He naturally made a large point that Barry Goldwater was "the grandson of the peddler." This brought no pleasure to the crowd. Main Street was taking Wall Street; Newport Beach, California, would replace Newport; and General Goldwater, Air Force Reserve, possessed sufficient cachet to negotiate the move; but not the grandson of the peddler. Dirksen however went on and on, making a sound like the whir of the air conditioning in a two-mile tunnel.

When he was done, they blew Dirksen down, the high screams of New Year's Eve went off, a din of screamers, rattles, and toots, a clash of bands, a dazzle of posters in phosphorescent yellow and orange and gold, the mad prance of the state standards, wild triumphant pokes and jiggles, war spears, crusader's lances, an animal growl of joy, rebel cries, eyes burning, a mad nut in each square jaw, *Viva-Olé, Viva-Olé*, bugle blasts and rallying cries, the call of heralds, and a fall from the rafters of a long golden rain, pieces of gold foil one inch square, hundreds of thousands of such pieces in an endless gentle shimmer of descent. They had put a spot on the fall—it was as if sunlight had entered every drop of a fine sweet rain. I ran into Mike Wallace on the floor. "The guy who thought of this was a genius," said Mike. And the sounds of the band went up to meet the rain. There was an ummistakable air of beauty, as if a rainbow had come to a field of war, or Goths around a fire saw visions in a cave. The heart of the beast had loosed a primitive call. Civilization was worn thin in the center and to the Left the black man raised his primitive cry; now to the far Right were the maniacal blue eyes of the other primitive. The jungles and the forests were readying for war. For a moment, beauty was there—it is always there as tribes meet and clans gather for war. It was certain beyond certainty now that America was off on a ride which would end—was it God or the Devil knew where.

But the ride did not begin for another seven hours and seven nominations. Knowland seconded Goldwater's nomination; and Clare Boothe Luce, Charlie Halleck, Senator Tower. Then Keating nominated Rockefeller, a twenty-two-minute demonstration, decent in size but predictably hollow. More seconding speeches. Next came Scranton's turn. Dr. Milton Eisenhower, Ike's younger brother, did the nominating. It was good, it was clear, but there was not much excitement any more. One knew why the older Eisenhower had wanted the younger Eisenhower to be President. One also knew why he had not come very near—he gave a hint of Woodrow Wilson. Then the demonstration for Scranton. It was respectable, it let loose a half hour of music, it had fervor, the Scranton supporters died pure, an enjoyable demonstration. But the music was softer. Instead of *Viva-Olé* and the bugle blasts and rallying cries of the crusaders, one now heard *Boys and Girls Together*, or *Hail, Hail, the Gang's All Here*. And the Scranton posters did not have the deep yellow and deep orange of the phalanxes who had jammed the gorge for Goldwater; no, they bore blue and red letters on white, or even black on white, a gray photograph of Scranton on a white background with letters in black—the sign had been designed by Brooks Brothers, you may bet. Even some of the lapel buttons for Scranton revealed a camp of understatement, since they were five inches in diameter, yet Scranton's name was in letters one-eighth of an inch high. It made one think of *The New Yorker* and the blank ordered harmoniums of her aisles and text.

Now went the nominations hour after hour like the time between four in the morning and breakfast at a marathon dance. Here came the nominating speeches and the pumped-up state demonstrations on the floor which spoke of plump elderly tourists doing the hula in Hawaii. Then would come a team of seconding speeches, the weepers and the wringers, the proud of nose and the knotty of nose, the kickers and the thumpers, the ministerial bores and the rabbinical drones, the self-satisfied, the glad-to-be-there, the self-anointed, the unctuous, the tooth suckers, the quaverers.

Fong was nominated, and Margaret Chase Smith, first woman ever to be nominated for President. Now she had a lock on the footnotes in the history books. Romney was nominated, and Judd, defeated Congressman Walter H. Judd of Minnesota, given a grand-old-man-of-the-party nominating speech. The band played *Glory, Glory, Hallelujah*. Just after World War II, early in 1946, Judd had been one of the first to talk of war with Russia. Last came Lodge who scratched himself. The nominations were done. The balloting could begin. They cleared the floor of the Press.

We had been there off and on for seven hours, circling the delegations, talking where we could, a secondary sea of locusts. All through the seven hours of this afternoon and evening, there was the California delegation. They could not be ignored. They sat in the front rows off the center aisle just beneath the speaker on the podium. They wore yellow luminescent Goldwater shirts, the sort of sleeveless high-colored shirts which highway workers wear to be phosphorescent at night. On the floor there were a thousand sights and fifty conversations those seven hours, but there was nothing like the California delegation. In California Rockefeller had lost to Goldwater by less than three percent of the vote, and, losing, had lost all the delegates. California had eighty-six delegates—all eighty-six by the rules of the victory were for Goldwater. So there were eighty-six yellow shirts right down front. Winning California, the Right had also won the plums of the convention, the distribution of tickets in the gallery, central placement on the floor, the allegiance of the Cow Palace cops. They had won the right to have their eighty-six faces at the center of the convention.

Most of the California delegation looked like fat state troopers or prison guards or well-established ranchers. A few were thin and looked like Robert Mitchum playing the mad reverend in *Night of the Hunter*. One or two were skinny as Okies, and looked like the kind of skinny wild-eyed gas-station attendant who works in a small town, and gets his picture in the paper because he has just committed murder with a jack handle. Yes, the skinny men in the California delegation leered out wildly. They looked like they were sitting on a body—the corpse of Jew Eastern Negritudes—and when the show was over, they were gonna eat it. That was it—half the faces in the California delegation looked like geeks. They had had it and now they were ready to put fire to the big tent.

There was one man who stood out as their leader—he had the face to be a leader of such men. Of course he looked not at all like a robber baron, the pride of Pinkerton, and a political boss all in one, no, nor was he in the least like an amalgam of Wallace Beery and fat Hermann Goering, no he was just Bill Knowland, ex-Senator William F. Knowland, Lord of the China Lobby, and honcho number one for Barry in Northern and Southern Cal.

So began the balloting. In twenty minutes there was another demonstration. The California standard, a white silk flag with a beast, some mongrel of bear and wild boar, danced in the air as if carried by a knight on a horse. The chairman for South Carolina intoned, "We are humbly grateful that we can do this for America. South Carolina casts sixteen votes for Senator Barry Goldwater." Barry was in. Four years of work was over. Final score: 883 for Goldwater. Scranton, 214. Rockefeller had 114, Romney 41. Smith received 27, Judd 22, Lodge 2, and Fong had 5.

When the voting was done, when the deliriums were down, an ooh of pleasure came up from the crowd, like the ooh for an acrobat. For Scranton accompanied by his wife was walking down the ramp to the podium, down the high ramp which led from the end-arena exits to the speaker's stand. It was a walk of a hundred feet or more, and Scranton came down this ramp with a slow measured deferential step, like a boy carrying a ceremonial bowl.

He made a clear speech in a young rather vibrant voice. He was doing the thing he was best at. He was making a gesture his elders would approve. He called on Republicans "not to desert our party but to strengthen it."

They cheered him modestly and many may have thought of his comments about Goldwater. On different days through June and July he had said: "dangerously impulsive," "spreading havoc across the national landscape," "a cruel misunderstanding of how the American economy works," "injurious to innumerable candidates," "chaos and uproar," "talking off the top of his head." "Hypocrisy . . ." says our friend Burke, "delights in the most sublime speculations; for never intending to go beyond speculation, it costs nothing to have it magnificent." "I ask . . ." Scranton said. He asked his delegates to make Goldwater's nomination unanimous.

Anywhere but in politics the speed with which the position had been shifted would be sign of a monumental instability. But politics was the place where finally nobody meant what they said—it was a world of nightmare; psychopaths roved. The profound and searing conflicts of politicians were like the quarrels between the girls in a brothel—they would tear each other's hair one night, do a trick together the next. They had no memory. They had no principles but for one—you do not quit the house. You may kill each other but you do not quit the house.

One could imagine the end of an imaginary nightmare: some time in the future, the Iron Ham (for such had become the fond nickname attached to President Barry Goldwater) would be told, thinking back on it all, that Billy-boy Scranton should be removed for some of the things he had said, and old Eisenhower, our General Emeritus, would find it in himself to say at a press conference on TV that while removal could not in itself be condoned, that is for high political figures, still it was bad, of course, policy, for people to have gotten away with insulting the President even if it was in the past and in the guise of free speech which as we all know can be abused. They would shave Scranton's head. Like a monk would he take the walk. And Old Ike would walk with him, and tell Willy S. a joke at the end, and have his picture taken shaking hands. Then, back to the White House for a two-shot drinking beer with Barry, the Iron Ham. After it was over, Barry would go back to the people who had put the ring in his nose.

. . . They should not think it amongst their rights to cut off the entail, or commit waste on the inheritance, by destroying at their pleasure the whole original fabric of their society; hazarding to leave to those who come after them a ruin instead of a habitation.

— BURKE, *Reflections on the Revolution in France*

Goldwater: "There have been several suggestions made. I don't think we would use any of them. But defoliation of the forests by low-yield atomic weapons could well be done. When you remove the foliage, you remove the cover."

— *New York Post*, May 27, 1964

Driving away from the Cow Palace after the nomination, I could hear Goldwater on the car radio. He was celebrating. He was considerably more agreeable than Dick Nixon celebrating — no all-I-am-I-owe-to-my-mother-and-father-my-country-and-church; no, Goldwater was off instead on one of his mild rather tangy excursions, "I feel very humble," he said, and you could feel the itch in the long johns and the hair in the nose, a traveling salesman in an upper berth, belt of bourbon down the hatch — as Mrs. Goldwater entered the room, he cried out, "Hi, honey," and added just a touch mean and small-town, "You didn't cry very much tonight."

"No," said Mrs. Goldwater, "wait till tomorrow."

The questioning went back and forth. He was all voice and very little mind, you could tell he had once been so bright as to invent and market a novelty item called Antsy Pants, men's white shorts with red ants embroidered all over them. But he had a voice! It made up for the mind. Lyndon Johnson's hambone-grits-and-turnip-greens was going to play heavy to this; Goldwater on radio was sweet and manly, clean as Dad in the show of new shows, One Man's Dad. They asked him, *Senator, you said that you would not wage a personal campaign against the President.* Yes, said Goldwater. *Well, sir,* said the interviewer now, *today you called President Johnson the biggest faker in the U.S.* Butters of ecstasy in the interviewer's mouth. *It's going to be a hard-hitting campaign, I assume then?* "Oh," said Goldwater, "I think you'll find some brickbats flying around."

The dialogue went on: *Could you tick off just a few of the major issues you think will be in the campaign against the Democrats?* "I think," said Goldwater, "law and dis — the abuse of law and order in this country, the total disregard for it, the mounting crime rate is going to be another issue — at least I'm going to make it one, because I think the responsibility for this has to start someplace and it should start at the Federal level with the Federal courts enforcing the law.

"I noticed one tonight in the evening paper, for example — a young girl in New York who used a knife to attack a rapist is now getting the worst of the deal and the rapist is probably going to get the Congressional Medal of Honor and sent off scot-free," said Goldwater, neglecting to tell us that the girl had had her indictment dismissed, and the alleged rapist was already up on a charge of attempted rape. Goldwater now said in the sort of voice Daddy employs when he is ready to use the strap, "That kind of business has to stop in this country and, as the President, I'm going to do all I can to see that women can go out in the streets of this country without being scared stiff." Yes, he would. He was a Conservative and he was for States' Rights. It was just that he wasn't for *local* rights.

"By this wise prejudice we are taught to look with horror on those children of their country, who are prompt rashly to hack that aged parent in pieces, and put him into the kettle of magicians, in hopes that by their poisonous weeds, and wild incantations, they may regenerate the paternal constitution, and renovate their father's life."

— BURKE, *Reflections on the Revolution in France*

Next day was the last day of the convention. Bill Miller was nominated for Vice-President. He was not a very handsome man nor did his manner seem particularly agreeable, but then the thought obtruded itself that the President of the United States was now in a more dramatic statistical relation to violent death than a matador. So a candidate would not necessarily look for too appealing a Vice-President — it might encourage notions of succession in the mind of an assassin. One would look instead for deterrents. William Miller was a deterrent.

III

A little later on the last day, Nixon made the speech of introduction for Goldwater. In the months ahead, when the bull in Barry swelled too wild and he gave promise of talking again of Negro assailants getting Medals of Honor, they would send in Nixon to calm him down. The Eastern Establishment, hydra head, was not dead after all; they still had Nixon. He was the steer to soothe the bull. Poor Barry. He had tried to lose Nixon in Cleveland, he had said, "He's sounding more like Harold Stassen every day." Nixon however was as easy to lose as a plain wife without prospects is easy to divorce.

"My good friend and great Republican, Dick Nixon . . ." was how Goldwater began his historic acceptance speech. It had come after a rich demonstration of happiness from the delegates. A boxcar of small balloons was opened in the rafters as Goldwater came down the ramp with his wife, his sons, his daughters. The balloons tumbled in thousands to the floor where (fifty balloons being put out each second by lighted cigarettes) a sound like machine-gun fire popped its way through the cheers. Fourth of July was here once more. He looked good, did Goldwater. Looking up at him from a position just beneath the speaker's stand, not twenty feet away, it was undeniable that Barry looked as handsome as a man who had just won the five-hundred-mile race in Indianapolis, had gone home to dress, and was now attending a party in his honor. He was even, protect the mark, elegant.

Then he began his speech. Today, the voice for large public gatherings had dignity. It was not a great voice, as Churchill's voice was great; there were no majesties nor storms of complexity, no war of style between manner and the obligation to say truth; but it was a balanced manly voice which would get votes. His speech was good in its beginning.

Now my fellow Americans, the tide has been running against freedom. Our people have followed false prophets. . . . We must, and we shall, set the tide running again in the cause of freedom. . . . Every breath and every heartbeat has but a single resolve, and that is freedom. . . . Tonight there is violence in our streets, corruption in our highest offices, aimlessness among our youth, anxiety among our elderly . . . despair among the many who look beyond material success toward the inner meaning of their lives.

As the speech went on, the mind went out again on a calculation that this candidate could win. He was humbug—H. L. Hunt's idea of freedom would not be very close to the idea of freedom in the minds of the children who were for Barry, no, nor William Knowland's idea either, no, nor the Pinkertons, the hawkshaw *geist* of the F.B.I., nor the fourteenth and fifteenth floor. Goldwater was a demagogue—he permitted his supporters to sell a drink called Gold Water, twenty-five cents a can for orange concentrate and warm soda—let no one say it went down like piss—he was a demagogue. He was also sincere. That was the damnable difficulty. Half-Jew and blue-eyed—if you belonged in the breed, you knew it was manic-depressive for sure: a man who designed his own electronic flagpole to raise Old Glory at dawn, pull her down at dusk—he had an instinct for the heart of the disease—he knew how to bring balm to the mad, or at least to half the mad; Goldwater would have much to learn about Negroes. But one thing was certain: he could win. He would be breadwinner, husband and rogue to the under-privileged of the psyche, he would strike a spark in many dry souls for he offered release to frustrations deeper than politics. There-fore, he could beat Lyndon Johnson, he could beat him out of a variety of cause, out of natural flood or hurricane, in an epidemic of backlash, or by an epidemic of guilt—how many union workers fed to the nose with exhortations that Johnson was good for take-home pay might rise and say to themselves, "I've been happy with less." Indeed I knew Goldwater could win because something in me leaped at the thought; a part of me, a devil, wished to take that choice. For if Goldwater were President, a new opposition would form, an underground—the time for secret armies might be near again. And when in sanity I thought, Lord, give us twenty more years of Lyndon Johnson, nausea rose in some cellar of the throat, my stomach was not strong enough to bear such security; and if true for me, true for others, true perhaps for half or more of a na-tion's vote. Yet what of totalitarianism? What of war? But what of war? And the answer came back that one might be better a little nearer to death than the soul dying each night in the plastic encir-clements of the new architecture and the new city, yes better, if death had dimension and one could know the face of the enemy and leave a curse. What blessing to know the face of the enemy by the end of the second third of the twentieth century.

And what of the Negro if Goldwater won? What of all the small-town Southern sheriffs who wished to wipe their hands in the black man's hair? And a fury, a white fury, burst out of the mind and said, "No white sheriff is necessarily so very much worse than the worst Negro," no, the mad light of the black hoodlum might be get-ting equal geek to geek to the worst of the California delegation. Then came a memory of James Baldwin and Diana Sands on a show called *Night Line* where television viewers could make a tel-ephone call to the guests. Baldwin had received a call from a liberal which went, "I'd like to help, and I'm asking you how." "Don't ask me, baby," said Baldwin, "ask yourself." "You don't under-stand," said the liberal, "I know something about these matters, but it's getting confusing for me. I'm asking you in all sincerity where you think my help could be best offered." "Well, baby," said Baldwin, "that's *your* problem." And Diana Sands, pinky extended in total delicate black-lady disgust, put the receiver back in the cradle. "You see," said Baldwin, talking to Les Crane, the master of ceremonies, "I remember what an old Negro woman told me once down South. She said, 'What the white man will someday learn is that there is no remission of sin.' That I never forgot," said Jimmy, "because you see it's perfectly possible the white will not be forgiven, not for a single cut or whipping or lynch mob or rape of a black woman," his voice now as soft and reminiscent of the wind as some African man of witchcraft. And I had to throttle an impulse to pick up the phone and call Baldwin, and say, "You get *this*, baby. There's a shit storm coming like nothing you ever knew. So ask yourself if what you desire is for the white to kill every black so that there be total remission of guilt in your black soul." And the mind went out still again.

The country was in disease, it was conceivably so ill that a butcher could operate with dirty hands and have magic sufficient to do less harm than the hospital with its wonder drugs and the new pestilence. (As the oil goes out, the earth turns cold, an arid used-up space, a ground for jumping off Texas to the used-up pits of the moon.) Still, you could not keep Americans from madness; our poetry was there, our symbolic logic: $AuH_2O + GOP + 64 =$ Victory! color of orange juice, Go, Go, Goldwater. Mrs. Goldwater's maiden name was Johnson, a portent of triumph to Barry? *Viva-Olé*. Eager to slay.

The country was in disease. It had been in disease for a long time. There was nothing in our growth which was organic. We had never solved our depression, we had merely gone to war, and going to war had never won it, not in our own minds, not as men, no, we had won it but as mothers, sources of supply; we did not know that we were equal to the Russians. We had won a war but we had not really won it, not in the secret of our sleep. So we had not really had a prosperity, we had had fever. *Viva-Olé*. We had grown rich because of one fact with two opposite interpretations: there had been a cold war. It was a cold war which had come because Communism was indeed a real threat to freedom, or it had come because capitalism would never survive without an economy geared to war; or was it both—who could know? who could really know? The center of our motive was the riddle wrapped in the enigma— was the country extraordinary or accursed? No, we had not even found our Communist threat. We had had a secret police organization and an invisible government large enough by now to occupy the moon, we had hunted Communists from the top of the Time-Life Building to the bottom of the Collier mine; we had not found that many, not that many, and had looked like Keystone cops. We had even had a Negro Revolution in which we did not believe. We had had it, yes we had had it, because (in the penury of our motive) we could not afford to lose votes in Africa and India, South America and Japan, Vietnam, the Philippines, name any impoverished place: we were running in a world election against the collective image of the Russ, and so we had to give the black man his civil rights or Africa was so much nearer to Marx. But there had not been much like love in the civil rights. Just Dirksen. So we were never too authentic. No.

We had had a hero. He was a young good-looking man with a beautiful wife, and he had won the biggest poker game we ever played, the only real one — we had lived for a week ready to die in a nuclear war. Whether we liked it or not. But he had won. It was our one true victory in all these years, our moment; so the young man began to inspire a subtle kind of love. His strength had proved stronger than we knew. Suddenly he was dead, and we were in grief. But then came a trial which was worse. For the assassin, or the man who had been arrested but was not the assassin — we would never know, not really — was killed before our sight. In the middle of the funeral came an explosion on the porch. Now, we were going mad. It took more to make a nation go mad than any separate man, but we had taken miles too much. Certainties had shattered. Now the voice of our national nerves (our arts, our events) was in a new state. Morality had wed itself to surrealism, there were cockroaches in all the purple transistors, we were distractable. We had an art of the absurd; we had moral surrealism. Our best art was *Dr. Strangelove* and *Naked Lunch, Catch-22; Candy* was our heroine; Jack Ruby our aging juvenile; Andy Warhol, Rembrandt; our national love was a corpse in Arlington; and heavyweight champion turned out to be Cassius Clay; New York was the World's Fair plus the Harlem bomb — it would take a genius to explain they were the same — and Jimmy Baldwin said, "That's *your* problem," on the Les Crane show at one a.m. Even the reverends were salty as the sea.

Yes, our country was fearful, half mad, inauthentic. It needed a purge. It had a liberal Establishment obeisant to committees, foundations, and science — the liberal did not understand that the center of science was as nihilistic as a psychopath's sense of God. We were a liberal Establishment, a prosperous land — we had a Roman consul among us — the much underrated and much disliked Lyndon Johnson was become a power in the land and doubtless a power upon the land; civilization had found its newest helmsman in the restraints, wisdom, and corruption of a major politician, of an organization boss to whom all Mafias, legit and illegit, all syndicates, unions, guilds, corporations and institutions, cadres of conspiracy and agents for health, Medicare, welfare, the preservation of anti-biotics, and the proliferation of the Pentagon could bend their knee. The Establishment (the Democratic Establishment and the reeling columns of the Republican Establishment, falling back upon the center in the thundering confusion of Barry Goldwater's break-through) had a new leader, a mighty Caesar had arisen, Lyndon Johnson was his name, all hail, Caesar. Caesar gave promise to unify the land. But at what a cost. For if the ideology were liberal, the methodology was total — to this political church would come Adlai Stevenson and Frank Sinatra, the President of U.S. Steel and the President of the Steel Worker's Union, there would be photographs of Johnson forty feet high in Atlantic City — Big Bub-ber Lyndon — and parties in which minority groups in native cos-tume would have their folk dance: could one see the ghost of Joe Stalin smiling on his pipe?

Yes, if we all worked to beat Barry, and got behind Lyndon and pushed, radicals and moderate Republicans, Negroes and Southern liberals, college professors and Cosa Nostra, café society and Beatniks-for-Johnson, were we all then going down a liberal super-highway into the deepest swamp of them all? For Johnson was intelligent enough to run a total land, he had vast competence, no vi-sion, and the heart to hold huge power, he had the vanity of a Ren-aissance prince or a modern dictator, whereas Barry might secretly be happier with his own show daily on radio. If Goldwater were elected, he could not control the country without moving to the center; moving to the center he would lose a part of the Right, sat-isfy no one, and be obliged to drift still further Left, or moving back to the Right would open schisms across the land which could not be closed. Goldwater elected, America would stand revealed, its latent treacheries would pop forth like boils; Johnson elected, the drift would go on, the San Francisco Hiltons would deploy among us. Under Goldwater, the odds were certainly greater that nuclear war would come, but under Johnson we could move from the threat of total war to war itself with nothing to prevent it; the anti-Goldwater forces which might keep the country too divided to go to war would now be contained within Johnson. Goldwater promised to lead the nation across the edge of a precipice, Johnson would walk us through the woods, perchance to quicksand itself. Goldwater would open us to the perils of our madness, Johnson would continue our trip into the plague. Goldwater could acceler-ate the Negro Revolution to violence and disaster — Johnson might yet be obliged to betray it from within. And what a job could be done! Who in such a pass should receive the blessing of a vote — the man who inspired the deepest fear, or the man who encouraged us to live in a lard of guilt cold as the most mediocre of our satisfied needs?

Still, the more Goldwater talked, the less impressive became his voice. When he went on too long, his voice grew barren. One could never vote for him, one could not vote for a man who made a career by crying Communist—that was too easy: half the pigs, bullies, and cowards of the twentieth century had made their fortune on that fear. I had a moment of rage at the swindle. I was tired of hearing about Barry Goldwater's high fine courage. Yesterday, on the floor, talking to a young delegate from Indiana, I had said, "Did it ever occur to you that Fidel Castro might have more courage than Barry Goldwater?"

"Yes, but Castro is a criminal mentality," said the boy.

I had cut off the argument. I was too close to losing my temper. Would the best of the young in every hick town, washed by the brainwater of the high school and the Legion, come to join this conservative crusade because Goldwater made an appeal to freedom, to courage, to change? What a swindle was in the making, what an extinction of the best in Conservative thought. They were so righteous, these Republicans. Goldwater might end with more warfare, security, and statism than any Democrat had ever dared; as a conservative, he would fail altogether (doubtless!) but certain he was to do one thing: he would march into Cuba. That was too much. One could live with a country which was mad, one could even come to love her (for there was agony beneath the madness), but you could not share your life with a nation which was powerful, a coward, and righteously pleased because a foe one-hundredth our size had been destroyed. So one got up to leave at this—we would certainly be strong enough to march into Cuba.

Then Goldwater uttered his most historic words: "Extremism in the defense of liberty is no vice. . . . Moderation in the pursuit of justice is no virtue," and I sat down and took out my notebook and wrote in his words, since I did not know how famous they would become. And thought: Dad, you're too much. You're really too much. You're too hip, baby. I have spent my life seeking to get four-letter words into U.S. magazines, and now you are ready to help me.

And as I left the arena, there was a fire engine and the cry of a siren and the police with a gaunt grim look for the end of the week. There had been a fire burning, some small fire.

On the way out, outside the Cow Palace, a wet fog was drifting, and out beyond the exits, demonstrators from CORE were making a march. They had been out there every day of the convention: Monday, Tuesday, Wednesday, and Thursday now, each day had demonstrated, carrying their placards, marching in a circle two abreast, singing *We Shall Overcome*, shouting, "Goldwater Must Go," marching round and round like early Christians in the corrals waiting to be sent to the arena, while about them, five, six, ten deep, was a crowd of the Republican curious, some with troubled faces, some with faces troubled by no more than appetite, hounds staring at the meat, these white girls and Negro boys walking side by side, the girls pale, no lipstick, nunlike, disdainful, wearing denim shirts and dungarees; the Negroes tall and sometimes handsome, not without dignity, bearded almost all, the wild Negro girl in the center screaming savage taunts at the watching crowd, rude as Cassius Clay with a high-yaller mouth, and the crowd dreaming of an arena where lions could be set on these cohabiting blacks and whites, and the blacks and whites in the marching circle with their disdainful faces. Yes, kill us, says the expression on the face of the nunlike girl with no lipstick, you will kill us but you will never digest us: I despise you all. And some of the old Wasps are troubled in their Christian heart, for the girl is one of theirs, no fat plain Jewess with a poor nose is this one, she is part of the West, and so their sense of crisis opens and they know like me that America has come to a point from which she will never return. The wars are coming and the deep revolutions of the soul.

The Argument Reinvigorated

Assume I am a lecturer in the fields of Fellowship surrounding Literature (American) and am trying to draw some grand design in twenty minutes on a talk devoted to "The Dynamic of American Letters." Knowing attention is iron for the blood of a Fellow, I will not be so foolish as to perish without a look at the topical and the interesting. No, I will use "The Dynamic of American Letters" as preparation for a lightning discussion of Herzog and Terry Southern, with a coda on the art of the absurd. Let me then have my first sentence as lecturer: "There has been a war at the center of American letters for a long time." That is not so poor. The look of absolute comprehension on the face of the audience encourages the lecturer to go on.

The war began as a class war; an upper-middle class looked for a development of its taste, a definition of its manners, a refinement of itself to prepare a shift to the aristocratic; that was its private demand upon culture. That demand is still being made by a magazine called *The New Yorker*. This upper-class development of literature was invaded a long time ago, however, back at the cusp of the century, by a counter-literature whose roots were found in poverty, industrial society, and the emergence of new class. It was a literature which grappled with a peculiarly American phenomenon—a tendency of American society to alter more rapidly than the ability of its artists to record that change. Now, of course, one might go back two thousand years into China to find a society which did not alter more rapidly than its culture, but the American phenomenon had to do with the very rate of acceleration. The order of magnitude in this rate had shifted. It was as if everything changed ten times as fast in America, and this made for extraordinary difficulty in creating a literature. The sound, sensible, morally stout delineation of society which one found in Tolstoy and Balzac and Zola, in Thackeray and in Trollope, had become impossible. The American novelist of manners had to content himself with manners—he could not put a convincing servant into his work, and certainly not a workingman, because they were moving themselves in one generation out from the pantry into the morning dress of the lady in the parlor and up from the foundry to the master of the factory. The novelist of manners could not go near these matters—they promised to take over all of his book. So the job was left to Howells, Stephen Crane, to Dreiser, and in lesser degree to such writers as Norris, Jack London, Upton Sinclair—let us say it was left to Dreiser. A fundamental irony of American letters had now presented itself. For in opposition to Dreiser was the imperfectly developed countertradition of the genteel. The class which wielded the power which ran America, and the class which most admired that class, banded instinctively together to approve a genteel literature which had little to do with power or the secrets of power. They encouraged a literature about courtship and marriage and love and play and devotion and piety and style, a literature which had to do finally with the *excellence* of belonging to their own genteel tradition. Thus it was a literature which borrowed the forms of its conduct from European models. The people who were most American by birth, and who had the most to do with managing America, gave themselves a literature which had the least to say about the real phenomena of American life, most particularly the accelerated rate, the awful rate, of growth and anomaly through all of society. That sort of literature and that kind of attempt to explain America was left to the sons of immigrants who, if they were vigorous enough, and fortunate enough to be educated, now had the opportunity to see that America was a phenomenon never before described, indeed never before visible in the record of history. There was something going on in American life which was either grand or horrible or both, but it was going on—at a dizzy rate—and the future glory or doom of the world was not necessarily divorced from it. Dreiser labored like a titan to capture the phenomenon; he became a titan; Thomas Wolfe, his only peer as giant (as the novelist-as-giant), labored also like a titan, but for half as long and died in terror of the gargantuan proportions of the task. Yet each failed in one part of the job. They were able to describe society—Wolfe like the greatest five-year-old who ever lived,* an invaluable achievement, and Dreiser like some heroic tragic entrepreneur who has reasoned out through his own fatigue and travail very much how everything works in the iron mills of life, but is damned because he cannot pass on the knowledge to his children. Dreiser and Wolfe were up from the people, and Dreiser particularly came closer to understanding the social machine than any American writer who ever lived, but he paid an unendurable price—he was forced to alienate himself from manner in order to learn the vast amount he learned. Manner insists one learn at a modest rate, that one learn each step with grace before going on to the next. Dreiser was in a huge hurry, he had to learn everything—that was the way he must have felt his mission, so there is nothing of manner in his work; which is to say, nothing of tactics.

If the upper-class quite naturally likes a literature which is good for them, a literature at the surface perhaps trivial, but underneath amusing, elucidative, *fortifying*, it is because this kind of literature elaborates and clarifies the details of their life, and thus adjusts their sense of power, their upper-class sense of power, which is invariably lubricated by a sense of detail. So too does that other class of readers in American literature, that huge, loose, all but unassociated congregation of readers—immigrant, proletarian, entrepreneur—wish in turn for a literature which is equally good for them. That is where Dreiser had to fail. He was only half-good for such readers. He taught them strategy as Americans had never gotten it before in a novel. If they were adventurers, he was almost as useful to them as Stendhal was exceptionally useful to a century of French intellectuals who had come to Paris from the provinces. But not quite. Dreiser, finally, is not quite as useful, and the difference is crucial. Because a young adventurer reads a great novel in

---

*This Argument was delivered, originally, as a talk to The American Studies Association and the M.L.A. This remark brought laughter from the audience. Since I did not wish to insult the memory of Wolfe, it would have been happier and perhaps more accurate to have said: like the greatest fifteen-year-old alive.

the unvoiced hope it is a grindstone which sharpens his axe sufficiently to smash down doors now locked to him. Dreiser merely located the doors and gave warnings about the secret padlocks and the traps. But he had no grindstone, no manner, no eye for the deadly important manners of the rich, he was obliged to call a rich girl "charming"; he could not make her charming when she spoke, as Fitzgerald could, and so he did not really prepare the army of his readers for what was ahead. His task was doubly difficult—it was required of him to give every upstart fresh strategy and tactics. No less than the secret sociology of society is what is needed by the upstart and that strategy Dreiser gave him. But tactics—the manners of the drawing room, the deaths and lifes of the drawing room, the cocktail party, the glorious tactics of the individual kill—that was all beyond him. Dreiser went blind climbing the mountains of society, so he could not help anyone to see what was directly before him—only what had happened and what was likely to come next.

That was the initial shape of the war, Naturalism versus the Genteel Tradition it has been called, and one might pose Henry James against Dreiser, but James is sufficiently great a writer to violate the generalizations one must make about the novel of manners which must always—precisely because it deals with manners—eschew the overambitious, plus extremes of plot—which James of course did not. So let us say the war was between Dreiser and Edith Wharton, Dreiser all strategy, no tactics; and Wharton all tactics. Marvelous tactics they were—a jewel of a writer and stingy as a parson—she needed no strategy. The upper-class writer had all strategy provided him by the logic of his class. Maybe that is why the war never came to decision, or even to conclusion. No upper-class writer went down into the pits to bring back the manner alive of the change going on *down* there, certainly not Edith Wharton, not James Branch Cabell, of course not, nor Hergesheimer nor even Cather or Glasgow, not Elinor Wylie, no, nor Carl Van Vechten, and no diamond in the rough was ever reshaped by the cutters of Newport. The gap in American letters continued. Upper-class writers like John Dos Passos made brave efforts to go down and get the stuff and never quite got it, mainly in Dos Passos's case because they lacked strategy for the depths—manners may be sufficient to delineate the rich but one needs a vision of society to comprehend the poor, and Dos Passos had only revulsion at injustice, which is ultimately a manner. Some upper-class writers like Fitzgerald turned delicately upon the suppositions of their class, lost all borrowed strategy and were rudderless, were forced therefore to become superb in tactics, but for this reason perhaps a kind of hysteria lived at the center of their work; lower-class writers like Farrell and Steinbeck described whole seas of the uncharted ocean but their characters did not push from one milieu into another, and so the results were more taxonomic than apocalyptic.

Since then the war has shifted. No writer succeeded in doing the single great work which would clarify a nation's vision of itself as Tolstoy had done perhaps with *War and Peace* or *Anna Karenina*, and Stendhal with *The Red and the Black*, no one novel came along which was grand and daring and comprehensive and detailed, able to give sustenance to the adventurer and merriment to the rich, leave compassion in the icechambers of the upper class and energy as alms for the poor. (Not unless it was *Tropic of Cancer*.) Dreiser came as close as any, and never got close at all, for he could not capture the moment, and no country in history has lived perhaps so much for the moment as America. After his heroic failure, American literature was isolated — it was necessary to give courses in American literature to Americans, either because they would not otherwise read it, or because reading it, they could not understand it. It was not quite vital to them. It did not save their lives, make them more ambitious, more moral, more tormented, more audacious, more ready for love, more ready for war, for charity and for invention. No, it tended to puzzle them. The realistic literature had never caught up with the rate of change in American life, indeed it had fallen further and further behind, and the novel gave up any desire to be a creation equal to the phenomenon of the country itself; it settled for being a metaphor. Which is to say that each separate author made a separate peace. He would no longer try to capture America, he would merely try to give life to some microcosm in American life, some metaphor — in the sense that a drop of water is a metaphor of the seas, or a hair of the beast is for some a metaphor of the beast — and in that metaphor he might — if he were very lucky — have it all, rich and poor, strategy and tactics, insight and manner, detail, authority, the works. He would have it all for a particular few. It was just that he was no longer writing about the beast but, as in the case of Hemingway (if we are to take the best of this), about the paw of the beast, or in Faulkner about the dreams of the beast. What a paw and what dreams! Perhaps they are the two greatest writers America ever had, but they had given up on trying to do it all. Their vision was partial, determinedly so, they saw that as the first condition for trying to be great — that one must not try to save. Not souls, and not the nation. The desire for majesty was the bitch which licked at the literary loins of Hemingway and Faulkner: the country could be damned. Let it take care of itself.

And of course the country did. Just that. It grew by itself. Like a weed and a monster and a beauty and a pig. And the task of explaining America was taken over by Luce magazines. Those few aristocratic novelistic sensibilities which had never seen the task of defining the country as one for them—it was finally most unamusing as a task—grew smaller and smaller and more and more superb. Edith Wharton reappeared as Truman Capote, even more of a jewel, even stingier. Of writers up from the bottom there were numbers: Dreiser's nephews were as far apart as Saul Bellow and James Jones. But the difference between the two kinds of writers had shifted. It had begun to shift somewhere after the Second World War, and the shift had gone a distance. One could not speak at all now of aristocratic writers and novelists whose work was itself the protagonist to carry the writer and his readers through the locks of society; no, the work had long since retreated, the great ambition was gone, and then it was worse, even the metaphor was gone, the paw of the beast and the dreams of the beast, no, literature was down to the earnest novel and the perfect novel, to moral seriousness and Camp. Herzog and Candy had become the protagonists.

Frank Cowperwood once amassed an empire. Herzog, his bastard great-nephew, diddled in the ruins of an intellectual warehouse. Where once the realistic novel cut a swath across the face of society, now its reality was concentrated into moral seriousness. Where the original heroes of naturalism had been active, bold, self-centered, close to tragic, and up to their nostrils in their exertions to advance their own life and force the webs of society, so the hero of moral earnestness, the hero Herzog and the hero Levin in Malamud's *A New Life*, are men who represent the contrary—passive, timid, other-directed, pathetic, up to the nostrils in anguish: the world is stronger than they are; suicide calls.

Malamud's hero is more active than Herzog, he is also more likeable, but these positive qualities keep the case from being so pure. There is a mystery about the reception of *Herzog*. For beneath its richness of texture and its wealth of detail, the fact remains: never has a novel been so successful when its hero was so dim. Not one of the critics who adored the book would ever have permitted Herzog to remain an hour in his house. For Herzog was defeated, Herzog was an unoriginal man, Herzog was a fool—not an attractive God-anointed fool like Gimpel the Fool, his direct progenitor, but a sodden fool, over-educated and inept, unable to fight, able to love only when love presented itself as a gift. Herzog was intellectual but not bright, his ideas not original, his style as it appeared in his letters unendurable—it had exactly the leaden-footed sense of phrase which men laden with anxiety and near to going mad put into their communications. Herzog was hopeless. We learned nothing about society from him, not even anything about his life. And he is the only figure in the book. His wives, his mistress, his family, his children, his friends, even the man who cuckolds him are seen on the periphery of a dimming vision. Like all men near to being mad, his attention is within, but the inner attention is without genius. Herzog is dull, he is unendurably dull—he is like all those bright pedagogical types who have a cavity at the center of their brain.

Yet the novel succeeds. There is its mystery. One reads it with compassion. With rare compassion. Bored by Herzog, still there is a secret burning of the heart. One's heart turns over and produces a sorrow. Hardly any books are left to do that.

Of course, Herzog is alive on sufferance. He is a beggar, an extraordinary beggar who fixes you with his eye, his breath, his clothing, his dank near-corrupt presence; he haunts. Something goes on in Herzog's eye. It says: I am debased, I am failed, I am near to rotten, and yet something just as good and loving resides in me as the tenderest part of your childhood. If the prophet Elijah sent me, it is not to make you feel guilt but to weep. Suddenly, Herzog inspires sorrow—touch of alchemy to the book—Herzog is at the center of the modern dilemma. If we do not feel compassion for him, a forceful compassion which sends blood to warm the limbs and the heart, then we are going to be forced to shoot him. Because if Herzog does not arouse your compassion there is no other choice—he is too intolerable a luxury to keep alive in his mediocrity unless he arouses your love. The literary world chose to love him. We were not ready to shoot Herzog. It all seemed too final if we did. Because then there would be nothing left but Camp, and Camp is the art of the cannibal, Camp is the art which evolved out of the bankruptcy of the novel of manners. It is the partial thesis of these twenty minutes that the pure novel of manners had watered down from *The House of Mirth* to the maudlin middle reaches of *The Rector of Justin;* had in fact gone all the way down the pike from *The Ambassadors* to *By Love Possessed.* So, one does not speak of the novel of manners any longer—one is obliged to look at the documentary, *In Cold Blood*—or one is obliged to look at satire. The aristocratic impulse turned upon itself produced one classic—Terry Southern's *The Magic Christian.* Never had distaste for the habits of a mass mob reached such precision, never did wit falter in its natural assumption that the idiocies of the mass were attached breath and kiss to the hypocrisies, the weltering grandeurs, and the low stupidities of the rich, the American rich. The aristocratic impulse to define society by evocations of manner now survived only in the grace of any cannibal sufficiently aristocratic to sup upon his own family. *The Magic Christian* was a classic of Camp.

Note then: The two impulses in American letters had failed, the realistic impulse never delivered the novel which would ignite a nation's consciousness of itself, and the aristocratic impulse clawed at the remaining fabric of a wealthy society it despised and no longer wished to sustain. Like a Tinguely machine which destroys itself, Camp amused by the very act of its destruction. Since it was also sentimental, the artifacts were necrophiliac.

Literature then had failed. The work was done by the movies, by television. The consciousness of the masses and the culture of the land trudged through endless mud.

The American consciousness in the absence of a great tradition in the novel ended by being developed by the bootlicking pieties of small-town newspaper editors and small-town educators, by the worst of organized religion, a formless force filled with the terrors of all the Christians left to fill the spaces left by the initial bravery of the frontiersman, and these latterday Christians were simply not as brave. That was one component of the mud. The other was the sons of the immigrants. Many of them hated America, hated it for what it offered and did not provide, what it revealed of opportunity and what it excluded from real opportunity. The sons of these immigrants and the sons' sons took over the cities and began to run them, high up in the air and right down into the ground, they plucked and they plundered and there was not an American city which did not grow more hideous in the last fity years. Then they spread out—they put suburbs like blight on the land—and piped mass communications into every home. They were cannibals selling Christianity to Christians, and because they despised the message and mocked at it in their own heart, they succeeded in selling something else, a virus perhaps, an electronic nihilism went through the mass media of America and entered the Christians and they were like to being cannibals, they were a tense and livid people, swallowing their own hate with the tranquilizers and the sex in the commercials, whereas all the early cannibals at the knobs of the mass-media made the mistake of passing on their bleak disease and were left now too gentle, too liberal, too programmatic, filled with plans for social welfare, and they looked and talked in Show

Biz styles which possessed no style and were generally as unhealthy as Christians who lived in cellars and caves.

Yes, the cannibal sons of the immigrants had become Christians, and the formless form they had evolved for their mass-media, the hypocritical empty and tasteless taste of the television arts they beamed across the land encountered the formless form and the all but tasteless taste of the small-town tit-eating cannibal mind at its worst, and the collision produced schizophrenia in the land. Half of America went insane with head colds and medicaments and asthmas and allergies, hospitals and famous surgeons with knives to cut into the plague, welfares and plans and committees and cooperations and boredom, boredom plague deep upon the land; and the other part of America went ape, and the motorcycles began to roar like lions across the land and all the beasts of all the buried history of America turned in their circuit and prepared to slink toward the market place, there to burn the mother's hair and bite the baby to the heart. One thought of America and one thought of aspirin, kitchen-commercials, and blood. One thought of Vietnam. And the important art in America became the art of the absurd.

There will be talk before this book is done of the nature of the art of the absurd, there will be perhaps even an attempt to explain it, but for now we have come to another explanation. For a good deal follows about the writing of contemporaries; there is criticism, some of it very critical. But then, good writing is not an act to excite tolerance because it is good, but anguish because it is not better. Who can swear there has not been something catastrophic to America in the failure of her novelists? Maybe we are the last liberators in the land, and if we continue to thrive on much less than our best, then the being of all of us may be deadened before we are done.

That is a statement which sups on the essence of extravagance, and yet it is the distance of the bridge to be built. It may be necessary that a communication of human experience, of the deepest and most unrecoverable human experience, must yet take place if we are to survive. Such at least is the covert opinion beneath the criticism which now follows.

Punching Papa: *A Review of That Summer in Paris*

There is an irony which usually defeats the memoir and makes it an inferior art. The man who can tell a good story in company about his friends is usually not able find a prose which can capture the nuances of his voice. Invariably, the language is leached out — the account tends to have a droning episodic quality as if some movie queen were recounting the separate toils of her lovers to a tape recorder.

Now the worst to be said for *That Summer in Paris* is that Morley Callaghan has not altogether avoided this blight. Using himself as a character of reasonable dimensions, an honest sensible hard-nosed ego-bastard, a talented short-story writer, a good husband, a good Irish Catholic, a good college boxer, and a good expatriate, his memoir is built on the premise that catgut is good for stringing pearls. So one is taken by Callaghan for a three-to-five-page description of each of his separate meetings with Maxwell Perkins, Sherwood Anderson, Ford Madox Ford, Josephine Herbst, Sinclair Lewis, Robert McAlmon, Sylvia Beach, James Joyce, Pauline Hemingway, Michael Arlen, Ludwig Lewisohn, Allen Tate, Edward Titus, Joan Miró, and Zelda Fitzgerald. It is dim writing. One has only to compare the chapter he gives to Sinclair Lewis (one of the more elaborate cameos) against some equivalent number of pages Wolfe devoted to a similar portrait, and the result is no contest. A deadness comes back from Callaghan's echo. His short portraits are written at the level of a conversation with somebody who might tell you he met Truman Capote.

"Well," you might respond, "what is he like?"

"Well," says your friend, "he's small, you know, and he's kind of bright."

If one knows some of the people mentioned, or is obsessed with the period, then Morley Callaghan's memoir will satisfy. But it is not a good book. It is in fact a modest bad dull book which contains a superb short story about Hemingway, Fitzgerald, and Callaghan. One can push so far as to say it is probably the most dramatic single story about Hemingway's relation to Fitzgerald in the literature. If Callaghan had been ready to stop at this, he could have had a long short story or a short memoir which might have become a classic. Instead he attenuated his material over a run of 255 pages, and so reminds one of a remark Fitzgerald once made to Callaghan. Talking about *The Great Gatsby*, he said the book had done reasonably well but was hardly a best seller. "It was too short a book," Fitzgerald said. "Remember this, Morley. Never write a book under sixty thousand words."

That's it. Callaghan has remembered, and has proceeded to stretch it out. As literature, it's a mistake. Financially, Fitzgerald's advice might still prove wise. The author now has a book instead of a story; the value of a movie sale is increased. The story about Hemingway, Fitzgerald, and Callaghan done by John Huston, produced by Sam Spiegel, could make a very good movie. For the first time one has the confidence that an eyewitness has been able to cut a bonafide trail through the charm, the mystery, and the curious perversity of Hemingway's personality. One gets a good intimation of what was very bad in the man, and the portrait is reinforced by the fact that Callaghan was not out to damage the reputation — on the contrary, he is nearly obsessed by the presence of taint in a man he considers great.

In turn, Fitzgerald is also admired. In fact he is even loved as a friend, loved perhaps more than Hemingway. Yet Callaghan fixes his character for our attention. Like many an American writer to come after him, Fitzgerald was one of those men who do not give up early on the search to acquire more manhood for themselves. His method was to admire men who were strong. In this sense he was a salesman. When the beloved object did not smile back, Fitzgerald, like Willy Loman, looked into an earthquake. We are offered Fitzgerald at just such a moment.

Talking to Callaghan one day, Fitzgerald referred to Hemingway's ability as a boxer, and remarked that while Hemingway was probably not good enough to be heavyweight champion of the world, he was undoubtedly as good as Young Stribling, the light-heavyweight champion. "Look, Scott," said Callaghan, "Ernest is an amateur. I'm an amateur. All this talk is ridiculous." Unconvinced, Fitzgerald asked to come along to the gym at the American Club and watch Hemingway and Callaghan box. But Callaghan has let the reader in earlier on one small point. Hemingway, four inches taller and forty pounds heavier than Callaghan, "may have thought about boxing, dreamed about it, consorted with old fighters and hung around gyms," but Callaghan "had done more actual boxing with men who could box a little and weren't just taking exercise or fooling around."

So on an historic afternoon in June in Paris in 1929, Hemingway and Callaghan boxed a few rounds with Fitzgerald serving as timekeeper. The second round went on for a long time. Both men began to get tired, Hemingway got careless. Callaghan caught him a good punch and dropped Hemingway on his back. At the next instant Fitzgerald cried out, "Oh, my God! I let the round go four minutes."

"All right, Scott," Ernest said. "If you want to see me getting the shit knocked out of me, just say so. Only don't say you made a mistake."

According to Callaghan's estimate, Scott never recovered from that moment. One believes it. For months later, a cruel and wildly inaccurate story about this episode appeared in the *Herald Tribune* book section. It was followed by a cable sent collect by Fitzgerald at Hemingway's insistence. "HAVE SEEN STORY IN HERALD TRIBUNE. ERNEST AND I AWAIT YOUR CORRECTION. SCOTT FITZGERALD."

Since Callaghan had already written such a letter to the paper, none of the three men could ever forgive each other.

As the vignettes, the memoirs, and the biographies of Hemingway proliferate, Callaghan's summer in Paris may take on an importance beyond its literary merit, for it offers a fine clue to the logic of Hemingway's mind, and tempts one to make the prediction that there will be no definitive biography of Hemingway until the nature of his personal torture is better comprehended. It is possible Hemingway lived every day of his life in the style of the suicide. What a great dread is that. It is the dread which sits in the silences of his short declarative sentences. At any instant, by any failure in magic, by a mean defeat, or by a moment of cowardice, Hemingway could be thrust back again into the agonizing demands of his courage. For the life of his talent must have depended on living in a psychic terrain where one must either be brave beyond one's limit, or sicken closer into a bad illness, or, indeed, by the ultimate logic of the suicide, must advance the hour in which one would make another reconnaissance into one's death.

That may be why Hemingway turned in such fury on Fitzgerald. To be knocked down by a smaller man could only imprison him further into the dread he was forever trying to avoid. Each time his physical vanity suffered a defeat, he would be forced to embark on a new existential gamble with his life. So he would naturally think of Fitzgerald's little error as an act of treachery, for the result of that extra minute in the second round could only be a new bout of anxiety which would drive his instinct into ever more dangerous situations. Most men find their profoundest passion in looking for a way to escape their private and secret torture. It is not likely that Hemingway was a brave man who sought danger for the sake of the sensations it provided him. What is more likely the truth of his long odyssey is that he struggled with his cowardice and against a secret lust to suicide all of his life, that his inner landscape was a nightmare, and he spent his nights wrestling with the gods. It may even be that the final judgment on his work may come to the notion that what he failed to do was tragic, but what he accomplished was heroic, for it is possible he carried a weight of anxiety within him from day to day which would have suffocated any man smaller than himself. There are two kinds of brave men: those who are brave by the grace of nature, and those who are brave by an act of will. It is the merit of Callaghan's long anecdote that the second condition is suggested to be Hemingway's own.

The Killer: *A Story*

"Now," he said to me, "do you think you're going to bear up under the discipline of parole?"

"Yessir," I said.

He had white hair even though he was not more than fifty-two. His face was red. He had blue eyes. He was red, white, and blue. It was a fact I noticed before. They had this coloring. Maybe that was why they identified with the nation.

"In effect you're swearing that you won't take a drink for eight months."

"I know, sir, but I haven't had a drink inside for four years." Which was a lie. Three times I had come in with my cellmate on part of a bottle. The first time I was sick. The second time we had a fight, a quiet fight which I lost. He banged my head on the floor. Without noise. The third time we had sex. Democratic sex. We did each other.

"You understand that parole is not freedom."

"Yessir."

They asked these questions. They always asked the same questions, and they always got the same answers. It had nothing to do with what you said. It had nothing to do with how you shaved or how you combed your hair because you combed your hair the way everybody else did, and the day you went up to Board you shaved twice. Maybe, it had to do with how many shaving cuts you had, but I didn't have any. I had taken care, wow. Suppose it had to do with the way you moved. If two of the three men on the parole board liked the way you moved, you were all right, provided they didn't like the way you moved too much. Sex. No matter who I'm with, man or woman, always get a feeling off them. At least I used to. I always could tell if they were moving inside or moving away, and I could tell if anything was going on inside. If we ever touched, I could tell better. Once I was in a streetcar and a girl sat down next to me. She was a full barrel. A very fat girl. Pretty face. I don't like fat. Very fat people have no quick. They can always stop. They can stop from doing a lot of things.

This girl and me had a future however. Her hip touched. I could feel what I did to her. From side of my leg, through my pants, and her dress, through some kind of corset, cheap plastic corset, something bad, through that, through her panties, right into her, some current went out of me, and I could feel it in her, opening up future. She didn't do a thing, didn't move. Fixed.

Well, five minutes, before I got off at my stop. In those minutes I was occupied by a project with that girl where we projected five years. I knew what I could do to her. I say without exaggeration I could take her weight down from one hundred eighty to one-eighteen in a year and it would have been a pleasure because all that fat was stored-up sugar she was saving. For somebody. She was stingy, congealed like lard, but I had the current to melt that. I knew it would not be hard to pick her up. If I did, the rest would happen. I would spend a year with her. It is difficult to pick up a fat girl, but I would have used shock treatment. For example, I would have coughed, and dropped an oyster on her skirt. I think it is revolting to do something like that, but it would have worked with this fat girl because disgust would have woke her up. That's the kind of dirt sex is, in the mind of somebody fat and soft and clammy. Sex to them is spit and mucus. It would have given me the opportunity to wipe it off. I could trust my fingers to give a touch of something. The point to the entire operation (people watching in the streetcar, me standing with my handkerchief, apologizing) would be that my fingers would be doing two things at once, proper and respectful in the part of my hand everybody else could see, flame through the handkerchief on her lap. I would have begun right there. For the least I would get her name. At the end of the five minutes I turned to take a look at her, and under that fat face, in the pretty face which could be very attractive, I could see there was a dumb look in her eyes that nothing was going to improve. That stopped me. Putting in a year on a girl like that would be bad unless she was all for me at the end. Stupidity is for nothing, not even itself. I detest stupidity in women — it sets me off. So I got off the car. Didn't even look at the girl. After she gets married to somebody fat and stupid like herself she will hate any man who looks like me because of that five minutes. Her plastic corset must have had a drug-store smell after I got off the trolley car. Think of plastic trying to smell.

I tell this as an example. On the outside it used to be that I never sat down next to anybody that I didn't feel them even when we didn't touch and two or three times a week, or even a day, I would be close to the possibilities of somebody like the fat girl. I know about certain things. I know with all policemen, detectives, correction officers, turnkeys, hacks, parole-board officials, that sex is the problem with them. Smartest cellmate I had said one time like a philosopher, "Why, man, a judge will forgive any crime he is incapable of committing himself." My friend put it right. Sex is a bitch. With police. They can't keep their hands off. They do, but then it builds tension. For some it's bad. They can get ready to kill. That's why you comb your hair. Why you must look neat. You have to be clean. Above sex. Then a cop can like you. They ask you those questions knowing how you will answer. Often they know you are lying. For example they know that you will take a drink in the next six months. What is important is not that you are lying, but the kind of lie they hear in your voice. Are you afraid of them? Are you afraid they will see down into your lying throat? Then you are okay. They will pass you. If you are afraid of them, you're a good risk. But if you think they are stupid, faintest trace of such a thought in yourself, it comes through. Always one of them will be sensitive to condescension. It gets them ready to kill. A policeman never forgives you when you get him ready to kill. Obviously he can't do it, especially in a room performing official duty with a stenographer at the side. But the adrenalin goes through him. It is bad to take a flush of adrenalin for nothing. All that murder and nowhere to go. For example when you're standing up talking to a parole board it's important the way you stand, how tight your pants are. Good to be slim, trim, shipshape, built the way I am, provided you are modest. Do not project your groin forward or your hips back. It is best if your pants are not tight-fit. Younger juvenile delinquents actually make this sort of mistake. It is not that they are crazy so much as egotistical. They think older men will like them so much they will give them parole in order to look them up. A mistake. Once read in the newspapers about a Russian soldier who picked up a German baby and said, "It's beautiful," but then he got angry because he remembered the baby's father had been shooting his children, so he killed the baby. That's a cop. If you strut, even in good taste and subtle, they will start to get a glow where it is verboten, and they will like you, they will get a little rosy until they sense it goes nowhere, and wow the sex turns. Gets ready to kill you. If cops have an adrenalin wash for their trouble, you are remembered badly. It is much better to be slim, trim, ship-shape, and a little peaked-looking, so they can see you as a thrifty son, which is the way they must have seen me because they gave parole that day, and I was out of there in a week. Out of prison. Out of the can. I think I would have died another year. Liver sickness or go berserk.

Now you may ask can police be so dumb as to let me go on an armed-robbery sentence, six years unserved out of ten. Well, they saw me as thrifty. I was careful that day with voice and posture. But how can police be so stupid as to think in categories like thrifty? That's easy, I can answer. Police are pent up, they're apes, they're bulls. Bulls think in categories.

2

Well, I've been feeling small for four years now. Prison is a bitch for people like me. It cuts your—I don't want to use doubtful language. It's a habit you build up inside. Some do use language that way. Some lifers. Spades. People who don't give a damn. They're playing prison as if it is their life, the only one they are going to have. But I am conservative in temperament. I comb my hair every morning, I comb it the same way. Minor matter you may say, but it isn't for me. I like to comb my hair when I feel like it. Animal of the woods. I have the suspicion—some would call it superstition—that combing my hair can spoil some good ideas. I would never say this to a hack but why is it not possible that some ideas live in your hair, the way the hair curls. I have very wavy hair when it is left to itself. Whenever I get a haircut, I have the feeling I'm losing possibilities I never got around to taking care of. Put it this way: when I comb my hair, it changes my mood. So naturally I prefer to comb it when I want to. In prison forget that. Comb your hair the same time same way every day. Look the same. If you're smart, keep your mood the same way. No ups. Nor downs. Don't be friendly. Don't be sullen. Don't offer company. Don't keep too quiet. If you stay safe, in the middle, and are the same thing every day you get a good report. The reason I get parole first time out, six years off a ten-year sentence is that I was a model prisoner which means just this: you are the same thing every day. Authorities like you if you are dependable. Be almost boring. I think what it may be about is that any man in authority finds his sleep important to him. People in authority can't stand the night. If you wear a uniform and you go to bed to sleep and a certain prisoner never bothers your dreams, you'll say a good word for him when it comes time to making out reports.

Of course you are not popular. Necessarily. My bunky shakes my hand when I get this good news, but I can see he is not happy in every way. So I complain about details. I am not to possess liquor at home, nor am I to frequent any bar even once, even at Christmas. Moreover, I am not to eat in any restaurant which serves liquor.

"What if you don't drink? But just eat there?"

"I'm not to go into any premises having a liquor license."

"A restaurant that don't serve liquor is a tearoom or a hash house."

"Crazy," I say. I don't like such expressions, but this is perfect to express my sentiments.

"Well, good luck."

It is possible we are thinking of the same things, which is the three times he got a bottle into the cell and we drank it together. The first time sick, second time we had a fight, third time sex. I remember I almost yelled in pain when my rocks got off, because they wouldn't stop. I was afraid I'd hurt myself. It had been so long. It seemed each time I took liquor something started in me that was different from my normal personality. By normal I mean normal in prison, no more. You wouldn't want a personality like that on the outside any more than you would want to smell like a laundry bag. But so far as inside personality went, I couldn't take liquor and keep the same. So if I started drinking on the secret when outside, I was in trouble. Because my style of personality would try to go back to what it was before, and too many eyes would be on me. My parole officer, people in the neighborhood. The parole board was getting me a job. They just about picked out the room where you lived. They would hear about it even if I didn't get into a rumble when I was drunk. If I kept a bottle in my room, I would have to hide it good. The parole officer has been known to come around and pay a friendly visit which is to say a sneak visit. Who could enjoy the idea of him sniffing the air in my room to see was there liquor on the breeze? If they caught me drinking in the eight months, back I would be sent to here. A gamble, this parole. But I was glad to take it, I needed out. Very much. Because there was a monotony in me. It had been coming in day after day. I didn't have the feeling of a current in me any more, of anything going. I had the feeling if I sat down next to a girl like the fat girl now, and our legs touched, she would move away cause there was a blank in me which would pass into her. Something repulsive. There was something bad in me, something very dull. It wasn't in my body, it wasn't even in my mind, it was somewhere. I'm not religious, but it was somewhere. I mean I didn't know if I could keep control or not. Still, I couldn't have done it the other way. Eight more months. I might have flipped. Talking back to a hack, a fight. I'd have lost good time. There is only one nightmare in prison. It's that you don't get out, that you never get out because each time you come close the tension has built up in you so that you have to let it break out, and then your bad time is increased. So it's like being on the wrong escalator.

"Take it slow, take it easy," said my bunky. "Eight months goes by if you get yourself some sun."

"Yeah, I'm going to sleep in the sun," I said. "I'm going to drink it."

"Get a good burn your first day out, ha-ha. Burn the prison crap out of your pores."

Maybe the sun would burn the dullness away. That's what I was thinking.

The Last Night: *A Story*

NOTE TO THE READER: *Obviously a movie must be based on a novel, a story, a play, or an original idea. I suppose it could even derive from a poem. "Let's do* The Wasteland," *said a character of mine named Collie Munshin. The novel may be as much as a thousand pages long, the play a hundred, the story ten, the original idea might be stated in a paragraph. Yet each in its turn must be converted into an art form (a low art form) called a treatment. The treatment usually runs anywhere from twenty to a hundred pages in length. It is a bed of Procrustes. Long stories have their limbs lopped off. Too brief tales are stretched. The idea is to present for the attention of a producer, a director, or a script reader, in readable but modest form, the line of story, the gallery of characters, the pith and gist of your tale.*

But one's duty is to do this without much attempt at style and no attempt at high style. The language must be functional, even cliché, and since one's writing prepares the ground for a movie script, too much introspection in the characters is not encouraged. "Joey was thinking for the first time that Alice was maybe in love with him" is barely acceptable. An actor on contract could probably manage to register that emotion in a closeup. Whereas,

. . . the little phrase, as soon as it struck his ear, had the power to liberate in him the room that was needed to contain it; the proportions of Swann's soul were altered; a margin was left for a form of enjoyment which corresponded no more than his love for Odette to any external object, and yet was not, like his enjoyment of that love, purely individual, but assumed for him an objective reality superior to that of other concrete things,

would bake the clay of a producer's face a little closer to stone. A producer is interested in the meat and bone of a story. His question as he reads a treatment is whether he should go on to assign a writer to do a screenplay of this story with specific dialogue and most specific situations added, or whether he should ask for another treatment with new characters and plot, or whether indeed he should write off the loss and quit right now. So a treatment bears the same relation to a finished screenplay as the model for a wind tunnel does to the airplane. Since a treatment is functional, any excellence must be unobtrusive. In fact, a good director (George Stevens) once told me that good writing in a treatment was a form of cheating because it introduced emotional effects through language which he might not as a director be able to repeat on film.

So, thus modestly, I present here a treatment of a movie. It is based on an original idea. It is a short treatment. Only a few of the scenes are indicated. As an example of the art of the treatment, it is not characteristic, for it is written in somewhat formal prose, but it may have the virtue of suggesting a motion picture to your imagination.

Best wishes. See you in the morning after this last night. — N. M.

We're going to describe a movie which will take place twenty years from now, forty years from now, or is it one hundred years from now? One cannot locate the date to a certainty. The world has gone on just about the way we all expected it would go on. It has had large and dramatic confrontations by heads of state, cold wars galore, economic crises resolved and unresolved, good investment, bad investment, decent management and a witch's bag full of other complexities much too numerous ever to bring into a movie. The result has been a catastrophe which all of us have dreaded, all of us expected, and none of us has been able to forestall. The world in twenty or forty years — let us say it is thirty-six — has come to the point where without an atomic war, without even a hard or furious shooting war, it has given birth nonetheless to a fearful condition. The world has succeeded in poisoning itself. It is no longer fit to inhabit. The prevalent condition is fallout radiation, anomalous crops, monstrous babies who grow eyes in their navels and die screaming with hatred at the age of six weeks, plastics which emit cancerous fumes, buildings which collapse like camphor flakes, weather which is excruciatingly psychological because it is always too hot or too cold. Governments fall with the regularity of pendulums. The earth is doomed. The number of atom bombs detonated by the Americans, Russians, English, French, the Algerians, Africans, the Israelis and the Chinese, not to mention the Turks, Hindus and Yugoslavians, have so poisoned existence that even the apples on the trees turn malignant in the stomach. Life is being burned out by a bleak fire within, a plague upon the secrets of our existence which stultifies the air. People who govern the nations have come to a modest and simple conclusion. The mistakes of the past have condemned the future. There is no time left to discuss mankind's guilt. No one is innocent of the charge that all have blighted the rose. In fact, the last President to be elected in the United States has come to office precisely by making this the center of his plank: that no one is innocent. The political reactions have been exceptional. Earlier in the century the most fundamental political notion was that guilt could be laid always at the door of one nation and one nation only. Now a man had been elected to one of the two most powerful offices in the world on the premise that the profound illness of mankind was the fault of all, and this victory had prepared the world for cooperative action.

Shortly after the election of this last of the American Presidents, the cold war was finally ended. Russia and America were ready to collaborate, as were Algeria and France, China, England, Western Europe, India and Africa. The fact had finally been faced. Man had succeeded in so polluting the atmosphere that he was doomed to expire himself. Not one in fifty of the most responsible government scientists would now admit that there were more than twenty years left to life. It was calculated that three-quarters of the living population would be gone in five years from the various diseases of fallout. It was further calculated that of the one-quarter remaining women and men, another three-quarters would be dead in the two following years. What a perspective — three-quarters of the people dead in five years, another three-quarters lost in two, one in sixteen left after seven years to watch the slow extinction of the rest. In the face of this fact, led by a President who was exceptional, who was not only the last but perhaps the greatest of America's leaders, the people of the world had come together to stare into the grim alternatives of their fate. All men and women who continued to live on earth would expire. Five hundred thousand at least could survive if they were moved to Mars, perhaps even as many as one million people could be saved, together with various animals, vegetables, minerals and transportable plants. For the rocketeers had made fine advances. Their arts and sciences had developed enormously. They had managed to establish a company of astronauts on Mars. Nearly one thousand had perished earlier on the Moon, but on Mars over a hundred had managed to live; they had succeeded in building a camp out of native vegetation found on the surface. Dwellings had been fabricated from it and, in triumph, a vehicle constructed entirely from materials found on Mars had been sent back to earth, where men and women received it with extravagant hope.

No space here, or for that matter in the movie, to talk of the endless and difficult negotiations which had gone on. The movie could begin perhaps with the ratification of the most astounding piece of legislation ever to be passed in any country. In this case the piece of legislation had been passed by every nation in the world. It was a covenant which declared that every citizen in each nation was going to devote himself to sending a fleet of rocket ships to Mars. This effort would be herculean. It would demand that the heart of each nation's economy be turned over completely to building and equipping ships, selecting the people, training them, and having the moral fortitude to bid them goodbye. In a sense, this universal operation would be equivalent to the evacuation of Dunkirk but with one exception: three-quarters of the British Expeditionary Force was removed safely from the beach. In this case, the world could hope to send up to Mars no more than one million of its people, conceivably less.

It was calculated that the operation must be accomplished in eighteen months — the spread of plague dictated this haste, for half of the remaining members of mankind might be dead in this time and it was felt that to wait too long would be tantamount to populating the ships with human beings too sick, too weak, too plague-ridden to meet the rigors of life on Mars.

It was indeed a heroic piece of legislation, for the people on earth had had the vision to see that all of them were doomed, and so the majority had consented to accept a minority from within themselves to go out further across space and continue the species. Of course, those who were left would make some further effort to build new rocket ships and follow the wave of the first million pioneers, but the chances of this were unlikely. Not only would the resources of the world be used at an unprecedented rate to build a fleet of ten thousand rocket ships capable of carrying one hundred persons each out so far as Mars, but, in fact, as everyone knew, the earth would be stripped of its most exceptional people, its most brilliant technicians, artists, scientists, athletes and executives, plus their families. Those who were left could hardly hope to form a nucleus or a new cadre brilliant enough to repeat the effort. Besides, it was calculated that the ravages of the plague would already be extreme by the time the fleet departed. The heroism of this legislation resided therefore in the fact that man was capable of regarding his fate and determining to do something exceptional about it.

Now the President of the United States, as indicated earlier, was an unusual man. It was a situation right for a dictator, but he was perhaps not only the most brilliant but the most democratic of American Presidents. And one of the reasons the separate nations of the world had been able to agree on this legislation, and the Americans in particular had voted for it, was that the President had succeeded in engaging the imagination of the world's citizens with his project, much as Churchill had brought an incandescence to the morale of the English by the famous speech where he told them he could offer them nothing but blood, sweat, toil and tears. So this President had spared no detail in bringing the citizens of America face to face with the doom of their condition. There were still one hundred million people alive in America. Of that number, one hundred thousand would voyage to Mars. One person in a thousand then could hope to go. Yet there were no riots in the streets. The reason was curious but simple. The President had promised to stay behind and make every effort to train and rally new technicians for the construction of a second fleet. This decision to remain behind had come from many motives: he had recognized the political impossibility of leaving himself — there was moreover sufficient selflessness in the man to make such a course tasteless to him — and, what was also to the point, his wife, whom he loved, was now incurably sick. It had been agreed that the first of the criteria for selection to the fleet was good physical condition, or at least some reasonable suggestion of health, since everyone on earth was now ill in varying degree.

In the first six months after the worldwide ratification of what had already become known as the Legislation For A Fleet, an atmosphere of cooperation, indeed almost of Christian sanctity and good will, came over the earth. Never before in the memory of anyone living had so many people seemed in so good a mood. There was physical suffering everywhere — as has been mentioned, nearly everyone was ill, usually of distressing internal diseases — but the pain now possessed a certain logic, for at least one-half the working force of the world was engaged directly or indirectly in the construction of the Fleet or the preparations surrounding it. Those who were to travel to Mars had a profound sense of mission, of duty and humility. Those who knew they would be left behind felt for the first time in years a sensation of moral weightlessness which was recognized finally as the absence of guilt. Man was at peace with himself. He could even feel hope, because it was, after all, not known to a certainty that those who were left behind must inevitably perish. Some still believed in the possibility of new medical discoveries which could save them. Others devoted themselves to their President's vow that the construction of the second fleet would begin upon the departure of the first. And, with it all, there was in nearly everyone a sense of personal abnegation, of cooperation, of identification with the community.

It was part of the President's political wisdom that the people who were chosen for the American Fleet had also been selected geographically. Every town of ten thousand inhabitants had ten heroes to make the trip. Not a county of five thousand people scattered over ten thousand square miles of ranches was without its five men, women, and children, all ready. And, of course, for each person chosen there were another ten ready to back them up in case the first man turned ill, or the second, or the third. Behind these ten were one hundred, directly involved in the development, training and morale of each voyager and his ten substitutes. So participation in the flight reached into all the corners of the country, and rare was the family which had nothing to do with it. Historians, writing wistfully about the end of history, had come to the conclusion that man was never so close to finding his soul as in this period when it was generally agreed he was soon to lose his body.

Now, calculate what a blow it was to morality, to courage, and the heart of mankind when it was discovered that life on Mars was not supportable, that the company of a hundred who had been camping on its surface had begun to die, and that their disease was similar to the plague which had begun to visit everyone on earth, but was more virulent in its symptoms and more rapid in its results. The scientific news was overwhelming. Fallout and radiation had poisoned not only the earth but the entire solar system. There was no escape for man to any of the planets. The first solar voyagers to have journeyed so far away as Jupiter had sent back the same tragic news. Belts of radiation incalculably fierce in their intensity now surrounded all the planets.

The President was, of course, the first to receive this news and, in coordination with agreements already arrived at, communicated it to the Premier of the Soviet Union. The two men were already firm friends. They had succeeded, two and a half years before, in forming an alliance to end the Cold War, and by thus acting in concert had encouraged the world to pass the Legislation For A Fleet. Now the Premier informed the President that he had heard the bad news himself: ten of the one hundred men on Mars were, after all, Russians. The two leaders met immediately in Paris for a conference which was brief and critical in its effect. The President was for declaring the news immediately. He had an intimation that to conceal such an apocalyptic fact might invite an unnamable disaster. The Premier of Russia begged him to wait a week at least before announcing this fact. His most cogent argument was that the scientists were entitled to a week to explore the remote possibility of some other solution.

"What other could there possibly be?" asked the President.

"How can I know?" answered the Premier. "Perhaps we shall find a way to drive a tunnel into the center of the earth in order to burn all impurities out of ourselves."

The President was adamant. The tragic condition of the world today was precisely the product, he declared, of ten thousand little abuses of power, ten thousand moments in history when the leaders had decided that the news they held was too unpleasant or too paralyzing for the masses to bear. A new era in history, a heroic if tragic era, had begun precisely because the political leaders of the world now invited the citizens into their confidence. The President and the Premier were at an impasse. The only possible compromise was to wait another twenty-four hours and invite the leaders of Europe, Asia, South America and Africa to an overnight conference which would determine the fate of the news.

The second conference affected the history of everything which was to follow, because all the nations were determined to keep the new and disastrous news a secret. The President's most trusted technical adviser, Anderson Stevens, argued that the general despair would be too great and would paralyze the best efforts of his own men to find another solution. The President and Stevens were old friends. They had come to power together. It was Stevens who had been responsible for some of the most critical scientific discoveries and advances in the rocketry of the last ten years. The Legislation For A Fleet had come, to a great extent, out of his work. He was known as the President's greatest single friend, his most trusted adviser. If he now disagreed with the President at this international conference, the President was obliged to listen to him. Anderson Stevens argued that while the solar system was now poisoned and uninhabitable, it might still be possible to travel to some other part of our galaxy and transfer human life to a more hospitable star. For several days, scientists discussed the possibilities. It was admitted that no fuel or system of booster propulsion was sufficiently powerful to take a rocket ship beyond the solar system. Not even by connecting to booster rockets already in orbit. But then it was also argued that no supreme attempt had yet been made and if the best scientific minds on earth applied themselves to this problem the intellectual results were unforeseeable. In the meantime, absolute silence was to be observed. The program to construct the Martian Fleet was to continue as if nothing had happened. The President acceded to this majority decision of the other leaders, but informed them that he would hold the silence for no more than another week.

By the end of the week, Anderson Stevens returned with an exceptional suggestion: a tunnel ten miles long was to be constructed in all haste in Siberia or the American desert. Pitched at an angle, so that its entrance was on the surface and its base a mile below the earth, the tunnel would act like the muzzle of a rifle and fire the rocket as if it were a shell. Calculated properly, taking advantage of the earth's rotation about its own axis and the greater speed of its rotation about the sun, it was estimated that the rocket ship might then possess sufficient escape velocity to quit the gravitational pull of the sun and so move out to the stars. Since some of the rocket ships were already close to completion and could be adapted quickly to the new scheme, the decision was taken to fire a trial shot in three months, with a picked crew of international experts. If the ship succeeded in escaping the pull of the sun, its crew could then explore out to the nearest stars and send back the essential information necessary for the others who would follow.

Again the question of secrecy was debated. Now Stevens argued that it would be equally irresponsible to give people hope if none would later exist. So, suffering his deepest misgivings, the President consented to a period of silence for three months while the tunnel was completed. In this period, the character of his administration began to change. Hundreds and then thousands of men were keeping two great secrets: the impossibility of life on Mars, and the construction of the giant cannon which would fire an exploratory ship to the stars. So an atmosphere of secrecy and evasion began to circle about the capital, and the mood of the nation was affected. There were rumors everywhere; few of them were accurate. People whispered that the President was dying. Others stated that the Russians were no longer in cooperation with us, but engaged in a contest to see who could get first to Mars. It was said that the climate of Mars had driven the colonists mad, that the spaceships being built would not hold together because the parts were weakened by atomic radiation. It was even rumored—for the existence of the tunnel could not be hidden altogether—that the government was planning to construct an entire state beneath the surface of the earth, in which people could live free of radiation and fallout. For the first time in three or four years, the rates of the sociological diseases — crime, delinquency, divorce and addiction — began again to increase.

The day for the secret test arrived. The rocket was fired. It left the earth's atmosphere at a rate greater than any projectile had yet traveled, a rate so great that the first fear of the scientists was substantiated. The metal out of which the rocket was made, the finest, most heat-resistant alloy yet devised by metallurgists, was still insufficient to withstand the heat of its velocity. As it rose through the air, with the dignitaries of fifty countries gathered to watch its departure, it burst out of the earth, its metal skin glowing with the incandescence of a welding torch, traced a path of incredible velocity across the night sky, so fast that it looked like a bolt of lightning reversed, leaping lividly from the earth into the melancholy night, and burned itself out thirty miles up in the air, burned itself out as completely as a dead meteor. No metal existed which could withstand the heat of the excessive friction created by the extreme velocity necessary to blast a ship through the atmosphere and out beyond the gravitational attractions of the sun and its planets. On the other hand, a rocket ship which rose slowly through the earth's atmosphere and so did not overheat could not then generate enough power to overcome the pull of the sun. It seemed now conclusive that man was trapped within his solar system.

The President declared that the people must finally be informed, and in an historic address he did so inform them of the futility of going to Mars and of the impossibility of escape in any other way. There was nothing left for man, he declared, but to prepare himself for his end, to recognize that his soul might have a life beyond his death and so might communicate the best of himself to the stars. There was thus the opportunity to die well, in dignity, with grace, and the hope that the spirit might prove more miraculous and mighty than the wonders man had extracted from matter. It was a great speech. Commentators declared it was perhaps the greatest speech ever delivered by a political leader. It suffered from one irrevocable flaw: it had been delivered three months too late. The ultimate reaction was cynical. "If all that is left to us is our spirit," commented a German newspaper, "why then did the President deny us three useful months in which to begin to develop it?"

Like the leaden-green airless evening before an electrical storm, an atmosphere of depression, bitterness, wildness, violence and madness rose from the echoes of this speech. Productivity began to founder. People refused to work. Teachers taught in classrooms which were empty and left the schools themselves. Windows began to be broken everywhere, a most minor activity, but it took on accelerated proportions, as if many found a huge satisfaction in throwing rocks through windows much as though they would proclaim that this was what the city would look like when they were gone. Funerals began to take on a bizarre attraction. Since ten to twenty times as many people were dying each day as had died even five years before, funeral processions took up much of the traffic, and many of the people who were idle enjoyed marching through the streets in front of and behind the limousines. The effect was sometimes medieval, for impromptu carnivals began to set themselves up on the road to the cemetery. There were speeches in Congress to impeach the President and, as might conventionally be expected, some of the particular advisers who had counseled him to keep silence were now most forward in their condemnation of his act.

The President himself seemed to be going through an exceptional experience. That speech in which he had suggested to mankind that its best hope was to cultivate its spirit before it died seemed to have had the most profound effect upon him. His appearance had begun to alter: his hair was subtly longer, his face more gaunt, his eyes feverish. He had always been unorthodox as a President, but now his clothing was often rumpled and he would appear unexpectedly to address meetings or to say a few words on television. His resemblance to Lincoln, which had in the beginning been slight, now became more pronounced. The wits were quick to suggest that he spent hours each day with a makeup expert. In the midst of this, the President's wife died, and in great pain. They had been close for twenty years. Over the last month, he had encouraged her not to take any drugs to dull the pain. The pain was meaningful, he informed her. The choice might be one of suffering now in the present or later in eternity. In anguish she expired. On her deathbed she seared him with a cruel confession. It was that no matter how she had loved him for twenty years, she had always felt there was a part of him never to be trusted, a part which was implacable, inhuman and ruthless. "You would destroy the world for a principle," she told him as she died. "There is something diabolical about you."

On the return from her funeral, people came out to stand silently in tribute. It was the first spontaneous sign of respect paid to him in some months, and riding alone in the rear of an open limousine, he wept. Yet, before the ride was over, someone in the crowd threw a stone through the windshield. In his mind, as he rode, was the face of his wife, saying to him some months before, "I tell you, people cannot bear suffering. I know that I cannot. You will force me to destroy a part of your heart if you do not let me have the drugs."

That night the chief of America's Intelligence Service came to see the President. The Russians were engaged in a curious act. They were building a tunnel in Siberia, a tunnel even larger than the American one, and at an impossible angle; it went almost directly into the earth and then took a jog at right angles to itself. The President put through a call to Moscow to speak to the Premier. The Premier told the President that he had already made preparations to see him. There was a matter of the most extreme importance to be discussed: the Russians had found a way to get a rocket ship out of the solar system.

So, the two men met in London in a secret conference. Alone in a room, the Premier explained the new project and his peculiar position. Slowly, insidiously, he had been losing control in his country, just as the President had become progressively more powerless in America. Against the Premier's wishes, some atomic and rocket scientists had come together on a fearsome scheme which the Army was now supporting. It had been calculated that if an ordinary rocket ship, of the sort which belonged to the Martian Fleet, were fired out from the earth, it would be possible to blast it into the furthest reaches of our own galaxy, provided—and this was most important—a planet were exploded at the proper moment. It would be like the impetus a breaking wave could give to a surfboard rider. With proper timing the force released by blowing up the planet would more than counteract the gravitational pull of the sun. Moreover, the rocket ship could be a great distance away from the planet at the moment it was exploded, and so the metal of its skin would not have to undergo any excessive heat.

"But which planet could we use?" asked the President.

The two men looked at one another. The communication passed silently from one's mind to the other. It was obvious. With the techniques available to them there was only one planet: the earth.

That was what the Russian tunnel was for. A tunnel going deep into the earth, loaded with fissionable material, and exploded by a radio wave sent out from a rocket ship already one million miles away. The detonation of the earth would hurl the rocket ship like a pebble across a chasm of space.

"Well," says the President, after a long pause, "it may be possible for the Fleet to take a trip after all."

"No," the Premier assured him, "not the Fleet." For the earth would be detonated by an atomic chain reaction which would spew radioactive material across one hundred million miles of the heavens. The alloy vuranel was the only alloy which could protect a rocket ship against the electronic hurricane which would follow the explosion. There was on earth enough vuranel to create a satisfactory shield for only one ship. "Not a million men, women, and children, but a hundred, a hundred people and a few animals will take the trip to a star."

"Who will go?" asks the President.

"Some of your people," answers the Premier, "some of mine. You and me."

"I won't go," says the President.

"Of course you will," says the Premier. "Because if you don't go, I don't go, and we've been through too much already. You see, my dear friend, you're the only equal I have on earth. It would be much too depressing to move through those idiotic stars without you."

But the President is overcome by the proportions of the adventure. "You mean we will blow up the entire world in order that a hundred people have some small chance — one chance in five, one chance in ten, one chance in a hundred, or less — to reach some star and live upon it. The odds are too brutal. The cost is incalculable."

"We lose nothing but a few years," says the Premier. "We'll all be dead anyway."

"No," says the President, "it's not the same. We don't know what we destroy. It may be that after life ceases on the earth, life will generate itself again, if only we leave the earth alone. To destroy it is monstrous. We may destroy the spirit of something far larger than ourselves."

The Premier taps him on the shoulder. "Look, my friend, do you believe that God is found in a cockroach? I don't. God is found inside you, and inside me. When all of us are gone, God is also gone."

"I don't know if I believe that," answers the President.

Well, the Premier tells him, religious discussion has always fascinated him, but politics are more pressing. The question is whether they are at liberty to discuss this matter on its moral merits alone. The tunnel in Siberia had been built without his permission. It might interest the President to know that a tunnel equally secret is being constructed near the site of the old Arizona tunnel. There were Russian technicians working on that, just as American technicians had been working in Siberia. The sad political fact is that the technicians had acquired enormous political force, and if it were a question of a showdown tomorrow, it is quite likely they could seize power in the Soviet Union and in America as well.

"You, sir," says the Premier, "have been searching your soul for the last year in order to discover reasons for still governing. I have been studying Machiavelli because I have found, to my amusement, that when all else is gone, when life is gone, when the promise of future life is gone, and the meaning of power, then what remains for one is the game. I want the game to go on. I do not want to lose power in my country. I do not want you to lose it in yours. I want, if necessary, to take the game clear up into the stars. You deserve to be on that rocket ship, and I deserve to be on it. It is possible we have given as much as anyone alive to brooding over the problems of mankind in these last few years. It is your right and my right to look for a continuation of the species. Perhaps it is even our duty."

"No," says the President. "They're holding a gun to our heads. One cannot speak of the pleasures of the game or of honor or of duty when there is no choice."

He will not consent to destroying the earth unless the people of earth choose that course, with a full knowledge of the consequences. What is he going to do, asks the Premier. He is going to tell the world, says the President. There must be a general world-wide election to determine the decision.

"Your own people will arrest you first," says the Premier. He then discloses that the concept of exploding the earth to boost the power of the rocket had been Anderson Stevens' idea.

The President picks up the phone and makes a call to his press chief. He tells him to prepare the television networks for an address he will deliver that night. The press chief asks him the subject. The President tells him he will discuss it upon his return. The press chief says that the network cannot be cleared unless the President informs him now of the subject. It will be a religious address, says the President.

"The networks may not give us the time," says the press chief. "Frankly, sir, they are not certain which audiences share your spiritual fire."

The President hangs up. "You are right," he tells the Premier. "They will not let me make the speech. I have to make it here in London. Will you stand beside me?"

"No, my friend," says the Russian, "I will not. They will put you in jail for making that speech, and you will have need of me on the outside to liberate your skin."

The President makes the address in London to the citizens of the world. He explains the alternatives, outlines his doubts, discusses the fact that there are technicians ready to seize power, determined to commit themselves to the terrestrial explosion. No one but the people of the earth, by democratic procedure, have the right to make this decision, he declares, and recommends that as a first step the people march on the tunnel sites and hold them. He concludes his address by saying he is flying immediately back to Washington and will be there within two hours.

The message has been delivered on the network devoted to international television. It reaches a modest percentage of all listeners in the world. But in America, from the President's point of view the program took place at an unfortunate time, for it was the early hours of the morning. When he lands in Washington at dawn, he is met by his Cabinet and a platoon of M.P.'s, who arrest him. Television in America is devoted that morning to the announcement that the President has had a psychotic breakdown and is at present under observation by psychiatrists.

For a week, the atmosphere is unendurable. A small percentage of the people in America have listened to the President's speech. Many more have heard him in other countries. Political tensions are acute, and increase when the Premier of the Soviet Union announces in reply to a question from a reporter that in his opinion the President of the United States is perfectly sane. Committees of citizens form everywhere to demand an open investigation of the charges against the President. It becomes a rallying cry that the President be shown to the public. A condition close to civil war exists in America.

At this point, the President is paid a visit by Anderson Stevens, the scientist in charge of the rocket program, the man who has lately done more than any other to lead the Cabinet against the President. Now they have a conversation behind the barred windows of the hospital room where the President is imprisoned. Anderson Stevens tells the President that the first tunnel which had been built for the star shot was, from his point of view, a ruse. He had never expected that rocket ship, which was fired like a bullet, to escape from the earth's atmosphere without burning to a cinder. All of his experience had told him it would be destroyed. But he had advanced the program for that shot because he wished to test something else — the tunnel. It had been essential to discover how deeply one could dig into the crust of the earth before the heat became insupportable for an atomic bomb. In effect, the tunnel had been dug as a test to determine the feasibility of detonating the earth. And so that shot which had burned up a rocket ship had been, from Stevens' point of view, a success, because he had learned that the tunnel could be dug deep enough to enable a superior hydrogen bomb to set off a chain reaction in the fiery core of the earth. The fact that one hundred rocketeers and astronauts, men who had been his friends for decades, had died in an experiment he had known to be all but hopeless was an indication of how serious he was about the earth bomb shot. The President must not think for a moment that Stevens would hesitate to keep him in captivity, man the ship himself, and blow up the earth.

Why, then, asks the President, does Stevens bother to speak to him? Because, answers Stevens, he wants the President to command the ship. Why? Because in some way the fate of the ship might be affected by the emotions of everybody on earth at the moment the earth was exploded. This sounded like madness to some of his scientific colleagues, but to him it was feasible that if life had a spirit and all life ceased to exist at the same moment, then that spirit, at the instant of death, might have a force of liberation or deterrence which could be felt as a physical force across the heavens.

"You mean," says the President, "that even in the ruthless circuits of your heart there is terror, a moral terror, at the consequence of your act. And it is me you wish to bear the moral consequence of that act, and not you."

"You are the only man great enough, sir," says Anderson Stevens, bowing his head.

"But I think the act is wrong," says the President.

"I know it is right," says Stevens. "I spent a thousand days and a thousand nights living with the terror that I might be wrong, and still I believe I am right. There is something in me which knows that two things are true—that we have destroyed this earth not only because we were not worthy of it, but because it may have been too cruel for us. I tell you, we do not know. Man may have been mismated with earth. In some fantastic way, perhaps we voyaged here some millions of years ago and fell into a stupidity equal to the apes. That I don't know. But I do know, if I know anything at all, because my mind imprisoned in each and every one of my cells tells me so, that we must go on, that we as men are different from the earth, we are visitors upon it. We cannot suffer ourselves to sit here and be extinguished, not when the beauty which first gave speech to our tongues commands us to go out and find another world, another earth, where we may strive, where we may win, where we may find the right to live again. For that dream I would kill everyone on earth. I would kill my children. In fact I must, for they will not accompany me on the trip. And you," he says to the President, "you must accompany us. You must help to make this trip. For we as men may finally achieve greatness if we survive this, the most profound of our perils."

"I do not trust myself," says the President. "I do not know if my motive is good. Too many men go to their death with a hatred deep beyond words, wishing with their last breath that they could find the power to destroy God. I do not know — I may be one of those men."

"You have no choice," says Anderson Stevens. "There are people trying to liberate you now. I shall be here to shoot you myself before they succeed. Unless you agree to command the ship."

"Why should I agree?" says the President. "Shoot me now."

"No," says Stevens, "you will agree, because I will make one critical concession to you. I do it not from choice, but from desperation. My dreams tell me we are doomed unless you command us. So I will let you give the people their one last opportunity. I will let you speak to them. I will put my power behind you, so that they may vote."

"No," says the President, "not yet. Because if such an election were lost, if the people said, 'Let us stay here and die together, and leave the earth to mend itself, without the sound of human speech or our machines,' then you would betray me. I know it. You would betray everyone. Some night, in some desert, a rocket ship would be fired up into the sky, and twenty hours later, deep in some secret tunnel, all of us would be awakened by the last explosion of them all. No. I will wait for the people to free me first. Of necessity, my first act then will be to imprison you."

After this interview between Stevens and the President, the ruling coalition of Cabinet officers and technicians refused, of course, to let the people see the President. The response was a virtually spontaneous trek of Americans by airplane, helicopter, automobile, by animal, by motorcycle, and on foot, toward the tunnel site the President had named. The Army was quickly deployed to prevent them, but the soldiers refused to protect the approaches to the tunnel. They also asked for the right to see the President. The Cabinet capitulated. The President was presented on television. He announced that the only justification for the star ship was a worldwide general election.

The most brilliant, anguished, closely debated election in the history of the world now took place. For two months, argument licked like flame at the problem. In a last crucial speech the night before the election, the President declared that it was the words of a man now in prison, Anderson Stevens, which convinced him how he would vote. For he, the President, had indeed come to believe that man rising out of the fiery grave of earth, out of the loss of his past, his history, and his roots, might finally achieve the greatness and the goodness expected of him precisely because he had survived this, the last and the most excruciating of his trials. "If even a few of us manage to live, our seed will be changed forever by the self-sacrifice and nobility, the courage and the loss engraved on our memory of that earth-doomed man who was our ancestor and who offered us life. Man may become human at last." The President concluded his speech by announcing that if the people considered him deserving of the honor, he would be the first to enter the ship, he would take upon himself the act of pressing that button which would blow up the earth.

The answer to this speech was a solemn vote taken in favor of destroying the world, and giving the spaceship its opportunity to reach the stars.

The beginning of the last sequence in the movie might show the President and the Premier saying goodbye. The Premier has discovered he is now hopelessly ill, and so will stay behind.

The Premier smiles as he says goodbye. "You see, I am really too fat for a brand-new game. It is you fanatics who always take the longest trips."

One hundred men and women file into the ship behind the President. The rocket is fired and rises slowly, monumentally. Soon it is out of sight. In the navigation tower within the rocket the President stares back at earth. It is seen on a color television screen, magnified enormously. The hours go by and the time is approaching for the explosion. The radio which will send out the wave of detonation is warmed up. Over it the President speaks to the people who are left behind on earth. All work has of course ceased, and people waiting through the last few hours collect, many of them, in public places, listening to the President's voice on loudspeakers. Others hear it in radios in their rooms, or sprawled on the grass in city parks. People listen in cars on country crossroads, at the beach, watching the surf break. Quietly, a few still buy tickets for their children on the pony rides. One or two old scholars sit by themselves at desks in the public library, reading books. Some drink in bars. Others sit quietly on the edge of pavements, their feet in the street. One man takes his shoes off. The mood is not too different from the mood of a big city late at night when the weather is warm. There is the same air of expectation, of quiet, brooding concentration.

"Pray for us," says the President to them, speaking into his microphone on that rocket ship one million miles away. "Pray for us. Pray that our purpose is good and not evil. Pray that we are true and not false. Pray that it is part of our mission to bring the life we know to other stars." And in his ears he hears the voice of his wife, saying through her pain, "You will end by destroying everything."

"Forgive me, all of you," says the President. "May I be an honest man and not first deluded physician to the Devil." Then he presses the button.

The earth detonates into the dark spaces. A flame leaps across the solar system. A scream of anguish, jubilation, desperation, terror, ecstasy, vaults across the heavens. The tortured heart of the earth has finally found its voice. We have a glimpse of the spaceship, a silver minnow of light, streaming into the oceans of mystery, and the darkness beyond.

Poems

You're not large enough
    for a whale
and much too fat
    to be a shark
said I to my love.
              Porpoise
was her reply

Sleek pig
  thought the mind
  of my eye

  Sleek pigs
    are porpoises
    said she
  and began to cry.

THE EXECUTIONER'S SONG

I think if I had three good years to give
    in study at some occupation
    which was fierce and new
    and full of stimulation
I think I would become
            an executioner
    with time spent out in the field
    digging graves for bodies I had made
            the night before.
You see: I am bad at endings
My bowels move without honor
    and flatulence is an affliction
    my pride must welcome with gloom
It comes I know from preoccupation
    much too much with sex
Those who end well do not spend their time
    so badly on the throne

For this reason I expect the task
    of gravedigger welcomes me
I would like to kill well and bury well
Perhaps then my seed would not shoot
    so frantic a flare
If I could execute neatly
    (with respect for whatever romantic
                        imagination

gave passion to my subject's crime)
and if I buried well
(with tenderness, dispatch, gravity
and joy that the job was not jangled—
giving a last just touch of the spade
to the coffin
                in order to leave it
quivering
                like a leaf—for forget not
coffins quiver as the breath goes out
and the earth comes down)

Yes if I could kill cleanly
and learn not to turn my back
on the face of each victim
as he chooses
                what is last to be seen
in his eye,
           well, then perhaps,
then might I rise so high upon occasion
as to smite a fist of the Lord's creation
into the womb of that muse
which gives us poems
Yes, then I might
For one ends best when death is clean
   to the mind
                and calm in its proportions
   fire in the orchard and flame at the root

DAIMON RUNS REVISITED

There was a meet for the boys
The moolahs, the mozzers, the Maf, the Coast and the
    Nose
even the bonze and the dunes.
They were in to get acquaints for a new soft commodtz
and general affiliation.

How, said the Coaster to the Nostrand
do you think soft sell began?
Well, I'll tell you, said the Maf, we said to the dunes
Whaderya trying to shove that shit
    down people's troat for?
Slip it up their stroonz
    you asshole
Strike a match!

Said the dunes to the Maf,
Whaderya want to give me a hardon for?
you have hurt my feels
how much can the heart of my feels take
before the heart of some other Guinea's feels
    is forced to break?
Listen, said the dunes to the Maf—you're a dunze
Don't get hit!

So they had a ruining
They had the runs.
That was some thunder.
Those fartsaroons came close to eating all the prunes.

ESPRIT DE SOMMELIER

Waiter!

Yessir!

Are you
  Diner's Club?

No sir,
  we are not
  Upper Mediocrity

Well fuck
    you

Thank you sir
we are quite aristocracy

Which
aristocracy?

Quiet aristocracy, sir,

Oh, well thank you.
Say did you know
that cops are like
ladies in a
    bad mood?

Ha, ha.
  that is funny, sir
  so, that is very
  funny. You must
  bitter please join
  our Quit Aristocracy
    credit club.

Mon dieu, Feinspan,
  it's you.

Yessir, will presumption
  never cease?

THE SHORTEST NOVEL
OF THEM ALL

At first she thought she could kill him in three days.

She did nearly. His heart proved nearly unequal to her compliments.

Then she thought it would take three weeks. But he survived.

So she revised her tables and calculated three months.

After three years, he was still alive. So they got married.

Now they've been married for thirty years. People speak warmly of them. They are known as the best marriage in town.

It's just that their children keep dying.

A WALTZ

Paper covers rock
  rock breaks scissor
  scissor cuts paper

A woman can always
  take a man

A fag may always
  take a woman

A man may always
  take a fag

Circles bore me.

They obey
    too many laws

Epitaph for a man of parts

I do not think there was an occasion
        in my life
    which did not have
            me
        fatally
    misquoted

Dr. Hu
speaks
twenty-three
  languages.

What loneliness.

A Universal Cure for Illness
don't go to bed
until you
fall
in
it

The most
  eligible
  bachelor
  in London
  is a category
  conceived
  by presumptive
    witches
    weary
    of doing
    without
  their widow's weeds—
  whispered
    the epigram
  to the boutonniere.

Go fix the flowers fuck-face
    was the King's reply

It's amazing
    how many
    ladies
    never crack
    a book
    it hurts
        the spine.

BOITES

I love Bobby, Bobby's divine
  The Windsors came to
    see him
  and the Duke
    kept calling for
  Bye Bye Blackbird
  over and over again.
  It was a glorious night.
  I borrowed mascara
    from the Duchess
  before we were done
  we were crying
    so hard
    even the Duke.
How were we to know
  that in five years
    give ten
  the West
    Old World
  would shiver from blight
  and I would turn
    to a Prince
    of the Congo
  saying: embrace me
    darkest delight
  for in your firmament
  are stars.

when he sang
  Blackbird
    bye-bye
for can it be
  we heard
  the chord
  of the cannibal
sharpening his knife
  on a blooded stone
  and wept for you
    as well as us.

Oh blackbird
  do not banish us
  banish not
    the lovers
    of Bobby

Young winners
  make weak old losers
  said Bobby
    removing his mask
  to show
  he was now
    King
  of our
    Congo.

IN THE JARDIN EXOTIQUE OF EZE

In the Jardin Exotique of Eze
the cactus come up from the sea
like an anemone wooing a spider
or a pygmy with a blowgun dart.
Silently they smell the breeze,
      invertebrate,
their memory as long as the tripe of the Mediterranée.
Was it once or never? that a God from deep waters
             dreaming of the moon
fell in love with a gleam from the midnight sky
who, intoxicated with herself
and the rapture of the depths,
like a daughter most fortunate in family,
beautiful, spoiled, innocent of alarm,
wandered down an alley
dark as the pitch of blackest frustration
and there was trapped by the sound of need
in the murmur of an ape.
So did that God of dark waters woo a moon beam
and from their love leave a seed
on the spume of the wrack
which washes a desert shore.
Cactus,
    mad psychotic bulb of light and dark
        spy of the deep sea
        intimate of the moon
your form inspires nausea
for love which dares too much
and has no soil but sand
flowers spines of lunar hatred
shapes tubers on the leaf
and gives no wine but visions from peyote
of ether and her gardens
which burn in gloom
of poison, bliss, the death of suns
and phosphorescent nights.

WHY ARE WE IN VIETNAM?

Mailer's first extended piece of fiction since An American Dream *was published by Putnam's in 1967 and remains available in their Berkley Medallion paperback edition. The novel had originally been intended, Mailer has explained, to focus upon the hostilities between a band of young cultural dropouts and an American community which they held under siege. But he began first to write of the earlier lives of two of the band's leaders — D.J. and Tex — and ended up with* Why Are We in Vietnam? *Critical commentary has been largely directed at the issue raised by the title, since the action of the book takes place not in Vietnam but in Dallas and Alaska, and at the heavy dimension of literary allusion in the narrative. The two chapters excerpted here depict Rusty Jethroe and his son D.J. on their Alaskan hunting expedition, itself a status symbol in Rusty's American business executive world, breaking loose from the conventional party and hunting on their own. The failure of this attempt at fusion through separation sets up the next excerpted chapter, where D.J. and his friend Tex also break off from the party, this time to expose themselves to the natural forces in their world as nakedly as possible.*

Chap Eight

Rusty has been studying the map. He and D.J. are map readers (at your service, coordinates) and compass hounds. He even bought D.J. a Keuffel & Esser surveyor's transit, tripod, and tape for his fourteenth birthday. He knows they now have eleven miles to make before dark and five to six hours to do it in — long twilight still, endless ass of ass-end summer long Alaskan twilight, and he's not worried a bit at that, he's free, man, loose, loose as Henry with a goose, shedding those corporation layers, all that paper ass desk shit and glut, dictating larynx ass machines, six-button Tphones, buzzer shit (conference table alcohol — where is your buzz), dead-ass hour shit, and he's free of Luke the Fink with his Washington up your ass connections, he's being bad Rusty and it's years, man, he wants to holler hallo for a grizzer any size big ass beast.

They go, putting on the miles, walking ten yards apart, crossing bare ridgelines when they feel they far enough away from Luke to take the chance, then ducking back to timber when they hear whirlybird Cop Turd glomming over the next hill, yeah, Luke has put in a call, round up those strays, shit, no one is going to round them up. And after an hour, a good sweat on each, father and son sweat, a little alike, a little diff, Rusty got just a hint of sweet rot in his smell but when the balls is back in as now he's okay, many a hero smell worse than old Rust, and they go like two combat wolves, eyes to the left, eyes to the right, slow relaxed sweep, looking, listening to the *mood*, man, their steps keen off each little start of sound, squirrels on a split ass, working upwind through the timber, skirting all the alder, briers, snag-brush, working their way into the wind as if they going to *smell* that bear. And when they stop to rest, they are real good, man, tight as combat buddies, they pick a spot under an overhang rock at their back so no bear can come up behind and the touch, just the feather on your ass touch, of danger, cause grizzer could be anywhere near, is ozone bubble in the nose, that oo oo oo of the nose when you going to meet a real hot fuck in an hour and you know she there waiting for you, whoo-ee, whoo-ee, humping a sweet pump by the railroad track beautiful big-ass Texas night. Rusty starts to talk. They looking out off a ledge onto a view of stone ice peaks twenty miles away, could be Colorado, not Alaska in September, and those mountains full of evergreen dropping in long fat sweet ass sweet husband fat-ass type of lines, the rolling stands of evergreen looking like fur on the ass of the grizzer, yeah, those soft humps of mountains are like sleeping bears, big haunches of hibernation, Hiram, and Rusty starts to point out the local flora, the tall saxifrages like the boykinia, the sowdock, fireweed, horsetail, he been pointing them out all along as they were going, just a quiet little voice, "That's white bell of heather over there, D.J." or "Hot damn, look at the height of those horsetails," "White mountain avens, boy, pretty flower that," "Purple rhododendrons, up in the Circle! Wait till I tell your mother I saw purple rhododendrons in the Arctic Circle." Oh, there's cow parsnip and climbing bells, yellow arctic poppies, more of a fine white little flower he calls saxifrage again. "Know what saxifrage means, kid?"

"You tell me."

"Rock buster. That little white flower is a rock buster. Any saxifrage is strong enough to grow and split a rock." And D.J. reels with that, cause he thinks of the little green shoot (or is it white? underground, just nipple tit out of the seed) getting its white nose into the smallest crack of the rock and pushing and the rock pushing back, and it swelling to crack the rock, and the rock not cracking, how can a soft shoot move rock? Yeah, well it sends out the word to the root and the root pulls into the basic ass power of the earth and draws a force, a subterranean thunder, Wanda, and womb, woom woom woom, one little blast of swell, that shoot is harder than rock for one micromillionth of a second, it got a hard on, Herbert, and the rock stone pussy cracks, and up comes boykinia the local saxifrage. Just rock buster. D.J. is humper-ding with sweet pores of thought. Damn.

"That's monkshood," says Rusty.

About then was when they first sat looking out across a canyon and a long field of tundra turning red and yellow already and a pioneer tree in the middle of it.

"Man, you like to be a tree by yourself in the middle of a field?" asks Rusty.

"Now you know I really don't know," says D.J. confessing ignorance for the first time since thirteen.

"My grandmammy, your great-grandmother Eula Spicer Jethroe, used to be a witch, so evehbody claims. She used to tell me when I was a little three-year-old still shit ass in my breeches that I must never sleep under a pioneer tree, cause it is full of sorrow and alone and bats piss on it at midnight, therefore it stands by itself getting messages, all kind of special messages, and if you sleep under it, you witched by it, you get the messages too."

"What are they?"

"I don't know. Old Eula Spicer Jethroe wouldn't say." Yeah, they laughed. D.J. said, oh, cautious as they come, "Rusty . . . sir . . . how do you know the names of all this grass . . . herb . . . all this."

"Why I spent a half hour talking to Luke asking the names. That's the only good half hour I had with him. Cause that used to be my hobby. When I was your age I used to be a walking compendium of Texas wild flowers."

"Say, you never let on."

"Well, D.J., my daddy had more time, you know. Him and me were close, you know cause it was all that time, depression, East Texas depression years, cold heart times. He had no work so we went hunting for meat. Then two years later he hit a well and the Jethroes was rich again, but those two years I saw sights, learned things. We used to camp out in a lean-to right on the plains. Coyotes. Oh, that's a cry."

"I've heard it hunting."

"Yeah, but in a lean-to set up so the rain don't blow in the open end, and starting a fire in the rain, know how to do that?"

"No, sir."

"Well, you got to look for a stump that's protected by overhang, or the underside of a tree branch that's rotten, you got to find dry punk, that dry perfumy sort of rot stuff in a tree, and that's your tinder and your paper all in one. If it's dry, it will get wet twigs to burn. So, that we used to do, daddy and me, used to camp out there four days in a row, trailing across that plain till an animal got in range, not so easy when the plain is bare, you hear, and we had to make the shots count too, I learned a lot from my daddy, he taught me one thing I'm going to teach you now—the only time a good man with a good rifle is in trouble is when he steps from sunlight into shadow, cause there's two or three seconds when you can't see."

"I know that daddy," says D.J.

"Yeah, but you never made a principle of it. That's the difference."

"Yessir, yessir."

"Listen, know the worst thing I ever saw. It was a poor deer being killed by an eagle. Some hunter had wounded the deer—the eagle finished the job or was about to when I couldn't stand to watch no more and shot the eagle and put the poor deer out of its miz. But that eagle had swooped in, plucked out one eye of the deer, fluttered up a little you know like a Nigger strutting his ass feathers, and then plucked the other eye. It was going to go for the nuts next. Terrible creature the eagle. I've heard they even pull the intestine out of a carcass like a sailor pulling rope with his mouth. It got me so upset to recognize that E Pluribus Unum is in the hands of an eagle that I almost wrote an open letter to the Congress of America. Can you imagine your daddy getting that ape shit? But I think it's a secret crime that America, which is the greatest nation ever lived, better read a lot of history to see how shit-and-sure a proposition that is, is nonetheless represented, indeed even symbolized by an eagle, the most miserable of the scavengers, worse than crow."

On and on they go for half an hour, talking so close that D.J. can even get familiar with Rusty's breath which is all right. It got a hint of middle-aged fatigue of twenty years of doing all the little things body did not want to do, that flat sour of the slightly used up, and there's a hint of garlic or onion, and tobacco, and twenty years of booze gives a little permanent rot to the odor coming off the lining of the stomach, and there's even a speck of caries, one bit of dental rot almost on the agreeable side (for face it, fellow Americans, there are secret freaked-out grope types who dig dental rot if its subtle kind of high clean funky smell, how often, after all, does a nose get near a living nerve?) but with all this detraction, fatigue, booze, Nick the Teen, garlic and cavity, it's still a good breath, it got muscle and a big happy man with that clean odorless white

American flesh (hey assholes out there, is this D.J. addressing you a Texas youth for sure or is he a genius of a crippled Spade up in Harlem making all this shit up, better wonder, work your bronze, this is a problem — whose consciousness you getting, overlap on the frequencies, Percival? shit, D.J. is going to make you fly up your own ass before you get to read him right, it's love to have the consciousness of D.J., Texas youth, better believe, cause it's easier for D.J. to imitate a high I.Q. Harlem Nigger time to time, since D.J. knows New York, yeah, he passed through, MacDougal Street you wait and see, than for a Harlem Nigger ever to know all this secret Texas shit. Well, place your bets, worry your head audience of D.J. there is no security in this consciousness, and you are going to die some day and there is no security in that, well, before you buy your casket Mr. Rot Gut wait till you get to know Tex and his own daddy Gottfried Hyde Senior, the undertaker, there's a piece of woo, and point coming here, point your nose, auditor, is that D.J. riding on currents of love can take all the smell of his daddy's breath and love him still, cause that's love — you can go to the end of the other's breath and still forgive him. If you husbands and wives out there in receiving land cannot do that, well, hump your shrug, all is not hopeless, maybe you still in love if only with limp dick and just one lip of the pussy, or two lips of cunt dry as adhesive tape. Woo-ee!) D.J. takes his consciousness and by act of will zooms with Superman moves of his brain projectile back to ledge, back to rock, and Rusty pointing across the valley to a caribou upwind from them, a caribou just standing near the pioneer tree, and Rusty lifts his rifle, breathes, waits to feel D.J.'s mood, waits, puts down his rifle. "Shall we let it go?"

"Yeah."

"Yeah, son. Shit, let's let old caribou go. He suffering anyway."

And that old caribou is standing with his nose in the moss, digging his nose in, and his haunches are hicking and twitching and his stump tail is wiggling like a baby's running nose. Alaska flies are murdering him, he stands, suffers, then makes a dash for two hundred yards to escape the flies, stands, looks for damp in the tundra, holds it, suffers the flies, then runs again, on up to the ridge where there will be wind maybe, maybe there will be wind, and he can clear his head from thirty fly bite on the minute. And Rusty and D.J. watching have been waiting for fifteen minutes, and there's fine cool in them now, they're off the fever of hunting and into the heart of it, the cool, letting that caribou go has got them so ready for bear they could believe in man-bear radar, it's as if now they know, cause the pitch of secret tune is pure that grizzer is near, something big is by. And as they step out, they have not gone

one-half of a mile before they find a track, fresh bear track on the wet earth of a high mountain rivulet, and their hearts hold, cause track is big, Rusty could put the soles of both his big hunting shoes inside that one bear's foot, and mark of the claws in front is long, two inches long of claws, this is grizzer, grizzer baby, never black bear, not with claws two inches long. Now they feel the size. They've been thinking of grizzer as a big big man, about as frightening as a stone-black seven-foot three-hundred-pound Nigger, but grizzer is bigger than that, grizzer is right up there with the hippopotami and the small elephants, and the big elephants, yeah, that's how it feels, now they feel alone and in the woods with some fast dark boxcar size of beast moving somewhere around in relation to them. Shit! And the Cop Turd comes by overhead shaking the silence, and failing to see them in the woods, and Rusty says in a hoarse little clearing of his throat (just like a little clearing in the forest) "Hey, now, D.J., we're on bear traveling trail." And through the brush ahead is a path, looks like it's been grooved by many a grizzer working down the same route through the brush, and there and here, bark rubbed from trees, familiar intimate family rub of itching hide and itching bear asshole rubbing against that old corncob bark. Yeah, some nappy mountain of grizzly has been lumbering and slinging his legs along here. And D.J. breathes death—first time in his life—and the sides of the trail slam onto his heart like the jaws of a vise cause that grizzer could come erupting out of the brush, could a grizzer travel at speed through that brush? it's death D.J.'s breathing, it comes like attack of vertigo when stepping into dark and smelling pig shit, that's what death smells to him, own pig shit smell, terrible fear right out of his lungs and pores, mucous lining of now flappy-ass organs, and back of fear like man riding chariot pulled by eight wild pigs in harness is crazy-ass murder, cause D.J. for first time in his life is hip to the hole of his center which is slippery desire to turn his gun and blast a shot into Rusty's fat fuck face, thump in his skull, whawng! and whoong! with the dead-ass butt of his Remington 721, D.J. is shivering on the death in this hot-ass vale of breath, cause each near-silent step of his toe on the tail sounds a note, chimes of memory, angel's harp of ten little toes picking out the blows of Rusty's belt on his back, he five years old and shrieking off the fuck of his head, cause the face of his father is a madman ass, a power which wishes to beat him to death—for what no longer known—a child's screaming in the middle of, and so interrupting, a Hallelujah Sir Jet Throne fuck? nobody know now, D.J. just remembers the beating, screaming, pleading, smell of pig shit in his five-year-old pants, and death, coming in like oscillations red and green waves pulsating

576   *The Long Patrol*

from oscilloscope, murder came red and green, stop, go, Rusty's eyes in to kill on D.J. — fat five-year-old spoiled beautiful little fuck in the middle between husband and wife, hola, Olatunji, vale of breath on the vise in his heart and first seed of tumor, figure-toi, could that be? — little pretty seed of backed-up murder passed from valve asshole Rusty's heart to the seat of D.J.'s brain, for Hallie rushed in then, picked up decanter whiskey, flung it through on a line through window, and glass crackled all scythe and lightnings, and spell broke, murder weather cracked in thunder, and D.J. all pig shit smell and five-year-old ass and back burning like the flesh in the burns of Hell run all screaming into Hallie's arms, little man saved by cunt, virility grew with a taint in the armature of the phallic catapult, call it tumor if that's what D.J.'s got in his brain, cause brilliance is next to murder, man, brilliance is green and gold light on the body and wings of horseflies hovering over the rot and gray-gold and red of degenerating meat. Whoo! Death is on him, memory of father near to murdering the son, breath of his own murder still running in the blood of his fingers, his hands, all murder held back, and then on the trail came a presence, no longer the fear of death but concentration, murder between the two men came to rest, for murder was outside them now, same murder which had been beaming in to D.J. while he thinking of murdering his father, the two men turned to contemplate the beast. Which was there? There before! No. Nothing to be seen. All calm now, as if they walking into the flat ass calm of a flat still sea, stepping in deeper on every step, their bodies in different states of immersion every breath, the late sun throwing out orange-lavender, and lead of color near to immersions now infusions of purple in deep of the wood, and each step took them into different domain, for D.J.'s nose was like a king surveying the principalities of the realm, bleed you not, Sigismunde, calm to calm they stepped on in along the trail, each step a rock God laid on water, hot horseshit Hercules, and hum the smells in that wood, Prince of Pals, they took one step through a kingdom of pines, mad genius pine trees, prescribing their aromatic antiseptic prescription for all things, incense saying come to me I am all, I am siren of the North, nerve of the Arctic Circle with affiliates down to the Equator, I'm a brain, man, pine needles my calling card.

Next step, in they're plunged into some rot, some stump of dwarf birch, bark rubbed ass of raw by tail of bear or moose of caribou antlers eight years ago! like that! and dying over the years, cause a ring of bark had been cut and the skin of such dying tree go to rot beneath the trunk, fell down. Into the open mouth of that remaining stump came the years of snow, sun, little jewels of bird shit, cries of sap from the long dying roots, the monomaniacal electric yodeling of insects, and wood rotting into rotting wood, into gestures of wood, into powder and punk all wet and stinking with fracture between earth and sky, yeah, D.J. could smell the break, gangrene in the wood, electric rot cleaner than meat and sick shit smell and red-hot blood of your flesh in putrefaction, but a confirmed wood gangrene nonetheless, Burbank, a chaos of odor on the banks of the wound, nothing smells worse than half-life, life which has no life but don't know it—thank you, Mr. Philosopher, just show me the hemorrhoids of the academy, and on that rock! . . . Next step was into a pool of odor which came from the sweets of the earth, sweet earth smell speaking of endless noncontemplative powers, beds of rest, burgeonings, spring of life, a nectar for the man's muscles on the odor of that breath, yeah, D.J. was breathing his last, he was in the vale of breath, every small smell counted, it was the most fucking delicious moment of his life up to that point, for there are those who know and those who do not know when a very bad grizz is near to you (a final division of humanity) and D.J. knew, and D.J. was in love with himself because he did not wish to scream or plead, he just wished to encounter Mr. D., big-ass grizz, and the next step put his nose into an aisle of forest scents, herbs offering each their high priest of here, here is the secret lore and the cold fires of the temple, and leaf mold, wet molderings, some kind of forest goodbye weeded in from the messages of the wind, sending back to the peasant, back to the farm, then moss, new greenings, the odor of forest beginnings like baby ass powder and tiny flowers, the tenderness of the tip where life began, and some sweet wine of old funk in the moss as well, some odor of dwarf's armpits wiped with velvet, thank you, milady.

That was when the griz came.

Around a turn in the trail, by the side of a ledge, he'd been waiting, listening to the tick snap and twig crack of their boots, and he came at them from thirty yards away with the roar of nothing D.J. ever heard, like a foghorn fire siren about to burst, cause some congested hell in a whirlwind has come thundering with rocks down a hill out of its foghorn throat and D.J. heard the crazy wild ass moan of every animal they'd gunned down and the tear and blast of all flesh from all fat exploded knockout Magnums, what a cry came out of that shit ass beast, and frozen like prisoners in the searchlight, hypnotized half up to sky, and the air shivered as if a .105 howitzer just gone off, the grizzer came at them on the heuuuuuu of the cry, two red coal little eyes of fire, wall of fur coming fast as a locomotive barreling on that trail, and D.J. in some sweet cool of rest below all panic and paralysis dropped to one knee, threw up Remington, had a sail of light at the top of his head of far-gone tree and sky, and pulled off the trigger to smash a shot into that wall of fur, almost leisurely, like shotputting a rock into a barrel, his eye not even to the scope, you could not miss if your arm had the strength to get the gun up. And Rusty fired from behind and that animal didn't stop, it kept coming on down like a twelve-foot surf of comber bamming right for your head, and D.J.'s heart and his soul sweet angel bird went up the elevator of his body and all balls but flew out before he slammed bolt and fired again at grizzer not ten yards away flame of the muzzle meeting flame from grizzer's red flame ass red mouth, grizzer kerwhonked half in air from the blast, took leap, hop, howl, one mad bound off trail, leaving a wake of hot caves, gamy earth, fur went by so near, yeah, one flash of blood on his honey hide, and then he went booming down the mean crazy slope of the ledge, twisting D.J.'s neck, so fast was the move. Then grizzer was gone.

Well, now they had a pretty, didn't they? How sweet seemed Big Luke's precaution stay in open with the bear. Now they had to climb down that fucking ledge and somewhere down, down there in all that thicket and brush and owl shit slunk and precipitous slope was Mr. D., the Red Ball Express, half-dead or not nearly dead at all, awful bad. They are doing their best not to chatter, cackle, or carry on like birdwomen now. "Never heard of a grizzer charging like that," said Rusty's voice, weak as piss over pebbles.

"They gone ape shit just as Big Luke say." Hoarse adolescent big phlegm voice.

"Yeah." Humps.

"Yeah." Humps. Echo in the silences.

"I wish I had my Ruger right now," said Rusty, big-ass State Trooper style. "A rifle's too slow for tight-ass quarters."

"Was you going to bring it?"

"I almost took it up from Ding Bat today."

The Ruger 44 Magnum is Rusty's twelve-inch barrel pistol, detachable stock, comes highly recommended for bear in the brush. "That fucking Luke," says Rusty, "sticking us around the chimney—who's to know we'd end up here?"

They are waiting for the other to be first to say, "Let us go back to camp and come out tomorrow with the Ruger and the mob." But they can't, and the moment they are silent, echo of the event opens silence after silence—they are close to puking they are so scared. D.J. feels shit yellow between his toes, his bowels slosh internal bilge, every bit of hard shit in him has broken down to squirts like spit and dishwater rumblings. A pall is on the woods. He can smell nothing but randy ammonia in his armpits. Yeah. And like lightning which cut across the sleeper's bed so close that sleeper was turned and flung to the floor, so the memory of Mr. D. (D for Death) Grizzer's mad-ball charge is like a stroke across the strings of nerve in his life — say, it will come back and back again.

Yeah, recollected in memory, it comes back to D.J. eating in the Dallas ass manse, and he shivers — no man cell in him can now forget that if the center of things is insane, it is insane with force, heuuuuuu goes the bellow of the grizzer in the salt of his meat and sorrow. But bearable. Cause they went down for the grizzer after all — here is how — 58% of D.J. wanted nothing but to leave Mr. Wounded Grizzer and get the fuck out, in fact that 58% was pulling on his liver and gut. But D.J. is a head man. Which is not to say he gives head, but is ruled by his head. A creature of will. That will now says to sixteen-year-old flesh, "Go back without looking for this griz and Tex will ride your ass to shit."

That's it. D.J. face the anger of God before he look into the contempt and contumely of that State of Texas personified by Gottfried Tex Hyde Jr. Whooee.

"Well, dad, let's start down after the animal."

"Right, son," and Rusty smiles with lips like two wet soda crackers flapping at each other.

And the grizz is there. Forty shit-eating minutes later, their back wet, legs trembling like horse just run the mile and a quarter, their hands slippery with coward oil (clam juice and sweat, you bird watcher) faces scratched like two bitches been working them over with *long* nails, lad, rifle stocks scratched, their knees, thighs, ribs and butts a congregate of bruises (which congregate is the established plural for bruises, look it up, turd pedant) their lungs fired from fear, funk, exhaustion and the anticipation that each step could back them into a wound-ass grizzer, they worked their collective father and son ass down the steep slope below the edge, farting through catbrier brush, dwarf alder brush, blueberry cranberry brush, rocks, slick-ass rocks, sharp-ass rocks to cut their hands, ghost trees with roots half-exposed on the near precipices of the slope, trees taking on witches' arms for shapes, limbs beseeching the North — O, power above the Circle, incantations and greetings from this witches' tree.

Well, they went down one at a time following a trail of blood as thick and clean as Sherwin-Williams Red. D.J. would go first and Randy would cover him — combat men flushing out a sniper. Then Randy would make his trip and pass D.J., D.J. meanwhile scanning about him in a 360 degree circle which meant thirty feet of visibility here, one hundred there, and wonder. Cause the blood led down and down, as if Mr. D., his insides a rocket of exploded works, was plunging like a cannonball to the bottom of something, and yet. All grizzers crazy. What if Mr. D. went down and then circled up to take them from behind? So D.J. scanned three hundred and sixty degrees about, waited till Rusty beckoned from below and then started his scratch-ass descent on the trail of the griz, passing Rusty with the high hard sobs of lungs working too hard, and Rusty sobbing back. What a fucking dual coward-ass twin sweat and sob that was. Wham! That Texas will carries Texas cowards to places they never dreamed of being. Vava, va va voom!

After forty minutes they made rendezvous. The griz was lying in a beat-down circle of brush which he must have tromped out forty or fifty times while going through one of the bends of his wounds, and he had set down like a tabby cat on its stomach, forelegs tucked under him, peaceful, looking to be stuffed bear served on a red plate ten feet in diameter, for that blood beneath was monumental in its pool. They came on him from a hundred feet above, and Rusty was for pouring in some lead just to make shit-and-sure, but peace was coming off that bear—it was like the moment a gull sets on water—and so Rusty contented himself—being a camera-conscious flash-bulb poking American—to heist a little stone and bap that bear on the hide. Old Griz raised its head a little. Not dead yet. And its mouth looked to laugh as if between the mill-stones of two huge pains (or was it three huge gears from three huge wounds?) something very funny has occurred, as if he was saying, "You put your palm sweat on that stone, mother-fucker, and I'm taking your sweat with me."

Rusty raised his gun, but D.J. touched the rifle slightly with a little salute, and started walking down toward the bear.

"Come back," Rusty whispered, "you're out of your fucking head," for D.J. was holding his rifle in one hand swinging down around his thigh. "You cover me, daddy," said D.J. to avoid a fishwife family gone-for-gooney while that poor huge beast was going. D.J. just had to see him up close.

At twenty feet away, D.J.'s little cool began to evaporate. Yeah, that beast was huge and then huge again, and he was still alive—his eyes looked right at D.J.'s like wise old gorilla eyes, and then they turned gold brown and red like the sky seen through a ruby crystal ball, eyes were transparent, and D.J. looked in from his twenty feet away and took a step and took another step and another step and something in that grizzer's eyes locked into his, a message, fellow, an intelligence of something very fine and very far away, just about as intelligent and wicked and merry as any sharp light D.J. had ever seen in any Texan's eyes any time (or overseas around the world) those eyes were telling him something, singeing him, branding some part of D.J.'s future, and then the reflection of a shattering message from the shattered internal organs of that bear came twisting through his eyes in a gale of pain, and the head went up, and the bear now too weak to stand up, the jaws worked the pain.

Then the gale subsided. The peace came back to the eye, pain fading like the echo of the last good note, and that wild wicked little look of intelligence in the eye, saying something like, "Baby, you haven't begun," and when D.J. smiled, the eyes reacted, they shifted, they looked like they were about to slide off the last face of this presence, they looked to be drawing in the peace of the forest preserved for all animals as they die, the unspoken cool on tap in the veins of every tree, yes, griz was drawing in some music of the unheard burial march, and Rusty—wetting his pants, doubtless, from the excessive tension—chose that moment to shoot, and griz went up to death in one last paroxysm, legs thrashing, brain exploding from new galvanizings and overloadings of massive damage report, and one last final heuuuuuu, all forgiveness gone. And coughed blood out of his throat as he died.

D.J. didn't speak to Rusty on the way back. And when they hit camp at dark, Big Luke so relieved he couldn't even read various prescribed riot acts, they asked at last who had got the bear, and D.J., in the silence which followed, said, "Well, we both sent shots home, but I reckon Rusty got it," and Rusty didn't contradict him—one more long silence—and Rusty said, "Yeah, I guess it's mine, but one of its sweet legs belongs to D.J." Whew. Final end of love of one son for one father.

Next morning, crack ass of dawn, Rusty was overseeing the transfer of that dead and now dressed grizzer from his dried blood patch up the winch to the helicopter. And they figured the bear in his natural state had stood nine hundred pounds and more counting the claws.

Chap Ten

Listen, did you know, creep technician, about the superconductivity of metals at absolutely low temperatures? yeah, fab, you get down at three degrees or four degrees of absolute zero (and that's *the* zero, man—lower you cannot go) guess what—there is five metals, no more, which become super superconductors. Take a ring of Thallium, that soft shit, put it at 240° abs. for absolute, run a bar magnet through the middle of the ring, run it out again, and the current that's induced won't stop running around the ring for months. So employ your new knowledge, take a cunt, put her near Absolute Zero, work up a ring of troth (this is a wedding, you nut) composed of Old Thallium, Mother Mercury, Lemuel Lead, Timothy Tin, or Ike Indium, any one of those soft spooky witch metal elements will do, cool it till it's as cold as that beauteous cunt out near Absolute Zero, and then, man, hold your hairy jewels, cause a shock is coming up, why you just take and run and plunge your dick through the near absolute zero ring, zing into that gone ice snatch, whoo-ee! whoo-ee! pull it out before you rock stone ice pinnacle prick. You just set up a current, man, is going to keep that cunt in charge for months. Whoever said your gong was not a magnet? Oo la la, Françoise, your trou de merde is inoubliable for it is like the Camembert my mozzaire used to make when we were young, Boonkie.

Fuck this noise, why is D.J. hovering on the edge of a stall? Make your point! But D.J. is hung because the events now to be recounted in his private tape being made for the private ear of the Lord (such is the hypothesis now forging ahead) are hung up on a moment of the profoundest personal disclosure, in fact, dig, little punsters out in fun land, D.J. cannot go on because he has to talk about what Tex and him were presented with there all alone up above the Arctic Circle, and that's where the root of the hangnail grows, it all happens faster in the Arctic C, there's gathering of ionization on those polar caps, those auroral regions are electric, man, more ground charge than the rest of earth, cause the messages are coming in, the M.E.F. (Magnetic-Electro Fief—don't forget) is charging the joint by night, those ice ass pinnacles of the Brooks Range are vibrating to the modulations of the waves, a crystal oscillator is every mountain has got ice on its tip, and there's lots of mountains and lots of ice, pick up on this—the boys, you will remember, dear grassed-out auditor, have just finished cooking their breakfast, and aware of game all about them, half-clean themselves from the walk, half-fouled with the emanated nauseas of medium assholes and Rusty high-grade asshole, disillusioned with Big Luke's Cop Turd copping out on the big game hunter's code and oath, and just in a general state of mixed shit, for the walk up to here has done them only a minim of good. They have not cleaned the pipes, not yet. They are still full of toilet plunger holes seen in caribou, and shattered guts and strewn-out souls of slaughtered game meats all over the Alaska air and Tex feels like he's never going to hunt again which is not unhorrendous for him since he's natural hunter, but then with one lightning leap from the button on his genius belt to the base of his brainpan he gets the purification ceremony straight in his head, and announces to D.J. that they gonna wrap their weapons and lash them in a tree, and then they going to walk through the forest and up to the peak with their Randall bowies, and their binocs, and packs, but nothing to protect themselves with except the knife. They each know even as he says it that this is how you get the fear, shit, disgust and mixed shit tapeworm out of fucked-up guts and overcharged nerves. But D.J. is in a grab for your dick competition snit that he didn't think of this first, so says, "Let's leave the Randalls behind, too."

And Tex replies, "A man can't go without a knife."

"Do it or don't do it," says D.J., "but don't finger fuck yore ass."

Man, this is striptease shit. "Then we don't take our binocs," says Tex.

"Then don't take our packs."

No sleeping bags.

No food.

No compass.

Man, they got some of that mixed shit out of them already. About the time they cache all belongings, they own clean fear now, cause they going to live off the land. And they as light as if they lost gravity. D.J. could take a ten-foot spring. If it wasn't cold ass this morning, he'd be ready to go naked. Oh, that country looks big and mean up ahead.

But they got to take a backward step. Cause their ass is freezing half to death. You ever count on the weather in Brooks Range, kiss your own fever blister, mister (you know how you got it) that weather is like a bitch with hot and cold water running in her bush. Right now it's running icy shock cold. They push up not two hundred yards after we left them caching their gear, going through the boreal-montane, not two hundred yards through a forest getting skinny in its Arctic birch and alder, hardly a black spruce left, and squat, they at the edge, they at timberline again, and the ridge of the hill they been climbing is there, bare, twenty yards ahead of them, and they top that, and look down on a long valley, more forest, and then ahead to the beginning of a range of snow-topped mountains, bare-ass peaks, bare as the bald head of an egg, bare and white as the crest on a wave, and more mountains behind them, and more behind, like an arrow across the morning blue shooting for two hundred miles or more across mountains no man ever saw from the center, only from the air, and nothing but snow, even now in September nothing but snow, land as white as a desert and deserted, just peaks. And it rings back at them like a stone on a shield, no, better block that metaphor, drop it altogether, Lady Ethel, it rings back like a finger wet on the rim of the best piece of glass on Park Avenue, New York, yeah — D.J. ain't been East for nothing — those mountains are a receptacle, man, a parabolic reflector, an avatar, a bowl of resonance, listen to the boys totter just at the icy look of them, and they know they got to go back a little on their newfound principles, they got to take a bedroll and grub, their pup tent, the matches, a rope, shit, they can't go clean, they even take the binoculars, but mixed shit does not flow in again to the reservoir of their heart because celestial mechanics is built on equations and going with nothing into the forest is not necessarily more loaded with points of valor than going with rudimentary bag and forage yet without arms into mountain snow. September, and that land ahead is white as a sheet! So they still clean, and lost thirty minutes pulling down lashed gear from the tree and lashing it up again to keep grizzer from cleaning them out before they return, but now they really off, they up over the ridge, down into the forest draw, and climb up again, and one hour and twenty minutes later they are on the edge of the snow, that same snow which looked to be near as an arrow shot away. But now the sun is out, and it is hot, man, up to 65° and more which is hot in that snow and the dazzle is like sunlight on the water.

"That dazzle," said D.J., pushing into the sluggish kind of mealy new wet powder, not fluff, not sludge, just a bit of going heavy, three inches deep here, no more, here at the beginning of a snowfield, one thousand miles wide (or near to that) and two hundred miles north across the mountains onto tundra again, "that dazzle," said D.J., "is like sunlight on water."

"Shit," said Tex.

"Yeah, man, it's like the dazzle on the water outside of Herod's court in Caesarea, ever hear of that?"

"Shee-it," said Tex.

"Well, you ain't no I.Q. competitor."

"Fuck, I ain't. I compete you in anything."

"Never mess with me, ignoramus."

"Why," said Tex, "tell me about Herod and his fuck hole in Caesarea. When you done I'm gone to do a Caesarea up your ass."

"You ain't seen the day you was strong enough to unzip it out of your pants around me, pussy kisser."

"Pick the dingleberries out of your teeth. Who was Herod?"

"Herod was a royal goat fucker, you cocksucker."

"I," said Tex, "never sucked a cock in my life, but I'm going to make you the first. I'm going to suck your cock and bite it off and send the bloody abomination to your momma."

"Oh, man, you'd be a cha-cha faggot if you wasn't so ugly."

Hey, hey, is this the way they really talk? And at sixteen and seventeen. Well, yes, they is geniuses, D.J. been telling you. And all that pederastic palaver? Hell, yes. They is crazy about each other. They even prong each other's girls when they can, but fear not, gentle auditor, they is men, real Texas men, they don't ding ding ring a ling on no queer street with each other, shit, no, they just talk to each other that way to express Texas tenderness than which there is nothing more tender than a flattened pan-fried breaded paper-thin hard-ass Texas steak. And don't forget those French fries and the dead fly in the red crud rim of the bottle ketchup, not to mention the citric acid in the salad dressing—we ain't got those gut bucket skillet flat Texas ass stomachs for nothing. Listen, fellow Americans, and D.J. here to tell you, don't get upset by the boys' last dialogue, they so full of love and adventure and in such a haste to get all the mixed glut and sludge out of their systems that they're heating up all the foul talk to get rid of it in a hurry to enjoy good air and nature, cause don't forget they up in God's attic, that country way upstairs, Brooks Range here, to say not too far from Mount Michelson, that's a mount, and so fret not those of ye who live for the quiet of Sunday on our quiet streets, those boys would not talk that way to your daughter or your sister, no, sir, they would just ruminate privately a little, and do their best to fuck her.

Yeah, and now they don't talk for half an hour, and just walk along climbing in the barest parts of the snow which is three inches and two and not too bad, but for the drifts where it is foot and more, and then Tex, all quiet and cool, puts a light grip of a hand on D.J., and whispers, "Shut up, now, there's a wolf on the ridge."

And that wolf is a sight. He's a white wolf and he weigh in at one hundred and plus and plus, just a long big high beast of a white police dog the size of a Dalmatian and more. And that wolf is doing nothing, he's just running along the ridge, and taking a bound now and then and his big white fur goes up in the air and separates just as lithe and quick ass from the snow. There's times you can see nothing more than a mouth, nose and eyes, black outline black as paint, two ovals, two green-gold eyes, black stub of a nose, air so clear you can see the shine in the cavity of the black nostrils, and then the mouth, black outline, red gums, red as cut-open flesh, and white teeth, fangs. They suddenly aware they got no gun, and this wolf not much beyond one hundred yards away on the ridge is alert to something, could it be them? and they raise hackles and try to hold them down, cause those hackles are transmitting waves, and oh, shit, that wolf just turned, he's putting his radar on their waves, whoo, he's zero on them, can't see, but can sense, he takes one step their direction like feeling the pulsing up of the field — what they giving off, murder or a meal? He can't determine, so here comes another step. Animal murder is near. Everything is all silent suddenly. Nature is just as timid shit as a slum street — the boys did not know before how silent silence could be, thought it was silent in the snow, but there had been sparrows, yeah, scutterings of squirrels, yeah, white snow mice, sounds all over, now none. Each of those boys rings up the voltage in their resolve, like let that fuck wolf try to come to them, and they will give him a time, they thinking of how to kick his nuts in, choke his throat, dig into his eyes to his brain (that is if he is biting one and other does the rescue) man, they're fired, and that electric fire goes off them. Two waves of murder, human and animal, meet across the snow in a charge as fantastic and beautiful as Alexander Nevsky, thank you very much, and wolf stops dead, knocked on his psychic ass, what a pity psychic struggle cut no ice with silver iodide or movies be cheaper to make: that wolf slides off them and goes ambling down the ridge, no longer leaping and swinging at how loose, hippy-dippy, juggler balls and ass he is, no, the wolf he older, he been put down, that's no good for any presumptive continuer of his own species.

But the D.J. wave and the Tex Hyde wave which Lupo II decided to slide away from has gone wave zinging into the air where Mr. Lobster with wings, Thing with a claw, E Pluribus, old man Eagle fuck, yeah old man Eagle comes a zooming down out of the air in plummet, gray feather mass, white neck, black head, black claws, black as teakwood, man, whoo-ee, what a drop, the boys they practically clapping, he comes from five hundred feet right down like Magnum Lightning Zero down to the back of Lupo II who turns just in time, opens those teeth, wheels, stands on hind feet, swings two forelegs, left right, cuff, cuff, and M Lightning Zero, our eagle, hereafter MLZ, thank you, splats into a flat out, wings out, hovers, like an *eagle*, man, wings arched and fluttering just a tickle to stay in place above the wolf, he just gliding in the air one spot, his claws like lightning, zap! zap! — they miss each other, wolf and eagle, but that opening of the wings to brake out from the plummet when Lupo II took his wheel, turn, and fight, oh man, it was a shock to the heart, cause death stood out in those wings, if you'd been a bug in the shadow of those wings you'da called out, "Bury me clean, Armageddon is here." And D.J. thinks just once of his dad, and eagle story he told him and knows MLZero is going for the eyes, and wolf he's just going for the meal, and in comes MLZ and L II stands him off, miss and miss, and again they try, wolf giving a sobbing scream like, "I'm going to kill you, mother-fucker." And old Magnum LZ he got a screech like a den of hooknosed women when one of their pocketbooks is missing, so it's sob and scream, and attack and parry, come in on a shot, brake, claw air, veer off, do a spin back, and Mr. Wolf like a boxer picking off horseflies in the air, cuff, cuff, coot, coot, suddenly it's bullshit and bullshit, cause they each missing the other, old eagle he staying just out of range, Magnum Z. Lightning that's all the fuck he is, Tuckerman, and finally they done, and M.Z. Lightning humps his wings and heads on down the air carrying on like a crow, and L II nominating himself as winner, sets on his hind end and lets up a call which starts low, calls in all the beasty guts for miles around, tells them of the taste of fresh game, goes up higher than a coloratura into ascents of panic and power and warning and a call to the mountain ring and then tries to hit High E above High C for nothing, to show he's a virtuoso, and fails to make it, good for him, and slides all down into bronchitis again and the smell of his own shit ass wolf hide in a hole in hibernation not so far away. And the boys understood every sound of it. And if Tex had had a gun, he would have imitated every sound of it. But they don't have a gun and once again they feel just as clean and on-edge and perfect as would you, sedentary send-in-terror auditor of this trip, when you, sir, are about to insert the best piece of cock you ever mustered up into a cunt which is all fuck for you, and your nose is ozone you so clean and perfect, well, they feeling like that every instant now, whoo-ee! whoo-ee; they can hardly hold it in, cause this mother nature is as big and dangerous and mysterious as a beautiful castrating cunt when she's on the edge between murder and love, forgive the lecture, Pericles, but the smell is everywhere, the boys are moving on smell, snow smell, better believe it, good here, not so good there — move along, this is sweet, hold up, rotten shit around the bend, some clutch of mice, no more, but their scampering set up the wrong scratchy little tickler cymbal along the snow fluff and make some smell go wrong somewhere else, something like that. Man, it's terrifying to be free of mixed shit. And they got the unfucked heaven of seeing twelve Dall ram on an outcropping of snow two miles away across two ridges, and those Dall ram solemn head and light foot make their way down a slope, heading into valleys for winter and for feed, it's a procession, and through the binocs they are so white and their horns, oh, man, the underside is yellow golden rosy color that gives D.J. twiddles in the gut (twiddles being of course nothing but mother-of-pearl butterflies in cameo, Sir Lancelot) and the sun is on that snow and space! man. You could be Cleopatra on a barge and twenty galley slaves, and the sun on the water is a feather in your nose. Olé, olé.

Then they hear the helicopter. Man conceived of fucking in order to get fucked. There is no doubt of that. So, off they plunge, trying always to keep a ridge between them and the copter, and looking for streams so they leave no track, and already they've left a track. Well, for the next two hours right into two in the afternoon, it's no action, just pain, they going in deeper into Brooks Range and Cop Turd buzzing about, looking here, looking there, but never too far away. And then around two P.M. he departs, figuring, they hope, that Cop Turd finally decided the hints of trail they left might be animal. No, that ain't it, Cop Turd must have set down long enough to examine their steps—hell, CT is out of gas, Al Bell with his Bell 47J is out of gas. That all—he'll be back.

Then they discover a valley. It's for the boys, better believe it. A bowl below snow level, maybe two miles by one mile, meadows and wood, tundra and rock, and clearings and shapings, could be the Colorado Rockies it's so sweet right in the middle of the beginning of all that snow and wilderness, tucked between ridges of snow, and so the boys work a trail in a false direction into a creek, back up on their steps a mile (you try walking backward a mile) and slip into the forested bowl leaving behind the fields of snowfields and see for a last sight one pale pink fox go springing through the snow to pin a field mouse in snow and Arctic grass, flip, flop, oops and out, nub, nudge, you're dead mouse and a little echo out in the air, one small sorrow. And then some squirrels dart from the wood, run out by the fox, coax him to chase, and go back up a stand of black spruce at the edge of the bowl, black spruce again after the boys thought the biome was dead and finished. And a wing of sparrows go rip-titting and coo-cawing after Fox cause he can't catch Squirrel, and Fox he humps and scratches and whines and cries, he cries, dig, cause Squirrel won't come down to get killed. Maybe he's thinking of the children at home on a starve.

Man, our two little hunt boys, Killer I and Killer II, are excruciated. They near to being sick from the sweet they want to laugh so hard at Mr. Egomaniac Fox—come on down, Squirrel, be a good fellow. Yeah, they feel so good they stop for an inst, head to head, toe to toe, and mill it up, each taking ten good lumps to the gut.

"Hurt?" screams Tex.

"No, sir."

"Why not?"

"Cause I'm a Royal Commando, sir." And they cackle. But the moment they stop (1) the King of Mountain Peak M.E.F. shit,

(2) Mr. Awe and (3) Mr. Dread — that troika — that Cannibal Emperor of Nature's Psyche (this is D.J. being pontiferous, for we are contemplating emotion recollected in tranquillity back at the Dallas ass manse, RTPY — Remembrance Things Past, Yeah, you remember?) yeah the CE of NP, Cannibal Emperor for sure, Mr. Sender, who sends out that Awe and Dread is up on their back clawing away like a cat because they *alone*, man, you dig? why, they just dug, they all *alone*, it's a fright wig, man, that *Upper* silence alone is enough to bugger you, whoo-ee, all the twiddles have turned to plummets and they don't even know from what, and then know, it's their laughing up in the silence. They turning everything on in the wrong way, and they ready to retreat. And mixed shit is ready to drop in again on the lip of their liver.

But that meadow is beautiful. Arctic flowers, more white mountain aven with yellow centers, and the tundra gone to red and yellow and berries, dwarf huckleberries, cranberries, which they eating to calm Mr. A and Mr. D and the Cannibal, Mr. Sender, and the tart comes up out of the berry, one fine vein of sugar drawn from sour ice. And earth, taste of sunlight the sentimental might declare, but the troika is on them again, Cannibal Emperor to the fore, whoa whoa what I dread, they can but hardly breathe, and D.J. first to dig into the dimensions of the message which is simple, yes, direct — bear is nearby. That is it — a bear is near. And Tex don't argue — all in a funk without a gun, they pick a tree, they up it fifteen feet, high as they can go, they wait there on the edge of the meadow, the minutes go by. And then they remember they have left the packs behind and down they go all shaking, up the tree they work again, getting the packs up, and before they once more in the upper whippy weak crack snap branches of the black spruce like pegs, not much better to sit on, well, lo, behold, bear, there bear, out at other edge of the meadow and he don't see them, no, nor smell upwind from them, they ready to swear they smell him.

Now, bit by bit, they cool, get back cock. Because they safe, yeah, man, safe unless the branch break, and Mr. Bear he's all right, because their mind-ass transmitter after Awe-Dread Bombardment from Mr. Sender is chucked down to relaxed little beeps (the boys is quietened now from being up in the Brooks Range all alone — you in need of a great cool-out — you try it) and because the boys are relaxed, half in soft fear, half sweet fatigue — ain't slept, remember? they just now look, and what do you think Grizzer is doing?

Well, he after a meal, man, and he like every fat ass in the world: when he eating, you could ring a fire siren under his nuts and he never miss a beat in the gourmandize, he's humping up on all the berries—they ain't been too many this season, remember?—and so he grab with a paw and hooks in about two hundred buffalo berries at a pop, and swallows, and lets blue juice and red juice run out of the sides of his black wet leather mouth, and then raises one paw in the air and wipes said mouth on his shoulder as if he imitating a weight lifter sniffing his own armpits, then griz burps, yeah, old bear burps and spits out the next mouth of berries, and then he sighs (and they chilling him with their pistol eyes, so young and up tight with trying not to breathe they could be airline hostesses serving Frank Sinatra African rock-tail frozen ass lobster) yeah, and fighting silently over who holds the binocs, and daring each other to climb down the tree and watch from the ground, and then each of them being not up to the dare, and not certain—does private honor of Texas good heart and clean shit require they touch boot leather to ground?—but while they debating in the lowest whisper ever heard, "You go," no "Fuck, you go," it gets too fascinating and they just watch some more, because Old Bear has the burps, and now he out in the tundra with his dark mahogany hide digging up sod and scrubbing at roots, and he works at that like a gardener, digging in one of his big mitts, bigger in plan than a volume of *Encyclopaedia Britannica*, Dallas edition (which is bigger than the standard edition, natch) he's all claws in the sod and turf of poor old skinny misery tundra, he like a rake, yeah, he just cuts out pieces of turf and turns them over. The underneath is tundra root of all variety, thick as nerves and shoots, thick as lamp wire, thick as your finger, and Grizzer just eats away at this mat looking just like a roast beef hash, crust, black and almost charred, digging into the mat of the earth and contemplating what the dirt and the nerve roots and the accumulated experience of the various bugborers and slugs have to say. And in the middle of this, sitting sad and munching slow after slowly uprooting, expunging, and devouring five square yards of peat with many a heavy sigh and one or two fine from the heart burps, Griz suddenly decides his ass is on an itch and he looks to scratch it, and flings away his mat, and works his butt on the tundra, scraping and scratching and rolling on his back, and thumping and bumping his ass, and then he gets up like a fat woman and walks off in a grump to the other end of the meadow and sidles to a young tree and takes a bite out of the bark on the trunk about seven feet up, just rising on his hind legs sort of lazy and taking a deep easy bite, mean and pleasurable, like a businessman copping a goose on a bare-ass nightclub waitress, yum! and then he turn around, old Griz, and shove his insatiable ass against the bark of the tree, and he rub and he slide and he shimmy like you rubbing a Turkish towel up the crack of your own sweet potato, and then he grunt and lie down and go to sleep right there.

And the boys wait, ten minute, twenty minute, the squirrels flitting, mice heads popping in the tundra, sparrow settling on the back of Grizzer, indeed! and a hint of the wind spring up in the afternoon and see a white hare, hop, hump, hop, he gone, looking like white Benny bump tail on a caribou, and a marmot in a burrow, and a weasel so Tex would swear, D.J. do not see it. Then they decide to go down and keep working downwind from sleeping Grizzer, but griz starts to stir. And over the ridge which they can just see through the binocs, up in snow country again out of the bowl, is a sight they hear first and cannot believe cause a hundred or more, maybe many more, caribou are passing on the ridge and that convention of antlers looks just so fine and unbelievable as a forest on a march. And while the boys watch they hip into a little aggregate of fact which is those antlers (known in plural as a calliope of antlers) are a-zigging and a-jogging and a-twigging because there are lines of dance shaping and reshaping around three or four caribou gentlemen known as Bull Fuck 1, Bull Fuck 2, etc., each of them with cows and kids, but there's a vigorish in the air, a rumble to be heard among these beasts, they stepping and hopping like rutting season is near, and two of them BF 1 and BF 3 stop for a second in the brisk September afternoon air and hunker down their hind legs, and then give each other a clout with their antlers like football linemen making contact, slap, snap, sharp and fast, then they break off like they've had a taste of goodies to come but must go back to march route, and all this, especially the clear crack of antler clatter, sharp as shoulder guards hitting each other in loud clear hill ringing echo has done one bit of work, Grizzer he's up, he shakes, he wheels in a circle once, twice, then he off like a bull locomotive driving up to the ridge, and busts up and out of the bowl and makes a mad-ass charge at the procession of caribou, and they who have been traveling in the deep of their noncarnivorous communion to new forage, new land, new love, and winter quarters, are off now on a tear, as are the boys, now down from the tree and scrambling up the ridge to have a look at the sight of hundreds plus of beast all running silently through the snow and Grizzer after them cutting through the middle of that calliope of antlers scattering like fish, then regrouping out and around Mr. Bear and taking off and they all getting away, of course, of course, except for one calf who stumble in fright and griz right down on young beast and with one paw at the neck and the other on the flank, goes in with mouth open to rip her belly and get the living blood and taste of live entrail, whatever that may be, whatever taste to have fat-ass Grizzer so avid ass for it, and when calf breaks loose half for an instant, pain springing it near to free, why, Grizzer flips her down again and having had his taste of her live, kills her now by slamming his teeth through the big muscles of her back right through to the spine and vertebrae which he crunches in two closing his big mouth and she breaks like a stick of wood and is there lifeless and her death goes out over the ridge and slips into the bowl and the afternoon takes a turn and is different having just passed through one of those unseen locks of the day, everything is altered, not saying how.

And Grizzer he eats awhile, and paws at flesh, he feeling fat and sort of food disgusted, and then works a little half-ass at covering the carcass over, but he's not heart in it, and after a while just contents himself by taking a piss at the head, and a big bear drop of baubles at the tail, Griz like a baron hasn't learned to read or write but sure knows sealing wax, let me put my humper monicker mooney on this. And goes off, Griz #2 about as different from Griz #1 with the big eye dying that D.J. would kiss LBJ on the petoons just to have a rifle to take down Griz 2 and see how he look when he die, similar or very different as if the center of all significant knowledge right there.

The bear is gone, and they down from the tree and exploring the bowl, but modestly, stepping in the big cool, feeling clean but weak, and too sweet, sweet as caribou. Instinct take them up the bowl and onto snow ridge and there is a caribou, mother of the dead calf, and she hardly look up when she see them, she just stand with her head down and her nose on the flesh of her dead, pushing off the snow and bits of dirt Griz 2 left, and her hooves in passing and by accident go through the bear bauble old Baron Bear has left and kicks her into a fright as if hate was suddenly stinging her feet, and she circles about in a dance, but never takes her nose off as if she is going to smell on through to the secret of flesh, as if something in the odor of her young dead was there in the scent of the conception not ten months ago when some bull stud caribou in moonlight or sun illumined the other end of the flesh somewhere between timber slide and lightning there on the snow, some mystery then recovered now, and woe by that mother caribou nuzzled in sorrow from her nose while the sky above blue as a colorless sea went on and sun burned on her, flies came, last of the flies traveling over the snow and now running a shuttle from Baron Bear's pile of bauble to the nappy spotty hide of caribou mother, she twitching and jumping from the sure spite of the sting but not relinquishing her nose and the dying odor of her yearling calf and D.J.'s head full spun with that for new percipience, since could it be odor died last of all when one was dead? and took a separate route, and where could that lead his mind, for the secret of D.J.'s genius is that he pure American entrepreneur, and so his mind will always follow a lead. Never been a businessman yet wasn't laughed at in the beginning, you bet. And here was the lead about the death of odor but then, just then, a flight of cranes went over, one hundred, two hundred, so now there were hundreds and hundreds, yes, men, they could no longer count numbers flying overhead in formations of V and diamond and echelon and hovering on course, two hundred like one, and birds wrapped up in the mission to go south carrying some part of the sky in their thousand wings as if the very beginning of autumn, seed of the fall, for North America below in all the weeks to come was in the high cawing and wing beat clear up to the fanning and vibrating of reeds some high long-gone sound such as summer coming to the very end.

That was all they saw that day. They traveled over ridges, slid down new snow on slopes and went in further. A still was on them. The cranes had emptied the pocket of this territory and they moved on seeing not a tree nor an animal nor a sight but for the glaciers ahead and the loud crack of their boom in the late afternoon, and the ridgelines, the ridgelines now beginning to dance in the late afternoon with transparencies behind turns of transparency and sunlight rising up straight from the snow in lines of razzle reflection, their eyes gritted, and afternoon chill was still good on them yes, and yes, for the colors began to go from snow gold and yellow to rose and blue, coral in the folds of the ridges when the sun still hit, coral bright as the underside of the horn of the Dall ram and there were two, a couple, high again on the farthest ridge, first animal they'd seen in hours and then they saw one more. It was after they put up a tent. They came to one more bowl with a few trees, a hint of bare ground, and a crazy salty pond, mud and salt at its edges but very sure of itself in the snow hills like all that Northern land so ready to declare it has a purpose when none to be seen, and they put up a lean-to in grove of black spruce, last black spruce this side of the Pole, D.J. ready to swear, and lit a fire and cooked grub, roast beef hash, yeah, beans, bread, coffee, chocolate bar, so tired they jawed the food like cattle plodding, and lay down side by side drawing heat from the fire up the blankets into their legs, boots tied to a stay overhead, heat of the fire putting iron back into their body like the iron and fire of faith for those black spruce twigs and short branches and rotten punk for start (which punk D.J. had not forgot was from the lore of his father of whom he could not yet think) fuel for the fire out of the soil of this land up on the top, cold bare electric land of North, magnetic-electro fief of the dream, and D.J. full of iron and fire and faith was nonetheless afraid of sleep, afraid of wolves, full of beauty, afraid of sleep, full of beauty, yeah, he unashamed, for across the fire and to their side the sun was setting to the west of the pond as they looked north, setting late in the evening in remembering echo of the endless summer evening in these woods in June when darkness never came for the light never left, but it was going now, September light not fading, no, ebbing, it went in steps and starts, like going down a stair from the light to the dark, sun golden red in its purple and purple red in the black of the trees, the water was dark green and gold, a sigh came out of the night as it came on, and D.J. could have wept for a secret was near, some mystery in the secret of things—why does the odor die last and by another route?—and he knew then the meaning of trees and forest all in dominion to one another and messages across the continent on the wave of their branches up to the sorrow of the North, the great sorrow up here brought by leaves and wind some speechless electric gathering of woe, no peace in the North, not on the top of the rim, and as the dark came down, a bull moose, that King Moose with antlers near to eight feet wide across all glory of spades and points, last moose of the North, came with his dewlap and his knobby knees and dumb red little eyes across the snow to lick at salt on the other side of the pond, and sunlight in the blood of its drying caught him, lit him, left him gilded red on one side as he chomped at mud and salt, clodding and wads dumping from his mouth to plop back in water, like a camel foraging in a trough, deep in content, the full new moon now up before the sun was final and down silvering the other side of this King Moose up to the moon silhouettes of platinum on his antlers and hide. And the water was black, and moose dug from it and ate, and ate some more until the sun was gone and only the moon for light and fire of the boys and he looked up and studied the fire some several hundred of feet away and gave a deep caw pulling in by some resonance of this grunt a herd of memories of animals at work and on the march and something gruff in the sharp wounded heart of things bleeding somewhere in the night, a sound somewhere in that voice in the North which spoke beneath all else to Ranald Jethroe Jellicoe Jethroe and his friend Gottfried (Son of Gutsy) "Texas" Hyde. They were alone like that with the moose still staring at them. And then the moose turned and crossed the bowl the other way and plodded through the moonlight along the ridges of snow, moonlight in his antlers, gloom on his steps. And the boys slept.

THE ARMIES
OF THE NIGHT

New American Library published The Armies of the Night,
History as a Novel, The Novel as History *in 1968, after it first
appeared in the March* Harper's *and the April* Commentary *of
that year. A Signet paperback edition of the book is now
available. A narrative, nonfiction account of his participation in
the 1967 march on the Pentagon, the book marked the turn of a
tide of popular criticism in Mailer's favor. He was awarded both
a National Book Award and a Pulitzer Prize for it, and even* Time
*magazine, whose most recent vilification served as a frontispiece
to the narrative, joined in the chorus of critical praise. His device
of projecting himself as a third person whose actions and
thoughts could be analyzed from the vantage point of narrative
distance evidently was a key discovery for Mailer, since he was to
use it in his next two books. The present excerpt consists of the
remarkably closely knit first six chapters of the book, plus a single
chapter from a later section which glosses the earlier material.*

Part I: Thursday Evening

CHAPTER 1: PEN PALS

From the outset, let us bring you news of your protagonist. The following is from *Time* magazine, October 27, 1967.

A Shaky Start

Washington's scruffy Ambassador Theater, normally a pad for psychedelic frolics, was the scene of an unscheduled scatological solo last week in support of the peace demonstrations. Its antistar was author Norman Mailer, who proved even less prepared to explain Why Are We in Vietnam? than his current novel bearing that title.

Slurping liquor from a coffee mug, Mailer faced an audience of 600, most of them students, who had kicked in $1,900 for a bail fund against Saturday's capers. "I don't want to grandstand unduly," he said, grandly but barely standing.

It was one of his few coherent sentences. Mumbling and spewing obscenities as he staggered about the stage — which he had commandeered by threatening to beat up the previous M.C. — Mailer described in detail his search for a usable privy on the premises. Excretion, in fact, was his preoccupation of the night. "I'm here because I'm like LBJ," was one of Mailer's milder observations. "He's as full of crap as I am." When hecklers mustered the temerity to shout "Publicity hound!" at him, Mailer managed to pronounce flawlessly his all-purpose noun, verb and expletive: "**** you."

Dwight Macdonald, the bearded literary critic, was aghast at the barroom bathos, but failed to argue Mailer off the platform. Macdonald eventually squeezed in the valorous observation that Ho Chi Minh was really no better than Dean Rusk. After more obscenities, Mailer introduced Poet Robert Lowell, who got annoyed at requests to speak louder, "I'll bellow, but it won't do any good," he said, and proceeded to read from *Lord Weary's Castle*.

By the time the action shifted to the Pentagon, Mailer was perky enough to get himself arrested by two Marshals. "I transgressed a police line," he explained with some pride on the way to the lockup, where the toilet facilities are scarce indeed and the coffee mugs low-octane.

Now we may leave *Time* in order to find out what happened.

CHAPTER 2: IN THE DEN

On a day somewhat early in September, the year of the first March on the Pentagon, 1967, the phone rang one morning and Norman Mailer, operating on his own principle of war games and random play, picked it up. That was not characteristic of Mailer. Like most people whose nerves are sufficiently sensitive to keep them well-covered with flesh, he detested the telephone. Taken in excess, it drove some psychic equivalent of static into the privacies of the brain; so he kept himself amply defended. He had an answer service, a secretary, and occasional members of his family to pick up the receiver for him — he discouraged his own participation on the phone — sometimes he would not even speak to old friends. Touched by faint intimations of remorse, he would call them back later. He had the idea — it was undeniably oversimple — that if you spent too much time on the phone in the evening, you destroyed some kind of creativity for the dawn. (It was taken for granted that nothing respectable would come out of the day if the morning began on the phone, and indeed for periods when he was writing he looked on transactions via telephone as Arabs look upon pig.)

Still, Mailer had a complex mind of sorts. Like a later generation which was to burn holes in their brain on Speed, he had given his own head the texture of a fine Swiss cheese. Years ago he had made all sorts of erosions in his intellectual firmament by consuming modestly promiscuous amounts of whiskey, marijuana, seconal, and benzedrine. It had given him the illusion he was a genius, as indeed an entire generation of children would so come to see themselves a decade later out on celestial journeys of LSD.

Now, however, that he had again an actively working brain only partially hampered by old bouts of drugs (which revealed their ravages in occasional gaps like the absolutely necessary word for an occasion failing utterly to arrive on time, or a critical crossroad of memory being forever obliterated so that for the safety of his life he could not remember whether some old beloved had helped him or betrayed him on a specific occasion—no small hole *that*, for a novelist!) yes, Mailer was bitter about drugs. If he still took a toke of marijuana from time to time for Auld Lang Syne, or in recognition of the probability that good sex had to be awfully good before it was better than on pot, yes, still!—Mailer was not in approval of any drug, he was virtually conservative about it, having demanded of his eighteen-year-old daughter, a Freshman now at Barnard, that she not take marijuana, and never LSD, until she had completed her education, a mean promise to extract in these apocalyptic times.

Such were the sort of contradictions one could discover. As a corollary of his detestation of the telephone was his necessity to pick it up once in a while. Mailer had the most developed sense of image; if not, he would have been a figure of deficiency, for people had been regarding him by his public image since he was twenty-five years old. He had in fact learned to live in the sarcophagus of his image—at night, in his sleep, he might dart out, and paint improvements on the sarcophagus. During the day, while he was helpless, newspapermen and other assorted bravos of the media and the literary world would carve ugly pictures on the living tomb of his legend. Of necessity, part of Mailer's remaining funds of sensitivity went right into the war of supporting his image and working for it. Sometimes he thought his relation to this image was not unlike some poor fellow who strains his very testicles to bring in emoluments for his wife yet is never favored with carnal knowledge of her. In any event, Mailer worked for the image, and therefore he detested the portrait of himself which would be promulgated if no one could *ever* reach him. So, on impulse, thereby sharpening his instinct as a gambler, he took spot plunges: once in a while he would pick up his own phone.

On this morning in September, 1967, he lost his bet.

No, let us leave it to history whether he lost his bet or eventually won it. But for our record, it had best be stated that his immediate reaction was one of woe—he did not wish to speak to the man on the other end. That man was an author named Mitchell Goodman. Mitch Goodman, as everyone called him, was a worthy fellow, and

Mailer had only good things to say of him, indeed Mailer had even given a blurb to Goodman's war novel, a brooding poetic work about World War II which had taken something like eight years to write and had been a book deserving of a blurb. (Although Mailer, with Swiss cheese for memory, could not at the instant recollect the title.) That was not necessarily here nor there. The reason Mailer did not wish to speak to Goodman was that he knew that (1) Goodman had a better character than he did and (2) was going to ask something which would not be easy to refuse but would be expensive to perform. Besides, Goodman was the sort of clear conscience which insists upon being solemn, as if the powers of the universe, concerned that worldly balance not disappear altogether, had decided that if men of good conscience were cheerful, all men might like to grow into good conscience and then the ball game would most certainly be over.

In fact Mailer had known Goodman for twenty years. They had been, if he recollected properly, almost in the same year at Harvard (Mailer was Harvard '43 — his 25th Reunion was coming up), they were both from Brooklyn, both married young. They had met in Paris in 1947, Goodman then a tall powerful handsome dark-haired young man with a profound air of defeated gloom. (He looked the way J. D. Salinger would have looked if J. D. Salinger had been tall enough and beefed-up enough to play football, and had fumbled *Catcher in the Rye*.) He was married to a charming and most attractive dark-haired English girl with a characteristic space between her two front teeth. Everyone called her Dinny. Everyone in Paris liked her. She was pure as a bird, delicate yet firm in conscience. Since one did not see them again for years except at parties now and then, it took years to realize that the Denise Levertov of whom everyone spoke as an exceptional and splendid poet was the same Dinny. Bless her, she was still cheerful. Bless Mitch — he was still gloomy. They had been married for twenty years. Of how many could that be said? Not of Mr. Mailer.

In fact, the last time Mailer had heard of Mitch Goodman was when the latter had led a small group of protesters out of the large hotel banquet hall where Hubert Humphrey was about to address the assorted literati and book reviewers of the American writing world at the National Book Award festivities in March, 1967. Mailer had not attended. He had been boycotting the affair for several years — not that it mattered to anyone, but Mailer thought it was the least he could do, since none of his books had ever been considered for an award, let alone given one. But he remembered being glad he had not attended, for if he had, would he have been ready to walk out with Mitch Goodman or not? The war in Viet-

602   *The Long Patrol*

nam was probably to be protested on every occasion, and any attempt to twist Hubert Humphrey's nose was, in all favorable winds, a venture to applaud, but the exodus from the National Book Award's assembly, as one might have predicted, was small, pilgrim small, by reports not unfarcical: Jules Feiffer walked out with the demonstrators, then sneaked back to go to a party for Humphrey. Feiffer's comet had not been in ascendance since.

If one was going to take part in a literary demonstration, it had better work, since novelists like movie stars like to keep their politics in their pocket rather than wear them as ashes on the brow; if it is hard for people in the literary world to applaud any act braver or more self-sacrificing than their own, it is impossible for them to forgive any gallant move which is by consensus unsuccessful. The measure of the failure on this occasion had been that Bernard Malamud, who won the 1966 award in fiction for his novel *The Fixer*, did not boycott the Vice-President, but on the contrary had given his prepared speech in its proper place. Since Malamud was also opposed to the war in Vietnam, Goodman's action presumably had failed to light an outstanding fire in the sympathizers.

Here, therefore, was Mailer now on the phone with an old friend and lugubrious conscience whose instinct for the winning move was not—on the face—spectacular. Mailer hated to put in time with losers. Like many another man of varied affairs considered worthy by some, worthless by others, there had been all too many years when he had the reputation of being a loser; it had cost him much. While he could hardly, at this stage of his career, look back on a succession of well-timed and generally established triumphs, his consolation in those hours when he was most uncharitable to himself is that taken at his very worst he was at least still worthy of being a character in a novel by Balzac, win one day, lose the next, and do it with boom! and baroque in the style. If he had lost many painful engagements, he had also won a few, and the damnable habit of consorting with losers was that they passed their subtle problems on.

Quickly, the conversation, therefore, took a harsh turn. Before it had been going two minutes, Mailer was scolding Goodman; that was predictable enough, given the request. Goodman had just finished telling Mailer that there was going to be a March on Washington in about a month, and Mailer had hardly finished saying he doubted if he would attend since he had no desire to stand in a large meadow and listen to other men make speeches (still furious was Mailer at SANE for an occasion two years ago when they had wanted $50 in contribution from him for a protest in Washington, but did not think enough—or were too dismayed—of the text of a speech he had given in Berkeley about the war in Vietnam to invite him to speak) so, no he did not think he would go to Washington, when Goodman interrupted by saying, "This is going to be different, Norman. Did you read the circular from the Mobilization Committee?"

"I get many circulars, and they're all badly written," Mailer said in a cranky voice.

"Well, this one is a departure," said Mitch Goodman. "Some of us are going to try to invade the corridors of the Pentagon during office hours and close down some of their operation."

Mailer received such news with no particular pleasure. It sounded vaguely and uneasily like a free-for-all with students, state troopers, and Hell's Angels flying in and out of the reports — exactly the sort of operation they seemed to have every other weekend out on the Coast. He felt one little bubble of fear tilt somewhere about the solar plexus.

"Yes, this sounds more interesting," he growled.

"Well, I think it will be," said Goodman. "Anyway, Norman, what I'm calling you about is something else: our group called Resist. On Friday, the day before the Pentagon, we're going to have a demonstration at the Department of Justice to honor students who are turning in their draft cards."

This is about where Mailer began to scold Goodman. He went on for a breath or two on the redundancy of these projects. When was everyone going to cut out the nonsense and get to work, do their own real work? One's own literary work was the only answer to the war in Vietnam. As he was talking, Mailer began to realize that he had not done any real writing in months — he had been making movies — but then it didn't matter, he had done as much in the way of protest about this war as anyone, his speech at Berkeley in 1965 had attacked Johnson at a time when lots of the mob now so much against the war were still singing "Hello, Lyndon." Mailer, filled with such righteous recollections, was therefore scolding Goodman at near to full pedal, when the organ came to a sudden stop. The thought that he was beginning to sound like a righteous old toot came just as suddenly into his head. Mailer had never had a particular age — he carried different ages within him like different models of his experience: parts of him were eighty-one years old, fifty-seven, forty-eight, thirty-six, nineteen, et cetera, et cetera — he now went back abruptly from fifty-seven to thirty-six. "All right, Mitch," he said, "I don't know what I'm arguing for, I'm sure you'll need all your strength to melt some of the real hard heads."

Mitch Goodman chuckled at the other end. It was the first hint between them of memories of somewhat more idealistic days in Paris.

"Mitch, I'll be there," said Mailer, "but I can't pretend I'm happy about it."

A week later some girl called to ask if he would write a form letter to go out under his signature supporting these students. Mailer answered in effect that he was hanging in on this affair by his fingernails and would not try to break them by sending a letter.

A week after that another girl called to ask if he would speak on Thursday night in Washington at a theater with Robert Lowell and Dwight Macdonald and Paul Goodman, not Mitch Goodman this time, *Paul* Goodman. Mailer asked who might be running the meeting. Ed de Grazia was doing that — Mailer knew the name — the thought of seeing de Grazia offered a small but definite pleasure. Warily, he accepted. There would now be three days out of his week, Thursday to speak, Friday at the Department of Justice, and Saturday — it came upon him that something actually was going to be attempted at the Pentagon, and he — if he knew himself — would end up, no matter how, part of such a party. It was going to prove a wasteful weekend he decided with some gloom — he could have spent it more profitably cutting his new movie. He had made a film about cops and crooks (actually about detectives and suspects) which came to more than six possible hours of film and would have to be cut down to three hours or two and a half. Some of the rushes were surprising in their promise; he looked forward to cutting the film; he had directed it and acted in it. In fact he had played a chief of detectives, Lieutenant Francis Xavier Pope, and had been not unbelievable in places. Well, farewell to Francis X. Pope, cheers to you, dear Pentagon: Mailer wished as the Washington weekend approached that the Washington weekend were done.

CHAPTER 3: TERMINALS

Thursday afternoon, Dwight Macdonald was on the same plane from New York to Washington, but Mailer and he did not see each other. This could, of course, be made symbolic of the happenings which were to follow at the Ambassador by night, but the probability is that an airplane, serving as some sort of dentist's chair without a drill, does not encourage one's powers of recognition. (In any case they were to meet later at a party, Macdonald, Robert Lowell, Paul Goodman and Mailer.) Ed de Grazia, who was to be M.C. at the Ambassador until dispossessed, was kind enough to meet the novelist at the airport and take him to the Hay-Adams. (People, of course, had been willing to put the guest up. Washingtonians with a spare bedroom and loyal to the cause were not nonexistent after all, but a man who has six children of his own does not necessarily wish to spend his idle moments talking to another man's children on the weekend.) En route, de Grazia explained a little of the temper in the town. It was not in focus, he murmured.

De Grazia was a slim elegant Sicilian with a subtle diffidence in his manner, terribly hesitant, almost a stammer, but he was a Sicilian and somehow inspired the confidence that he knew where the next bit of information might reside. Besides, he bore a pleasant resemblance to the way Frank Sinatra looked ten years ago.

Leading lawyer for the Mobilization's Legal Defense Committee, and an old friend from times so recent as the trial in Boston of *Naked Lunch*, where Mailer and he had met, de Grazia as counsel for the book, Allen Ginsberg and Mailer as witnesses to its literary merits, de Grazia expected to be busy on Saturday. No one had any idea of how many arrests would be made, nor of how much violence there would be, neither on the side of the police, nor the demonstrators.

It was a bright late afternoon in Washington, much like a day of Indian summer in September on Cape Cod, the air was good; after New York, surprisingly good. But the car was a convertible, the top was down, and in the shade of taller buildings, waiting for a light, an October cold was in the breeze. Bright and sunny and a hint of cold to bring a whiff of the sinister from the wind. So came idle thoughts: how incredible if in two days one was going to be dead!

The difficulty, de Grazia was explaining, was that there was no center to the March. Unlike the move on Washington in 1963 for civil rights, there was now no central supervisory or coordinating committee to which all organizations would defer, or with whom they would even promise to maintain communication. Something like fifty thousand people were going to arrive and nearly all of them would be unaffiliated or disaffiliated. Nor was the government revealing quite what they were going to do. At the thought of their august power, a vacuum was certainly present in the center of Mailer and de Grazia's mood. Listening to de Grazia talk of the negotiations about the route of march from the Lincoln Memorial to the Pentagon, Mailer learned that first there would be a meeting at Lincoln Memorial similar to the assembly in 1963 when Martin Luther King had said, "I have a dream," and many had whispered that someday he would be President.

Now, for this morning meeting four years later at Lincoln Memorial no one anticipated too much trouble, but afterward tens of thousands of virtually leaderless people were going to walk over Memorial Bridge to Virginia and from there advance to the Pentagon over a road which had still not been selected, no agreement on the route of march having yet been negotiated between the government and the war protesters. There were three roads, de Grazia explained, and the government wished the marchers to use the narrowest of the three. That was one source of trouble. Another—he hesitated. Was what? Well, in discussing police arrangements, which is to say, dispositions of city police, U.S. Marshals, and National Guard, the government representative had indicated there would be other units as well. When queried, the official had given one of those delicate technological replies: he was, he said, not volunteering to indicate what the specific unit might be. "That sounds like paratroopers," said de Grazia. As it turned out, he was right. "Hey, hey," said Mailer, "aren't they just a little bit worried." But *they* were not alone. The sound of paratroopers still had its magic ring. "I want to go out to see it on Saturday," said de Grazia, "but I guess I'll have to stay at the Defense Center." "Oh, that's where you belong," said the Participant, "somebody's got to be there to get us out."

It was now after six, after the rush hour, but in Washington it still seemed like late afternoon and endlessly peaceful. As the afternoon goes on, Washington seems more and more a tender Southern city. The light psychic rust of its iron will, the sense of suffocation (conceivably one chokes to death in Washington more slowly than anywhere else—for some, it takes thirty years) the faded scent of its inhibition, its severity and its concealed corruption (like entering a drawing room plumped with rich middle-aged ladies) all this seemed absent in the golden hovering of such leisurely twilight. Mailer sighed; like most New Yorkers, he usually felt small in Washington. The capital invariably seemed able to take the measure of men like him.

But as Mailer had come to recognize over the years, the modest everyday fellow of his daily round was servant to a wild man in himself: the gent did not appear so very often, sometimes so rarely as once a month, sometimes not even twice a year, and he sometimes came when Mailer was frightened and furious at the fear, sometimes he came just to get a breath of air. He was indispensable, however, and Mailer was even fond of him for the wild man was witty in his own wild way and absolutely fearless—once at the edge of paralysis he had been ready to engage Sonny Liston. He would have been admirable, except that he was an absolute egomaniac, a Beast—no recognition existed of the existence of anything beyond the range of his reach. And when he appeared, it was often with a great speed; he gave little warning. Certainly he gave no warning as the Historian checked in at the Hay-Adams, changed his clothes and prepared to give a few thoughtful remarks a little later that night at the Ambassador Theater on the essential insanity of our venture in Vietnam, such remarks designed presumably to encourage happy participation for Saturday's move to invest the Pentagon.

CHAPTER 4: THE LIBERAL PARTY

There was a party first, however, given by an attractive liberal couple. Mailer's heart, never buoyant at best, and in fact once with justice called "sodden" by a critic, now collected into a leaden little ball and sank, not to his feet but his stomach. He was aware for the first time this day of a healthy desire to have a drink for the party gave every promise of being dreadful. Mailer was a snob of the worst sort. New York had not spoiled him, because it had not chosen to, but New York had certainly wrecked his tolerance for any party but a very good one. Like most snobs he professed to believe in the aristocracy of achieved quality — "Just give me a hovel with a few young artists, bright-eyed and bold" — in fact, a party lacked flavor for him unless someone very rich or social was present. An evening without a wicked lady in the room was like an opera company without a large voice. Of course there were no wicked ladies when he entered this room. Some reasonably attractive wives to be certain, and a couple of young girls, too young for him, they were still in the late stages of some sort of extraordinary progressive school, and were innocent, decent-spirited, merry, red-cheeked, idealistic, and utterly lobotomized away from the sense of sin. Mailer would not have known what to do with such young ladies — he had spent the first forty-four years of his life in an intimate dialogue, a veritable dialectic with the swoops, spooks, starts, the masks and snarls, the calm lucid abilities of sin, sin was his favorite fellow, his tonic, his jailer, his horse, his sword, say he was not inclined to flirt for an hour with one bright seventeen-year-old or another when they conceived of lust as no more than the gymnasium of love. Mailer had a diatribe against LSD, hippies, and the generation of love, but he was keeping it to himself. (The young girls, incidentally, had been brought by de Grazia. Not for nothing did de Grazia bear a resemblance to Sinatra.)

But we are back with the wives, and the room has not yet been described. It was the sort of room one can see at many a faculty party in places like Berkeley, the University of Chicago, Columbia—the ground of common being is that the faculty man is a liberal. Conservative professors tend to have a private income, so their homes show the flowering of their taste, the articulation of their hobbies, collections adhere to their cabinets and odd statements of whim stand up in the nooks; but liberal instructors, liberal assistant professors, and liberal associate professors are usually poor and programmatic, so secretly they despise the arts of home adornment. Their houses look one like the other, for the wives gave up herculean careers as doctors, analysts, sociologists, anthropologists, labor relations experts—great servants of the Social Program were lost when the women got married and relinquished all for hubber and kids. So the furnishings are functional, the prevailing hues of wall and carpet and cloth are institutional brown and library gray, the paintings and sculpture are stylized abstract, hopeless imitation I. Rice Pereira, Leonard Baskin, Ben Shahn, but bet your twenty-five dollars to win an assured ten dollars that the artist on the wall is a friend of the host, has the right political ideas, and will talk about literature so well, you might think you were being addressed by Maxim Gorky.

Such were the sour and near to unprintable views of the semidistinguished and semi-notorious author as he entered the room. His deepest detestation was often reserved for the nicest of liberal academics, as if their lives were his own life but a step escaped. Like the scent of the void which comes off the pages of a Xerox copy, so was he always depressed in such homes by their hint of oversecurity. If the republic was now managing to convert the citizenry to a plastic mass, ready to be attached to any manipulative gung ho, the author was ready to cast much of the blame for such success into the undernourished lap, the overpsychologized loins, of the liberal academic intelligentsia. They were of course politically opposed to the present programs and movements of the republic in Asian foreign policy, but this political difference seemed no more than a quarrel among engineers. Liberal academics had no root of a real war with technology land itself, no, in all likelihood, they were the natural managers of that future air-conditioned vault where the last of human life would still exist. Their only quarrel with the Great Society was that they thought it temporarily deranged, since the Great Society seemed to be serving as instrument to the Goldwater wing of the Republican party, a course of action so very irrational to these liberal technologues that they were faced with bitter necessity to desert all their hard-earned positions of leverage on real power in the Democratic party, a considerable loss to suffer merely because of an irrational development in the design of the

Great Society's supermachine. Well, the liberal technologues were not without character or principle. If their living rooms had little to keep them apart from the look of waiting rooms of doctors with a modern practice, it was exactly because the private loves of the ideologues were attached to no gold standard of the psyche. Those true powers of interior decoration — greed, guilt, compassion and trust — were hardly the cornerstones of their family furnishings. No, just as money was a concept, no more, to the liberal academic, and needed no ballast of gold to be considered real, for nothing is more real to the intellectual than a concept! so position or power in society was, to the liberal technologue, also a concept, desirable, but always to be relinquished for a better concept. They were servants of that social machine of the future in which all irrational human conflict would be resolved, all conflict of interest negotiated, and nature's resonance condensed into frequencies which could comfortably phase nature in or out as you please. So they were servants of the moon. Their living rooms looked like offices precisely because they were ready to move to the moon and build Utope cities there — Utope being, one may well suppose, the only appropriate name for pilot models of Utopia in Non-Terrestrial Ecologically Sub-Dependent Non-Charged Staging Areas, that's to say dead planets where the food must be flown in, but the chances for good civil rights and all-out social engineering are one hundred percent zap!

As is invariably the case with sociological ruminations the individual guests at this party disproved the general thesis, at least in part. The hostess was small, for example, almost tiny, but vivid, bright-eyed, suggestive of a fiery temper and a childlike glee. It was to pain Mailer later to refuse her cooking (she had prepared a buffet to be eaten before the move to the theater) but he was drinking with some devotion by then, and mixing seemed fair neither to the food nor the bourbon. It was of course directly unfair to the hostess: Mailer priding himself on his good manners precisely because the legend of his bad manners was so prevalent, hated to cause pain to a hostess, but he had learned from years of speaking in public that an entertainer's first duty was to deliver himself to the stage with the maximum of energy, high focus, and wit — a good heavy dinner on half a pint of bourbon was likely to produce torpor, undue search for the functional phrase, and dry-mouthed maunderings after a little spit. So he apologized to the lady, dared the look of rejection in her eye which was almost balanced on a tear — she was indeed surprisingly adorable and childlike to be found in such a liberal academic coven — and tried to cover the general sense of loss by marshaling what he assumed his most radiant look, next assuring her that he would take a rain check on the meal.

"Promise?"

"Next time I'm in Washington," he lied like a psychopath. The arbiter of nicety in him has observed with horror over many a similar occasion that he was absolutely without character for any social situation in which a pause could become the mood's abyss, and so he always filled the moment with the most extravagant amalgams of possibility. Particularly he did this at the home of liberal academics. They were brusque to the world of manners, they had built their hope of heaven on the binary system and the computer, 1 and 0, Yes and No—they had little to do therefore with the spectrum of grace in acceptance and refusal; if you did not do what they wished, you had simply denied them. Now Mailer was often brusque himself, famous for that, but the architecture of his personality bore resemblance to some provincial cathedral which warring orders of the church might have designed separately over several centuries, the particular cathedral falling into the hands of one architect, then his enemy. (Mailer had not been married four times for nothing.) If he was on many an occasion brusque, he was also to himself at least so supersensitive to nuances of manner he sometimes suspected when in no modest mood that Proust had lost a cell mate the day they were born in different bags. (Bag is of course used here to specify milieu and not the exceptional character of the mothers, Mme. Proust and Mrs. I. B. Mailer.) At any rate, boldness, attacks of shyness, rude assertion, and circumlocutions tortured as arthritic fingers working at lace, all took their turn with him, and these shuttlings of mood became most pronounced in their resemblance to the banging and shunting of freight cars when he was with liberal academics. Since he—you are in on the secret—disapproved of them far more than he could afford to reveal (their enmity could be venomous) he therefore exerted himself to push up a synthetic exaggerated sweetness of manner, and his conversations with liberal ideologues on the consequence consisted almost entirely of overcorrections of the previous error.

"I know a friend of yours," says the ideologue. A nervous voice from the novelist for answer. "Yes? Who?" Now the name is given: it is X.

Mailer: I don't know X.

The ideologue proceeds to specify a conversation which M held with X. M recollects. "Oh, yes!" he says; "of course! X!" Burbles of conversation about the merits of X, and his great ebullience. Actually X is close to flat seltzer.

There had been just this sort of dialogue with a stranger at the beginning of the party. So Mailer gave up quickly any thought of circulation. Rather, he huddled first with Dwight Macdonald, but Macdonald was the operative definition of the gregarious and could talk with equal facility and equal lack of personal observation to an Eskimo, a collector from the New York Department of Sanitation, or a UN diplomat—therefore was chatting happily with the world fifteen minutes after his entrance. Hence Mailer and Robert Lowell got into what was by all appearances a deep conversation at the dinner table sometime before food was laid out, Mailer thus doubly wounding the hostess with his later refusal.

We find, therefore, Lowell and Mailer ostensibly locked in converse. In fact, out of the thousand separate enclaves of their very separate personalities, they sensed quickly that they now shared one enclave to the hilt: their secret detestation of liberal academic parties to accompany worthy causes. Yes, their snobbery was on this mountainous face close to identical—each had a delight in exactly the other kind of party, a posh evil social affair, they even supported a similar vein of vanity (Lowell with considerably more justice) that if they were doomed to be revolutionaries, rebels, dissenters, anarchists, protesters, and general champions of one Left cause or another, they were also, in private, *grands conservateurs*, and if the truth be told, poor damn émigré princes. They were willing if necessary (probably) to die for the cause—one could hope the cause might finally at the end have an unexpected hint of wit, a touch of the Lord's last grace—but wit or no, grace or grace failing, it was bitter rue to have to root up one's occupations of the day, the week, and the weekend and trot down to Washington for idiot mass manifestations which could only drench one in the most ineradicable kind of mucked-up publicity and have for compensation nothing at this party which might be representative of some of the Devil's better creations. So Robert Lowell and Norman Mailer feigned deep conversation. They turned their heads to one another at the empty table, ignoring the potentially acolytic drinkers at either elbow, they projected their elbows out in fact like flying buttresses or old Republicans, they exuded waves of Interruption Repellent from the posture of their backs, and concentrated on their conversation, for indeed they were the only two men of remotely similar status in the room. (Explanations about the position of Paul Goodman will follow later.)

Lowell, whose personal attractiveness was immense (since his features were at once virile and patrician and his characteristic manner turned up facets of the grim, the gallant, the tender and the solicitous as if he were the nicest Boston banker one had ever hoped to meet) was not concerned too much about the evening at the theater. "I'm just going to read some poems," he said. "I suppose you're going to speak, Norman."

"Well, I will."

"Yes, you're awfully good at that."

"Not really." Harumphs, modifications, protestations and denials of the virtue of the ability to speak.

"I'm no good at all at public speaking," said Lowell in the kindest voice. He had indisputably won the first round. Mailer the younger, presumptive, and self-elected prince was left to his great surprise—for he had been exercised this way many times before— with the unmistakable feeling that there was some faint strain of the second-rate in this ability to speak on your feet.

Then they moved on to talk of what concerned them more. It was the subject first introduced to Mailer by Mitch Goodman. Tomorrow, a group of draft resisters, led by William Sloane Coffin, Jr., Chaplain at Yale, were going to march from their meeting place at a church basement, to the Department of Justice, and there a considerable number of draft cards would be deposited in a bag by individual students representing themselves, or their groups at different colleges, at which point Coffin and a selected few would walk into the Department of Justice, turn the cards over to the Attorney General, and await his reply.

"I don't think there'll be much trouble at this, do you?" asked Lowell.

"No, I think it'll be dull, and there'll be a lot of speeches."

"Oh, no," said Lowell with genuine pain, "Coffin's not that kind of fool."

"It's hard to keep people from making speeches."

"Well, you know what they want us to do?" Lowell explained. He had been asked to accompany a draft resister up to the bag in which the draft cards were being dropped. "It seems," said Lowell, with a glint of the oldest Yankee light winging off like a mad laser from his eye, "that they want us to be *big buddy*."

It was agreed this was unsuitable. No, Lowell suggested, it would be better if they each just made a few remarks. "I mean," said Lowell, beginning to stammer a little, "we could just get up and say we respect their action and support it, just to establish, I suppose, that we're there and behind them and so forth."

Mailer nodded. He felt no ease for any of these suggestions. He did not even know if he truly supported the turning in of draft cards. It seemed to him at times that the students who disliked the war most should perhaps be the first to volunteer for the Army in order that their ideas have currency in the Army as well. Without them, the armed forces could more easily become Glamour State for the more mindless regions of the proletariat if indeed the proletariat was not halfway to Storm Troop Junction already. The military could make an elite corps best when the troops were homogenized. On the other hand, no soldier could go into combat with the secret idea that he would not fire a gun. If nothing else, it was unfair to friends in his outfit; besides it suggested the suicidal. No, the iron of the logic doubtless demanded that if you disapproved of the war too much to shoot Vietcong, then your draft card was for burning. But Mailer arrived at this conclusion somewhat used up as we have learned from the number of decisions he had to make at various moral crossroads en route and so felt no enthusiasm whatsoever for the preliminary demonstration at the Department of Justice tomorrow in which he would take part. To the contrary, he wondered if he would burn or surrender his own draft card if he were young enough to own one, and he did not really know the answer. How then could he advise others to take the action, or even associate his name? Still, he was going to be there.

He started to talk of these doubts with Lowell, but he could hear the sound of his own voice, and it offended him. It seemed weak, plaintive, as if his case were—no less incriminating word—phony, he did not quite know why. So he shut up.

A silence.

"You know, Norman," said Lowell in his fondest voice, "Elizabeth and I really think you're the finest journalist in America."

Mailer knew Lowell thought this—Lowell had even sent him a postcard once to state the enthusiasm. But the novelist had been shrewd enough to judge that Lowell sent many postcards to many people—it did not matter that Lowell was by overwhelming consensus judged to be the best, most talented, and most distinguished poet in America—it was still necessary to keep the defense lines in good working order. A good word on a card could keep many a dangerous recalcitrant in the ranks.

Therefore, this practice annoyed Mailer. The first card he'd ever received from Lowell was on a book of poems, *Deaths for the Ladies and other disasters* it has been called, and many people had thought the book a joke which whatever its endless demerits, it was not. Not to the novice poet at least. When Lowell had written that he liked the book, Mailer next waited for some word in print to canonize his thin tome; of course it never came. If Lowell were to begin to award living American poets in critical print, two hundred starving worthies could with fairness hold out their bowl before the escaped Novelist would deserve his turn. Still, Mailer was irked. He felt he had been part of a literary game. When the second card came a few years later telling him he was the best journalist in America, he did not answer. Elizabeth Hardwick, Lowell's wife, had just published a review of *An American Dream* in *Partisan Review* which had done its best to disembowel the novel. Lowell's card might have arrived with the best of motives, but its timing suggested to Mailer an exercise in neutralsmanship— neutralize the maximum of possible future risks. Mailer was not critically equipped for the task, but there was always the distant danger that some bright and not unauthoritative voice, irked at Lowell's enduring hegemony, might come along with a long lance and presume to tell America that posterity would judge Allen Ginsberg the greater poet.

This was all doubtless desperately unfair to Lowell who, on the basis of two kind cards, was now judged by Mailer to possess an undue unchristian talent for literary logrolling. But then Mailer was prickly. Let us hope it was not because he had been beaten a little too often by book reviewers, since the fruit of specific brutality is general suspicion.

Still Lowell now made the mistake of repeating his remark. "Yes, Norman, I really think you are the best journalist in America."

The pen may be mightier than the sword, yet at their best, each belong to extravagant men. "Well, Cal," said Mailer, using Lowell's nickname for the first time, "there are days when I think of myself as being the best writer in America."

The effect was equal to walloping a roundhouse right into the heart of an English boxer who has been hitherto right up on his toes. Consternation, not Britannia, now ruled the waves. Perhaps Lowell had a moment when he wondered who was guilty of declaring war on the minuet. "Oh, Norman, oh, certainly," he said, "I didn't mean to imply, heavens no, it's just I have such *respect* for good journalism."

"Well, I don't know that I do," said Mailer. "It's much harder to write"—the next said with great and false graciousness—"a good poem."

"Yes, of course."

Chuckles. Headmastersmanship.

Chuckles. Fellow headmastersmanship.

They were both now somewhat spoiled for each other. Mailer got up abruptly to get a drink. He was shrewd enough to know that Lowell, like many another aristocrat before him, respected abrupt departures. The pain of unexpected rejection is the last sweet vice left to an aristocrat (unless they should happen to be not aristocrats, but secret monarchs—then watch for your head!).

Next, Mailer ran into Paul Goodman at the bar—a short sentence which contains two errors and a misrepresentation. The assumption is that Goodman was drinking alcohol but he was not; by report, Goodman never took a drink. The bar, so-called, was a table with a white tablecloth, set up near the archway between the dining room where Lowell and Mailer had been talking and the living room where most of the party was being enacted—to the tune of ten couples perhaps—so the bar did not qualify as a bar, just a poor table with a cloth to support Mailer's irritated eye. Finally he did not run into Goodman. Goodman and Mailer had no particular love for one another—they tended to slide about each other at a party. In fact, they hardly knew each other.

Their lack of cordiality had begun on the occasion of a piece written by Goodman for *Dissent* which had discussed Washington in the early days of the Kennedy Administration. Goodman had found much to displease him then, and kept referring to the "wargasms" of this Kennedy Administration which wargasms he attached with no excessive intellectual jugglery to the existential and Reichian notions of the orgasm which Mailer had promulgated in his piece *The White Negro*. (Goodman was a sexologue—that is, an ideologue about sex—Mailer was then also a sexologue; no war so rich without quarter as the war between two sexologues.) Goodman, at any rate, had scored off Mailer almost at will, something to the general effect that the false prophet of the orgasm was naturally attached to the false hero of Washington who went in for wargasms. Writing for a scholarly Socialist quarterly like *Dissent*, it was hard to miss. The magnetic field of *Dissent*—hostile to Kennedy at the time—bent every wild shot to the target. So Mailer wrote a letter in reply. It was short, sought to be urbane, and was delivered exactly to the jugular, for it began by asserting that he could not judge the merits of Goodman's intellectual points since the other had made a cardinal point of emphasizing Mailer's own incapacity to reason and Goodman was doubtless correct, but Mailer did nonetheless feel competent to comment on the literary experience of encountering Goodman's style and that was not unrelated to the journeys one undertook in the company of a laundry bag . . . Great ferment in scholarly Socialist quarters! A small delegation of the Editors assured Mailer they would print his letter if he insisted, but the hope was that he would not. Mailer had always thought it senseless to undertake an attack unless you made certain it was printed, for otherwise you were left with a determined enemy who was an unmarked man, and therefore able to repay you at leisure and by the lift of an eyebrow. Mailer acceded however. He was fond of the Editors of *Dissent*, although his private mixture of Marxism, conservatism, nihilism, and large parts of existentialism could no longer produce any polemical gravies for the digestive apparatus of scholarly Socialist minds; nonetheless Mailer had never been asked to leave the Board, and would not have resigned on his own since that would have suggested a public attack on the ideas of people with whom he had no intellectual accord but of whom he was personally fond.

Nonetheless, from that day, Mailer and Goodman slid around one another at parties and waved languid hands in greeting. It was just as well. Each seemed to have the instinct a discussion would use up intellectual ordnance best reserved for articles. Besides, they had each doubtless read very little of the other.

Mailer, of course, was not without respect for Goodman. He thought Goodman had had an enormous influence in the colleges and much of it had been, from his own point of view, very much to the good. Paul Goodman had been the first to talk of the absurd and empty nature of work and education in America, and a generation of college students had formed around the core of his militancy. But, oh, the style! It set Mailer's teeth on edge to read it; he was inclined to think that the body of students who followed Goodman must have something de-animalized to put up with the style or at least such was Mailer's bigoted view. His fundamental animus to Goodman was still, unhappily, on sex. Goodman's ideas tended to declare in rough that heterosexuality, homosexuality, and onanism were equal valid forms of activity, best denuded of guilt. Mailer, with his neo-Victorianism, thought that if there was anything worse than homosexuality and masturbation, it was putting the two together. The super-hygiene of all this mental prophylaxis offended him profoundly. Super-hygiene impregnated the air with medicated Vaseline — there was nothing dirty in the damn stuff; and sex to Mailer's idea of it was better off dirty, damned, even slavish! than clean, and without guilt. For guilt was the existential edge of sex. Without guilt, sex was meaningless. One advanced into sex against one's sense of guilt, and each time guilt was successfully defied, one had learned a little more about the contractual relation of one's own existence to the unheard thunders of the deep — each time guilt herded one back with its authority, some primitive awe — hence some creative clue to the rages of the deep — was left to brood about. Onanism and homosexuality were not, to Mailer, light vices — to him it sometimes seemed that much of life and most of society were designed precisely to drive men deep into onanism and homosexuality; one defied such a fate by sweeping up the psychic profit which derived from the existential assertion of yourself — which was a way of saying that nobody was born a man; you earned manhood provided you were good enough, bold enough.

This most conservative and warlike credo could hardly have

meaning to a scientific humanist like Goodman for whom all obstacles to the good life derived precisely from guilt: guilt which was invariably so irrational—for it derived from the warped burden of the past. Goodman therefore said hello mildly to Mailer, who answered in as mild a voice, and that was all they had to say. Lowell, following, expressed his condolences to Goodman on the recent death of his son, and Mailer after depressing the hostess by his refusal to eat, went on to talk to Macdonald.

That was most brief. They were old friends, who had a somewhat comic relation, for Macdonald—at least as Mailer saw it—was forever disapproving of the younger author until the moment they came together at one or another party or meeting. Then Macdonald would discover he was glad to see Mailer. In fact, Macdonald could hardly help himself. Of all the younger American writers, Mailer was the one who had probably been influenced most by Macdonald, not so much from the contents of Macdonald's ideas which were always going in and out of phase with Mailer's, but rather by the style of Macdonald's attack. Macdonald was forever referring the act of writing to his sense of personal standards which demanded craft, care, devotion, lack of humbug, and simple *a fortiori* honesty of sentiment. All this was a little too simple for Mailer's temper. Nonetheless, Macdonald had given him an essential clue which was: look to the feel of the phenomenon. If it feels bad, it *is* bad. Mailer could have learned this as easily from Hemingway, as many another novelist had, but he had begun as a young ideologue—his mind had been militant with positions fixed in concrete, and Macdonald's method had worked like Zen for him—at the least it had helped to get his guns loose. Macdonald had given the hint that the clue to discovery was not in the substance of one's idea, but in what was learned from the style of one's attack. (Which was one reason Mailer's style changed for every project.) So, the younger author was unquenchably fond of Macdonald, and it showed. Not a minute would go by before he would be poking Macdonald's massive belly with a finger.

But for now, they were ill at ease. Macdonald was in the process of reviewing Mailer's new novel *Why Are We in Vietnam?* for *The New Yorker*, and there was an empty space in the presence of the mood. Mailer was certain Macdonald did not like the new novel, and was going to do a negative review. He had seemed professionally unfriendly these past few weeks. The Novelist would have liked to assure the Critic that the review could not possibly affect their good feeling for one another, but he did not dare, for such a remark would break a rule, since it would encourage Macdonald to talk about what was in his review, or at worst trick him into an unwilling but revealing reply. Besides, Mailer did not trust himself to speak calmly about the matter. Although Macdonald would not admit it, he was in secret carrying on a passionate love affair with *The New Yorker* — Disraeli on his knees before Victoria. But the Novelist did not share Macdonald's infatuation at all — *The New Yorker* had not printed a line in review of *The Presidential Papers, An American Dream,* or *Cannibals and Christians,* and *that,* Mailer had long ago decided, was an indication of some of the worst things to be said about the magazine. He had once had a correspondence with Lillian Ross who asked him why he did not do a piece for *The New Yorker.* "Because they would not let me use the word 'shit,' " he had written back. Miss Ross suggested that all liberty was his if only he understood where liberty resided. True liberty, Mailer had responded, consisted of his right to say shit in *The New Yorker.* So there was old rage behind the arms-length bantering about Dwight's review of Norman's book, and Mailer finally left the conversation. Macdonald was beginning to like him again, and that was dangerous. Macdonald was so full of the very beans of that old-time Wasp integrity, that he would certainly bend over much too far backward if for a moment while reviewing the book he might have the thought he was sufficiently fond of Norman to conceivably be giving him too-gentle treatment. "No," thought the Novelist, "let him keep thinking he disapproves of me until the review is written."

Among his acquaintances at the party, this now left de Grazia. As has been indicated, they were old friends of the most superficial sort, which is to say that they hardly knew each other, and yet always felt like old friends when they met. Perhaps it was no more than the ability of each man to inspire an odd sense of intimacy. At any rate they never wasted time in needless conversation, since they were each too clever about the other to be penned in position by an evasion.

"How would you like to be the first speaker of the evening?" de Grazia asked.

"There'll be nothing interesting to follow me."

De Grazia's eyes showed pleasure. "Then I thought of starting with Macdonald."

"Dwight is conceivably the world's worst speaker." It was true. Macdonald's authority left him at the entrance to the aura of the podium. In that light he gesticulated awkwardly, squinted at his text, laughed at his own jokes, looked like a giant stork, whinnied, shrilled, and was often inaudible. When he spoke extempore, he was sometimes better, often worse.

"Well," said de Grazia, "I can't start with Lowell."

"No, no, no, you must save him."

"That leaves Goodman."

They nodded wisely. "Yes, let's get rid of Goodman first," said Mailer. But then the thought of that captive audience tuned to their first awareness of the evening by the pious drone of Goodman's voice injured every showman's instinct for the opening. "Who is going to be M.C.?" Mailer asked.

"Unless you want to, I thought I might be."

"I've never been an M.C.," said Mailer, "but maybe I should be. I could warm the audience up before Goodman drops them." De Grazia looked uneasily at Mailer's bourbon. "For Christ's sakes, Ed," said Mailer.

"Well, all right," said de Grazia.

Mailer was already composing his introductory remarks, percolating along on thoughts of the subtle annoyance his role as Master of Ceremonies would cause the other speakers.

CHAPTER 5: TOWARD A THEATER OF IDEAS

The guests were beginning to leave the party for the Ambassador, which was two blocks away. Mailer did not know this yet, but the audience there had been waiting almost an hour. They were being entertained by an electronic folk rock guitar group, so presumably the young were more or less happy, and the middle-aged dim. Mailer was feeling the high sense of clarity which accompanies the light show of the aurora borealis when it is projected upon the inner universe of the chest, the lungs, and heart. He was happy. On leaving, he had appropriated a coffee mug and filled it with bourbon. The fresh air illumined the bourbon, gave it a cerebrative edge; words entered his brain with the agreeable authority of fresh minted coins. Like all good professionals, he was stimulated by the chance to try a new if related line of work. Just as professional football players love sex because it is so close to football, so he was fond of speaking in public because it was thus near to writing. An extravagant analogy? Consider that a good half of writing consists of being sufficiently sensitive to the moment to reach for the next promise which is usually hidden in some word or phrase just a shift to the side of one's conscious intent. (Consciousness, that blunt tool, bucks in the general direction of the truth; instinct plucks the feather. Cheers!) Where public speaking is an exercise from prepared texts to demonstrate how successfully a low order of consciousness can beat upon the back of a collective flesh, public speaking being, therefore, a sullen expression of human possibility metaphorically equal to a bugger on his victim, speaking-in-public (as Mailer liked to describe any speech which was more or less improvised, impromptu, or dangerously written) was an activity like writing; one had to trick or seize or submit to the grace of each moment, which, except for those unexpected and sometimes well-deserved moments when consciousness and grace came together (and one felt on the consequence, heroic) were usually occasions of some mystery. The pleasure of speaking in public was the sensitivity it offered: with every phrase one was better or worse, close or less close to the existential promise of truth, *it feels true*, which hovers on good occasions like a presence between speaker and audience. Sometimes one was better, and worse, at the same moment; so strategic choices on the continuation of the attack would soon have to be decided, a moment to know the blood of the gambler in oneself.

Intimations of this approaching experience, obviously one of Mailer's preferred pleasures in life, at least when he did it well, were now connected to the professional sense of intrigue at the new task: tonight he would be both speaker and master of ceremonies. The two would conflict, but interestingly. Already he was looking in his mind for kind even celebrative remarks about Paul Goodman which would not violate every reservation he had about Goodman's dank glory. But he had it. It would be possible with no violation of truth to begin by saying that the first speaker looked very much like Nelson Algren, because in fact the first speaker was Paul Goodman, and both Nelson Algren and Paul Goodman looked like old cons. Ladies and Gentlemen, without further ado let me introduce one of young America's favorite old cons, Paul Goodman! (It would not be necessary to add that where Nelson Algren looked like the sort of skinny old con who was in on every make in the joint, and would sign away Grandma's farm to stay in the game, Goodman looked like the sort of old con who had first gotten into trouble in the YMCA, and hadn't spoken to anyone since.)

All this while, Mailer had in clutch *Why Are We in Vietnam?* He had neglected to bring his own copy to Washington and so had borrowed the book from his hostess on the promise he would inscribe it. (Later he was actually to lose it — working apparently on the principle that if you cannot make a hostess happy, the next best charity is to be so evil that the hostess may dine out on tales of your misconduct.) But the copy of the book is now noted because Mailer, holding it in one hand and the mug of whisky in the other, was obliged to notice on entering the Ambassador Theater that he had an overwhelming urge to micturate. The impulse to pass urine, being for some reason more difficult to restrain when both hands are occupied, there was no thought in the Master of Ceremonies' mind about the alternatives — he would have to find The Room before he went on stage.

That was not so immediately simple as one would have thought. The twenty guests from the party, looking a fair piece subdued under the fluorescent lights, had therefore the not unhaggard look of people who have arrived an hour late at the theater. No matter that the theater was by every evidence sleazy (for neighborhood movie houses built on the dream of the owner that some day Garbo or Harlow or Lombard would give a look in, aged immediately they were not used for movies anymore) no matter, the guests had the uneasiness of very late arrivals. Apologetic, they were therefore in haste for the speakers to begin.

Mailer did not know this. He was off already in search of The Room, which, it developed was up on the balcony floor. Imbued with the importance of his first gig as Master of Ceremonies, he felt such incandescence of purpose that he could not quite conceive it necessary to notify de Grazia he would be gone for a minute. Incandescence is the *satori* of the Romantic spirit which spirit would insist — this is the essence of the Romantic — on accelerating time. The greater the power of any subjective state, the more total is a Romantic's assumption that everyone understands exactly what he is about to do, therefore waste not a moment by stopping to tell them.

Flush with his incandescence, happy in all the anticipations of liberty which this Götterdämmerung of a urination was soon to provide, Mailer did not know, but he had already and unwitting to himself metamorphosed into the Beast. Wait and see!

He was met on the stairs by a young man from *Time* magazine, a stringer presumably, for the young man lacked that I-am-damned look in the eye and rep tie of those whose work for *Time* has become a life addiction. The young man had a somewhat ill-dressed look, a map showed on his skin of an old adolescent acne, and he gave off the unhappy furtive presence of a fraternity member on probation for the wrong thing, some grievous mis-deposit of vomit, some hanky panky with frat-house tickets.

But the Beast was in a great good mood. He was soon to speak; that was food for all. So the Beast greeted the *Time* man with the geniality of a surrogate Hemingway unbending for the Luce-ites (Loo-sights was the pun) made some genial cryptic remark or two about finding Herr John, said cheerfully in answer to why he was in Washington that he had come to protest the war in Vietnam, and taking a sip of bourbon from the mug he kept to keep all fires idling right, stepped off into the darkness of the top balcony floor, went through a door into a pitch-black men's room, and was alone with his need. No chance to find the light switch for he had no matches, he did not smoke. It was therefore a matter of locating what's what with the probing of his toes. He found something finally which seemed appropriate, and pleased with the precision of these generally unused senses in his feet, took aim between them at a point twelve inches ahead, and heard in the darkness the sound of his water striking the floor. Some damn mistake had been made, an assault from the side doubtless instead of the front, the bowl was relocated now, and Master of Ceremonies breathed deep of the great reveries of this utterly non-Sisyphian release—at last!!—and thoroughly enjoyed the next forty-five seconds, being left on the aftermath not a note depressed by the condition of the premises. No, he was off on the Romantic's great military dream, which is: seize defeat, convert it to triumph. Of course, pissing on the floor was bad; very bad; the attendant would probably gossip to the police (if the *Time* man did not sniff it out first) and The Uniformed in turn would report it to The Press who were sure to write about the scandalous condition in which this meeting had left the toilets. And all of this contretemps merely because the management, bitter with their lost dream of Garbo and Harlow and Lombard, were now so pocked and stingy they doused the lights. (Out of such stuff is a novelist's brain.)

Well, he could convert this deficiency to an asset. From gap to gain is very American. He would confess straight out to all aloud that he was the one who wet the floor in the men's room, he alone! While the audience was recovering from the existential anxiety of encountering an orator who confessed to such a crime, he would be able—their attention now riveted—to bring them up to a contemplation of deeper problems, of, indeed, the deepest problems, the most chilling alternatives, and would from there seek to bring them back to a restorative view of man. Man might be a fool who peed in the wrong pot, man was also a scrupulous servant of the self-damaging admission; man was therefore a philosopher who possessed the magic stone; he could turn loss to philosophical gain, and so illumine the deeps, find the poles, and eventually learn to cultivate his most special fool's garden: *satori*, incandescence, and the hard gem-like flame of bourbon burning in the furnaces of metabolism.

Thus composed, illumined by these first stages of Emersonian transcendence, Mailer left the men's room, descended the stairs, entered the back of the orchestra, all opening remarks held close file in his mind like troops ranked in order before the parade, and then suddenly, most suddenly saw, with a cancerous swoop of albatross wings, that de Grazia was on the stage, was acting as M.C., was—no calling it back—launched into the conclusion of a gentle stammering stumbling—small orator, de Grazia!—introduction of Paul Goodman. All lost! The magnificent opening remarks about the forces gathered here to assemble on Saturday before the Pentagon, this historic occasion, let us hold it in our mind and focus on a puddle of passed water on the floor above and see if we assembled here can as leftists and proud dissenters contain within our minds the grandeur of the two—all lost!—no chance to do more than pick up later—later! after de Grazia and Goodman had finished dead-assing the crowd. Traitor de Grazia! Sicilian de Grazia!

As Mailer picked his way between people sitting on the stone floor (orchestra seats had been removed—the movie house was a dance hall now with a stage) he made a considerable stir in the orchestra. Mailer had been entering theaters for years, mounting stages—now that he had put on weight, it would probably have been fair to say that he came to the rostrum like a poor man's version of Orson Welles, some minor note of the same contemplative presence. A titter and rise of expectation followed him. He could not resist its appeal. As he passed de Grazia, he scowled, threw a look from Lower Shakespearia "Et tu Bruté," and proceeded to slap the back of his hand against de Grazia's solar plexus. It was not a heavy blow, but then de Grazia was not a heavy man; he wilted some hint of an inch. And the audience pinched off a howl, squeaked on their squeal. It was not certain to them what had taken place.

Picture the scene two minutes later from the orchestra floor. Paul Goodman, now up at the microphone with no podium or rostrum, is reading the following lines:

> . . . these days my contempt
> for the misrulers of my country
> is icy and my indignation raucous.

It is impossible to tell what he is reading. Off at the wing of the stage where the others are collected—stout Macdonald, noble Lowell, beleaguered de Grazia, and Mailer, Prince of Bourbon, the acoustics are atrocious. One cannot hear a word the speaker is saying. Nor are there enough seats. If de Grazia and Macdonald are sitting in folding chairs, Mailer is squatting on his haunches, or kneeling on one knee like a player about to go back into the ball game. Lowell has the expression on his face of a dues payer who is just about keeping up with the interest on some enormous debt. As he sits on the floor with his long arms clasped mournfully about his long Yankee legs, "I am here," says his expression, "but I do not have to pretend I like what I see." The hollows in his cheeks give a hint of the hanging judge. Lowell is of a good weight, not too heavy, not too light, but the hollows speak of the great Puritan gloom in which the country was founded—man was simply not good enough for God.

At this moment, it is hard not to agree with Lowell. The cavern of the theater seems to resonate behind the glare of the footlights, but this is no resonance of a fine bass voice—it is rather electronics on the march. The public address system hisses, then rings in a random chorus of electronic music, sounds of cerebral mastication from some horror machine of Outer Space (where all that electricity doubtless comes from, child!) then a hum like the squeak in the hinges of the gates of Hell—we are in the penumbra of psychedelic netherworlds, ghost-odysseys from the dead brain cells of adolescent trysts with LSD, some ultrapurple spotlight from the balcony (not ultraviolet—ultrapurple, deepest purple one could conceive) there out in the dark like some neon eye of the night, the media is the message, and the message is purple, speaks of the monarchies of Heaven, madnesses of God, and clamvaults of people on a stone floor. Mailer's senses are now tuned to absolute pitch or sheer error—he marks a ballot for absolute pitch—he is certain there is a profound pall in the audience. Yes, they sit there, stricken, inert, in terror of what Saturday will bring, and so are unable to rise to a word the speaker is offering them. It will take dynamite to bring life. The shroud of burned-out psychedelic dreams is in this audience, Cancer Gulch with open maw—and Mailer thinks of the vigor and the light (from marijauna?) in the eyes of those American soldiers in Vietnam who have been picked by the newsreel cameras to say their piece, and the happy healthy never unintelligent faces of all those professional football players he studies so assiduously on television come Sunday (he has neglected to put his bets in this week) and wonders how they would poll out on a sentiment for the war.

HAWKS 95   DOVES 6

NFL Footballers Approve Vietnam War

Doubtless. All the healthy Marines, state troopers, professional athletes, movie stars, rednecks, sensuous life-loving Mafia, cops, mill workers, city officials, nice healthy-looking easy-grafting politicians full of the light (from marijuana?) in their eye of a life they enjoy—yes, they would be for the war in Vietnam. Arrayed against them as hard-core troops: an elite! the Freud-ridden embers of Marxism, good old American anxiety strata—the urban middle-class with their proliferated monumental adenoidal resentments, their secret slavish love for the oncoming hegemony of the computer and the suburb, yes, they and their children, by the sheer ironies, the sheer ineptitude, the *kinks* of history, were now being compressed into more and more militant stands, their resistance to the war some hopeless melange, somehow firmed, of Pacifism and closet Communism. And their children—on a freak-out from the suburbs to a love-in on the Pentagon wall.

It was the children in whom Mailer had some hope, a gloomy hope. These mad middle-class children with their lobotomies from sin, their nihilistic embezzlement of all middle-class moral funds, their innocence, their lust for apocalypse, their unbelievable indifference to waste: twenty generations of buried hopes perhaps engraved in their chromosomes, and now conceivably burning like faggots in the secret inquisitional fires of LSD. It was a devil's drug—designed by the Devil to consume the love of the best, and leave them liver-wasted, weeds of the big city. If there had been a player piano, Mailer might have put in a quarter to hear "In the Heart of the City Which Has No Heart."

Yes, these were the troops: middle-class cancer-pushers and drug-gutted flower children. And Paul Goodman to lead them. Was he now reading this?

> Once American faces
> were beautiful to me
> but now they look cruel
> and as if they had narrow thoughts.

Not much poetry, but well put prose. And yet there was always Goodman's damnable tolerance for all the varieties of sex. Did he know nothing of evil or entropy? Sex was the superhighway to your own soul's entropy if it was used without a constant sharpening of the taste. And orgies? What did Goodman know of orgies, real ones, not lib-lab college orgies to carry out the higher program of the Great Society, but real ones with murder in the air, and witches on the shoulder. The collected Tory in Mailer came roaring to the surface like a cocked hat in a royal coach.

"When Goodman finishes, I'm going to take over as M.C.," he whispered to de Grazia. (The revery we have just attended took no more in fact than a second. Mailer's melancholy assessment of the forces now mounting in America took place between two consecu-

tive lines of Goodman's poem—not because Mailer cerebrated that
instantly, but because he had had the revery many a time before—
he had to do no more than sense the audience, whisper Cancer
Gulch to himself and the revery went by with a mental ch-ch-ch
Click! reviewed again.) In truth, Mailer was now in a state. He had
been prepared to open the evening with apocalyptic salvos to announce the real gravity of the situation, and the intensely peculiar
American aspect of it—which is that the urban and suburban middle class were to be offered on Saturday an opportunity for glory—
what other nation could boast of such option for its middle class?
Instead—lost. The benignity and good humor of his planned opening remarks now subjugated to the electronic hawking and squab-
bling and *hum* of the P.A., the maniacal necessity to *wait* was on
this hiatus transformed into a violent concentration of purpose, all
intentions reversed. He glared at de Grazia. "How could you do
this?" he whispered to his ear.

De Grazia looked somewhat confused at the intensity. Meetings
to de Grazia were obviously just meetings, assemblages of people
who coughed up for large admissions or kicked in for the pitch; at
best, some meetings were less boring than others. De Grazia was
much too wise and guilty-spirited to brood on apocalypse. "I
couldn't find you," he whispered back.

"You didn't trust me long enough to wait one minute?"

"We were over an hour late," de Grazia whispered again. "We
had to begin."

Mailer was all for having the conversation right then on stage: to
hell with reciprocal rights and polite incline of the ear to the speaker. The Beast was ready to grapple with the world. "Did you think
I wouldn't show up?" he asked de Grazia.

"Well, I was wondering."

In what sort of mumbo-jumbo of promise and betrayal did de
Grazia live? How could de Grazia ever suppose he would not
show up? He had spent his life showing up at the most boring and
onerous places. He gave a blast of his eyes to de Grazia. But Macdonald gave a look at Mailer, as if to say, "You're creating disturb-
ance."

Now Goodman was done.

Mailer walked to the stage. He did not have any idea any longer
of what he would say, his mind was empty, but in a fine calm, taking for these five instants a total rest. While there was no danger of
Mailer ever becoming a demagogue since if the first idea he offered
could appeal to a mob, the second in compensation would be sure
to enrage them, he might nonetheless have made a fair country orator, for he loved to speak, he loved in fact to holler, and liked to

hear a crowd holler back. (Of how many New York intellectuals may that be said?)

"I'm here as your original M.C., temporarily displaced owing to a contretemps" — which was pronounced purposefully as contre-tempse — "in the men's room," he said into the microphone for opening, but the gentle high-strung beast of a device pushed into a panic by the electric presence of a real Beast; let loose a squeal which shook the welds in the old foundation of the Ambassador. Mailer immediately decided he had had enough of public address systems, electronic fields of phase, impedance, and spooks in the circuitry. A hex on collaborating with Cancer Gulch. He pushed the microphone away, squared off before the audience. "Can you hear me?" he bellowed.

"Yes."

"Can you hear me in the balcony?"

"Yes."

"Then let's do away with electronics," he called out.

Cries of laughter came back. A very small pattern of applause. (Not too many on his side for electrocuting the public address system, or so his orator's ear recorded the vote.)

"Now I missed the beginning of this occasion, or I would have been here to introduce Paul Goodman, for which we're all sorry, right?"

Confused titters. Small reaction.

"What are you, dead-heads?" he bellowed at the audience. "Or are you all" — here he put on his false Irish accent — "in the nature of becoming dead ahsses?" Small laughs. A whistle or two. "No," he said, replying to the whistles, "I invoke these dead asses as part of the gravity of the occasion. The middle class plus one hippie surrealistic symbolic absolutely insane March on the Pentagon, bless us all," beginning of a big applause which offended Mailer for it came on "bless" and that was too cheap a way to win votes, "bless us all — shit!" he shouted, "I'm trying to say the middle class plus shit, I mean plus revolution, is equal to one big collective dead ass." Some yells of approval, but much shocked curious rather stricken silence. He had broken the shank of his oratorical charge. Now he would have to sweep the audience together again. (Perhaps he felt like a surgeon delivering a difficult breech — nothing to do but plunge to the elbows again.)

"To resume our exposition," a good warm titter, then a ripple of laughter, not unsympathetic to his ear; the humor had been unwitting, but what was the life of an orator without some bonus? "To resume this orderly marshalling of concepts" — a conscious attempt at humor which worked less well; he was beginning to recognize for the first time that bellowing without a mike demanded a more forthright style — "I shall now *engage* in confession." More Irish accent. (He blessed Brendan Behan for what he had learned from him.) "A public speaker may offer you two opportunities. Instruction or confession." Laughter now. "Well, you're all college heads, so my instruction would be as pearls before — I dare not say it." Laughs. Boos. A voice from the balcony: "Come on, Norman, say something!"

"Is there a black man in the house?" asked Mailer. He strode up and down the stage pretending to peer at the audience. But in fact they were illumined just well enough to emphasize one sad discovery — if black faces there were they were certainly not in plenty. "Well ah'll just have to be the *impromptu* Black Power for tonight. Woo-eeeeee! Woo-eeeeee! HMmmmmmmm." He grunted with some partial success, showing hints of Cassius Clay. "Get your white butts moving."

"The confession. The confession!" screamed some adolescents from up front.

He came to a stop, shifted his voice. Now he spoke in a relaxed tone. "The confession, yeah!" Well, at least the audience was awake. He felt as if he had driven away some sepulchral phantoms of a variety which inhabited the profound middle-class schist. Now to charge the center of vested spookery.

"Say," he called out into the semidarkness with the ultrapurple light coming off the psychedelic lamp on the rail of the balcony, and the spotlights blaring against his eyes, "say," all happiness again, "I think of Saturday, and that March and do you know, fellow carriers of the holy unendurable grail, for the first time in my life I don't know whether I have the piss or the shit scared out of me most." It was an interesting concept, thought Mailer, for there was a difference between the two kinds of fear — pursue the thought, he would, in quieter times — "we are up, face this, all of you, against an existential situation — we do not know how it is going to turn out, and what is even more inspiring of dread is that the government doesn't know either."

Beginning of a real hand, a couple of rebel yells. "We're going to try to stick it up the government's ass," he shouted, "right into the sphincter of the Pentagon." Wild yells and chills of silence from different reaches of the crowd. Yeah, he was cooking now. "Will reporters please get every word accurately," he called out dryly to warm the chill.

But humor may have been too late. *The New Yorker* did not have strictures against the use of sh*t for nothing; nor did Dwight Macdonald love *The New Yorker* for nothing, he also had strictures against sh*t's metaphorical associations. Mailer looked to his right to see Macdonald approaching, a book in his hands, arms at his side, a sorrowing look of concern in his face. "Norman," said Macdonald quietly, "I can't possibly follow you after all this. Please introduce me, and get it over with."

Mailer was near to stricken. On the one hand interrupted on a flight: on the other, he had fulfilled no duty whatsoever as M.C. He threw a look at Macdonald which said: give me this. I'll owe you one.

But de Grazia was there as well. "Norman, let me be M.C. now," he said.

They were being monstrous unfair, thought Mailer. They didn't understand what he had been doing, how good he had been, what he would do next. Fatal to walk off now—the verdict would claim he was unbalanced. Still, he could not hold the stage by force. That was unthinkably worse.

For the virtuous, however, deliverance (like buttercups) pops up everywhere. Mailer now took the microphone and turned to the audience. He was careful to speak in a relaxed voice. "We are having a disagreement about the value of the proceedings. Some think de Grazia should resume his post as Master of Ceremonies. I would like to keep the position. It is an existential moment. We do not know how it will turn out. So let us vote on it." Happy laughter from the audience at these comic effects. Actually Mailer did not believe it was an existential situation any longer. He reckoned the vote would be well in his favor. "Will those," he asked, "who are in favor of Mr. de Grazia succeeding me as Master of Ceremonies please say aye."

A good sound number said aye.

Now for the ovation. "Will those opposed to this, please say no." The no's to Mailer's lack of pleasure were no greater in volume. "It seems the ayes and no's are about equal," said Mailer. (He was thinking to himself that he had posed the issue all wrong— the ayes should have been reserved for those who would keep him in office.) "Under the circumstances," he announced, "I will keep the chair." Laughter at this easy cheek. He stepped into the middle of such laughter. "You have all just learned an invaluable political lesson." He waved the microphone at the audience. "In the absence of a definitive vote, the man who holds the power, keeps it."

"Hey, de Grazia," someone yelled from the audience, "why do you let him have it?"

Mailer extended the microphone to de Grazia who smiled sweetly into it. "Because if I don't," he said in a gentle voice, "he'll beat the shit out of me." The dread word had been used again.

"Please, Norman," said Macdonald retreating.

So Mailer gave his introduction to Macdonald. It was less than he would have attempted if the flight had not been grounded, but it was certainly respectable. Under the military circumstances, it was a decent cleanup operation. For about a minute he proceeded to introduce Macdonald as a man with whom one might seldom agree, but could never disrespect because he always told the truth as he saw the truth, a man therefore of the most incorruptible integrity. "Pray heaven, I am right," said Mailer to himself, and walked past Macdonald who was on his way to the mike. Both men nodded coolly to each other.

In the wing, visible to the audience, Paul Goodman sat on a chair clearly avoiding any contaminatory encounter with The Existentialist. De Grazia gave his "It's tough all over" smile. Lowell sat in a mournful hunch on the floor, his eyes peering over his glasses to scrutinize the metaphysical substance of his boot, now hide? now machine? now, where the joining and to what? foot to boot, boot to earth — cease all speculations as to what was in Lowell's head. "The one mind a novelist cannot enter is the mind of a novelist superior to himself," said once to Mailer by Jean Malaquais. So, by corollary, the one mind a minor poet may not enter . . .

Lowell looked most unhappy. Mailer, minor poet, had often observed that Lowell had the most disconcerting mixture of strength and weakness in his presence, a blending so dramatic in its visible sign of conflict that one had to assume he would be sensationally attractive to women. He had something untouchable, all insane in its force; one felt immediately there were any number of causes for which the man would be ready to die, and for some he would fight, with an axe in his hand and a Cromwellian light in his eye. It was even possible that physically he was very strong — one couldn't tell at all — he might be fragile, he might have the sort of farm mechanic's strength which could manhandle the rear axle and differential off a car and into the back of a pickup. But physical strength or no, his nerves were all too apparently delicate. Obviously spoiled by everyone for years, he seemed nonetheless to need the spoiling. These nerves — the nerves of a consummate poet — were not tuned to any battering. The squalls of the mike, now riding up a storm on the erratic piping breath of Macdonald's voice, seemed to tear along Lowell's back like a gale. He detested tumult — obviously. And therefore saw everything which was hopeless in a rife situation: the dank middleclass depths of the audience, the strident squalor of the mike, the absurdity of talent gathered to raise money—for what, dear God? who could finally know what this March might convey, or worse, purvey, and worst of all—to be associated now with Mailer's butcher boy attack. Lowell's eyes looked up from the shoe, and passed one withering glance by the novelist, saying much, saying, "Every single bad thing I have ever heard about you is not exaggerated."

Mailer, looking back, thought bitter words he would not say: "You, Lowell, beloved poet of many, what do you know of the dirt and the dark deliveries of the necessary? What do you know of dignity hard-achieved, and dignity lost through innocence, and dignity lost by sacrifice for a cause one cannot name. What do you know about getting fat against your will, and turning into a clown of an arriviste baron when you would rather be an eagle or a count, or rarest of all, some natural aristocrat from these damned democratic states. No, the only subject we share, you and I, is that species of perception which shows that if we are not very loyal to our unendurable and most exigent inner light, then some day we may burn. How dare you condemn me! You know the diseases which inhabit the audience in this accursed psychedelic house. How dare you scorn the explosive I employ?"

And Lowell with a look of the greatest sorrow as if all this *mess* were finally too shapeless for the hard Protestant smith of his own brain, which would indeed burst if it could not forge his experience into the iron edge of the very best words and the most unsinkable relation of words, now threw up his eyes like an epileptic as if turned out of orbit by a turn of the vision—and fell backward, his head striking the floor with no last instant hesitation to cushion the blow, but like a baby, downright sudden, savagely to himself, as if from the height of a foot he had taken a pumpkin and dropped it splat on the floor. "There, much-regarded, much-protected brain, you have finally taken a blow," Lowell might have said to himself, for he proceeded to lie there, resting quietly, while Macdonald went on reading from "The White Man's Burden," Lowell seeming as content as if he had just tested the back of his cranium against a policeman's club. What a royal head they had all to lose!

CHAPTER 6: A TRANSFER OF POWER

The evening went on. It was in fact far from climax. Lowell, resting in the wing on the floor of the stage, Lowell recuperating from the crack he had given his head, was a dreamy figure of peace in the corner of the proscenium, a reclining shepherd contemplating his flute, although a Washington newspaper was to condemn him on Saturday in company with Mailer for "slobbish behavior" at this unseemly lounging.

Now Macdonald finished. What with the delays, the unmanageable public address system, and the choppy waters of the audience at his commencement, for Mailer had obviously done him no good, Macdonald had been somewhat less impressive than ever. A few people had shown audible boredom with him. (Old-line Communists perhaps. Dwight was by now one of the oldest anti-Communists in America.)

> Take up the White Man's burden —
> Ye dare not stoop to less —
> Nor call too loud on Freedom
> To cloak your weariness;
> By all ye cry or whisper,
> By all ye leave or do,
> The silent, sullen peoples
> Shall weigh your Gods and you.

read Macdonald from Kipling's poem, and the wit was in the selection, never the presentation.

He was done. He walked back to the wings with an air of no great satisfaction in himself, at most the sense of an obligation accomplished. Lowell's turn had arrived. Mailer stood up to introduce him.

The novelist gave a fulsome welcome to the poet. He did not speak of his poetry (with which he was not conspicuously familiar) nor of his prose which he thought excellent — Mailer told instead of why he had respect for Lowell as a man. A couple of years ago, the poet had refused an invitation from President Johnson to attend a garden party for artists and intellectuals, and it had attracted much attention at the time for it was one of the first dramatic acts of protest against the war in Vietnam, and Lowell was the only invited artist of first rank who had refused. Saul Bellow, for example, had attended the garden party. Lowell's refusal could not have been easy, the novelist suggested, because artists were attracted to formal afternoons of such elevated kind since that kind of experience was often stimulating to new perception and new work. So, an honorific occasion in full panoply was not easy for the mature artist to eschew. Capital! Lowell had therefore bypassed the most direct sort of literary capital. Ergo, Mailer respected him—he could not be certain he would have done the same himself, although, of course, he assured the audience he would not probably have ever had the opportunity to refuse. (Hints of merriment in the crowd at the thought of Mailer on the White House lawn.)

If the presentation had been formal up to here, it had also been somewhat graceless. On the consequence, our audience's amusement tipped the slumbering Beast. Mailer now cranked up a vaudeville clown for finale to Lowell's introduction. "Ladies and gentlemen, if novelists come from the middle class, poets tend to derive from the bottom and the top. We all know good poets at the bot'—ladies and gentlemen, here is a poet from the top, Mr. Robert Lowell." A large vigorous hand of applause, genuine enthusiasm for Lowell, some standing ovation.

But Mailer was depressed. He had betrayed himself again. The end of the introduction belonged in a burlesque house—he worked his own worst veins, like a man on the edge of bankruptcy trying to collect hopeless debts. He was fatally vulgar! Lowell passing him on the stage had recovered sufficiently to cast him a nullifying look. At this moment, they were obviously far from friends.

Lowell's shoulders had a slump, his modest stomach was pushed forward a hint, his chin was dropped to his chest as he stood at the microphone, pondering for a moment. One did not achieve the languid grandeurs of that slouch in one generation—the grandsons of the first sons had best go through the best troughs in the best eating clubs at Harvard before anyone in the family could try for such elegant note. It was now apparent to Mailer that Lowell would move by instinct, ability, and certainly by choice, in the direction most opposite from himself.

"Well," said Lowell softly to the audience, his voice dry and gentle as any New England executioner might ever hope to be, "this has been a zany evening." Laughter came back, perhaps a little too much. It was as if Lowell wished to reprove Mailer, not humiliate him. So he shifted, and talked a bit uneasily for perhaps a minute about very little. Perhaps it was too little. Some of the audience, encouraged by earlier examples, now whistled. "We can't hear you," they shouted, "speak louder."

Lowell was annoyed. "I'll bellow," he said, "but it won't do any good." His firmness, his distaste for the occasion, communicated some subtle but impressive sense of his superiority. Audiences are moved by many cues but the most satisfactory to them is probably the voice of their abdomen. There are speakers who give a sense of security to the abdomen, and they always elicit the warmest kind of applause. Mailer was not this sort of speaker; Lowell was. The hand of applause which followed this remark was fortifying. Lowell now proceeded to read some poetry.

He was not a splendid reader, merely decent to his own lines, and he read from that slouch, that personification of ivy climbing a column, he was even diffident, he looked a trifle helpless under the lights. Still, he made no effort to win the audience, seduce them, dominate them, bully them, amuse them, no, they were there for him, to please *him*, a sounding board for the plucked string of his poetic line, and so he endeared himself to them. They adored him—for his talent, his modesty, his superiority, his melancholy, his petulance, his weakness, his painful, almost stammering shyness, his noble strength—*there* was the string behind other strings.

> O to break loose, like the chinook
> salmon jumping and falling back,
> nosing up to the impossible
> stone and bone-crushing waterfall—
> raw-jawed, weak-fleshed there, stopped by ten
> steps of the roaring ladder, and then
> to clear the top on the last try,
> alive enough to spawn and die.

Mailer discovered he was jealous. Not of the talent. Lowell's talent was very large, but then Mailer was a bulldog about the value of his own talent. No, Mailer was jealous because he had worked for this audience, and Lowell without effort seemed to have stolen them: Mailer did not know if he was contemptuous of Lowell for playing *grand maître*, or admiring of his ability to do it. Mailer knew his own version of *grand maître* did not compare. Of course no one would be there to accept his version either. The pain of bad reviews was not in the sting, but in the subsequent pressure which, like water on a joint, collected over the decade. People who had not read your books in fifteen years were certain they were missing nothing of merit. A buried sorrow, not very attractive, (for bile was in it and the bitterness of unrequited literary injustice) released itself from some ducts of the heart, and Mailer felt hot anger at how Lowell was loved and he was not, a pure and surprising recognition of how much emotion, how much simple and childlike bitter sorrowing emotion had been concealed from himself for years under the manhole cover of his contempt for bad reviews.

Pity the planet, all joy gone
from this sweet volcanic cone;
peace to our children when they fall
in small war on the heels of small
war—until the end of time
to police the earth, a ghost
orbiting forever lost
in our monotonous sublime.

They gave Lowell a good standing ovation, much heartiness in it, much obvious pleasure that they were there on a night in Washington when Robert Lowell had read from his work—it was as nice as that—and then Lowell walked back to the wings, and Mailer walked forward. Lowell did not seem particularly triumphant. He looked still modest, still depressed, as if he had been applauded too much for too little and so the reservoir of guilt was still untapped.

Nonetheless, to Mailer it was now *mano a mano*. Once, on a vastly larger scale of applause, perhaps people had reacted to Manolete not unlike the way they reacted to Lowell, so stirred by the deeps of sorrow in the man, that the smallest move produced the largest emotion. If there was any value to the comparison then Mailer was kin to the young Dominguin, taking raucous chances, spitting in the eye of the bull, an excess of variety in his passes. But probably there was no parallel at all. He may have felt like a matador in the flush of full competition, going out to do his work after the other torero has had a triumph, but for fact he was probably less close in essence now to the bullfighter than the bull. We must not forget the Beast. He had been sipping the last of the bourbon out of the mug. He had been delayed, piqued, twisted from his purpose and without anything to eat in close to ten hours. He was on the hunt. For what, he hardly knew. It is possible the hunt existed long before the victim was ever conceived.

"Now, you may wonder who I am," he said to the audience, or bellowed to them, for again he was not using the mike, "and you may wonder why I'm talking in a Southern accent which is phony"—the Southern accent as it sounded to him in his throat, was actually not too bad at this moment—"and the reason is that I want to make a presentation to you." He did not have a notion of what he would say next, but it never occurred to him something would not come. His impatience, his sorrow, his jealousy were gone, he just wanted to live on the edge of that rhetorical sword he would soon try to run through the heart of the audience. "We are gathered here"—shades of Lincoln in hippieland—"to make a move on Saturday to invest the Pentagon and halt and slow down its workings, and this will be at once a symbolic act and a real act"—he was roaring—"for real heads may possibly get hurt, and soldiers will be there to hold us back, and some of us may be arrested" — how, wondered the wise voice at the rear of this roaring voice, could one ever leave Washington now without going to jail? — "some blood conceivably will be shed. If I were the man in the government responsible for controlling this March, I would not know what to do." Sonorously — "I would not wish to arrest too many or hurt anyone for fear the repercussions in the world would be too large for my bureaucrat's heart to bear — it's so full of shit." Roars and chills from the audience again. He was off into obscenity. It gave a heartiness like the blood of beef tea to his associations. There was no villainy in obscenity for him, just — paradoxically, characteristically — his love for America: he had first come to love America when he served in the U.S. Army, not the America of course of the flag, the patriotic unendurable fix of the television programs and the newspapers, no, long before he was ever aware of the institutional oleo of the suffocating American ideas he had come to love what editorial writers were fond of calling the democratic principle with its faith in the common man. He found that principle and that man in the Army, but what none of the editorial writers ever mentioned was that that noble common man was obscene as an old goat, and his obscenity was what saved him. The sanity of said common democratic man was in his humor, his humor was in his obscenity. And his philosophy as well — a reductive philosophy which looked to restore the hard edge of proportion to the overblown values overhanging each small military existence — viz: being forced to salute an overconscientious officer with your back stiffened into an exaggerated posture. "That Lieutenant is chickenshit," would be the platoon verdict, and a blow had somehow been struck for democracy and the sanity of good temper. Mailer once heard a private end an argument about the merits of a general by saying, "his spit don't smell like ice cream either," only the private was not speaking of spit. Mailer thought enough of the line to put it into *The Naked and the Dead*, along with a good many other such lines the characters in his mind and his memory of the Army had begun to offer him. The common discovery of America was probably that Americans were the first people on earth to live for their humor; nothing was so important to Americans as humor. In Brooklyn, he had taken this for granted, at Harvard he had thought it was a by-product of being at Harvard, but in the Army he discovered that the humor was probably in the veins and the roots of the local history of every state and county in America — the truth of the way it really felt over the years passed on a river of obscenity from small-town storyteller to storyteller there down below the bankers and the books and the educators and the legislators — so Mailer never felt more like an American than when he was naturally obscene—all the gifts of the American language came out in the happy play of obscenity upon concept, which enabled one to go back to concept again. What was magnificent about the word shit is that it enabled you to use the word noble: a skinny Southern cracker with a beatific smile on his face saying in the dawn in a Filipino rice paddy, "Man, I just managed to take me a noble shit." Yeah, that was Mailer's America. If he was going to love something in the country, he would love that. So after years of keeping obscene language off to one corner of his work, as if to prove after *The Naked and the Dead* that he had many an arrow in his literary quiver, he had come back to obscenity again in the last year—he had kicked goodbye in his novel *Why Are We in Vietnam?* to the old literary corset of good taste, letting his sense of language play on obscenity as freely as it wished, so discovering that everything he knew about the American language (with its incommensurable resources) went flying in and out of the line of his prose with the happiest beating of wings—it was the first time his style seemed at once very American to him and very literary in the best way, at least as he saw the best way. But the reception of the book had been disappointing. Not because many of the reviews were bad (he had learned, despite all sudden discoveries of sorrow, to live with that as one lived with smog) no, what was disappointing was the crankiness across the country. Where fusty conservative old critics had once defended the obscenity in *The Naked and the Dead*, they, or their sons, now condemned it in the new book, and that *was* disappointing. The country was not growing up so much as getting a premature case of arthritis.

At any rate, he had come to the point where he liked to use a little obscenity in his public speaking. Once people got over the shock, they were sometimes able to discover that the humor it provided was not less powerful than the damage of the pain. Of course he did not do it often and he tried not to do it unless he was in good voice—Mailer was under no illusion that public speaking was equal to candid conversation; an obscenity uttered in a voice too weak for its freight was obscene, since obscenity probably resides in the quick conversion of excitement to nausea—which is why Lyndon Johnson's speeches are called obscene by some. The excitement of listening to the American President alters abruptly into the nausea of wandering down the blind alleys of his voice.

This has been a considerable defense of the point, but then the point was at the center of his argument and it could be put thus: the American corporation executive, who was after all the foremost representative of Man in the world today, was perfectly capable of burning unseen women and children in the Vietnamese jungles, yet felt a large displeasure and fairly final disapproval at the generous use of obscenity in literature and in public.

The apology may now be well taken, but what in fact did Mailer say on the stage of the Ambassador before the evening was out? Well, not so very much, just about enough to be the stuff of which footnotes are made, for he did his best to imitate a most high and executive voice.

"I had an experience as I came to the theater to speak to all of you, which is that before appearing on this stage I went upstairs to the men's room as a prelude to beginning this oratory so beneficial to all"—laughs and catcalls—"and it was dark, so—ahem—I missed the bowl—all men will know what I mean. Forgiveness might reign. But tomorrow, they will blame that puddle of water on Communists which is the way we do things here in Amurrica, any-one of you pinko poos want to object, lemme tell ya, the reason nobody was in the men's room, and it so dark, is that if there been a light they'd had to put a CIA man in there and the hippies would grope him silly, see here, you know who I am, why it just came to me, ah'm so phony, I'm as full of shit as Lyndon Johnson. Why, man, I'm nothing but his little old alter ego. That's what you got right here working for you, Lyndon Johnson's little old *dwarf* alter ego. How you like him? How you like him?" (Shades of Cassius Clay again.)

And in the privacy of his brain, quiet in the glare of all that sound and spotlight. Mailer thought quietly, "My God, that is prob-ably exactly what you are at this moment, Lyndon Johnson with all his sores, sorrows, and vanity, squeezed down to five foot eight," and Mailer felt for the instant possessed, as if he had seized some of the President's secret soul, or the President seized some of his— the bourbon was as luminous as moonshine to the spores of insani-ty in the flesh of his brain, a smoke of menace swished in the air, and something felt real, almost as if he had caught Lyndon Johnson by the toe and now indeed, bugger the rhyme, should never let him go.

"Publicity hound," shouted someone from the upper balcony.

"Fuck you," cried Mailer back with absolute delight, all the force of the Texas presidency in his being. Or was it Lucifer's fire? But let us use asterisks for these obscenities to emphasize how happily he used the words, they went off like fireworks in his ora-tor's heart, and asterisks look like rocket-bursts and the orbs from Roman candles ***. F*ck you he said to the heckler but with such gusto the vowel was doubled. F*-*ck you! was more like it. So, doubtless, had the President disposed of all opposition in private session. Well, Mailer was here to bring the presidency to the public.

"This yere dwarf alter ego has been telling you about his imbroglio with the p*ssarooney up on the top floor, and will all the reporters please note that I did not talk about defecation commonly known as sheeee-it!"—full imitation of LBJ was attempted there—"but to the contrary, speak of you-rye-nation! I p*ssed on the floor. Hoo-ee! Hoo-ee! How's that for Black Power full of white p*ss? You just know all those reporters are going to say it was sh*t tomorrow. F*ck them. F*ck all of them. Reporters, will you stand up and be counted?"

A wail of delight from the students in the audience. What would the reporters do? Would they stand?

One lone figure arose.

"Where are *you* from?" asked Mailer.

"Washington *Free Press*." A roar of delight from the crowd. It was obviously some student or hippie paper.

"Ah want *The Washington Post*," said Mailer in his best Texas tones, "and the *Star*. Ah know there's a *Time* magazine man here for one, and twenty more like him no doubt." But no one stood. So Mailer went into a diatribe. "Yeah, people," he said, "watch the reporting which follows. Yeah, these reporters will kiss Lyndon Johnson's *ss and Dean Rusk's *ss and Man Mountain McNamara's *ss, they will rush to kiss it, but will they stand up in public? No! Because they are the silent assassins of the Republic. They alone have done more to destroy this nation than any force in it." They will certainly destroy me in the morning, he was thinking. But it was for this moment worth it, as if two very different rivers, one external, one subjective, had come together; the frustrated bile, piss, pus, and poison he had felt at the progressive contamination of all American life in the abscess of Vietnam, all of that, all heaped in lighted coals of brimstone on the press' collective ear, represented one river, and the other was the frustrated actor in Mailer—ever since seeing *All the King's Men* years ago he had wanted to come on in public as a Southern demagogue.

The speech went on, and a few fine things possibly were said next to a few equally obscene words, and then Mailer thought in passing of reading a passage from *Why Are We in Vietnam?* but the passage was full of plays of repetition on the most famous four-letter word of them all, and Mailer thought that was conceivably redundant now and so he ended modestly with a final, "See you on Saturday!"

The applause was fair. Not weak, but empty of large demonstration. No standing ovation for certain. He felt cool, and in a quiet, pleasant, slightly depressed mood. Since there was not much conversation between Macdonald, Lowell, and himself, he turned after a moment, left the stage, and walked along the floor where the audience had sat. A few people gathered about him, thanked him, shook his hand. He was quiet and reserved now, with genial slightly muted attempts to be cordial. He had noticed this shift in mood before, even after readings or lectures which had been less eventful. There was a mutual embarrassment between speaker and audience once the speaker had left the stage and walked through the crowd. It was due no doubt to the intimacy — that most special intimacy — which can live between a speaker and the people he has addressed, yes they had been so intimate then, that the encounter now, afterward, was like the eye-to-the-side maneuvers of client and whore once the act is over and dressing is done.

Mailer went on from there to a party of more liberal academics, and drank a good bit more and joked with Macdonald about the superiority of the introduction he had given to Lowell over the introduction Dwight had received.

"Next time don't interrupt me," he teased Macdonald, "and I'll give you a better introduction."

"Goodness, I couldn't hear a word you said," said Macdonald, "you just sounded awful. Do you know, Norman, the acoustics were terrible on the wing. I don't think any of us heard anything anyone else said."

Some time in the early morning, or not so early, Mailer got to bed at the Hay-Adams and fell asleep to dream no doubt of fancy parties in Georgetown when the Federal period in architecture was young. Of course if this were a novel, Mailer would spend the rest of the night with a lady. But it is history, and so the Novelist is for once blissfully removed from any description of the hump-your-backs of sex. Rather he can leave such matters to the happy or unhappy imagination of the reader.

Part III: Saturday Matinée

CHAPTER 1: THE NEXT STEP

Next morning, Macdonald and Lowell met Mailer in the dining room of the Hay-Adams for breakfast. There was a crowd about now. In the lobby, a mood prevailed of well-dressed people come together for a collective celebration — a homecoming game or civic testimonial, or class reunion. Everybody was saying hello to people they had not seen in years, and everybody looked good. The thousand days of John Kennedy had done much to change the style of America; nowhere perhaps more than to the sartorial sense of the liberals and Left Wing intellectuals now gathering for breakfast — some drabness had quit them since the fifties, some sense of power had touched them with subtle concomitants of power — a hint of elegance. The city was awake. On the way to the hotel last night, somewhat after midnight, Mailer thought the streets of downtown Washington held a hint of Times Square in early morning hours, that same offering of fevers not abated, echo of voices a block away which promised violence — if not for tonight, then for another. The whores were out: not a common sight in Washington. The Capital was usually about as lively at 1 A.M. as the center of Cincinnati late at night, but now there were motorcycles gunning up and down the avenues with their whine of constant climax looping into the new whine of higher climax — one waits for them to explode, they never do, they go gunning for the night. The air was violent, yet full of amusement; out of focus. Mailer had no idea whether this atmosphere was actually now typical of Washington on Friday night (as lately of more than one other quiet American city) or whether this mood came in with the weekend migrants from New York; or if indeed some of the Under-Thirties in Washington were warming up to repel the invasion. There was a hint of hurricane calm, then wind-bursts, gut-roars from the hogs. If the novelist had never heard of Hell's Angels or motorcycle gangs, he would still have predicted, no, rather *invented* motorcycle orgies, because the orgy and technology seemed to come together in the sound of 1200 cc's on two wheels, that exacerbation of flesh, torsion of lust, rhythm in the pistons, stink of gasoline, yeah, oil as the last excrement of putrefactions buried a million years in Mother Earth, yes indeed, that funky redolence of gasoline was not derived from nothing, no, doubtless it was the stench of the river Styx (a punning metaphor appropriate to John Updike no doubt) but Mailer, weak in Greek, had nonetheless some passing cloudy unresolved image now of man as Charon on that river of gasoline Styx wandering between earth and the holy mills of the machine. Like most cloudy metaphors, this served to get him home — there is nothing like the search for a clear figure of speech to induce gyroscopic intensity sufficient for the compass to work.

Actually, Mailer had not been that drunk. Speak of the river Styx, the whiskey earlier that evening had worked like balming oil for the collective ego of Macdonald, Lowell, and Mailer. In the late afternoon they had all been naturally weary when speeches were done, but not unsatisfied with themselves. "It was a good day, wasn't it, Norman," Lowell kept asking. In the best of gentle moods, his nerves seemed out of their rack, and his wit had plays of light, his literary allusions always near to private, were now full of glee. In one sprawling bar-restaurant where they went at random to drink, a plump young waitress with a strong perfume, who looked nonetheless a goddess of a bucket for a one-night stand, caught Mailer the novelist's eye — he flirted with the sense of gravity Buddhists reserve for the cow. "Good God, Norman, what do you see in her?" Macdonald had to know. Mailer, conceivably, could have told him, but they talked instead of cheap perfume — why it was offensive to some, aphrodisiac to others.

Lowell remarked, "I like cheap perfume, Norman, don't you?" But he said this last as if he were talking about some grotto in Italy he had blundered into all by himself. It was a difficult remark to make without some faint strain of dry-as-sachet faggotry, but Lowell brought it off. The mixture of integrity (Cromwellian axe of light in the eye!) in company with his characteristic gentleness, enabled him to make just about any remark without slithering. It was as if he had arrived at the recognition, nothing lost, that cheap perfume might be one of the hundred odd scents of mystery in the poet's apothecary — let us not, however, forget the smell of gasoline which Mailer in his turn had pondered. Gasoline and cheap perfume — half the smell in American adventure.

But in fact what must have been contributing to his good mood was the knowledge that Norman Mailer seemed to like him. Robert Lowell gave off at times the unwilling haunted saintliness of a man who was repaying the moral debts of ten generations of ancestors. So his guilt must have been a tyrant of a chemical in his blood always ready to obliterate the best of his moods. Just as danger is a Turk to a coward and the snub a disembowelment to the social climber, so Lowell was vulnerable to not being liked by anyone remotely a peer. In the poet's loneliness — the homely assumption is that all talent is lonely to the degree it is exalted — Lowell was at the mercy of anyone he considered of value, for only they might judge his guilt, and so relieve the intolerable dread which accompanies this excessive assumption of the old moral debts of the ancestors. Who knows what they might be? We may only be certain that the moral debt of the Puritan is no mean affair: agglutinations of incest, abominations upon God, kissing the *sub cauda* of the midnight cat—Lowell's brain at its most painful must have been equal to an overdose of LSD on Halloween.

There had been, however, a happy conversation somewhat earlier and it had made a difference in Lowell's good mood. As they were coming down the steps from the Department of Justice in the now late cold October afternoon, Lowell had said, "I was most impressed with your speech, Norman."

"Well, glad you liked it, Cal," Mailer said, "for I think your speech produced it."

"My speech did?"

"I was affected by what you said. It took me out of one mood and put me in another."

"What sort of mood, Norman?"

"Well, maybe I was able to stop brooding over myself. I don't know, Cal, your speech really had a most amazing impact on me." Mailer drawled the last few words to drain any excessive sentimental infection, but Lowell seemed hardly to mind.

"Well, Norman, I'm delighted," he said, taking Mailer's arm for a moment as if, God and knightdom willing, Mailer had finally become a Harvard dean and could be addressed by the appropriate limb. "I'm delighted because I liked *your* speech so much."

These repetitions would have been ludicrous if not for the simplicity of feeling they obviously aroused in so complex a man as Lowell. Through the drinks and the evening at dinner, he kept coming back to the same conversation, kept repeating his pleasure in Mailer's speech in order to hear Mailer doggedly reaffirm his more than equal pleasure in Lowell's good words. Mailer was particularly graceless at these ceremonious repetitions by which presumably New England mandarins (like old Chinese) ring the stately gong of a new friendship forming.

In fact the dinner was what delivered Lowell's decision to remain for the March on the Pentagon. On the whole, he had come down for the event at the Department of Justice, he had in fact a dinner party at his home in New York on Saturday night, and he did not wish to miss it. That was obvious. For whatever reason Lowell had evidently been looking forward for days to Saturday evening.

"I wonder if I could get the plane back by six tomorrow," he kept asking aloud. "If we're arrested, I don't suppose there's much chance of that at all."

Mailer had not forgotten the party to which he was, in his turn, invited. Repeat: it had every promise of being wicked, tasty and rich. "I think if we get arrested early," he said, "we can probably be released among the first."

"By six?"

"No, Cal," said Mailer, the honest soul, "if you get arrested, you had better plan on not making dinner before nine."

"Well, should we get arrested? What do you think of the merits?"

They talked about it for a while. It was Mailer's firm conclusion that this was probably the way they could best serve the occasion. "If the three of us are arrested," he said, "the papers can't claim that hippies and hoodlums were the only ones guilty."

No conclusion was reached that night. Over breakfast they were ready to take it up again. It was evident that none had thought about it too much; also obvious there was nothing particularly to think about. Over the years they had all been bored by speeches, polemics and political programmings which invariably detailed the sound-as-brickwork logic of the next step in some hard new Left program. Existentially, it hardly mattered whether the logic came from a Communist, Trotskyist, Splinter Marxist, union organizer, or plain Social Democrat. While the ideals of such speakers were sometimes as separated as a flush in one hand is from a full house in the other, there was dependably a false but uxorious confidence in the adenoidal whine of the speaker as he shifted gears in his larynx the better to drive the certain efficacy of the program into the ears of his audience. Thus, at their worst, had Communist speakers used these gears of the larynx to defend the Moscow-Berlin pact in 1939. So had Trotskyists worked in and out of the knots of the thesis of the degenerated worker's state—a thesis which seemed less absurd to Mailer in 1967 than to Sidney Hook in 1947, but the Trotskyists had been as full of the unbreakable logic of the next step as the Communists, so they had succeeded in smashing the bones of their own movement into the hundred final slivers of American Marxism, miniscule radical sects complete each with their own special martyred genius of a Marxicologist. There had been the enlightened polemics of the cultivated socialism of the Committee for Cultural Freedom which had been brought by the sound-as-brickwork-logic-of-the-next-step in good Socialist *Anti-*Communism to so incisive an infestation by the CIA that it now called up pictures of the cockroaches in a slum sink; not all the wines of the Waldorf could wash out a drop of that! Yes, and the labor movement, and the confidence once held by Communists and

Trotskyists, Splinterites, and Reutherites, that the labor union would prove the strong back to jack the country up from the Depression to that luminous plane where Peace and Justice, Equality and Freedom would reign. The labor movement lifted the country and carried it to a field of plenty, but it was a football field where professionals played, and America watched on Sunday full of Peace before the rainbow of the color set, feeling Justice when their side won, knowing Equality since everyone presumably had an unimpeded view of his own set, and Freedom in abundance for a man could always turn his set off, yes, the labor unions now sat closer to the Mafia than to Marx.

Well, Macdonald, Lowell, and Mailer knew all this, they did not have to talk or argue, they had learned what politics they had, each in his own separate way, and so they did not need to discuss the sound-as-brickwork-logic-of-the-next-step. The March tomorrow would more or less work or not work. If it didn't, the Left would always find a new step—the Left never left itself unemployed (that much must be said for the conservative dictum that a man who wants to, can always find work) if the March did more or less succeed, one knew it would be as a result of episodes one had never anticipated, and the results might lead you in directions altogether unforeseen. And indeed how could one measure success or failure in a venture so odd and unprecedented as this? One did not march on the Pentagon and look to get arrested as a link in a master scheme to take over the bastions of the Republic step by step, no, that sort of sound-as-brickwork-logic was left to the FBI. Rather, one marched on the Pentagon because . . . because . . . and here the reasons became so many and so curious and so vague, so political and so primitive, that there was no need, or perhaps no possibility to talk about it yet, one could only ruminate over the morning coffee. What possibly they shared now between them at the morning table of the Hay-Adams was the unspoken happy confidence that politics had again become mysterious, had begun to partake of Mystery; that gave life to a thought the gods were back in human affairs. A generation of the American young had come along different from five previous generations of the middle class. The new generation believed in technology more than any before it, but the generation also believed in LSD, in witches, in tribal knowledge, in orgy, and revolution. It had no respect whatsoever for the unassailable logic of the next step: belief was reserved for the revelatory mystery of the happening where you did not know what was going to happen next; that was what was good about it. Their radicalism was in their hate for the authority—the authority was the manifest of evil to this generation. It was the authority who had covered the land with those suburbs where they stifled as children while watching the adventures of the West in the movies, while looking at the guardians of dull genial celebrity on television; they had had their minds jabbed and poked and twitched and probed and finally galvanized into surrealistic modes of response by commercials cutting into dramatic narratives, and parents flipping from network to network—they were forced willy-nilly to build their idea of the space-time continuum (and therefore their nervous system) on the jumps and cracks and leaps and breaks which every phenomenon from the media seemed to contain within it.

The authority had operated on their brain with commercials, and washed their brain with packaged education, packaged politics. The authority had presented itself as honorable, and it was corrupt, corrupt as payola on television, and scandals concerning the safety of automobiles, and scandals concerning the leasing of aviation contracts—the real scandals as everyone was beginning to sense were more intimate and could be found in all the products in all the suburban homes which did not work so well as they should have worked, and broke down too soon for mysterious reasons. The shoddiness was buried in the package, buried somewhere in the undiscoverable root of all those modern factories with their sanitized aisles and automated machines; perhaps one place the shoddiness was buried was in the hangovers of a working class finally alienated from any remote interest or attention in the process of the work itself. Work was shoddy everywhere. Even in the Warren Commission.

Finally, this new generation of the Left hated the authority, because the authority lied. It lied through the teeth of corporation executives and Cabinet officials and police enforcement officers and newspaper editors and advertising agencies, and in its mass magazines, where the subtlest apologies for the disasters of the authority (and the neatest deformations of the news) were grafted in the best possible style into the ever-open mind of the walking American lobotomy: the corporation office worker and his high school son.

The New Left was drawing its political aesthetic from Cuba. The revolutionary idea which the followers of Castro had induced from their experience in the hills was that you created the revolution first and learned from it, learned of what your revolution might consist and where it might go out of the intimate truth of the way it presented itself to your experience. Just as the truth of his material was revealed to a good writer by the cutting edge of his style (he could thus hope his style was in each case the most appropriate tool for the material of the experience) so a revolutionary began to uncover the nature of his true situation by trying to ride the beast of his revolution. The idea behind these ideas was then obviously that the future of the revolution existed in the nerves and cells of the people who created it and lived with it, rather than in the sanctity of the original idea.

Castro's Cuba was of course a mystery to Mailer. He had heard much in its favor, much he could hardly enjoy. That was not necessarily to the point. Revolutions could fail as well by Castro's method as by the most inflexible Comintern program; what seemed significant here, was the idea of a revolution which preceded ideology; the New Left had obviously adopted the idea for this March.

The aesthetic of the New Left now therefore began with the notion that the authority could not comprehend nor contain nor finally manage to control any political action whose end was unknown. They could attack it, beat it, jail it, misrepresent it, and finally abuse it, but they could not feel a sense of victory because they could not understand a movement which inspired thousands and hundreds of thousands to march without a coordinated plan. The bureaucrats of the Old Left had not been alone in their adoration of the solid-as-brickwork-logic-of-the-next-step; no, the bureaucrats of the American Center, now liked it as much, and were as aghast at any political activity which ignored it.

These Leviathan ruminations and meditations on the nature of the March coming up, and the reasons for their participation without much discussion now completed, ch-ch-ch-click! in the touch of the tea cup on Mailer's lip, let us move on to the event concerning us — that first major battle of a war which may go on for twenty years; let us even consider there is one interesting chance (one chance of a thousand) that in fifty years the day may loom in our history large as the ghosts of the Union dead.

MIAMI AND THE SIEGE OF CHICAGO

For the second time in 1968, New American Library issued a Mailer hit. Miami and the Siege of Chicago *is a double account of the two national political conventions, that of the Republicans in Miami, which nominated Richard Nixon, and that of the Democrats in Chicago, which, of course, nominated Hubert Humphrey. The two accounts were published as a single text in the November* Harper's *under the title "Miami Beach and Chicago." Signet has issued the paperback. The book was nominated for a National Book Award—the only time an author has had two books nominated in the same year—and its accounts of the conventions compare favorably with the two earlier Mailer essays: "Superman Comes to the Supermarket" in* The Presidential Papers *and "In the Red Light" in* Cannibals and Christians. *Taken together, the four accounts add up to an analysis of the decade's political history, and some day should probably be issued as a single volume. The present excerpts are designed to provide highlights — the book is not as tightly unified as* Armies — *and slightly more space has been allowed here to the stormy Chicago experience.*

Miami Beach, August 3 – 9

CHAPTER 1

They snipped the ribbon in 1915, they popped the cork, Miami Beach was born. A modest burg they called a city, nine-tenths jungle. An island. It ran along a coastal barrier the other side of Biscayne Bay from young Miami—in 1868 when Henry Lum, a California 'forty-niner, first glimpsed the island from a schooner, you may be certain it was jungle, cocoanut palms on the sand, mangrove swamp and palmetto thicket ten feet off the beach. But by 1915, they were working the vein. John S. Collins, a New Jersey nurseryman (after whom Collins Avenue is kindly named) brought in bean fields and avocado groves; a gent named Fisher, Carl G., a Hoosier—he invented Prestolite, a millionaire—bought up acres from Collins, brought in a work-load of machinery, men, even two elephants, and jungle was cleared, swamps were filled, small residential islands were made out of baybottom mud, dredged, then relocated, somewhat larger natural islands adjacent to the barrier island found themselves improved, streets were paved, sidewalks put in with other amenities—by 1968, one hundred years after Lum first glommed the beach, large areas of the original coastal strip were covered over altogether with macadam, white condominium, white luxury hotel and white stucco flea-bag. Over hundreds, then thousands of acres, white sidewalks, streets and white buildings covered the earth where the jungle had been. Is it so dissimilar from covering your poor pubic hair with adhesive tape for fifty years? The vegetal memories of that excised jungle haunted Miami Beach in a steam-pot of miasmas. Ghosts of expunged flora, the never-born groaning in vegetative chancery beneath the asphalt came up with a tropical curse, an equatorial leaden wet sweat of air which rose from the earth itself, rose right up through the baked asphalt and into the heated air which entered the lungs like a hand slipping into a rubber glove.

The temperature was not that insane. It hung around 87 day after day, at night it went down to 82, back to the same 87 in the A.M.—the claims of the News Bureau for Miami Beach promised that in 1967 temperature exceeded 90° only four times. (Which the Island of Manhattan could never begin to say.) But of course Miami Beach did not have to go that high, for its humidity was up to 87 as well—it was, on any and every day of the Republican Convention of 1968, one of the hottest cities in the world. The reporter was no expert on tropical heats—he had had, he would admit, the island of Luzon for a summer in World War II; and basic training in the pine woods of Fort Bragg, North Carolina, in August; he had put in a week at Las Vegas during July—temperatures to 110; he had crossed the Mojave Desert once by day; he was familiar with the New York subway in the rush hour on the hottest day of the year. These were awesome immersions—one did not have to hit the Congo to know what it was like in a hothouse in hell—but that 87° in Miami Beach day after day held up in competition against other sulphuric encounters. Traveling for five miles up the broken-down, forever in-a-state-of-alteration and repair of Collins Avenue, crawling through 5 P.M. Miami Beach traffic in the pure miserable fortune of catching an old taxi without air conditioning, dressed in shirt and tie and jacket—formal and implicitly demanded uniform of political journalists—the sensation of breathing, then living, was not unlike being obliged to make love to a 300-pound woman who has decided to get on top. Got it? You could not dominate a thing. That uprooted jungle had to be screaming beneath.

Of course it could have been the air conditioning: natural climate transmogrified by technological climate. They say that in Miami Beach the air conditioning is pushed to that icy point where women may wear fur coats over their diamonds in the tropics. For ten miles, from the Diplomat to the Di Lido, above Hallandale Beach Boulevard down to Lincoln Mall, all the white refrigerators stood, piles of white refrigerators six and eight and twelve stories high, twenty stories high, shaped like sugar cubes and ice-cube trays on edge, like mosques and palaces, shaped like matched white luggage and portable radios, stereos, plastic compacts and plastic rings, Moorish castles shaped like waffle irons, shaped like the baffle plates on white plastic electric heaters, and cylinders like Waring blenders, buildings looking like giant op art and pop art paintings, and sweet wedding cakes, cottons of kitsch and piles of dirty cotton stucco, yes, for ten miles the hotels for the delegates stood on the beach side of Collins Avenue: the Eden Roc and the Fontainebleau (Press Headquarters), the Di Lido and the De Lano, the Ivanhoe, Deauville, Sherry Frontenac and the Monte Carlo, the Cadillac, Caribbean and the Balmoral, the Lucerne, Hilton Plaza, Doral Beach, the Sorrento, Marco Polo, Casablanca, and Atlantis, the Hilyard Manor, Sans Souci, Algiers, Carillon, Seville, the Gaylord, the Shore Club, the Nautilus, Montmartre, and the Promenade, the Bal Harbour on North Bay Causeway, and the Twelve Caesars, the Regency and the Americana, the Diplomat, Versailles, Corona-do, Sovereign, the Waldman (dig!), the Beau Rivage, the Crown Hotel, even Holiday Inn, all oases for technological man. Deep air conditioning down to 68°, ice-palaces to chill the fevered brain—when the air conditioning worked. And their furnishings were monumentally materialistic. Not all of them: the cheaper downtown hotels like the Di Lido and the Nautilus were bare and mean with vinyl coverings on the sofas and the glare of plastic off the rugs and tables and tiles, inexpensive hotel colors of pale brown and buff and dingy cream, sodden gray, but the diadems like the Fontaine-bleau and the Eden Roc, the Doral Beach, the Hilton Plaza (Headquarters for Nixon), the Deauville (Hq for Reagan) or the Americana—Rockefeller and the New York State delegation's own ground—were lavish with interlockings, curves, vaults and runs of furnishings as intertwined as serpents in the roots of a mangrove tree. All the rivers of the very worst taste twisted down to the delta of each lobby in each grand Miami Beach hotel—rare was the cen-tral room which did not look like the lobby of a movie palace, imi-tation of late-Renaissance imitations of Greek and Roman statues, imitations of baroque and rococo and brothel Victorian and Art Nouveau and Bauhaus with gold grapes and cornucopias welded to the modern bronze tubing of the chair, golden moldings which ran like ivy from room to room, chandeliers complex as the armature of dynamos, and curvilinear steps in the shape of amoebas and pal-ettes, cocktail lounge bars in deep rose or maroon with spun-sugar white tubes of plaster decor to twist around the ceiling. There was every color of iridescence, rainbows of vulgarity, aureoles of gorgeous taste, opium den of a middle-class dollar, materialistic as meat, sweat, and the cigar. It is said that people born under Taurus and Capricorn are the most materialistic of us all. Take a sample of the residents in the census of Miami B. — does Taurus predominate more than one-twelfth of its share? It must, or astrology is done, for the Republicans, Grand Old Party with a philosophy rather than a program, had chosen what must certainly be the materialistic capital of the world for their convention. Las Vegas might offer competition, but Las Vegas was materialism in the service of electricity — fortunes could be lost in the spark of the dice. Miami was materialism baking in the sun, then stepping back to air-conditioned caverns where ice could nestle in the fur. It was the first of a hundred curiosities — that in a year when the Republic hovered on the edge of revolution, nihilism, and lines of police on file to the horizon, visions of future Vietnams in our own cities upon us, the party of conservatism and principle, of corporate wealth and personal frugality, the party of cleanliness, hygiene, and balanced budget, should have set itself down on a sultan's strip.

That was the first of a hundred curiosities, but there were mysteries as well. The reporter has moved through the convention quietly, as anonymously as possible, wan, depressed, troubled. Something profoundly unclassifiable was going on among the Republicans and he did not know if it was conceivably good or a concealment of something bad — which was the first time a major social phenomenon like a convention had confused him so. He had covered others. The Democratic Convention in 1960 in Los Angeles which nominated John F. Kennedy, and the Republican in San Francisco in 1964 which installed Barry Goldwater, had encouraged some of his very best writing. He had felt a gift for comprehending those conventions. But the Republican assembly in Miami Beach in 1968 was a different affair — one could not tell if nothing much was going on, or to the contrary, nothing much was going on near the surface but everything was shifting down below. So dialogue with other journalists merely depressed him — the complaints were unanimous that this was the dullest convention anyone could remember. Complaints took his mind away from the slow brooding infusion he desired in the enigmas of conservatism and/or Republicanism, and any hope of perspective on the problem beyond. The country was in a throe, a species of eschatological heave. The novelist John Updike was not necessarily one of his favorite authors, but after the assassination of Robert F. Kennedy, it was Updike who had made the remark that God might have withdrawn His blessing from America. It was a thought which could not be forgotten for it gave insight to the perspectives of the Devil and his political pincers: Left-wing demons, white and Black, working to inflame the conservative heart of America, while Right-wing devils exacerbated Blacks and drove the mind of the New Left and liberal middle class into prides of hopeless position. And the country roaring like a bull in its wounds, coughing like a sick lung in the smog, turning over in sleep at the sound of motorcycles, shivering at its need for new phalanxes of order. Where were the new phalanxes one could trust? The reporter had seen the faces of too many police to balm his dreams with the sleep they promised. Even the drinks tasted bad in Miami in the fever and the chill.

CHAPTER 3

Unless one knows him well, or has done a sizable work of preparation, it is next to useless to interview a politician. He has a mind which is accustomed to political questions. By the time he decides to run for President, he may have answered a million. Or at least this is true if he has been in politics for twenty years and has replied to an average of one hundred-fifty such queries a day, no uncharacteristic amount. To surprise a skillful politician with a question is then approximately equal in difficulty to hitting a professional boxer with a barroom hook. One cannot therefore tell a great deal from interviews with a candidate. His teeth are bound to be white, his manner mild and pleasant, his presence attractive, and his ability to slide off the question and return with an answer is as implicit in the work of his jaws as the ability to bite a piece of meat. Interviewing a candidate is about as intimate as catching him on television. Therefore it is sometimes easier to pick up the truth of his campaign by studying the outriggers of his activity. Therefore the reporter went to cover the elephant.

It was, as expected, a modest story in a quiet corner of International Airport in Miami. Not more than ten reporters and a dozen photographers showed up. And a band, and a quorum of Nixonettes wearing blue dresses and white straw hats with a legend "NIXON'S THE ONE." A publicity puff was handed around which informed the Press that the beast was named Ana (for Anaheim, California) and was 52" high, 2½ years old, weighed 1,266 lbs. and had been given to Nixon by the happy citizens of the town—Ana!

Ana came in on a Lockheed 100, a hippo of a four-motor plane with four-bladed propellers. The cargo door was in the rear, and as the musicians, Don Goldie and his Dixieland Band, white musicians from the Hilton-Miami—accordion, tuba, trombone, snares, clarinet, banjo, and trumpet—began to play, and the six Nixonettes began to strut (they looked to be high school juniors) and the plane to unload, so the black cloud on the horizon moved over, and began its drop, black tropical rain so intense even photographers had to take shelter, and a dozen, then another dozen of musicians, Nixonettes, cameramen, photographers, and animal handlers piled into a small 6 × 8 Hertz trailer later to be used for the elephant. In the steam of the interior, the day took on surreal and elegant proportions—two dozen amateurs and professionals on call for one baby elephant (said to be arriving in her tutu) were equal across the board to the logic of one political convention; by the time the rain stopped five minutes later and the elephant crate was unloaded, hoisted on a fork lift off the carrier, brought near the trailer and opened, everyone gave a cheer to Ana who came out nervously from her crate, but with a definite sense of style. She took a quick look at the still photographers surrounding her, and the larger movie cameras to which certain humans were obviously connected, stepped on the still-wet steaming runway, threw a droll red-eye at her handler, dropped a small turd to X the spot of her liberation from the crate (and as a marker in case she wanted later to retrace her steps) then did a good Republican handstand, trunk curved as graciously as a pinkie off a teacup. To which the media corps responded with approval, Nixonettes squealing, Don Goldie Band playing Dixieland, still cameras clicking, movie cameras ticking within the gears of their clockwork, Dade County police grinning as they stood to one side (four men—all armed). Then Ana from Anaheim walked on her hind legs. To much approval. She curtsied, bowed, turned in a circle, obviously pleased with herself, then stretched out her trunk in the general area of everybody's midsection. "Hey, chum, watch your peanuts," a man called out.

It went on for a period, the Nixonettes having their pictures taken, one girl who was not a high school junior but most likely a professional model taking care to see she was in the picture often, and all the girls kept trying to put a straw Nixon hat on Ana, but the hat kept falling off. After ten minutes, the handlers tried to coax Ana into the Hertz trailer, but she was not about to, not yet, so they walked her around a hangar, brought her back, then slipped her 1200-lb. bulk into the box with a bit of elephant handler's legerdemain. The arrival was over.

It had been pleasant; in truth, more pleasant than the reporter had expected. It had not been tense, not even with the four armed cops. The air had been better than one might have thought. So it was a warning to one's perspective and proportion: the Nixon forces and the Nixon people were going to be in command of small subtleties he had not anticipated. It was his first clue to the notion that there was a new Nixon. He could have read a dozen articles which said the same thing and paid no mind, for the men who wrote them were experts and so were wrong in their predictions as often as they were right. Experts he would disregard — so far as he was able — but Ana had been happy doing her handstand: that was an unexpected fact he would have to absorb into the first freshets of his brooding. Of course the reporter had once decided (using similar methods) that Barry Goldwater could win the 1964 election. This, at least, was the method at its extreme. Still, a happy elephant spoke of luck for Nixon, or at the least, agreeable management down the line.

CHAPTER 7

That evening at the Fountainebleau, on the night before the convention was to begin, the Republicans had their Grand Gala, no Press admitted, and the reporter by a piece of luck was nearly the first to get in. The affair was well-policed, in fact strict in its security, for some of the most important Republican notables would be there, but strolling through the large crowd in the lobby the reporter discovered himself by accident in the immediate wake of Governor Reagan's passage along a channel of security officers through the mob to the doors of the Gala. It was assumed by the people who gave way to the Governor that the reporter must be one of the plainclothesmen assigned to His Excellency's rear, and with a frown here, judicious tightening of his mouth there, look of concern for the Governor's welfare squeezed onto his map, offering a security officer's look superior to the absence of any ticket, he went right in through the ticket-takers, having found time in that passage to observe Governor Reagan and his Lady, who were formally dressed to the hilt of the occasion, now smiling, now shaking hands, eager, tense, bird-like, genial, not quite habituated to eminence, seeking to make brisk but not rude progress through the crowd, and obviously uneasy in the crowd (like most political figures) since a night in June in Los Angeles. It was an expected observation, but Mr. and Mrs. Reagan looked very much like an actor and actress playing Governor and Wife. Still Reagan held himself sort of uneasily about the middle, as if his solar plexus were fragile, and a clout would leave him like a fish on the floor.

Once inside the ballroom, however, the reporter discovered that the Governor had been among the first guests to enter. His own position was therefore not comfortable. Since there were no other guests among whom to mix (nothing but two hundred and forty empty tables with settings for two thousand people, all still to come in) and no cover to conceal him but small potted trees with oranges attached by green wire, since Security might be furious to the point of cop-mania catching him thus early, there was no choice but to take up a stand twenty feet from the door, his legs at parade rest, his arms clasped behind, while he scrutinized the entrance of everybody who came in. Any security officer studying him might therefore be forced to conclude that he belonged to *other* Security. Suffice it, he was not approached in his position near the entrance, and for the next thirty minutes looked at some thousand Republicans coming through the gate, the other thousand entering out of view by an adjacent door.

It was not a crowd totally representative of the power of the Republican Party. Some poor delegates may have been there as guests, and a few other delegates might have chosen to give their annual contribution of $1,000 for husband and wife here ($500 a plate) rather than to some other evening of fund raising for the party, indeed an air of sobriety and quiet dress was on many of the Republicans who entered. There were women who looked like librarians and schoolteachers, there were middle-aged men who looked like they might be out for their one night of the year. The Eastern Establishment was of course present in degree, and powers from the South, West, Midwest, but it was not a gang one could hold up in comparative glitter to an opening at the Met. No, rather, it was modesty which hung over these well-bred subscribers to the Gala.

Still, exceptions noted, they were obviously in large part composed of a thousand of the wealthiest Republicans in the land, the corporate and social power of America was here in legions of interconnection he could not even begin to trace. Of necessity, a measure of his own ignorance came over him, for among those thousand, except for candidates, politicians and faces in the news, there were not ten people he recognized. Yet here they were, the economic power of America (so far as economic power was still private, not public) the family power (so far as position in society was still a passion to average and ambitious Americans) the military power (to the extent that important sword-rattlers and/or patriots were among the company, as well as cadres of corporations not unmarried to the Pentagon) yes, even the spiritual power of America (just so far as Puritanism, Calvinism, conservatism and golf still gave the Wasp an American faith more intense than the faith of cosmopolitans, one-worlders, trade-unionists, Black militants, New Leftists, acid-heads, tribunes of the gay, families of Mafia, political machinists, fixers, swingers, Democratic lobbyists, members of the Grange, and government workers, not to include the *Weltanschauung* of every partisan in every minority group). No, so far as there was an American faith, a belief, a mystique that America was more than the sum of its constituencies, its trillions of dollars and billions of acres, its constellation of factories, empyrean of communications, mountain transcendant of finance, and heroic of sport, transports of medicine, hygiene, and church, so long as belief persisted that America, finally more than all this, was the world's ultimate reserve of rectitude, final garden of the Lord, so far as this mystique could survive in every American family of Christian substance, so then were the people entering this Gala willy-nilly the leaders of this faith, never articulated by any of them except in the most absurd and taste-curdling jargons of patriotism mixed with religion, but the faith existed in those crossroads between the psyche and the heart where love, hate, the cognition of grace, the all but lost sense of the root, and adoration of America congregate for some.

Their own value was in this faith, the workings of their seed from one generation into the next, their link to the sense of what might be life-force was in the faith. Yes, primitive life was there, and ancestral life, health concealed in their own flesh from towns occupied and once well-settled, from farms which prospered, and frontiers they had — through ancestors — dared to pass. They believed in America as they believed in God — they could not really ever expect that America might collapse and God yet survive, no, they had even gone so far as to think that America was the savior of the world, food and medicine by one hand, sword in the other, highest of high faith in a nation which would bow the knee before no problem since God's own strength was in the die. It was a faith which had flared so high in San Francisco in 1964 that staid old Republicans had come near to frothing while they danced in the aisle, there to nominate Barry, there to nominate Barry. But their hero had gone down to a catastrophe of defeat, blind in politics, impolite in tactics, a sorehead, a fool, a disaster. And if his policies had prevailed to some degree, to the degree of escalating the war in Vietnam, so had that policy depressed some part of America's optimism to the bottom of the decade, for the country had learned an almost unendurable lesson — its history in Asia was next to done, and there was not any real desire to hold armies on that land; worse, the country had begun to wear away inside, and the specter of Vietnam in every American city would haunt the suburb, the terror of a dollar cut loose from every standard of economic anchor was in the news, and some of the best of the youth were mad demented dogs with teeth in the flesh of the deepest Republican faith.

They were a chastened collocation these days. The high fire of hard Republican faith was more modest now, the vision of America had diminished. The claims on Empire had met limits. But it was nonetheless uncommon, yes bizarre, for the reporter to stand like an agent of their security as these leaders of the last American faith came through to the Gala, for, repeat: they were in the main not impressive, no, not by the hard eye of New York. Most of them were ill-proportioned in some part of their physique. Half must have been, of course, men and women over fifty and their bodies reflected the pull of their character. The dowager's hump was common, and many a man had a flaccid paunch, but the collective tension was rather in the shoulders, in the girdling of the shoulders against anticipated lashings on the back, in the thrust forward of the neck, in the maintenance of the muscles of the mouth forever locked in readiness to bite the tough meat of resistance, in a posture forward from the hip since the small of the back was dependably stiff, loins and mind cut away from each other by some abyss between navel and hip.

More than half of the men wore eyeglasses, young with old — the reporter made his count, close as a professional basketball game, and gave up by the time his score was up to Glasses 87, No Glasses 83. You could not picture a Gala Republican who was not clean-shaven by eight A.M. Coming to power, they could only conceive of trying to clean up every situation in sight. And so many of the women seemed victims of the higher hygiene. Even a large part of the young seemed to have faces whose cheeks had been injected with Novocain.

Yet he felt himself unaccountably filled with a mild sorrow. He did not detest these people, he did not feel so superior as to pity them, it was rather he felt a sad sorrowful respect. In their immaculate cleanliness, in the somewhat antiseptic odors of their astringent toilet water and perfume, in the abnegation of their walks, in the heavy sturdy moves so many demonstrated of bodies in life's harness, there was the muted tragedy of the Wasp — they were not on earth to enjoy or even perhaps to love so very much, they were here to serve, and serve they had in public functions and public charities (while recipients of their charity might vomit in rage and laugh in scorn), served on opera committees, and served in long hours of duty at the piano, served as the sentinel in concert halls and the pews on the aisle in church, at the desk in schools, had served for culture, served for finance, served for salvation, served for America—and so much of America did not wish them to serve any longer, and so many of them doubted themselves, doubted that the force of their faith could illumine their path in these new modern horror-head times. On and on, they came through the door, the clean, the well-bred, the extraordinarily prosperous, and for the most astonishing part, the almost entirely proper. Yes, in San Francisco in '64 they had been able to be insane for a little while, but now they were subdued, now they were modest, now they were looking for a leader to bring America back to them, their lost America, Jesusland.

"Nelson Rockefeller is out of his mind if he thinks he can take the nomination away from Richard Nixon," the reporter said suddenly to himself. It was the first certitude the convention had given.

CHAPTER 10

The room filled slowly. By the time Nixon began, it was apparent that 500 seats had been an excessive estimate. Perhaps half of them were filled, certainly no more than two-thirds. It was nonetheless a large press conference. Nixon came in wearing a quiet blue-gray suit, white shirt, black and blue close-figured tie, black shoes, and no handkerchief for the breast pocket. He stepped up on the dais diffidently, not certain whether applause would be coming or not. There was none. He stood there, looked quietly and warily at the audience, and then said that he was ready for questions.

This would be his sole press conference before the nomination. He was of course famous for his lack of sparkling good relation with the Press, he had in fact kept his publicity to a functional minimum these past few months. The work of collecting delegates had been done over the last four years, particularly over the last two. Their allegiance had been confirmed the last six months in his primary victories. He had no longer anything much to gain from good interviews, not at least until his nomination was secured; he had everything to lose from a bad interview. A delegate who was slipping could slide further because of an ill-chosen remark.

To the extent that the Press was not Republican, and certainly more than half, privately, were not, he would have few friends and more than a few determined enemies. Even among the Republicans he could expect a better share of the Press to go to Rockefeller. Even worse, for the mood of this conference, he did not, in comparison with other political candidates, have many reporters who were his personal friends. He was not reputed to smoke or drink so he did not have drinking buddies as Johnson once had, and Goldwater, and Bill Miller, and Humphrey; no brothel legends attached to him, and no outsize admiration to accompany them; no, the Press was a necessary tool to him, a tool he had been obliged to employ for more than twenty years but he could not pretend to be comfortable in his use of the tool, and the tool (since it was composed of men) resented its employment.

Probably Nixon had agreed to this conference only to avoid the excess of bad feeling which no meeting with the Press would be likely to cause. Still, this was an operation where his best hope was to minimize the loss. So he had taken the wise step of scheduling the conference at 8:15 in the morning, a time when his worst enemies, presumably the heavy drinkers, free lovers, and free spenders on the Reagan Right and Far Left of the press corps, would probably be asleep in bed or here asleep on their feet.

Nonetheless his posture on the stage, hands to his side or clasped before him, gave him the attentive guarded look of an old ball player—like Rabbit Maranville, let us say, or even an old con up before Parole Board. There was something in his carefully shaven face—the dark jowls already showing the first overtones of thin gloomy blue at this early hour—some worry which gave promise of never leaving him, some hint of inner debate about his value before eternity which spoke of precisely the sort of improvement that comes upon a man when he shifts in appearance from looking like an undertaker's assistant to looking like an old con seriously determined to go respectable. The Old Nixon, which is to say the young Nixon, used to look, on clasping his hands in front of him, like a church usher (of the variety who would twist a boy's ear after removing him from church). The older Nixon before the Press now— the *new* Nixon—had finally acquired some of the dignity of the old athlete and the old con—he had taken punishment, that was on his face now, he knew the detailed schedule of pain in a real loss, there was an attentiveness in his eyes which gave offer of some knowledge of the abyss, even the kind of gentleness which ex-drunkards attain after years in AA. As he answered questions, fielding them with the sure modest moves of an old shortstop who hits few homers but supports the team on his fielding (what sorrow in the faces of such middle-aged shortstops!) so now his modesty was not without real dignity. Where in Eisenhower days his attempts at modesty had been as offensive as a rich boy's arrogance, for he had been so transparently contemptuous of the ability of his audience to *witness* him, now the modesty was the product of a man who, at worst, had grown from a bad actor to a surprisingly good actor, or from an unpleasant self-made man—outrageously rewarded with luck—to a man who had risen and fallen and been able to rise again, and so conceivably had learned something about patience and the compassion of others.

When the reporter was younger, he might have said, "Nixon did not rise again; they raised him; if a new Nixon did not exist, they would have had to invent him." But the reporter was older now — presumably he knew more about the limits of the ruling class for inventing what they needed; he had learned how little talent or patience they had. Yes, at a certain point they might have decided, some of them at any rate, to dress Richard Nixon for the part again, but no one but Nixon had been able to get himself up from the political deathbed to which his failure in California had consigned him. He was here, then, answering questions in a voice which was probably closer to his own than it had ever been.

And some of the answers were not so bad. Much was Old Nixon, extraordinarily adroit at working both sides of a question so that both halves of his audience might be afterward convinced he was one of them. ("While homosexuality is a perversion punishable by law, and an intolerable offense to a law-abiding community, it is life-giving to many of those who are in need of it," he might have said if ever he had addressed a combined meeting of the Policemen's Benevolent Association and the Mattachine Society.) So he worked into the problem of Vietnam by starting at A and also by starting at Z which he called a "two-pronged approach." He was for a negotiated settlement, he was for maintaining military strength because that would be the only way to "reach negotiated settlement of the war on an honorable basis." Later he was to talk of negotiations with "the next superpower, Communist China." He spoke patiently, with clarity, gently, not badly but for an unfortunate half-smile pasted to his face. The question would come, and he would back-hand it with his glove or trap it; like all politicians he had a considered answer for every question, but he gave structure to his answers, even a certain relish for their dialectical complexity. Where once he had pretended to think in sentimentalities and slogans, now he held the question up, worked over it, deployed it, amplified it, corrected its tendency, offered an aside (usually an attempt to be humorous) revealed its contradiction, and then declared a statement. With it all, a sensitivity almost palpable to the reservations of the Press about his character, his motive, and his good intention. He still had no natural touch with them, his half-smile while he listened was unhappy, for it had nowhere to go but into a full smile and his full smile was as false as false teeth, a pure exercise of will. You could all but see the signal pass from his brain to his jaw. "SMILE," said the signal, and so he flashed teeth in a painful kind of joyous grimace which spoke of some shrinkage in the liver, or the gut, which we would have to repair afterward by other medicine than good-fellowship. (By winning the Presidency, perhaps.) He had always had the ability to violate his own nature absolutely if that happened to be necessary to his will—there had never been anyone in American life so resolutely phony as Richard Nixon, nor anyone so transcendentally successful by such means—small wonder half the electorate had regarded him for years as equal to a disease. But he was less phony now, *that was the miracle*, he had moved from a position of total ambition and total alienation from his own person (at the time of Checkers, the dog speech) to a place now where he was halfway conciliated with his own self. As he spoke, he kept going in and out of focus, true one instant, phony the next, then quietly correcting the false step.

Question from the Press: *You emphasized the change in the country and abroad. Has this led you to change your thinking in any shape or form specifically?*

Answer: *It certainly has.* (But he was too eager. Old Nixon was always ready to please with good straight American boyhood enthusiasm. So he tacked back, his voice throttled down.) *As the facts change, any intelligent man* (firm but self-deprecatory, he is including the Press with himself) *does change his approaches to the problems.* (Now sharp awareness of the next Press attitude.) *It does not mean that he is an opportunist.* (Now modestly, reasonably.) *It means only that he is a pragmatist, a realist, applying principles to the new situations.* (Now he will deploy some of the resources of his answer.) *For example . . . in preparing the acceptance speech I hope to give next Thursday, I was reading over my acceptance speech in 1960, and I thought then it was, frankly, quite a good speech. But I realize how irrelevant much of what I said in 1960 in foreign affairs was to the problems of today.* (The admission was startling. The Old Nixon was never wrong. Now, he exploited the shift in a move to his political left, pure New Nixon.) *Then the Communist world was a monolithic world. Today it is a split world, schizophrenic, with . . . great diversity . . . in Eastern Europe* (a wholesome admission for anyone who had labored in John Foster Dulles' world.) *. . . after an era of confrontation . . . we now enter an era of negotiations with the Soviet Union.*

While he was never in trouble with the questions, growing surer and surer of himself as he went on, the tension still persisted between his actual presence as a man not altogether alien to the abyss of a real problem, and the political practitioner of his youth, that snake-oil salesman who was never back of any idea he sold, but always off to the side where he might observe its effect on the sucker. The New Nixon groped and searched for the common touch he had once been able to slip into the old folks with the ease of an incubus on a spinster. Now he tried to use slang, put quotes around it with a touching, almost pathetic, reminder of Nice-Nellyism, the inhibition of the good clean church upbringing of his youth insisting on exhibiting itself, as if he were saying with a YMCA slick snicker, "After we break into slang, there's always the danger of the party getting *rough*." It was that fatal prissiness which must have driven him years ago into all the militaristic muscle-bending witch-hunting foam-rubber virilities of the young Senator and the young Vice President. So, now he talked self-consciously of how the members of his staff, counting delegates, were "playing what we call 'the strong game.' " SMILE said his brain. FLASH went the teeth. But his voice seemed to give away that, whatever they called it, they probably didn't call it "the strong game," or if they did, *he* didn't. So he framed little phrases. Like "a leg-up." Or "my intuition, my 'gut feelings,' so to speak." Deferential air followed by SMILE — FLASH. Was it possible that one of the secrets of Old Nixon was that his psyche had been trapped in rock-formations, nay, geological strata of Sunday school inhibitions? Was it even possible that he was a good man, not a bad man, a good man who had been trapped by an early milieu whose habits had left him with such innocence about three-quarters of the world's experience that he had become an absolute monster of opportunism about the quarter he comprehended all too well? Listening to Nixon now, studying his new modesty, it was impossible to tell whether he was a serious man on the path of returning to his own true seriousness, out to unite the nation again as he promised with every remark: "Reconciliation of the races is a primary objective of the United States," or whether the young devil had reconstituted himself into a more consummate devil, Old Scratch as a modern Abe Lincoln of Modesty.

Question from the Press: *A little less than six years ago, after your defeat for the Governorship of California, you announced at the ensuing press conference that that was going to be your last news conference. Could you recall for us this morning two or three of the most important points in your own thinking which made you reverse that statement and now reach for political office on the highest level?*

Answer: *Had there not been the division of the Republican Party in 1964 and had there not been the vacuum of leadership that was created by that division and by that defeat, I would not be here today. . . . I believe that my travels around the country and the world in this period of contemplation and this period of withdrawal from the political scene* (some dark light of happiness now in his eye, as if withdrawal and contemplation had given him the first deep pleasures, or perhaps the first real religious pleasures of his life) *in which I have had a chance to observe not only the United States but the world, has led me to the conclusion that returning to the arena was something that I should do* (said almost as if he had heard a voice in some visitation of the night)—*not that I consider myself to be an indispensable man.* (Said agreeably in a relaxed tone as if he had thought indeed to the bottom of this and had found the relaxation of knowing he was not indispensable, an absurd vanity if one stares at Nixon from without, but he had been Vice President before he was forty, and so had had to see himself early, perhaps much too early, as a man of destiny. Now, reservation underlined, he could continue.) *But something that I should do* (go for the Presidency) *because this is the time I think when the man and the moment in history come together.* (An extraordinary admission for a Republican, with their Protestant detestation of philosophical deeps or any personification of history. With one remark, Nixon had walked into the oceans of Marx, Spengler, Heidegger, and Tolstoy; and Dostoevski and Kierkegaard were in the wings. Yes, Richard Nixon's mind had entered the torture chambers of the modern consciousness!)

I have always felt that a man cannot seek the Presidency and get it simply because he wants it. I think that he can seek the Presidency and obtain it only when the Presidency requires what he may have to offer (the Presidency was then a mystical seat, mystical as the choice of a woman's womb) *and I have had the feeling* (comfortably pleasant and modest again—no phony Nixon here) *and it may be a presumptuous feeling, that because of the vacuum of leadership in the Republican Party, because of the need for leadership particularly qualified in foreign affairs, because I have known not only the country, but the world as a result of my travels, that now time* (historical-time—the very beast of the mystic!) *requires that I reenter the arena.* (Then he brought out some humor. It was not great humor, but for Nixon it was curious and not indelicate.) *And incidentally, I have been very willing to do so.* (Re-enter the arena.) *I am not being drafted. I want to make that very clear. I am very willing to do so. There has never been a draft in Miami in August anyway.* (Nice laughter from the Press—he has won them by a degree. Now he is on to finish the point.) . . . *I believe that if my judgment —and my intuition, my "gut feelings" so to speak, about America and American political tradition—is right, this is the year that I will win.*

The speech had come in the middle of the conference and he kept fielding questions afterward, never wholly at ease, never caught in trouble, mild, firm, reasonable, highly disciplined — it was possible he was one of the most disciplined men in America. After it was over, he walked down the aisle, and interviewers gathered around him, although not in great number. The reporter stood within two feet of Nixon at one point but had not really a question to ask which could be answered abruptly. "What, sir, would you say is the state of your familiarity with the works of Edmund Burke?" No, it was more to get a sense of the candidates presence, and it was a modest presence, no more formidable before the immediate Press in its physical aura than a floorwalker in a department store, which is what Old Nixon had often been called, or worse — Assistant Mortician. It was probable that bodies did not appeal to him in inordinate measure, and a sense of the shyness of the man also appeared — shy after all these years! — but Nixon must have been habituated to loneliness after all those agonies in the circus skin of Tricky Dick. Had he really improved? The reporter caught himself hoping that Nixon had. If his physical presence inspired here no great joy nor even distrust, it gave the sense of a man still entrenched in toils of isolation, as if only the office of the Presidency could be equal (in the specific density of its importance) to the labyrinthine delivery of the natural man to himself. Then and only then might he know the strength of his own hand and his own moral desire. It might even be a measure of the not-entirely dead promise of America if a man as opportunistic as the early Nixon could grow in reach and comprehension and stature to become a leader. For, if that were possible in these bad years, then all was still possible, and the country not stripped of its blessing. New and marvelously complex improvement of a devil, or angel-in-chrysalis, or both — good and evil now at war in the man, Nixon was at least, beneath the near to hermetic boredom of his old presence, the most interesting figure at the convention, or at least so the reporter had decided by the end of the press conference that Tuesday in the morning. Complexities upon this vision were to follow.

Chicago, August 24 – 29

CHAPTER 1

Chicago is the great American city. New York is one of the capitals of the world and Los Angeles is a constellation of plastic, San Francisco is a lady, Boston has become Urban Renewal, Philadelphia and Baltimore and Washington wink like dull diamonds in the smog of Eastern Megalopolis, and New Orleans is unremarkable past the French Quarter. Detroit is a one-trade town, Pittsburgh has lost its golden triangle, St. Louis has become the golden arch of the corporation, and nights in Kansas City close early. The oil depletion allowance makes Houston and Dallas naught but checkerboards for this sort of game. But Chicago is a great American city. Perhaps it is the last of the great American cities.

The reporter was sentimental about the town. Since he had grown up in Brooklyn, it took him no time to recognize, whenever he was in Chicago again, that the urbanites here were like the good people of Brooklyn – they were simple, strong, warm-spirited, sly, rough, compassionate, jostling, tricky and extraordinarily good-natured because they had sex in their pockets, muscles on their back, hot eats around the corner, neighborhoods which dripped with the sauce of local legend, and real city architecture, brownstones with different windows on every floor, vistas for miles of red-brick and two-family wood-frame houses with balconies and porches, runty stunted trees rich as farmland in their promise of tenderness the first city evenings of spring, streets where kids played stick-ball and roller-hockey, lots of smoke and iron twilight. The clangor of the late nineteenth century, the very hope of greed, was in these streets. London one hundred years ago could not have looked much better.

Brooklyn, however, beautiful Brooklyn, grew beneath the skyscrapers of Manhattan, so it never became a great city, merely an asphalt herbarium for talent destined to cross the river. Chicago did not have Manhattan to pre-empt top branches, so it grew up from the savory of its neighborhoods to some of the best high-rise architecture in the world, and because its people were Poles and Ukrainians and Czechs as well as Irish and the rest, the city had Byzantine corners worthy of Prague or Moscow, odd tortured attractive drawbridges over the Chicago River, huge Gothic spires like the skyscraper which held the Chicago *Tribune*, curves and abutments and balconies in cylindrical structures thirty stories high twisting in and out of the curves of the river, and fine balustrades in its parks. Chicago had a North Side on Lake Shore Drive where the most elegant apartment buildings in the world could be found — Sutton Place in New York betrayed the cost analyst in the eye of the architect next to these palaces of glass and charcoal colored steel. In superb back streets behind the towers on the lake were brownstones which spoke of ironies, cupidities and intricate ambition in the fists of the robber barons who commissioned them — substantiality, hard work, heavy drinking, carnal meats of pleasure, and a Midwestern sense of how to arrive at upper-class decorum were also in the American grandeur of these few streets. If there was a fine American aristocracy of deportment, it was probably in the clean tough keen-eyed ladies of Chicago one saw on the streets off Lake Shore Drive on the near North Side of Chicago.

Not here for a travelogue — no need then to detail the Loop, in death like the center of every other American city, but what a dying! Old department stores, old burlesque houses, avenues, dirty avenues, the El with its nineteenth-century dialogue of iron screeching against iron about a turn, and caverns of shadow on the pavement beneath, the grand hotels with their massive lobbies, baroque ceilings, resplendent as Roman bordellos, names like Sheraton-Blackstone, Palmer House, red fields of carpet, a golden cage for elevator, the unheard crash of giant mills stamping new shapes on large and obdurate materials is always pounding in one's inner ear — Dreiser had not written about Chicago for nothing.

To the West of the Lake were factories and Ciceros, Mafia-lands and immigrant lands; to the North, the suburbs, the Evanstons; to the South were Negro ghettos of the South Side — belts of Black men amplifying each the resonance of the other's cause — the Black belt had the Blackstone Rangers, the largest gang of juvenile delinquents on earth, 2,000 by some count — one could be certain the gang had leaders as large in potential as Hannibal or Attila the Hun — how else account for the strength and wit of a stud who would try to rise so high in the Blackstone Rangers?

Further South and West were enclaves for the University of Chicago, more factories, more neighborhoods for Poles, some measure of more good hotels on the lake, and endless neighborhoods — white neighborhoods which went for miles of ubiquitous dingy wood houses with back yards, neighborhoods to hint of Eastern Europe, Ireland, Tennessee, a gathering of all the clans of the Midwest, the Indians and Scotch-Irish, Swedes, some Germans, Italians, Hungarians, Rumanians, Finns, Slovaks, Slovenes — it was only the French who did not travel. In the Midwest, land spread out; not five miles from the Loop were areas as empty, deserted, enormous and mournful by night as the outer freight yards of Omaha. Some industrial desert or marsh would lie low on the horizon, an area squalling by day, deserted by night, except for the hulking Midwestern names of the boxcars and the low sheds, the warehouse buildings, the wire fences which went along the side of unpaved roads for thousands of yards.

The stockyards were like this, the famous stockyards of Chicago were at night as empty as the railroad sidings of the moon. Long before the Democratic Convention of 1968 came to the Chicago Amphitheatre, indeed eighteen years ago when the reporter had paid his only previous visit, the area was even then deserted at night, empty as the mudholes on a battlefield after a war has passed. West of the Amphitheatre, railroad sidings seemed to continue on for miles, accompanied by those same massive low sheds larger than armories, with pens for tens of thousands of frantic beasts, cattle, sheep, and pigs, animals in an orgy of gorging and dropping and waiting and smelling blood. In the slaughterhouses, during the day, a carnage worthy of the Disasters of War took place each morning and afternoon. Endless files of animals were led through pens to be stunned on the head by hammers, and then hind legs trussed, be hoisted up on hooks to hang head down, and ride along head down on an overhead trolley which brought them to Negroes or whites, usually huge, the whites most often Polish or Hunkies (hence the etymology of Honkie—a Chicago word) the Negroes up from the South, huge men built for the shock of the work, slash of a knife on the neck of the beast and gouts of blood to bathe their torso (stripped of necessity to the waist) and blood to splash their legs. The animals passed a psychic current back along the overhead trolley—each cut throat released its scream of death into the throat not yet cut and just behind, and that penultimate throat would push the voltage up, drive the current back and further back into the screams of every animal upside down and hanging from that clanking overhead trolley, bare electric bulbs screaming into the animal eye and brain, gurglings and awesome hollows of sound coming back from the open plumbing ahead of the cut jugular as if death were indeed a rapids along some underground river, and the fear and absolute anguish of beasts dying upside down further ahead passed back along the line, back all the way to the corrals and the pens, back even to the siding with the animals still in boxcars, back, who knew—so high might be the psychic voltage of the beast—back to the farm where first they were pushed into the truck which would take them into the train. What an awful odor the fear of absolute and unavoidable death gave to the stool and stuffing and pure vomitous shit of the beasts waiting in the pens in the stockyard, what a sweat of hell-leather, and yet the odor, no, the titanic stench, which rose from the yards was not so simple as the collective diarrhetics of an hysterical army of beasts, no, for after the throats were cut and the blood ran in rich gutters, red light on the sweating back of the red throat-cutters, the dying and some just-dead animals clanked along the overhead, arterial blood spurting like the nip-ups of a little boy urinating in public, the red-hot carcass quickly encountered another Black or Hunkie with a long knife on a long stick who would cut the belly from chest to groin and a stew and a stink of two hundred pounds of stomach, lungs, intestines, mucosities, spleen, exploded cowflop and pigshit, blood, silver lining, liver, mother-of-pearl tissue, and general gag-all would flop and slither over the floor, the man with the knife getting a good blood-splatting as he dug and twisted with his blade to liberate the roots of the organ, intestine and impedimenta still integrated into the meat and bone of the excavated existence he was working on.

Well, the smell of the entrails and that agonized blood electrified by all the outer neons of ultimate fear got right into the grit of the stockyard stench. Let us pass over into the carving and the slicing, the boiling and scraping, annealing and curing of the flesh in sugars and honeys and smoke, the cooking of the cow carcass, stamp of the inspector, singeing of the hair, boiling of hooves, grinding of gristle, the waxpapering and the packaging, the foiling and the canning, the burning of the residue, and the last slobber of the last unusable guts as it went into the stockyard furnace, and up as stockyard smoke, burnt blood and burnt bone and burnt hair to add their properties of specific stench to fresh blood, fresh entrails, fresh fecalities already all over the air. It is the smell of the stockyards, all of it taken together, a smell so bad one must go down to visit the killing of the animals or never eat meat again. Watching the animals be slaughtered, one knows the human case — no matter how close to angel we may come, the butcher is equally there. So be it. Chicago makes for hard minds. On any given night, the smell may go anywhere — down to Gary to fight with the smog and the coke, out to Cicero to quiet the gangs with their dreams of gung ho and mop-up, North to Evanston to remind the polite that *inter faeces et urinam* are we born, and East on out to Lake Michigan where the super felicities in the stench of such earth-bound miseries and corruptions might cheer the fish with the clean spermy deep waters of their fate.

Yes, Chicago was a town where nobody could ever forget how the money was made. It was picked up from floors still slippery with blood, and if one did not protest and take a vow of vegetables, one knew at least that life was hard, life was in the flesh and in the massacre of the flesh—one breathed the last agonies of beasts. So something of the entrails and the secrets of the gut got into the faces of native Chicagoans. A great city, a strong city with faces tough as leather hide and pavement, it was also a city where the faces took on the broad beastiness of ears which were dull enough to ignore the bleatings of the doomed, noses battered enough to smell no more the stench of every unhappy end, mouths—fat mouths or slit mouths—ready to taste the gravies which were the reward of every massacre, and eyes, simple pig eyes, which could look the pig truth in the face. In any other city, they would have found technologies to silence the beasts with needles, quarter them with machines, lull them with Muzak, and have stainless steel for floors, aluminum beds to take over the old overhead trolley—animals would be given a shot of vitamin-enrichment before they took the last ride. But in Chicago, they did it straight, they cut the animals right out of their hearts—which is why it was the last of the great American cities, and people had great faces, carnal as blood, greedy, direct, too impatient for hypocrisy, in love with honest plunder. They were big and human and their brother in heaven was the slaughtered pig—they did not ignore him. If the yowls and moans of his extinction was the broth of their strength, still they had honest guts to smell him to the end—they did not flush the city with Odorono or Pinex or No-Scent, they swilled the beer and assigned the hits and gave America its last chance at straight-out drama. Only a great city provides honest spectacle, for that is the salvation of the schizophrenic soul. Chicago may have beasts on the street, it may have a giant of fortitude for Mayor who grew into a beast—a man with the very face of Chicago—but it is an honest town, it does not look to incubate psychotics along an air-conditioned corridor with a vinyl floor.

CHAPTER 3

At this party, McCarthy looked weary beyond belief, his skin a used-up yellow, his tall body serving for no more than to keep his head up above the crowd at the cocktail party. Like feeder fish, smaller people were nibbling on his reluctant hulk with questions, idiotic questions, petulant inquiries he had heard a thousand times. "Why?" asked a young woman, college instructor, horn-rimmed glasses, "Why don't we get out of Vietnam?" her voice near hysterical, ringing with the harsh electronics of cancer gulch, and McCarthy looked near to flinching with the question and the liverish demand on him to answer. "Well," he said in his determinedly mild and quiet voice, last drop of humor never voided—for if on occasion he might be surrounded by dolts, volts, and empty circuits, then nothing to do but send remarks up to the angel of laughter. "Well," said Senator McCarthy, "there seem to be a few obstacles in the way."

But his pale green eyes had that look somewhere between humor and misery which the Creation might offer when faced with the bulldozers of boredom.

Years ago, in 1960, the reporter had had two glimpses of Eugene McCarthy. At the Democratic convention in Los Angeles which nominated John F. Kennedy, McCarthy had made a speech for another candidate. It was the best nominating speech the reporter had ever heard. He had written about it with the metaphor of a bullfight:

> '. . . he held the crowd like a matador . . . gathering their emotion, discharging it, creating new emotion on the wave of the last, driving his passes tighter and tighter as he readied for the kill. "Do not reject this man who made us all proud to be called Democrats, do not leave this prophet without honor in his own party." McCarthy went on, his muleta furled for the naturales. "There was only one man who said let's talk sense to the American people. He said, the promise of America is the promise of greatness. This was his call to greatness . . . Do not forget this man . . . Ladies and gentlemen, I present to you not the favorite son of one state, but the favorite son of the fifty states, the favorite son of every country he has visited, the favorite son of every country which has not seen him but is secretly thrilled by his name." Bedlam. The kill. "Ladies and gentlemen, I present to you Adlai Stevenson of Illinois." Ears and tail. Hooves and bull. A roar went up like the roar one heard the day Bobby Thomson hit his home run at the Polo Grounds and the Giants won the pennant from the Dodgers in the third playoff game of the 1951 season. The demonstration cascaded onto the floor, the gallery came to its feet, the sports arena sounded like the inside of a marching drum.'

Perhaps three months later, just after his piece on that convention had appeared, and election time was near, he had met Senator McCarthy at another cocktail party on Central Park West to raise money for the campaign of Mark Lane, then running for State Assemblyman in New York. The reporter had made a speech himself that day. Having decided, on the excitements of the Kennedy candidacy and other excitements (much marijuana for one) to run for Mayor of New York the following year, he gave his maiden address at that party, a curious, certainly a unique political speech, private, personal, tortured in metaphor, sublimely indifferent to issues, platform, or any recognizable paraphernalia of the political process, and delivered in much too rapid a voice to the assembled bewilderment of his audience, a collective (and by the end very numb) stiff clavicle of Jewish Central Park West matrons. The featured speaker, Senator McCarthy, was to follow, and climbing up on the makeshift dais as he stepped down, the Senator gave him a big genial wide-as-the-open-plains Midwestern grin.

"Better learn how to breathe, boy," he whispered out of the corner of his mouth, and proceeded to entertain the audience for the next few minutes with a mixture of urbanity, professional elegance, and political savvy. That was eight years ago.

But now, near to eight years later, the hour was different, the audience at this cocktail party in Cambridge with their interminable questions and advice, their over-familiarity yet excessive reverence, their desire to touch McCarthy, prod him, *galvanize* him, seemed to do no more than drive him deeper into the insulations of his fatigue, his very disenchantment—so his pores seemed to speak—with the democratic process. He was not a mixer. Or if he had ever been a mixer, as he must have been years ago, he had had too much of it since, certainly too much since primaries in New Hampshire, Wisconsin, Indiana, Oregon, and California—he had become, or he had always been, too private a man for the damnable political mechanics of mixing, fixing, shaking the hands, answering the same questions which had already answered themselves by being asked. And now the threat of assassination over all, that too, that his death might come like the turn of a card, and could a man be ready? The gloomy, empty tomb-like reverberations of the last shot shaking rough waves doubtless through his own dreams, for his eyes, sensitive, friendly, and remote as the yellow eyes of an upper primate in a cage, spoke out of the weary, sagging face, up above the sagging pouches, seeming to say, "Yes, try to rescue me—but as you see, it's not quite possible." And the reporter, looking to perform the errand of rescue, went in to talk about the speech of 1960 in Los Angeles, and how it was the second best political speech he had ever heard.

"Oh," said McCarthy, "tell me, what was the best?"

And another questioner jostled the circle about McCarthy to ask another question, the Secret Service man in the gray suit at McCarthy's elbow stiffening at the impact. But McCarthy held the questioner at a distance by saying, "No, I'd like to listen for awhile." It had obviously become his pleasure to listen to others. So the reporter told a story about Vito Marcantonio making a speech in Yankee Stadium in 1948, and the Senator listened carefully, almost sadly, as if remembering other hours of oratory.

On the way out the door, in the press of guests and local party workers up to shake his hand before he was gone, a tall bearded fellow, massive chin, broad brow for broad horn-rimmed glasses, spoke out in a resonant voice marred only by the complacency of certain nasal intrigues. "Senator, I'm a graduate student in English, and I like your politics very much, but I must tell you, I think your poetry stinks."

McCarthy took it like a fighter being slapped by the referee across the forearms. "You see what it is, running for President," said the laughter in his eyes. If he worshipped at a shrine, it was near the saint of good humor.

"Give my regards to Robert Lowell," said the reporter. "Say to him that I read 'The Drunken Fisherman' just the other day."

McCarthy looked like the victim in the snow when the St. Bernard comes up with the rum. His eyes came alight at the name of the poem . . . "I will catch Christ with a greased worm," might have been the line he remembered. He gave a little wave, was out the door.

Yet the reporter was depressed after the meeting. McCarthy did not look nor feel like a President, not that tall tired man with his bright subtle eyes which could sharpen the razor's edge of a nuance, no, he seemed more like the dean of the finest English department in the land. There wasn't that sense of a man with vast ambition and sufficient character to make it luminous, so there was not that charisma which leaves no argument about the nature of the attempt.

CHAPTER 9

Later that day, early in the evening, McCarthy went into a meeting with Steve Smith, Teddy Kennedy's brother-in-law, and told him that he was willing to withdraw from the race if Kennedy would enter, and that he would instruct his delegates that they were free; further, he would suggest that they give their support to Kennedy.

Would there be anything he desired in return?

No, he was not asking for anything in victory or defeat. (McCarthy was obviously a fanatic—he was seeking to destroy politics-is-property.)

Smith thanked him, told him he would relay his message to Teddy Kennedy, made some comment on the munificence of the offer, perhaps thinking to himself that it came a little late, and left.

Perhaps two hours after this, the reporter encountered McCarthy by chance in a Chicago restaurant on the North Side.

The Senator, sitting at a long table in the corner of the main dining room, a modest room (for the restaurant was situated in a brownstone) had his back comfortably to the wall, and was chatting over the coffee with his guests. The atmosphere was sufficiently relaxed for the reporter and his friend, another reporter who had been doing a story on McCarthy for *Look*, to come up past the Secret Service without great strain and greet the Senator. Neither of the reporters was to know anything about the meeting with Steve Smith until some days later, but it was likely McCarthy had come to some decision—at the least, he was more relaxed than at any time the reporter had seen him in Chicago. Perhaps it was the friends he was with, big Irishmen like himself for the most part, a couple of them present with their wives, or at least such was the reporter's impression, for he was introduced to more than a half-dozen people in the aftermath of meeting the Senator and some were big genial Irishmen with horn-rimmed glasses and some were lean Irishmen with craggy faces, and one was an Irishman from Limerick with a Dublin face, one-third poet, one-third warrior, one-third clerk. Perhaps it was the company, but the reporter had never seen McCarthy in such a mood. The benign personality of the public meetings, agreeable but never compelling, was gone—the personality which suggested that serious activity had something absurd about it—gone. The manner which declared, "I'm a nice guy, and look what I got into"—gone!

Speaking with the license a man has when his dinner is interrupted, McCarthy struck back to the conversation twelve weeks earlier in a living room in Cambridge, "Still waiting for me to repeat that 1960 speech?"

"Well, Senator," said the reporter—he was trying to become sufficiently presumptuous to say, "if you could make a speech like that on the war in Vietnam tonight when the peace plank is debated . . ."

But McCarthy cut him off. "That was then. We don't retain all our abilities necessarily. Once the ability leaves you, how do you regain it?" It was impossible to tell if he was mocking the reporter or mocking himself. "I used to be angry then," he said across the table with an evil look of amusement, as if recording these remarks for posterity as well, his yellow eyes gleaming in the light, "but I can't seem to get angry again. It's a gift to get angry when you wish to get angry, Mailer."

"A grace I would say, sir."

If the table had been laughing at McCarthy's sallies, they chuckled now with his. The Senator's friends looked tough and were tough-minded, but they were obviously open to wit from any corner.

"Then you also want to ask yourself if you should get people angry." McCarthy went on in a voice of the hardest-tempered iro-ny. "Once you get them angry, you've got to get them quieted down. That's not so easy. Lyndon, for instance, has never under-stood the problem. He thinks politicians are cattle, whereas in fact most politicians are pigs. Now, Norman, there's a little difference between cattle and pigs which most people don't know. Lyndon doesn't know it. You see, to get cattle started, you make just a lit-tle noise, and then when they begin to run, you have to make more noise, and then you keep driving them with more and more noise. But pigs are different. You have to start pigs running with a great deal of noise, in fact the best way to start them is by reciting Latin, very loudly, that'll get them running — then you have to quiet your voice bit by bit and they'll keep moving. Lyndon has never under-stood this."

These gnomic remarks now concluded, the reporter had no idea precisely what the Senator was talking about. He had been expand-ing a metaphor, and images of the stockyards, the convention, the war on the streets, the expression on the face of Humphrey dele-gates and McCarthy delegates, and some tidal wave of contempt at the filthy polluted plumbing of things was in the remark. In the laughter which followed, the reporter was silent.

"It's a funny thing about pigs," McCarthy went on. "They have an odd way of keeping warm in winter if they find themselves out-side. You see, pigs don't know if they're cold, provided their nose is warm. So they stand around in a circle with their nose between the hind legs of the pig in front of them. Wouldn't you call that a curious relationship?"

"Oh, Senator, I would call that a Satanic relationship."

McCarthy joined in the laughter. Hard was his face, hard as the bones and scourged flesh of incorruptibility, hard as the cold stone floor of a monastery in the North Woods at five in the morning. The reporter leaned forward to talk into his ear.

"You see, sir," he said, "the tragedy of the whole business is that you should never have had to run for President. You would have been perfect for the Cabinet." A keen look back from Mc-Carthy's eye gave the sanction to continue. "Yessir," said the re-porter, "you'd have made a perfect chief for the F.B.I!" and they looked at each other and McCarthy smiled and said, "Of course, you're absolutely right."

The reporter looked across the table into one of the hardest, clean-est expressions he had ever seen, all the subtle hints of puffiness and doubt sometimes visible in the Senator's expression now gone, no, the face that looked back belonged to a tough man, tough as the harder alloys of steel, a merciless face and very just, the sort of black Irish face which could have belonged to one of the hanging judges in a true court of Heaven, or to the proper commissioner of a police force too honest ever to have existed.

The reporter left. But the memory of McCarthy at this table persisted. And the memory of his presence, harder than the hardest alloys of steel. But not unjust. What iron it must have taken to be annealed in Lyndon's volcanic breath. Yes, the reporter had met many candidates, but McCarthy was the first who felt like a President, or at least felt like a President in that hard hour after he had relinquished the very last of his hopes, and so was enjoying his dinner.

CHAPTER 11

A moment:

The following is a remark by Dino Valente, an electric guitarist. It ran as the headline in an advertisement in the *East Village Other* for an album of his records.

"You take this electrical power out of the wall and you send it through the guitar and you bend it and shape it and make it into something, like songs for people and that power is a wonderful thing."

Yes, the Yippies were the militant wing of the Hippies, Youth International Party, and the movement was built on juice, not alcoholic juice which comes out of the mystery of fermentation — why, dear God, as fruits and grains begin to rot, does some distillate of this art of the earth now in decomposition have the power to inflame consciousness and give us purchase on visions of Heaven and Hell? — no, rather, we are speaking of the juice which comes from another mystery, the passage of a metallic wire across a field of magnetism. That serves to birth the beast of all modern technology, electricity itself. The Hippies founded their temple in that junction where LSD crosses the throb of an electric guitar at full volume in the ear, solar plexus, belly, and loins. A tribal unity had passed through the youth of America (and half the nations of the world) a far-out vision of orgiastic revels stripped of violence or even the differentiation of sex. In the oceanic stew of a non-violent, tribal ball on drugs, nipples, arms, phalluses, mouths, wombs, armpits, short-hairs, navels, breasts and cheeks, incense of odor, flower and funk went humping into Breakthrough Freak-out Road together, and children on acid saw Valhalla, Nepenthe, and the Taj Mahal. Some went out forever, some went screaming down the alleys of the mad where cockroaches drive like Volkswagens on the oilcloth of the moon, gluttons found vertigo in centrifuges on consciousness, vomitoriums of ingestion; others found love, some manifest of love in light, in shards of Nirvana, sparks of satori — they came back to the world a twentieth-century tribe wearing celebration bells and filthy garments. Used-up livers gave their complexions a sickly pale, and hair grew on their faces like weeds. Yet they had seen some incontestable vision of the good — the universe was not absurd to them; like pilgrims they looked at society with the eyes of children: society was absurd. Every emperor who went down the path was naked, and they handed flowers to policemen.

It could hardly last. The slum in which they chose to live — for they were refugees in the main from the suburbs of the middle class — fretted against them, fretted against their filth, their easy casual cohabiting, their selflessness, which is always the greatest insult to the ghetto, for selflessness is a luxury to the poor, it beckons to the spineless, the undifferentiated, the inept, the derelict, the drowning — a poor man is nothing without the fierce thorns of his ego). So the Hippies collided with the slums, and were beaten and robbed, fleeced and lashed and buried and imprisoned, and here and there murdered, and here and there successful, for there was scattered liaison with bikers and Panthers and Puerto Ricans on the East Coast and Mexicans on the West. There came a point when, like most tribes, they divided. Some of the weakest and some of the least attached went back to the suburbs or moved up into commerce or communications; others sought gentler homes where the sun was kind and the flowers plentiful; others hardened, and like all pilgrims with their own vision of a promised land, began to learn how to work for it, and finally, how to fight for it. So the Yippies came out of the Hippies, ex-Hippies, diggers, bikers, drop-outs from college, hipsters up from the South. They made a community of sorts, for their principles were simple — everybody, obviously, must be allowed to do (no way around the next three words) his own thing, provided he hurt no one doing it — they were yet to learn that society is built on many people hurting many people, it is just who does the hurting which is forever in dispute. They did not necessarily understand how much their simple presence hurt many good citizens in the secret velvet of the heart — the Hippies and probably the Yippies did not quite recognize the depth of that schizophrenia on which society is built. We call it hypocrisy, but it is schizophrenia, a modest ranch-house life with Draconian military adventures; a land of equal opportunity where a white culture sits upon a Black; a horizontal community of Christian love and a vertical hierarchy of churches — the cross was well-designed! a land of family, a land of illicit heat; a politics of principle, a politics of property; nation of mental hygiene with movies and TV reminiscent of a mental pigpen; patriots with a detestation of obscenity who pollute their rivers; citizens with a detestation of government control who cannot bear any situation not controlled. The list must be endless, the comic profits are finally small—the society was able to stagger on like a 400-lb. policeman walking uphill because living in such an unappreciated and obese state it did not at least have to explode in schizophrenia—life went on. Boys could go patiently to church at home and wait their turn to burn villages in Vietnam. What the Yippies did not recognize is that their demand for all-accelerated entrance into twentieth-century Utopia (where modern mass man would have all opportunities before him at once and could thus create and despoil with equal conscience—up against the wall mother-fucker, let me kiss your feet) whether a vision to be desired or abhorred, was nonetheless equal to straight madness for the Average Good American, since his liberated expression might not be an outpouring of love, but the burning of his neighbor's barn. Or, since we are in Chicago, smashing good neighbor's skull with a brick from his own back yard. Yippies, even McCarthyites, represented nothing less by their presence than the destruction of every saving hypocrisy with consequent collision for oneself—it is not so easy to live every day of your life holding up the wall of your own sanity. Small wonder the neighborhood whites of Chicago, like many small-town whites in other places, loved Georgie Wallace—he came in like cavalry, a restorer of every last breech in the fort.

Somber thoughts for a stroll through Lincoln Park on a Sunday afternoon in summer, but the traffic of the tourists and the curious was great; one had to leave the car six blocks away. Curiosity was contained, however, in the family automobile: the burghers did not come to the park. Young tourists and cruisers were there in number, tough kids, Polish and Irish (not all plainclothesmen) circulating around the edges of the crowd, and in the center of the southern part of Lincoln Park where the Yippies had chosen to assemble on an innocuous greensward undistinguished from similar meadows in many another park, a folk-rock group was playing. It was an orderly crowd. Somewhere between one and two thousand kids and young adults sat on the grass and listened, and another thousand or two thousand, just arrived, or too restless to sit, milled through an outer ring, or worked forward to get a better look. There was no stage—the entrance of a flatbed truck from which the entertainers could have played had not been permitted. So the musicians were half hidden, the public address system—could it work off batteries?—was not particularly clear. For one of the next acts it hardly mattered—a young white singer with a cherubic face, perhaps eighteen, maybe twenty-eight, his hair in one huge puff ball teased out six to nine inches from his head, was taking off on an interplanetary, then galactic, flight of song, halfway between the space music of Sun Ra and "The Flight of the Bumblebee," the singer's head shaking at the climb like the blur of a buzzing fly, his sound an electric caterwauling of power come out of the wall (or the line in the grass, or the wet plates in the batteries) and the singer not bending it, but whirling it, burning it, flashing it down some arc of consciousness, the sound screaming up to a climax of vibrations like one rocket blasting out of itself, the force of the noise a vertigo in the cauldrons of inner space—it was the roar of the beast in all nihilism, electric bass and drum driving behind out of their own non-stop to the end of mind. And the reporter, caught in the din—had the horns of the Huns ever had noise to compare?—knew this was some variety of true song for the Hippies and adolescents in the house, in this enclave of grass and open air (luxury apartments of Lake Shore Drive not five football fields away) crescendos of sound as harsh on his ear, ear of a generation which had danced to "Star Dust," as to drive him completely out of the sound, these painted dirty under-twenties were monsters, and yet, still clinging to recognition in the experience, he knew they were a generation which lived in the sound of destruction of all order as he had known it, and worlds of other decomposition as well; there was the sound of mountains crashing in this holocaust of the decibels, hearts bursting, literally bursting, as if this were the sound of death by explosion within, the drums of physiological climax when the mind was blown, and forces of the future, powerful, characterless, as insane and scalding as waves of lava, came flushing through the urn of all acquired culture and sent the brain like a foundered carcass smashing down a rapids, revolving through a whirl of demons, pool of uproar, discords vibrating, electric crescendo screaming as if at the electro-mechanical climax of the age, and these children like filthy Christians sitting quietly in the grass, applauding politely, whistles and cries of mild approval when the song was done, and the reporter as affected by the sound (as affected by the recognition of what nihilisms were calmly encountered in such musical storm) as if he had heard it in a room at midnight with painted bodies and kaleidoscopic sights, had a certainty which went through gangs and groups and rabble, tourists and consecrated saints, vestal virgins with finger bells, through the sight of Negroes calmly digging Honkie soul, sullen Negroes showing not impressed, but digging, cool on their fringe (reports to the South Side might later be made) through even the hint of menace in the bikers, some beaks alien to this music, come to scoff, now watching, half turned on by noise so near to the transcendencies of some of their own noise when the whine of the gears cohabited with the pot to hang them out there on the highway singing with steel and gasoline, yeah, steel and gasoline exactly equal to flesh plus hate, and blood plus hate; equations were pure while riding the balance of a machine, yes, even the tourists and the college boys who would not necessarily be back contributed nonetheless to the certainty of his mood. There was a mock charade going on, a continuation of that celebration of the Yippie Convention yet to come, when Pigasus, a literal pig, would be put in nomination. Vote Pig in '68, said the Yippie placards, and now up at the stage, music done, they announced another candidate to a ripple of mild gone laughter across the grass, Humphrey Dumpty was the name, and a Yippie clown marched through the crown, a painted egg with legs, "the next President of the United States," and in suite came a march of the delegates through an impromptu aisle from the stage to the rear of the crowd. A clown dressed like a Colorado miner in a fun house came first; followed Miss America with hideous lipsticked plastic tits, star of rouge on her cheeks; Mayor Daley's political machine—a clown with a big box horizontal to his torso, big infant's spoon at the trough on top of the box, and a green light which went on and off was next; then the featured delegate, the Green Beret, a clown with a toy machine gun, soot, and red grease on his face, an Australian bush hat on his head. Some sort of wax vomit pop-art work crowned the crown. Yes, the certainty was doubled. Just as he had known for one instant at the Republican Gala in Miami Beach that Nelson Rockefeller had no chance of getting the nomination, so he knew now on this cool gray Sunday afternoon in August, chill in the air like the chill of the pale and the bird of fear beginning to nest in the throat, that trouble was coming, serious trouble. The air of Lincoln Park came into the nose with that tender concern which air seemed always ready to offer when danger announced its presence. The reporter took an unhappy look around. Were these odd unkempt children the sort of troops with whom one wished to enter battle?

CHAPTER 17

There have been few studies on the psychological differences between police and criminals, and the reason is not difficult to discover. The studies based on the usual psychological tests fail to detect a significant difference. Perhaps they are not sufficiently sensitive.

If civilization has made modern man a natural schizophrenic (since he does not know at the very center of his deliberations whether to trust his machines or the imperfect impressions still afforded him by his distorted senses and the more or less tortured messages passed along by polluted water, overfertilized ground, and poisonously irritating air) the average man is a suicide in relation to his schizophrenia. He will suppress his impulses and die eventually of cancer, overt madness, nicotine poisoning, heart attack, or the complications of a chest cold. It is that minority — cop and crook — which seeks issue for violence who now attract our attention. The criminal attempts to reduce the tension within himself by expressing in the direct language of action whatever is most violent and outraged in his depths; to the extent he is not a powerful man, his violence is merely antisocial, like self-exposure, embezzlement, or passing bad checks. The cop tries to solve his violence by blanketing it with a uniform. That is virtually a commonplace, but it explains why cops will put up with poor salary, public dislike, uncomfortable working conditions and a general sense of bad conscience. They know they are lucky; they know they are getting away with a successful solution to the criminality they can taste in their blood. This taste is practically in the forefront of a cop's brain; he is in a stink of perspiration whenever he goes into action; he can tolerate little in the way of insult, and virtually no contradiction; he lies with a simplicity and quick confidence which will stifle the breath of any upright citizen who encounters it innocently for the first time. The difference between a good cop and a bad cop is that the good cop will at least do no more than give his own salted version of events — the bad cop will make up his version. That is why the police arrested the pedestrians they pushed through the window of the Haymarket Inn at the Conrad Hilton: the guiltier the situation in which a policeman finds himself, the more will he attack the victim of his guilt.

There are — it is another commonplace — decent policemen. A few are works of art. And some police, violent when they are young, mellow into modestly corrupt, humorous and decently efficient officials. Every public figure with power, every city official, high politician, or prominent government worker knows in his unspoken sentiments that the police are an essentially criminal force restrained by their guilt, their covert awareness that they are imposters, and by a sprinkling of career men whose education, rectitude, athletic ability, and religious dedication make them work for a balance between justice and authority. These men, who frighten the average corrupt cop as much as a priest frightens a choirboy, are the thin restraining edge of civilization for a police force. That, and the average corrupt cop's sense that he is not wanted that much by anyone.

What staggered the delegates who witnessed the attack—more accurate to call it the massacre, since it was sudden, unprovoked and total—on Michigan Avenue, was that it opened the specter of what it might mean for the police to take over society. They might comport themselves in such a case not as a force of law and order, not even as a force of repression upon civil disorder, but as a true criminal force, chaotic, improvisational, undisciplined, and finally—sufficiently aroused—uncontrollable.

Society was held together by bonds no more powerful proportionately than spider's silk; no one knew this better than the men who administered a society. So images of the massacre opened a nightmare. The more there was disorder in the future, the more there would be need for larger numbers of police and more the need to indulge them. Once indulged, however, it might not take long for their own criminality to dominate their relation to society. Which spoke then of martial law to replace them. But if the Army became the punitive force of society, then the Pentagon would become the only meaningful authority in the land.

So an air of outrage, hysteria, panic, wild rumor, unruly outburst, fury, madness, gallows humor, and gloom hung over nominating night at the convention.

CHAPTER 21

The National Guard was out in force. On the side streets of the hotel, two-and-a-half-ton Army trucks were parked, jamming every space. Traffic was cut off. The Daley-dozers, named yesterday by a newspaper man, those Jeeps with barbed-wire grids in front of their bumpers, were lined in file across Michigan Avenue just south of the Hilton, and he crossed over to Grant Park with the sound of Army vehicles revving up, the low coughing urgency of carburetors flooded and goosed and jabbed and choked by nervous drivers, feet riding the accelerator and clutch while their truck waited in place. The huge searchlights near the Hilton were shining from a height of ten or fifteen feet, from a balcony or a truck, he could not see the glare, but they lit up the debris and clangor of Michigan Avenue, the line of soldiers on the sidewalk of Michigan Avenue just off the edge of Grant Park, the huge pent crowd, thousands here, facing the line of troops. For some reason or other, a hydrant had been opened on Michigan Avenue in the hollow square formed by lines of National Guard and police barriers before the Hilton, and the lights of the searchlight reflecting from the wet street gave that dazzle of light and urgency and *glamour* unique to a movie company shooting in a city late at night, crowds dazzled themselves by their own good luck in being present.

At that moment, he had a sign of what to do, which is to say, he had an impulse. His impulses, perhaps in compensation for his general regime of caution were usually sufficiently sensational to need four drinks for gasoline before they could even be felt. Now without questioning the impulse, he strode down the line of troops walking under their raised guns, not a foot away from their faces, looking (he supposed—perhaps he even did) like an inspecting officer, for he stared severely or thoughtfully or condescendingly into each separate soldier's face with that official scrutiny of character which inspecting officers had once drilled into him. He was in fact fulfilling an old military dream. Since some of the soldiers did not like what he was doing, not altogether! and shifted their rifles abruptly with loud claps of their hand like stallions now nervous and therefore kicking the boards of their stall with abrupt and warning displeasure, he had the obverse pleasure of finding his nerve was firm again, he was sublimely indifferent to the possibility that any of these soldiers might give him a crack on the head with their rifle.

In the middle of examining this line—it must have been two hundred soldiers long, some weary, some bored, some nervous, some curious or friendly, some charged with animosity; nearly all sloppy in their uniforms which he noticed with displeasure—he was indeed an inspecting officer—he passed by the speaker's stand, a park table, or something of the sort, on which a dozen men were standing, one with a microphone attached by a wire to a big portable bullhorn held by another demonstrator. The speeches were going on, and a couple of guitarists appeared ready to perform next.

A woman he knew, who worked on the McCarthy staff, approached him. "Will you speak?" she asked.

He nodded. He felt more or less ready to speak and would have answered, "Yes, just as soon as I conclude this inspection," if some saving wit in a corner of his brain had not recognized how absurd this would seem to her.

So he concluded his inspection, taking the time to regard each soldier in that long line, and felt as if he had joined some private victory between one part of himself and another—just what, would have been tedious to consider at the moment, for he felt charged, ready, full of orator's muscle.

A Yippie wearing a dirty torn sweater, his hair long, curly, knotted, knuckled with coils and thrusting vertically into the air, hair quite the match of Bob Dylan's, was running the program and whispered hello cordially, worked him to the center of this ridiculously small platform, perhaps the area of two large bathtubs put side by side, and told him he would speak as soon as the electric guitarists were done.

He stood then in the center between two guitars who were singing a loud wild banging folk rock, somewhat corny, a patriotic song of the Left whose title eluded him. He did not like the song usually, but up on the platform, flanked by the singers, the bullhorn being held just back of his head turned out to the crowd, he felt insulated by the sound, blasted with it completely and so somehow safe with it, womb-safe with it, womb-cushioned — did the embryo live in such a waterfall of uproar each time the mother's digestion turned over? His mind was agreeably empty as he waited, good sign generally that he was ready to deliver a real speech.

When the song ended and he was given the mike after a generous introduction and a sweet surge of applause beefed up to its good point precisely by the introduction of the youth in the dirty sweater and the hair like Bob Dylan, he spoke out to the crowd just long enough to tell them he wanted to speak first to the soldiers. Then he turned his back, and the loudspeaker turned with him, and he talked to the line of troops he had not long ago passed, introducing himself as a novelist whose war novel some of them might possibly have read since it was famous in many barracks for its filthy passages and four-letter words, although not nearly so famous as another work, *From Here to Eternity*, with whose author he was often confused. He did not wish to disappoint the soldiers, he said, but he was not that fine author, Mr. James Jones, but the other, the one who had written the other book.

These remarks given and enjoyed by him, he then talked to the soldiers as a man who had been a soldier once. "As I walked down your line, inspecting you, I realized that you are all about the kind of soldier I was nearly twenty-five years ago, that is to say, not a very good soldier, somewhat unhappy with the Army I found myself in." But, he went on, the war in which he himself had fought had not bothered his sense of what might be right the way this war in Vietnam must bother them. And he went on to talk about how American soldiers could take little pride in a war where they had the superiority and yet could not win, and he thought that was because they were ashamed of the war. Americans were conceivably the best fighting soldiers in the world if they could ever find a war which was the most honorable war in the world for them, but the war in Vietnam was the worst war for them, and so they could not fight with enthusiasm. At their best, Americans were honest; so they needed an honest war.

It would have been a first rate talk to give to fighting troops. In the general excitement of this occasion he did not necessarily arrive at the central point—the soldiers before him had no wish to serve in Vietnam. That was why they were in the National Guard. Still, his speech to the troops pleased him, it warmed him for his next address which he was able to begin by turning around in place 180°, the loudspeaker doing the same, and now addressing his remarks to the crowd in the park. They were seated in a semicircle perhaps two hundred feet in diameter, a crowd of several thousand at least, with an attention he knew immediately was superb, for it was tender as the fatigue of shared experience and electric as the ringing of pain from a new bruise.

He began once again by paying his respects, explaining how he had missed one fray and then another, not certain if for the best or worst of motives. They were polite even to this, as if a manifest of honesty in a speaker was all they had come to hear. But he had seen them, he explained, over these few days, taking beatings and going back, taking beatings, going back; so he now found himself in this park talking to them (although he had had no such intention earlier). They were fine troops, he declared, they were the sort of troops any general would be proud to have. They had had the courage to live at war for four days in a city which was run by a beast.

A roar of delight came back from them. He felt the heights of the Hilton behind him, the searchlights, and the soldiers. Before him, these revolutionary youth—they were no longer the same young people who had gone to the Pentagon at all. They were soldiers.

"Yes, this is a city run by a beast, and yet we may take no pleasure in it," he said, "because the man is a giant who ended as a beast. And that is another part of the horror. For we have a President who was a giant and ended also as a beast. All over the world are leaders who have ended as beasts; there is a beastliness in the marrow of the century," he said, or words like that and went on, "Let us even have a moment of sorrow for Mayor Daley for he is a fallen giant and that is tragic," and they cheered Daley out of good spirit and some crazy good temper as if Mayor Daley was beautiful, he had given them all this—what a great king of the pigs! and somebody yelled, "Give us some of that good grass, Norman," and he bellowed back, "I haven't had pot in a month." They all roared. "Four good bourbons is all you need," said the demagogue, and the troops were in heaven.

The exchange fired him into his next thought. He repeated again that he had not been ready to march, repeated his desire to avoid arrest or a blow on the head, and "Write! Write!" they yelled back, "You're right, baby, do the writing!" But now, he went on, the time had come for Democratic delegates to march. He had not gone, he said, on the vigil and march from the stockyards to the hotel, because "that was in the wrong direction." Demagogue's metaphor, demagogue's profit. They cheered him richly. No, tomorrow, he told them (the idea coming to his mind at just this instant) he was going to try to get three hundred delegates to march with them to the Amphitheatre. He would march along then! But he would not if there were less than three hundred delegates! Because if little more than a tenth of the Democratic Party was not ready to go out with their bodies as a warrant of safekeeping for all of them, then there was no sense in walking into still one more mauling. They had taken enough. If there was not real outrage in the Democratic Party, then it was time they knew that as well; they could then prepare to go underground. A roar came back again from the new soldiers seated on the grass.

Were there delegates here, he asked? Candles waved in the dark—he was aware of them for the first time. "Spread the word," he called out, "I'll be here tomorrow."

Then he went on to speak of that underground. He would try to explain it. The other side had all the force, all the guns, all the power. They had everything but creative wit. So the underground would have to function on its wit, its creative sense of each new step. They must never repeat a tactic they had used before, no matter how successful. "Once a philosopher, twice a pervert," he bawled out. And in the middle of the happy laughter which came back, he said, "Voltaire!" and they were happy again. It was as good a speech as he had ever made.

For example, he continued, the march tomorrow with three hundred delegates would be a new tactic, and might offer a real chance of reaching the police barriers outside the Amphitheatre, where they could have a rally and quietly disband. That could make the point, for the Mayor had refused to let them even get near until now. Of course if the police chose to attack again tomorrow, well, three hundred Democratic delegates would also be in the crowd—so the nation would know that the authority was even determined to mop up its own. So he would march, he repeated, if the delegates would go, but he was damned, he told the crowd, if he was about to give cops the chance to maul him for nothing after he had made a point of here insulting the Mayor; no, he would not take that chance unless a tenth of the Democratic delegates were also willing to take a chance. On that note, he stepped down, and took a walk forward through the crowd, stopping to shake hands every step with the young men and women on the grass. Some were well-dressed, some were near to wearing rages, some looked as dusty and war-like as Roger's Rangers, others were small and angelic. Everything from ghosts of Robin Hood's band to the worst of the descendants of the worst Bolshevik clerks were here in the Grant Park grass at five in the morning and McCarthyites and McGovernites, and attractive girls, and college boys, and a number of Negroes, more now than any day or night before, and they were shaking hands with him, Black Power was revolving a hint in its profound emplacements. There were kooks and plainclothesmen and security and petty thieves and provocateurs with calculating faces and mouths just out of balance, eyes that glinted with a telltale flick; but there were also more attractive adolescents and under-twenties in this crowd than in any like crowd of New Left and Yippies he has seen before, as if the war had indeed been good for them. And he was modest in the warmth of their greeting, and not honored with himself, for they were giving him credit he did not possess—they were ready to forgive all manner of defection on the pleasure of a good speech.

So he circulated, talking, came back to the platform to make one quick amendment. Delegates in the crowd had told him three hundred was too great a number to seek in so short a time. It would not be possible to reach them all. Two hundred was a better expectation. So he relayed that information to the crowd, and added that he would be back in this Park at noon.

He returned to the hotel, pleased with his project, and aware of one whole new notion of himself. All courage was his and all determination, provided he could lead. There seemed no rank in any Army suitable for him below the level of General—extraordinary events deliver exceptional intuitions of oneself. No wonder he had spent so many years being General of an army of one. It was something to discover the secret source of the river of one's own good guts or lack of them. And booze was no bad canoe. He went to bed prepared for heroic events on the morrow.

CHAPTER 22

He was to receive instead a lesson in the alphabet of all good politick: which is, that a passion is nothing without a good horse to carry you in visit over your neighbor's lands. He went to sleep at six A.M. prepared to visit different leaders as soon as he had finished his next speech at noon; by six in the evening he hoped they would be ready for the march, all delegates assembled.

Be prepared for total failure.

If this were essentially an account of the reporter's actions, it would be interesting to follow him through the chutes on Thursday, but we are concerned with his actions only as they illumine the event of the Republican Convention in Miami, the Democratic Convention in Chicago, and the war of the near streets. So his speech to the Yippies and children assembled was of value, since he learned for the record of his report that they were a generation with an appetite for the heroic, and an air not without beauty had arisen from their presence; they had been better than he thought, young, devoted, and actually ready to die—they were not like their counterparts ten years ago. Something had happened in America, some forging of the steel. He had known while speaking that if it came to civil war, there was a side he could join. At what a cost! At what a cost!

But such discoveries are unsettling. He lay in bed not able to sleep; he lay in fact on the edge of a twilight slumber rich as Oriental harems in the happiness of their color, but he was thus celebrating too soon, because by nine o'clock in the morning, the last of his liquor now beautifully metabolized, he was in that kind of unhappy shape on which comedy is built. Quick calisthenics, a shower, a shave, and the urgency of his mission, did not quite give him a brain the equal of three hours in slumber. He would begin to think well for a minute, then lapse into himself like a mind become too weak for the concentration of consecutive thoughts.

We can spare the day, and report the lesson. He made his speech in Grant Park at noon, talked then to reporters, then to delegates (who had been in the Park) at the Hilton, discussed problems, arranged to meet them again, and never was able to keep the meetings. He could never get to see McCarthy quite alone, nor McGovern, lost hours on the hope he might talk to the New York delegation, did not know how to reach Peterson of Wisconsin, could have wept at the absence of a secretary, or a walkie-talkie, since phones refused to function, or beginning to work, could reach no soul. He ran back and forth over Chicago, sent messages—by whomever he could find, to the Park; he would be back at three, he would be back at four, he saw Murray Kempton who was ready to march all alone if only to interpose himself between the police and the body of one demonstrator (Kempton was indeed to be arrested later in the day) he saw others, lost connection with delegates who had volunteered to help, was helpless himself in his lack of sleep, was too early or too late for each political figure he wished to find, he was always rushing or waiting in hallways—he learned the first lesson of a convention: nothing could be accomplished without the ability to communicate faster than your opponent. If politics was property, a convention was a massive auction, and your bid had to reach the floor in time.

So he was defeated. He could put nothing together at all. Hungover, drained, ashen within, and doubtless looking as awful as Rockefeller at Opa Locka or McCarthy in Cambridge, he went back to Grant Park in the late afternoon to make a speech in which he would declare his failure, and discovered the Park instead was near empty. Whoever had wanted to march had gone off already with Peterson of Wisconsin, or later with Dick Gregory. (Perhaps a total of fifty Democratic delegates were in those walks.) Now the Park was all but deserted except for the National Guard. Perhaps a hundred or two hundred onlookers, malcontents, hoodlums, and odd petty thieves sauntered about. A mean-looking mulatto passed by the line of National Guard with his penknife out, blade up, and whispered, "Here's my bayonet." Yes, Grant Park was now near to Times Square in Manhattan or Main Street in L.A. The Yippies were gone; another kind of presence was in. And the grass looked littered and yellow, a holocaust of newspapers upon it. Now, a dry wind, dusty and cold, gave every sentiment of the end of summer. The reporter went back to his room. He had political lessons to absorb for a year from all the details of his absolute failure to deliver the vote.

CHAPTER 23

Let us look at the convention on the last night. Two hours before the final evening session the Progress Printing Company near the stockyards finished a rush order of small posters perhaps two feet high which said: CHICAGO LOVES MAYOR DALEY. They were ready to be handed out when the crowds arrived tonight; thousands of workers for the city administration were packed into the spectators' gallery, then the sections reserved for radio, TV and periodicals. The crowd fortified with plastic tickets cut to the size of Diner's Club cards, and therefore cut to the size of the admission pass one had to insert in the signal box to enter, had flooded all available seats with their posters and their good Chicago lungs-for-Daley. The radio, television and periodical men wandered about the outer environs of the Amphitheatre and were forced to watch most of the convention this night from the halls, the ends of the tunnels, the television studios.

Daley had known how to do it. If he had been booed and jeered the first two nights and openly insulted from the podium on Wednesday, despite a gallery already packed in his favor, he was not going to tolerate anything less than a built-in majesty for to-night. Power is addicted to more power. So troughs of pigs were sweet to him as honey to a mouse, and he made certain of the seats.

Shortly after convening, the convention showed a movie thirty-two minutes long, entitled "Robert Kennedy Remembered," and while it went on, through the hall, over the floor, and out across the country on television, a kind of unity came over everyone who was watching, at least for a little while. Idealism rarely moved politicians—it had too little to do with property. But emotion did. It was closer to the land. Somewhere between sorrow and the blind sword of patriotism was the fulcrum of reasonable politics, and as the film progressed, and one saw scene after scene of Bobby Kennedy growing older, a kind of happiness came back from the image, for something in his face grew young over the years—he looked more like a boy on the day of his death, a nice boy, nicer than the kid with the sharp rocky glint in his eye who had gone to work for Joe McCarthy in his early twenties, and had then known everything there was to know about getting ahead in politics. He had grown modest as he grew older, and his wit had grown with him—he had become a funny man as the picture took care to show, wry, simple for one instant, shy and off to the side on the next, but with a sort of marvelous boy's wisdom, as if he knew the world was very bad and knew the intimate style of how it was bad, as only boys can sometimes know (for they feel it in their parents and their school-teachers and their friends). Yet he had confidence he was going to fix it—the picture had this sweet simple view of him which no one could resent for somehow it was not untrue. Since his brother's death, a subtle sadness had come to live in his tone of confidence, as though he were confident he would win—if he did not lose. That could also happen, and that could happen quickly. He had come into that world where people live with the recognition of tragedy, and so are often afraid of happiness, for they know that one is never in so much danger as when victorious and/or happy—that is when the devils seem to have their hour, and hawks seize something living from the gambol on the field.

The reporter met Bobby Kennedy just once. It was on an after-noon in May in New York just after his victory in the Indiana primary and it had not been a famous meeting, even if it began well. The Senator came in from a conference (for the reporter was being granted an audience) and said quickly with a grin, "Mr. Mailer, you're a mean man with a word." He had answered, "On the contrary, Senator, I like to think of myself as a gracious writer."

"Oh," said Senator Kennedy, with a wave of his hand, "that too, that too!"

So it had begun well enough, and the reporter had been taken with Kennedy's appearance. He was slimmer even than one would have thought, not strong, not weak, somewhere between a blade of grass and a blade of steel, fine, finely drawn, finely honed, a fine flush of color in his cheeks, two very white front teeth, prominent as the two upper teeth of a rabbit, so his mouth had no hint of the cruelty or calculation of a politician who weighs counties, cities, and states, but was rather a mouth ready to nip at anything which attracted its contempt or endangered its ideas. Then there were his eyes. They were most unusual. His brother Teddy Kennedy spoke of those who "followed him, honored him, lived in his mild and magnificent eye," and that was fair description for he had very large blue eyes, the iris wide in diameter, near to twice the width of the average eye, and the blue was a milky blue like a marble so that his eyes, while prominent, did not show the separate steps and slopes of light some bright eyes show, but rather were gentle, indeed beautiful — one was tempted to speak of velvety eyes — their surface seemed made of velvet as if one could touch them, and the surface would not be repelled.

He was as attractive as a movie star. Not attractive like his brother had been, for Jack Kennedy had looked like the sort of vital leading man who would steal the girl from Ronald Reagan every time, no, Bobby Kennedy had looked more like a phenomenon of a movie star — he could have filled some magical empty space between Mickey Rooney and James Dean, they would have cast him sooner or later in some remake of *Mr. Smith Goes to Washington*, and everyone would have said, "Impossible casting! He's too young." And he was too young. Too young for Senator, too young for President, it felt strange in his presence thinking of him as President, as if the country would be giddy, like the whirl of one's stomach in the drop of an elevator or jokes about an adolescent falling in love, it was incredible to think of him as President, and yet marvelous, as if only a marvelous country would finally dare to have him.

That was the best of the meeting — meeting him! The reporter spent the rest of his valuable thirty minutes arguing with the Senator about Senator McCarthy. He begged him to arrange some sort of truce or liaison, but made a large mistake from the outset. He went on in a fatuous voice, sensing error too late to pull back, about how effective two Irish Catholics would be on the same ticket for if there were conservative Irishmen who could vote against one of them, where was the Irish Catholic in America who could vote against two? and Kennedy had looked at him with disgust, as if offended by the presumption in this calculation, his upper lip had come down severely over his two front white teeth, and he had snapped, "I don't want those votes." How indeed did the reporter presume to tell him stories about the benightedness of such people when he knew them only too well. So the joke had been a lame joke and worse, and they got into a dull argument about McCarthy, Kennedy having little which was good to say, and the reporter arguing doggedly in the face of such remarks as: "He doesn't even begin to campaign until twelve."

They got nowhere. Kennedy's mind was altogether political on this afternoon. It did not deal with ideas except insofar as ideas were attached to the name of bills, or speeches, or platforms, or specific debates in specific places, and the reporter, always hard put to remember such details, was forced therefore to hammer harder and harder on the virtues of McCarthy's gamble in entering the New Hampshire primary until Kennedy said, "I wonder why you don't support Senator McCarthy. He seems more like your sort of guy, Mr. Mailer," and in answer, oddly moved, he had said in a husky voice, "No, I'm supporting you. I know it wasn't easy for you to go in." And even began to mutter a few remarks about how he understood that powerful politicians would not have trusted Kennedy if he had moved too quickly, for his holding was large, and men with large holdings were not supportable if they leaped too soon. "I know that," he said looking into the Senator's mild and magnificent eye, and Kennedy nodded, and in return a little later Kennedy sighed, and exhaled his breath, looked sad for an instant, and said, "Who knows? Who knows? Perhaps I should have gone in earlier." A few minutes later they said goodbye, not unpleasantly. That was the last he saw of him.

The closest he was to come again was to stand in vigil for fifteen minutes as a member of the honor guard about his coffin in St. Patrick's. Lines filed by. People had waited in line for hours, five hours, six hours, more, inching forward through the day and through the police lines on the street in order to take one last look at the closed coffin.

The poorest part of the working-class of New York had turned out, poor Negro men and women, Puerto Ricans, Irish washerwomen, old Jewish ladies who looked like they ran grubby little newsstands, children, adolescents, families, men with hands thick and lined and horny as oyster shells, calluses like barnacles, came filing by to bob a look at that coffin covered by a flag. Some women walked by praying, and knelt and touched the coffin with their fingertips as they passed, and after a time the flag would slip from the pressure of their fingers and an usher detailed for the purpose would readjust it. The straightest line between two points is the truth of an event, no matter how long it takes or far it winds, and if it had taken these poor people six hours of waiting in line to reach that coffin, then the truth was in the hours. A river of working-class people came down to march past Kennedy's coffin, and this endless line of people had really loved him, loved Bobby Kennedy like no political figure in years had been loved.

The organ played somewhere in the nave and the line moved forward under the vast—this day—tragic vaults of the cathedral so high overhead and he felt love for the figure in the coffin and tragedy for the nation in the years ahead, the future of the nation seemed as dark and tortured, as wrenched out of shape, as the contorted blood-spattered painted sculpture of that garish Christ one could find in every dark little Mexican church. The horror of dried blood was now part of the air, and became part of the air of the funeral next day. That funeral was not nearly so beautiful; the poor people who had waited on line on Friday were now gone, and the mighty were in their place, the President and members of the Congress, and the Establishment, and the Secret Service, and the power of Wall Street; the inside of St. Patrick's for the length of the service was dank with the breath of the over-ambitious offering reverence—there is no gloom so deep unless it is the scent of the upholstery in a mortician's limousine, or the smell of morning in a closed Pullman after executives have talked through the night.

CHAPTER 24

The movie came to an end. Even dead, and on film, he was better and more moving than anything which had happened in their convention, and people were crying. An ovation began. Delegates came to their feet, and applauded an empty screen—it was as if the center of American life was now passing the age where it could still look forward; now people looked back into memory, into the past of the nation—was that possible? They applauded the presence of a memory. Bobby Kennedy had now become a beloved property of the party.

Minutes went by and the ovation continued. People stood on their chairs and clapped their hands. Cries broke out. Signs were lifted. Small hand-lettered signs which said, "Bobby, Be With Us," and one enormous sign eight feet high, sorrowful as rue in the throat—"Bobby, We Miss You," it said.

Now the ovation had gone on long enough—for certain people.

So signals went back and forth between floor and podium and phone, and Carl Albert stepped forward and banged the gavel for the ovation to end, and asked for order. The party which had come together for five minutes, after five days and five months and five years of festering discord, was now immediately divided again. The New York and California delegations began to sing the "Battle Hymn of the Republic," and the floor heard, and delegations everywhere began to sing, Humphrey delegations as quick as the rest. In every convention there is a steamroller, and a moment when the flattened exhale their steam, and "Mine eyes have seen the glory of the coming of the Lord!" was the cry of the oppressed at this convention, even those unwittingly oppressed in their mind, and not even knowing it in their heart until this instant, now they were defying the Chair, clapping their hands, singing, stamping their feet to mock the chairman's gavel.

Carl Albert brought up Dorothy Bush to read an appreciation the convention would offer for the work of certain delegates. The convention did not wish to hear. Mrs. Bush began to read in a thin mean voice, quivering with the hatreds of an occasion like this, and the crowd sang on, "Glory, Glory, Hallelujah, his truth goes marching on," and they stamped their feet and clapped their hands, and were loose finally and having their day as they sang the song which once, originally, had commemorated a man who preached civil disorder, then mutiny, and attacked a fort in his madness and was executed, John Brown was also being celebrated here, and the Texas and Illinois delegations were now silent, clapping no longer, sitting on their seats, looking bored. Every delegate on the floor who had hated the Kennedys was now looking bored, and the ones who had loved them were now noisier than ever. Once again the party was polarized. Signs waved all over the floor, "Bobby, We'll Remember You," "Bobby, We'll Seek Your Newer World," and the ever-present, "Bobby, We Miss You." Yes they did, missed him as the loving spirit, the tender *germ* in the living plasma of the party. Nothing was going to make them stop: this offering of applause was more valuable to them than any nutrients to be found in the oratorical vitamin pills Hubert would yet be there to offer. The demonstration went on for twenty minutes and gave no sign of stopping at all. Dorothy Bush had long ago given up. Carl Albert, even smaller than Georgie Wallace, was now as furious as only a tiny man can be when his hard-earned authority has turned to wax — he glared across the floor at the New York delegation like a little boy who smells something bad.

However did they stop the demonstration? Well, convention mechanics can be as perfect as the muscle in a good play when professionals have worked their football for a season. Mayor Daley, old lover of the Kennedys, and politically enough of an enigma six months ago for Bobby to have said in his bloodwise political wisdom, "Daley is the ballgame," Mayor Daley, still flirting with the Kennedys these last three days in his desire for Teddy as Vice President, now had come to the end of this political string, and like a good politician he pulled it. He gave the signal. The gallery began to chant, "We love Daley." All his goons and clerks and beef-eaters and healthy parochial school students began to yell and scream and clap, "We love Daley," and the power of their lungs, the power of the freshest and the largest force in this Amphitheatre soon drowned out the Kennedy demonstrators, stuffed their larynxes with larger sound. The Daley demonstration was bona fide too— his people had suffered with their Mayor, so they screamed for him now and clapped their hands, and Mayor Daley clapped his hands too for he also loved Mayor Daley. Simple narcissism gives the power of beasts to politicians, professional wrestlers and female movie stars.

At the height of the Daley demonstration, it was abruptly cut off. By a signal. "Shut your yaps" was an old button, no matter how the signal came. In the momentary silence, Carl Albert got his tongue in, and put Ralph Metcalfe (Daley's Black Man) who was up on the podium already, into voice on the mike, and Metcalfe announced a minute of silence for the memory of Martin Luther King. So New York and California were naturally obliged to be silent with the rest, the floor was silent, the gallery was silent, and before the minute was up, Carl Albert had slipped Dorothy Bush in again, and she was reading the appreciation of the convention for certain delegates. Business had been resumed. The last night proceeded.

OF A FIRE
ON THE MOON

In the spring of 1969, just as Mailer was announcing his plans to run for Mayor of New York, the news story broke that he had been commissioned by Life *magazine to cover the attempt to land American astronauts on the moon. The fee was quoted as being nearly a million dollars, thus ruining Mailer's attempt to launch a fund-raising drive for his campaign. He did cover the moonshot, three installments appeared in* Life *(August 29 and November 14, 1969, and January 9, 1970), and the full book was published by Little, Brown late in 1970. Paperback arrangements have not yet been announced. The book resembles* Armies *and* Miami and Chicago *in its narrative design, and the excerpts in this collection have been chosen to permit comparison between the three "Norman Mailers" of the books, but* Of a Fire on the Moon *is basically different. For years, Mailer has written of the cultural effects of technology, but for the first time here, he tries to cut into the cultural origins of technology, to illuminate it from the inside. Nothing like it has ever been attempted by a serious American writer.*

Part I: Aquarius

CHAPTER 5, A DREAM OF THE FUTURE'S FACE

Early on the afternoon of July 21, the Lunar Module fired its ascent motor, lifted off Tranquility Base, and in a few hours docked with Columbia. Shortly after, the astronauts passed back into the Command Module and Eagle was jettisoned. It would drift off on a trajectory to the sun. A little before midnight, out of communication for the last time with Mission Control, traveling for the final orbit around the back of the moon, Apollo 11 ignited the Service Module engine and accelerated its speed from 3,600 miles to 5,900 miles per hour. Its momentum was now great enough to lift it out of the moon's pull of gravity and back into the attractions of the earth — the spacecraft was therefore on its way home. Since the trip would take sixty hours, a quiet two and a half days were in store and Aquarius decided to get out of Nassau Bay and visit some friends.

His host and hostess were wealthy Europeans with activities which kept them very much of the time in Texas. Since they were art collectors of distinction, invariably served a good meal, and had always been kind to him, the invitation was welcome. To go from the arid tablelands of NASA Highway 1 to these forested grounds now damp after the rain of a summer evening was like encountering a taste of French ice in the flats of the desert. Even the trees about the house were very high, taller than the tallest elms he had seen in New England—"Wild pigs used to forage in this part of Houston," said his host, as if in explanation, and on the lawn, now twice-green in the luminous golden green of a murky twilight, smaller tropical trees with rubbery trunks twisted about a large sculpture by Jean Tinguely which waved metal scarecrow arms when a switch was thrown and blew spinning faucets of water through wild stuttering sweeps, a piece of sculpture reminiscent of the flying machines of La Belle Epoque, a hybrid of dragon and hornet which offered a shade of the time when technology had been belts and clanking gears, and culture was a fruit to be picked from a favored tree.

The mansion was modern, it had been one of the first modern homes in Houston and was designed by one of the more ascetic modern architects. With the best will, how could Aquarius like it? But the severity of the design was concealed by the variety of the furniture, the intensity of the art, the presence of the sculpture, and the happy design in fact of a portion of the house: the living room shared a wall with a glass-in atrium of exotics in bloom. So the surgical intent of the architect was partially overcome by the wealth of the art and by the tropical pressure of the garden whose plants and interior tree, illumined with spotlights, possessed something of that same silence which comes over audience and cast when there is a moment of theater and everything ceases, everything depends on—one cannot say—it is just that no one thinks to cough.

There had been another such moment when he entered the house. In the foyer was a painting by Magritte, a startling image of a room with an immense rock situated in the center of the floor. The instant of time suggested by the canvas was comparable to the mood of a landscape in the instant just before something awful is about to happen, or just after, one could not tell. The silences of the canvas spoke of Apollo 11 still circling the moon: the painting could have been photographed for the front page—it hung from the wall like a severed head. As Aquarius met the other guests, gave greetings, took a drink, his thoughts were not free of the painting. He did not know when it had been done—he assumed it was finished many years ago—he was certain without even thinking about it that there had been no intention by the artist to talk of the moon or projects in space, no, Aquarius would assume the painter had awakened with a vision of the canvas and that vision had he delineated. Something in the acrid breath of the city he inhabited, some avidity emitted by a passing machine, some tar in the residue of a nightmare, some ash from the memory of a cremation had gone into the painting of that gray stone — it was as if Magritte had listened to the ending of one world with its comfortable chairs in the parlor, and heard the intrusion of a new world, silent as the windowless stone which grew in the room, and knowing not quite what he had painted, had painted his warning nonetheless. Now the world of the future was a dead rock, and the rock was in the room.

There was also a Negro in his host's living room, a man perhaps thirty-five, a big and handsome Black man with an Afro haircut of short length, the moderation of the cut there to hint that he still lived in a White man's clearing, even if it was on the very edge of the clearing. He was not undistinguished, this Negro, he was a professor at an Ivy League college; Aquarius had met him one night the previous year after visiting the campus. The Negro had been much admired in the college. He had an impressive voice and the deliberate manner of a leader. How could the admiration of faculty wives be restrained? But this Black professor was also a focus of definition for Black students in the college — they took some of the measure of their militancy from his advice. It was a responsible position. The students were in the college on one of those specific programs which had begun in many a university that year — students from slum backgrounds, students without full qualification were being accepted on the reasonable if much embattled assumption that boys from slums were easily bright enough to be salvaged for academic life if special pains were taken. Aquarius had met enough of such students to think the program was modest. The education of the streets gave substantial polish in Black ghettos — some of the boys had knowledge at seventeen Aquarius would not be certain of acquiring by seventy. They had the toughness of fiber of the twenty-times tested. This night on the campus, having a simple discussion back and forth, needling back and forth, even to even — so Aquarius had thought — a Black student suddenly said to him, "You're an old man. Your hair is gray. An old man like you wants to keep talking like that, you may have to go outside with me." The student gave an evil smile. "You're too old to keep up with me. I'll whomp your ass."

It had been a glum moment for Aquarius. It was late at night, he was tired, he had been drinking with students for hours. As usual he was overweight. The boy was smaller than him, but not at all overweight, fast. Over the years Aquarius had lost more standards then he cared to remember. But he still held on to the medieval stricture that one should never back out of a direct invitation to fight. So he said with no happiness, "Well, there are so many waiting on line, it might as well be you," and he stood up.

The Black boy had been playing with him. The Black boy grinned. He assured Aquarius there was no need to go outside. They could talk now. And did. But what actors were the Blacks! What a sense of honor! What a sense of the gulch! Seeing the Black professor in this living room in Houston brought back the memory of the student who had decided to run a simulation through the character of Aquarius' nerve. It was in the handshake of both men as they looked at each other now, Aquarius still feeling the rash of the encounter, the other still amused at the memory. God knows how the student had imitated his rise from the chair. There had been a sly curl in the Black man's voice whenever they came across each other at a New York party.

Tonight, however, was different. He almost did not recognize the professor. The large eyes were bloodshot, and his slow deliberate speech had become twice-heavy, almost sluggish. Aquarius realized the man had been drinking. It was not a matter of a few shots before this evening, no, there was a sense of somebody pickling himself through three days of booze, four days of booze, five, not even drunk, just the heavy taking of the heaviest medicine, a direct search for thickening, as if he were looking to coagulate some floor between the pit of his feelings at boil and the grave courtesies of his heavy Black manner. By now it showed. He was normally so elegant a man that it was impossible to conceive of how he would make a crude move—now, you could know. Something raucous and jeering was still withheld, but the sourness of his stomach had gotten into the sourness of his face. His collar was a hint wilted.

He had a woman with him, a sweet and wispy blond, half plain, still half attractive, for she emitted a distant echo of Marilyn Monroe long gone. But she was not his equal, not in size, presence, qualifications—by the cruel European measure of this richly endowed room, she was simply not an adequate woman for a man of his ambitions. At least that was the measure Aquarius took. It was hard not to recognize that whatever had brought them together, very little was now sustaining the project. The Black man was obviously tired of her, and she was still obviously in love with him. Since they were here enforcedly together, that was enough to keep a man drinking for more than a day. Besides—if he was a comfortable house guest of these fine Europeans, he might nonetheless wish to leave the grounds. Being seen with her on Houston streets would not calm his nerves.

But there were other reasons for drinking as well. America had put two White men on the moon, and lifted them off. A triumph of White men was being celebrated in the streets of this city. It was even worse than that. For the developed abilities of these White men, their production, their flight skills, their engineering feats, were the most successful part of that White superstructure which had been strangling the possibilities of his own Black people for years. The professor was an academic with no mean knowledge of colonial struggles of colored peoples. He was also a militant. If the degree of his militancy was not precisely defined, still its presence was not denied. His skin was dark. If he were to say, "Black is beautiful" with a cultivated smile, nonetheless he was still saying it. Aquarius had never been invited to enter this Black man's vision, but it was no great mystery the Black believed his people were possessed of a potential genius which was greater than Whites. Kept in incubation for two millennia, they would be all the more powerful when they prevailed. It was nothing less than a great civilization they were prepared to create. Aquarius could not picture the details of that civilization in the Black professor's mind, but they had talked enough to know they agreed that this potential greatness of the Black people was not to be found in technology. Whites might need the radio to become tribal but Blacks would have another communion. From the depth of one consciousness they could be ready to speak to the depth of another; by telepathy might they send their word. That was the logic implicit in CPT. If CPT was one of the jokes by which Blacks admitted Whites to the threshold of their view, it was a relief to learn that CPT stood for Colored People's Time. When a Black friend said he would arrive at 8 P.M. and came after midnight, there was still logic in his move. He was traveling on CPT. The vibrations he received at 8 P.M. were not sufficiently interesting to make him travel toward you—all that was hurt were the host's undue expectations. The real logic of CPT was that when there was trouble or happiness the brothers would come on the wave.

Well, White technology was not built on telepathy, it was built on electromagnetic circuits of transmission and reception, it was built on factory workers pressing their button or monitoring their function according to firm and bound stations of the clock. The time of a rocket mission was Ground Elapsed Time, GET. Every sequence of the flight was tied into the pure numbers of the time-line. So the flight to the moon was a victory for GET, and the first heats of the triumph suggested that the fundamental notion of Black superiority might be incorrect: in this hour, it would no longer be as easy for a militant Black to say that Whitey had built a palace on numbers, and numbers killed a man, and numbers would kill Whitey's civilization before all was through. Yesterday, Whitey with his numbers had taken a first step to the stars, taken it ahead of Black men. How that had to burn in the ducts of this Black man's stomach, in the vats of his liver. Aquarius thought again of the lunar air of technologists. Like the moon, they traveled without a personal atmosphere. No wonder Blacks had distaste for numbers, and found trouble studying. It was not because they came — as liberals necessarily would have it — from wrecked homes and slum conditions, from drug-pushing streets, no, that kind of violence and disruption could be the pain of a people so rich in awareness they could not bear the deadening jolts of civilization on each of their senses. Blacks had distaste for numbers not because they were stupid or deprived, but because numbers were abstracted from the senses, numbers made you ignore the taste of the apple for the amount in the box, and so the use of numbers shrunk the protective envelope of human atmosphere, eroded that extrasensory aura which gave awareness, grace, the ability to move one's body and excel at sports and dance and war, or be able to travel on an inner space of sound. Blacks were not the only ones who hated numbers — how many attractive women could not bear to add a column or calculate a cost? Numbers were a pestilence to beauty.

Of course this particular Black man, this professor, was in torture, for he lived half in the world of numbers, and half in the wrappings of the aura. So did Aquarius. It was just that Aquarius was White and the other Black — so Aquarius could not conceal altogether his pleasure in the feat. A little part of him, indefatigably White, felt as mean as a Wasp. There was something to be said after all for arriving on time. CPT was excellent for the nervous system if you were the one to amble in at midnight, but Aquarius had played the host too often.

"You know," said the professor, "there are no Black astronauts."

"Of course not."

"Any Jewish astronauts?"

"I doubt it."

The Black man grunted. They would not need to mention Mexicans or Puerto Ricans. Say, there might not even by any Italians.

"Did you want them," asked Aquarius, "to send a Protestant, a Catholic, and a Jew to the moon?"

"Look," said the Black professor, "do they have any awareness of how the money they spent could have been used?"

"They have a very good argument: they say if you stopped space tomorrow, only a token of the funds would go to poverty."

"I'd like to be in a position to argue about that," said the Black. He sipped at his drink. It trickled into his system like the inching of glucose from a bottle down a rubber tube. "Damn," he said, "are they still on the moon?"

"They took off already," said Aquarius.

"No trouble?"

"None."

If the Blacks yet built a civilization, magic would be at its heart. For they lived with the wonders of magic as the Whites lived with technology. How many Blacks had made a move or inhibited it because the emanations of the full moon might affect their cause. Now Whitey had walked the moon, put his feet on it. The moon presumably had not spoken. Or had it, and Richard Nixon received the favor and Teddy Kennedy the curse? Was there no magic to combat technology? Then the strength of Black culture was stricken. There would not be a future Black civilization, merely an adjunct to the White. What lava in the raw membranes of the belly. The Black professor had cause to drink. The moon shot had smashed more than one oncoming superiority of the Black.

ii

That night Aquarius had trouble falling asleep, as if the unrest of the Black professor at the passage of men's steps on the moon had now passed over to him. Nothing in the future might ever be the same — that was cause for unrest — nor could the future even be seen until one could answer the obsessive question: was our venture into space noble or insane, was it part of a search for the good, or the agent of diabolisms yet unglimpsed? It was as if we had begun to turn the pocket of the universe inside out.

He had had at the end a curious discussion with the Black professor. "It's all in the remission of sin," the Black man had said. "Technology begins when men are ready to believe that the sins of the fathers are not visited on the sons. Remission of sin — that's what it's all about," he said in his Black slow voice.

Yes, if the sons were not punished, then the father might dare, as no primitive father had dared, to smash through a taboo. If the father was in error, or if he failed, the sons would be spared. Only the father would suffer. So men were thereby more ready to dare the gods. So that love on the cross which had requested that the sons not pay for the sins of the fathers had opened a hairline split which would finally crack the walls of taboo. And the windowless walls of technology came through the gap. Back to Sören the Dane. You could not know if you were a monster or a saint of the deep.

In the Nineteenth Century, they had ignored Kierkegaard. A middle-class White man, living on the rise of Nineteenth Century technology was able to feel his society as an eminence from which he could make expeditions, if he wished, into the depths. He would know all the while that his security was still up on the surface, a ship—if you will—to which he was attached by a line. In the Twentieth Century, the White man had suddenly learned what the Black man might have told him—that there was no ship unless it was a slave ship. There was no security. Everybody was underwater, and even the good sons of the middle class could panic in those depths, for if there were no surface, there was no guide. Anyone could lose his soul. That recognition offered a sensation best described as bottomless. So the Twentieth Century was a century which looked to explain the psychology of the dream, and instead entered the topography of the dream. The real had become more fantastic than the imagined. And might yet possess more of the nightmare.

Lying there, unable to sleep, lost in the caverns of questions whose answers never came (Mr. Answer Man, what is the existential equivalent of infinity?—Why insomnia, Sandy, good old insomnia) Aquarius knew for the first time in years that he no longer had the remotest idea of what he knew. It was the end of the decade, and the fashion was rising in New York literary lakes to inquire after the nature of the decade to come. He had been a poor prophet of the Sixties, but it was not a century for prophets—poor as he had been, he had still been one of the few who had some sense of what was coming. He had known that marijuana was on its way, and Hip, and the Kennedys, and a time of upheaval, and in the center of the Establishment: loss of belief. Now they asked him what he thought of the Seventies. He did not know. He thought of the Seventies and a blank like the windowless walls of the computer city came over his vision. When he conducted interviews with himself on the subject, it was not despair he felt, or fear—it was anesthesia. He had no intimations of what was to come and that was conceivably worse than any sentiment of dread, for a sense of the future, no matter how melancholy, was preferable to none—it spoke of some sense of continuation in the projects of one's life. He was adrift. If he tried to conceive of a likely perspective in the decade before him, he saw not one structure to society but two: if the social world did not break down into revolutions and counterrevolutions, into police and military rules of order with sabotage, guerrilla war and enclaves of resistance, if none of this occurred, then there would certainly be a society of reason, but its reason would be the logic of the computer. In that society, legally accepted drugs would become a necessity for accelerated cerebration, there would be inchings toward nuclear installation, a monotony of architectures, a pollution of nature which would arouse technologies of decontamination odious as deodorants, and transplanted hearts monitored like spaceships—the patients might be obliged to live in a compound reminiscent of a Mission Control Center where technicians could monitor on consoles the beatings of a thousand transplanted hearts. But in the society of computer-logic, the atmosphere would obviously be plastic, air-conditioned, sealed in bubble-domes below the smog, a prelude to living in space stations. People would die in such societies like fish expiring on a vinyl floor. So of course there would be another society, an irrational society of the dropouts, the saintly, the mad, the militant and the young. There the art of the absurd would reign in defiance against the computer.

In the society of the irrational would be found the weather of the whirlpool. Accelerations and torpor would ride over one another with eyes burned out by visions no longer recalled, motorcycles would climb the trees, a night of freakings when all the hair would be burned for the bonfire of the goat, and bald as the moon would be the skins of the scalp. Hare Krishna! A part of the American world, gassed by the smog of computer logic, would live like gurus, babas and yogas in the smallest towns, the small towns of America would be repopulated with the poets of the city, and mysticism would live next to murder, for murder was love in freak newspeak, and the orgy was the family. Because the computer was the essence of narcissism (the computer could not conceive of its inability to correct its own mistakes) a view of the Seventies suggested a technological narcissism so great that freak newspeak was its only cure—only the threat of a murderous society without could keep computer society from withering within. How those societies would mingle! Acid and pot had opened the way.

Yet even this model of the future was too simple. For the society of the rational and the world of the irrational would be without boundaries. Computersville had no cure for skin disease but filth in the wound, and the guru had no remedy for insomnia but a trip to the moon, so people would be forever migrating between the societies. Sex would be a new form of currency in both worlds—on that you could count. The planner and the swinger were the necessary extremes of the computer city, and both would meet in the orgies of the suburbs. But was this a vision of the future or the vertigo of the early hours?

Aquarius got out of bed. He was a disciplinarian about insomnia. Having suffered from it years before, he had learned how to live with an occasional bad night. He took no pill, he took no drink, he looked to ride it out. Sometimes he indulged in a game of formal optimism, carrying over from artillery training the injunction to bracket a target. So now if his sense of the future was too pessimistic—he could only hope it was too dark!—he would look for the formal opposite: try to regard science as reasonable, religion as rewarding. He could see—sitting in a kitchen chair, reading by a lamp—how new religions might crystallize in the Seventies, they could give life, for their view of God might be new. And science . . . But he could not regard science apart from technology. Aquarius began to think of Dr. George Mueller.

iii

He had had an interview with the head of the Manned Space Program when he was back at Kennedy. Once a professor of electronics, Mueller had become the second highest man in NASA, indeed nobody was higher than him but Dr. Thomas O. Paine, yet Mueller was in appearance a very modest man, an archetype to Aquarius of the technician. Mueller—whose name was pronounced Miller—was not tall, certainly he was not short, he was slim in weight, in fact without excess weight, he looked forty-five although he had to be older, and he had a long thin face, a high forehead, straight black hair which he combed straight back—so his black horn-rimmed glasses jutted forth, so did the blade of his nose, the blade of his jaw. He spoke with mild icky-dicky Midwest expletives like "Golly gee, gee whiz, gosh!" that modest but central sense of presence one might find in a YMCA secretary on the night desk—the manner friendly, impersonal, and on an astral plane, a manner to indicate that of course one is used to talking to all sorts of people—golly gee, you ought to see some of the characters who come in here.

Mueller had the reputation of being tremendously determined when he wanted to get something done, and one could believe it, for he emitted the gently but total impersonality of a man for whom obstacles if irrational were unforgivable. Perhaps for this reason he was curiously reminiscent of Hugh Hefner. The publisher of *Playboy* was a little in relation to ordinary men like a guy who had been to the moon and back and Dr. Mueller could have been his older brother.

Aquarius met him in Mueller's motel at Cocoa Beach, a room as modest as his pretensions. There had been a photographer taking pictures. Mueller apologized, explaining that he had been so busy for so many years that he had hardly had a picture taken—now they had discovered there weren't enough pictures of him for the NASA files. So he posed for a few more, in some degree as pleased and flustered as a man walking into a room, and crack! flashbulbs! they are giving him a birthday party.

Yet once the interview began, Mueller was sensitive to every change about him. Did Aquarius, searching for his next question, feel some intensity of motive or charge of energy, then Mueller was there to respond as quickly as the needle on any of the measuring instruments he had used in all the electrical labs of his youth and academic career. Dart! would go his head; up! would fly a finger; sway! would swing his torso. How alert he must have been to signs of overload or impedance in all the human circuits about his field position in the room. Yes, Dr. George Mueller was certainly one full academic counterpart to the Black professor. Having seen Apollo-Saturn rise from the drawing board to an orbit of the moon, it was as natural for him to live with comfort in the future as it was flesh and drink for the Black to brood upon the past. So Mueller was looking beyond this landing to the uses of space in the future. He talked of rocket shuttles which could be fired up to rendezvous with space stations in orbit and yet be able to return through the heats of reentry to land at spaceports in order to be used again; he spoke of lowering the cost of transport in space from $100,000 a pound to $200 a pound; he outlined future projects for nuclear power plants on the moon whose heats would melt the permafrost and so make available a supply of water. The electrical output of the power plant could then separate the water into hydrogen and oxygen—some of that product would be used to make Lox and LH_2 for rocket fuels; the rest would be mixed with nitrogen extracted from the rocks so they would have the elements necessary to create a livable atmosphere within an enclosed space. Perhaps they would even grow plants. Would it be Aristotle Onassis or Richard Burton who would be first to spring for a bouquet of moon roses?

The space station orbiting the earth could go in for a "total earth sensing program," doubtless as comprehensive for the earth, Aquarius decided, as a thorough physical examination conducted daily for a man. The space station would also set up a high-energy physics laboratory. It would certainly accelerate every technique in the manufacture of cameras, telescopes, radars, lasers, and that was just the beginning. Mueller went on in full sentences. He had spoken of these matters a hundred times, but like all high bureaucrats he was equal to a professional actor in his ability to repeat the same dialogue with verve another hundred times. If any reporter had brought a tape recorder, he could by transcribing Mueller's remarks directly have had a printable feature story for a Sunday section. As though unwinding a scroll, Mueller indicated the possibility of a new wonder with each paragraph. Since the space stations would have a weightless environment at their command, it would be possible to grow crystals which would be molecularly perfect. As a corollary, one would be able to build up flawless diamonds of any size. Before Aquarius could ask if the diamond would be as big as the Ritz, Mueller assured him in his cheerful small-town voice that the diamond could be as big as a basketball anyhow—such a cargo might be worth much more than two hundred dollars a pound. Thus the perspective of space factories returning the new imperialists of space a profit was now near to the reach of technology. Forget about diamonds! The value of crystals grown in space was incalculable: gravity would not be pulling on the crystal structure as it grew, so the molecules would line up in lattices free of shift or sheer. Such a perfect latticework could serve to carry messages for a perfect computer. Computers the size of a package of cigarettes would then be able to do the work of present computers the size of a trunk. So the mind could race ahead to see computers programming go-to-school routes in the nose of every kiddie car—the paranoid mind could see crystal transmitters sewn into the rump of every juvenile delinquent— doubtless, everybody would be easier to monitor. In the Systematized Detection Systems of the future, Big Brother could get superseded by Moon Brother—the major monitor of them all might yet be sunk in a shaft on the back face of the lunar sphere.

The possibilities of the new technology glowed in the enthusiasms of Mueller's voice. "Ball bearings," he said holding up a finger like an antenna to focus all scattered waves of random thought, "it's fascinating to consider what possibilities are opened in the manufacture of ball bearings." He went on the explain in his careful considerate feature-story paragraphs that ball bearing which were cast in a weightless environment would come out as perfect spheres; the deviation on their skin need be no greater than the thickness of a molecule. Earth ball bearings were of course imprecise. In the instant it took the shot to cool, gravity was pulling on the molten ball. So to obtain precision they must be polished, a relatively imprecise technique.

Aquarius was to think again of the ball bearings after he said good-by to Dr. Mueller. Such creations of a weightless environment could yet prove monumental for the manufacturer, since ball bearings were as crucial to every load-bearing or load-transporting machine as the valves of the human heart to the flow of blood. Out of the imperfections of ball bearings (which were located after all around the center of every high-speed moving part) came the multiplication of all the other imperfections, since each moving part added the scope of its imprecision to the next moving part. Once perfect ball bearings could be installed, the action of the machines might become a whole order of efficiency closer to the laws of physics, rather than to the adjustments and counterbalances of engineering. That meant a world of future machines whose view of present-day machines might be equal to nothing less than our view of Piltdown man. Or would it merely mean that plastic could now be employed for the ball bearings in order to maintain the built-in obsolescence of machines? Indeed the center of the problem of capitalism's morale was in the perfect ball bearing. Machines built on perfect ball bearings would have a life duration so much greater than present machines that modern capitalism living with the vice of built-in obsolescence as the poison-stimulant to its blood, would be face to face with problems greater and more inescapable than automation. For once space explorers, seeking economic justification, would be forced to develop perfect ball bearings, there use would be bound to explode the sustaining fevers and indulgences of the economy. What then would they all do? Then, capitalism would be as much at war with itself over the continuing nature of the economy as world communism was at war with itself over the direction of its ideology.

So the mood of space which remained with Aquarius after talking to Mueller, that mood elegant and austere as the perfect laws of physical principle, was still a force for disruption. Sitting in the spaced-out colors of Dun Cove, inhabiting the shank end of ruminations like this, was the thought that the moon shot was conceivably the first voyage of the very cancer of the world, for indeed the first journeys of the cancer cell in a body, taken from the point of view of the cancer cell, were certainly bold and dangerous. Not by little effort did a cell leave its own organ and learn how to survive in another. Cancer cells, seen in relation to ordinary cells, were often extraordinary in the variety of their form, as different as a view of Las Vegas at night is different from a village in the Bluegrass, or as different as the internal works of Apollo were in comparison to the works of the family car. Did that account for the curious depression, the sobriety mixed in so many faces with the pride of the achievement? Aquarius did not know.

That was still another reason why he did not perceive the decade to come with any clear picture of events. A dull sense of disaster pushed at the compass of the picture. He was not so certain the decade would have a life like other decades. If space was benign, then on we would continue into space, and the artists would yet be voyaging with the astronauts—think of that happy day when he would nominate himself to be first writer to visit the moon. (Not a chance! NASA would opt for Updike!)

But what if space were not so benign? What if we did not act upon space, explore into space, but space rather acted upon us, drew us toward her dispositions, her plans for us, her intent upon human life, what if we thought we moved up but were drawn up, what if the moon was as quiet as the fisherman when he lays the fly on the water . . .

Having journeyed to the center of his gloom, Aquarius went to sleep. In his dreams a country doctor he had known for years murmured, "I don't know about all of this. Recognize that the moon could be some kind of catchall simple as the tonsils to protect us here on earth. Maybe those craters come from catching all the cess." In his dream Aquarius answered back, "It depends on your idea of God, that's what it must depend on." Out into sleep he went again, ringings of ether in his ear.

iv

In the morning after breakfast, he found himself rereading a transcript of the postlaunch briefing, a curious activity, but he was like a man on the cusp of a clue. To fall asleep in pursuit of the answer to a mystery was to awaken with the fire in a new place. It had burned beneath the ground while he was sleeping. So he dallied over the substance of the transcript as if some hint of smoke could linger here in the words of men taken down for posterity four hours after the launch.

PUBLIC AFFAIRS OFFICER *I'd like to introduce Mr. Rocco A. Petrone, Director of Launch Operations for the Kennedy Space Center and Launch Director for the Apollo* II *flight, Rocco?*

PETRONE *Thank you. Well, this is our sixth Saturn V, the Apollo aboard, to go up in a row on time. But I'm not saying, of course—this meant a lot more to us. This is the big one. This is the one we've been working for eight years. The mission is just getting started. I'm sure you all know. But the first step in this historic mission has been just the step we've wanted to take.*

Every detail of the launch, Aquarius recollected, had been Petrone's responsibility. Four hours after lift-off, matters now comfortably out of his hands, he was by the evidence of the transcript as tired as a boxer in his dressing room after a fifteen-round fight.

PETRONE *From the moment of truth here, from the moment of ignition and lift-off, lots and lots of equipment have to work for a number of starts to come on our side. We had a few difficulties in the count. I'm sure they already fed it to you. I'd be glad to answer questions. I'm pleased to say that the team was able to handle the problems, keeping the count rolling, and very obviously start this historic mission off. I say on the right first step, which I can assure you is most pleasing to me. And for the team that's worked so hard to get to this point . . .*

PUBLIC AFFAIRS OFFICER *Okay, thanks, Rock.*

At NASA, the elegance was in the design of the engineering systems rather than in the manners of the men. Which future student of language, unfamiliar with Saturn V, Apollo II or lift-off, would have any idea, encountering this scrap of Petrone's transcript, that the man was describing the emotions he felt after having led thousands of men in Launch Control through the nine hundred hours, the ninety and the nine hours of the preparations and countdowns which put his ship into the air. Who was to know by such a speech — thought Aquarius sipping his breakfast tea — that Petrone had beem midwife to the most momentous week, and the mightiest hour. Yes, and that was not so ridiculous if one recognized that to believe in progress and believe in God as well might make it necessary to conceive of our Lord as a vision of existence who conceivably was obliged to compete with other visions of existence in the universe, other conceptions of how life should be. But this had brought him to the heart of the question. It was as if his mind, knowing the style of his thoughts, had directed him to the transcript in the confidence that his sense of irony once aroused, his sense of apocalypse could never be far behind. He was, after all, quick to hunt for reason in absurdity. So to read the language of men who were not devoid of mechanical genius and yet spoke in language not even fit for a computer, of events which might yet dislocate eternity, was a fine irony — the banality of the verbal reaction was an indication of the disease of our time, so advanced in one lobe, so underdeveloped in the other, a fine irony! Unless one was encountering the very desperation of the Lord — there might not be time to develop men to speak like Shakespeare as they departed on heavenly ships.

To believe in God and to believe in progress — what could that mean but that the desire for progress existed in the very creation of man, as if man were designed from the outset to labor as God's agent, to carry God's vision of existence across the stars. If this were true then the intent of the Lord could hardly be to reveal His goodness to us; rather He must employ us to reveal His vision of existence *out there*, somewhere out there where His hegemony came to an end and other divine conceptions began to exist, or indeed were opposed to us. If God finally was the embodiment of a vision which might cease to exist in the hostilities of the larger universe, a vision which indeed might be *obliged* to prevail or would certainly cease to exist, then it was legitimate to see all of human history as a cradle which had nurtured a baby which had now taken its first step. Intended by divine will to travel across the heavens, we were now at least on our way to the moon, and who could know if we were ahead or behind of some schedule the Lord had presented us, a schedule which presumably each man and woman alive would keep in the depths of their unconscious along with everything else most vital for the preservation of life. A large and uncomfortable thought, for if it were so, then the flight of Apollo II was a first revelation of the real intent of History. So this much, anyway, had been revealed: one could not make a judgment on the value or absurdity of devoting such effort to go to the moon unless one was ready to recognize that eschatology had conceivably been turned on its head. For if eschatology, that science of "the four last things: death, judgment, heaven and hell," was now to be considered in the light of God's need for supermen to negotiate His passage quickly through the heavens, then how much more value might He give to courage than to charity, how much harsh judgment to justice itself if the act to be considered was not expeditious but merely just, yes if speed were of the essence then Hell's Angels were possibly nearer to God than the war against poverty.

This last suggested a step Aquarius was not prepared to take: the idea was as disruptive to a liberal philosophical system as tartar emetic and mustard to a glutton. For it offered a reason why the heroes of the time were technologists, not poets, and the art was obliged to be in the exceptional engineering, while human communication had become the routine function. It was because the Power guiding us had desired nothing less. He was looking to the day when all of mankind would yet be part of one machine, with mechanical circuits, social flesh circuits, and combined electromagnetic and thought-transponder circuits, an instrument of divine endeavor put together by a Father to whom one might no longer be able to pray since the ardors of His embattled voyage could have driven Him mad.

Sweet thoughts for Aquarius to have as a sequel to the ascent, but the questions were grand at least, they could occupy the consciousness of the century. It was somehow superior to see the astronauts and the flight of Apollo II as the instrument of such celestial or satanic endeavors, than as a species of sublimation for the profoundly unmanageable violence of man, a meaningless journey to a dead arena in order that men could engage in the irrational activity of designing machines which would give birth to other machines which would travel to meaningless places as if they were engaged in these collective acts of hugely organized but ultimately pointless activity because they had not the wit, goodness, or charity to solve their real problems, and so would certainly destroy themselves if they did not have a game of gargantuan dimensions for diversion, a devilish entertainment, a spend-spree of resources, a sublimation, yes, the very word, a sublimation of aggressive and intolerably inhuman desires, as if like a beast enraged with the passion of gorging nature, we looked now to make incisions into the platinum satellite of our lunacy, our love, and our dreams.

Aquarius would have given much to find a truly revealing face at NASA, for that could have given a clue to these questions, but it was in the logic of such endeavor that no answers be apparent on the surface. If it would take the rest of the century to begin to disclose the real intent of the act, no lightning raid on the evidence, no single happy disclosure, could possibly offer a reply.

Still, Aquarius preferred the first assumption, that we were the indispensable instruments of a monumental vision with whom we had begun a trip. On that conclusion he would rest his thoughts. Having come back at last to earth from the orbits of the dream with such a hypothesis in his pocket, Aquarius was a little more ready to head for home, the writing of a book and conceivably the pouring of a drink. The study of more than one technical manual awaited him.

Part III: The Age of Aquarius

CHAPTER 1, THE HANGING OF THE HIGHWAYMAN

There was a melancholy to the end of a century. The French, who were the first to specify a state for every emotion, would speak of the *fin de siècle*. It was the only name to give his own mood, for Aquarius was in a depression which would not lift for the rest of the summer, a curious depression full of fevers, forebodings, and a general sense that the century was done — it had ended in the summer of 1969.

If he had had his extraordinary night of insomnia in Houston, and had thought his way out, well, that was just for one night. The woes of these hot weeks sat upon him as he slept and as he worked. He was used to writing in moods so bad he could assume he was passing through a swamp at midnight — some of his best work had come out of periods worse than this, and some of his worst efforts had emerged from hours which had been too pleasant. It was almost as if he had to suffer while working in order to come closer to exercising some more ultimate faculty of judgment. It was a terror to write if one wished to speak of important matters and did not know if one was qualified — sometimes the depressions helped to give sanction to the verdicts taken. It was not so unreasonable. The question is whether it is better to trust a judge who travels through his own desolations before passing sentence, or a jurist who has a good meal, a romp with his mistress, a fine night of sleep, and a penalty of death in the morning for the highwayman.

To write was to judge, and Aquarius may never have tried a subject which tormented him so.

ii

He had come home the day before the astronauts came back to earth. There were splashdown parties promised all over Houston, and he was tempted to remain, for there would be portraits in plenty to paint of Texas drinking and poolside brawls, but he was also in a panic to get back and start work — his first deadline was not three weeks off. Each extra day at this end could be a reprieve at the other. Still much in the middle of the event, mental digestions churning, he returned to the bosom of his family.

The house was sour; the milk gave every intimation that it had curdled. His wife and he were getting along abominably. They had had hideous phone calls these last few weeks while he was away. Several times, one or the other had hung up in the middle of a quarrel. It was impossible to believe, but they each knew—they were coming to an end. They could not believe it for they loved their two sons as once they had loved each other, but now everything was wrong. It was sad. They had met on a night of full moon, and would end in the summer of the moon. Sometimes his wife seemed as if deranged by Apollo's usurpation of the moon. She was extraordinarily sensitive to its effects; she was at best uneasy and at worst unreachable when the moon was full. Through the years of their marriage Aquarius had felt the fullness of the moon in his own dread, his intimations of what full criminality he might possess, had felt the moon in the cowardice not to go out on certain nights, felt the moon when it was high and full and he was occasionally on the side of the brave. And she was worse. Call her Pisces for the neatness of the scheme. Beverly, born sign of Pisces. She was an actress who now did not work. An actress who does not work is a maddened beast. His lovely Pisces, subtle at her loveliest as silver, would scream on nights of the full moon with a voice so loud she sounded like an animal in torment. They were far and away the noisiest house on the street.

It hardly mattered in Provincetown. That was the land of the free. At the very tip of Cape Cod, a fishing town curled around a spiral of land whose sand dunes separated the bay and the sea, it was a town of Portuguese and Yankees in winter, of artists, faggots, hippies, bikers, debs, dikes, off-course jets, groupies, and beefed-up beer-drinking tourists from Jersey in summer, not to mention hordes of middle-class professionals with progressive views and artistic liens. An isthmus of quiet in the calm months, it was no island of the mind in July, no, it was the Wild West of the East, and it took forty-five minutes in the middle of August to drive a car half a mile down the one-lane main street. Marijuana was as available in Provincetown in the hideous hocks of summer as popcorn is plentiful in a drive-in movie in Iowa. Aquarius, of course, had none of it, not these years, not when working. He could not afford it. His brain was always lost for the following day. But now he had to work in its presence. There was hardly a dentist, a psychoanalyst, a townie, or a narco agent who was not turned on half the time, and the drinking parties among the most sedate began at five and ended at five with the dawn coming up his window on the bay, the gulls croaking their readjustments to all the twisted vertebrae of sand and sea. Stoned out of the very head of sensation, the summer populace was still groping and brooding and pondering its way down the gray and lavender beach in the red-ball dawn, sun coming over the water in one long shot of fire — Provincetown was the only place in the East he knew where the land spiraled so far around that you could see the sun rise out of the dunes in the east and set in water to the west. What a town! There was not one of his wrong and ill-conceived books he had not written in part here, and all of his good books as well, all of this books. He had learned how to work in summer if he had to, but one needed the skill of a contemplative who pitched his tent by a hot dog stand. So he hated his beloved Provincetown this summer above all.

It had been bad from the moment he was back. One of the early nights after his return, perhaps two or three days after splashdown, he had taken his wife and one of his best friends to a restaurant for dinner. The friend was Eddie Bonetti, a battered knob-nosed working writer out of South Boston, handsome as an old truck to those who knew him well, a small rugged prodigy of talent who had boxed a few fights professionally and been given working lessons in the gym by Willie Pep. Bonetti wrote poetry, perhaps he was the best working poet in Provincetown, certainly the best Aquarius had heard, and he had written a very good short novel about an old Italian making wine, a manuscript which was always on the edge of getting published by editors who were almost ready to put up with its brevity and its chastity — like many an Italian before him, Eddie Bonetti did not swear in print.

"Norman, I'm so fucking glad you're back," he declared for the fourth time in his loudest voice five minutes after they sat down in the restaurant.

Bonetti stored his talent in many places. He had acted in two of Aquarius' movies, memorable in a small part in one, unforgettable in another. He had played an axe murderer who killed his wife after fifteen years of marriage; Aquarius was fond of saying that Bonetti was as good an actor as Emil Jannings for one night in his life. But that had been in passing. Bonetti also grew the best tomatoes in town, and had been known to play his flute to them in the middle of the night. Eddie was also capable while riding a bicycle down the main street (if he saw a friend driving behind him) of jumping his bike off the street across the sidewalk and into the bushes, where he would take a wild dive over the handlebars into the grass, just to give his friends the craziest laugh of the week. Bonetti could say, "I'm worried about my heart," and fall immediately on his back, there to wink at you. Bonetti was a prodigy of talent.

But he was drunk this night. He was drunk before the evening began. Because he had a big punchy sepulchral voice even in the quietest of times, it was booming everywhere tonight on his drinks. "Fuck, Norman, I didn't know whenna fuck you were gonna get back," he bellowed again in his best Savin Hill South Boston tones and the carnal communicant quavered like an organ pipe with a crazy nonstop overtone in the clean white tablecloth Wasp spa to which they had gone, an error of incomparable dimension, for Eddie in his dungarees and blue sweat shirt was as funky as the upholstery in the last used car on the lot. His clothes were in line for nine out of ten restaurants in town, but not where they were now — indeed Aquarius had picked it to obtain some afterthoughts on the moon shot. But Bonetti had a good century-old stiffening of his drunken proletarian senses when they walked in. No restaurant was going to put *him* down. So Aquarius, proud Aquarius, iconoclast of the last two decades, was obliged to act as a middle-class silencer, "Will you keep your voice down," he blasted in a hopeless murmur.

"Norman, this place is filled with drunken assholes. Fucking drunken assholes."

"Eddie, I'll give you two to one you can't go through the meal without saying fuck."

"Norman, I don't want to take your money."

The bet was made. Eight dollars to four dollars. Before three minutes had passed, Bonetti had lost. Aquarius bet him again. Another two minutes and Eddie said, "These shrimp are fucking good shrimp."

Down eight dollars, his good mood cracked. Bonetti's wife was meeting them later. She worked as a waitress while Bonetti wrote — the lost eight dollars was now salt in his sores. Bonetti lived with his wounds. So he grew morose, and the meal took solid conservative steps. The Wasps at the neighboring tables recovered a few of the harmonies which had been blasted out of their bite. The sense of being stitched across the back by rays of displeasure abated. Aquarius did not know how many pinholes had been left in him, but the air in the restaurant was like the awful air of America on its perpetual edge, nihilisms gathering at the poles, dreams of extermination in all the camps. He looked at the Wasp at the adjoining table, a sturdy worthy with silver-rimmed glasses, red righteous ire in the flat red washes of his cheeks, the mottling of his neck. Two mature ladies with silver-rimmed glasses and silver curls and cones of marcel in their beauty parlor lacquer sat in court upon his specimen of the great unwashed, Bonetti, eating lobster right next to them. He felt suddenly as if he had betrayed Eddie —

to calm him down was to leave him a target for every wild nihilism of the Wasp, that same laser of concentration and lack of focus on consequence which had taken us up to the moon.

Later, Aquarius was livid. At another place, listening to music, Bonetti's wife joined them, and he told her with keen cruelty, "I hope Eddie bleeds over those eight bucks. He ruined the meal." What he could not give voice to was a voice large and endless in its condemnations of himself and all the friends of his generation and the generations which had followed, an indictment of the ways they had used their years, drinking, deep into grass and all the mind illuminants beyond the grass, princelings on the trail of the hip, so avid to deliver the sexual revolution that they had virtually strained on the lips of the great gate. They had roared at the blind imbecility of the Square, and his insulation from life, his furious petulant ignorance of the true tremor of kicks, but now it was as if the moon had flattened all of his people at once, for what was the product of their history but bombed-out brains, bellowings of obscenity like the turmoil of cattle, a vicious ingrowth of informers, police agents, militants, angel hippies, New Left totalists, entropies of vocabulary where they would all do their thing—but "thing" was the first English word for anomaly—an unholy stew of fanatics, far-outs, and fucked-outs where even the few one loved were intolerable at their worst, an army of outrageously spoiled children who cooked with piss and vomit while the Wasps were quietly moving from command of the world to command of the moon, Wasps presenting the world with the fact after prodigies of discipline, while the army he was in, treacherous, silly, overconfident and vain, haters and despisers of everything tyrannical, phony, plastic and overbearing in American life had dropped out, goofed and left the goose to their enemies. Who among all the people he knew well had the remotest say on the quality of these lunar expeditions whose results might yet enter the seed of them all with concentrates worse than their collective semen already filled with DDT. An abominable army. A debauch. And he hated his good friend Eddie Bonetti for this, hated him for drinking at the post. "You've been drunk all summer," he felt like saying to him, "and *they* have taken the moon." Yes, there was a wild nihilism in his own army: the people were regurgitating the horrors of the centuries, looking to slip the curse out of their seed and into the air, while the curse reentered their seed through every additive in every corporate food. And on the other side, heroes or monsters, the Wasps had put their nihilism into the laser and the computer, they were out to savage or save the rest of the world, and were they God's intended? Looking at his drunken own, Aquarius did not know. He was one judge who would write willy-nilly out of his desolations this year.

CHAPTER 2, "THE WORLD IS BIGGER INFINITELY"

To make everything worse, he was forced to see the end of the mission on television. He had applied months ago to cover the splashdown from the *Hornet*, but NASA and the Pentagon limited that number of reporters to a pool of three. So the end of the greatest week was seen by him in his living room in Provincetown, glaring at the television set—there was nothing to see. The sky was fogged. He was left to watch a succession of commentators. Since this came after days of watching TV in Houston, days of hearing the score of *Yellow Submarine* inserted behind old color movies of Gemini 6 and 7 doing a space ballet, he felt drowned. The flavonoids and the plasticoids had taken over. It was his name for TV men. He sometimes thought they came from a species which did not seem to have blood precisely, but some high concentration of haemoglobin-flavonoid in cryogenic plasma. If someone came on their show and cut off their arm or their nose, they would grow another one—plasticoid-flavonoid was a mutation which came from years of talking into microphones and passing on the remark somebody else had just handed you.

So he felt somehow deprived of the last beauties of the Command Module and the flight plan. Reentry was now the most predictable part of the mission and if, in relative terms, it was safe, still with that part of his brain which would insist on remaining a technological child of his century, he had to admire the splendors of the design for reentry. There would after all have been never a trip to the moon if there had not been a means to get back to earth discovered years ago—the atmosphere surrounding the planet offered the friction of a Carborundum wheel toward any object which approached from space. The heat generated was sufficient to consume everything but an occasional meteor. Yet a means had been evolved for safe reentry. Apollo 11 would come back at the speed it left, come back at seven miles a second, 25,000 miles an hour. The Command Module would separate from the Service Module back of it, and the Service Module would burn in the atmosphere to leave only the little cone ten and a half feet high, twelve feet ten inches wide, the mini-cathedral holding the three astronauts strapped in their couches, just ten and a half feet to come back out of three hundred and sixty-three feet, that alone to come back out of all that mighty ship of Apollo-Saturn which had first gone up. The Command Module would come skipping into the atmosphere on a carefully measured route, guided by its thrusters, which were controlled in turn by the computer, or in event of malfunction, by the men. Approaching base-first, its rounded circular base slapping into the atmosphere like a flat stone popping along the surface of a pond, it would sear a path through the sky from eighty miles up and fifteen hundred miles away from the site of splashdown, singeing through the outer air in an incandescent deceleration down to a horizontal speed of a few hundred feet a second, slow enough for a pair of drogue parachutes to open and turn its horizontal path down over to a line of descent. That would occur four miles up. At ten thousand feet, the drogue chute would be released and three little pilot chutes would deploy three larger parachutes, each of a diameter of eighty-three feet. They would slow the vertical descent from one hundred seventy-five miles an hour to twenty-two miles an hour, and the Command Module, swinging on suspension lines one hundred and twenty feet below her three canopies (which had previously been packed in a ring around her docking tunnel), would be deposited in the water in an area within a few miles of the carrier *Hornet*. Immediately, a built-in cutter would sever the parachute lines. If the Command Module ended upside down in the water—a position called Stable II—then three inflatable bags in the forward compartment, blown up by compressors on board, would proceed to float the cone over so she was riding on her base. Swimmers, dropped from approaching helicopters, would attach a flotation collar, and bring up a raft. The astronauts would emerge from the hatch. After decontamination procedures they would be lifted in a sling to the helicopters and brought to the *Hornet*. It was neat. It had been as carefully worked out as the deployment of the Navy of Recovery over thousands of miles of the Pacific. Still, the foundation of all reentry remained the heat shield at the base of the Command Module, nothing but an epoxy resin, a species of phenolic plastic injected in a honeycomb screen. It was not even three inches thick at its widest but it would bear a reentry temperature of 5000 degrees Fahrenheit, hotter than the fiercest kiln, hotter than the melting point of all metals but tantalum and tungsten and they in alloy with anything but themselves would also have softened, so the heat shield of phenolic epoxy was a virtuoso piece of engineering. Indeed, it left no residual problem of cooling down from high temperatures once velocity had slowed. The material heated in chips which turned white-hot, charred, melted, and then flaked away leaving no ember behind, but only a chip of fresh material to be charred in its turn. The epoxy once gone, the spaceship was through reentry as well, its brazed-steel honeycomb heat shield back of that char layer no hotter than 600 degrees at touchdown, and the interior of the Command Module remained at 75 degrees. Yet on the way down, the spacecraft would gleam like a comet, a pale violet flame would flare behind it for hundreds of yards in a galaxy of molecules, a nebula of heat and light.

Well, none of that would he see. Not the flames of reentry on this cloudy day, nor the firing of the mortars on the Command Module to pop those first drogue parachutes far out beyond the turbulence of their immediate wake, no, nor would he have an eyewitness sense of the scene on board the *Hornet* — first instrument of rescue for the Wasp! — no, the news pool was providing all news of the *Hornet*. For the heat and energy of the reception one would have to depend on the atmosphere of the handouts from the press pool. They had accumulated every day in the mimeograph rack in the News Center at Houston, and he had taken a sheaf before he left. Now, he leafed through them while watching the plasticoids and the flavonoids on the TV screen, and President Nixon waiting upon the bridge of the *Hornet* with the Admiral. The Press Release, he decided, was an undiscovered literary form; indeed was it not the seed-bull of Camp?

ii

WUI − 017 NASA − 017 PRESS PD FROM WUI PRESS CENTER USS
HORNET 14TH LOS ANGELES ▼IMES
FROM CHARLES HILLINGER ABORD THE USS HORNET

ABOARD THE HORNET — THE SHIP'S SKIPPER APPEARED ON TV STANDING BEFORE A CHART OF THE MID-PACIFIC WITH A POINTER IN HAND . . .

"EACH OF US MUST BE DOUBLY VIGILANT IN PERFORMING OUR DUTIES ON JULY 24," DECLARED CAPT. CARL J. SIEBERLICH, 48, WHOSE HOME ASHORE WITH HIS WIFE, TRUDY, AND THREE CHILDREN IS IN THE MIRALESTE AREA OF PALOS VERDES PENINSULA, CALIF.

"THE THREE MOST IMPORTANT PEOPLE IN THE WORLD AT THAT TIME IN HISTORY WILL COME ABOARD OUR SHIP. WE ARE THE LAST LINK IN A VERY IMPORTANT CHAIN."

. . . .

. . . .

He did not know if he learned any more when word came back to him of the splashdown parties. Like a true journalist he was on the phone for full sessions with his informants, and the accounts had that essential wonder which speaks of the exaggeration of the journalist overcome by the exaggeration of events. In deference to the mission it had been a quiet week in Nassau Bay until splashdown — night after night it was as if no one connected with NASA dared to get too drunk for fear of fudged responses in the morning. A few hours after splashdown, however, the parties began; they had begun in effect from the moment technicians from the Staff Support rooms began to fill the Mission Operations Control Room, and people wet cigars and waited for the astronauts to come in on the helicopter and land on the carrier, and when they did, little flags came out and were waved in everyone's hand. The aisles jammed between the consoles with scores of personnel who now were crowding in the door.

From there, parties spread in all directions. Out through the computer-designed suburbs around the Manned Spacecraft Center spread the celebrations, and up the highway to Houston. There was a large and formal ball in Houston that night at the Marriott Hotel from seven to nine, put together by the twenty-five main contractors in the Apollo Program, North American, Grumman and General Electric to lead the rest, a huge orchestration and libation with paté de foie gras, pigs in blankets, shrimp and eggs and olives, and ice carvings on the tables of antelope, pumpkin and dolphin tails, plus two thousand guests, the cream (selected by the twenty-five corporations) of nabobs from NASA king contractors, and bona-fide River Oaks Houston. It was a proper party, and the bar closed at nine-thirty. There were even ladies wearing red-white-and-blue Ed White scarves (autographed by every astronaut) which were sold by astronauts' wives to make money for the "Ed White Memorial Fund."

Word was out, however, of another party which had begun in the Nassau Bay Motor Inn, the motel off NASA Highway Number i with the round red velvet beds where Aquarius had stayed weeks before. There everybody was welcome — $1.50 bought barbecue beef and drinks were $1.15 if you did not bring your own. Three thousand people came not in beards and not with sideburns, rather in short-sleeve shirts with neckties, the ladies in cocktail dresses, scarce were the ladies in décolletage and mini-skirts and pants suits — it was a regiment of office workers, engineers, technicians, secretaries, and people wandering in off the highway, the sun burning the pool until nightfall, then the night itself with all of young NASA-land driving into the great trough of all-out recreation, rebel yells finally tearing the Texas air. At seven-thirty in the evening two men threw a blond into the pool. A man followed immediately. The heats of the party were on. A go-go dancer got up on the diving board and worked to the gut rhythm of a band called the Astronauts—six Blacks. The Blacks were finally at NASA. Men climbed up the diving board, went flying past the go-go girls and into the pool, beer cans followed, and broken whisky bottles, chairs and shoes and pieces of clothing, bodies thumped in with the splat of mortars, and toilet paper was slung over the bushes and the lawn. A bouncer with a fire extinguisher went prowling the corridors in the main body of the inn looking for teeny boppers who had jammed the elevator. It went on until four in the morning.

Listening to his informants, Aquarius had a pang for not being there, as if some knowledge more revelatory than the rest might have come his way, some better sense of what resided in the computer men of the windowless walls, but he did not really know that it would have mattered any more than being on the *Hornet*. What did it matter finally if one were anywhere but on the moon for this story? God or Devil at the helm—that was the question behind the trip, and any vulgarities or fine shows of spirit on the good carrier *Hornet*, any verdict decided by the detritus in the pool on the morning after, would hardly reveal the core of the event. That core was buried in the nerve ends of everyone's life. One might as well judge the event from an armchair, for a species of apocalypse was upon us. This was, after all, repeat, the year in which a couple had fornicated on the stage and we had landed on the moon, this was the decade in which we had probed through space, and who knew which belts of protection had been voided and what precisely they had protected. A revolution was in the air which could overthrow every living establishment, an organization of society was also building which might march men daily through aisles monitored by computer probes, there to measure the individual deviations and developments of the night. That was equally on its way. We had contracted for a lunar program in 1961 and what a decade had followed! The times were loose, and no scientist alive could prove that the moon was wholly a dead body any more than they could show that death was a state of being totally dead. Teddy Kennedy's car went off the bridge at Chappaquiddick with Mary Jo Kopechne and the hopes of the Democratic Party went with them as a proper end to a period which had begun with the suicides of Ernest Hemingway and Marilyn Monroe; the younger brother of Martin Luther King was found dead in his swimming pool the day after men walked the moon. And Provincetown was like a province of the moon in these days of a moon-crazy summer through which he was obliged to work, marriage with Pisces foundering around him, Provincetown, where Eugene O'Neill had lived in the dunes and Anna Christie's father cursed "that ole debbil sea." Did the seagulls call these bronze mornings of August dawn with a special fright across the long flats? He could not rid himself altogether of the thought that the moon might be a resting place for more than the hounds of the tide. Perhaps the mysterious magnetosphere had been designed to hold back all those streams of ignoble dead who did not deserve the trip, perhaps the belts of protection were now being voided in all of afterlife, and so anomalies were rising from hell—he was obliged to wonder if man had finally become a cancer in the forms of the Lord. Yet, equally, the fullness of the moon in Provincetown these nights after the landing was more radiant with lunacy than ever. What if the moon had been drawing us to her for years, what if the plastic amphitheaters of NASA were nothing less than the intimations of her call? It was obvious that if he were without compass to the designs of the Father, then of course he had no clue to the nature of the moon: she could be a disguise of Heaven or as easily the Infernal Shades. For another man, such thoughts might have been dangerous, as dangerous as for Aquarius to drive a sports car with a loose wheel down a mountain road, but it was his profession to live alone with thoughts at the very edge of his mental reach. If brooding over unanswered questions was the root of the mad, however, and sanity was the settling of dilemmas, then with how many questions could one live? He would answer that it was better to live with too many then too few. Rave on, he would. He would rave on.

CHAPTER 3, A BURIAL
BY THE SEA

The strain of the summer did not abate. He went back to Houston in the middle of August to see the astronauts at a press conference when they came out of quarantine, and they looked astonishingly the same as they had in the last conference eleven days before they left for the moon. He had long held the theory that experts were men who had the least sensitivity to their subject and so experienced the smallest difficulty in memorizing a huge number of facts concerning their topic. He had only to think of some of the sports writers, literary critics and pornographers he had known, to be confirmed in his thesis. Now he wondered if that was why the astronauts were the first experts in walking on the moon.

Back in New York next evening, he was again a student of TV as he watched the dinner party President Nixon gave for the crew of Apollo II and several thousand NASA men, contractors and guests.

When Nixon got up to speak, Aquarius' host switched on a projector loaded with a color film of a boy and girl making love. But the television set was made to serve as the screen. Soon a vagina fluttered butterfly wings over the nose and mouth of the speaker. The laughter that came up from the toils and locks of the company's hard-hearted plumbing was close to apocalyptic. With astonishment Aquarius found himself laughing as hard as the rest. Jokes at the expense of Nixon usually bored him. If Aquarius thought Nixon's most striking effect upon America was as a blood-letter who would reduce all passions, Aquarius was on the other hand not so certain that America had not needed a leech for its fever. From across a political divide, he admired what he had come to decide was Nixon's grasp on political genius — to be so unpopular and yet successful — that was genius! So Aquarius was bored with liberals who thought politics was equal to loathing Nixon. But the sight of that young and wide-open pussy fluttering back and forth over the dish antenna of Richard Nixon's endlessly inquiring face touched off some explosion of frustrations in all of them, battered, bewildered, dislocated New Yorkers roaring now like college kids doubly in love with themselves for the success of the prank.

Back in Provincetown, however, marriages were breaking up as fast as tires blowing a long race. The most astonishing couples — a man and woman, for example, who had been married unhappily and most tenaciously for twenty years — were breaking up. He counted at least five such surprising dissolutions where one, or at most two, might be par for a warm season. He didn't know if all those marriages had ended because the principals felt ridiculous before the serious actions of men in other places this summer, or whether the marriages had smashed on the outraged waves of some unmeasurable radiation from the roiled invisible waters of Tranquility Base.

As if answer to the moon landing, the Woodstock Music Festival came and went, and four hundred thousand children sat in the rain for two days and nights and listened to rock music, the electronic amplifications elevating the nerves beneath the fingernails of the musicians to the Holy of Holies; Sharon Tate, three friends, and an employee, plus her unborn baby seven months in the womb, were murdered in a guttering of blood all over the walls of her jewel-box of a dwelling in the whimpering Hollywood hills. He felt no shock in further weeks to come when Manson and his family were arrested, for like many novelists Aquarius had a few stray powers of divination, and had projected a novel two years before about a gang of illumined and drug-accelerated American guerrillas who lived in the wilds of a dune or a range and descended on Provincetown to kill. A year later, parts of four girls had been found in a common grave in Truro eight miles away. They would bring to trial a young man from the town who was steeped by report in no modest depths of witchcraft. Yes, drugs to expand consciousness were detonating the banks of fires burning beneath these hundreds of years, and Provincetown was country for witches: here the Pilgrims had landed, here first in the weeks before they moved to Plymouth, Provincetown was the beginning of America for Americans, an immense quadrangle of motel to prove it now on the ground where the Pilgrims first sailed around the point, anchored, and rowed an explorer's boat to shore.

ii

His friends, the Bankos, buried a car as Labor Day approached. They had purchased a heap for the summer, purchased it with a request of the salesman that he sell them a piece of well-used automobile which would manage to survive through August and into the first weeks of September, but it died before Labor Day was on them, bearings gone, valves gone, oil pan cracked, and broken crankshaft—it was gone. Something in the mood of the summer brought every neighbor in for the burial. The sculptor Jack Kearney became the master of the rites, and poets living near became sacramental officers of the day. Friends came with drinks, while Harold McGinn, local contractor with bulldozer and earth digger, was there to scoop a hole six feet by eight feet by eight feet deep. A rope was put up to hold the neighbors and children from cavorting too near the abyss. And the car, a two-tone sedan of apricot and cream of a long-gone year with mourns of chromium now pitted by salt air and eight years of sun, such faded vehicle, was pushed back by the pallbearers, Aquarius among them, to land with its rear bumper, trunk and differential in the hole and its hood to the sky. The bulldozer leaned it up to a near vertical, and the pallbearers shoveled in earth and tamped sand at the base of the hole. Children ate cake and candy. A boy dressed in the black robes of a Byzantine priest read somber verses from Virgil, the Latin passing like a wash of coagulants over the car still settling in its half-buried grave, and Heaton Vorse in a cape and long-brimmed loose-hinged hat read from the Song of Solomon, sounds of mirth going up as the lines fell like hoops on the promontories of the apricot and cream Ford.

> I compare you, my love,
>   to a mare of Pharoah's chariots.
> Your cheeks are comely with ornaments,
> Your neck with strings of jewels.

Vorse was the son of Mary Heaton Vorse, a lady radical who had participated in such events as the Paterson strike now fifty years gone, and Heaton Vorse had a long Yankee nose which virtually touched his plank of a chin. He read to the Ford:

> Your navel is a rounded bowl,
> That never lacks mixed wine.
> Your belly is a heap of wheat,
>   encircled with lilies.
> Your two breasts are like two fawns,
>   twins of a gazelle.
> Your neck is like an ivory tower.
> Your eyes are pools in Heshbon.

The crowd applauded, and Aquarius felt the proper warmth a funeral should evoke, a sorrow in the pit of merriment and the humor of the very sad—all these Provincetown neighbors out to applaud the burial of an old oil-soaked beast, and the Bankos circulated beer while children ran around the edge of the event, impatient for the ceremony to cease so that they might begin to paint the half of the auto protruding from earth. A child reached in through the open window and turned a switch. The windshield wipers went on in a flick. "My God, it's not dead yet," said a voice. But as if in a throe of its last effluents, the washers began to spurt a final lymph.

Eddie Bonetti read his poem, "Duarte Motors giveth, and terminal craftsmanship taketh away." Bonetti had worked all summer on a truck, finding the pieces he needed in the town dump, had worried over the Chevrolet manual for pickup trucks of the year of his buy the way a medical student in first-year anatomy goes through strings of flesh which might be nerves, Bonetti had lived with the mysteries of a working transmission through all of this summer, a dungeon of grease by evening to the groans of his pale blond Missouri wife, and Eddie read in his deep cockeyed booming voice, eloquent as the wind which announces a shift in the omens, played with his poetic humors, which moved ponderous phrases through turns of silver by shift of weight, and his poem continued, honoring this buried friend, conceived in cynicism and sold in exhortation on the floor of Duarte Motors, agent of promises too huge for its fealty to the domains of work, too large for its embarkation back into the particulars of the soil. It was a heroic poem for the occasion (bound to have been printed if it had not been lost) and Aquarius, finding himself drunk unexpectedly on this afternoon of curious frolic, unable for once to resist the noise and calls of the last of summer and the ferments of the town, had come wandering out of his studio to attend half aghast, half sympathetic, to the idiocies of his friends—they would chop up a lawn mower to serve a salad.

The last of the poets, Walter Howard, was reading Numbers 16.

> But if the Lord creates something new, and the ground opens its mouth and swallows them up, with all that belongs to them, and they go down alive into Sheol, then you shall know that these men have despised the Lord.

The children were out with brushes and paints, drawing figures, figure-drippings, and inchoate totems on the vertical roof of the car, and Kearney was limning the exposed bottom of the crankcase and chassis with lights of green luminescent pigment in slashes through the grease, hints of war paint—slowly the radiant ribbings of an insert's belly emerged from the dark and open works.

> And as he finished speaking all these words, the ground under them split asunder and the earth opened its mouth and swallowed them up with their households. And all the men that belonged to Korah and all their goods.

Now the children were slinging paint through the open windows onto the vinyl of an old upholstery. Aquarius watched his wife at the other end of the lawn and knew again as he had known each day of this summer that their marriage was over. Something had touched the moon and she would be never the same. The sense of love as a balm for the vacuums of the day was departed from them—they were sealed from one another, a run of seven years was done, and his heart throbbed like a bruise in the thigh.

So he mourned the hour as well as any man would when his pains were not small, even mourned for the beast who cried out in Banko's half-burned Ford, mourned him like the skull of poor Yorick, and came back often in the next day and the next to watch Kearney the sculptor work with his torch and goggles to weld bumpers and angles of chromium into mandibles and legs while insect's antennae reached up in a mute's catalepsy to the sky. And they put floodlights at the base. The funeral had ended in an artifact for the summer of the moon in the East End of Provincetown not a hundred feet off the street which runs around the bay, not a half-mile in from the edge of town, Metamorphosis, titled by Kearney, a massive Yorick of half a Ford standing twelve feet high, first machine to die with burial in the land of the Pilgrims and the cod.

iii

And in those days, men will seek death and will not find it; they will long to die and death will fly from them.

That was from Revelations 8:7 and gives a clue to Aquarius' thoughts at the funeral. It was a day for more than a little to seek to die, for his work had him studying colonizations on the moon, conversion of oxygen from moon rocks, and cities of moon-based energy derived from radiations of the sun. Moon vegetables huge in size would grow in the reduced gravity of the field, the plants to thrive in hydroponic waters (also extracted from moon rocks) while algae proliferated in gardens of new-made atmosphere beneath a dome. The effort of these colonies would offer no less than the cheap manufacture on the moon vacuum of products of mass consciousness—electronics, communications, pharmaceuticals, yes, Sartre might be right and consciousness the conversion of Being to Nothingness, yes, the tools of the future mind seemed to be forged best in a vacuum—soon they would be orbiting rocket trains of cancer patients to take the cure in space, for the growth of malignancy was slowed apparently by radiation in weightless condition. Pain appeared at the thought of a new species of men born in lunar gravity, bodies grown in lunar gravity—what form would appear to their figures, pilot men of an electrical and interplanetary world which could speak across the ages of a failure of human potential, a smashing of mood, some loss of that other means of communication which once had lived in the carnal grasp of the roots of that earlier human so much closer to an animal in the ecological scheme, early human who had survived pregnancy, birth, first-year diseases, syphilis, loss of teeth—what a strength and substance to that earlier and lost human race Aquarius brooded as the dirt flew in on the dead Ford, what a nice balance of food consumed and material used, equilibrium of lives, and deaths, and wastes in fair balance, as opposed to the oncoming world of parallel colostomies draining into the same main line, and the air of earth cities become carbon monoxide and lead, sulphur dioxide and ash, nitrogen oxide and other particulates of the noxious, earth staggering with sewages which did not rot, synthetics, aluminums, oils and pesticides, fertilizers, detergents and nuclear spews, acids and plastics and salt in the soil, cakes of suffocation in the rivers, hazes of nitrogen effluent to cut off the light from the sky, a burgeoning of artificials to addict the crops, another year of pollutions to choke the planet. And the population ready to double in four decades, no, less. One knew with the worst sense of bottoms disgorging into bottomless bottoms that if the military-industrial establishment was beginning to accept the idea that funds might be taken eventually from them and given over to the solution (or the barest hope of a solution!) to the critical symptoms of ecology, the nauseas of pollution, then the statistics presented to their private councils must have been incredible indeed. Was the end of the world at hand? Was that the message they now received? Io, Europa, Ganymede and Callisto!—we might be safer far on the moons of Jupiter. What did we know of what we did? Why the very organs of disease which once would kill a man were now delivered by surgeons to the womb of the open day, organs of disease reborn for an instant in a half-life, yes, cancer organs removed probably became the cancer communicants of ether yet unglimpsed.

Only a generation ago, they would have thought it was the essence of an insane heart to personify an organ, attribute a soul to the part, believe that a cancer of liver or cancer of lung was not extinguished so soon as its malignancy was removed. It would have been considered the core of psychosis to speak of the postoperative cancer communicants of the organ removed. Yet we were infants who tickled the navel of the moon while suffocating in the loop of our diaper. A line from a poem of Hemingway burned across the funeral festivities of the day.

> In the next war
> we shall bury the dead in cellophane
> The host shall come packaged
> in cellophane.

He broke up with his wife on Labor Day night and knew they would not be together for many a month, many a year, maybe forever. In the morning, after a night of no sleep, he was on a plane to Houston and sifting of haystacks of technological fact for the gleam of a needle or a clue. And no computer named HAYSTAQ to serve as horse.

iv

It was a long September. He went back and forth between Houston and the mournful memories of the land of the Pilgrims and the cod. Pisces was away, and traveling. In the mend of Indian summer with the crowds gone and the rose-hip bushes in bloom on the dunes, their flowers artful as violet in a pearl, he bought a Land Rover for consolation and took long rides through lands of sand back of town, a corner of Sahara. In the bay, the flats at low tide heard the singing of the clams — dreams of glory at the majesty of oceans emerged in a sigh, a whistle, one could not quite hear the buried song of the clam. And the light dazzled across mirrors of inch-deep water and luminosities of glistening sand — he could almost have packed the literary equipment in for one good year of oil and gesso ground.

There were contracts however. Prose was never so much prose as when constructed with obligation. The more he visited Houston, the more he knew with what unhappiness is not automatic to tell that he might have blundered in accepting the hardest story of them all, for it was a sex-stripped mystery of machines which might have a mind, and mysterious men who managed to live like machines, and more than once in airplanes, high enough above the clouds to give a hint of other worlds in the gatherings and demarcations of airy attenuated farewell, he came to think again, as he had brooded again and again, on that simple conception of God as an embattled vision which had terrified him from the hour he first encountered the thought around one of the bends of marijuana fifteen years ago. Every other one of his notions had followed from that, for if God were a vision of existence at war with other visions in the universe, and we were the instruments of His endeavor just so much as the conflicting cells of our body were the imperfect instrument of our own will, then what now was the condition of God? Was He trapped in the wound of nature, severed from our existence as completely as the once exquisite balances of the shattered ecology? had that vision He wished to carry across the universe depended altogether upon human mind and flesh in sensuous communication with nature? had radio-by-machine been the cancer of communication? had the savage lived in a set of communions with the invisible messages of nature which we had pulverized with our amplifiers? These days Aquarius carried Frazer's *Golden Bough* on long trips by plane.

Bechuana warriors wear the hair of a hornless ox among their own hair because the ox, having no horns, is hard to catch . . . a South African warrior who twists tufts of rat hair among his own curly black locks will have just as many chances of avoiding the enemy's spear as the nimble rat has of avoiding things thrown at it . . . When you are playing the one-stringed lute, and your fingers are stiff, the thing to do is catch some long-legged field spiders and roast them, and then rub your fingers with the ashes; that will make your fingers as lithe and nimble as the spiders' legs—at least so think the Galalereese. To bring back a runaway slave an Arab will trace a magic circle on the ground, stick a nail in the middle of it and attach a beetle by a thread to the nail, taking care that the sex of the beetle is that of the fugitive. As the beetle crawls round and round, it will coil the thread about the nail, thus shortening its tether and drawing nearer to the center at every circuit. So by virtue of homeopathic magic the runaway slave will be drawn back to his master.

It was the magic of savage metaphor, the science of symbol, it married spiders' legs to the music of the fingers and the useful frenzy of the rat to the sensors in his hair. It made a wedding between the spiraled-in will of insects forced to focus on a point of tether and the loss of any will-to-escape in the slave. It was pretty, poetic and nonsensical, it was nonsensical. Unless it were not. What if some real exchange between insects, trees, crops, and grains, between animals and men, had lived with real if most distorted power in the first hours of history? What if that Vision of the Lord which had gone out to voyage among the stars had obtained the power to be carried up by the artwork of a bounteous earth exquisite in the resonance of all psyches in its field?—what if radio, technology, and the machine had smashed the most noble means of presenting the Vision to the universe?

What if God wrestled for the soul of man in some greased arena with the Devil, who was now fortified by every emanation from baleful stars beyond the sun—could that be so? What if God, losing cruelly here, and yet gaining there, was in a combat just so crude as the counts of point in a contest. What if, for the sake of a premise, one would assume that the Devil was reconstructing nature with every electronic, plastic, surgery and computer and so had forced the Lord in desperation to descend into the earth and come back with His life in the grass of that most mysterious marijuana, a drug which made one aware of life in the veins at what severe price was not yet known? What if God, aghast at the oncoming death of man in man-deviled pollution, was finally ready to relinquish some part of the Vision, and substitute a vision half machine, and half of man, rather than lose all? What indeed if the Lord was allowing Himself to be consumed so that the angels and swine of His children who swallowed Him promiscuously each day and night on drugs were able to embark on journeys into the land of the dead, little journeys in through the first gates of the palace of death, and thus giving Himself to the children in the milk of their drugs was, yes, consumed by them each night and thereby relinquished the largest dreams of His future. Such thoughts were an agony of pain if one held them truly, for responsibility was then like a burning of blood, and the time of apocalypse was certainly near. A war of the millennia might yet rest on the shoulders of the young. What an abattoir of brain-splattered substance if they consumed their smack and left the world dirtier than when they began.

Or was it the Devil who had insinuated marijuana into every pot and every garage? Or was the Devil being consumed as well by computers and transistors, by agents of far-off stars? There was also an hour when questions trampled upon questions to leave the ground of thought as much a mire as the gray greasy boot-trampled soil of the moon. Sometimes he even thought that pot and hash and LSD had opened the way to the moon, for they might have voided the spiritual belts of real protection. Perhaps as the runaway slave came back to the master who kept the beetle on a string, so the drugged odysseys of inner space might have altered the zones of the outer. Again and again, staring out his airplane window he would say good-by to these thoughts and stare at clouds.

In the several trips to Houston, he was like a man looking for the smallest sign. For the moon book which he had begun that summer idled now in the gap of Pisces' absence, and he did not know where to put his feet. One lifted a book like a boulder out of the mud of the mind, and his mind was a pit of wrenched habits and questions which slid like snakes. Where did you put your feet so that finally you might begin?

He found the answer at last in company with his favorite saying. "Trust the authority of your senses," Aquinas had said. He could repeat it again, for there was an object at last for his senses, there in the plastic vaults and warehouses of the Manned Spacecraft Center at Houston was a true object, a rock from the moon. Looking at it, answers came, answers strong enough to send him back to Provincetown for the fall and winter haul of his book, and a little of the spring. He finished in fact on a day when Apollo 13 was limping back to earth in wounded orbit with two fuel cells gone, its Lunar Module Aquarius never to reach the moon, yes, he finished in an hour when he did not know if the astronauts would return in safety or be lost, but he had written the ending in his mind long before; it came on the day he stood in quiet before that object from the moon, that rock which gave him certitude enough to know he would write his book and in some part applaud the feat and honor the astronauts because the expedition to the moon was finally a venture which might help to disclose the nature of the Lord and the Lucifer who warred for us; certainly, the hour of happiness would be here when men who spoke like Shakespeare rode the ships: how many eons was that away! Yes, he had come to believe by the end of this long summer that probably we had to explore into outer space, for technology had penetrated the modern mind to such a depth that voyages in space might have become the last way to discover the metaphysical pits of that world of technique which choked the pores of modern consciousness—yes, we might have to go out into space until the mystery of new discovery would force us to regard the world once again as poets, behold it as savages who knew that if the universe was a lock, its key was metaphor rather than measure.

Marvelous little moon rock. What the Devil did it say?

It was not so much. They led Aquarius through one back room after another, and up and down a stone stair or two. The week of exhibiting the rock at MSC was over—it was now on its way to the Smithsonian—and special favors were needed this particular afternoon to obtain a peek. But he reached a place at last he had been in months before, the room with the plate-glass window across its middle where magazine writers had hounded Armstrong until Armstrong confessed that man explored out as salmon swim upstream, and there on the other side of the glass was no astronaut today, but a small case vacuum-tight on the other side of the divide. He saw the lunar piece through not one glass but two, rock in a hermetically tight glass bell on the other side of another glass with still another hermetic seal. Yet she was not two feet away from him, this rock to which he instinctively gave gender as she— and *she* was gray, gray as everyone had said, gray as a dark cinder and not three inches across nor two inches high nor two inches for width, just a gray rock with craters the size of a pin and craters the size of a pencil point, and even craters large as a ladybug and rays ran out from the craters, fine white lines, fine as the wrinkles in an old lady's face, and maybe it was the pain of all these months of a marriage ending and a world in suffocation and a society in collapse, maybe it was just the constant sore in his heart as the blood pumped through to be cleared of love, but he liked the moon rock, and thought—his vanity finally unquenchable—that she liked him. Yes. Was she very old, three billion years or more? Yet she was young, she had just been transported here, and there was something young about her, tender as the smell of the cleanest hay, it was like the subtle lift of love which comes up from the cradle of the newborn, and he wondered if her craters were the scars of a war which had once allowed the earth to come together in the gathered shatterings of a mighty moon—there was something familiar as the ages of the bone in the sweet and modest presence of this moon rock, modest as a newborn calf, and so he had his sign, sentimental beyond measure, his poor dull senses had something they could trust, even if he and the moon were nothing but devils in new cahoots, and child of the century, Nijinsky of ambivalence, hanging man Aquarius, four times married and lost, moved out of MSC with the memory of the moon, new mistress, two feet below his nose, and knew he would live with the thought of a visit. All worship the new science of smell! It was bound to work its way through two panes of glass before three and a half billion more years were lost and gone.

DATE DUE

PRINTED IN U.S.A.